1986

Ethnic Plurality in India

INDIA 1974

Miles

0   300

Srinagar
JAMMU
and
KASHMIR
Rawalpindi
Amritsar
HIMACHAL
PRADESH
Chandigarh   Simla
PUNJAB
PAKISTAN
HARYANA
Delhi
SIKKIM
ARUNACHAL
PRADESH
Jaipur
UTTAR
PRADESH
NEPAL
BHUTAN
ASSAM   NAGALAND
RAJASTHAN
Lucknow
Kanpur
Patna
BIHAR
MEGHALA
BANGLADESH
MANIPUR
TRIPURA
GUJARAT
Bhopal
MADHYA PRADESH
Jamshedpur
WEST
Ranchi   BENGAL
Dacca
MIZORAM
Ahmedabad
Diu
Daman
Nagpur
Dadra and Nagar
Haveli
Calcutta
Bombay
MAHARASHTRA
ORISSA
Bhubaneswar
Srikakulam
Arabian
Sea
Hyderabad
KARNATAKA
Bay of Bengal
GOA
ANDHRA
PRADESH
Anantapur
Laccadive,
Minicoy,
and
Aminidivi Is.
Bangalore
Mysore
Madras
Pondicherry
KERALA
TAMIL
NADU
Cochin
Andaman
and
Nicobar Is.
Trivandrum
Cape Comorin
SRI
LANKA
Colombo

Indian Ocean

Ethnic Plurality

in India

R. A. Schermerhorn

University of Arizona Press
Tucson, Arizona

About the Author . . .

R. A. Schermerhorn began his study of Indian minorities in 1959 while serving as Visiting Professor of Sociology on a Fulbright grant at the University of Lucknow. At the Indian Institute of Technology in Kanpur from 1968 to 1970, he completed his research under the sponsorship of the U.S. Aid for International Development. Professor Schermerhorn joined the faculty of Western Reserve University (now Case Western Reserve University) in 1948 and retired as Professor Emeritus in 1972. He received his Ph.D. from Yale in 1931, after earning his Master's degree at Northwestern University. Among his publications are *These Our People, Minorities in American Culture,* 1949; *Society and Power,* 1961; *Comparative Ethnic Relations,* 1970; and *Communal Violence in India: A Case Study,* 1976.

THE UNIVERSITY OF ARIZONA PRESS

Library of Congress Cataloging in Publication Data

Schermerhorn, Richard Alonzo, 1903-
    Ethnic plurality in India.

    Bibliography: p.
    Includes index.
    1. Ethnology—India. 2. Minorities—India.
3. India—Social life and customs. I. Title.
DS430.S28   301.45'0954   77-75662
ISBN 0-8165-0612-4
ISBN 0-8165-0578-0 pbk.

Dedicated to all my former students
at home or abroad, whose continual
challenges have helped to keep me honest.

Contents

MAPS

FIGURES

TABLES

Acknowledgments

Without the counsel and assistance of many benefactors, I could not have hoped to see this study reach publication. Though I cannot name them all, I would like to thank Marvin B. Sussman for making my sojourns to India possible, and both the U.S. Educational Foundation in India and the Kanpur Indo-American Program for financial support of research activities. More specifically, I should especially single out Gilbert Oakley, Jr., for encouragement in the form of travel grants; C. N. R. Rao for subvention of a demographic exploration; Ashish Bose for locating suitable personnel; Joginder Singh Sodhi for research assistance; C. D. Misra for demographic guidance; Jerry St. Dennis for a number of demographic calculations; A. K. Saran for documents from the Indian Institute of Advanced Study; Niharranjan Ray for a copy of his book on the Sikh Gurus; S. F. Desai for field orientation in the Parsi community; B. J. Israel for extensive correspondence on Jewish life; Richard W. Taylor for judicious guidance to leaders and literature in the Christian community; V. A. Sangave for permission to quote extensively from his volume on the Jaina community; R. Vijaya Kumar for liaison with outstanding leaders among the Scheduled Castes and for literature on neo-Buddhism; Irma Johnson of the M.I.T. library and Grace Korewick of the Honnold Library, Claremont Colleges, for supererogatory assistance.

To the following persons, who read the manuscript and offered countless valuable corrections or suggestions for improvement, I owe gratitude not easily measured: K. N. Sharma, Ali Ashraf, D. N. Dhanagare, P. N. Rastogi, Bhavani Mannheim, Ravindra K. Jain, Harry Izmirlian, Jr., Lelah Dushkin, Theodore P. Wright, Jr., Satish K. Arora, Noel P. Gist, Schifra Strizower, Ketayun Gould, Christine Inglis, William H. Newell, Irwin Deutscher, and Mattison Mines. This list does not include the many interviewees who were promised anonymity but who gave of their time so freely and generously.

I must also extend thanks to Marshall Townsend of the University of Arizona Press for diligent and assiduous efforts to improve this work and for his stern insistence that I exercise redoubled criticism of the manuscript on my own. His advice has had a salutory effect on me and, I hope, on this book as well. In addition, I must express both obligation and admiration to Marie Webner of the Press editorial staff for her corrections, suggestions, and admonitions which have clarified and enhanced the substance of the manuscript incalculably.

I salute them all in grateful acknowledgment; and where I have failed to accept their sage advice, I hereby absolve them from responsibility for what follows. I must answer for it unequivocally.

Finally to Helen, my ever-present guardian of time and schedule, my usual obeisance for her thankless task.

R. A. SCHERMERHORN

SPECIAL THANKS

Special thanks are also due to the following authors and publishers for permission to quote at some length from their works:

To Asia Publishing House for permission to quote from S. A. Husain's book, *The Destiny of Indian Muslims*, Bombay, 1965, pp. 19-20, 22, 128, and 131-132.

To F. G. Bailey and to the Manchester University Press for permission to quote from his *Tribe, Caste and Nation*, Manchester, 1960, pp. 159, 160, and 191.

To Gerald Berreman for permission to quote from his article, "Stratification, Pluralism and Interaction, A Comparative Analysis of Caste," in Anthony de Reuck and Julie Knight, eds., *Caste and Race: Comparative Approaches*, A CIBA Foundation Volume, London, J. and A. Churchill, Ltd., 1967, p. 54.

To R. Chandidas for permission to use his table on Sectoral Distribution of Scheduled Castes and Scheduled Tribes in the labor force, appearing in the *Economic and Political Weekly* 4 (No. 4, June 14, 1969).

To Noel P. Gist for permission to quote from the volume by him and Roy Dean Wright, *Marginality and Identity, Anglo-Indians as a Racially-Mixed Minority in India*, Publication 3, Monographs and Theoretical Studies in Sociology and Anthropology, in Honour of Nels Anderson. General Editor, K. Ishwaran. Leiden, E. J. Brill, 1973, p. 17.

To the Institute of Advanced Study, Simla, for permission to quote from an Inaugural Address of S. C. Dube, Director of the Institute, at a Conference on the status of tribals in India, July 1969.

To Corliss Lamont, husband of the late Helen B. Lamb, for permission to quote from her article, published before her death, "The Indian Business Communities and the Evolution of an Industrialist Class," in *Pacific Affairs* 28 (No. 2, June 1955), pp. 103, 108-109, 112, and 115. This article is republished in a posthumous volume: Helen B. Lamb, *Studies on India and Vietnam*, New York, Monthly Review Press, 1976.

To Orient Longman for permission to quote from the work of M. A. Karendikar, *Islam in India's Transition to Modernity*, Bombay, 1968, p. 377.

To Bhai Jodh Singh for permission to quote from his chapter entitled "Structure and Character of Sikh Society," in *Sikhism and Indian Society*, Transactions of the Indian Institute of Advanced Study, Vol. 4, Simla, 1967, pp. 43-44.

To Myron Weiner for permission to quote from his volume, *State Politics in India*, Princeton University Press, 1968, pp. 39-40.

Introduction

In the study of any society not his own, the social scientist worth his salt is startled from time to time by the realization of his enormous presumption in reaching supposedly authentic conclusions.[1] This difficulty is compounded when he approaches his task at the macrolevel and when his field of research is India, a society of such complex diversity that it almost defies his efforts at understanding. Linguistically the task is hopeless; there is no philologist so erudite that he has simultaneous and equal familiarity with the fourteen official languages and the hundreds of dialects. Vernacular knowledge is commonly limited to local or, at most, to regional affairs. Anthropological studies, traditionally micro and intensive, have explored such zones and have rewarded us with multiple in-depth closeups, each with its own unique configuration. To the extent that we are versed in these plural ethnographies, we are able to peer over the rim of each subculture. Transcending these small-scale views are a number of recent macroperspectives by anthropologists: Bernard Cohn's *India: the Social Anthropology of a Civilization,* David Mandelbaum's *Society in India,* or Milton Singer's *When a Great Tradition Modernizes: An Anthropological Approach to Indian Civilization.*

In other disciplines, the economists and political scientists have each factored out a selected set of activities that occur in a nationwide network and have attempted a systematic account of the way people function at such levels; local affairs may then appear as derivatives of larger societal patterns like "the economy" or "the polity." In India, as elsewhere, the economists have a longer history and more firmly established prestige, but the political scientists are gaining on them. For macroanalyses it would be hard to better the Rudolphs' *The Modernity of Tradition, Political Development in India* or Rajni Kothari's *Politics in India.*

Benchmarks for guiding all explorations also come from the historians, who might have been expected to produce a comprehensive account of India's developing society as a recognizable entity. Handicapped, however, by the gap between traditions of the literate elite and popular localisms, as well as by the uncertainties of chronology in earlier times, historians have also had to wrestle with the obstacles of plural perspectives – the Brahmanic, the Muslim, the

---

1. The same is true, of course, when he observes his own society, except that his realization comes less often and with less poignancy.

[1]

British, the post-independence revisionist, and all the rest. The very enormity of their task has often led historians not to attempt to portray a well-rounded whole but to take refuge in specialization: histories of religion, philosophy, literature, art, dynasties, regions, or a selected period carved out of the 4,000 years of Indian history.

But specialization haunts us all. It was with a special focus on ethnic relations that I made two forays into India. The first, under the Fulbright program, was at the University of Lucknow in 1959-60; the second was sponsored by the Aid for International Development in their Kanpur Indo-American Program at the Indian Institute of Technology in Kanpur during 1968-70. Having explored to some degree the intergroup relations of ethnic and racial minorities in the United States,[2] I naturally gravitated toward the study of the same (or what I assumed to be analogous) phenomena in India. In discussion with colleagues among Indian social scientists, and after some immersion in historical and anthropological documentation, I decided to abandon intensive study for extensive and to accept the risk of superficiality by attempting a broader macroview. If, I argued, the presently undeveloped field of ethnic relations were now opened up as a promising area for future research in India, it could achieve more impetus by showing its variable implications for *different* minorities in their modes of adjustment to the actions of a dominant group than by monographic analysis of the same sort for a single minority. Years of struggle to find an appropriate framework for assessing the relationships of ethnic groups to total societies convinced me that macrostudy would be much more fruitful in the effort to find our bearings and gain maximum perspective from which to estimate the appropriateness of future consolidation of knowledge. For this purpose, profiles rather than intensive microstudies would be a more promising approach, especially when oriented toward the larger changes in society.

How could I accomplish such profiles within my remaining year and a half in India without adequate funds and while on a limited teaching schedule? I recalled the bold advice of C. Wright Mills:

> Let every man be his own methodologist; let every man be his own theorist, let theory and method again become part of the practice of a craft. Stand for the primacy of the individual scholar; stand opposed to the ascendancy of research teams of technicians. Be one mind that is on its own confronting the problems of man and society.[3]

By continually re-examining the issues, I finally decided to combine a sociohistorical approach with repeated reliance on what the anthropologists would call key informants, supplemented throughout by whatever field observations I would have time for. Guiding all these was the conceptual framework already developed in *Comparative Ethnic Relations*, which would

---

2. In *These Our People, Minorities in American Culture,* Boston, D.C. Heath, 1949.

3. C. Wright Mills, *The Sociological Imagination* (New York, Oxford University Press, 1959), p. 224. Note the word "ascendancy." Mills was not a total iconoclast, nor was he denying that team research has a place in advancing sociological knowledge. Rather, he was opposed to making it the *dominant* method and obviously gave it a *secondary* place.

help to furnish a selective set of themes to be explored and matters that could be omitted without serious loss.[4]

The sociohistorical investigation included the examination of books, pamphlets, journal articles, newspaper stories and summary accounts, social surveys, research monographs,[5] census data, government reports, and extensive private correspondence. As a matter of tactics I focused on the literature of each minority before interviewing one of the key informants from that particular group to familiarize myself with relevant issues and to avoid false assumptions in verbal exchange. As a matter of strategy I tried to alternate frequently between informants and the literature so that respondents might suggest written sources previously unknown and the literature might suggest new questions for informants still to be interviewed. Continual shift between interviews and the literature could thus perform several functions at once: it could furnish continual correction for errors in the data or their interpretation, it could provide opportunities for serendipity and, with good fortune, for validation of provisional conclusions.

Key informants were divided into two categories: (1) those from a particular minority group reputed by social scientists or prominent figures within their own community to be highly conversant with its history and activities; (2) specialists who had made the same group an object of central investigation, sometimes over an entire lifetime, but who were not members of the community they studied. The specialists were academicians; the minority members, with one or two exceptions, were not.[6] Informants in the first category were interviewed before results were written up; the same was true of nearly all informants in the second category, though some could not be interviewed until the preliminary version was completed. On finishing the first draft about each minority, I submitted it to another independent authority (again, a specialist) for a thoroughgoing editorial critique. (Three of these authorities were Western or Westernized members of the minority in question.) The result was another set of deletions, emendations, and changes of emphasis in the final draft.

Although this procedure lacks the strictness and precision demanded by so many methodologists, it seems suited to macroresearch under limited time requirements, just as their more rigid exactions are feasible for microanalysis. The use of key informants together with specialists to furnish modalities of ethnic behavior and ideology on a societal scale is to place confidence in their ability to synthesize a wide set of observations, many extending back over years of time. This is a process of *distillation* which we have all taken for granted without properly exploiting it, except for the microstudies of the anthropologist. It is time for a deliberate extension of this procedure to broader areas of investigation.

---

4. Cf. R.K. Merton, *Social Theory and Social Structure* (Glencoe, Ill., Free Press, 1957), pp. 54-55, for comments on the usefulness of theory for parsimonious choice in research.

5. Some of these were graduate theses and dissertations at Indian universities; others at American universities could not be examined until a return to the United States in 1970.

6. Where academic "outsiders" were unavailable, "insiders" had to be accepted. The insiders then had to be scrutinized more severely for what American historians have called "filiopietistic" bias, just as "outsiders" were inspected for antiminority prejudice. Unquestionably, filiopietistic partiality was encountered more frequently.

Locating key informants was not difficult. I began with suggestions from academic colleagues (often the best leads). Then I perused the literature and news stories, had informal discussions with rank-and-file members of the minorities themselves, and accepted recommendations made by other key informants (often familiarly acquainted with leaders in communities not their own). Visits to one government bureau not infrequently led to others; discussion with one politician brought to light others with similar or contrasting viewpoints. In the end I had more possibilities than I could possibly interview. I therefore limited the choice to (1) informants who were bilingual and had command of at least one vernacular in addition to English (with some exceptions for Anglo-Indians and Christians); (2) interviewees from the same community having different occupations; (3) respondents from different geographical areas when possible.

The key informants interviewed were four businessmen (one head of a chamber of commerce, one officer of a trade association, one restaurant owner, and one general trader), two physicians, a former municipal councillor, three members of legislative assemblies, a member of the Lok Sabha, two officials from different bureaucracies in New Delhi, vice-chancellor of a university, dean of a college, three university professors in active service and one in retirement, two school principals, one primary teacher, one librarian, one retired army officer, one dramatist, one journalist, three priests, three clergymen, three prominent lay figures including a personnel officer, a nurse, a prominent woman leader, and two officials in national minority organizations. These informants were interviewed in the following cities: New Delhi, Amritsar, Ahmedabad, Lucknow, Kanpur, Bombay, Calcutta, Bangalore, Hyderabad, Madras, and Trivandrum. At least three key informants were interviewed from each of the minority communities and, in the case of the Christians (with whom I had previous connections), the number was substantially larger if respondents from an earlier research (1960) were counted. All interviewees could be classified as middle-class;[7] caste backgrounds were not verified.

Interviews lasted from two to four hours for each informant; in some cases it was necessary to have more than one session. No one refused to be interviewed, and no questions seemed to arouse resistance. Disagreement among respondents was infrequent; specialists consulted later were usually able to resolve such issues when they arose. If not, the uncertainty was either reported or omitted. Specialists in the history and social analysis of each separate minority who were not members of it were academicians or had previous connections with some institution of higher learning. Both field informants and specialists were promised anonymity.[8] In all cases the same leading questions from the interview guide were used for both categories of respondents. Together with the literature, this made possible a triangulation of comparison.

---

7. Without replies from respondents in the lower brackets, there is doubtless some loss of perspective. To fill this gap would, however, require interviewing with the aid of interpreters in many vernaculars and multiple sociolinguistic adjustments.

8. By agreement, this stipulation was abandoned in a single case where the informant also served as field guide.

Preferred temporal sequence for the inquiry was the following: first an initial search of the literature for a historical and cross-sectional introduction; next, the use of the identical interview guide[9] for interviewing each key informant; then, a return to documentary sources, including those suggested by the respondent, adding of new questions from the reading and first interview to the second interrogation, and so on throughout a series. Ideally I planned to complete all interviews for each single minority before approaching an outside specialist, but the vagaries of time and travel did not always permit this. Some specialists were seen before having a parley with all the key informants for that particular community. I made it a practice, however, to interview the specialist late in the process rather than early. The chief complicating factor, of course, was the necessity to keep in mind the requirements for all ten minorities at each planning stage. This marred the symmetry of schedule for any one of them and required continual shift of focus from one minority representative to another. Ecological concentration simplified this occasionally where a single minority was dominant, like the Sikhs in Amritsar, or where two communities were clustered, like the Anglo-Indians and Chinese in Calcutta or the Jews and Parsis in Bombay. These were exceptional cases, at least partly nullified by my guiding principle of dispersing the interviews into different geographical regions.[10] As a rule it became imperative to interview informants from several minorities in the same city — a process compounded at the most intensive level in Delhi where, fortunately enough, it was also possible to check documentary sources.

Supplemental guidance came in different forms. It was possible, for example, to attend a statewide conference for Scheduled Castes and an all-India convention of Roman Catholic Christians; on both occasions new key informants were located and fresh literature obtained. On another occasion a respondent invited me to a recreational evening for Anglo-Indians conducted by their Association. I was also able to attend a national Gandhi commemorative conference and a memorial meeting for the University of Bombay; both these occasions presented opportunities to discuss problems and issues with perceptive observers. During the write-up of my results, I was able to organize a few ideas into lecture form and, on occasion, present them to university audiences at Gorakhpur, Ranchi, Aligarh, Lucknow, and Bombay, where critical discussions were most profitable. An even more salutory critique resulted from reading a similar paper at the national meeting of the Indian Sociological Society in Delhi (1969), where there was opportunity to compare notes informally with a number of colleagues in private sessions.

For many reasons, this is a work of uneven quality, and no one can be more sensible of its vulnerabilities than I. At times I was totally unable to locate any research literature at all, as in the case of the Chinese, for whom I found it necessary to draw on parallel studies in southeast Asia. At the other end of the scale, there are three well-conceived systematic studies of minorities (for Jews, Jains, and Anglo-Indians) on which I have drawn heavily (the reader may think

---

9. A copy of this guide may be found in the appendix.

10. Excessive clustering of the Chinese in Calcutta prevented completion of more than one interview from an informant in any other city.

too heavily). In all other cases there are monographs on selected themes, local conditions, or subgroupings that leave many gaps in our knowledge. It is obvious that the use of informants will have differential value in the three cases. Yet without these informants, the interpretive dimension would be lacking; even with a substantial theoretical framework, the application of that scheme to a succession of ethnic groups on the basis of a documentary fill-in, although more organized and focused than a one-dimensional summary, would still lack the insights and nuances that appear in social intercourse with persons directly and intimately involved with the activities and events under study. Continuous reliance on such respondents has, in my experience, been fairly convincing evidence that the anthropologist's approach in these matters is not only valid for microstudies but for macroinvestigations as well, especially where informants are properly chosen. What one Australian ethnographer has said about her own research in small communities seems surprisingly relevant to more panoramic views as well:

> Though the neat tables which a structured questionnaire makes possible appear more scientific than the less precise generalities of subjective observation, the latter may prove to be more accurate in the event, since it becomes increasingly more difficult, over a period, to hide felt attitudes and responses from the trained inquirer.[11]

My own confidence in the validity of such an approach increased with its use, as corroboration of views from different informants proved the rule rather than the exception, at least for the major issues. Some disagreement on details was, of course, expected. But it was gratifying to find how hard some of the soft data were.

The chief failures in an exploratory venture of this kind are those of omission. Needless to say, I consider this volume no more than a first step toward more thorough analysis of ethnic relations in India. If it proves to be a gateway for more conclusive and substantial research in an opening field of investigation, rich in promise for both theory and practice in the subcontinent, I shall feel amply rewarded.

Throughout I have stressed the importance of integration as characterized in my previous work,[12] the process itself depending in large part on reciprocal interpretations by dominant and subordinate groupings.[13]

The last few pages of each minority profile will furnish a concrete example of how the acts of interpretation generate integration, conflict, and their interrelation. Interviewing of key informants assures contemporaneity for these interpretative processes; but widespread historical changes in the future could alter such responses appreciably. This is the nemesis of all social analysis.

---

11. Lorna Lippman, *Words or Blows. Racial Attitudes in Australia,* Ringwood, Victoria, Australia, Penguin Books Australia Ltd., 1973, p. 77.

12. *Comparative Ethnic Relations,* New York, Random House, 1970, p. 83 (and see Fig. 2, Chap. 1, below).

13. Ibid., pp. 15-16.

Each epoch (historically defined) will imprint a selective direction to the ongoing events of the period. This was especially true of the so-called "emergency period" that gripped India from June 16, 1975, to January 20, 1977, when the regime displayed a conspicuous flurry of attention to minority problems. For example: the prime minister visited a number of tribal areas ordinarily neglected, in one case distributing land ceremonially to thirty landless families in Maharashtra; other gifts of land to landless Untouchables and tribal units were reported in Gujarat, Himachal Pradesh, Kerala and Uttar Pradesh. State level grievance committees were set up for Scheduled Castes and Scheduled Tribes in half a dozen states, and a national ordinance prohibiting bonded labor was passed by Parliament. Strong restrictions on unbridled moneylending exploitation of tribals in Orissa were enacted, while Maharashtra canceled tribal debts. Special outlays for the two "weaker sections" were programmed for the Fifth National Plan. All of these provisions were specifically economic programs.

The role of cultural values in intergroup relations received only fleeting attention in comparison, as in Bihar where grass-roots consultations on public issues with Scheduled Tribes in Chotanagpur were organized toward the end of 1976. As for the Muslims, they received attention only in non-economic issues. For example, the late President Fakhruddin Ali Ahmed promised future sponsoring of Urdu in a public address to his Muslim coreligionists in Lucknow, while in New Delhi a joint celebration of Ali Jinnah's birthday by both India and Pakistan was at least a symbolic act for easing tensions. Whether all these events were manipulative gestures of tokenism in an appeal for votes or signs of a more long-ranging commitment to benevolence, only future historians can judge. Whether Morarji Desai, Indira Gandhi's successor, proves to be as surreptitiously anti-Muslim as he was in 1969[14] also remains to be seen.

---

14. See my monograph *Communal Violence in India: A Case Study* (Consultative Committee of Indian Muslims, Broadview, Illinois, 1976) for data on this subject.

Chapter 1

Comparative Perspectives

India has been the scene of the mixing of peoples for thousands of years. The ethnic relations reviewed briefly in the present volume constitute the last stage of a long interactive process that now stretches toward an uncertain future. A great many authorities have interpreted the contemporary stage as a transition from "traditional" to "modern" or "Western" modes of life, a perspective that partly reveals while partly concealing the nature of the fundamental movement. For purposes of ethnic analysis I believe that M. G. Smith's threefold typology of societal organization is a more useful perspective.

INCORPORATION OF ETHNIC GROUPS

In Smith's view, societies adopt three well-defined modes of incorporating their internal ethnic divisions. The first mode, called *differential,* encompasses two or more ethnic units on an unequal basis with power and privilege rating from high to low for the groups involved. The second, the so-called *equivalent,* mode is one in which the ethnic units are exclusive corporate groups, each with equivalent standing in the society as a whole. In this mode, individuals can only participate in the political system as members or representatives of their respective groups; it is this membership that confers eligibility for them to enter into such public activity. An ungrouped man is not a citizen. Finally, the third or *uniform* mode of incorporation nullifies or cancels out ethnic membership as a prerequisite for political activity and includes all, regardless of ethnic origin, in the universal category of citizenship. (See Smith, 1971, p. 434ff.)

Twentieth century examples of the three modes are the Republic of South Africa for the mode of *differential* or unequal incorporation; Malaya, Canada, and Switzerland as examples of *equivalence;* and France or the United States illustrating the *uniform* mode.

In India the three modes appear to follow each other historically. In two or more millennia, invasions and conquests formed a series of larger or smaller kingdoms, each with its own priorities of partiality for some subject peoples in preference to others. In this first stage of differential incorporation (covering most of India's history, extending well into the British period), the turbulence of intermittent military incursions was counterbalanced by two forms of order: regional and local hierarchies of caste that maintained their form and shape no matter what forms of conquest engulfed their people; and permeation of most areas by the Great Tradition of Brahmanic Hinduism which, especially in the Vedanta, could provide a religious ideological unity that legitimated multiple forms of worship and belief. But the differential mode of incorporation remained through it all and, in fact, was reincarnated over centuries into the particularisms of caste, occupation, and kinship at specific levels, while still admitting broader application at the level of wider linguistic boundaries.

For a time the British colonial administrators followed the pattern of differential incorporation, but as their power became sufficiently relaxed to permit their subjects a limited franchise, they moved farther and farther in the direction of the equivalent mode. Under this arrangement, separate electorates were established for Muslims and other ethnic groups. Independent India, however, with the adoption of its new constitution abolished the equivalent mode at one stroke in favor the the uniform mode, which eliminated the requirement of membership in an intermediate collective group and threw open the status of citizenship to all individuals regardless of ascriptive affiliation.[1] Universal franchise became a symbol of the new equality.

What is significant for our problem is the vulnerability of the third mode of uniform incorporation. In comparison with the first mode, which lasted through most of Indian history, and the second mode, which was of such short duration that it could hardly serve as a satisfactory transition to the universal equality of the third, the last mode of uniform incorporation has been tested for no more than a generation. Although Gandhi and a few other nationalist leaders fought hard and successfully for the new dispensation, the egalitarian ideal embedded in it violates the cultural norm of hierarchy presupposed in the caste system, and the attempt to establish a neutral plane where all citizens are Indians without regard to region or language (not to speak of religion) is in many ways unnatural. Nirad Chaudhuri declares, for example, that he enjoys setting the foreign visitor straight when he uses the word "Indian" by contradicting him flatly and denying that the word has the meaning that aliens attribute to it. It is more accurate, he claims, to speak of "Bengali, Punjabi, Hindustani, Marathi, Tamil, Sikh, Muslim and so on. As to the word 'Indian,' it is only a geographical definition and a very loose one at that." A few pages later he admits that "Indian" may have the following attenuated meaning: "A legally recognized citizen of the new sovereign State called the Republic and Union of India, it being clearly understood that I do not consider that all the citizens of this State belong to one

---

1. It can be plausibly argued that vestigial remains of the second or equivalent mode continued in the special provisions reserving seats in legislatures for Scheduled Castes and Tribes, or quotas in the bureaucracy. Theoretically, however, these benefits are regarded as temporary and as aids to promoting equality of citizenship guaranteed by the third mode.

nation. In their case, *de jure* nationality is not the same as *de facto* nationality." (Chaudhuri, 1965, pp. 27, 30).

Thus Chaudhuri bears witness to the equivocal status of citizenship. We do well to note that it was superimposed as a mode of incorporation, and rather suddenly at that, upon an entire subcontinent where deeply ingrained beliefs and inclinations were strongly opposed to its central thrust. Not only was the new egalitarian type of inclusion a questionable pattern, but the individualism which was a part of it contradicted group norms long taken for granted. The shift of incorporation, therefore, is of central importance for ethnic analysis in India, since it permeates all the relations that come under scrutiny. As a theme, it will recur frequently in the discussion that follows.

ANALYSIS OF ETHNIC RELATIONS: A FRAMEWORK

The scientific analysis of ethnic relations needs, at the outset, to transcend a mere series of descriptions. The object of its inquiry must be viewed as a special case of societal relations in their broadest and most generic sense, not a separate and unrelated field of investigation. By implication it follows that, in order to make a selection of the phenomena to be studied, it is necessary to choose those that permit comparison with similar phenomena in other settings. This cross-cultural demand will be met here in two ways: first, by classifying ethnic minority groups into types that appear throughout the entire modern world; and second, by enlarging the scope of the exploration to the "study of total societies" in order to relate such smaller groupings to their encompassing wholes. Eventually, of course, at least a tentative sorting or assigning of rubrics to the societies themselves will be required.

I have advanced a schematic framework in some detail elsewhere for this sort of analysis (Schermerhorn, 1970) and will pare down the substance of the earlier exposition to the following statements: The way we classify ethnic minorities should give us an inkling of their relationship to environing societies. I suggest that this can best be done by employing *categories of duration*. Such categories permit us to have capsule versions of successive events that repeat themselves at different times and places. Ethnic groups take their rise (that is, become differentiated or distinguishable) from such recurrent historical patterns that link them with total societies. I call these the *intergroup sequences*.

Six intergroup sequences deserve mention: (1) the emergence of pariahs, (2) the emergence of indigenous isolates, (3) annexation, (4) migration, (5) colonization, and (6) religious cleavage. [2]

The first sequence (emergence of pariahs) occurs in such Asian societies as Tibet, Korea, Japan, and India. Particularly in the last two countries the lowest stratum has been composed of people supposedly unclean and degraded, with their status defined in religious tradition as "inevitable, immutable, and in some

---

2. In the 1970 volume I outlined only the first five of these sequences, but, after doing research in India, I felt the need to add the sixth sequence because of its salient importance in the subcontinent.

way deserved" (J. Price, 1966, p. 9). However, both countries officially abolished pariah status in law, Japan in 1871 and India at the time of her independence in 1949-50. Since then the Buraku of Japan and the Scheduled Castes of India have struggled to implement legal equality in the face of continuing discrimination sanctioned by custom. It so happens that in India the Scheduled Castes constitute the largest minority, numbering 79,995,896, or 14.6 percent of the total population (1971 census).

The second sequence (emergence of indigenous isolates) is found in all those countries of the world where an aggregate of nonliterate people are surrounded or dominated by a literate, usually considerably urbanized, sector of the population. The comparative isolation of the relatively secluded ethno-linguistic groups is shattered by continual contact with outsiders whose economic and political institutions have such impact and diffusion that insularity is broken down and participation in the wider world continually fostered. At times, this provokes formerly separated groups into mobilizing a unified political movement to improve their lot. In India, this diversified sector, designated as the Scheduled Tribes, numbers 38,015,162, or some 6.94 percent of the population.

The third sequence, annexation, has little relevance for India unless Goa, annexed or "liberated" in 1961, is included. Goa will probably not qualify as a minority, however, unless and until it makes increasingly greater claims on the central government for preferential treatment, greater autonomy, or both. It will consequently receive no attention in these pages.

Migration, the fourth sequence, has been of more consequence for India in the past than in modern times. Historically, the two religious communities who migrated to India in the early Christian era were the Jews (only some 16,000 remained in India as of 1971) and the Parsis (91,266 in 1971). In the twentieth century, however, India has not attracted migrants in the way that other Asian countries have done. Perhaps only the Chinese should be mentioned at all, and their numbers were quite small in 1971 (between 14,000 and 53,000). (See Chap. 12 below for a discussion of demographic uncertainties.) I am omitting the tiny refugee colony from Tibet since they were involuntary migrants. This question will probably be raised: Why not include the Christians with the Jews and Parsis in a migrant category since the first Christians are reputed to have entered India in the first century of the present era? There are two reasons for not doing so. The vast majority of Indian Christians are not descendants of the early migrants but of later converts, mostly of the nineteenth and twentieth centuries; Jews and Parsis, however, are genetically related to the first settlers from their communities. In the second place, the Indian public perceives the Christians as somehow bound up with the influx of Westerners (more specifically, the colonial power), not with an ancient influx of pilgrims from the Mediterranean basin. It therefore seems more fitting to subsume the Christians within the fifth sequence.

This sequence is entitled "colonization," but the pertinence of such a term requires explanation. As a form of social control, colonization is a special form of conquest. In earlier times the leading form of dominance was to establish kingdoms by conquest, but in the last two or three centuries, it has been to set up colonies through paramount authority in distant lands. Recognizing that the two forms belong together and represent simply the distinction between the distant and more recent past, I include both Muslims and Christians as derivatives from the fifth sequence. The Muslims who came as conquering Turks, Afghans, and Moguls brought not only soldiers and courtiers but religious leaders who spread the doctrines of Islam throughout the subcontinent. The success of their efforts can be seen from the fact that in 1971, in spite of the tragedy of partition, the Muslims in India numbered 61,417,934, or 11.21 percent of the population. Like Islam, Christianity was a proselyting faith. In the high tide of British rule during the nineteenth and early twentieth centuries, a striking influx of new priests and missionaries from Europe and America multiplied converts to a peak of numbers which leveled off at the time of independence. By 1971 they were listed as 14,223,382, or 2.6 percent of the nation's population.[3] A far more direct consequence of the colonization sequence was racial mixture between males of the dominant group and females of the subordinates. Offspring of the two, popularly known as half-castes, Eurasians, or Anglo-Indians, have occupied a marginal status, not only in India but in Burma, Indonesia, and elsewhere. Experiencing rejection from both sides, this minority first attached itself closely to the colonial rulers but found this a handicap after independence, when they were despised for "bootlicking" the imperialists. Some attempted an escape by emigration; those who have remained in India (something like 250,000 in 1968)[4] have ambivalent reactions to integration.

The sixth sequence, religious cleavage, refers to the splitting off of religious sects or communities under the influence of charismatic leaders who initiated new directions in worship and belief. The two largest of these internal cleavages in India deserve attention because they point up parallels and differences with other religious minorities that lack a Hindu base. The Jains and the Sikhs thus took their rise from religious cleavage, the former numbering 2,604,646 and the latter 10,378,797, according to the 1971 census.

The present volume will be devoted to an analysis of the ten minorities just reviewed and their encounter with the rest of Indian society considered as a whole:

1. Scheduled Castes	(Emergence of pariahs)
2. Scheduled Tribes	(Emergence of indigenous isolates)
3. Jains 4. Sikhs	(Religious cleavage)
5. Muslims 6. Christians 7. Anglo-Indians	(Colonization, or conquest)
8. Jews 9. Parsis 10. Chinese	(Migrations, bygone and recent)

---

3. Some Christian leaders are bound to protest at their inclusion with the sequence of colonization. They can rightly assert that the history of Christianity in India predates both Zoroastrianism and Judaism and is, like Judaism, an Eastern religion. Most Indians, however, will not see it in this light. For them it appears as a Western importation which flourished to a peak of success in the colonial period but not afterward. In W. I. Thomas' oft-quoted phrase, "If men define situations as real, they are real in their consequences." Most Indians define the Christians as derivatives of colonialism, and this is their common meaning.

4. Unofficial estimate by Frank Anthony in the *Review* (New Delhi), October 1968, p. 11. Both the 1961 and 1971 census omitted the Anglo-Indians from enumeration. See Chapter 9 below for further discussion of demographic uncertainties.

There are many other candidates for inclusion in these pages, but their omission can be tentatively justified. Linguistic minorities are perhaps the most obvious examples. The Constitution of India provides definite safeguards for these groups, especially where members reside in areas dominated by speakers of other languages. Special officers are appointed to oversee their condition and assure their rights to the use of their own tongue in schooling insofar as possible. By the very nature of the case, these are fractionated groups of such minor size that it is nearly impossible to treat them on a societal basis. On the other hand, it is not entirely satisfactory to regard the linguistic *States* as minorities since they are formal units of government. It is true that a strong movement for State secession arose in Tamil Nadu, but this demand has been fluctuating rather than steady, and the militant Dravida Munnetra Kazhagam (DMK) takes an equivocal position. I therefore omit the linguistic States as minorities. Further strengthening this viewpoint is the fact that the dire forecasts of Selig Harrison (1960) about the dangerous divisiveness inherent in the linguistic sectors of India have not come true. There have been disturbances in Telengana, of course, but though language is certainly one issue, economic realities seem more impelling.[5]

Other possibilities will occur to Indian readers. Why not include Kabir-panthis, Chaitanyas, Lingayats, Smartas, and other similar groups? There are two reasons for excluding them. First, their influence is so local and weak that they are unknown to most Indians. Second, these religious offshoots do not seem to constitute true communities. As R. E. Park (1952, p. 66) has put it, "A community is not only a collection of people, but it is a collection of institutions. Not people, but institutions, are final and decisive in distinguishing the community from other social constellations." Hence, the presence of a religious institution by itself is not sufficient to qualify such groups as true communities; however, the ten minorities listed above do qualify in this respect. It must be admitted that this classification is a matter of degree rather than a sharp distinction, and it is certainly possible to draw the line somewhat differently from the way I have done here. The Lingayats, for example, have many elements of a true community and are almost as well organized politically as the Sikhs.[6] However, for the reasons just advanced, this book will omit smaller religious sects and caste groupings. Only in the case of those negatively defined in caste terms — the Avarnas — will caste or sectarian status be a major issue.

TERMINOLOGY AND ITS IMPLICATIONS

The selection of minority groups for attention here rests upon prior criteria of definition. Before proceeding further, these definitions must be made explicit.

---

5. Cf. "Andhra, Keeping the Lid on Telengana," *Economic and Political Weekly* 4 (No. 5, Feb. 1, 1969), 279-80.

6. Cf. the analysis of the Lingayats by Stephen A. Oren (1969). At any rate, throughout this volume I shall use the terms "community" and "ethnic group" synonymously. For example, Allen Grimshaw comments quite properly, "The term 'community' has the meaning in India of 'ethnic group,' namely a group with distinctive racial or cultural characteristics. The term has no ecological referent" (Grimshaw, 1959, p. 227).

First, the term "society." For the purpose at hand, I shall circumscribe this meaning to correspond with Talcott Parsons' third category of societies as primitive, intermediate, and modern (Parsons, 1966, p. 3). In the modern world it is further appropriate to define a society as a nation-state: that is, a social unit territorially distinguished from other such units, having a set of governmental institutions of a central character preeminent over local political controls, and empowered to act for the entire unit in external relations (Smith, 1957, p. 766). Such societies are, in Gerhard Lenski's terms, "imperfect systems" (Lenski, 1966, p. 34).

A second term requiring attention is "ethnic group." With rare exceptions, all societies in the modern world contain subsections or subsystems distinct from the rest of the population in a positive degree. The most fitting generic term for such a fraction of the whole is "ethnic group." To specify more exactly, I define an ethnic group as a collectivity existing within a larger society, having real or fictional common ancestry, memories of a shared historical past, and a cultural focus on one or more symbolic elements defined as the epitome of their peoplehood. Examples of such symbolic elements are kinship patterns, physical contiguity (as in localism or sectionalism), religious affiliation, language or dialect forms, tribal affiliation, nationality, phenotypical features, or any combination of these. A necessary accompaniment is some consciousness of kind among members of the group. This would place it in Robert Bierstedt's category of "societal group" (Bierstedt, 1963, pp. 295ff.). Finally, the group should have its origin identified with one of the intergroup sequences so that its historical matrix can be established in space and time.[7]

Still more important is the term "minority group." To clarify its meaning, it is helpful to take a prior glance at the dimensions of size and power that determine its usage (Fig. 1.1). It is quite possible, of course, to employ the term "minority" for group B, but then it would be necessary to add the adjective "dominant." To avoid confusion, the constant use of qualifiers, and continual departure from common usage, I prefer to restrict the term "minority group" to those of the D type rather than the B type and to employ the term "majority

More Powerful Groups (Dominant)

	Size	Power	
Group A	+	+	Majority Group
Group B	–	+	Elite

Less Powerful Groups (Subordinate)

	Size	Power	
Group C	+	–	Mass Subjects
Group D	–	–	Minority Group

AD and BC = typical intergroup configurations.

Fig. 1.1 A Fourfold Typology of Groups

---

7. This is a somewhat broader meaning than C.A. Price's "ethnic division" which has, as its denotation, a constellation originating in Europe. The usage adopted here has a greater generality and would include what Price calls a "folk" (Price, 1963, pp. 3-13).

group" for the A type rather than the C type. The designation "mass subjects" may seem awkward, but the paradigm makes it instantly clear.

Ethnic groups may have greater or lesser power in a given society: in Figure 1.1 they run the entire gamut from A to D. In most cases, however, each separate society has a single dominant group[8] along with a number of subordinate ones. It follows that an overwhelming preponderance of ethnic groups are in subordinate rather than dominant positions, and it therefore seems justifiable to drop the adjective "subordinate" as a practical measure, since it is clearly redundant. Unless called for by special considerations, it seems best to use the term "ethnic group" without a qualifier for subordinates in C and D groupings, adding the word "dominant" only when pertinent.

Combining the characteristics of size, power, and ethnicity, it is then appropriate to use "minority group" to signify any ethnic group in category D, implying that such a group forms less than half the population of a given society, that is, an appreciable subsystem with limited access to roles and activities central to the economic and political institutions of the society. On the other hand, if ethnics form an actual majority of the population but are in a status of subordination (group C), they can then be designated as mass ethnics.

On the basis of these definitions, the groups enumerated above (the Scheduled Castes, the Scheduled Tribes, Jains, Sikhs, Muslims, Christians, Anglo-Indians, Jews, Parsis, and Chinese) are singled out as the chief minority groups within India. Each is also definable as an ethnic group when considered as a collective whole, though subdivisions may also bear this title on occasion, as in the case of a single Scheduled Tribe. This issue and related matters will receive more detailed attention in the chapters to follow.

Still another term requires closer attention, namely, "dominant group." This may be defined as the collectivity within a society that has preeminent authority to function both as guardian and sustainer of the controlling value system and as prime allocator of rewards in the society. It may be a group of greater or lesser extensity: that is, a restricted elite, incumbents of a governmental apparatus, an ethnic group, a temporary or permanent coalition of interest groups, or a majority.

Is there a dominant group in India and, if so, what is it? To determine the answer to this question, let us try an experiment. First let us enumerate the population figures for the ten minority groups outlined above, obtain their sum, and subtract this number from the total population of India. Disregarding the linguistic divisions as such and the tiny sects of mainly local influence, we obtain the results shown in Table 1.1. By the process of elimination, Table 1.1 gives us the extent or measure of the majority relative to the total, but there are two items the calculation cannot give: the composition of the majority, and whether, in terms of our definition, this majority is a genuine dominant group. A reliable estimate of the first should furnish a clue for determining the second.

What population groups, therefore, make up this majority of nearly 350 million? On the assumption that the Scheduled Castes can be excluded from the

---

8. Students of the Middle East will immediately think of a notable exception: Lebanon, with two dominant groups of approximately equal power, Muslims and Christians. But it is difficult to pinpoint other cases.

TABLE 1.1

Minority Populations, 1971

Group	Population	Percentage of Total
Scheduled Castes	79,995,896	
Scheduled Tribes	38,015,162	
Jains	2,604,646	
Sikhs	10,378,797	
Muslims	61,417,934	
Christians	14,223,382	
Anglo-Indians	250,000*	
Jews	16,000†	
Parsis	91,000	
Chinese	53,000‡	
Total Minority	207,046,083	37.79
* * * * * * * * * * * * * * * * *		
All-India	547,949,809	100.
Total Minority	− 207,046,083	37.79
Majority	340,903,726	62.21

*Unofficial estimate.
† Unofficial estimate from Strizower, 1971, p. 5.
‡ Maximal figure (see Chap. 12 below).

category of Sudras in the varna classification,[9] this would make the majority (almost entirely Hindu) an aggregation of the four varnas: Brahmans, Kshatriyas, Vaisyas, and Sudras. Since, however, Sudras occupy a lowly and subservient position vis-à-vis the upper castes (with occasional exceptions like the Lingayats of southern India), it seems a mistake to include them within the all-India dominant group just because they happen to form part of the majority.

If the Sudras are eliminated, this leaves the upper three varnas (the "caste Hindus") as the true dominant group. There is admittedly a margin of error inherent in the varna classification since, at the local level, the jati or subcaste is far more accurate. Although varna has its ambiguities and lacks the same denotation in different Indian regions, it has pragmatic justification in dealing with the nation as a whole. As M. N. Srinivas comments, "Translating jati into varna terms has its hazards, though it is unavoidable when discussing India as a whole. Listing all the jatis involved in a given process would not only distract from readability but would also assume that we have the necessary information. Vague terms have their uses" (Srinivas, 1966, p. 69).

---

9. This is the practice in southern India where caste practices are more strict. But even in other areas where this is not the case, the same attitude is implied by referring to the ex-untouchables as Avarnas. And as Marc Galanter observes, "Even where untouchables are popularly regarded as Sudras, they cannot be equated with them since there are non-touchable groups which belong to this category" (Galanter, 1963, pp. 551-52).

Subtracting the Sudra population (estimated at 312,002,621)[10] from the majority of 340,903,726 would leave 28,901,105 as the remainder, the approximate population of the three upper varnas. On the basis outlined above, this would qualify as India's dominant group. The nearly 29 million in this aggregation constitute only 5 percent of the all-India population; thus, on the basis of Table 1.1, we conclude that the dominant group is an elite rather than a majority. It is not composed of an ethnic group as here defined, but there would be enough solidarity or "we-feeling" vis-à-vis the lower orders to give cohesion and relative identity to its members.

On the other hand, is this a dominant group in terms of our definition? That the three upper varnas, particularly the Brahmans, are the guardians and sustainers of the controlling value system is quite evidently true insofar as religious values are concerned. Conversely, to the extent that Western values have replaced those of tradition, it is primarily educated caste Hindus who are in the vanguard. Where disagreement or controversy over values takes place, it is usually the leaders from upper varnas who exchange the arguments and outline the alternatives. For the most part, the lower castes simply follow along. On the other dimension (that is, the allocation of rewards), it would be hard to deny that caste Hindus have assumed this responsibility – not collectively, to be sure, but as leaders in their sphere of activity. For example, if we take a simple criterion, like that of C. Wright Mills, and inquire who are the people occupying the top positions in business, government, and the military, the great majority of these decision-makers (who are really allocating rewards whether they realize it or not) are caste Hindus, granting rare exceptions. Certainly in the universities and professional organizations, the upper varnas rule supreme. In political parties, the preponderance is not so great, since one can rise in these ranks without extensive education and the lower castes have numerical voting strength; yet the predominance of Brahmans, even among Communist political leaders, is a matter of frequent comment. In India as a whole, one would not go far wrong in assuming that, when major decisions are made, it is caste Hindus who make them.

To use the term "elite" for this dominant group is to enlarge the usual meaning somewhat. André Béteille, for example, restricts the term elite to (1) members of the Indian Administrative Service, (2) officers in the upper echelons of the Army, (3) managers of large corporations, (4) top leaders of political parties, (5) members of cabinets, and of parliament at the Centre (New Delhi), (6) professionals of the upper ranks, and, in general, (7) elected politicians.

---

10. The basis for this estimate rests, first of all, on Harold Isaac's figure of 250 million as the Sudra population relative to 1961 census statistics (H. R. Isaacs, 1964, p. 26). Transposing his Sudra-all-India ratio to the corresponding 1971 figures results in a Sudra calculation of 312,002,621, the best approximate statistics now available. Isaacs arrives at his own figure by using a special base for his calculations. Since he does not subtract minority populations from his totals, his statistics for upper caste groups are higher, proportionately, than those given above. He is convinced, however, of the validity of a very high figure for the Sudras and quotes Ambedkar's estimate that they comprise 75 to 80 percent of the population (Ambedkar, 1946; H. R. Isaacs, personal correspondence). The calculations given here for 1971 would make the Sudras only 56.96 percent of the all-India population.

Extending this notion broadly, I then submit that it is the pool from which Béteille's elite is drawn that constitutes the dominant group in India and that equally well deserves the appellation of elite. This pool (the upper varnas) is the source of recruitment for the nation's leaders, and, in view of India's history, probably no other source could be expected. It is doubtful, too, whether any other source can really be expected for generations to come.

THE GREAT DIVIDE IN THE DOMINANT GROUP

It would be false, however, to leave the impression that the dominant group of upper caste members is a unified whole. Probably its most significant feature is a bifurcation into contrasting divisions which are not so openly in conflict (yet) as simply divergent in background, interests, and goals. For convenience I am calling the subgroupings the "parochial neo-traditionals" and the "conditionally Westernized."[11] The line between the two is not hard and fast because a considerable number actually take positions identified first with one camp and then with the other. But different socialization is usually a reliable indicator of their basic values.

The "parochial neo-traditional" division is overwhelmingly large and can be estimated as close to 90 percent of the dominant group. Its members are in most elective political posts but seldom in the very top cabinet or administrative offices. Persons in the "parochial neo-traditional" sector tend to have the following characteristics which, in combination, form an ideal type. The majority of them had their education (at whatever level) primarily in the vernacular. They are more attracted to local or regional than to Western culture. A possible exception to this rule is the cinema, which presents popular culture with a Western veneer, although many themes and slogans of Indian films are rooted in indigenous tradition reinforced by censorship. Males of the "parochial neo-traditional" persuasion prefer Indian to Western garb. Vegetarianism retains a strong hold on dietary habits, while caste restrictions and practices remain potent in the home, no matter how often they are violated in public. Adults observe pujas fairly regularly, along with an occasional pilgrimage sometimes dressed up as a vacation. Neo-traditionals pay deference and honor to swamis, rishis, and gurus, along with a fairly regular use of astrology to guide important decisions. In agricultural regions, political participation tends to follow the leadership of local landowners, while in the cities it is more diversified, though essentially conservative. Most members in this category have strong susceptibility to patriotic appeals couched in Hindu slogans, and they tend to share the suspicion that Muslims or Christians lack nationalist commitment. Social techniques like gherao, bandh, dharna, satyagraha — in fact, a wide variety of agitational methods, often erupting into violence — were regarded, at least before Indira Gandhi's emergency decrees of June 1975, as legitimate means of last resort. Most neo-traditionals conform to Parliamentary enactments and

---

11. These are variants on Merton's familiar dichotomy of locals and cosmopolitans (Merton, 1968, pp. 441-74).

court orders as a matter of habit without necessarily accepting the ideology underlying them. They usually ignore members of lower castes or Untouchables as much as possible unless upper level politicians make a temporary display of favoritism toward them.

Although not every member of the parochial neo-traditional aggregate shares all these characteristics, yet, by and large, they do so sufficiently to make the traits just outlined into a recognizable societal pattern familiar in most regions of India.

The second, or "conditionally Westernized" division has a set of character-istics quite opposite in most respects. Educated almost universally in English medium if not "public" schools, the members are fluent in the English language[12]; they prefer Western to regional culture (though music and dancing are frequent exceptions). People in this category consume meat and alcohol without a qualm, though in other respects they maintain an Indian diet. Males almost uniformly wear Western clothing. Nearly all members are secular-minded or agnostic in religious belief, failing to practice the rituals and ceremonies they knew in their youth; they often disparage or deride the holy men of Hinduism and are inclined to scoff at astrology. In rural areas, they pragmatically follow the strongest local political party, while rationalizing preferences in philo-sophical language; in the cities they choose their political stance on a more deliberate ideological basis. For the most part, patriotic appeals touch them only lightly except during national conflicts like the Indo-Pakistani wars. They are convinced secularists in politics and have no difficulty regarding Muslims or Christians as loyal patriots. In general they disapprove the use of public agitational techniques like gherao or satyagraha — not on religious grounds but as a matter of law and order.

The conditionally Westernized have been convinced parliamentarians in the past, though many did not acquiesce in the restrictions on the Constitution put forward in 1975-76 (for example, legitimizing indefinite preventive detention or enlarging the powers of the prime minister at the expense of the president). Much like their neo-traditional opposite numbers, they ignore the Scheduled Castes except on ceremonial occasions, although they are more likely to defend the equality of citizens under the law than the neo-traditionals are. However, this rhetoric is rarely followed by action to implement such sentiments.

These sharp divergencies within the dominant group give rise to special problems of national integration. In the long run, such integration will come about either through a compromise between the two subdivisions, or the victory of one over the other. If it is numbers that count, there is little question who will win. As governmental power becomes more centralized, however, numbers will doubtless lose their importance while policy pronouncements from on high gain more prominence.

---

12. The 1951 census shows 1 percent of the population literate in English, which makes the above assertion that 90 percent of the dominant group are in the parochial neo-traditional division educated in the vernacular, quite a conservative estimate, since a literal rendering would give 99 percent; I am therefore allowing a wide margin of error. Though comparable figures for English literacy are not available for either 1961 or 1971, it is fair to assume that less English was used at the later dates than in 1951. (Cf. W. H. Morris-Jones, 1967, p. 55.)

A GUIDE TO MINORITY GROUP INTEGRATION[13]

One of the main purposes of this volume is to determine the extent to which the ten ethnic minorities under scrutiny are integrated into the national life. To accomplish this aim, it is necessary to define what is meant by integration and then to specify some way or ways of identifying and verifying it. By integration I mean a process whereby units or elements of a society are brought into an active and coordinated compliance with the ongoing activities and objectives of the dominant group in that society. An index to the presence (not necessarily complete fulfillment) of this process is the agreement between dominant and subordinate groups on collective goals for the subordinates, for instance, assimilation or pluralism. The most satisfactory way of portraying such relationships is by the use of paired opposites: centripetal and centrifugal. Every minority will have as its modal intergroup goal either closer relations with the dominant group and acceptance of its standards (way of life) — a centripetal aim — or some type of separation, either physical or cultural, from the dominant group and more inclusive societal bonds — a centrifugal goal. The crucial factor here is not simply the choice the minority makes between one or the other, but *the agreement or disagreement of the dominant group with the goals embraced by the subordinates.* These varying views of goals are depicted in Figure 1.2.

It must be emphasized that every cell, whether A, B, C, or D, represents a simultaneous judgment on the part of each party to the encounter. The terms "centripetal" and "centrifugal" in the lower part of each cell refer to subordinates' definition of their *own* goals, but, when found in the upper part of the cell, these terms refer to the goals which the superordinates believe that the subordinates *should* take. In either case they are normative ideologies. The A and B cells represent *agreement* on goals, smoothing the way toward integration, and C and D indicate fundamental *disagreement* on goals, which reveals a strong propensity toward conflict. The diagram must be taken as a guide rather than a hard and fast classification. For instance, it lacks the overt-covert dimension that might prove decisive when considering whether such ideologies are flaunted or concealed. Furthermore, Figure 1.2 as it stands furnishes a necessary but not sufficient criterion for assessing integration. It represents only an intervening factor in a wider causal matrix of sociocultural historical forces that carry their own momentum. But whatever its limitations, it proves useful in the chapters that follow, at least as a first approximation to an answer for this question: Is the minority integrated into the larger society? Empirical observation will show us what can and what cannot be expected from this line of exploration. At the level of total societies, any conclusions along these lines can be further sharpened and refined by such extended research as public opinion polls, which have not been available for this study.

At the outset, some passing observations may be valuable to the reader who approaches Figure 1.2 for the first time. For those puzzled or uncertain about the validity of the B cell where *both* parties stress centrifugal goals, an example may clarify why such a juxtaposition could make for integration. This conclusion

---

13. What follows is a condensation of the treatment given this issue in Schermerhorn (1970, pp. 77-85).

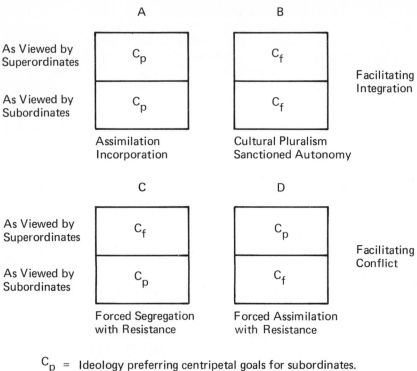

Fig. 1.2   Reciprocal Goal Definitions of Centripetal and Centrifugal Trends of Subordinates (as Viewed by Themselves and Superordinates)

follows from the assumption that integration involves satisfaction of the minority group's modal tendency, no matter whether this be centripetal or centrifugal. Some groups are better satisfied by autonomy, others by assimilation or full incorporation. For example, an Indian sociologist writing about his compatriots in Great Britain begins by telling about the integration of Parsis into the fabric of Indian life, namely that "they have preserved their religion, culture, and their social identity. In contact with others, they act as a caste. By a paradox they have become integrated through voluntary segregation." He then adds, significantly, "This is the form of integration which Indian immigrants in the United Kingdom desire" (Desai, 1963, preface). What he does not say, but certainly implies, is that in India, the dominant group looks favorably on this "voluntary segregation" and that he hopes for the same consideration from the British people.

INDIA AS AN ASIAN SOCIETY

Reflecting on the characteristics of Asian regions, I submit that most nations in the area (including the countries of both south and southeast Asia) show a fairly strong preference for patterns of the B type (cultural pluralism) rather than the A type (assimilation). The reasons for this are a bit obscure, though it appears, on the face of it, that the very diversity and multiplicity of ethnic groups in Asian societies make assimilation an impractical goal, so that a mutual, if often brittle, tolerance among coeval groups developed. Many times even a common language is lacking, and, without such a medium of communication, wholesale assimilation is clearly out of the question.

On the other hand, it is a defensible proposition that India has a more intense preference for the B pattern (sanctioned autonomy) than other nations of the zone. The long history of the caste system, habituating people to the idea that the proper way to deal with social differences is to embody them in particularistic custom and ritual for each variety of human grouping, is a trend that reaches its apogee in Indian civilization. Thus caste becomes a model for stabilizing human relationships, a model with normative force in all segments of society. As already noted, the Parsis fit into this pattern fairly comfortably and, as noted below, the Christians are clearly moving in that direction. Indigenous groups like Jains and Sikhs have already reached an analogous equilibrium with many caste features. Even the Jewish community has been characterized in caste terms (Strizower, 1959). A kind of benevolent plurality is deeply rooted in Indian life. Whether this is the product of charitable Hindu values or mutual exhaustion after a series of conflicts is a question that must be left to the historians, though it is not impossible to see both factors playing an important part.

Much has been written about the similarity of "developing nations" as, for example, in Clifford Geertz's *Old Societies and New States* (1963). But one can go too far in this direction. There is an Asian type of culture and civilization quite distinct from, let us say, the sub-Saharan type in Africa, though both are lumped together in the indiscriminate category of "developing nations." Throughout their long history, Asian societies have had far more cultural contacts, more intermingling of peoples with a long succession of invasions and conquests by alien rulers from afar, often with highly contrasting forms of ethos. If Ralph Linton's thesis is correct, it is just this mixture of influences with its fermentation of ideas and practices that gives rise to urban empires with the development of writing, complex technical exploits, and widespread trade across boundary lines. The increased communication and consequent diffusion of ideas, inventions, and arts brings with it an emergent we call civilization (Linton, 1936, Chap. 3). In sub-Saharan Africa, environmental confines sharply restricted such cross-fertilizing influences to contiguous (and hence culturally similar) peoples. As I have noted elsewhere:

> . . . the interior of Africa has been cut off from the main streams of diffusion (and hence from interstimulation) by two important geographical barriers. First there are few good harbors on its seacoasts; and second,

there is a lack of navigable rivers that reach far into the continent, the sudden drop from a high plateau to lower land causing huge falls in the rivers. [Schermerhorn, 1949, p. 52]

This lack of communication had the effect of suspending sub-Saharan cultures in a nonliterate level, and, without the stimulus of conquering empires from distant areas, an almost unrelieved plurality of small tribal kingdoms remained typical.[14] In Asia, where interregional exchanges of trade and military campaigns took place with great frequency and over vast distances, a succession of urban empires absorbed some tribal units and pushed others to peripheral frontiers. These dominions, with their great and little traditions, remained typical in Asia from ancient times to the intrusion of European colonialism. The ruling stratum in these empires was a literate elite of courtiers, priests, military leaders, and whatever hangers-on proved useful to the rulers, be they traders or artisans. Below were the unlettered mass of peasants who supplied the food and the manpower for the regime. Over time, the gap between upper and lower strata became still wider as the advantages of the aristocracy and the deprivations of the plebeians multiplied and accumulated. Tradition crystallized the pattern into hereditary orders, and with it the assumption of inherent superiority for the elite.

With the coming of colonialism, the contrast between Asia and Africa visibly emerged. In Asia the elite strata became Westernized political leaders, while in Africa a totally new elite was brought into being through the process of Western education. After independence, the political elite of Asian nations had the confidence and assurance that come with habitual dominance, while the new men of authority in Africa struggled to establish an unaccustomed legitimacy to replace that of the now-deposed chiefs. Arbitrary exercise of raw power by relatively inexperienced heads of government proved a serious disadvantage in post-colonial Africa. In Asia, however, the ruling groups were so calmly convinced of their superiority that they often took advantage of their traditional status by totally ignoring the deprivations of lower classes, who belonged in their view to an inferior order of beings and who would not retaliate. This ascriptive ethos took its most extreme form in India, where the caste system was buttressed by an ideology of transmigration that extended status relations into the next world. A legitimized condescension is deeply ingrained in the elite of all Asian societies but shows itself with greatest clarity in India. It is impossible to analyze the minority situation in the subcontinent without recognizing this pervasive sentiment. It has special relevance in the next two chapters, where it is exemplified in its clearest form in the Scheduled Castes.

---

14. There were, of course, occasional local empires like the Zulu but few that impinged on sub-Saharan Africa from the outside until the Arab overruns. This distinguished lower Africa from Mediterranean Africa, which was continuously subject to cross-currents of interchange with maritime peoples.

BIBLIOGRAPHY

Ambedkar, B. R., *Who Were the Shudras?*, Bombay, Thatcher, 1946.

Bierstedt, Robert, *The Social Order,* New York, McGraw-Hill, 1963.

Chaudhuri, N. C., *The Continent of Circe, An Essay on the Peoples of India,* Bombay, Jaico Publishing House, 1965.

Desai, Rashmi, *Indian Immigrants in Britain,* London, Oxford University Press, 1963.

Galanter, Marc, "Law and Caste in India," *Asian Survey* 3 (Nov. 1963), 554-59.

Geertz, Clifford, ed., *Old Societies and New States,* New York, Free Press, 1963.

Grimshaw, Allen D., "The Anglo-Indian Community: The Integration of a Marginal Group," *Journal of Asian Studies* 18 (Feb. 1959), 227-40.

Harrison, Selig, *India: The Most Dangerous Decades,* Princeton, Princeton University Press, 1960.

Isaacs, Harold, *India's Ex-Untouchables,* New York, John Day, 1964.

Lenski, Gerhard, *Power and Privilege. A Theory of Social Stratification,* New York, McGraw-Hill Co., 1966.

Linton, Ralph, *The Study of Man,* New York, Appleton-Century Co., 1936.

Merton, Robert K., *Social Theory and Social Structure,* New York, Free Press, 1968 (enlarged edition).

Morris-Jones, W. H., "Language and Region within the Indian Union," in *India and Ceylon, Unity and Diversity,* edited by Philip Mason, London, Oxford University Press, 1967.

Oren, Stephen A., Religious Groups as Political Organizations: A Comparative Analysis of Three Indian States, unpublished Ph.D. dissertation, Columbia University, 1969.

Park, Robert E., *Human Communities,* New York, Free Press, 1952.

Parsons, Talcott, *Societies, Evolutionary and Comparative Perspectives,* Englewood Cliffs, N. J., Prentice-Hall, 1966.

Price, Charles A., *Southern Europeans in Australia,* Melbourne, Oxford University Press, 1963.

Price, John, "A History of the Outcaste: Untouchability in Japan," in *Japan's Invisible Race, Caste in Culture and Personality,* edited by George De Vos and Hiroshi Wagatsuma, Berkeley, University of California Press, 1966.

Schermerhorn, R. A., *These Our People, Minorities in American Culture,* Boston, D. C. Heath, 1949.

Schermerhorn, R. A., *Comparative Ethnic Relations,* New York, Random House, 1970.

Smith, M. G., "Social and Cultural Pluralism," *Annals of New York Academy of Science* 83, Art. 5 (Jan. 20, 1957), 763-85.

Smith, M. G., "Some Developments in the Analytic Framework of Pluralism," in *Pluralism in Africa,* edited by Leo Kuper and M. G. Smith, Berkeley, University of California Press, 1971.

Srinivas, M. N., *Social Change in Modern India,* Berkeley, University of California Press, 1966.

Strizower, Schifra, "Jews as an Indian Caste," *Jewish Journal of Sociology* 1 (April 1959), 43-57. Reprinted in *Religion, Culture and Society*, edited by Louis Schneider, New York, John Wiley & Sons, 1964.

Strizower, Schifra, *The Bene Israel of Bombay,* New York, Schocken Books, 1971.

Chapter 2

Scheduled Castes: Permanent Pariahs?

India's largest minority, the Scheduled Castes, deserves first place in any review of intergroup relations on the subcontinent — not merely because of its commanding size but because its presence is an inescapable reality quite unmatched by that of other minorities. With the exception of tribal areas with their own populations, every community in India has its Untouchables[1] whose work is needful but despised, its people in demand as laborers, though they themselves are segregated. These baseborn members of the lowly pariahs, 79, 995, 896 as of the 1971 census, constituted more than 14 percent of the all-India population at that time. Especially since independence, the members of these depressed classes are making advances, both political and economic, that are fateful for India's future.

On the face of it, this sector of the population may seem to be a mere aggregate with nothing more than an adventitious unity. However, there are defensible reasons for calling it a minority, some of which have been mentioned

---

1. At the outset, a word about terminology. Although untouchability is constitutionally banned and therefore has no legal existence, educated members of this caste background do not hesitate to use the term "Untouchable," nor shall I. However, the word "Harijan" is offensive to educated Scheduled Caste persons in spite of the fact that Gandhi coined the word as a theological euphemism. As one of the M.P.'s from the Scheduled Castes put it, " 'Harijan' is a bad word introduced by Mahatma Gandhi. In Hindi it means a boy whose father's name is unknown, hence 'children of God.' In the Hindu temples there were, as you know, the devadassi, the girls who took part in the worship ceremonies and also served the priests. Sometimes they gave birth to children and these children were called 'Harijan.' That's why we don't like the name" (H. Isaacs, 1964, p. 41). Though the historical truth of this assertion is denied by scholars, the fact that it is believed by Untouchables gives it validity in their eyes. In the present volume, therefore, I shall avoid the term "Harijan" unless quoted and shall use four other terms interchangeably: "Scheduled Castes," "Untouchables," "outcastes," and the traditional "depressed classes." For the relation of these terms to each other and to the related "backward classes," see A. Béteille (1967), pp. 83-87.

in Chapter 1. Certainly the Scheduled Castes, taken as a whole, are increasing their consciousness of a common solidarity and are attempting to implement the legal equality already granted in spite of popular resistance and the residual forms of discrimination still sanctioned in custom. Official decrees and the floodgates of franchise have heightened their self-awareness and have begun to transform them into a minority group oriented to the struggle for power. In this sense they form a recognizable subsystem of Indian society with limited access to roles and activities characteristic of economic and political institutions as others engage in them. The salience of Untouchables in the national scene makes them a visible target for caste Hindus and is a growing source of concern to their own members (a subject elaborated later in this chapter).

THE COMPARATIVE DIMENSION

As an observable phenomenon, the Scheduled Castes of India have their parallels elsewhere in Asia, notably in Japan where their counterpart, the Buraku, though considerably smaller in size — about 2 percent of the national population (Wagatsuma and De Vos, 1967, p. 117) — bears a relation to the dominant majority uncommonly similar to the situation faced by the outcastes of India. Other examples like these appear, with less clearness of outline, in Tibet and Korea; thus, it has been possible to classify them all together in the first intergroup sequence listed above, "the emergence of pariahs." How these pariah groups were formed in the first place is historically obscure; in both Japan and India, popular views on the subject are much alike. ". . . to the outcaste group is attributed an origin other than that of the majority. . . . In India the untouchables are considered to be descendants of aboriginal tribes conquered by the Aryan invaders. . . [and] in Japan they are popularly held to come from various separate 'races,' including Koreans" (Price, 1967, p. 8).

To fill the gap left by our historical ignorance, a number of writers have advanced theories of greater or lesser plausibility to account for the origin of caste in general and pariah status in particular. Their hypotheses fall into two explanatory themes: a conquest theory and a religious theory. The conquest theory asserts that a people victorious in war enslaved a population of subjects possessing a different culture and physical appearance. Either because the differences were so great, or because overwhelming force was needed to suppress the vassals, conquerors came to despise and fear them, coercing them into menial tasks and eventually placing them beyond the pale of close or intimate contact. The religious theory, on the other hand, envisions a slow and leisurely growth of hallowed ideas about ritually pure (and impure) acts, objects, or persons in the society. Purity may focus on the upper reaches of the community, as in the Pacific Islands where the chief is so sacred that his person is taboo. Conversely, purity and impurity may both be emphasized, the former imputed to the sanctified priests at the top while impurity fastens on the polluted menials at the bottom and on their occupations (De Vos, 1967, pp. 340ff.).

No doubt there is truth in both theories; De Vos (1967, pp. 340ff.) supplements them by outlining hypotheses about the psychological elements inhering in religious feelings about pollution and contamination. It is not necessary to enter into details of his analysis, but it is useful for our purposes here to emphasize the way assignment of rank by religious sanction luxuriates into an intricate graded hierarchy in India. In complexity of social structure and doctrinal apologetics, the Indian system is definitely unique. However, in the sense that it defines the lowest stratum as polluted objects of avoidance, it is not without parallels; such beliefs are shared in a number of Asian countries.[2] With the possible exception of an obscure preliterate African tribe (Nadel, 1954), caste is essentially an Asian phenomenon with examples in Ceylon and Pakistan (Leach, 1959), as well as in the countries already mentioned. However, caste does not proliferate into multiform hierarchies with elaborate provincial variations except in India, where it likewise reaches maximum rigidity as a stratified system.

THE LOWEST STRATUM AND ITS SETTING

The term "Scheduled Castes" originates in the British desire to define the so-called depressed classes in such a way that they could be distinguished on an all-India basis for census purposes. They were categorized or "scheduled" in the 1930s as "Hindu castes, contact with whom entails purification on the part of high-caste Hindus," a de jure definition. Lists or schedules of such castes were drawn up for the purpose of singling out those groups suffering civil and religious disabilities, in order that some provision could be made for their impairments in the hope of removing them. The custom of putting all such lowly castes into a census schedule continued after independence, with the under-standing that details of the schedule would be revised at each decennial census.[3]

It is significant that the definition actually used did not refer to inherent characteristics of the group but only to its regularized relations with other groups. And, as Lelah Dushkin declares,

> Another major feature of the system is that it is by definition temporary and is supposed to last only as long as it is needed. In theory, the protective caste criterion is used to ensure members of the lowest castes a share of power and opportunity for advancement until they can hold their own without it. However, no guidelines have been established for determining when this goal has been reached, and the only provision with a legal time limit on it has been extended each time it was about to expire. [Dushkin, 1972, p. 169]

From a statistical point of view, the category of Scheduled Castes leaves much to be desired. In some cases, it is based on a caste assessment, while in others (as in south India) this criterion would have been too inclusive; thus, in South India

---

2. The reader will doubtless observe a number of similarities between the position of outcastes in India and the blacks in the United States. Gerald Berreman (1960, 1967) outlined these resemblances in plausible fashion, although, by using the term "caste" for both cases, he concealed a number of salient differences, such as the racial one. For a critique of this usage, see my article (Schermerhorn, 1972).

3. Scheduled Tribes, however, did not appear on a schedule until after independence, when the method of their scheduling was defined by the Constitution (see Chap. 4 below).

only the most illiterate and poverty-stricken of the "backward classes" were incorporated (Dushkin, 1972; Béteille, 1967).

In addition to problems of enumeration, there are analytical difficulties. McKim Marriott (1968) contends, for example, that there is an unbroken chain of continuity between the highest and lowest castes, that a caste's position in the hierarchy depends on the transactions of food-giving and service-giving. In general, food givers are higher and food receivers are lower; those who give a service are lower, and those who receive it are higher. It is these reciprocal transactions that Marriott sees as defining the twin notions of purity and pollution. On the basis of his analysis it is possible to construct a matrix of the castes in a village from the Brahman at the top, who gives the most frequently, to the sweeper at the bottom, who serves most often.

Any generalization from Marriott's research is open, however, to criticism on two counts. First, the entire thesis rests on investigation of a single village with no replication in other parts of India to test its wider validity. Second, Marriott rests his whole case on a single set of criteria; that is, he restricts his questions put to the villagers to a single narrow range, such as "Who gives food to whom?" or "Who serves whom?" On this limited basis it may be possible to construct a really elegant continuum that ostensibly represents the working of the system. Had other questions been used to broaden the inquiry, however, the pattern would not have been so neat. Results would have tended to show more and more some marked discontinuity, particularly at the lower end of the scale. The following might have been asked: "Who are given the facilities of the village well?" "Who are denied such facilities?" "Who are permitted to enter the local temple?" "Who are forbidden such entry?" "Who deal with carcasses of dead animals?" "Who are prohibited to engage in such dealings?" "Who are not permitted to live in the main area of the village but are confined to a separate area avoided by others?" If such questions had been used, the sharp break between the Untouchables and the other castes would have been revealed as a palpable, living reality, in striking contrast with the smooth logical construct based on a single criterion.

As already indicated in Chapter 1, the use of *varna* as a point of reference has justifiable relevance when applied to India as a whole (see Chap. 1, p. 17). At the bottom of the Sudra level or below it (depending on which region is doing the defining) are the Untouchables as the most defiled of all, the ones who can pollute all others. In the traditional view, ". . . pollution signifies involvement with life substance and process, which is to be avoided so far as is possible and proper. Polluting things or processes include birth, death, sexual intercourse, bodily excretions, harmful actions, and so on" (Orenstein, 1968, p. 115). Purity seems to denote spirituality, or at least the absence of any biological involvement. Pure things are defiled by polluted things, but the effects of pollution may be removed by exposure to purity (ibid.).

In Hindu law,[4] then, all human beings are polluted to some extent because of the life processes in which they engage. However, the amount of "normal" pollution varies with ritual rank; those of upper varnas have less and those of

---

4. This, of course, is the Brahman version since the Brahmans established and promulgated it.

lower rank more. To preserve their purity, upper varnas avoid all contact with Untouchables. Untouchables are almost without exception restricted to special quarters in rural areas (on the border or outside of each village) and are also prohibited from using the common well or entering the local temple.

It is at the village level that the limited meaning of caste, the *jati,* is basic. Varnas are an all-India phenomenon and serve as categories of reference for the subcastes or jatis that vary from region to region or village to village. Table 2.1 shows the distribution in a single Punjab village.

From the varna point of view, the jatis are local variations of caste categories; from the jati point of view, the varnas are summations of occupational clusters having differential rank. Ritual criteria more or less determine such ranking and appear to have arisen after the jatis originated, eventually defining them in religiolegalistic terms. Endogamy was the rule within each jati and hypergamy[5] the exception.

After independence, extensive migration to towns and cities increased economic pressures, which then changed traditional occupations. Among the Scheduled Castes, 72.2 percent of their rural population is engaged in agriculture, 37.7 percent as cultivators and 34.46 percent as agricultural laborers (intermittent daily work).[6] In one instance, leather workers of Untouchable status (the Jatavs of Agra) migrated to the city, where their standard of living rose appreciably (Lynch, 1968). Such an occurrence is, of course, highly exceptional.

SOLIDARITY AND ENCLOSURE

Consciousness of kind among Scheduled Castes is definitely a variable for the very reason that group identity is more often found at the jati than at the varna level. Cases still exist, particularly in south India, where the stringent intercaste rules prohibiting eating together, taking water from each other, or intermarriage are more rigidly enforced *within* Scheduled Caste groups than among caste Hindus. However, the tide is definitely running in the opposite direction. Among the changes bringing about an awakening of group consciousness among Scheduled Castes in widely different regions are (1) the influence of Gandhi who popularized the campaign for abolishing untouchability and aroused the masses to a new sense of dignity and importance in the cause of national emancipation; (2) the inspiration of Ambedkar, a living example of what an educated Untouchable could accomplish in political action for his people, many of whom he also took with him into the Buddhist fold;[7] (3) the launching of universal

---

5. Hypergamy denotes the marriage of a male belonging to an upper caste to a female of a lower caste. This practice seems to be declining today. For an account of variability in the practice of hypergamy, see K. N. Sharma (1956).

6. Census of India, 1961, Vol. 1, Part V-A(i).

7. I have seen pictures of Ambedkar displayed in the huts of Untouchables in Uttar Pradesh and Andhra Pradesh, and in a political gathering of Scheduled Castes in Mysore. Yet I have been unable to discover Gandhi's picture in these or other places frequented by Untouchables.

TABLE 2.1

Castes at the Local Level in North Punjab*

	Jati	Varna	
	Brahman (priests)	Brahman	The "Twice-Born" caste Hindus
	Rajput (warrior landlords)	Kshatriya	
	Arora (merchants)	Vaisya	
	Khatri (merchants)		
	Jat (cultivators)	Sudra (upper level)	
	Bhati (cultivators)		
	Saini (gardener-cultivators)		
A	Sonar (goldsmiths)		B†
	Ramgaria (carpenters)	Sudra (lower level)	
	Sareri (cotton-carders)		
	Kumhar (potters)		
	Jhinwar (water-carriers)		
	Mahsi (basket-makers)		
	Nai (barbers)		
	Ramdasi (leather workers and agricultural laborers)‡	Untouchable	Avarnas
	Ad Dharmi (leather workers and agricultural laborers)‡		
	Balmiki (scavengers)		

*Table adapted from J.E. Schwartzberg (1968, p. 98) with varna designations added. The aid of Professor K.N. Sharma is gratefully acknowledged.

†The large number of jatis below line AB gives a false impression of an unusually large proportion of people, but in this village the bulk of the population is above line AB.

‡Local schisms within the Chamar subcaste.

franchise after adoption of the Constitution, a powerful stimulus to caste solidarity through uniting at the polls for village, district, state, and national candidates; (4) special appeals of politicians from all parties directed at Scheduled Caste voters as such, including the explicit role of the Republican Party organized to promote the interests of Untouchables at the polls. Each of these influences had its special impact, and their convergent effect heightened the sense of solidarity the Scheduled Castes began to feel with each other.

Contributing to this in a special way is the degree of enclosure characteristic of the minority group. In general, the greater the enclosure (separation of the group from the rest of the society) the easier it is for the dominant group to make the minority a target of coercion, since there are few cross-pressures to mitigate a show of force; yet, it may equally result in ignoring the minority altogether. Conversely, a maximal enclosure makes it possible for the subordinate group to gather its forces unobserved for resistance and attack *or* to withdraw from all dealings with outsiders and avoid them completely. Only sufficient knowledge of antecedent events would supply guidelines for determining which alternatives might be activated.

How can we go about determining the actual degree of enclosure in such a minority group? A tentative answer is to find reliable indicators defining such enclosure. Probably the most significant ones would be (1) endogamy, (2) ecological concentration, (3) institutional duplication, (4) associational clustering, (5) rigidity and clarity of group definition, and (6) segmentary relations of group members with outsiders.[8]

Applying these criteria to the present case, it takes very little demonstration to show that the Scheduled Castes rank high on all indicators. The endogamous barrier between them and members of the upper castes is probably as absolute as any human regulation can be, even recognizing that extramarital unions are excluded from the rules. As for ecological concentration, any observation of Indian villages will confirm the separation of outcaste living quarters from the rest of the community as a practically invariable rule. Since some 90 percent of the Scheduled Castes are rural rather than urban dwellers, their enclosure in hut complexes cut off from the rest of the villages affects the overwhelming majority and is a fact of life widely taken for granted.

In the matter of institutional duplication, the distinction is not so great, though still present to a marked degree. Probably the most complete separation occurs in religious institutions, where the outcastes are still excluded from local temples, even though the law stipulates that the temples be kept open. The de facto situation has changed little since the 1940s when Ambedkar wrote that Untouchables and caste Hindus may have worshiped at the same cults of Rama, Krishna, Vishnu, and Siva but went on to declare, "The fact is that even as followers of recognized cults they cannot be said to have a common religion. The exact and appropriate expression would be to say that they have a similar religion. A common religion means a common cycle of participation. Now, in the observance of the cults there is no such common cycle of participation. The Hindus and the Untouchables practice their cults in segregation so that notwithstanding the similarity of their cults they remain as separate as two aliens do" (Ambedkar, 1946, pp. 183-84).

Before independence the Untouchables were not only excluded from religious institutions but, on a wide scale, from political and economic ones as well. Although this situation has changed – today the Scheduled Castes not only vote but attend the village school – there are still vestiges of social and psychological rejection that set them apart and limit their participation. In politics, one observer in a rural district noted:

> . . . the Harijans must vote for the candidates selected by the employing landlord. In every village I visited, I heard stories of persecution of the Harijan electorate, ranging from forcible confinement of voters to murders. [S. Bannerjee, 1969]

As for the village school, the observer was told by a teacher of Scheduled Caste origin,

---

8. For an exact comparison of different minorities on this dimension, it would be necessary to give each indicator an operational definition facilitating the use of numerical values to treat each of the six items as a variable. Not all of the six indicators are quantifiable (for example, numbers 5 and 6). Furthermore, precise data are lacking in India at the present time to give numerical measures on the other four indicators; enormous expense would be necessary to obtain them on an all-India basis. Hence, we are limited, at this point, to making use of well-established social observations, historical data, and statements by authorities.

"When I went to school for the first time, I was greeted by shouts of 'Chamar, Chamar!' from my schoolmates," says Powar, a school teacher from Bankner. As usual, he was not allowed to drink water from the common tap in the school. [ibid.]

Clubs or societies among the Scheduled Castes are so rare that is is difficult to speak of associational clustering. And though Untouchable members are approached by political or religious organizations of outsiders like the DMK or the Arya Samaj,[9] it is for ulterior purposes of which they are the willing or unwilling tools.

In addition, the social definition of the outcastes is so sharp and unyielding that it constitutes a clear stigma-boundary. So notorious is the label that it overrides achieved status. When a group of Mahars (Marathi Untouchables) from one village converted to Buddhism, they felt forced to leave the village for employment since they now shared the double disrepute of being Untouchable while at the same time attempting to escape their caste duties through wholesale conversion. Though they now called themselves Buddhists, there was little doubt that the villagers still regarded them as Mahars, and renegade Mahars at that (Miller and Kale, 1972, pp. 317-59). The rigidity of group definition is quite unbroken by any endeavor to redefine status by converting to a non-Hindu religion. A similar situation will appear in the discussion of the Christian minority below (Chap. 8).

A final indicator of enclosure is segmentary relations of members with outsiders, which is present to a marked degree among the Scheduled Castes in rural villages where they come in contact with caste Hindus only in specified occupational activities. Such is the licit relationship at the local level where demands of the work task govern interpersonal transactions between high and low castes. Members of the depressed classes who migrate to the city and who are unable to find industrial employment not infrequently revert to their old occupations: sweeping, scavenging, leather work, and so forth. Thus, to a considerable degree, even in the cities segmentary relations with those of higher rank tend to continue.

It is hard to escape the conclusion that the Untouchables occupy an enclave that is maximally enclosed. Those who are not segregated are so ostracized that they live in the society but not of it. Probably no other minority of India, with the possible exception of the tribals, is so effectively insulated from the ongoing collective life of the nation. Were it not for expanding communication links between communities and for the rising clamor of politics, the dissociation of Scheduled Castes from the rest of India would closely resemble conditions in pre-Gandhian days.

CONTROL BY THE DOMINANT GROUP

Structural separation of Untouchables from the caste Hindus is enforced by a de facto monopoly of power in the hands of the upper castes. Far too much emphasis has been placed in the past on the caste system as an arrangement ruled

---

9. A Hindu society dedicated to the reform of Hinduism.

by consensus, while the way this "consensus" has been imposed on the lower orders has been neglected. The full implication of religious revolts against Brahmanism throughout history is not always presented by writers whose upper caste presuppositions could well prevent them from noting what is obvious to outside observers.

Thus Gerald Berreman, while recognizing that the caste system must encompass some shared understandings in order to function at all, nevertheless declares:

> . . . all caste systems are held together in large measure by considerations of relative power among castes — power expressed physically, economically, politically and socially. . . . In this they resemble plural societies, with the dominant caste(s) exercising the power which maintains the *status quo*, just as does the dominant group in a plural society. . . . There is invariably an official rationale which indicates that the system functions by mutual consent — by consensus. Malfunctioning or change is likely to be attributed, therefore, to alien intervention. Actually, it is more often a result of changed power relations among groups, with consequent attempts by some of these groups to realize formerly suppressed aspirations. [Berreman, 1967, p. 54, By permission]

The exercise of this power by caste Hindus shows marked variability; placed on a continuum it would show its highest force in rural areas where it is informal, direct, and unrestrained, and a minimal pressure in metropolitan centers where it is more formal, indirect, and covert. The Scheduled Castes have full visibility in the villages and are an easy target, but in the cities they find it fairly easy to become anonymous and to elude continuous surveillance.

It is also in the villages that the economic power of the landlords and moneylenders is imposed most heavily on cultivators and landless laborers. Public opinion in these communities is likely to favor such authority figures; to oppose them is to lay oneself open to severe reprisals, and most villagers are sufficiently vulnerable to avoid taking that risk.

As long as Untouchables remain in the small community, they are restricted to traditional or, at best, low menial occupations. "In the villages in which they live they cannot engage in any trade or occupation,[10] for owing to untouchability no Hindu will deal with them" (Elayaperumal Report, Part II, p. 76). And in the cities, it is reported that unions in both private and public sectors discriminate against the Scheduled Castes to such a degree that the Parliamentary Committee investigating the condition of Untouchables specifically recommended that they be given the right to organize their own unions (Elayaperumal Report, Parts IV and V, pp. 105-06).[11] There is also some

---

10. The reference here is obviously to commercial and other high caste jobs.

11. This committee, commissioned in 1965, reported back to Parliament in 1969. Most, if not all, members of the committee were from the Scheduled Castes, which raises the question of bias. One must be on the alert to such criticism, though careful reading of the entire report shows it to be thoroughly documented, including several accounts of official obstruction to fact-finding in individual cases. As for the opinions expressed, there is no question that group interests have their influence, but as one Scheduled Caste official told the writer, "If I try to support or defend any of my people in trouble, I am accused of being communal. Yet I find only too often that no one else will exert himself in their behalf."

evidence that resistance to outcaste entry into new occupations originates in a number of Sudra castes competing for the same jobs.

COLONY TO NATION: LEGAL AND SOCIAL CONSEQUENCES

Two views on the future of Untouchables developed before independence. The first was the charity policy; the second, the activist-cum-compensation policy.

Gandhi himself espoused the charity policy, beginning his appeal by proclaiming untouchability as India's greatest sin which must be abolished in a revitalized and purified nation.[12] He set a prime example by adopting an Untouchable girl as daughter in his own household. In public life he founded the Harijan journal, proclaimed Harijan Day, helped organize Harijan boards, and founded the Harijan Sevak Sangh (HSS) to promote reform of untouchability and minister to the needs of the depressed classes. The very name Harijan Sevak Sangh signified a society of those dedicated to serving the Untouchables. The HSS set in motion many systematic efforts to provide scholarships, medical aid, village wells, and trade schools for Scheduled Caste members in different regions. This program has continued down to the 1970s.

Ambedkar vigorously opposed the charity view, regarding it as a palliative. He attacked the philanthropy of the Harijan Sevak Sangh as a paternalistic condescension by those of upper status to the lowly, benighted people beneath. The social distance between upper and lower castes was perpetuated, in Ambedkar's view, by such a policy. He took keen pleasure in pointing out that the HSS once had Untouchables on its board, only to drop them from their positions. Gandhi himself approved the exclusion of outcastes from membership in the organization, and this policy finally became official (Ambedkar, 1946, p. 142).

In place of charity, Ambedkar advocated an activist-cum-compensation policy of his own. During negotiations with the British, he pleaded for separate electorates for the depressed classes, a plan which the British partly approved at the second session of the Round Table Conference in 1932. When Gandhi opposed the plan with a fast unto death, Ambedkar retracted and accepted a place for Untouchables in the general electorate (Poona Pact). However, he contended that under this new scheme only Untouchable candidates acceptable to the prejudiced upper castes could be nominated or elected: that is, only those favored by the Congress party, nearly a monopoly at the time, which was dominated by upper caste leaders (Ambedkar, 1946, pp. 40-102).

Since, in his view, the lowest disadvantaged castes now had their path to political action effectively blocked, Ambedkar turned to another familiar strategy, formerly advanced by the British as part of their colonial program. This was the policy of compensation, also trenchantly named "protective discrimination." The policy assumes that the disabilities suffered by the outcastes can be compensated for in the long run by granting them special privileges of a temporary nature. Examples of these privileges were educational scholarships,

---

12. For a systematic appraisal of Gandhi's oft-changing views on caste, see D. Dalton (1967).

reserved seats in legislatures, and specially designated places in the government bureaucracy. Since Ambedkar was chairman of the committee to draft the Constitution, he had the rare opportunity to see that his ideas were embodied in the document, subject to the concurrence of the Constituent Assembly. Two steps followed. The first was an enunciation of the principle of equality – a major assumption without which the whole notion of compensation would have no meaning. The second was to follow up with enabling clauses that permitted Parliament to make a special case for those who suffered from prominent disabilities. The relevant passages appear in Part III, Articles 14-19, of the Constitution.[13]

Part III, Article 15 (4), places the stamp of approval on methods of educational compensation previously instituted by the British from the 1920s onward in the states (see map of British Colonial India) of Madras, Bihar, Bengal, Bombay, Central Provinces, Punjab, United Provinces, and the princely states of Baroda, Travancore, Cochin, and Mysore (*Handbook on Scheduled Castes and Scheduled Tribes,* 1968, pp. 94-99).

Compensation as a tool of government action thus rested on British precedent. Certainly Ambedkar regarded it as a powerful mechanism for equalizing the skills and achievements of the depressed classes in comparison with the upper castes. He envisioned a two-pronged attack. The first would consist of government statutory regulations; the second would be political demands advanced by the Scheduled Castes organized as an interest group. He recognized, however, that the second tactic would be effective only after long and strenuous effort, even after he organized the Scheduled Caste Federation (later to become the Republican party). Owing to the uncertain fortunes of party activism, however, he fell back upon the compensatory technique as one already familiar to the citizenry; it required, of course, considerable confidence in the efficacy of direct government action.

Ambedkar's optimism in this respect, cautious as it was, has hardly been justified. For one thing, the whole semantics of the compensatory approach seems to derive from the Victorian vocabulary, where benevolence is condescending and the upper strata are conscious of leaving their elevated position to descend long enough for a donation of largesse to the lower orders. The attitude of pity accompanying the action thus maintains social distance while displaying generosity. The very nomenclature employed encourages such condescension: for instance, "backward classes," "the weaker sections of the people," "disabilities," "protection," "uplift," and many others.

Embedded in these innocent linguistic forms is a social *Weltanschauung* resembling the charity ideology, except that the new action called for is in the public rather than the private sector. As the compensatory policy became official, identified with government administration, three significant consequences followed.

First, the spelling out of rules and regulations for bureaucratic implementation of the policy gave the program an impersonality that often belied any humanitarian sentiments that might have initiated the plan. Secondly, by

---

13. Paragraph 4 in Article 15 and Paragraph 4 in Article 16 were both added by later amendment to the Constitution and cannot be directly attributed to Ambedkar, although they embody his ideas.

shifting responsibility for action to government agencies, the dominant caste Hindus could delegate the fulfillment of duties to other hands and absolve themselves of action on their own behalf; eventually it became possible to forget the whole thing. Evidence from public opinion polls is not available, but the sociological observer gets the unmistakable impression (confirmed by private interviews with qualified specialists) that the condition of depressed classes is widely ignored by the upper castes. Only when political leaders of the left bring such questions to public attention do they seem to receive recognition; even then it is common to accuse leftists of crass appeals for votes. Third and finally, the compensatory policy encourages dependency among those who benefit from it. With long habituation, immunities and special privileges grow into permanent crutches that prevent attainment of genuine equality through achievement. Leaning on these benefits can insidiously undermine the very qualities of dignity and autonomy that reformers have so long desired.[14]

Historically, the ghastly slaughter accompanying partition focused attention on the Muslims to the neglect of other minority groups. In the holocaust of those days, any disabilities suffered by the Scheduled Castes no doubt seemed trivial. In 1951, Ambedkar commented that the Congress party manifesto of that year was strongly slanted in the direction of the Muslims to the total neglect of the Scheduled Castes (Ambedkar, 1969, pp. 53-55). Three years later he quoted Nehru's memorable words, "I do not recognize that there is such a problem as that of the untouchables. There is a general problem of the economically poor and the problem of the untouchables is a part of that problem. It will take its place and receive its attention along with other problems. There is no occasion, no purpose in bestowing any special thought upon it" (ibid, p. 94). More than a decade later, Muslims were still capturing major attention in discussions about minorities. For example, G. S. Ghurye's lengthy work, *Social Tensions in India* (1968), analyzed minority conflicts throughout India, devoting his account primarily to Muslims in eight chapters out of fourteen and giving no space whatever to the Scheduled Castes. His selection appears to be representative, reflecting the views of the majority.

As India passed from colonial to national status, legitimation of its new government (an issue with explosive potential for all new states) was considerably complicated by the question of Untouchability. This issue evoked considerable ambivalence on the part of the public. Popular utterances of Gandhian leaders criticized the practice of Untouchability quite frequently, especially when recalling the memory of their revered leader. Yet it became painfully clear that such words found less and less echo among those who

---

14. Too much reliance on compensatory methods to solve the problems of the disadvantaged can go to ridiculous lengths. It is reported that the Sukhadia Ministry in Rajasthan announced in the fall of 1969 that it was raising the percentage of reserved government posts for Scheduled Castes and Scheduled Tribes from 12½ to 28. In previous years, however, the Rajasthan government had already reserved 30 percent of the vacancies for ex-Servicemen and 20 percent more for goldsmiths. With the new figure of 28 percent for "backward communities," a total 78 percent of all vacancies are on the reserved list before members of the general public have any chance at all. This is a *reductio ad absurdum*. Eventually its legality will doubtless be challenged, since the Supreme Court already ruled that not over 50 percent of such vacancies can be reserved (Kaul, 1969).

listened. The élan toward equality had already reached its high point with the adoption of the Constitution. A gradual descent to traditional values and practices soon followed. When weighed against the habits and sacred customs of centuries, the influence of Gandhi, however charismatic, could not tip the scales in such a radical new direction. No doubt the Constitution was a statement of principles. What was yet to be proved was its efficacy as a plan of action.

It may never be known how much private misgiving or secret opposition arose in response to the forthright declarations abolishing untouchability in the Constitution. Yet in all likelihood there must have been covert resistance among conservative Hindus who were, after all, more numerous than their liberal and Westernized colleagues. The latter, however, dominated the Constituent Assembly, voting for the declaration of rights and for the clause outlawing untouchability.

In contests that arose over reserved seats for Parliament and the state assemblies, it soon became apparent to the Congress party that it could maintain control by nominating Scheduled Caste candidates in the areas where they had a substantial share of the electorate. The subservient and lowly outcastes, swelling with pride at the sight of their fellows in places of honor, were inspired to support the Congress even though material benefits failed to follow. Congress leadership, drawn from the upper castes and large landholders in rural areas, could rest assured that their entrenched position would not be disturbed by successful agitation for lower caste rights. Occasional campaign rhetoric extolling generosity toward the depressed classes, coupled with inaction on behalf of law enforcement (upholding the newly established rights of Untouchables), revealed the ambivalence of party leaders.

UNTOUCHABILITY OFFENSES ACT

During early years of the new republic there was still enough forward momentum to press for legislation to implement the enabling clauses affecting untouchability in the Constitution. By 1955, Parliament passed the Untouchability Offenses Act (UOA), which was, in its own terms, "an Act to prescribe punishment for the practice of 'Untouchability,' for the enforcement of any disability arising therefrom, and for matters connected therewith." In effect, the statute was directed against "enforcement of any disability" and hence those acts perpetrated directly against specific persons, not merely against the usual social avoidances that did not involve transitive action. The Act prescribed punishment for restraining outcastes from entering temples, bathing in sacred waters, having access to shops, rivers, burial grounds, public conveyances, hotels, and restaurants; for preventing the observance of religious ceremonies, the use of jewelry and finery, admission to hospitals, and selling goods or services; and even punishment for use of boycott against Untouchables or excommunicating those who refused to practice Untouchability. These and other active offenses were made punishable by fine or imprisonment.

Those who have examined the evidence most thoroughly have concluded that the UOA has been notably ineffective in operation. The Elayaperumal Committee found that most state agencies had no check on the distribution of the UOA and therefore could not tell whether local officials had been reached or not. Of the 500 copies of the Act published by the state of Orissa in 1961 (six years after its passage), 483 were still lying about undistributed some four years later. The committee also found a large number of police officers who did not even know that the UOA was on the statute books. Investigating in Uttar Pradesh, the committee found in Sitapur district that not a single person in the rural areas knew that the UOA existed and that only two police officers out of thirty could tell anything at all about the provisions of the Act. In many states government officials were equally ignorant. In some cases the committee reported that "villagers" (doubtless Scheduled Caste members) complained that police officials seemed to know little or nothing about the new federal law forbidding the practice of untouchability (Elayaperumal Report, Part I, pp. 103-14).

Loopholes in the enforcement provisions and the general failure to implement the UOA, increasing with the years, have been amply demonstrated in meticulous detail by Marc Galanter (1969, 1972) and need not be repeated here. For the many reasons he advances, it seems fair to conclude that current legislation to enforce constitutional rights of the Scheduled Castes is generally ineffective. Apathy and indifference make it effectively a dead letter.[15]

---

15. In late November 1976, the truncated Lok Sabha (one without an opposition) passed a new Protection of Civil Rights Act closing two important loopholes in the UOA: prosecution is now noncompoundable (i.e., cannot be avoided by payment of a fee), and violation of the law under the new dispensation entails a *minimum* penalty, whereas the UOA specified only a *maximum* penalty. This is a definite improvement in the law itself, though whether these features will be implemented in practice remains to be seen *(Overseas Hindustan Times,* Dec. 2, 1976).

BIBLIOGRAPHY

Ambedkar, B. R., *Thus Spoke Ambedkar* (Selected Speeches), Vol. II, edited by Bhagwan Das, Jullundur, Bheem Patrika Publications, 1969.

Ambedkar, B. R., *What Congress and Gandhi Have Done to the Untouchables,* Bombay, Thacker & Co., 1946.

Bannerjee, Sumanta, "The Cast(e) Outs," *See* (No. 5, April-June 1969), 19ff.

Berreman, Gerald D., "Stratification, Pluralism and Interaction: A Comparative Analysis of Caste," in *Caste and Race: Comparative Approaches,* edited by Anthony de Reuck and Julie Knight, A CIBA Foundation Volume, London, J. and A. Churchill, 1967.

Béteille, André, "The Future of the Backward Classes: The Competing Demands of Status and Power," in *India and Ceylon: Unity and Diversity,* edited by Philip Mason, London, Oxford University Press, 1967.

Dalton, Dennis, "The Gandhian View of Caste and Caste after Gandhi," in *India and Ceylon: Unity and Diversity,* edited by Philip Mason, London, Oxford University Press, 1967.

De Vos, George, "Essential Elements of Caste: Psychological Determinants in Structural Theory," in *Japan's Invisible Race, Caste in Culture and Personality,* edited by George De Vos and Hiroshi Wagatsuma, Berkeley, University of California Press, 1967.

Dushkin, Lelah, "Scheduled Caste Politics," in *The Untouchables in Contemporary India,* edited by J. Michael Mahar, Tucson, Arizona, University of Arizona Press, 1972.

Elayaperumal Report, brief designation for *Report of the Committee on Untouchability, Economic and Educational Development of the Scheduled Castes,* Cyclostyled, New Delhi, Ministry for Law and Social Welfare, Government of India, 1969.

Galanter, Marc, "Untouchability and the Law," *Economic and Political Weekly* IV (Nos. 1 and 2, Jan. 1969), 131-70.

Galanter, Marc, "The Abolition of Disabilities – Untouchability and the Law," in *The Untouchables in Contemporary India,* edited by J. Michael Mahar, Tucson, Arizona, University of Arizona Press, 1972.

Ghurye, G. S., *Social Tensions in India,* Bombay, Popular Prakashan, 1968.

Handbook on Scheduled Castes and Scheduled Tribes, Government of India, Office of the Commissioner for Scheduled Castes and Scheduled Tribes, 1968.

Kaul, T. N., "Plight of Harijans in Rajasthan," *Times of India,* Oct. 3, 1969.

Leach, E. R., ed., *Aspects of Caste in South India, Ceylon and North-West Pakistan,* Cambridge, Cambridge University Press, 1959.

Lynch, Owen M., "The Politics of Untouchability: a Case from Agra, India," in *Structure and Change in Indian Society,* edited by Milton Singer and Bernard Cohn, Chicago, Aldine Publishing Co., 1968.

Marriott, McKim, "Caste Ranking and Food Transactions: A Matrix Analysis," in *Structure and Change in Indian Society,* edited by Milton Singer and Bernard Cohn, Chicago, Aldine Publishing Co., 1968.

Miller, Robert J., and Pramodh Kale, "The Burden on the Head is Always There," in *The Untouchables in Contemporary India,* edited by J. Michael Mahar, Tucson, Arizona, University of Arizona Press, 1972.

Nadel, S. F., "Caste and Government in Primitive Society," in *Journal of the Anthropological Society of Bombay* VIII (1954), 9-22.

Orenstein, Henry, "Toward a Grammar of Defilement in Hindu Sacred Law," in *Structure and Change in Indian Society*, edited by Milton Singer and Bernard Cohn, Chicago, Aldine Publishing Co., 1968.

Price, John, "A History of the Outcaste: Untouchability in Japan," in *Japan's Invisible Race, Caste in Culture and Personality*, edited by George De Vos and Hiroshi Wagatsuma, Berkeley, University of California Press, 1967.

Schermerhorn, R. A., "A Note on the Comparative View of Caste," *Phylon* 33 (No. 3, Fall 1972), 254-59.

Schwartzberg, Joseph E., "Caste Regions of the North Indian Plain," in *Structure and Change in Indian Society,* edited by Milton Singer and Bernard Cohn, Chicago, Aldine Publishing Co., 1968.

Sharma, K. N., "Hypergamy in Theory and Practice," *Journal of Research* (Kanpur) 3 (No. 1, 1956).

Wagatsuma, Hiroshi and George De Vos, "The Ecology of Special Buraku," in *Japan's Invisible Race, Caste in Culture and Personality,* edited by George De Vos and Hiroshi Wagatsuma, Berkeley, University of California Press, 1967.

Chapter 3

Scheduled Castes:
Mobility and Integration

The restrictions and boundaries that hold Untouchables in a lowly and despised position have not been completely irrevocable. Historically, there were times and occasions when bonds actually slackened, however mildly, and hopeful members ventured to escape. Such forms of release deserve attention. In earlier centuries the main avenue of deliverance was through the Hindu heresies: Jainism, Sikhism, and smaller sects; these will receive attention in the chapters below. Buddhism, too, was a temporary outlet, but it declined in numbers and importance within India until the twentieth century. Before the nineteenth century, perhaps the chief avenue of escape was through conversion to Islam, especially in Bengal in the thirteenth and fourteenth centuries where mass adoptions of the alien religion occurred (Spear, 1967, p. 34). In this chapter I shall examine only those attempts to escape traditional status that have occurred in the modern period, especially the twentieth century.

RELIGIOUS AVENUES OF ESCAPE

Movement into the Christian fold was, for a time, of primary importance. Though a more detailed account of growth in the Christian community will appear in Chapter 8 below, it is worth mentioning here that new adherents to that faith increased manyfold from the ranks of the depressed classes in the years before the 1930s. In Uttar Pradesh (then the United Provinces) where conversions to Christianity began well before the turn of the century, J. W. Pickett reports in 1933 that a quarter of a million sweepers had already become professing Christians. Mass movements into Christianity occurred simultaneously in the Deccan, where the number doubled and trebled before 1930. Only in the latter part of this period did more than a few scattered members of the upper castes enter the Christian ranks (Pickett, 1933, pp. 50-51). Although actual statistics on the proportion of new Christians from Untouchable ranks are unavailable, Pickett (1933, p. 56) and others who investigated mass movements into Christianity during the first third of the twentieth century refer to outcaste converts with unvarying frequency while mentioning enlistments from caste Hindus as exceptional and worthy of special comment. However, the conversion of multitudes from the depressed classes into Christianity declined after the 1930s with the growth of the nationalist movement and its attack on British colonialism with which Christianity was identified. In the years of agitation for Swaraj, it became so unpopular to become a Christian, let alone to be one, that this channel of escape lost its attraction for the Untouchables.

As *pukka* Indian manners and customs gained a new ascendancy in the 1940s and 1950s, the urge for a new religious status among the Scheduled Castes moved toward more indigenous patterns. This process was led by B. R. Ambedkar after he tried unsuccessfully to raise the status of Untouchables by agitating for the adoption of some upper caste practices and for the opening of the temples to the depressed classes. When all such measures failed, he "decided to reject all claims to Hinduism by converting to another religion" (Zelliot, 1972, p. 76). Late in his life this resolve crystallized into a firm decision to stage a public conversion to Buddhism; in Nagpur, on March 18, 1956, Ambedkar took with him 2,000 members of the Jatav (Untouchable) caste in a solemn ceremony pledging allegiance to the Buddha whose path of salvation was open to all without caste distinctions.[1] This symbolic act opened a kind of sluice gate into a new and attractive faith whose origins were completely Indian. In an incredibly short time a mass movement into Buddhism (especially among the Mahars of Maharashtra) attracted 3.5 million former Untouchables into the new fold. After the initial impetus, however, the formation of Buddhist societies, chiefly in western but also in northern and southern India, failed to show much continued growth. One reason for this failure was the "absence of a strong central organization and the lack of communication between local units" (Fiske, 1972, p. 123). Local chapters of Buddhist societies are reported to have internal vitality, but there seems to be little urgency or demand for further proselytization. The probable conclusion is that the Buddhist outlet for the Scheduled Castes will be used less and less in the future.[2]

CONTRAVENTION OF CASTE RULES

In the freer atmosphere of independent India following the adoption of the Constitution and the improved political role of the depressed classes, there developed a new willingness on the part of Scheduled Caste members to test the

---

1. Ambedkar (1957) adopted an interpretation of Buddhism strictly unique to him and considerably different from Hinayana and Mahayana versions adopted elsewhere, but especially relevant for the social condition of the Untouchables.

2. The 1971 Census reports that the Buddhists of India had a growth rate (1951-61) of 2267.01 percent but that this shrank to only 17.20 percent in 1961-71, a figure below the growth rate of the total population. (Census of India 1971, Series 1, Paper 2 of 1972. Religion, p. 22.)

legal and formal equality that was theirs. Even in the villages where the outcastes perform functional and menial roles of a polluted character, they have begun a continual probing of the traditional boundary lines defining "proper behavior." When these attempts are ignored or disregarded, they make possible new habits that violate the old regulations without arousing much public notice. In other cases, however, such deviations from the old caste rules, no matter how minor, excite and inflame the anger of caste Hindus, who react with heat or violence to what they regard as perfidy.

John Dollard (1938, pp. 19-20; quoted in Williams, 1947, p. 57) declares that "when there is an actual threat to the dominance of the in-group, socially legitimated hostilities may appear." It is not necessary, however, for the threat to be objective in the sense that it is independently verifiable. If the superordinates *perceive* a threat, it *is* one for them and they act accordingly. In fact, the very meaning of "threat" is inseparable from its social definition by a person or group. In the villages of India, any departure from authorized behavior by Scheduled Caste members may quickly be regarded as a threat to a whole system of approved conduct (dharma) and to those in a position to enforce it. The natural response is to suppress and restrain (by violence if necessary) those who step out of their "place" as defined by caste rules of immemorial sanctity. In reality, the reaction of the dominant group (caste Hindus) falls on a continuum from mild to savage sanctions.

If the examples of Japan and the United States have any parallel in India, we could hypothesize that, in the early stages of subordinate violation of traditional rules, attacks all come from the dominant group. However, both M. N. Srinivas and A. Béteille predict that, as the Scheduled Castes insist more and more on their rights, conflicts may become more numerous (Srinivas, 1966, p. 93; Béteille, 1967, p. 113). Béteille even predicts that "Where Harijans are more or less evenly matched in numerical strength with caste Hindus, a certain amount of tension or even violence is likely to become a part of the system." He does not say, however, whether this violence will be one-sided or reciprocal. If the experience of Japan and the United States has relevance here, the clashes and conflicts may proceed from an early stage in which the violence comes from the dominant group and may then gradually change to full engagement of both sides, with the minority initiating attacks independently (Totten and Wagatsuma, 1967, pp. 63ff.; Killian, 1968, pp. 147ff.).

DYNAMIC TRADITIONALISM VERSUS DISCREET MODERNITY

Members of the Scheduled Castes are experiencing rapid change and the tides of transition as they advance toward a new stage in the life of the nation. Alterations in the legal structure, rapid growth of an urban-cum-industrial economy, and widespread opportunities for advanced education quicken the pace. They open up avenues of escape which are more legitimate from the standpoint of the wider society. Four of these channels of mobility are so significantly interrelated that it should clarify matters to consider them all together. The first two are tendencies or processes that go by the names of Sanskritization and Westernization.

Sanskritization refers to lower caste adoption of upper caste (more particularly Brahman) behavior in order to buttress a claim to higher position in the caste hierarchy. The usual procedure is for an entire jati to make concerted changes in one or more of the following: occupation, customs, ritual practices, style of life, and ideology. After making these changes and continuing them for a long time (a generation or more), the low caste then makes a claim to higher position. This claim may or may not be accepted by others. The process is a slow one, and several decades or more may be required before the new caste label and status are legitimated by caste Hindus — often accompanied, to be sure, by trails of doubt. Rationalization of the higher status (higher than the traditional one) is not infrequently provided by a caste myth such as the following:

> Yes, we are drummers by occupation, but our ancestor was a Brahman who married a drummer woman. By rights, therefore, we should be Brahmans, but in such cases the high castes here go against the usual custom and assign the child the caste of his low caste parent rather than of his father, from whom a person inherits everything else.

So common is this mythologizing that Gerald Berreman, who gives the above example, declares, "I have not encountered a low caste group which did not claim high caste ancestry or origin" (Berreman, 1967, p. 310).

If Berreman's experience is germane to other parts of India and not to the northern region alone, the inference would be that successful Sanskritization is rare. Discussion of the issue by Srinivas (1966, p. 75) gives the distinct impression that it is only the intermediate castes that gain higher status by this method, since, he declares, ". . . it is only the two ends of the hierarchy which are fixed." Doubtless there are regional differences in this regard. In Madras, the outcaste toddy-tappers known as Shanans became Nadars, eventually recognized in both law and social esteem as having broken the pollution barrier (Rudolph, 1965).[3]

In India, the characteristics of Sanskritization may be summarized in the following descriptions: (1) a form of group rather than individual mobility; (2) a process typically marked by copying the style of life set by upper castes; (3) a program involving acceptance of the total hierarchy but not the status assigned to the lowly caste making higher claims; (4) a method using tradition as a stepping stone to a new and more prestigeful status (in the myths of "dynamic traditionalism," ideas from ancient writers and polytheistic beliefs are freely used); and (5) a plan with almost impossible chances of success for those at the bottom of the caste hierarchy.

The second mode of mobility is Westernization, often regarded as the polar opposite of Sanskritization. Without attempting a formal definition, I shall fall back on Béteille's (1967, p. 104) description of Westernization: "Broadly speaking, the process refers to the adoption by a community of Western elements in dress, habits, manners, and customs. An important agency of

---

3. Some attempts at Sanskritization were made by the Jatavs of Agra, but, as they were eventually relinquished in favor of other methods, I am not including them here. For the mixed experiences of the Jatavs, see other references to them in the present chapter.

Westernization in this sense is the modern educational system, which is associated with new norms and values, and new symbols of prestige." Since migration to the cities brings increased contact with customs and artifacts of the West, other writers feel that Westernization is chiefly, though not wholly, a matter of urbanization (Gould, 1961).

During the nineteenth and twentieth centuries, especially before independence, Westernization was largely a Brahman affair. A few Christians, including a number of Anglo-Indians, with higher education shared in the process, but it was chiefly the Brahmans who absorbed Western education and, with it, increasing place in the professions and the civil service. After 1948, Western education began to have much wider dissemination among all castes, including the very lowest. In fact, special reserved scholarships for Scheduled Caste students gave them certain advantages that were superior to those of the castes above them in the hierarchy.

Expenditures for the five-year plans indicate how important reserved scholarships became for the Westernization of the lower orders. In the First Plan, the combined expenditures of the Union Ministry of Education and the state governments on post-matriculation scholarships amounted to 5.46 crores of rupees.[4] In the Second Plan this amount went up to 18.28 crores, and in the Third Plan, to 31.81 crores. All of these were allotted to Scheduled Caste students. Another set of figures is perhaps more significant. In 1944-45, the number of post-matriculation scholarships for Scheduled Caste students was only 114, but by 1966-67 it had reached 89,907. Annual expense for these scholarships during the same period rose from 47,697 to 43,765,839 rupees (*Handbook on Scheduled Castes*, 1968, pp. 101, 106). This showing is impressive on any scale and shows that the commitment of government to educational improvement has been a growing one.

Not nearly so clear, however, is the extent of Westernization resulting from this outlay. To quantify such an ambiguous condition would be impossible. In view of the fact that some of this education was in vernacular tongues and some in English, it would be useful to discover the proportion of each. However, there are no systematic studies of Scheduled Caste students attaining higher education either during their school careers or in the period of later employment. Scholastic records, choice of vocation, later success in an occupation, employment or unemployment rates – all are unknown.[5] And as Harold Isaacs (1964, p. 81) further comments, "There are thousands of Scheduled Caste teachers now but no one knows how many."

---

4. One crore = 10 million.

5. It might be expected that the Ministry of Education which supplies the grants would require some knowledge of the results that accrue from such tremendous outlays in order to improve the program over the years. However, to my knowledge, the Ministry has initiated no research along these lines, nor has the Commissioner for Scheduled Castes and Scheduled Tribes included such data in annual reports. Such omissions are consistent with other forms of widespread avoidance of knowledge about Scheduled Caste conditions, whether due to disinterest or distaste is difficult to determine. For example, most research on the community life of Untouchables is done by foreign scholars, and it is practically impossible to find any social scientist of Indian origin who has specialized in this field of investigation.

From the occasional sampling by Isaacs, it appears that college and university posts are increasingly occupied by educated men from outcaste backgrounds but that they tend to lose their identifiability as they rise to these positions. If his information is representative, the concealing of identity is even more prevalent for Scheduled Caste members who "make it" into middle and upper echelons of business and commerce (Isaacs, 1964, pp. 92-93). It would seem that discretion is regarded as a necessary policy for Westernized former outcastes in the private sector. Isaacs' impression, though an unproved one, is that "Almost all educated ex-Untouchables move into government jobs" (Isaacs, 1964, pp. 92-93). Since the jobs are frequently theirs by reservation, they must declare their status to enter. Only after transfer or promotion can they hope to hide their identity.

The paradox of the situation existing in public sector employment is that, as long as the outcaste remains in his traditional occupation and place, he has a recognized social location, even though it is the lowest of all. If, however, he wishes to raise his status by entering Government employ, he must ordinarily do so by declaring his status in traditional terms; that is, he must stoop to conquer. As many of these men describe their experience, the stooping seems more obvious than any sense of conquering. On the other hand, if the Untouchable seeks employment in the private sector by taking advantage of his Constitutional rights, he tries to enter a condition of castelessness. While others are citizens with a caste location, he makes an effort to conceal his low caste origins by stressing his educational qualifications alone. In a sense, he is a citizen without caste anchorage, a kind of free-floating entity. As soon as he seeks employment in the private sector after climbing the educational ladder and becoming Westernized, he tends to take one of the alternatives: (1) he hides his identity; (2) he seeks a new identity by changing his religion to Buddhism; or (3) he seeks the same result in Christianity. The third possibility, as already mentioned, is less popular than it used to be a generation or so ago, and the second hardly conceals anything because the overwhelming majority of Indian Buddhists are former Untouchables, as everybody knows.

Westernization may therefore be summarized as (1) a form of individual rather than group mobility, (2) a process marked by imitation of the style of life introduced by Western models, (3) a mode of adaptation seeking to escape the handicaps of destiny by the contingent triumphs of opportunity, (4) a method that rejects Indian tradition in favor of an imported model that seems more favorable to economic and political advancement, and (5) a program that repudiates a fixed hierarchy in favor of equality of opportunity and the achievement ethic.

To state the contrast in another way: Sanskritization takes Brahmans and certain other high caste members as the typical reference group, whereas Westernization takes professionals or business leaders highly educated in the Western mode as the reference group.

Of these two patterns of mobility, Scheduled Castes have almost completely chosen Westernization, and in this choice they have been notably assisted by educational grants from the central government. For castes in the middle levels of the hierarchy, or even some of the well-placed Sudras, Sanskritization holds out some possibilities for advance, but for the Scheduled Castes it is hardly a choice at all. Even Westernization in one of its forms — migration to urban areas — has definite shortcomings; upper castes may leave the rural regions with ease, but the lower are often marooned on the land (Gould, 1961).[6] Sanskritization had a certain transient success in recent times among the Jatavs of Agra, but the group abandoned this tactic in favor of political gains and mass conversion to Buddhism (Lynch, 1968, pp. 209-40; Lynch, 1972, pp. 97-112). Politics as an important lever for manipulating the instruments of accomplishment has received little attention; it will now be considered in more detail.

POLITICAL MOBILITY: ITS DUAL POTENTIALS

A fact deserving more emphasis than it usually receives is the abruptness with which all Indian life was politicized with the sudden adoption of universal franchise. In order to win elections after independence, every group affiliation became endowed with new vigor and potency. Caste, faction, village, district, region, religion, and numerous other collectives were mobilized by politicians and parties for protean goals of every description. In this whirlpool of activity, Scheduled Castes entered with the rest to seek new victories, formerly unattainable.

The political structure enveloping the depressed classes had led to bifurcation of their activities in this field. Unable to secure the separate electorate demanded in pre-independence days, the Scheduled Castes had to settle for reservation of seats at state and national levels, which actually means that it is the non-Scheduled-Caste majority that elects the Scheduled Caste representatives from a slate of selected Scheduled Caste nominees. The major question then becomes: Who chooses the Scheduled Caste candidates, of whom there appear to be a fixed number in the reserved slots? (As we shall see, a few actually win unreserved seats, but their number is small.)

At this point there are two major possibilities, each with its own set of consequences. One is for Scheduled Caste members, through their own organization or political party, to nominate and work for the election of candidates belonging uniquely to them; the other is for other parties with upper caste leadership to co-opt leaders from the Scheduled Caste community whose popularity among their own people assures them of support and to nominate them under the aegis of party sponsorship. Such popular leaders are sometimes called "vote banks" and are much sought after by parties who want an attractive slate to increase their chances to elect great numbers of representatives with their own party affiliation. The Congress party, which has been largely dominant, has made good use of this method, though we shall see that others employ it too.

For these two processes, I shall borrow Ralph Turner's (1960) terminology and call the first (organization of one's own party) "contest mobility" and the second (co-optation of minority individuals by a political party for instrumental

---

6. This phenomenon may be primarily regional, for Srinivas asserts that lower castes seem drawn into urban centers to a high degree when all of India is considered (Srinivas, 1966, p. 67).

purposes) "sponsored mobility." In contest mobility, the group participates more directly in some form of militant action, and the candidate specifically represents group interests which, often enough, he has aroused in the first place. The minority group thus engages in an open competition or contest with other groups with the candidate as the spearhead of the group's effort in the struggle. In sponsored mobility, on the other hand, the candidate is likely to be what Lewin (1948) once called the "leader from the periphery." Such a leader would not be likely to be chosen by members of his own group, because he shows uncertain loyalty to their collective interests or goals. He would command a sufficient personal following among minority members, however, to prove attractive as a vote-getter to a party more intent on attaining power than on promoting an ideology. Quite often this candidate has greater popularity in the general electorate than he has among his own people. At any rate, he owes his elevation to outside sponsorship. In contest mobility the candidate is activistic, arousing and inspiring his followers to accept a particularistic political creed, to exert themselves in campaigns, and to press for strong demands. In sponsored mobility, however, the candidate plays a less active role; it is not so necessary for him to put forth extra effort because the party money and organization are employed for his benefit; he follows the tactics and strategy of party leaders who coach him in what he is expected to do. If elected, he owes his position more to the sponsoring organization than to his own efforts or that of the group whose tag he wears and whose reserved seat he occupies. He consequently becomes a party "regular" and is careful not to become too militant in the minority group's behalf, lest it antagonize the majority.

Under the system of reserved seats, there is only limited opportunity for Scheduled Caste members to increase their elected representatives above the number specified in the reserved schedule. The official allocation of seats in the Lok Sabha gives the Scheduled Castes 77 out of a total of 509, or 15 percent of Parliament. State assemblies vary more since some have much larger Scheduled Caste populations than others.[7]

Contest mobility in the form of collective political action has had a fluctuating series of minor victories and defeats. Ambedkar first organized his political party to mobilize the Untouchables into a pressure group in 1942. Naming it the Scheduled Caste Federation, he led the new party in an attempt to win reserved seats in Bombay State but without success in 1946 or, after independence, in 1952 and 1954. In 1956, the year in which he promoted mass conversions to Buddhism, Ambedkar revamped the organization and gave it a new title: the Republican party.[8] Entering an alliance with parties demanding a separate state of Maharashtra, the Federation won two reserved and two unreserved Lok Sabha seats and seventeen state assembly seats in 1957. This was the high tide of their success, for in 1962 the Republican party lost nearly all the

---

7. See *India, a Reference Annual,* 1968, pp. 123-24; and Census of India 1961, Vol. I, Part V-A(i).

8. Ambedkar died soon afterwards, in December 1956, two months before state elections. Since it was too late to employ the new name of the party in the 1957 election, the old label "Federation" served for the last time.

ground already gained, winning more seats (both national and state) in Uttar Pradesh than in Maharashtra, where they no longer had support of an alliance. That year the Hindu parties entered so many candidates in Uttar Pradesh that the Republican party, temporarily well organized and allied with Muslims, won seats in both reserved and unreserved categories. By 1967, with its notable decline in Congress fortunes, Republican representation in the Lok Sabha sank to a single seat, but they made important gains in state assemblies (along with other non-Congress parties), capturing six reserved, sixteen unreserved, and one Tribal seat on an all-India basis (L. Dushkin, 1972, pp. 198-201). Figures for the 1971 election in which Congress won a resounding victory (after the ordeal of Bangladesh) are unavailable to me, but the Scheduled Castes appear to have supported Indira Gandhi substantially and to have benefited by gaining offices both within the Congress and in the Ministries (ibid., p. 208n.). However, the fortunes of the Republican party do not appear to have kept pace with these other triumphs; in fact, the showing of Republican outcomes, set alongside those of other parties, is inconsequential by any standard (see Table 3.1).

By winning only one of seventy-seven reserved seats at the Centre, the Republican party revealed its weakness as an all-India organization. At the state level it has been somewhat more successful. B. K. Gaikwad (1966), who served as the president of the party for a number of years, listed accomplishments of the organization in Maharashtra in his public statement at the fifth session of the Republican party. He attributed these results directly to party activity, though he mentioned collaboration with the chief minister (then Y. B. Chavan) as aiding the cause. The following major achievements were claimed:

1.   Abolition of hereditary inferior village service (a kind of peonage).
2.   Extension of educational and economic privileges to the Buddhist converts formerly from the Scheduled Castes.

TABLE 3.1

**Party Distribution of Scheduled Caste Reserved Seats
in the Lok Sabha, 1967***

No. of Seats	Party
47	Indian National Congress
6	Dravida Munnetra Kazhagam
5	Bharatiya Jana Sangh
3	Swatantra Party
3	Socialist Party and Samyukta Socialist Party
2	Praja Socialist Party
2	Communist Party of India
2	Communist Party of India (Marxist)
1	Republican Party of India
1	Akali Dal
1	Bangla Congress
1	Forward Bloc
3	Independents
77 Total	

*Dushkin (1972), p. 202

3. Establishment of Ambedkar's birthday as a gazetted holiday in the state.
4. Distribution of continually increasing amounts of waste land to landless laborers, a large percentage of whom were from Scheduled Castes.

Outside Maharashtra, the Republican party has probably had its greatest impact in Uttar Pradesh, where the Scheduled Caste population is the largest of any state; in Madras (now Tamil Nadu), Andhra Pradesh, Mysore, and the Punjab, the party has also had minor influence. Interviews with members in a number of states make it evident that the party has been faction-ridden and therefore unable to exert even the potential strength of which it is capable. While the party platform varies from state to state, a more or less typical pronouncement from Uttar Pradesh, where the party had a temporary alliance with the Muslims and Scheduled Tribes, will give some idea of the aims pursued: (1) separate villages for Scheduled Castes; (2) separate electorates for the Scheduled Castes; (3) a university specifically organized for and run by personnel from the Scheduled Castes; (4) increased representation in civil service, police, and the military, with special emphasis on promotion to upper echelons; and (5) publicity for the persecution of Scheduled Caste members by caste Hindus, particularly in rural areas. The ideology accompanying these demands is openly defiant of public opinion, especially in the dogma expressed in the document, that the depressed classes are Mool Bharatis, that is, descendants of the original inhabitants of India who were conquered by the invading "uncultured" Aryans and kept in subjection ever since (Sunder *et al.,* 1968).[9]

When it is impossible to make significant political gains, the effort shifts to publicity campaigns. A set of formal demands on governmental bodies at all levels is presented with the aim of capturing attention in the mass media, thus ensuring that the public will be kept aware of the continued disabilities suffered by Untouchables. Such appeared to be the goal of the Mysore State Scheduled Castes Convention which I attended on July 8, 1969; this assembly approved a set of twenty demands, all the way from special implementation of specific Constitutional provisions to the granting of revenue posts to Scheduled Caste members in accordance with their proportion of the population (Charter of Demands, Mysore State Scheduled Castes Convention, 1969). These demands were duly submitted to the President and Prime Minister of India, as well as to the Governor and Chief Minister of Mysore. No more has been heard of the matter from these authorities since that date, but newspapers all over India carried the story when the action was first taken.

Similarly, in Andhra Pradesh, the Adi Andhra Convention of Scheduled Caste delegates sent a memorandum on December 6, 1968, to U Thant, Secretary-General of the United Nations, requesting that body to intervene in behalf of the Scheduled Castes of India who were being denied the human rights

---

9. Rewriting history in revivalistic style but in a different vein from the traditional mode is further illustrated by a prominent neo-Buddhist Dean of the Law School of Siddarth College, Bombay, who contends that the Panchamas once ruled Buddhist countries and, when these nations were conquered by Brahmanic India, the former were made into slaves and Untouchables (Borale, 1968). Ambedkar had still another theory, based largely on deductive reasoning, too involved for discussion here (Ambedkar, 1969).

outlined in the United Nations Charter of 1963. This document contained a short list of typical atrocities committed by upper caste members against the Untouchables of India (Scheduled Castes Memorandum to U.N.O., Hyderabad, 1968). This message received considerable publicity in India, though it appeared to gain little attention at the United Nations.[10]

In yet another instance, a deputation from the Republican party of India presented a charter of demands to the Prime Minister in Delhi on April 3, 1969, with the further threat that, if the demands were not accepted by April 14, the party would institute a nationwide satyagraha. This event had national coverage in the newspapers and created something of a temporary stir. The Prime Minister promised to consider the demands and make a decision if the satyagraha were postponed for six months (Republican Party of India, Minutes of Executive Committee, 1969). The six months passed without an announced decision by the Prime Minister and without the threatened satyagraha.

In sum, contest mobility as an organized form of political action has few achievements to its credit, whether winning legislative victories or capturing more than momentary public interest by circulating open demands to the authorities for dissemination by the media. Concerted action along these lines has hardly raised the status of Untouchables in any perceptible way.

Sponsored mobility is not so visible because it does not take place in the spotlight of open conflict. It consists largely of "deals" whereby popular figures among the Scheduled Castes are offered a chance to run for office under the aegis of a larger party that looks for "loyalty" in return. Table 3.1 above makes it quite clear that this is more likely to occur with the Congress party than with any other. The situation in Uttar Pradesh is a symbol of the way sponsored mobility operates, and Paul R. Brass (1968, p. 96) describes it in these words: "The Scheduled Caste vote has been a mainstay of the Congress in U. P. since independence. Until the 1962 election, the Republican party and its predecessor, the Scheduled Caste Federation, achieved no successes in U. P. politics. For the most part, the Scheduled Castes in U. P. have accepted the patronage of the Congress government and have given their votes to the Congress Party in return. *The Scheduled Caste leaders who have been given Congress tickets in the reserved constituencies are nonmilitant and have no power in the local or state Congress organizations* [italics added]. The numerous organizations in U.P. for the advancement of the Scheduled Castes have been content to serve as agencies for the distribution of Congress patronage." Clearly the Scheduled Caste candidates campaigning on Congress tickets have a co-opted status which has little social impact, either on the improvement of social and economic conditions among the Scheduled Castes in their own communities or on the policies of the Congress party itself.

It is instructive to get the reaction of one such MLA[11] to the pattern of sponsored mobility. In interviewing a Scheduled Caste Congress representative to

---

10. Soon after the United Nations passed the Charter on Human Rights, W. E. B. Du Bois in the United States submitted a similar memorandum on behalf of American blacks — with similar results.

11. Member of the legislative assembly of a state.

a southern state assembly, I inquired why he remained with the Congress when that party had been attacked both by Ambedkar and by more recent Untouchable militants as neglectful of the cause of his community. The MLA replied that, with members of the upper castes splitting their votes among so many parties, the great majority of Scheduled Caste members were voting for Congress; this gave any Congress politicians from the Untouchable ranks a great deal of leverage for accomplishment. He even went so far as to say that 98 percent of the Scheduled Caste electorate voted for Congress. As he expanded on his theme, however, he began complaining that upper caste Congress politicians still dominated the party and the assembly, preventing energetic action on behalf of the Scheduled Castes. This pointed up his ambivalence in a situation where his personal influence was presumably weak.

The discussion so far has omitted political behavior at local levels. This is because Scheduled Castes in a rural village, unless they are unusually numerous, do not participate so actively or so freely on behalf of local candidates as they do for others at more distant levels. As Myron Weiner (1968, pp. 39-40) has put it, "Where the so-called lower classes enter politics, they often do so not by moving into the local political arena but by leapfrogging directly into state politics. Landless laborers may hesitate to oppose their employers for control over local government but need not fear sanctions by supporting opposing candidates for more remote state assembly and parliamentary seats. Thus in Andhra Pradesh the landless laborers have almost never fought for control over village panchayats, but have often given their votes to Communist assembly and parliamentary candidates. Finally, it should be noted that the lower classes like other communities do not necessarily enter politics as a cohesive force, but typically split into factions which in turn are allied to existing factions within political parties."

Both these factors, the increased freedom to vote for state and national candidates, and the presence of factions, make admirable opening wedges for leftist appeals and have been so used. Acquaintance with southern universities convinces the observer that the student generation of the Scheduled Castes in states like Tamil Nadu and Mysore are strongly communist in ideology. Ironically, the fact is that the two major Communist parties are often led by Brahmans, which tends to prejudice many Scheduled Caste members against them. However, the Naxalites (Maoists) are free from this type of upper caste dominance which helps to explain the increasing attraction of the Naxalites, who also offer the satisfactions of violent revenge against exploiting landlords.

A PARADIGM OF MOBILITY

It is now possible to present, in condensed form, interconnections between the four types of mobility that have engaged our attention thus far. The modes of mobility are shown in Figure 3.1.

Both Sanskritization and Westernization are *cultural* processes with a quest for status rather than power. Sanskritization, however, is a collective phenomenon demanding combination, cooperation, and action in concert, with overtones reminiscent of Goffman's "impression management" (Goffman, 1959, Chap. 2).

Social categories	Collectivistic	Individualistic

Culture; Style of life; Prestige goal; Emulation	Sanskritization
	Neo-traditional
	Local, regional models
	Upper caste reference
	   group
	Group display
	Group cohesion
		Westernization
		Anti-traditional
		All-India urban models
		Western-educated
		   reference group
		Individual anonymity
		Alienation from group

Power and control; Use and acceptance of sanctions	Contest mobility
	Group political
	   activism
	Group commitment
	Group identification
	In-group authority
	In-group goals
		Sponsored mobility
		Co-optation by others
		Protected competition
		Formal group identifi-
		   cation only
		Out-group authority
		Out-group goals

Fig. 3.1 Modes of Mobility for Scheduled Castes

Westernization embodies individual ambition, an "inner-directed" personal drive (Riesman, 1950). Sanskritization and Westernization are forms of emulation, each with a face turned in a different direction: Sanskritization toward sanctified indigenous custom, Westernization toward secular, imported, and, in the context, innovative usage. In Sanskritization, group adherence and loyalty are conspicuous, whereas in Westernization, group bonds are increasingly rejected, the higher the climb, in favor of individual aspirations.

Both contest mobility and sponsored mobility have power as a central aim; culturological features are pushed into the background. Here too, however, is the familiar contrast between the collective and individualistic modes. Contest mobility assumes that group goals envelop and override those of the individual with a powerful contagion. Sponsored mobility is a matter of cool calculation, of utilizing the "main chance" and making oneself indispensable to the aims of an out-group more powerful than one's own. In contest mobility, commitment, identification, and authority derive from familiar, though extended, primary group relations; in sponsored mobility, the individual adopts a pragmatic, bargaining frame of mind in which he accepts the offer of the highest bidder from an out-group and in so doing, relinquishes his autonomy. Although emulation and power present contrasting forms, the most serious conflict appears if we draw a diagonal line between Westernization and contest mobility. Martin Orans (1965) speaks of this in the tribal context as the emulation-solidarity conflict, and Béteille (1967, p. 83) refers to the competing demands of status and power. It is the dilemma that plagues disadvantaged minorities in all societies: whether to give complete loyalty to the parental group at any cost, or to pursue individual ambitions that eventually separate persons from their ascriptive group.

VOCATIONAL NICHES: BUREAUCRACY AND ARMY

Although the great majority of the depressed classes are either landless laborers or dependent cultivators, those who migrate to the cities enter the industrial work force in considerable numbers and also enter a number of menial service occupations. Unfortunately, we know very little about the Scheduled Caste vocational structure in the urban scene. R. Chandidas has prepared a significant chart (see Table 3.2) of occupational figures on an all-India basis which gives a comparative overview in terms of primary, secondary, and tertiary occupations. Table 3.2 singles out Scheduled Castes and Scheduled Tribes separately, comparing them with the rest of the Indian population.

The breakdown in Table 3.2 makes it clear that the percentage of Scheduled Castes engaging in industrial labor (manufacturing) is not only extremely small but is only about one-half the percentage of the non-scheduled population in the

TABLE 3.2

Sectoral Distribution of Scheduled and Non-Scheduled Population by Percentage*

Sectoral Categories	Scheduled Castes	Scheduled Tribes	Non-Scheduled Population
Primary sector	72.20	87.88	66.73
Cultivators	37.74	68.15	54.20
Agricultural laborers	34.46	19.73	12.53
Secondary sector	12.19	6.60	14.43
Mining, quarrying, etc.	2.88	3.42	2.66
Household industry	6.56	2.47	6.81
Manufacturing other than household industry	2.75	0.71	4.96
Tertiary sector	15.61	1.52	18.84
Construction	1.08	0.31	1.19
Trade and commerce	1.14	0.39	5.12
Transportation and communication	0.96	0.27	1.90
Other services	12.43	4.55	10.63
Total for all sectors	100.00	100.00	100.00
Economically active population to total population	47.07	56.65	58.96
Inactive population to total population	52.93	43.35	41.04

*Chandidas, 1969. By permission.

same category. On the other hand, in the tertiary sector, the Scheduled Castes have almost as high a percentage as the non-scheduled population and actually surpass them in the so-called "other services." The deficit of the Scheduled Castes in the tertiary occupations is especially noticeable in trade and commerce, where they are at a disadvantage when compared with the castes that traditionally undertake these activities, often to the exclusion of all others.

For the moment, however, it is "other services" that demand closer attention. They make up nearly all of the tertiary category among the Scheduled Castes and show a higher percentage of workers than the Untouchables have in the secondary sector. It seems probable (on the basis of inference from incomplete data available) that the three occupations comprising a substantial share of the "other services" category are teaching, government service, and the military. As already noted, teachers from the Untouchable ranks apparently number in the thousands, although substantiation is unavailable (Isaacs, 1964, p. 72). Studies have been made, however, on the entrance of Scheduled Castes into administrative government posts and the army. Since these two occupations constitute secure havens of employment especially sought after by Untouchables, their presence in these particular vocational niches will be briefly sketched.

The actual number of Scheduled Caste employees in the bureaucracy is not large in proportion to their population,[12] but it is definitely a preferred vocation affording both security and prestige. The Scheduled Castes make up some 14 percent of the population; by reviewing the corresponding proportion of government employees from the Scheduled Castes, we can discover whether they have their share of posts. In the Indian Administrative Service (IAS) containing the upper reaches of bureaucratic workers, the percentage of Scheduled Caste employees increased from 1.63 percent in 1954 to 5.43 percent in 1967. In the Indian Police (national), the corresponding figures are 1.19 and 5.36 percent. If the calculation is by grade of service (Class I at the top and Class IV at the bottom), the results are: in Class I, the percentage of Scheduled Caste workers rose from 0.71 in 1957 to 1.77 in 1966. In Class II, the corresponding percentage went from 2.01 to 3.25. In Class III, it rose from 7.03 to 8.86, and in Class IV there was a drop from 22.10 (including sweepers) to 17.94 (excluding sweepers).[13] By 1966 the total number of Scheduled Caste employees in the central government (as listed in the above comparison) was 340,452, of whom about 60 percent were in the lowest echelon of Class IV (*Handbook,* 1968, pp. 88-89).

After independence, the number of reservations set aside for Scheduled Castes in the employ of the Government of India was 12½ percent for direct recruitment with open competition. The Centre recommended to the states that

---

12. The total, to my knowledge, is unavailable; it would require careful summation of central, state, and public sector employees, including a large number of state corporations. These records do not always show the number or percentage of Scheduled Caste workers.

13. Sweepers were included for the years 1957 and 1958, when the percentages read 22.10 and 20.83, respectively. From 1959 onward, sweepers were excluded, with the result that the percentage of Scheduled Caste workers in Class IV dropped to 17.24 in 1959.

they adopt a quota consonant with their own percentage of Scheduled Caste population and apply this percentage for Class III and IV posts. When there are insufficient qualified candidates for specific vacancies, which occurs more at higher than at lower levels, the posts may be de-reserved with the prior approval of the Ministry of Home Affairs. There are a number of other detailed regulations for various categories of recruitment or promotion, some of which have special provisions like relaxation of age limits, reduction in examination fees, lowering of physical and educational requirements, and so forth (*Handbook*, 1968, pp. 75-85).

Although it is true that the low educational level of the Untouchables limits the number of qualified candidates for upper posts, whether by recruitment or promotion,[14] other factors intervene to curtail the number of actual placements. In many areas of India, "there has been a great discontentment among the Scheduled Castes about the way the personality tests are being used to disqualify them" (Elayaperumal Report, IV and V, p. 99, henceforth referred to as E.R.).[15] Another obstacle appears in the unions of government employees who have shown open hostility to Scheduled Castes, opposing the reservations set aside for them in hiring and promotion. To compound the problem, "Scheduled Caste candidates are not in a position to approach the MLAs and MPs to get their grievances redressed as it is against the existing rules" (E.R. IV and V, p. 105).

Though the formal requirements for maintaining a proportional level of Scheduled Caste candidates are fairly close to the mark in the individual states (E.R. IV and V, pp. 331-33), problems of enforcement are especially evident at the state level. Investigation has shown a large number of cases where applicants from the Scheduled Castes were listed as available on the employment exchanges but the agencies seeking personnel either made no use of these lists or did not notify the exchanges of reserved posts that were theoretically open.[16] In some states like Madhya Pradesh and Rajasthan, there are many local districts with no Scheduled Caste employees at all, even in Class III and some Class IV levels (E.R. IV and V, pp. 167-68; 264-65). It is even reported that the chairman of one State Public Service Commission announced himself as totally opposed to the principle of reservation itself, although his office was charged with responsibility for implementing the regulations that reserved a special place for the Scheduled Castes (E.R. IV and V, p. 336).

Widespread public indifference, if not hostility, to vigorous action enforcing job reservations, appears to exist. For instance, it has been impossible for either the Elayaperumal Committee during its term of office, or the Commissioner for

---

14. One exception in the lower echelons was a paucity of applicants for stenographers' positions (Report of the Commissioner for Scheduled Castes and Scheduled Tribes, 1967-68, p. 22; henceforth referred to as RCSC.).

15. These tests employ oral interviews.

16. Those interested in details will find them in E.R. IV and V, pp. 126, 140-42, 160-61, 175-77, 186-88, 200, 211-13, 217-19, 224, 229, 252-54, 266-70, 278-80, 288-90, 302-03, 318-22, and 328-29. The states also neglect actual reporting, for the Commissioner writes, "None of the State Governments has furnished information regarding the representation of the Scheduled Castes and Scheduled Tribes in the services under them. The need for maintenance of such statistics has been stressed from time to time but to no avail" (RCSC, 1967-68, p. 24).

Scheduled Castes and Scheduled Tribes in recent years, to get information about the number of Scheduled Caste secretaries and other employees in services directly controlled by the Lok Sabha or Rajya Sabha. The Lok Sabha Secretariat informed the Elayaperumal Committee: "According to well established Parliamentary Convention this Sectt. does not furnish any material which is within the exclusive sphere of the speaker to any Committee appointed by the Government of India." Some years before, a similar reply went to the Commissioner who was called, in the letter addressed to him, an "outside authority" (E.R. IV and V, pp. 70-72). There appears to be no agency to which this information can be entrusted; executive privilege is here matched by legislative privilege.

Certain loopholes also allow laxity in implementing the rules for reservation of posts. For example, "The Ministry of Home Affairs have intimated in this connexion that the advice of the Ministry of Law is that neither the provisions of Article 16(4)[17] nor those of Article 335[18] of the Constitution are of a mandatory nature" (RCSC, 1967-68, p. 20). For want of a Supreme Court decision on the matter, this singular judgment of the Law Ministry has the force of law until reversed and is equivalent to the statement that the constitutional provisions relating to government employment of the Scheduled Castes are advisory only and without imperative force. There is certainly no penalty for evading the regulations on reservations. A second loophole is the precedent, followed by the bureaucracy, that when a *new* service is instituted, no reservation of posts is made for either Scheduled Caste or Scheduled Tribe members (RCSC, 1967-68, p. 16). The result of this practice is that newly organized sectors are filled by candidates from other communities which then form massive blocs that deny entry, possibly for years, to qualified candidates from the Scheduled Castes.

POSITIONS IN THE MILITARY

Although service in the Army, Navy, or Air Force is definitely government employment, discussion of its significance must occupy a special place because of the unique position held by the military in India. The Indian Army is a kind of transmission belt to the middle class since the recruits so often better their incomes and status positions by joining. For those low in the caste hierarchy, there is the added advantage of gaining an enhanced relationship with local police and municipal authorities. As a consequence, the Army, whose ranks are filled by enlistment, has a special attraction for the Scheduled Castes.

The Ministry of Defence does not make its statistics on composition of the Armed Forces available to the public, and the Commissioner for Scheduled Castes and Scheduled Tribes reports only percentage gains or losses in a given year for the depressed classes in the military. Without the absolute figures in

---

17. Relating to equality of employment opportunity and reservation of posts for Scheduled Castes and Scheduled Tribes.

18. Stating that claims of Scheduled Caste and Scheduled Tribe members shall be taken into consideration in making government appointments.

such cases, the percentages reveal only whether the direction is upward or downward for Scheduled Caste enlistment. Even this information may be misleading since the percentage figures report an upward trend, whereas other indicators (to be mentioned below) show the opposite.

The historical development of the armed forces in India places our limited data in perspective. Before the eighteenth century, the British made extensive use of Untouchables and tribals but began to drop this policy as the higher castes were increasingly attracted to British service. Only the Mahars in and around Bombay remained in considerable numbers. After 1857, with its revolt against British rule, a major change took place as the British "Punjabized" their army, taking in a greater number of Sikhs, including the Mazbhis, an Untouchable subcaste of the Sikh community. From this time on, the southern, western, and eastern sections of India not only saw less military activity but participated less in the armed forces under British command (again with the exception of the Mahars). World Wars I and II brought rapid changes as a result of the widespread tendency of armies everywhere to increase the number of lower status recruitments during intense warfare. Particularly in World War II, great numbers of Mahars, Mazbhis, Ramdasis, and Chamars were recruited, both as fighting men and as manual laborers.

After independence and the decline of warlike activity, there came a reorganization of the Indian Army with the President made head of the armed services, a broader base for recruitment set up, the enlistment period reduced to ten years, and a small ratio of commissioned officers assigned to each battalion. As the total size of the army decreased, so did the presence of Scheduled Caste enlisted men. The chief exception to this trend was the recruitment of Ramdasi Sikhs for the first time with the Chinese invasion of 1962. Eventually the branch of the services known as the Mazbhi and Ramdasi Sikhs (M. and R. Sikhs), under the prodding of caste-colleague politicians, changed its name to the Sikh Light Infantry to avoid the more obvious caste title. In the 1960s the chief representatives of the Scheduled Castes still left in the army were Mahars, Chamars, and the Sikh Mazbhis and Ramdasis. Other regions do not have salient military traditions and show less drive for recruitment.

To date, segregation of the outcaste groups mentioned in their own special regiments is a fact of life accepted by the military, the public, and by Scheduled Caste members themselves. It has a number of advantages in Indian society: (1) it makes possible public "records" of each unit which can be attributed to the entire caste group to enhance their fame; (2) both politicians and military officers seem to feel that segregation prevents "incidents" of violence; (3) segregation continues the policy of group assistance by the government and consequently gives caste members protection from both competition and insult. S. P. Cohen found officers who maintained that India, in the early stages of nationhood, had not yet reached the point where patriotism could fully take the place of caste or regional loyalties.[19]

The Elayaperumal Committee states that entrance of Scheduled Caste recruits into the Army on an all-India basis is minimal and that numbers have

19. S. P. Cohen, 1969. The above section on the Untouchables in the army is based on this article and S. P. Cohen, 1971, passim.

either remained static or declined somewhat during the last few years. They cite the annual examination by the Union Public Service Commission for vacancies in the Cadet Corps which, over a period of fifteen years, admitted 8,000 men to the Defence Services, of which the Scheduled Castes numbered only nine. The Committee calls for regular reservations in the Army on the same basis that is found in other government services. They also note the reply to a question on this subject in the Lok Sabha to the effect that all handicaps should be removed but that the officials did not favor any reservations for the Scheduled Castes (E.R. IV and V, pp. 72-76). Nevertheless, even if the government adopted a policy of reserving special places in the army for Scheduled Castes, it could have minimal effects simply because the military has adopted more and more technological methods, all of which require personnel with advanced scientific training. Such requirements will eliminate the groups with lower educational levels in the future, including the great bulk of Scheduled Caste candidates. The Navy and the Air Force have proceeded further in the technological direction than the Army and have therefore begun the process of elimination much sooner. The immediate prospects, then, for admission to the Armed Forces are not encouraging for young men in the Scheduled Castes, with exceptions in a few districts of the Punjab, Uttar Pradesh, and Maharashtra.

ASSESSMENT OF OVERALL POSITION

Comparison of the Scheduled Castes with the rest of the population on several dimensions will reveal something of their advance in vertical mobility. Though the data are scanty, enough exist to reach tentative conclusions.

In education, the literacy rate for Scheduled Castes in 1961 was 10.27 percent as compared with the national average of 24.0 percent. Figures vary from a low literacy rate of 4.72 for Scheduled Castes in Jammu and Kashmir to a high of 24.4 in Kerala, where it was slightly above the national average.[20]

A study by Jairamdas (1969) shows that deficiencies in primary school attendance of Scheduled Caste pupils are clearly marked in the Punjab and Uttar Pradesh; in middle schools, attendance is especially low in Bihar, Orissa, Punjab, Rajasthan, Uttar Pradesh, and West Bengal; in secondary schools the same states predominate, and in higher education, *all* states are deficient except Maharashtra.

A necessary supplement for any assessment of educational levels is to recognize that there are considerably higher rates for both literacy and schooling in urban areas. The data for both Delhi and Uttar Pradesh show these differences clearly. The probability is that the states where the percentage of urban Scheduled Caste population is highest would also show the highest percentage in school. The two states with the highest percentage of urban Scheduled Castes are Gujarat with 24.4 percent and Maharashtra with 21.8 percent. At the opposite extreme are Orissa with only 4.6 percent of its Scheduled Caste members in the urban category and Bihar with only 5.4 percent (1961 census).

Another important dimension for comparison is the economic level attained by the Scheduled Castes as a whole. A preliminary estimate of this position

---

20. Census of India, 1961, Vol. I, Part V-A(i).

comes from Table 3.2 above, where the percentage of landless laborers is three times as high among the Scheduled Castes as it is within the non-scheduled population. An important Bengal study throws further light on the position of these landless laborers. In this investigation, a team of researchers sampled data from 1,762 persons in twelve villages of four districts in West Bengal; 831 subjects came from the Scheduled Tribes, 464 from Scheduled Castes, and 467 from the non-scheduled population. Informants were asked their occupation, their father's occupation, and their grandfather's occupation. A few conclusions:

> In Grand Father's generation overwhelming numbers of persons were practicing 'cultivation' as major type of occupation.
>
> But in Ego's generation descendants of a considerable section of the population who had 'cultivation' as occupation has shifted towards 'day labour' as occupation, the reason being obvious – the paucity of land.
>
> Deviations towards occupations like 'service,' 'business,' etc., in Ego's generation is much less than deviation towards 'day labour.'
>
> The over-all trend of occupation pattern of the Ego's generation is the gradual increase of day labourers.
>
> The above types of trend are more perceptible among the Scheduled Tribes and Scheduled Castes than Other Communities.
>
> The above trend is supported by Census figures of 1961 relating to livelihood classes as well as interest and size of cultivable land.
>
> Instead of ascending type of occupational mobility, as is expected in these days of planned programme, the descending nature of mobility as revealed from the data gives an idea of the alarming situation in this respect. [Das, 1968, p. 44] [21]

Careful studies of this kind have not been made with adequate sampling methods elsewhere, but there are indications that the number of landless laborers is high enough to create serious problems in all Indian states, which in turn means an unusually high proportion of Scheduled Castes. Jayaprakash Narayan testifies to the manner in which the number of landless laborers is increased by citing the well-known fact that in many states, like Bihar, after independence "landowners pushed out tenants to take advantage of the proposed clause permitting resumption of land for personal cultivation" *(Times of India,* Aug. 17, 1969).[22] In Tamil Nadu, Thanjavur District, a news correspondent reports that "Harijans form 29 percent of the population and more than 80 percent of the 400,000 labourers," declaring also that the situation is regarded as increasingly desperate with the Communists making important inroads there *(The Hindu,* July 12, 1969). In similar vein it is reported for eastern Uttar Pradesh that "employed and unemployed landless farmers and Harijans are driven by poverty to migrate

---

21. Briefer studies in Madras, Punjab, Uttar Pradesh, and Chandigarh show a slight upward mobility in the direction of service occupations but a fairly static picture of mobility for sweepers and scavengers (RCSC, 1967-68, pp. 80-86).

22. J. P. Narayan (1969) indirectly supports the conclusions above on p. 43 by noting that rural violence used to be perpetrated by the landlord group on tenants and landless laborers but that now "the poor are beginning to hit back. This is what is new in the rural areas."

to Nepal where they are hired for planting paddy and harvesting the crop. The number of such seasonal migrants is estimated at 50,000. The number of people who emigrate to Assam, West Bengal, Bombay, Orissa, Bihar, and other States to work as labourers in coal mines and other industries runs into a lakh[23] or so per district" (*Times of India*, Oct. 1, 1969).

These examples do not demonstrate that landlessness is on the increase outside Bengal, but they are certainly consonant with such a conclusion[24] and show clearly that the high percentage of landless laborers among the Scheduled Castes in different areas throughout India has produced a potentially explosive situation. In the size of landholdings (where there are any) and in the quality of land held, the Scheduled Castes are also at a disadvantage. As Chandidas has shown, over half the Scheduled Castes' landholdings are of the smallest size, that is, below 2.5 acres, whereas in the non-scheduled population less than a third are such tiny holdings. At the other extreme, where proprietors own 30 acres or more, for every twenty-three non-scheduled owners there is one Scheduled Caste owner. Evidence also points to the fact that, when the outcastes have their own land, they possess the poorest and most uneconomical holdings (Chandidas, 1969, pp. 977-78).

In addition, it is not unknown for land allotted by legislative action to Scheduled Castes to find its way into the hands of upper caste farmers, as happened in Rajasthan. Reports from that state indicate: "Many years ago the State Government had decided to allot 418,000 bighas[25] of land to 120,000 landless Harijans. Committees have been set up at the tehsil level to make the allotments. Because hunger for land is acute and caste Hindus dominate the committees, Harijans seldom get a good piece of land" (Kaul, 1969).

Since the Scheduled Castes are in the lowest economic category, it is their standard of living that is most depressed.[26] As Jiwanlal Jairamdas (1969), Secretary of the Harijan Sevak Sangh, declared, "The weaker sections in general and the Scheduled Castes in particular are the victims of growing economic inequalities. They have not been assured of the basic amenities of life such as food, shelter, education and medical care. The incident of a poor mother throwing away her child in the river or starving father administering poison to his child put us all to shame and planning to ridicule."

Even the brief sketch presented here makes explicit how little mobility the Untouchables have gained *as a group*. Though a few thousand individuals have profited by educational advantages, political preferments, or bureaucratic reservations, advance of the group as a whole is doubtful. In the villages, where

---

23. One lakh equals 100,000.

24. Examination of the 1971 census produced unexpected confirmation of this trend. Data on the work force show that agricultural laborers were 16.71 percent of total workers in 1961 but 25.76 percent in 1971. Every state in India, without exception, shared a real increase (Census of India, 1971, Series 1, Paper 1 of 1971, Supplement, Provisional Population Totals and Table E, pp. 62-63). More detailed evidence appears in my article (Schermerhorn, 1974).

25. A bigha is five-eighths of an acre.

26. For welfare programs compared at state levels, see Schermerhorn, 1969.

the great majority live, there are signs of a real economic decline, whatever political gains may occur here and there. The political order seems to hold out some hope, but economic realities belie it. This tension is an augury of future change which could be violent.

INTEGRATION AS PROBLEMATIC

The status of Untouchables in Indian society is transitional; like the Buraku of Japan, they are legally emancipated from a stigmatized position that in actuality still incapacitates them for the attainment of full participation in the life of the wider society. Minorities of this order share a common historical succession which I have called the emergence of pariahs. Defined by a dominant group for centuries as a degraded suborder of mankind, restricted to a limited set of shameful, menial occupations that result in abject poverty and to residential quarters segregated from "respectable" society,[27] such outcastes have been formally destigmatized by governmental fiat through proclamations that are quite feebly implemented. New chances for political mobilization are then opened up for those whose lifetime habits of servility often render them notably ineffectual agents.

To what extent are the Scheduled Castes, as a minority of this character, integrated into Indian society? This will depend, of course, on the meaning we assign to integration. Repeating an earlier definition, I suggest that "integration is not an end-state but a *process* whereby units or elements of a society are brought into an active and coordinated compliance with the ongoing activities and objectives of the dominant group in that society" (Schermerhorn, 1970, p. 14).

Perhaps the major influences that affect integration are the degree of control over the subordinates' access to scarce values like power and wealth, together with the extent of group enclosure sustained by the minority. As we have seen, both these factors rate high, and in the villages they actually reinforce each other since the segregation of Scheduled Castes in their own quarters makes them a highly visible target for continued imposition of restrictions.

There is, however, an intervening factor that has so far been pushed into the background but now must receive explicit attention: What views do the dominants and the minority have about assimilation or its denial?

In the rapidly changing India of today relations between the dominant upper castes and the Scheduled Castes are basically those of conflict, where subordinates respond to segregation by pressing for greater participation in the system.[28] This condition is a product of structure, chiefly in the political and economic spheres. For integration to occur, either the upper or lower group

27. Such characteristics appear uniformly in the sequence designated as the emergence of pariahs. India, however, displays an additional, quite unique feature: the so-called "protective discrimination" or what is described above as compensatory practices intended to "make up for" disabilities but regarded as temporary.

28. In terms of Figure 1.2, the C alternative.

must change ideology. If the movement is toward assimilation or incorporation, it is the dominant group that has to change; if in the direction of sanctioned autonomy,[29] the subordinates must do so. As already mentioned, the ideological perspective of the Scheduled Castes depends strongly on guidance from outstanding leaders; the dominant upper castes are less dependent on leadership, for they can fall back on more widely diffused traditional views that permeate the populace as a whole.

Scheduled Caste leaders have quite divergent views on group goals. First of all there are those who desire to move toward assimilation, that is, who espouse more and more reservations for jobs. Inferentially this would imply a dispersed series of individual ascents rather than a group movement and would require long periods of time to show massive accomplishment. Since this plan would mean only a gradual rate of change, the upper castes might not oppose it too vigorously; in addition, it has the sanction of the constitution, renewals of the reservations are regular, and many bureaucratic regulations are now grown customary.

On the other hand, such forms of "protective discrimination" develop potentials for complacency, lack of initiative, and thralldom to the vagaries of government action. It gives one pause, for example, to find Scheduled Caste committee members expressing undisguised approval of Maharashtra's policy which states: "In the matter of promotion the Scheduled Caste candidates are judged with special sympathy and *promotion is not denied on the grounds of inefficiency* [italics added] unless they are considered to be definitely unfit or unless promotion is denied to them as a punishment" (E.R. IV and V, p. 191). As policies like these become known to other government servants and to the wider public, they will only confirm already existing stereotypes of the helpless, incompetent menials who are obviously out of place in their new surroundings.

There are signs, therefore, that the public can very easily become disenchanted with reserved positions of all kinds and refuse to support them any longer. A government servant interviewed by the writer told of once asking a Scheduled Caste politician, "How long do you think there should be reserved seats and posts?" The reply was prompt and emphatic, "For another hundred years at least." To which the official inquired sardonically, "Would ninety-nine years do?" From casual conversation with knowledgeable informants, I have gained the impression that the public is becoming impatient with the method of reservation and suspicious of politicians who keep it alive in order to garner votes. It may well become increasingly difficult to renew such privileges in the future. Many people seem to be wondering why criteria of merit cannot be applied to all without making special exceptions. No doubt some of this can be dismissed as prejudice rationalizing itself, but the view is held even among those who have devoted their lives to the cause of welfare among the depressed classes. A public opinion poll would be useful to verify or reject this hypothesis.

The full implications of any ideology that would prolong reservations (or increase them) are unexplored and too often unrecognized. In the first place, this view accepts individualistic premises; consequently, its realistic effect is to

---

29. Occasionally group demands actually focus on this possibility, as in the desire for separate villages noted above.

spur personal competition for a limited set of jobs in the occupational system, channeling energies toward egoistic goals that have quite minor group results until generations have passed. The "inner directed" strivers who get ahead will be those most successful in adopting the ways and life-styles of the upper echelons in society; this eventually could separate (in culture and loyalty) the upward mobile members from those they have left behind. In terms of Orans's "emulation-solidarity conflict," this ideology plumps for emulation and abandons solidarity (Orans, 1965, pp. 103-04, 127-46).

On the other hand, the very fact that competition is protected, that is, under the aegis of government surety, changes the competitive model into one of real though limited privilege. In the economic sphere it bears considerable likeness to sponsored mobility as we have noted it in the political arena. And, as already seen, it may be accepted reluctantly by the dominant group under the restraint of what are perceived to be only temporary rules and regulations. The upper castes seem to be moving in the direction of changing the system of reservations *in toto,* perhaps sooner rather than later.

Another implication of the ideology that stresses reservations is that, by focusing attention on the transitional competition of the actors, it ignores their actual destination in relation to the rest of society. As already emphasized, the ex-Untouchable who climbs to a higher place in the educational-occupational hierarchy often tries to lose his identity and remain anonymous. Having lost so many distinguishing marks of caste identity, he enters into a kind of social limbo without the anchorage and support experienced by caste Hindus. Consigning a whole generation of upward mobiles to this cloudy and ambiguous status is an unrecognized consequence of a policy oriented to the occupation of reserved seats and posts. In some respects, this policy also sanctions the uncritical adoption of Westernization.

Collective demands for group economic rewards, a quite different ideology, nevertheless has the same goal of passing from segregation to incorporation. This ideology, often with Communist or Socialist sponsorship, envisages mobility and goals of a collective nature. Although the public aim in seeking special reservations is essentially urban-oriented and an all-India phenomenon, the ideology of collective action for higher wages or taking over waste lands is *de facto* local and rural even though it is derived from labor union activity. Attempts to put the collective ideology into practice have been made primarily in Tamil Nadu, Kerala, Andhra Pradesh, and West Bengal. Revolutionary doctrines that support the strikes or occupation of surplus lands are, however, likely to be circulated by leaders outside the ranks of the Scheduled Caste population.[30] Whatever solidarity is achieved seems to be that of proletariat versus the landlords rather than the Untouchables versus the caste Hindus. If economic conditions worsen rapidly, or decline and then begin to rise, there is a strong probability that a Communist ideology will grow.

Is sanctioned autonomy a viable alternative? Perhaps the most prominent example is Ambedkar's decision to take his followers with him into Buddhism in

---

30. Bhagwan Das comments, "Russian Communists have been studying (the) Indian problem through the eyes of Communist leaders and writers of India who are predominantly Brahmins in their belief and conduct" (introduction to Ambedkar, 1963, II, p. 5).

1956. By leading them into a non-Hindu religion, he chose a voluntary form of separation that removed converts from the jurisdiction of caste regulations. Since Ambedkar's death, the great bulk of Mahars in Maharashtra have withdrawn into Buddhism, although this movement has had no more than minor consequences elsewhere. It is even reliably reported that in Tamil Nadu, when Buddhist priests were imported from Ceylon to serve the tiny neo-Buddhist community, the priests refused to stay and be associated with a group of such low status (statement by local informant).

Another separatist doctrine appears in the political demand of the Republican party for Scheduled Castes to have their own villages and towns where they can live without being molested or harassed by upper castes. For example, the President of the Adi Andhras in Hyderabad (a similar organization with similar goals) demonstrated the widespread influence of Republican party doctrine when he declared, "Let us have our own cities and towns. We must sever all connections with the Caste Hindus. Let them give us that piece of land required for us. Let us have our own State. We are by birth hard-working people and we can make any barren land into most fertile land" (Subrahmanyan, 1968).

This ideology of seclusion is somewhat extreme, since it espouses complete self-segregation. An implicit dialectic appears when the leaders seek greater political participation in order to attain complete autonomy. It might be expected that the dominant castes would be in accord with such a policy, since they have traditionally favored segregation for centuries. However, it was the *type* of segregation that paid rich dividends in the form of menial labor available to upper castes. The new demand for separate villages of a separate State is a real threat because it would entail mammoth expense, multiple shifts of habitation, and the loss of a menial labor force. Caste Hindus therefore do not take such programs seriously. An inverse relationship now appears: the higher the costs of a minority ideology to the dominant group, the weaker the effect it will have. Alternatively, it seems possible to state that the separate village alternative is especially vulnerable to cost variations.

It is significant that in Maharashtra the Scheduled Castes combine the best of both worlds, for they have not only converted to Buddhism but have successfully retained the demand for reservations. Although conversion moves in the direction of sanctioned autonomy, reservations show a long-term trend toward assimilation. The converts in that state now make up 7.05 percent of the population. Chiefly as the result of Republican party agitation, "13 percent of all classes to which direct recruitment is made have been reserved for Scheduled Caste *and Scheduled Caste converts to Buddhism*" [italics added] (E.R. IV and V, p. 191). This presents a quite different dialectical twist where, owing to sufficient political pressure, the minority group can demand certain rights that contradict the traditional definition of their status and can almost create a completely new legal definition even when this goes counter to current public opinion. However, unless there is equal mobilization of political power by Scheduled Castes elsewhere, this paradoxical result can hardly be expected in states outside Maharashtra.

The whole ideological picture is therefore a perplexing one. In the near future, the probabilities are not steady progression in one direction but weak predominance of one mode or oscillation between modes. Unanimity is too much to expect in the views of Scheduled Castes about their future aims; on the other hand, a single and consistent mode of ideological commitment would seem to be required if the minority is to advance. There is little sign that any such mandate is discernible today. Integration is therefore uncertain and problematical.

BIBLIOGRAPHY

Ambedkar, B. R., *The Buddha and His Dharma,* Bombay, Siddarth College Publication I, 1957.

Ambedkar, B. R., *The Untouchables, Who Were They and Why They Became Untouchables,* 2nd ed., Jetavan Mahavihara, Shravasti, Balrampur, Gonda, U. P., 1969.

Ambedkar, B. R., *Thus Spoke Ambedkar: Selected Speeches,* compiled by Bhagwan Das, Jullundur, Bheem Patrika Publications, 1963.

Anant, Santosh Singh, *The Changing Concept of Caste in India,* Delhi, Vikas Publishing House, 1972.

Berreman, Gerald D., "Concomitants of Caste Organization," in *Japan's Invisible Race: Caste in Culture and Personality,* edited by George De Vos and Hiroshi Wagatsuma, Berkeley, University of California Press, 1967.

Béteille, André, "The Future of the Backward Classes: The Competing Demands of Status and Power," in *India and Ceylon: Unity and Diversity,* edited by Philip Mason, London, Oxford University Press, 1967.

Borale, P. T., *Segregation and Desegregation in India,* Bombay, P. C. Manaktala & Sons, 1968.

Brass, Paul R., "Uttar Pradesh," in *State Politics in India,* edited by Myron Weiner, Princeton, Princeton University Press, 1968.

Chandidas, R., "How Close to Equality are Scheduled Castes?" *Economic and Political Weekly* 4 (No. 24, June 14, 1969), 975-80.

Charter of Demands, Mysore State Scheduled Castes (Untouchables) Convention, 1969, Bangalore, July 8, 1969.

Cohen, Stephen P., "The Untouchable Soldier: Caste, Politics, and the Indian Army," *Journal of Asian Studies* (No. 3, May 1969), 453-68.

Cohen, Stephen P., *The Indian Army, Its Contribution to the Development of a Nation,* Berkeley, University of California Press, 1971.

Das, A. K., *Trends of Occupation Patterns through Generations in Rural Areas of West Bengal,* Calcutta, Scheduled Castes and Tribes Welfare Department, Government of West Bengal, 1968.

Dollard, John, "Hostility and Fear in Social Life," *Social Forces* 17 (15-26), 1938), pp. 19-20. Quoted in Robin Williams,*The Reduction of Intergroup Tensions,* New York, Social Science Research Council, 1947, proposition 23, p. 57.

Dushkin, Lelah, "Scheduled Caste Politics," in *The Untouchables in Contemporary India,* edited by J. Michael Mahar, Tucson, University of Arizona Press, 1972.

Elayaperumal Report (E.R.): See below: Report of the Committee on Untouchability.

Fiske, Adele, "Scheduled Caste Buddhist Organizations," in *The Untouchables in Contemporary India,* edited by J. Michael Mahar, Tucson, University of Arizona Press, 1972.

Gaikwad, B. K., Speech on the Occasion of the 5th Session of the Republican Party of India held at Delhi, May 1, 1966, n. p.

Goffman, Erving, *The Presentation of Self in Everyday Life,* New York, Doubleday & Co., 1959.

Gould, Harold A., "Sanskritization and Westernization, A Dynamic View," *Economic Weekly* (No. 25, June 24, 1961).

Handbook on Scheduled Castes and Scheduled Tribes, Office of the Commissioner for Scheduled Castes and Scheduled Tribes, Delhi, Government of India, 1968.

Isaacs, Harold R., *India's Ex-Untouchables,* New York, John Day, 1964.

Jairamdas, Jiwanlal, "Fourth Five-Year Plan and the Scheduled Castes," Appendix XIII in Report of the Commissioner for Scheduled Castes and Scheduled Tribes, 1967-68, Vols. I and II, Delhi, Government of India, 1969.

Kaul, T. N., "Plight of Harijans in Rajasthan," *Times of India,* Oct. 3, 1969.

Killian, Lewis M., *The Impossible Revolution? Black Power and the American Dream,* New York, Random House, 1968.

Lewin, Kurt, *Resolving Social Conflicts,* New York, Harper & Row, 1948.

Lynch, Owen M., "The Politics of Untouchability: A Case from Agra, India," in *Structure and Change in Indian Society,* edited by Milton Singer and Bernard Cohn, Chicago, Aldine Publishing Co., 1968.

Lynch, Owen M., "Dr. B. R. Ambedkar – Myth and Charisma," in *The Untouchables in Contemporary India,* edited by J. Michael Mahar, Tucson, University of Arizona Press, 1972.

Narayan, Jayaprakash (Interview), "Rural Violence," *Times of India,* Aug. 17, 1969.

Orans, Martin, *The Santal: A Tribe in Search of a Great Tradition,* Detroit, Wayne State University Press, 1965.

Pickett, J. W., *Christian Mass Movements in India,* New York, Abingdon Press, 1933.

Report of the Committee on Untouchability: Economic and Educational Development of the Scheduled Castes, Cyclostyled, New Delhi, Ministry for Law and Social Welfare, Government of India, 1969.

Republican Party of India, Minutes of Executive Committee, 1969.

Riesman, David, in collaboration with Reuel Denny and Nathan Glazer, *The Lonely Crowd,* New Haven, Yale University Press, 1950.

Rudolph, Lloyd I., "The Modernity of Tradition: the Democratic Incarnation of Caste in India," *American Political Science Review* 59 (No. 4, Dec. 1965),

975-89; reprinted in *State and Society, A Reader in Comparative Political Sociology*, edited by Reinhard Bendix, Boston, Little, Brown & Co., 1968.

Scheduled Castes Memorandum to U.N.O., Approved at the Adi Andhra Convention held on December 6, 1968 at Hyderabad, A. P., India.

Schermerhorn, R. A., *Comparative Ethnic Relations,* New York, Random House, 1970.

Schermerhorn, R. A., "Scheduled Caste Welfare, Public Priorities in the States," *Economic and Political Weekly* 4 (No. 8, Feb. 22, 1969), 397-402.

Schermerhorn, R. A., "Minorities in the Census of India, 1971," *Demography India* 3 (No. 2, 1974), 315-27.

Spear, Percival, "The Position of the Muslims Before and After Partition," in *India and Ceylon: Unity and Diversity,* edited by Philip Mason, London, Oxford University Press, 1967.

Srinivas, M. N., *Social Change in Modern India*, Bombay, Allied Publishers, 1966.

Subrahmanyan, P. L., "Presidential Address," in Scheduled Castes Memorandum to U.N.O., Hyderabad, Bhim Bhavan, 1968.

Sunder, B. Sham, *et al., Bhim Sena,* Hyderabad, Mool Bharat Book Trust, 1968.

Totten, George O., and Hiroshi Wagatsuma, "Emancipation: Growth and Transformation of a Political Movement," in *Japan's Invisible Race: Case in Culture and Personality,* edited by George De Vos and Hiroshi Wagatsuma, Berkeley, University of California Press, 1967.

Turner, Ralph H., "Sponsored and Contest Mobility and the School System," *American Sociological Review* 25 (Dec. 1960).

Weiner, Myron, ed., *State Politics in India*, Princeton, Princeton University Press, 1968.

Williams, Robin M., Jr., *The Reduction of Intergroup Tensions*, New York, Social Science Research Council, 1947.

Zelliot, Eleanor, "Gandhi and Ambedkar: A Study in Leadership," in *The Untouchables in Contemporary India,* edited by J. Michael Mahar, Tucson, University of Arizona Press, 1972.

Chapter 4

Scheduled Tribes:
Isolates of Uncertain Future

Comprising a little over 6 percent of India's population, the minority probably least known, least understood, in least communication with the rest of the nation, and least assimilated now claims attention. The legal definition of the Scheduled Tribes can be established by government fiat,[1] but a sociological one is more difficult to formulate since, as André Béteille (1967, p. 87) remarks, "it is often very difficult to say of a particular social unit whether it is a tribe or a caste."

In spite of such difficulties, it is possible to say of Scheduled Tribes as a whole that they are substantially isolated from Hindu society by geography, economy, social structure, and cultural features. Many tribals (in most ways, the typical ones) live in areas secluded and remote from Hindu neighbors in hilly, forested, or mountainous areas not easily accessible by the usual forms of communication. More often than not such tribesmen engage in hunting, fishing, slash-and-burn agriculture, and cultivating without ploughs and without irrigation practices. They make limited use of storage facilities for food and are known for "quick consumption and generous distribution" when compared with the more sedentary caste groups of villages and towns (Mandelbaum, 1970, pp. 580-81).[2] The social structure of tribal communities is much less differentiated than that of jati society, which displays marked specialization. Tribesmen are distinguished from one another not so much by occupation (for they are much alike in this respect) as by kinship and lineage. Unlike caste

---

1. The Scheduled Tribes live in so-called Scheduled Areas, both terms definable in terms of presidential decree as described in the Constitution. Such decrees can be modified by future presidents. (See the Constitution of India, Fifth Schedule, Article 244 (1), Parts A, B, and C.) All descriptions in the present chapter are based on the presidential definitions embodied in the 1961 Census.

2. Characterization of tribals at this point is especially indebted to Mandelbaum's detailed distinctions (1970, Chap. 31).

villages, tribal communities may have kin of the same unit at all levels of society rather than in a specific hierarchical position. In fact, to speak of "levels" in tribal organization is hardly possible because of pervasive egalitarian patterns.

Unlike the caste villages where the division of labor makes the work of each jati revolve on the specific tasks of every other jati, tribesmen lack such group dependencies and the ritual ranking that accompanies them. Social units among tribals tend to be repetitive and alike without the diversity and variation of Hindu hierarchies. Emile Durkheim's "mechanical" pattern applies to tribal organization, whereas his "organic" model of interdependence properly belongs to the caste village (Durkheim, 1933). When a tribe incorporates outsiders, it brings them in as adopted equals, whereas Hindu society encompasses them as unequals low in the hierarchy if not outside it altogether. Because of their simpler subsistence economy, tribal populations have direct rather than indirect control over natural resources; there is no need for contractual forms of ownership or for differential legal controls reflecting specialized functions, because such plural functions are not needed.

Tribal languages are unwritten.[3] On the whole the cultural values of caste and tribe are quite distinct from each other. Since tribal communities place little value on surplus accumulation, they stress prompt consumption and immediate enjoyment; in comparison with Hindu villages, they are more hedonistic, relishing the pleasures of the senses without shame. There is no ascetic ideal (Mandelbaum, 1970, p. 582; Orans, 1965, pp. 52-53). Tribesmen also devalue the role of trader; its practice demands deferred gratification, refusal to share goods with others, and individualistic separation from the group, all of which repudiate deeply cherished views of tribal members. Furthermore, many tribes have suffered from exploitation by merchants and moneylenders. In religion, the tribesmen have their own deities or spirits but lack elaborate dogma about the transcendental world; nor do they have ornate temples for worship. Shamans are the most common type of religious leaders. Pragmatic results (rather than effects in a future life) are demanded of their faith.

Exceptions to all of these statements can be found simply because migration and acculturation have altered the lifeways of the "forest and hill peoples" sufficiently so that, to the eye of the social scientist, a number of tribal populations hardly have a distinctive character of their own any longer. As a collective whole, the tribals therefore live at many cultural levels with a wide range of values. However, most of these values are non-Hindu and some even anti-Hindu, as hinted above. Nevertheless, the great majority of tribal people are certainly not aboriginal, even though Hindus frequently continue to regard them as such.

THE COMPARATIVE DIMENSION

Such tribesmen in India are now entering into the mainstream of national life in increasing numbers. In this respect they resemble their counterparts throughout the world, caught up in the recurrent sequence mentioned in

---

3. Exceptions to this circumstance occur with the advent of outside teachers or instructors like missionaries.

Chapter 1 as the "emergence of indigenous isolates." To observe tribals in this light is to pass beyond the usual anthropological focus, which centers on each local group as a self-contained whole or on the process of acculturation described as individual adjustment to a changed mode of life with its often disorganizing effects. While not neglecting such a view entirely, I prefer, for purposes at hand, to shift attention to the total society and the ways in which tribesmen increase their rate of participation in that whole. This process is especially important for preliterate ethnolinguistic groups everywhere, because they start at a lower participant level than most groups in their environing societies and have a longer road to travel, compared with others, in order to become integrated. They suffer the further handicap of being regarded as alien outsiders who cannot be *expected* to advance beyond barbarism or some primitive level.

Such indigenous isolates, emerging into wider public life, are a common feature of Asian societies, particularly in the belt running from the southern borders of Tibet at Ladakh and extending eastward along the Himalayas through Nepal, Sikkim, Bhutan, Assam, then south through Burma, Thailand, Laos, Cambodia, Vietnam, and Malaysia. For many of these countries, tribals constitute a larger proportion of their population than they do in India. For example, in Burma, the Karens, Shans, Mon Wa, Kachins, and Chins, all separate from the Burmese majority in origin and language, form 23 percent of that nation's population. Other countries throughout southeast Asia have similar indigenous groups ranging from less than 5 percent to 14 or more percent of their total inhabitants (Hunter, 1966, p. 15).

As tribal groups, in all these territories, interact with their nontribal neighbors, it is important to assess in general terms what factors facilitate their integration into larger societies as the pace of change quickens and as intergroup contacts force new adjustments on both sides. Analysis of this issue here is a first step toward exploring what tentative answers are now available in the present state of our knowledge, at least for the subcontinent of India.

ENUMERATION AND LOCALE

The 1971 Census gives 38,015,162 as the population of the Scheduled Tribes of India. This comprises some 450 "communities" or tribal units of highly variable size, from the Gonds as the largest to the Andamanese as the smallest (Roy Burman, 1969b, pp. 3-4).

In physical makeup there seem to be two major racial strains in the tribal population: the Veddoid element, found among the tribes of southern and middle India, and the Paleo-Mongoloids of Assam and the North East Frontier Agency (Fürer-Haimendorf, 1967, pp. 187-88).

Linguistically, the tribes are fractionated into a maze of local dialects, although the plurality is less striking than it appears at first glance. The language groups break down into the following major divisions (by the 1961 census): the Austro-Asiatic cluster spoken by 6,192,495 persons, the Mon-Khmer by 377,993, the Munda by 5,814,496, the Tibeto-Burman by 3,183,505, the Dravidian by over 1.5 million, and the Aryan (mostly Bhili) by 2,439,611. Thus, the 1,549 languages listed by the 1961 census as mother tongues of Scheduled Tribes are local dialects, many of which are in related language groups (Fürer-Haimendorf, 1967, 189-98).

From a different point of view, the number of speakers of genuine tribal languages (as distinct from regional written languages) is given as 47.3 percent of the entire tribal population in 1961.[4] The remainder, or over half the Adivasis,[5] speak the same language as the nontribals of their area and, to this extent at least, are exposed to the same communication channels. Also noteworthy is the fact that 15.73 percent of the tribals are listed as bilingual, and these persons presumably speak one of the national languages in addition to their local mother tongue (Roy Burman, 1969b, p. 4). Thus, the bilinguals may share an enlarged world view, in contrast with their fellows who are restricted to a local dialect.

Geographically, the Scheduled Tribes live in areas of special concentration in contrast to the outcastes scattered through every one of the villages in all India. The usual geographical assignment of the Adivasis is threefold: tribes of the northeast, those of the middle belt (Chotanagpur along with other regions of Orissa and Madhya Pradesh), and southwest India among the Ghats and the surrounding hills. However, this tripartite division is too broad and lacks inclusiveness. Roy Burman's fivefold division (1969b, pp. 1-2) is more accurate:

(1) Northeast India, comprising Assam, North East Frontier Agency, Nagaland, Manipur, and Tripura.

(2) Sub-Himalayan region of north and northwest India comprising the northern submontane district of Uttar Pradesh and Himachal Pradesh as a whole, including the areas transferred from the Punjab.

(3) Central and eastern India comprising West Bengal, Bihar, Orissa, Madhya Pradesh, and Andhra Pradesh.

(4) South India comprising Tamil Nadu, Karnataka, and Kerala.

(5) Western India comprising Rajasthan, Gujarat, and Maharashtra.

These regional divisions can be given more specification by listing the tribal populations of the various states and their percentages in the total population. This information is presented in Table 4.1.

It will be observed that tribal populations form a clear majority in two states, Nagaland and the newly formed Arunachal Pradesh; in two Union Territories, Dadra and Nagar Haveli; and in Laccadive, Minicoy, and Amindivi Islands. Roy Burman also shows on the basis of 1961 statistics that in 187 taluks (revenue districts) throughout India, Scheduled Tribes form 50 percent or more of the inhabitants. What is still more significant is that "almost 50 percent of the Scheduled Tribes population of India live in pockets where they are the majority people" (Roy Burman, 1969b, p. 3).

---

4. This statistic is based on the assumption that all the speakers of tribal languages belong to tribal communities.

5. Hindi term for tribal people, in common use as appellation. It signifies "original inhabitants."

Scheduled Tribes as Isolates

TABLE 4.1

Tribal Population of States and Union Territories in Order of Size for
Tribal Aggregates, Together with Percentage of Scheduled Tribe
Populations in State Populations, 1971*

State or Union Territory	Tribal Population	Percentage of Tribals in State Population
Madhya Pradesh	8,387,403	20.14
Orissa	5,071,937	23.11
Bihar	4,932,767	8.75
Gujarat	3,734,422	13.99
Rajasthan	3,125,506	12.13
Maharashtra	2,954,249	5.86
West Bengal	2,532,969	5.72
Assam	1,919,947	12.84
Andhra Pradesh	1,657,657	3.81
Nagaland	457,602	88.61
Tripura	450,544	28.95
Arunachal Pradesh	369,408	79.02
Manipur	334,466	31.18
Tamil Nadu	311,515	0.76
Kerala	269,356	1.26
Karnataka	231,268	0.79
Uttar Pradesh†	198,565	0.22
Himachal Pradesh	141,610	9.09
Dadra and Nagar Haveli	64,445	86.89
Laccadive, Minicoy, and Amindivi Islands	29,540	92.86
Andaman and Nicobar Islands	18,102	15.72
Goa, Daman, and Diu†	7,654	0.89

(Chandigarh, Delhi, Pondicherry and the Punjab† have no tribals listed for
1971.)

*Compiled from Census of India, 1971, Paper 1 of 1972, Final Population. A glance at the
first four states listed will confirm the observation that the majority of Scheduled Tribes
live in central India (Cohn, 1971, p. 17).

†Notable variability in census reports appears for Uttar Pradesh, the Punjab, and Goa. In
1961, Uttar Pradesh had no tribals listed, but in 1971 had 198,565; in 1961 the Punjab
had 14,132 listed but none in 1971; Goa, Daman, and Diu had none listed in 1961 but
7,654 in 1971.

On a different demographic dimension, the religious affiliation of the
Adivasis, the Census has been highly inaccurate. Table 4.2, based on figures
drawn from the 1961 Census, demonstrates this bias. The term "others" in Table
4.2 refers in this context to tribal cults and religious practices of an indigenous
nature. On the face of it, these figures seem to show that only 4.5 percent of the
Scheduled Tribes are practicing their original religious forms and that nearly 90
percent are Hindus. The falsity of this report and the Hindu bias of the Census
are clearly shown by Fürer-Haimendorf, who writes that in the district where he
did his major research (Adilabad in Andhra Pradesh), there were 71,874 Gond
tribals in 1941, almost all of them professing a tribal religion. When, however, he

TABLE 4.2

Religious Affiliation of Scheduled Tribes in Rural Areas*

Religion	Number	Percentage to Total Rural Population of Tribals
Hindu	26,710,428	89.40
Christian	1,653,570	5.53
Buddhist	100,243	0.34
Muslim	61,015	0.20
Others	1,353,993	4.53

*Compiled from Census of 1961.

revisited the district in the 1960s, he could see "no change in Gond religion which would justify their classification as Hindus. Yet, in 1961 only two persons were returned under the head 'Other Religions' and there can be no doubt that all the Gonds were classified as Hindus." He also quotes from Census figures in other districts where similar mass disappearance of tribal religious adherents occurred, along with an equally sudden rise in the number of Hindus (Fürer-Haimendorf, 1967, pp. 196-97). The only conclusion possible, therefore, is that the proportion of Hindus in the tribal population remains unknown but is certainly far less than the Census shows.

In 1961 over 97 percent of the tribals were in rural areas.[6] This is a higher rural percentage than is true of any other Indian minority. At that time the Scheduled Tribes were 6.87 percent of India's *total* population, but they constituted 8.16 percent of the *rural* population. There were only three states in India where the percentage of Adivasis in the cities was as high as 5 percent of the tribals in that state: Gujarat, Tamil Nadu, and Karnataka.[7] Except for the limited number of hunters and food gatherers, the great majority of tribals are engaged in some form of agriculture. A significant difference appears when the Adivasis are compared with the Scheduled Castes on the occupational dimension. In 1961, for example, 68 percent of the work force among Scheduled Tribes were cultivators and 20 percent landless laborers; among the Scheduled Castes the corresponding figures were 38 and 34 percent. On the assumption that cultivators owned at least some land, a much greater proportion of the tribals would be actual proprietors, with a much smaller proportion landless laborers. This analysis does not take into account communal and kinship ownership in tribal areas, however, where agricultural conditions have some unique features, as will be noted below.

WHY A MINORITY GROUP?

If there are 450 tribal communities speaking literally hundreds of languages or dialects, it is only natural to raise this question: In what sense is it possible to

---

6. Computed from Census of India 1961, Vol. I, Part V-A(ii).

7. Census of India 1961, Vol. I, Part V-A(i).

regard this motley aggregation as a true minority? Does it have sufficient unity so that it is meaningful to regard it on a par with other ethnic minorities?

There will certainly be social scientists who deny that the tribals constitute a minority, and I can only hope to convince them on probabilistic grounds. First of all, in this study I am regarding all tribals as a collective whole because of the macrosociological approach essential to the present volume. It is when we look at total societies that we are forced to raise such questions as: What are the common features that set tribals off from nontribals? What are the factors that facilitate integration of tribals in the society as a whole, factors that they share not only with fellow tribals within India but with those of similar cultural and structural position in many other societies as well? I am not denying the relevance or importance of ethnographic studies that focus on the uniqueness of each tribe, but such microsociological investigations should neither monopolize nor exhaust the interests of science in such peoples. An opposite focus is equally legitimate when it centers on the societal (and generalizable) features of the situation. In spite of the plural cultural and linguistic variations from one unit to another, every one of these tribes faces the same dilemma of assimilation versus autonomy that is faced by every other tribe. Conversely, the nontribals forming the great majority face a similar question: How shall we come to terms with the tribals? And, what will be the policy for dealing with them?

Furthermore, the Scheduled Tribes, as a collective whole, correspond to the characteristics of a minority group as outlined in Chapter 1 above; that is, they are an ethnic group having their own symbolic features that distinguish them from the rest of the population, lacking both numerical and power dominance in the society as a whole. In addition, like other minorities, this group takes its rise from one of the six intergroup sequences (in this case, the "emergence of indigenous isolates"). Also, it is suggested that members of a minority have some consciousness of kind.

On this last point there may be objections that Scheduled Tribes have less self-awareness as a cohesive unit than any other minority in India. If all national minorities were placed on a continuum and if greater or lesser consciousness of kind were used as a variable, it would not be difficult to make out a convincing case that tribals would be placed at the lower end of the scale because of their rural isolation and their dispersion and separation from each other. This does not mean, however, that they lack a common consciousness altogether. In fact, I submit that a growing self-awareness is noticeable in many ways. The political demands made by such communities as the Nagas, a number of Assamese tribes, or the tribes of central India in the Jharkhand movement for a separate state all show that an awakening solidarity has started a vigorous development. According to Professor S. C. Dube, this feeling can be expected to increase in the future as the politicization of tribes continues and the communication channels are enlarged. A strong tribal image is emerging, he says: "Tribalness is now a powerful political factor, and to exploit its full potential tribal groups at different techno-economic levels and representing different cultural ethos and patterns are being linked politically. ... Separatist politics, often resulting in mass violence and senseless destruction of the infrastructure of development, befuddles economic and social issues and makes their solution increasingly difficult. But in recent years the short-run payoff of the politics of agitation and of separatism has been so great . . . that it is difficult to seal off the tribal areas from their pernicious influence. How can one expect greater political restraint from the tribals, who are recent entrants to the national political arena, when more mature parties and politicians throw all caution to the wind and involve these proud, sensitive, and volatile people in agitations and struggles aimed at furthering their personal or party interests?" (Dube, 1969, pp. 4-5; by permission).

A NOTE ON TRIBAL AGRICULTURE

Although the more assimilated groups like the Bhils of Rajasthan practice the same sort of cultivation as their nontribal neighbors, most of the Adivasis live in hilly or forested regions where a good many subsist on hunting, slash-and-burn agriculture (jhum, bewar), or both, as a matter of sheer survival. The peculiar conditions under which the tribals are frequently forced to work reduce their productivity to low levels and keep their standard of living depressed. As one investigating committee reported, "The terrain in the tribal areas is very undulating, and in most cases, it consists of steep slopes. Cultivation in such areas therefore results in the erosion of soil and reduction of fertility. The process is accentuated by winds, snow and turbulent watercourses in the hills. Scientific soil conservation on a large scale is therefore essentially necessary for the survival of the hill people. Government have set up soil conservation departments in the various States of India but the result so far achieved is not yet easily perceptible" (Bareh *et al.,* 1965, pp. 80-81).

The usual type of irrigation is useless in such areas; to be of any value, short channels and embankments (bunds) are the most efficient means for catching sufficient water, directing it properly, and providing storage for it. Such methods are not only difficult to adopt because of obstacles to construction but unusually costly, since they require individual adaptation on each plot. It is therefore unlikely that either state or central government will undertake the endless series of small operations that would be needed, or, alternately, will float a legion of diminutive loans to individual cultivators who would then repay over many years. Without such aids, however, the tribals continue to produce at low levels for lack of efficient irrigation methods.

Other handicaps affect the agriculture of tribal areas. These sections of the country are definitely susceptible to drought. For example, there are 199 districts with more than 8 percent tribal population, and only nineteen of these districts are in drought-free zones of assured irrigation, while forty-six are drought-prone districts. At times, famines have precipitated political agitation and protest, as in the Sarguja district of Madhya Pradesh in 1951 and the Mizo district of Assam in 1960 (Singh, 1969, pp. 3, 7). In Nagaland, the central government has made use of the air force to drop food and supplies to areas where famines exist or are impending (Anand, 1967, pp. 129-30). Such temporary measures that bring relief in an emergency cannot take the place of long-range planning for increasing the available water supply or encouraging the diversification of crops.

Land alienation also continually reduces the acreage available for tribal cultivation. As Bareh and his group discovered, at least 20 percent of the tribal population in Gujarat lost all their land through evictions or through changes brought about by the improper execution of the land-revenue acts. In Maharashtra, the legal procedure for registering title deeds is so complicated that few tribals can protect their holdings by this method; many have lost their properties while others remain vulnerable to loss because they cannot produce a proper legal claim. In Bihar, where alienation of land has been a major problem since the nineteenth century, the Chotanagpur Tenancy Act was passed in 1908 forbidding the sale of tribal lands to nontribals. Though this Act has been amended and strengthened several times, it still contains loopholes that allow transfers to take place — such as declaratory suits filed in the civil courts (Bareh *et al.,* 1965, pp. 75-76).

In addition to displacements brought about by landlords and moneylenders, tribal cultivators have lost land to large corporations. In central India, for example, mines and hydroelectric projects are likely to be located in tribal areas where huge tracts of land are appropriated by large-scale enterprises both private and public. Little thought appears to be given the tribal communities displaced by such operations (Das, 1969, pp. 1ff.). A few details illumine the effects of industrial progress on landholders who live in the path of mining, manufacturing plants, or dams for producing electric power. "Up to 1961, as many as 14,113 tribal families have been displaced in Bihar, West Bengal, Madhya Pradesh and Orissa to make room for dams, steel projects, fertiliser factory and the Heavy Engineering Corporation. The total areas of land from which the tribals have been displaced in the above places amount to 62,238 acres, but the area on which they have been rehabilitated amounts to only 8,314 acres" (Bareh *et al.,* 1965, p. 77). It is common where Adivasis are compensated for the loss of their land for them to receive less than nontribals of the same area who undergo similar deprivation. This process can be easily rationalized with the observation that many tribals, unaccustomed to a money economy, spend whatever cash compensation they receive on feasts, liquor, and the wares of itinerant traders, while at times the local moneylenders claim their dues in haste before it is too late. Often enough, the recipients of these cash sums are quickly impoverished and in worse condition than before (Das, 1969, p. 1).

In addition to these drawbacks, most tribal cultivators live on the poorest and most uneconomic landholdings, even though many are listed as proprietors (Bareh *et al.,* 1965, p. 77).

RELATIVE STATION IN SOCIETY

Although the evidence is scanty, the data available make it clear that the economic status of Adivasis is extremely low. "The income per capita of the tribals in Madhya Pradesh, Rajasthan and Gujarat was Rs. 104.6, Rs. 103.6 and Rs. 101.6 respectively as against Rs. 330 for the country in 1960-61" (Uppal, 1965).

In the matter of schooling and educational attainment, the data are more indicative. Except for the states of Assam and Nagaland where Christian mission schools have proliferated, literacy rates for tribals are low and attendance at the different school levels is poor. With the exception of North East Frontier Agency (N.E.F.A.), where complete statistics are not available, the all-India literacy rate for the Scheduled Tribes is 8.53 percent as compared with 10.27 for the Scheduled Castes and 24.0 for the nation as a whole (Census of India, 1961, Vol. 1, Part V-A).

There is, of course, a special reason why the Adivasis make a poor showing in the more advanced type of education; it is more or less inherent in the conservative attitudes holding them back from undertaking any novel programs too far removed from familiar habits. As one Block Development Officer observes, "The peculiar tribal customs and practices as well as the social structure create many problems when new trends are introduced. For example, the incapability of an Adivasi youth to separate from his wife temporarily for undergoing even a short training, away from his village to better his earnings, deprives him, of the benefits in spite of our best intentions. Lack of mutual trust between the couple is the reason behind it" (Kurup, 1965, p. 40). The same officer notes that handicrafts are not part of the tribals' usual skills. He writes, "In tribal areas, there is no traditional village industry except perhaps bamboo-craft. My experience in tribal area of the last 14 years is that the tribals are really not enthusiastic of taking up any cottage industry or craft to better their earnings. They prefer to do unskilled manual work rather than specializing in some skilled work" (ibid., p. 39).[8]

There are no reliable statistics on the employment picture for tribals in the cities, for their numbers are too limited. They have a tiny urban population outside the northeastern states or a few industrial centers like Jamshedpur, located in areas already tribal. And because of the scanty distribution of Adivasis as a whole in industrial occupations, coupled with their general lack of technical training,"the displaced tribals can be engaged only temporarily as labourers; but later when machines are brought, they become unemployed and without any moorings having been displaced from their lands" (Bareh *et al.*, 1965, pp. 64-65). Thus, the risk of unemployment is likely to be somewhat greater for tribals than for nontribals in industrial centers.

The data on representation of tribals in government service also reveal how limited their participation is. It is true that from 1957 to 1966, Scheduled Tribe workers increased in absolute numbers, which can be regarded as an encouraging sign. The total number of Adivasis in the service of the central government reached 106 in Class I by 1966, 80 in Class II, 12,356 in Class III, and 40,113 in Class IV. The last two figures may appear impressive, but percentages tell a different story. Scheduled Tribes form only 0.52 percent of all government workers in Class I, 0.27 percent in Class II, 1.10 percent in Class III, and 3.41 percent in Class IV; in comparison, their total population makes up over 6 percent of an all-India aggregate (*Handbook on Scheduled Castes and Scheduled Tribes*, 1968, pp. 92-93). In the Administrative Service (IAS) the percentage of

---

8. These comments reveal not only the conditions that make it difficult for many tribals to adopt work habits of the larger community but also the ethnocentric attitudes of official personnel doing the supervision. These attitudes will receive further attention below.

tribal officials is 1.90, and in the Indian Police Service it is 1.64 percent (ibid., pp. 90-91). Since theoretically there are reserved posts available for Adivasis in government service equal to their proportion of the population, it can be inferred that the poor showing indicated by these figures is not due to discrimination alone but to the unavailability of eligible candidates due to the generally low levels of education in most states.

FROM SECLUSION TO PARTICIPATION

Of all Indian minorities, the Scheduled Tribes have the highest degree of enclosure; they are what Martin Orans (1965, p. 126) once called the Santal, that is, an "encysted society." They come closest to the model of a "plural society" where the various units are compartmentalized into "analogous, parallel, non-complementary, but distinguishable sets of institutions" (van den Berghe, 1967, p. 3). Structural separation of tribals from nontribals is, of course, not absolute, and the designation "indigenous isolates" must be understood to mean "more isolated from the majority in comparison with other minorities." As already noted, the Adivasis are in areas usually inaccessible to outsiders, where roads are poor and railroads generally absent. They have a separate, frequently nonmonetary, barter economy; an unwritten language; limited or nonexistent participation in decision making affecting the entire nation; and, finally, experience or knowledge that is circumscribed within a local area and culture. Unlike the Scheduled Castes who reside in nearly every village so that they are spread out evenly over the society as a whole, the tribals are highly concentrated in a few regions, tapering off to the more accessible sections where the dominant group is preponderant.

In the case of developing countries like India, the government is "modernizing" society by social planning on a national scale, by trying to raise productivity along with the levels of living, and by equalizing in various ways the social and economic rewards. The ideals of rationality thus stand in the forefront of national aims. Societies taking on such tasks (Myrdal, 1968, Vol. I, pp. 57ff.) conceive of the indigenous isolates as "backward" peoples to be brought into the "mainstream" of a total life, integrating all scattered elements of the population into a "modern" configuration. However, this process may occur either as a by-product of industrial and political pursuits, or as a result of deliberate and planned intervention within the tribal areas. The distinction must be kept in mind in the analysis that follows.

Ideas of modernization must also avoid the simplistic notion that there are two sectors separate from each other: one modernized and the other traditional. In the present context, however, there is one sector partly modernized and partly traditional, serving as the transforming agent of another sector which is *less* modernized and *more* traditional (on a different cultural base). Finally, it is possible to observe the changes from the standpoint of the dominant group (regarding them as the agents) or to reverse the field and regard the isolated subordinates responding (and hence the reciprocal agents), interpreting the interaction from their point of view. I begin with the subordinate standpoint.

As the indigenous isolates, the tribals, get drawn into social, economic, and political participation, they increase their use of money, enter into wage labor in greater numbers, pay new taxes, travel more on improved roads and railroads, become familiar with new modes of mass communication, use novel tools and machines (often becoming dependent on them), emulate different religious practices, send their children to schools unfamiliar to the parents, and start voting and attending political rallies. In each of these novel activities, tribals increase their participation ratio, and in each they face the central question: to join or to separate? After initial isolation has broken down (often a phase in the distant past), there is no way to prevent the deluge of change. A steady accumulation of new habits occurs and, when it is rapid, threatens to overwhelm them. An increased contact with "modernizing" outsiders, however, has dialectical rather than unilateral consequences. For some tribes, greater interaction with nontribals increases the attractiveness of the alien culture and it becomes a model to be reproduced; for others, it leads to repugnance, antagonism, or withdrawal. In either case, some ambivalence occurs for many; conflict is attended by secret attraction and acceptance by concealed hatred. Figure 4.1 is drawn so as to bring out the dual possibilities inherent in the encounter, one centripetal, which leads to greater absorption into the wider society, the other centrifugal, which leads to separation or withdrawal.

Comment on this figure, which appeared in an earlier volume, can now be repeated: "... the assumption behind this rough sketch is that processes of integration or conflict become discernible for indigenous isolates only after a certain threshold of activation. Hence there may be a series of ethnic groups in a given society that are in different stages of the participation curve" (Schermerhorn, 1970, p. 132). For instance, the Bhils of Rajasthan and Gujarat are definitely in the activated phase, many of them highly skilled agriculturalists who raise cash crops like tobacco, cotton, and ground nut (Doshi, 1969, p. 8). At the opposite extreme are the Jawaras of the Andaman Islands who are not only quite isolated from others but who reject contacts with the outside world and reject its technology (Roy Burman, 1969a, p. 17). Between these two ends of the continuum are the great majority of tribes, most of them lying somewhere between the exposed marginal and the fully activated types. Some of the tribes that appear quite secluded and shut off from the world are nevertheless in areas literally teeming with nontribals whose presence is unrecognized until visitors enter the region and find them there. T. S. Negi (1969, p. 14) tells of the Kinnaur people in a remote area of Himachal Pradesh who appear cut off by mountainous terrain from the rest of India, but in their valley, "Today, against a total indigenous population of about 41,000, there are, more or less regularly living within the district all around the year, nearly thirty thousand outsiders. Mostly they are Government employees, labourers and businessmen." Furthermore, until the rate of population growth is checked, the search for more land will bring continued encroachments on tribal areas, and hence an increased amount of forced acculturation. This tendency will compel more and more tribesmen to make decisions either for centripetal acceptance or centrifugal aversion.

Figure 4.1 raises further problems: What are the factors or variables that determine whether the tribal response will move toward or against the wider society? If the movement is against the wider society, will it take the form of political activity or out-and-out violent rebellion? Since each local situation is complex enough to warrant intensive analysis, all that can be accomplished in

Fig. 4.1 Stages of Increased Participation for Indigenous Isolates (Dimensions of Communication and Institution)

COMMUNICATION DIMENSION

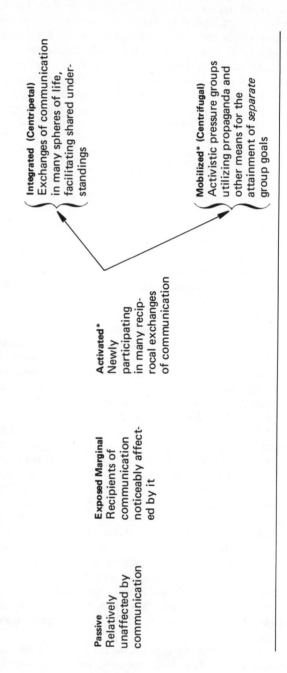

Passive
Relatively
unaffected by
communication

Exposed Marginal
Recipients of
communication
noticeably affect-
ed by it

Activated*
Newly
participating
in many recip-
rocal exchanges
of communication

Integrated (Centripetal)
Exchanges of communication
in many spheres of life,
facilitating shared understandings

Mobilized* **(Centrifugal)**
Activistic pressure groups
utilizing propaganda and
other means for the
attainment of *separate*
group goals

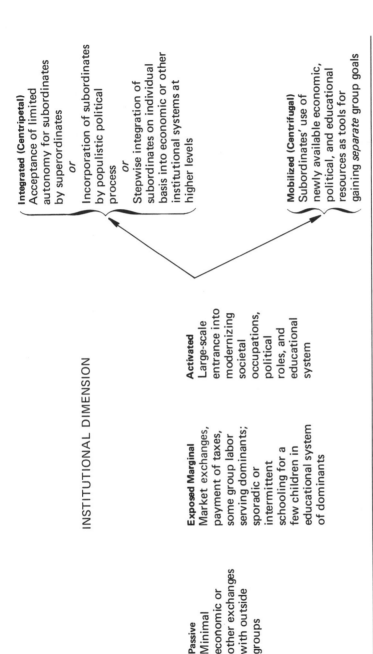

INSTITUTIONAL DIMENSION

Integrated (Centripetal)
Acceptance of limited autonomy for subordinates by superordinates

or

Incorporation of subordinates by populistic political process

or

Stepwise integration of subordinates on individual basis into economic or other institutional systems at higher levels

Mobilized (Centrifugal)
Subordinates' use of newly available economic, political, and educational resources as tools for gaining *separate* group goals

Activated
Large-scale entrance into modernizing societal occupations, political roles, and educational system

Exposed Marginal
Market exchanges, payment of taxes, some group labor serving dominants; sporadic or intermittent schooling for a few children in educational system of dominants

Passive
Minimal economic or other exchanges with outside groups

*This terminology substitutes Blalock's (1967) usage of "mobilize" for Deutsch's (1965) familiar one. Blalock asserts, "power is a multiplicative function of two very general types of variables, *total resources* and the degree to which these resources are *mobilized* in the services of those persons or groups exercising the power" (p. 110). "Activation" meaning intensive participation is here a synonym for Deutsch's "mobilization."

this brief overview is to identify the major influences and to indicate some combinations that seem likely clues for future research. What follows must be regarded as tentative and provisional. As more investigation focuses on this issue in the future, better grounded conclusions may be expected.

The first factor of importance is the patterned ethos of each tribal unit. Variability in this dimension is extensive. As one observer notes, "The Mompas are quiet, gentle, friendly and artistic. They are also fond of music, dance and drama. In contrast, the Daflas are unruly, turbulent and aggressive" (Haldipur, 1969, p. 3). Other things being equal, one would expect that the Mompas would have a greater chance for integration into the national whole than the Daflas. Yet there are external influences that belie the easy assumption of an equality of prior conditions. Asok Chanda, commenting on this same tribe, reports that among the Mompas, "even now portraits of Mao-tse-tung, delicately woven, can be seen in stray households, garlanded with oil lamps burning in front in reverence."[9]

A second variable of great importance is the nature of political rule imposed upon the tribals by an outside power. The actual structure of authority is a crucial element since it can vary tremendously from one area to another. During British rule, for example, there was one overarching principle of colonial dominion: the maintenance of order or the *Pax Britannica.* This principle dictated one policy for inaccessible tribes like those of the Garo Hills, and a different one for the tribes of Chotanagpur, who were in fairly close contact with Hindu neighbors and, prior to British occupation, under the authority of zamindars and moneylenders, with somewhat more distant Moghul rule. After the British brought the warrior tribes of the Garo Hills under control of their outposts, they protected these isolated peoples from further encroachment (and communication) by a series of British enactments that forbade plainsmen to enter the territory. The only outsiders allowed were Christian missionaries, possibly because they were supportive of law and order. The governmental structure in the Garo Hills (in present-day Meghalaya; see map of British Colonial India) was for years lightly imposed and permissive of autonomy, while prohibiting incursions from the plains (Kar, 1969, pp. 11-12). Such hill regions were known as "excluded areas," a term applied to similar hinterlands in Burma (Trager, 1966, p. 80).

The British penchant for law and order took a different turn in Chotanagpur, however, where a previous structure of external authority had already been imposed upon Oraon, Munda, and Santal peoples by zamindars and other landlords who not only encroached upon tribal land but made unlimited demands for *begar* or forced labor (Sahay, 1968, p. 290). In this case, all the British did was to reinforce the status quo (the already existing power structure), again so as to buttress law and order. But the consequences were quite different.

Events that followed pointed up the disparity of results in the two cases. The policy of protected isolation kept the Garos and other tribes of the northeast from encroachment until independence; it kept peace and order fairly well as long as the British were in control. But with the shift in government authority

---

9. *Times of India,* June 9, 1969.

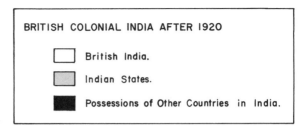

BRITISH COLONIAL INDIA AFTER 1920

☐ British India.

▨ Indian States.

■ Possessions of Other Countries in India.

from British to Indian hands, Naga revolt erupted and has continued to smolder ever since. In Chotanagpur, however, the two-tiered structure of authority allowed nontribals to exploit the tribals so incessantly that open rebellion of the tribals was suppressed by British arms (Orans, 1965, pp. 30-33).[10] With the coming of independence, conditions in Chotanagpur became more stabilized.

The Naga revolt after independence was not due solely to a change of rule, however. Another factor of great influence was the harsh exposure of Nagas to modern warfare as employed in guerrilla forays against the Japanese during World War II. Another was the arousal of nationalistic expectations when the British encouraged the formation of the Naga National [sic] Council after the war. A third was the signed agreement between the Council and representatives of the government of India, perceived by the Nagas as a promise to grant them independence after ten years, though not so interpreted by the government. Fourth, and perhaps equally important, was the charismatic leadership of Phizo who commanded the underground warfare of the Nagas for years until he was exiled to London and then directed rebellion from there (Puri, 1969, pp. 6ff.). All these convergent factors made open conflict highly probable, but none of the four was operative in Chotanagpur where events took a different turn.[11]

Among the tribes of south Bihar and northern Bengal, the impact of Christianity was followed by the rapid rise of industrialism in selected areas. These events awakened the central tribes to a whole set of novel expectations. After the failure of rebellion in the nineteenth century, the path of military revolt was rejected. As more Hindu tradesmen and farmers entered the region over the turn of the century, however, the number of exposed marginals steadily increased. An elite composed of the relatively more affluent and more educated (both in Christian and government schools) began their ascent to higher status. But, as Orans (1965, p. 100) put it, "... the effect of this increase in education was seen to be essentially divisive and as accelerating already existing tendencies." Correlative with this individual mobility and reinforcing the process was the arrival of the Tata Iron and Steel Company at Jamshedpur in 1908; other plants soon followed, and Chotanagpur was eventually dotted with both mines and factories. A selected number of the tribals (some of them the most educated) obtained factory positions and attained levels of living far above their fellow tribesmen on the land, while many of the land cultivators were displaced

---

10. Oddly enough, Indian nationalist anti-British opinion was strongly critical of colonial policy for protecting the tribals and isolating them, thus singling out the "excluded areas" plan as though it were the *only* British strategy for dealing with tribesmen; Indian leaders apparently overlooked the Chotanagpur regime, which was far more damaging to the tribals themselves (Fürer-Haimendorf, 1967, p. 185).

11. "Even until recently there did not exist any ethnic identity called the Naga. Various ethnic groups who used to identify themselves as Ao, Sema, Angami, Rengma, Kabui, Konyak, etc., were known by the term Naga to outsiders. There was no feeling of tribal solidarity . . . until after the withdrawal of the British Colonial Government. . . . Since then a few leaders among them with the alleged help of foreign missionaries started agitating for the separation of Naga territory from Indian Republic. Thus the formation . . . of the independent Government of India acted as a stimulant for the growth of tribalism among the Naga groups all of whom are at present inclined to identify themselves as members of a single Naga tribe" (Nag, 1968, p. 197).

by other industries and new towns which gobbled up their fields. The mobile individuals, particularly those attending Hindu-dominated schools, increasingly adopted Hindu practices, abjuring beef eating, abandoning tribal forms of recreation like excessive drinking and dancing, and rejecting witchcraft (ibid., pp. 51-54). This created a rift within the tribal community since the uneducated became ambivalent in their regard for the elite, acknowledging their prestige and importance, while simultaneously displaying envious hostility (ibid., pp. 54-55).

In the 1930s and 1940s, with the coming of independence, new opportunities for political participation opened up. An increasing proportion of the tribals were activated in the wider social system, and the franchise spurred the process on all sides. At this point, educated leaders initiated a movement to create a central state where tribals would take over the reins of government. This state was to be called Jharkhand, and the tribal political party devoted to its sponsorship was organized as the Jharkhand Party in 1951, with Jaipal Singh, an Oxford-educated Christian as the elected leader.[12]

The Jharkhand Party played on the long-smoldering grievances of the tribals, many of whom were reduced to tenancy and wage labor by landlords or moneylenders, while others were displaced by industries or mines. Also stimulated by the success of states like Andhra Pradesh or Nagaland in winning autonomy for themselves,[13] the party took on the enthusiasm of a mass movement; its leader, Jaipal Singh, "succeeded in bringing together Christians, non-Christians, urban and rural people under its common banner. The movement spread all over Chotanagpur and beyond, even among the Tea Garden labourers of North Bengal who were migrants from this area" (Sen, 1969, p. 3). Up to and including the early sixties, the Jharkhand Party elected many candidates to state assemblies and to Parliament. In all of Chotanagpur, the tribal party furnished lively competition for the Congress, often displacing it in critical elections. Congress leaders, alarmed at the loss of votes, convinced Jaipal Singh and other top figures in the Jharkhand Party that the tribals would make better gains for their constituents if they joined forces with the Congress; a merger of the two parties took place in 1963. This merger killed the agitation for a separate Jharkand state for the time being. Relinquishing this demand appears to have been the price paid.

After the Jharkhand Party joined the Congress, political action diverged in many directions. One important change was a shift from Christian to non-Christian leadership. In the fourth general election, "Among the 29 reserved Assembly seats in Bihar, 75.80 percent was won by non-Christian tribals against 24.20 percent by the Christian tribals. Among the five reserved parliamentary seats again, 80 percent of them were won by the non-Christians alone" (Vidyarthi, 1969, p. 9). In the majority of Bihar districts with substantial numbers of tribals, non-Christian candidates won in nearly every case. This raises the question, as Vidyarthi hints, of whether a Hindu model for acculturation is not reviving.

---

12. A less influential predecessor of the Jharkhand Party was the Adivasi Sabha formed in 1938. Jaipal Singh was elected its president in 1939.

13. The later addition of Maharashtra to the list of new states temporarily strengthened the tribals' case.

The Christian influence has not died out entirely, however. There are several attempts to rekindle the Jharkhand Party, and religious differences among leaders seem to be a function of generation level. "The older generation of leaders whose glories had waned in course of the last two decades were trying to revive it at the socio-cultural level. They wanted to keep the membership confined to the tribals only. The younger generation of leaders on the other hand were eager to have a full-fledged party uniting the different splinter groups of the Jharkhand Party that had cropped up. They wanted to extend the membership to non-tribals also who were not *Dikus*[14] and had settled in Chotanagpur for generations" (Sen, 1969, p. 4). Apparently it is the younger members who have higher education and come from Christian schools (Vidyarthi, 1969, p. 10).

After Jaipal Singh retired from politics, he still remained active and was prominent in the organization of a new semi-party, the Birsa Seva Dal in 1967. This association at first helped to supply legal aid and political pressure on behalf of Adivasis encountering such injustices as delays in payment of scholarships or difficulties in securing admission to postgraduate study. Gradually the Birsa Seva Dal developed in the direction of a more explicit political party, and, as it did so, it came under the increasing influence of the Communists, who supplied both money and leadership (Sen, 1969, p. 5). By and large, however, political unity among tribals in Chotanagpur has waned, and its divisions have split into cliques and factions. It seems likely that education of tribal youth in government schools is increasing more rapidly today than it is in Christian schools. Hinduization may therefore be expected to increase in Chotanagpur.

Such evidence suggests more general, though tentative, hypotheses. Tribes in border areas (other things being equal) are more difficult to integrate into the wider society than are tribes of the interior who are surrounded by the majority population, especially when the border regions are inaccessible by easy means of transportation. Being on the border, they are also likely to have fellow tribals on the other side of the line and are therefore subject to pressures of irredentism. In addition, their place on the border permits any foreign power hostile to the society in question to stimulate dissent or rebellion in the border group. Conversely, the border community may be used as a convenient springboard for fifth-column activity by the antagonistic foreign power. The Nagas exemplify all of these trends and have also been separated even more from Hindu society culturally by their strong adherence to Christianity, which brought in its train a high percentage of people educated in English medium schools. (Nagaland is the only state in which English is *the* official language.) All these factors exert a centrifugal pull on the Naga tribes, and their participation in guerrilla activity during World War II gave them confidence in the use of firearms that undoubtedly made open conflict more attractive to them than it did to most tribes of India.

Tribes of central India have a different relationship with their neighbors, although they share one characteristic with the Nagas — a strong Christian influence. Christian contact brings with it an increase in higher education and the consequent rise in "expectations." The term "awakening" is no more than a

14. Term of opprobrium meaning nontribals who are cheats or tyrants.

metaphor for awareness of new alternatives accompanying increase of external contacts with diverse cultural values and parallel growth of participation in novel situations. This "mental mobility" as Howard Becker has called it, is brought into play by anything that increases social contacts with outsiders: migration, religious conversions, urbanization, industrialization, and other like influences. All of these elements mentioned have had a strong impact on the Chotanagpur region, and their cumulative effect has been much stronger than it ever was in border areas. In Chotanagpur the Adivasis are totally surrounded by their Hindu neighbors and all links of communication (railways, bus lines, telegraph, telephone, newspapers, and radio) connect the people with the total society far more closely than is possible in the northeast.

Under the constant surveillance of their intimately juxtaposed Hindu fellow citizens, the tribes of central India have been restrained from using violence to achieve their ends; the memory of unsuccessful revolt in the past no doubt strengthens their caution. Also, close proximity to a politicized electorate (quite unmatched in the more isolated northeastern districts) has stimulated a desire to enter political rivalries where a plurality of tribal numbers in many districts is a potential weapon of great force. With the possible exception of the Gonds, the largest tribal groups in India live in Chotanagpur: the Mundas with over a million, the Oraons with nearly 1.5 million, and the Santal with well over 3 million. This almost brings the power of a separate electorate to the tribals as long as they remain united, and for a time they did so in the old Jharkhand Party.[15] As this unity became absorbed in the larger fold of the Congress, tribals lost their political impact as an organized group by accepting a new relationship that amounted to co-optation.

The mobility patterns introduced in Figure 3.1 of the previous chapter enable us to visualize the effect of the tribals' shift from contest mobility, illustrated by the large-scale support for the Jharkhand Party, to sponsored mobility where individual tribal politicians find a place for their talents in the all-encompassing Congress party. Figure 4.2, a variation of Figure 3.1, depicts the Adivasi situation.

Some features of the tribal situation differ from those of the Scheduled Castes as they were presented in the earlier figure of Chapter 3. Figure 4.2 has both manifest and less evident variations on a common theme when the reference shifts to the Scheduled Tribes. One manifest difference is the substitution of Hinduization for Sanskritization. Sanskritization assumes lower caste status as a *terminus a quo* and denotes the process by which the passage from lower to higher caste position is effected. Since the Adivasis are originally completely outside the caste system, they do not Sanskritize in the root meaning of that term, at least until they make the transition from tribe to caste.[16]

---

15. A weak and decentralized Jharkhand Party was reborn in 1970 or 1971, although the details are obscure. It produces a scattering of individual candidates with no more than local support in both Bihar and Orissa. Since it has lost the previous mass backing, I am disregarding its influence in the following paradigm.

16. Defending the use of "Sanskritization" for the tribal transition from non-caste to caste is D. N. Majumdar (1969, p. 3). To do this, however, he finds it necessary to redefine Sanskritization.

Social Categories	Collectivistic	Individualistic
Culture; Style of life; Prestige goal; Emulation	Hinduization Out-group traditional Local, regional models Upper caste reference group Group display Group cohesion	Westernization Anti-traditional All-India models Western-educated reference group Individual separation Alienation from group
Power and control; Use or acceptance of sanctions	Contest mobility Involvement with group encounter Self-chosen group commitment Total group identification In-group authority In-group goals	Sponsored mobility Protected competition Co-optation by others Ceremonial group identification Out-group authority Out-group goals

Fig. 4.2 Modes of Mobility for Tribals

Another difference is that Hinduization requires acceptance of cultural elements that may be traditional, but in quite a different social system.

There are less evident differences as well, but they are not visible in the figure. For example: (1) In the case of the Scheduled Tribes, Hinduization, unlike Sanskritization, seems to require an elite to lead the way toward new practices, others following after a lapse of time (Orans, 1965, pp. 36ff.), whereas Sanskritization utilizes concerted action by an entire group pervaded by consensus. (2) Since there is a greater cultural gap between tribals and the dominant group than exists between outcastes and the dominant group, it seems likely that tribals will experience more ambivalence in their choice of alternatives than will the Scheduled Castes. In other words, the pull of the old cultural traditions and language have greater weight among tribesmen than it will have for the lower jatis. (3) The Adivasis are under continual pressure from the dominant group to *change* their ways, in ways that are not applied to the outcastes. As Orans (1965, p. 126) observes, "Perhaps the oldest and most continuous of such pressures on the Santal has been governmental interference with Santal cow sacrifice and beef eating. Armed interference has been practiced everywhere and has not ceased under present democratic conditions." This pressure to change is in marked contrast with the situation of the Scheduled Castes, who are rather pressured to stay as they *are*.

Such added constraints create a double dilemma for tribesmen. In addition to the emulation-solidarity conflict which they share with outcastes and other minorities (symbolized by an imaginary line drawn diagonally between contest mobility and Westernization), they experience a conflict peculiarly their own between habits enjoined by their reference group of membership and quite different habits stressed by a reference group of power and authority,[17] the first nostalgically binding, the second often compulsorily enforced. This dilemma cannot be shown in Figure 4.2. However, the double dilemma (which is encountered by those in both marginal and activated stages of participation) creates a climate of uncertainty and accompanying habits that too frequently incapacitates tribals for activities in the wider community.

One hypothesis that can probably be derived from Figure 4.2 is that when contest mobility (exemplified by the Jharkhand Party) is replaced by sponsored mobility (where tribal candidates are taken under the wing of Congress sponsorship), there will be a corresponding increase in both Hinduization and Westernization on the part of the politicians who participate. Furthermore, since some of these "leaders" lean in one direction, some in the other, while still others try to combine the two, factionalism may also be expected to increase.

REVOLUTIONARY POTENTIAL

Another trend, so far unmentioned, is the incitement to violence, particularly among Adivasis in parts of southern India where it is interior tribes rather than those on the border that are activated. The following newspaper report pictures the situation:

In Srikakulam District [in Andhra Pradesh] the Naxalites are already well established with virtually the whole of 80,000 Girijan tribals of the Agency [Development Block Agency] under their sway. They are stated to have accumulated an arsenal of about 500 guns in addition to spears, bows and arrows, axes and abundant quantities of explosives. In clashing with rebel bands, police have so far seized about 250 country-made guns. Much more alarming is the slow but steady spread of Naxalite violence in other areas of Andhra Pradesh. Today Naxalites are active in at least 19 taluks spread over Visakhapatnam, East and West Godvari, Krishna, Guntur, Nellore, Anantpur, Warangal and Khammam districts. Over the past few weeks these rebel bands have conducted numerous raids mainly to secure arms and funds. Their targets are invariably landlords known to possess licensed arms. These raids have further consolidated the movement. [*The Statesman,* July 5, 1969]

The fact that revolutionary Naxalites have concentrated in Agency areas where tribals live shows that these constitute excellent regions of concealment where the dominant group does not intrude and where a buildup of semiguerrilla forces can proceed undisturbed.

Significantly, a 1969 study of rural conditions in India by the Home Ministry points up the explosive possibilities of poverty and deprivation with

---

17. Orans makes an ingenious distinction here between "rank concession" in which subordinates acknowledge the legitimacy of upper ranking for the dominant group, and "power concession" where the lowers bow to the authority of the stronger without any acceptance of value superiority. He quite properly insists that rank concession implies power concession but not vice versa (Orans, 1965, p. 125).

frequent allusions to the tribals who have been dispossessed, especially the Girijans in Andhra where "the State Government has considerably strengthened the police arrangements to control the insurgency. However, the basic cause of unrest, namely the defective implementation of laws enacted to protect the interests of the tribals, remains and unless this is attended to, it would not be possible to win the confidence of the tribals whose leadership has been taken over by the extremists."[18]

The Girijans, of course, are not representative of tribes in the southern region as a whole. There are some Kerala tribes (the Cherumans and Panyers) who have entered the caste system on the lowest rung in a gradual process of Hinduization (Fürer-Haimendorf, 1967, p. 183). However, there are quite a number of southern tribes in isolated areas who practice shifting cultivation. Under such conditions their lands are not coveted by outsiders, who tend to leave them alone. In the four states of Andhra Pradesh, Kerals, Karnataka, and Tamil Nadu, there are at least thirty-one tribes with a population of 226,200 who still practice shifting cultivation. Yet this amount is only 10 percent of the Adivasis in the four states, so that fully 90 percent are at least susceptible to displacement and alienation of their lands, as has occurred among the Girijans. Parallel difficulties exist among tribes of some forested areas where, for the protection of wild game, strict rules against hunting, fishing, gathering wood, or even collecting honey, are enforced by Forest Guards who, "housed in pukka houses totally unsuited to their surroundings, dominate the scene as petty dictators — a strange comment on the democratic decentralization which is being introduced in this State" (quoted in Moorthy, 1969, p. 24).

Consequently, incipient unrest occurs among a number of southern tribes, and, unless Tenancy Laws and Money Lenders Regulation Acts are strictly enforced (a prospect which none of the authorities regard as imminent), extremists will find equally receptive tribals in the Deccan. It is significant that in states like Andhra Pradesh or Tamil Nadu, tribes are so small and make up such a minute proportion of the state population that their votes would have little impact, even if mobilized. This situation contrasts with Bihar where tribal groups are large enough to swing elections or serve as the balance of power. With the political path blocked in scattered southern areas of sparse tribal residence, it is possible that violent means can come to be regarded as the only possible outlet.

FROM TRIBE TO CASTE

In his overview of the tribal situation in India, Fürer-Haimendorf (1967, p. 184) advances the thesis that Adivasis, faced by many encroachments on their lands and homes, tend to react in one of the following ways: (1) withdrawal to interior areas; (2) accepting subordinate position as tenants or day laborers; or (3) rebelling against outsiders. There is also a fourth possibility: namely, to resist encroachment successfully and become relatively successful agriculturalists, as many Bhils have apparently done. This last option seems to depend on a fairly large population base, as well as residence on the plains — a combination unmatched by the majority of tribal groups.

---

18. Quoted in *Times of India,* Dec. 8, 1969.

It is in the second and fourth alternatives that Hinduization is most likely to occur and that tribes will enter the caste system. Ideally, we would expect this process to be one of gradual incorporation in the centripetal direction shown in Figure 4.1. In terms of acculturation, D. N. Majumdar pictures three stages in the process of Sanskritization (here termed Hinduization), a model which he uses to typify what is happening to the Garos. In the first stage, the tribals give up "unclean" habits like beef eating, keeping of pigs and fowls, or the eating of pork and fowl. This is both a sign that the tribe wants acceptance in Hindu society and a claim to belong. Second is the abandonment of tribal deities and rites for the Hindu pantheon and the celebration of ceremonies associated with Hindu deities. These would now be performed by a Brahman priest. The third stage brings a relinquishing of clan organization and, in case it has been matrilineal, replacing it by the Hindu patrilineal system. To crown the entire process, Majumdar hints that the adoption of an Aryan language would complete detribalization in its totality (Majumdar, 1969, pp. 5-6).

Majumdar's scheme is a formal one in which some elements are supplied hypothetically in a given order. Such a smooth transition glosses over empirical details of a good many mixed forms revealed in historical and anthropological research. Almost without exception, such studies reveal that power and coercion play a greater part than Majumdar posits in his cultural framework. Assimilation of tribes into Hindu society has been going on since the sixty century B.C. as a by-product of conquest. With the coming of Ashoka and later rulers, forest and hill tribes were "warned that if they were to be the beloved of the Beloved of (other) Gods, they had best stop raiding the king's subjects and change their savage ways" (Mandelbaum, 1970, p. 587). Tribal-Hindu contacts appear to have been rather limited until the nineteenth century, however, and it was during that century that British rule slowed down the rate of assimilation; though colonial troops forced tribal raids to stop, the regime protected the practice of indigenous customs among their preliterate subjects. The movement toward Hinduization has accelerated in recent decades since the withdrawal of the British and now appears (with occasional exceptions) to be irreversible (ibid., 585-88). Instead of a gradual and even sequence, however, the transition has been marked by irregular and variable features.

For example, the Kond tribesmen of Orissa have had a changeable power relation to their Hindu neighbors, the Oriya. In the region known as the Kondmals, the Konds have a legend that Hindus have driven them out of lowlands and up into the hills. Certainly, the "Konds and Oriyas have competed for several centuries to win control over one another. Konds have tried to make Oriyas conform to their system of political relationships, in so far as the difference of caste would permit. Oriyas (in particular Warriors) have tried to make the Konds behave as a dependent caste, subordinate to themselves in just the same way as Baderi Pans are by tradition subordinate to Baderi Konds" (Bailey, 1960, p. 157).[19] The population of the Kondmal region is something

19. Baderi is the name of a village in the Kondmals. In this particular village, the tribal Konds have so far acculturated to Hindu ways that they have what appear to be castes of specialized occupations like smiths and herdsmen and an untouchable group of menials called Pans (Bailey, 1960, pp. 150-51). In other respects, however, they maintain their original kinship structure.

like two-thirds Kond to less than one-third Oriya, but "in spite of their numerical preponderance Konds have been subordinated to Oriyas and still are to some extent today." The larger villages are dominantly Oriya while the smaller ones have Kond majorities. Oriyas "occupy the best cultivating sites in the valleys, while the Konds occupy sites that are smaller and in remoter valleys. Since the Oriya villages are sited in the broader valleys, they lie along the lines of communication" (ibid., pp. 158-59). But the political relationships of Konds and Oriyas are contradictory, since the tribals are supposed to show fealty to the Oriya Sirdar but, in the new arena of universal franchise, have potentially enough votes to overpower the Oriyas of the district (ibid., p. 247). However, they have not yet fully exercised this influence and, at the time Bailey reported his findings (1960), there were still other perplexing complications:

> Oriyas treat Konds as a lower caste. No Oriya, other than the untouchables, will take food or water from a Kond. . . . But the Konds are not treated as untouchables by any clean caste Oriyas, who enter Kond houses and move freely about the villages where Konds live and permit Konds to draw water from wells which Oriyas use. . . . The ritual ranking of caste corresponds to some degree with political and economic ranking. Ritual ranking is sensitive to political and economic changes except at the extremes, where the Brahmin and the untouchables are placed. Both in the political and the economic system the Konds are not and never have been in the same position of dependence on the dominant Warrior group as the other inferior castes. There is a corresponding ambivalence in the symbolic behaviour of Konds toward Warriors whom they both accept and reject as their masters. [Bailey, 1960, pp. 159-60]

There are also contradictory norms in the political systems of Konds and Oriyas that help to maintain continual separation of the two communities. In the conflicts of the past, even though Konds could have conquered the Oriyas by sheer force of numbers, they could not fit the Oriyas into their political system simply because they could not make them over into relatives. And the Oriyas, who could have accommodated the Konds into a political structure, found it impossible to subdue them completely because they were too inferior numerically. In modern political terms, Bailey (1960, p. 266) believes that the distinction between tribe and caste is losing its utility.[20]

Similar mixed patterns appear among other tribes in transition. For example, the Bhumij of West Bengal do not live in isolated regions but have been in numerous villages, cheek by jowl with caste neighbors who apparently were

---

20. However, Bailey (1960) does try to elicit some general principles that apply to this situation: "If they have direct command over resources, and their access to the products of the economy are not derived mediately through a dependent status on others, then they are to be counted as a tribe, providing they fulfill a further condition: that they are a relatively large proportion of the total population in the area. If they fulfill the first condition but are a small part of the population, then they are a caste" (ibid, p. 265). "The (modern) system works toward cultural assimilation, while the traditional caste system promoted cultural disparity. . . . Caste in its traditional form can only flower in small-scale societies, and in the absence of extensive spatial mobility" (ibid., p. 191). (All Bailey quotations by permission.)

more recent arrivals in the area, although the two groups have been adjoined for centuries. In the past, Brahmans instructed many of the old chiefs in proper Kshatriya behavior,·a pattern followed by later Bhumij headmen and landowners of villages where they were often the dominant group. In some localities like Madhupur, the Bhumij as a whole regard themselves as a jati and are so regarded by other tribals. However, higher castes rank them low because they have not abandoned older habits of eating and drinking, widow remarriage, and burial of the dead. To the tribals of the region they are Kshatriyas; to Brahmans and twice-born Hindus they are pretenders who are unable to give up tribal ways. With the coming of independence and the special benefits open to Scheduled Tribes, there is a strong tendency to give up the maintenance of Kshatriya standards and opt for tribal status with its material and political privileges (Sinha, 1959; 1962; 1965).[21]

Another tribe, the Santal, are more affected by technological change; those who live in or near the city of Jamshedpur are especially apt to become part of the working force in the steel mills there. However, there is a split in the Santal community between those who pursue rank through economic improvement in the mills, a path that divides and individualizes their members, and those who seek to gain advantage for the group through political action which "requires cooperation and a solid front of opposition against competing societies. . . ." As the conflict between these two tendencies increases in intensity, it has produced an innovative process in which an old repugnance for Hindu practices is augmented by unfortunate experiences of the industrial world; this has led to revival of many distinctive traditional forms in a new "Great Tradition" that serves as an ideology for political activities and agitation (Orans, 1965, Chap. 8).

Consequently, the transition from tribe to caste takes many forms and may often remain at an intermediate stage for decades or generations. Appropriately, the Supreme Court of India declared in 1957 that "a person can be a Hindu and also be deemed a member of an aboriginal tribe" with respect to alienation of tribal lands (Galanter, 1966, p. 635).

IDEOLOGY AND INTEGRATION

Before concluding the present chapter, I return once again to the problem of integration as applied to the situation of Scheduled Tribes as a whole. In earlier reference to this issue, I commented that India has a strong preference for cultural pluralism rather than assimilation. But I must now emphasize that this is true at the *implicit level of culture:* it is like a presupposition taken for granted, buried deep in the Indian psyche without the need for verbalization.

However, the demands of India's new nationalism require strong assertion of an overriding unity; this makes the utterances of political leaders sound as though they favor a pervasive assimilation. Here at the *explicit* level of culture, in the limelight of public opinion, preference is expressed for a solvent in which the common character of Indian citizenship fuses all minorities into a unified

---

21. Surajit Sinha has a series of articles describing these changes among the Bhumij, all of which are briefly summarized by Mandelbaum (1970, pp. 603-10).

whole. Negatively, it takes the form of constant attacks on communalism as a destructive threat to the safety of the nation. It is impossible to document this preference fully, but one quotation from Nehru illustrates the point. In the Constituent Assembly debates preceding adoption of the Indian Constitution, he declared, "I do not think that it will be a right thing to go the way this country has gone in the past by creating barriers and by calling for protection. As a matter of fact nothing can protect such a minority or a group less than a barrier which separates it from the majority. It makes it a permanently isolated group and it prevents it from any tendency to bring it closer to the other groups in the country" (quoted by Ghurye, 1968, p. 122).

There is then a dialectical contrast between the popular belief that cultural separatism makes for constancy and order, and the opposite demand that citizenship be an overriding solidarity submerging everyone into an undifferentiated whole. It is hard to deny that, in a great many societies, cultural pluralism can and often does coexist with political unity. But the mixture can prove quite unstable, and there is always some danger, particularly in India, that public utterances, especially when delivered to make a strong impact on the electorate, may be only superficial in comparison with the deep convictions that are historically ingrained.

Ambivalence between traditional preference for a separatist solution and the nationalist political choice for a unified merger is nicely illustrated in the case of the Scheduled Tribes. S. L. Doshi in his Simla lecture (1969) maintained that Christians in India form a pluralistic society, the tribals of the central zone an assimilationist society, and the Nagas a secessionist society. While there is some truth in this statement (though details may be questioned), it does not touch on the central issue: How does the dominant group (caste Hindus) feel about it? Historical data show that for many years in central India, the relation between subordinate tribes and the dominant group was the one symbolized in our earlier paradigm (Figure 1.2), "forced assimilation with resistance." However, owing to the strenuous efforts of tribal defenders like Verrier Elwin, the central government adopted a public policy enunciated by Nehru (the so-called Tribal Panch Shila) advocating a cultural pluralist policy in the following terms: "People should develop along the lines of their own genius and we should avoid imposing anything on them. We should try to encourage in every way their own traditional arts and culture" (quoted in V. Elwin, 1969, foreword).

However, the fact that Elwin had to combat public opinion so long to get this view accepted at top levels convinced him that the wider electorate never fully accepted it, and there are frequent complaints from the tribals themselves that Block Development officers, who, after all, represent the government to the people, show disrespect for tribal customs and values, make no effort to learn the tribal language of their local area, and, in their contempt for the people under their charge, continually try to get transferred to other nontribal regions. The same is frequently true of schoolteachers whose lack of familiarity with Adivasi language and culture estranges them from the children under their care (Ratan, 1968-69, pp. 16-31; Rout, 1966-67, pp. 23-28). Perhaps these unsolicited reactions tell us more of what the dominant group thinks than resounding policy statements from the summit. It is a defensible hypothesis that the public at large regards tribals as uncouth primitives who are hardly acceptable in India until they have taken on the customs and lifeways of the surrounding Hindus. On the face of it, the current situation still resembles coercive assimilation.

Such a conclusion contradicts the judgment, already stated, that India has an implicit preference for sanctioned autonomy as a general rule. Is it true, then, that the dominant group in India is satisfied with cultural pluralism for *other* minorities but not for the Adivasi? This assertion is considerably strengthened if it can be shown (as it probably can) that the upper caste public is opposed to the Jharkhand goal of an autonomous state for Santals, Gonds, Mundas, Oraons, and others.

Nevertheless, a counter-argument is also plausible. There are certainly a few tribes who have been assimilated almost completely, to the manifest satisfaction of the surrounding Hindus. At least one social scientist hints that the Bhils of Rajasthan are now practically indistinguishable from the surrounding Hindus (Doshi, 1969, p. 14). Significantly, they now have jatis of their own. The list of their subcastes includes Bhil Gerasia, Dholi Bhil, Dungri Bhil, Mewasi Bhil, Rawal Bhil, Tadvi Bhil, Bhilala, and so forth (Bareh *et al.,* 1965, p. 20). The Bhils thus illustrate how a tribe may be integrated into the wider societal system by entering it eventually as a caste. In rural areas, this method is quite consistent with the usual forms of agricultural labor.[22] Throughout India as a whole, such entry would be at the lower end of the caste hierarchy, but in special locales it has been higher. The Cherumans and Panyers of Kerala, we are told, entered as Untouchables, but the "Meithis of Assam achieved a position comparable to that of the Kshatriya" (Fürer-Haimendorf, 1967, p. 183).[23]

Paradoxically, if, in order to enter the wider social system, tribals are constrained to come in the guise of caste, this only confirms our original proposition that a policy aimed at autonomy is really the one acceptable to the dominant group of caste Hindus. In the strict sense, this is not really assimilation, even though caste behaviors are adopted, for assimilation would mean the process by which the identity of groups is somehow fused together. Integration it certainly is, but not assimilation so long as a definite group identity is conserved in the process. It is the sort of a solution that has caste, rather than a Jharkhand autonomous state, as its vehicle. There is a wide variety of autonomous patterns and, in the case of caste adoption, we have one that has scant likeness to the Tribal Panch Shila enunciated by Nehru. Strict confirmation of this argument would, of course, require a scientific opinion poll.

---

22. However, Bhils of the Kherwara Tribal Development Block, fifty miles south of Udaipur, who are confined largely to relief work on the highway in a drought-stricken area, develop a deviating ethos of urban consumerism in default of agricultural opportunities. (See Bhasin and Malik, 1975.)

23. I received reports from the Nagpur area in 1969 to the effect that many Gonds there were converting to Neo-Buddhism in the wake of the Scheduled Castes. Unfortunately I have not been able to confirm this, but if these reports are correct, this would still show that the tribals had a preference for a cultural pluralist policy, albeit one that showed more defiance of public opinion.

BIBLIOGRAPHY

Anand, Major V. K., *Nagaland in Transition,* New Delhi, Associated Publishing House, 1967.

Bailey, F. G., *Tribe, Caste and Nation,* Manchester, Manchester University Press, 1960.

Bareh, Hamlet, *et al., Tribal Awakening: a Group Study,* Bangalore, Christian Institute for the Study of Religion and Society, 1965.

Béteille, André, "The Future of the Backward Classes: The Competing Demands of Status and Power," in *India and Ceylon: Unity and Diversity,* edited by Philip Mason, London, Oxford University Press, 1967.

Bhasin, Kamla, and Baljit Malik, "Liberation of Tribal Women," *Overseas Hindustan Times,* June 5, 1975.

Blalock, Hubert M., *Toward a Theory of Minority-Group Relations,* New York, John Wiley & Sons, 1967.

Cohn, Bernard, *India: The Social Anthropology of a Civilization,* Englewood Cliffs, New Jersey, Prentice-Hall, 1971.

Das, Nityananda, "National Projects and Displacement of Tribals," Seminar on the Tribal Situation in India, July 6-19, 1969. Simla, Indian Institute of Advanced Study (cyclostyled), 1969.

Deutsch, Karl W., *Nationalism and Social Communication,* rev. ed., Cambridge, Mass., M.I.T. Press, 1965.

Doshi, S. L., "Tribals: An Assimilationist Society and National Integration," Seminar on the Tribal Situation in India, July 6-19, 1969. Simla, Indian Institute of Advanced Study (cyclostyled), 1969.

Dube, S. C., Inaugural Address, Seminar on the Tribal Situation in India, July 6-19, 1969. Simla, Indian Institute of Advanced Study (cyclostyled), 1969.

Durkheim, Emile, *The Division of Labor in Society,* translated by George Simpson, Glencoe, Ill., Free Press, 1933.

Elwin, Verrier, *A Philosophy for N.E.F.A.,* 2nd ed., Shillong, North East Frontier Agency, 1969.

Fürer-Haimendorf, Christoph von, "The Position of the Tribal Populations in Modern India," in *India and Ceylon: Unity and Diversity,* edited by Philip Mason, London, Oxford University Press, 1967.

Galanter, Marc, "The Problem of Group Membership: Some Reflections on the Judicial View of Indian Society," originally published in *Journal of the Indian Law Institute* 5 (No. 4, July-September 1962, 331-58; republished in *Class, Status and Power: Social Stratification in Comparative Perspective,* 2nd ed., edited by Reinhard Bendix and Seymour M. Lipset, New York, Free Press, 1966, pp. 628-40.

Ghurye, G. S., *Social Tensions in India,* Bombay, Popular Prakashan, 1968.

Haldipur, R. N., "Problems of Administration of Tribes of North-East India," Seminar on the Tribal Situation in India, July 6-19, 1969. Simla, Indian Institute of Advanced Study (cyclostyled), 1969.

Handbook on Scheduled Castes and Scheduled Tribes, Government of India, Office of the Commissioner for Scheduled Castes and Scheduled Tribes, 1968.

Hunter, Guy, *Southeast Asia: Race, Culture and Nation,* New York and London, Oxford University Press, 1966.

Kar, P. C., "The Character and Consequences of Early British Administration in Garo Hills," Seminar on the Tribal Situation in India, July 6-19, 1969. Simla, Indian Institute of Advanced Study (cyclostyled), 1969.

Kurup, K. K., "Development of Adivasis Through Tribal Development Blocks," in *A Supplement to the Special Tribal Number of 'Vidyapith,'* Ahmedabad, October 18, 1965.

Majumdar, D. N., "A Study of the Tribe-Caste Continuum and the Process of Sanskritization among the Bodo-Speaking Tribes of the Garo Hills," Seminar on the Tribal Situation in India, July 6-19, 1969. Simla, Indian Institute of Advanced Study (cyclostyled), 1969.

Mandelbaum, David C., *Society in India,* vol. II, Berkeley, University of California Press, 1970.

Moorthy, O. K., "Tribal Situation in South India," Seminar on the Tribal Situation in India, July 6-19, 1969. Simla, Indian Institute of Advanced Study (cyclostyled), 1969.

Myrdal, Gunnar, *Asian Drama: An Inquiry into the Poverty of Nations,* 2 vols., New York, Pantheon (Random House), 1968.

Nag, Moni, "The Concept of Tribe in the Contemporary Socio-Political Context of India," in *Essays on the Problem of Tribe,* edited by June Helm, American Ethnological Society, Seattle (distributed by the University of Washington Press), 1968.

Negi, T. S., "The Tribal Situation in Himachal Pradesh," Seminar on the Tribal Situation in India, July 6-19, 1969. Simla, Indian Institute of Advanced Study (cyclostyled), 1969.

Orans, Martin, *The Santal,* Detroit, Wayne State University Press, 1965.

Puri, Rakshat, "Towards Security in the North-East: Transportation and Nationalism," Seminar on the Tribal Situation in India, July 6-19, 1969. Simla, Indian Institute of Advanced Study (cyclostyled), 1969.

Ratan, Ram, "Community Development in Action: Well Constructed," *Adibasi* (Bhubaneswar) 10 (No. 1, April 1968-69), 26-31.

Rout, Siba Prasad, "The Juang and Culture Change," *Adibasi* (Bhubaneswar) 8 (No. 1, April 1966-67), 23-28.

Roy Burman, B. K., "Integrated Area Approach to the Problems of the Hill Tribes of North-East India," Seminar on the Tribal Situation in India, July 6-19, 1969. Simla, Indian Institute of Advanced Study (cyclostyled), 1969a.

Roy Burman, B. K., "Tribal Demography in India: a Preliminary Appraisal," Seminar on the Tribal Situation in India, July 6-19, 1969. Simla, Indian Institute of Advanced Study (cyclostyled), 1969b.

Sahay, K. N., "Genesis and Development of the Early Christian Movement in Chotanagpur," *Journal of the Bihar Research Society* (Prof. S. H. Askri Felicitation Volume), 1968.

Schermerhorn, R. A., *Comparative Ethnic Relations,* New York, Random House, 1970.

Sen, Jyoti, "The Jharkhand Movement," Seminar on the Tribal Situation in India, July 6-19, 1969. Simla, Indian Institute of Advanced Study (cyclostyled), 1969.

Singh, K. Suresh, "Planning for Drought, Scarcity and Famine in Tribal Areas," Seminar on the Tribal Situation in India, July 6-19, 1969. Simla, Indian Institute of Advanced Study (cyclostyled), 1969.

Sinha, Surajit, "Bhumij-Kshatriya Social Movement in South Manbhum," *Bulletin of the Department of Anthropology,* Government of India 8 (1959), 9-32.

Sinha, Surajit, "Status Formation and Rajput Myth in Tribal Central India," *Man in India* 42 (1962), 35-80.

Sinha, Surajit, "Tribe-caste and Tribe-peasant Continue in Central India," *Man in India* 45 (1965), 57-83.

Trager, Frank M., *Burma from Kingdom to Republic: A Historical and Political Analysis,* New York, Frederick A. Praeger, 1966.

Uppal, R. C., "Programs of Education for Tribal People in India," in *A Supplement to the Special Tribal Number of 'Vidyapith,'* Ahmedabad, October 18, 1965.

van den Berghe, Pierre L., "Some Analytical Problems in the Study of Plural Societies," unpublished paper (mimeographed), 1967.

Vidyarthi, L. P., "Tribal Situation in India: An Appraisal of the Leadership Pattern Among the Tribes of Bihar," Seminar on the Tribal Situation in India, July 6-19, 1969. Simla, Indian Institute of Advanced Study (cyclostyled), 1969.

Chapter 5

Jains: The Unobtrusive Minority

Though diminutive in size with less than 1 percent of the population, the Jains have double prestige in India. In the first place, they are undoubtedly India's oldest religious minority and as such are venerated for their legendary position in history. It is for this reason that they occupy prior position here among minorities of religious cleavage. Secondly, as a group with more than their share of affluent business and industrial leaders, many renowned for their philanthropy, Jains have an elite status not unlike the Parsis, with whom they are often compared. In contrast with the Parsis, however, the Jains are indigenous to the civilization of India and have made a distinctive contribution by keeping alive for centuries the autochthonous idea of ahimsa, which Gandhi made so memorable and authoritative in the agitation for independence. Thus, while other minorities dealt with in this book are definitely transplantable, a number of them with colonies or subsocieties elsewhere, Jainism is so deeply embedded in Indian life that it is difficult to imagine it in any other society. Though there is some evidence that it once made its way to Ceylon (Sangave, 1959, p. 397), it apparently failed to live on when removed from its cultural home. In accordance with their doctrines, the Jains occupy a silent, gentle, and peaceful position in Indian life which has kept them out of the limelight without, however, diminishing their influence in the least.

CONTOURS OF THE COMMUNITY

The total population of the Jains in 1971 was 2,604,646[1] of whom 1,046,406 were rural and 1,558,240 were urban. There are Jains in every state of India; unlike the Sikhs, they are not highly concentrated in any one of them. However, over three-fourths of the Jains live in four states of India: Gujarat, Maharashtra, Rajasthan, and Madhya Pradesh (see Fig. 5.1). It is noteworthy, too, that Jains are more urban than rural, as shown by the 1971 enumeration: urban Jains

---

1. These and other figures below are taken and calculated from Census of India 1971, Series 1, Paper 2 of 1972. Religion and Union Table C-VII, Religion.

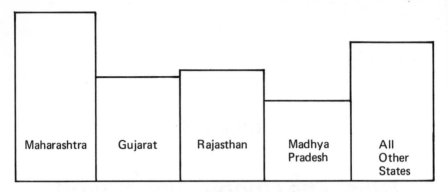

Fig. 5.1   Population Concentration of Jains by State
Jain concentrations by the 1971 census were Maharashtra, 703,664;
Gujarat, 451,578; Rajasthan, 513,548; Madhya Pradesh, 345,211;
all other states, 590,645.

number 1,558,240 or 59.83 percent of the total Jain population, whereas rural Jains account for 1,046,406 or 40.17 percent of all Jains. Among the religious minorities of India, Parsis and Jews are the most highly urbanized and the Jains are third in this respect.

In spite of their urbanization, there is evidence that the Jain community is holding its own numerically, in comparison with others. Thus, the ten-year percentage increase from 1961 to 1971 registered in the census was 24.8 for India as a whole, 23.69 for Hindus, 32.28 for Sikhs, 28.48 for Jains, 30.85 for Muslims, and 32.60 for Christians. The Jains are seen to be increasing more rapidly than Hindus but less rapidly than Muslims, Sikhs, or Christians. In the context of a long-term secular trend revealed by census enumerations going back to the nineteenth century, the Jains appear to have had a spurt of growth in the decennia 1921-31, 1951-61, and 1961-71 (see Fig. 5.2).

However, the recent increases do not appear large when a different index is used. Data showing the percentage of the total population belonging to the Jains are presented in Figure 5.3; they reveal only minute differences, and the trends do not parallel those of Figure 5.2. Only if 1891 be taken as the base year is it correct to conclude that "the proportion of Jains in the total population of India has declined" (Sangave, 1959, p. 434), but the percentage differences are so small that the inference is doubtful. In view of the comparison with other communities given above, it seems premature to conclude that a substantial decrease in the birthrate is taking place. Sangave also seems concerned about the deficiency of females in the Jain community, quoting the figure of 927 females per 1000 males in 1951 (ibid., p. 436). However, since the publication of Sangave's volume in 1959, the situation has changed: the 1971 census reports 940 females per 1000 males for that year.

There are no reliable data on income levels among the Jains, but there is little doubt that they occupy a high economic position relative to most

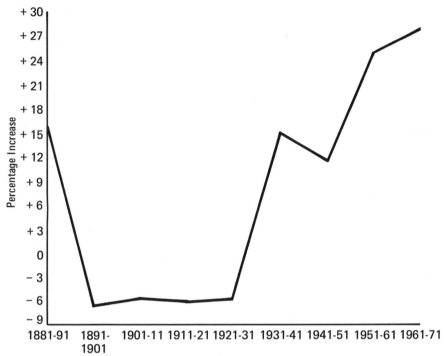

Fig. 5.2 Percentage Increase of the Jain Population in India, 1881-1971
Data from Sangave, 1959, pp. 433-34, supplemented by later census reports.

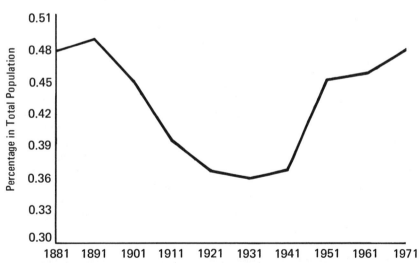

Fig. 5.3   Percentage of Jains in the Total Population of India, 1881-1971
Data from Sangave, 1959, p. 434, supplemented by later census reports.

communities. It is necessary, however, to dispel a long-standing misconception that Jains felt constrained by the doctrine of ahimsa to abandon agriculture, where they could easily kill many living things in the course of a day's work, and to transfer activities to commerce and moneylending, where such dangers could be avoided. This is a good deductive argument and is used by no less an authority than Jacobi (1914, vol. VIII, p. 473), but it has the misfortune of collision with the facts. From actual life situations it can be observed that Jains in the Karnataka today are *chiefly* farmers, and in Gujarat there are a considerable number as well. Historically, too, "we come across numerous references pertaining to agriculture in Jaina literature from which it could be seen that in general agriculture was not forbidden to Jainas" (Sangave, 1959, p. 278).

The reasons why commercial occupations predominate among the Jains are unknown, but such clustering has apparently come late in history. In early periods Jains came from a wide variety of vocations with a high proportion of Kshatriyas. In the twentieth century, however, it is reliably reported that Jains cluster in such occupations as moneylending, banking, the selling of jewelry and clothing, the grocery business, industrial management, and, increasingly, among the professions, with a sprinkling in the civil service. Most of these occupations imply at least a modest affluence (Sangave, 1959, pp. 277, 279). It is also true, in a sense, that Jainism is a highly complicated system of belief and therefore would have influence mainly in elite groups. Jacobi declares that "the small number of the Jains is explained by the fact that Jainism is not a religion of the uncultivated masses, but rather of the upper classes" (Jacobi, 1914, vol. VIII, p. 472).

THE DIVERGENT PATH

In the terms of reference adopted in our study of ethnic minorities, the Jains, like the Sikhs, share the intergroup sequence of religious cleavage. Similarities in the circumstances of their origin deserve mention at the outset. In both cases, an impetus to reform traditional practices of Brahmanism came from charismatic leaders who attacked the authority of Brahman priests and their monopoly of ceremony and ritual that held the key to salvation, or their lordly status in a caste hierarchy that relegated all others to inferior positions. In these respects, early Sikhism and early Jainism were alike in the object of their attack.

However, in their answers to the riddle of existence and especially in their notions about the path of salvation or the destination to be reached, they differed profoundly. While Nanak, the founder of Sikhism, with his *bhakti marga* or path of devotion, sought union with the godhead as the supreme good, he also denounced the ascetic calling and declared that the layman could achieve salvation without austerities and self-torture. The message of Jainism was almost the opposite. But in order to view both faiths in perspective, we must look for a moment at the context.

Historically, Jainism is far more ancient than Sikhism, reaching back to at least the sixth century B.C., which makes it roughly contemporary with the life of Gautama the Buddha in India, Confucius and Lao-tze in China, and Zoroaster in Persia (Hume, 1924, p. 42). Although the origin of Jainism is popularly ascribed to Mahavira who lived at this time, there is ample historical evidence to show (and Jain traditions confirm) that Mahavira himself was carrying on a religious practice and belief already spoken of as Jainism and that a previous ascetic named Parsva (also written Parsvanatha) had propounded a religious way of life eventually taken over by Mahavira, who gave it new life. Consequently, Mahavira became the apex figure of a religious movement that preceded him, a movement sharing a number of features with Buddhism. Historically, both Buddhism and Jainism are dubbed "the great heresies" of Hinduism; in their divergence from it, they had many negative criticisms of orthodoxy in common. Both religious movements opposed the use of sacrifices as useless in the quest for redemption, both denied the importance of the Vedas as revealed scriptures, both disowned the authority of Brahman priests and the hierarchy of caste in which they ruled supreme, both disputed the efficacy of moral effort, especially when defined as caste dharma, both renounced worship of the gods as having no value, since no gods exist who can aid man in his search for salvation. In both original Buddhism and early Jainism, each man had to seek out his own salvation without asking any help from the deity (Moore, 1925, Chapt. XII).[2]

Between the ninth and sixth centuries B.C., mendicant orders became very popular in India. In fact these peripatetic groups attained such prominence that "some men of commanding personality conceived the task of regulating the tendency to the ascetic life, not by checking it, or restricting it to a certain period of life, but by organizing the mendicants into communities governed by strict rules of conduct. Such men were the founders of Buddhism and Jainism" (Hoernle, 1926, vol. I, p. 260).

Of the two, Jainism is far older because its obscure founder Parsva lived in the ninth century B.C., some 250 years before Mahavira. Parsva especially abjured the killing of animals (himsa) in the Vedic sacrifices, while attacking the despotism of Brahmans in the caste system. He established a mendicant order open to members of all castes, to men and women alike. As for doctrine, Parsva enunciated four great vows, Ahimsa (non-injury), Satya (truth), Asteya (refraining from stealing), and Aparigraha (non-attachment to worldly things), emphasizing a life of renunciation and ascetic sacrifice as necessary for salvation. From a sociological point of view, even more important was the way Parsva organized the community of believers into four divisions: Yatis or Sadhus or Munis, who were male ascetics; Arjikas or Sadhvis, who were female ascetics; Sravakas, the male laity; and Sravikas, the female laity. Each of these divisions had its chief or leader with responsibility to see that it kept the rules of the

---

2. Buddhism, Jainism, and the related sect of the Ajivikas (mentioned below) "rejected the sacrificial polytheism of the Aryans and the monistic theories of the Upanishadic mystics. The personified natural forces of the former and the world-soul of the latter were replaced by cosmic principles, and the supernatural powers were relegated to an inferior or even negligible position. In fact, the three new religions represent a recognition of the rule of natural law in the universe" similar to the early trends in Ionia (Basham, 1951, p. 6).

order and maintained itself as a distinct organization. Later commentators, contrasting this well-arranged structure with the Buddhist monastic brotherhood without the same attention to the laity, attributed the persistence of Jainism as a living religion in India to lay participation; without this participation of the laity, Buddhism flourished only abroad (Sangave, 1959, p. 48).

Though the exact date of his birth is uncertain, Mahavira, the paramount leader of early Jainism, was born early in the sixth century B.C., a Kshatriya[3] of the Jnata clan in the town of Kundagrama, a suburb of Vaisali, twenty-seven miles north of present-day Patna. According to reports, he was the second son of Siddhartha and Trisala, both of whom were "pious Jains" and "worshippers of Parsva" who named their son Vardhamana. In time Vardhamana married Yasoda who bore him a daughter Anojja.[4] Siddhartha and Trisala died when Vardhamana was thirty years old, at which time Vardhamana became an ascetic monk, undergoing the usual Jain rites after obtaining permission from his brother to join the order. There followed twelve years of self-mortification, including the discarding of clothes as an encumbrance to the goal after thirteen months. At the end of the twelve-year period, Vardhamana attained kevala (omniscience, corresponding to the Bodhi of the Buddhists); thereafter he turned back to impart the wisdom already gained and lived another forty-two years teaching his eleven disciples.[5] Then at seventy-two he died at Pava and reached Nirvana just a few years before the death of Gautama, his contemporary. Here again the exact date is in question with estimates ranging from 527 to 480 B.C., though the latter date seems more probable (Jacobi, 1914, vol. VII, pp. 466-67).

In India of the sixth and fifth centuries B.C., wandering mendicants and ascetics seemed to fill the need of the people who were losing their faith in the traditional verities. It was a time of "theological anarchy" when orthodox views were crumbling (Basham, 1951, p. 100). Many popular terms were applied, quite loosely, to these wandering devotees: *acelaka* and *nigantha* (both referring to nakedness) and *ajivika* (lifelong dedicated). They came from both upper and lower castes and in this early period "the non-buddhist heterodox sects were not sharply differentiated." Some texts even place Mahavira "in the general category of the Ajivikas." Such peripatetic bands often, though not always, practiced nudity, admitted women into their groups, observed ahimsa and vegetarianism, and occasionally took vows of chastity (ibid., pp. 131, 96, 217, 103, 107, 123, 126).

During Mahavira's lifetime, a contemporary ascetic named Gosala attained such prominence that the term Ajivika came to be applied more and more to his followers alone. Close relations developed between Gosala with his disciples and Mahavira with his own; apparently, doctrines and practices of the two groups had much in common and for a time relations were friendly between them.

---

3. Both Mahavira and Gautama were Kshatriyas, leading some authorities to conjecture that the opposition to Brahman superiority came naturally from within the caste category next in line of authority.

4. A later subsect, the Digambaras, now deny that Mahavira ever married (Sangave, 1959, p. 53).

5. Note resemblance to the Buddhist Bodhisattva.

After some years, however, quarrels broke out, and eventually Mahavira forbade his followers to have any further dealings with Gosala and the Ajivikas;[6] this estrangement continued for some time, though gradual reconciliation seems to have occurred after the death of the two religious leaders.

INITIAL DOCTRINES

For the sake of convenience, it is useful to regard the early beliefs of Jainism as views expounded by Mahavira himself, and I accept this notion for the purposes of exposition. Nevertheless, it is only fair to warn the reader that this position oversimplifies the actual course of events. In realistic interpretation, Mahavira must be seen, first, as a remarkable synthesizer of earlier philosophies and practices and, then, as a designer of comprehensive arrangements whereby the greatest number of devotees could attain moksha. It is this peculiar blend or composite that captured the allegiance of his followers and helps to account for the wide appeal of Jainism in his own era.

In broadest terms, Jainist doctrines and beliefs are polar opposites of those held by the Sikhs. Mahavira glorified the ascetic life and denied the existence of a supreme deity; Nanak rejected ascetic austerities and regarded mystical union with the supreme God as the ultimate good. Mahavira gave laymen a subordinate place and looked upon acceptance of the monk's discipline as a necessary prerequisite for liberation; on the contrary, Nanak insisted that the everyday adult householder living a family life would be the carrier of the religious ideal, proving its relevance for everybody without need for renunciation from the world. Both of these religious paths represent religious cleavage from Brahmanism or popular Hinduism, but they diverge in opposite directions.

What then were the doctrines propounded by Mahavira? They cluster around three foci which can be stated separately but must be understood together: the nature of the world, the nature of karma, and the place and destiny of man. The world is not a universe, properly speaking, but a dualism of souls and matter. There is an indefinite series of soul forms of higher and lower degree; the gods to whom men pray are only souls like others, except that they have attained a higher state. But they are subject to death and rebirth as are the souls of men, and hence they cannot serve as the object of worship. There is no supreme God (Ishwara) over all. Matter, which is coeternal with souls, is a fine ethereal substance which clings to souls, drags them down to a lower estate, and pollutes them.[7] It is the union of soul with matter that brings about karma or the

---

6. One version of this quarrel has Mahavira condemning Gosala for refusing to adopt a vow of chastity (Hoernle, 1926, pp. 261-66); Basham (1951, p. 141) surmises that the story "may represent measures taken by the early Jaina community to counteract large-scale defections to the Ajivikas."

7. In these views, Mahavira incorporates much, if not most of the Samkhya philosophy which was already extant and later honored as one of the six recognized philosophies of Hinduism. (See Moore, 1925, pp. 277ff.) Here again is the trend toward an interpretation of natural law, one which took a really Calvinistic turn among the Ajivikas, who spoke of Niyati or fate as predetermining all events and "as the only determining factor in the universe" so that it "perhaps represents a more thorough recognition of the orderliness of nature than do the doctrines of either of its more successful rivals" (Basham, 1951, p. 6).

continual round of births and rebirths with all their attendant miseries. The souls of men (and of gods) are therefore in bondage until some way is found for the soul to rid itself of the matter that overburdens it. Liberation can only come when the passions that perpetuate the mixture are overcome and the soul escapes. Escape is only possible for those who practice the austerities of the ascetic life. But just as gods are embodied souls differing from man only in degree, not in kind, so the way to salvation is also a continuum where the difference between monks and laymen is correspondingly one of degree. To all, Mahavira preached the three excellences or three jewels of right faith, right knowledge, and right conduct; to attain these, five vows are to be kept: (1) Not to kill, (2) Not to lie, (3) Not to steal, (4) To abstain from sexual intercourse, and (5) To renounce all interest in worldly things, especially to keep no property. Monks are in a position to keep these vows strictly, while the laymen do so as far as possible (avoiding all intentional killing, for instance). The laymen are considered, therefore, as potential ascetics and are encouraged to take this view of themselves, even when it is recognized that full possession of such a status may have to be postponed to a future life. Such a doctrine proved to be one of Mahavira's most successful creations, for it brought about a close relationship between laymen and monks, with the lay status "preliminary and, in many cases, preparatory to the state of a monk." This rapprochement between the two grades, where duties differ in degree rather than in kind, had a great deal to do with the survival of Jainism for over 2,000 years and the retention of highly difficult self-renunciatory practices for the select during that time (Jacobi, 1914, p. 470).

SECTARIAN DIVISIONS

These early doctrines were simple, and so was the organization of the original Jain community. As later commentators have remarked, ahimsa is the first vow and all others are only parts of it. But later changes brought about divisions and subdivisions that split the Jains into separate and even opposing camps. Most important of such schisms is the partition of their total body of believers into the major subsects of Digambaras and Svetambaras. The time when this separation occurred is not a fixed date but must have occurred prior to the first century A.D. (Sangave, 1959, p. 52). Digambara signifies "sky clad," that is, without clothing, and Svetambara means "white clad." These terms, which originally referred to external symbols setting off one group of monks from another, came to stand for a whole range of doctrinal and behavioral differences cumulative over time.[8] It is a part of Digambara tradition that only ascetics who

---

8. When it is remembered that the proliferation of legend and myth had hundreds, nay thousands, of years to germinate and flourish, the end products must be recognized as highly influential in their era, though absent in the early stages. Such, for example, is the notion of the Tirthankaras which does not appear to be part of Mahavira's own message. This dogma holds that in ancient times there were twenty-four Tirthankaras (those who guide the people to attain liberation), of whom Rshabhdeva was the first, Parsva the

give up clothing can eventually attain liberation, that women cannot attain salvation in this life, and that a monk who attains kevala or omniscience needs no food to continue living. Svetambaras deny these allegations. There are lesser issues on which there is disagreement: Svetambaras assert that Mahavira's embryo was removed from the womb of Devananda (a Brahman mother) to that of Trisala or Priyarkarini (a Kshatriya mother). Digambaras reject this doctrine. Svetambaras have an extensive collection of canonical literature, but the Digambaras repudiate these books because they believe the ancient sacred volumes of the Jains actually disappeared. Svetambaras maintain that Mallinatha, the nineteenth Tirthankara, was a female, whereas Digambaras insist he was a male. Svetambaras have the images of Tirthankaras in the temples fully clothed, but Digambaras represent them as nude (ibid., pp. 52-53).

In the fourth century B.C., during a serious famine, a monk by the name of Bhadrabahu (mentioned as the eighth successor of Mahavira) led a party of several thousand followers to Mysore, which became the nucleus of the Jain community in south India. Although Bhadrabahu's name is linked with the precursors of the Svetambaras (Sangave, 1959, p. 51), to this day the overwhelming majority of southern Jains are Digambaras. This had led to another hypothesis which has a certain plausibility, though based on inference rather than direct evidence. The judgment is based on the geographic features of Mysore, to wit, "In that warmer region, where less clothes are needed, a stricter asceticism has been observed than by the Jains in the north. The two sections split definitely about the year 82 A.D. on the troublesome question of wearing clothes. Ever since that date most of the Jains who live in the cooler regions north of the Vindhya Mountains have belonged to the white-clad Svetambara sect, while the Jains in the southern half of India have belonged to the naked Digambara sect. But Muhammedan invaders have compelled the Digambara Jains to wear at least a loin cloth" (Hume, 1924, p. 52). The fact that in the twentieth century "there are no indigenous Svetambaras in South India" (Sangave, 1959, p. 109) may be confirming evidence for this hypothesis. Certainly Maharashtra and Gujarat constitute the population centers of the Svetambaras, while the Karnataka and Deccan areas have a high concentration of Digambaras. In the north and east there is more mixture of the two divisions.

In addition to doctrinal differences between the two sects, there are also variant practices, which are compared in Table 5.1.

VICISSITUDES OF HISTORICAL DEVELOPMENT

For hundreds of years, Jains were influential in royal courts where many laymen held high positions and monks were venerated by monarchs who were frequently converted to Jain beliefs. Documentary evidence of these trends is scattered and unsystematic, but sufficient data exist to show that Jainism had its

---

twenty-third, and Mahavira the last or twenty-fourth. These eventually assumed divine status in Jain ceremonies, with the Tirthankaras in the form of images accorded reverence and worship (Sangave, 1959, p. 47).

TABLE 5.1

Differential Usages of Jain Subsects*

Digambaras	Svetambaras
1. Temple pujari (priest) is a Jain (p. 244)	1. Temple pujari (priest) is a Hindu (Brahman) (p. 244)
2. A layman has to pass through 53 ceremonies unique to Digambaras (pp. 258-59)	2. A layman has to pass through 16 ceremonies unique to Svetambaras (p. 263)
3. Tirthakshetras (places of pilgrimage) unique to Digambaras: Gajapantha, Kunthalagiri, Mangitungi, Badaveni, Sravanabelgola† (p. 273)	3. Tirthakshetras (places of pilgrimage) unique to Svetambaras: Abu mountain, Sankhesvara, Kulapakat (p. 273)
4. Three all-India Jaina conferences (p. 293)	4. One all-India Jaina conference (p. 293)
5. Fewer ascetics than Svetambaras (p. 337)	5. More ascetics than Digambaras (p. 337)
6. Wearing of sacred thread (p. 357)	6. No wearing of sacred thread (p. 357)
7. A few outcasted people from "Dasa" caste groups prohibited from worship in the temples or giving meals to ascetics (p. 338)	7. No outcasted people (p. 338)
8. Fewer marriages with Hindus than occur among Svetambaras (p. 355)	8. More marriages with Hindus than occur among Digambaras (p. 355)
9. Fewer marriages celebrated with Hindu rituals than occur among Svetambaras (pp. 354-55)	9. More marriages celebrated with Hindu rituals than occur among Digambaras (pp. 354-55)
10. Total of 87 castes and subcastes (p. 45)	10. Only 38 castes and subcastes altogether (p. 75)

*Compiled from Sangave, 1959. Page references after each item refer to this source.
†Some Tirthakshetras are accepted by both groups: Sammeda sikhara mountain, Pavapura, Giranaro, and Satrunjaya (p. 273).

golden age far in the past and that a marked descent from a climax of influence occurred considerably before the British era.

Mahavira's own epoch and the two centuries following it saw the dynasties of Magadha (modern south Bihar) to be staunch followers of Jainism.[9] Later, Asoka (273-32 B.C.) promoted official tolerance for heretical sects like Buddhists or Ajivikas and, in official documents, he also mentions the Jains in

---

9. This account deliberately omits a traditional report of early Jainism which traces it back to Vedic or pre-Vedic times. When such a tradition arose is uncertain, but its claim for the hoary antiquity of Jainism is far from firmly established. On the basis of the dogma regarding the cycle of time and three characters (Rshabha, Arishtanemi, and Ajinatha) mentioned in the Vedas, Jain theologians have propounded the view that in the

the same general category.[10] After the reign of Asoka, Kalinga (present-day Orissa) was governed by a patron of the Jain faith as an adjunct of imperial rule in the second century B.C. Migration of the Jains farther north or northwest helped establish firm strongholds for the faith in Mathura and Ujjain from the second century B.C. to the fifth century A.D. In south India, after the death of Bhadrabahu in 297 B.C.,[11] Jainism made inroads into the Ganga kingdom of the first and second centuries A.D. and many other later monarchies in the south like the Kadamba, Chalukya, Rashtrakuta, Hoysala, Alupa, and several other minor states. In a number of these, Jainism became the state religion. During the same period it flourished in Gujarat, where it was officially sponsored by Rashtrakuta and Chalukya kings and especially favored at the time of the Baghelas in the thirteenth century A.D., when the remarkable temples at Satrunjaya, Giranara, and Abu were built (Sangave, 1959, pp. 379-85).

However, persecutions began even before this time and became a menace to the faith in southern India by the seventh century A.D., when King Sundara of the Pandhya dynasty initiated a pogrom of the Jains that took more than 8,000 lives, all of the victims being impaled on stakes (Sangave, 1959, p. 409). Another report states that "a Jaina king, Kuna, became converted to Saivism in the middle of the 7th century and, if we may trust the sculptures at Trivatur in Arcot, slew with the most horrible severity thousands of his former co-religionists who refused to follow his example. Even if the account of the persecution be exaggerated, there is no doubt that after this time the prosperity of Jainism in the south steadily declined" (Stevenson, 1915, p. 18). Actually, attacks came from many sides: from Brahmans, Lingayats, and Saivites in the south and from Brahmans and Muslims in the west. Thus, Ala-ud-din who conquered Gujarat in 1297-98 destroyed much that the Jains had built up. "He razed many of their temples to the ground, massacred their communities and destroyed their libraries. Many of the most beautiful Mohammedan mosques in India have woven into their fabric stones from Jaina shrines which the ruthless conquerors had destroyed" (ibid., p. 18). In like vein we read that the Brahmans forcibly converted a Jain temple at Pandharpura in Maharashtra into a Hindu

---

present half of the cyclical age, twenty-four Tirthankaras preached Jainism, the oldest of them (Rshabha) beginning before the Vedas were written, and the other two becoming the second and third Tirthankaras (Sangave, 1959, p. 375). Thus, "The Jaina firmly believe that theirs is the oldest religion in India, and delight to quote many passages from the Veda which prove to them that Jainism existed before the Vedas were written and cannot therefore be an offshoot of Brahmanism, as most scholars believe" (Stevenson, 1915, p. 50).

10. "... since Asoka mentions the Ajivikas before the Nigranthas or Jainas, the former sect seemed to the king to be either more influential or more worthy of support than the latter" (Basham, 1951, p. 150). The report that Asoka supplied the Ajivikas with hermitages indicates that he gave them considerable support. Significantly, Asoka's name is omitted from the king lists of both Buddhists and Jains; he was apparently regarded with disfavor "perhaps on account of his patronage of the Ajivikas" (ibid., p. 157).

11. Some scholars believe that Bhadrabahu revived a nucleus of Jainism that started much earlier in the south (Sangave, 1959, p. 381).

temple, transforming the idol of Lord Neminatha (the twenty-second Tirthankara) into that of the Hindu god Vitobha. Similarly, the Jains declare that the Hindus have converted temples of Jainism at Kolhapur into Hindu temples of Ambabai and Vishnu by brute force (Sangave, 1959, p. 272).

Significantly, "In the Central Provinces the best Jaina temples are found in very remote spots and it is suggested that they were built at times when the Jainas had to hide in such places to avoid Hindu persecution. In North India from time to time fanatic kings indulged in savage outbursts of cruelty and committed genuine acts of persecution directed against Jainas or Buddhists as such. Thus the persecution of the Jainas in different parts of India hastened their decline which had already gained some momentum due to the loss of royal patronage and slackness of the monastic order" (Sangave, 1959, p. 410). In some parts of India the Jains were also the target of Muslim attack, but they were protected up to the last in Rajput kingdoms where they were state officers at many levels including ministers and even generals (ibid., p. 386).

RESPONSES TO THE OUTER WORLD

The stark contrast between the militant stance of the Sikh leader Guru Gobind Singh and the moderation, even meekness, among the Jains in the face of mistreatment and cruelty is a measure of the difference in the doctrines and life-styles of the two religious communities. While Sikhism exalted the laity and a this-worldly ethic, Jainism elevated the ascetic order to the highest place, which made ahimsa and withdrawal from the world into major virtues. No matter how much they were tormented, the Jains never persecuted others, for this would have violated their deepest convictions. It is even suggested that Jains developed a special strategy to mollify their persecutors, particularly among the Hindus. We are told, for instance, that "under these circumstances the Jainas took the shelter of Brahmanical greed and began to employ the Brahmins for the performance of their social ceremonies, so as to preserve themselves in that way. The Practice has continued and even in the present day Brahmins are employed by some Jainas to assist in the performance of marriage and other ceremonies at various stages in certain parts of the country" (Sangave, 1959, p. 405).

During the turbulent years of persecution, not only were the ascetic orders weakened, but the laity, already divided into sects, subsects, castes, and other divisions, were demoralized and in disarray. In this crisis there arose, within the community, spontaneous leaders called Bhattarakas who rallied the people and re-established order in many ways. They encouraged the laity to rejuvenate their faith and practice by exhortation and organized centers of education for the purpose. In time they became the chief functionaries among the Digambaras, acting as counselors and adjusters of disputes, performing quasi-judicial functions, supervising conduct of the faithful in accordance with sacred rules set forth in religious literature, and, in many cases, performing the duties of a sarpanch by overseeing the observance of caste duties and restrictions (Sangave, 1959, p. 291). This institution of the Bhattarakas (for that is what it became) lasted well into the twentieth century, although it lost its force and declined in a great many districts (ibid., pp. 330-34).

A different type of response came in the wake of the Moghul empire. By this time, Gujarat had become the major center for Svetambaras, and it was in Ahmedabad that the encounter between them and the Muslims stimulated the rise of a non-idolatrous Jain sect called the Lonkas in the fifteenth century. Reformers of the Lonkas retained their rejection of idolatry and expanded their numbers to become the much larger and more influential Sthanakavasi subsect of the Svetambaras (Sangave, 1959, pp. 56-58). Since the Sthanakavasis do not believe in idol worship (which had become a prominent feature of the temples), they denied themselves temples altogether and worshiped only in the monasteries (upas rayas), a practice still continued today (ibid., p. 242). An offshoot of the Sthanakvasis in 1817 became the smaller but stricter non-idolatrous subsect known as the Terapanthi.[12]

EVOLUTION AS ELABORATION

So far I have mentioned in passing such features as idol worship, caste, and plural subdivisions without noting the fact that none of these appear in the simple doctrines and practices of the early Jain community. Historically, however, the process of change from the simple to the complex within the religious brotherhood was not only the familiar evolutionary trend toward differentiation so characteristic of social movements but, in addition, had a prominent thrust toward multiplication and expansion of profuse detail in most areas of practice and belief. Sharing with the ascetic branches of Hinduism their meditative culture, the Jain monks and writers alike embellished their ideas with numberless refinements; this process could well have been heightened by widespread preoccupation with devotional speculation. These phenomena, so characteristic of Indian philosophy and religion, are reminiscent of Linton's discourse on elaboration. He points out:

Some societies have developed an extreme elaboration and formalization of the rules governing the behavior of their members toward each other. Such elaborations contribute somewhat to the ease of social intercourse, but they impose a real burden upon the individual both in the labor of learning them and in the constant attention and frequent thwarting of personal inclinations which they call for. Even if they make for greater ease of existence within the society, they do not seem to give the society as a whole any noticeable advantage over other societies in which the regulations are less elaborate and formal. . . . In the field of religion this tendency toward needless elaboration is even more marked. The variety of religious beliefs and practices is almost infinite, yet the system developed by each society appears to meet all its members' needs. Some groups have developed elaborate creeds and philosophies, while others have barely attempted to rationalize the rites which they perform, yet the satisfaction to the worshipper seems to be the same in both cases. It would be hard to find a greater contrast than between the simple creed of early Islam and

---

12. Not to be confused with the subsect Terapanthi among the Digambaras.

the contemporary Hindu philosophy, yet each served its purpose and the Mohammedans conquered the Hindus. In rare cases the elaboration of certain phases of culture is even carried to the point where it becomes actively injurious and endangers the existence of the society. [Linton, 1936, pp. 88-89]

This sort of elaboration can be expected in an inward-facing community like the Jains. Not only did their ascetic practices and meditative absorption encourage the spinning out of highly complex and esoteric ideas, but *a fortiori* such trends attained new extremes when they relinquished all pretense at proselytizing and became more self-contained than ever (Sangave, 1959, pp. 11-12, 22). It is not certain when this change occurred historically; certainly in earlier periods there is ample evidence that Jain ascetics converted kings and princes to their doctrines. Perhaps the urge to convert others gradually waned after widespread persecutions took such a heavy toll. It is certain that we hear no more of the conversion of rulers or princes after the Moghul period, and it would make an interesting historical study to enquire into the latest references that speak of royal conversion to Jainism.[13]

Amplification and elaboration of Jain culture and institutions is therefore a dominant theme in what follows. At times the elements are absorbed from the surrounding Hindu culture before transmutation into Jain patterns and forms; at other times they are self-generated, taking original doctrines or practices and drawing them out into myriad shapes and filaments.

PROLIFERATION OF BELIEFS AND PRACTICES

In the beginning, Jainism taught that souls corrupted by matter were chained to the wheel of rebirth; they could only be liberated by following right faith, right knowledge, and right conduct, much as in original Buddhism. From this point on, elaboration begins.

Speculation on the nature of soul and of matter precipitates a current of ideas that literally overflow. The next step is to affirm that the inherent quality of souls (their pure state) is to be the lightest of all substances and to rise to the highest point in the universe. Only when mixed or compounded with karma or matter is the soul dragged down to a lower position, where it remains in bondage until released. However, it is not undifferentiated karma that sullies and defiles the soul, but there are different types of karma, each with its own effect: for example, the knowledge-obscuring, the conation-obscuring, and age. In all, there are eight main divisions of karma and 148 subdivisions, all of which drag the soul into lower regions of bondage (Sangave, 1959, p. 204). Just as there are types of karma, there are also classes of souls, as shown in Figure 5.4.

---

13. It is still a matter of note that the Jains preferred to live in princely states. By 1941, 60 percent of the Jains in India were still in princely states, while only 40 percent were in the provinces. It also seems true that Jains are clustered more in predominantly Hindu areas and less in Muslim ones (Sangave, 1959, p. 3).

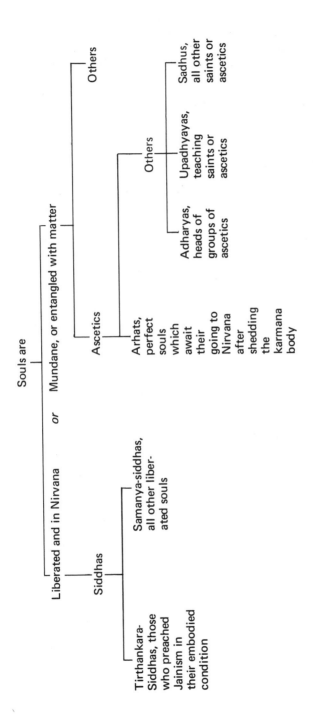

Fig. 5.4 Types of Souls in Jainist Doctrine From Jaini, 1940, p. 4.

In order to attain salvation one must first have right belief, which eventually involves acceptance of the seven principles or tattvas of Jainism: soul, non-soul, influx of karma, and so forth. There are eight Angas (pillars, requirements) which support the tattvas, such as freedom from doubt, freedom from desire for worldly comforts, and the like. There are also three types of ignorance from which one must be free, and there are eight kinds of pride from which one must be delivered (Sangave, 1959, pp. 208-09).

As already noted, early Jainism regarded the gods as only souls in a higher state of being but still subject to bondage and rebirth; prayer to them had no efficacy. There was only to be reverence for those who had attained liberation — the Jinas or Tirthankaras; devotion was due them as an ideal that all seekers of salvation could use as a model for their own conduct. This neutralization of polytheism had little appeal for the masses looking for divine favor and aid. As elaboration took hold, many objects of worship came to be recognized for the laity. First of all we hear of four ways to worship the Tirthankaras: (1) Nama worship — hearing or uttering the name of the god; (2) Sthapana worship — worshiping the material representation (idol worship); (3) Dravya worship, or adoring those who are to become Tirthankaras; and (4) Bhava worship, or that which is accorded the Tirthankara in his essence as an omniscient being. Of these the second type attained the most popularity among Jain laymen (Sangave, 1959, p. 240), and this relaxation of the earlier practical atheism brought a renascence of polytheism in popular Jainism. In one direction there is deification of superhuman beings like Yakshas and Sasanadevatas, who are supposed to have been the entourage of the Tirthankaras; they are invoked whenever worship is given to the Tirthankaras. Among the Svetambaras, more influenced by Hinduism than the Digambaras, there are also sixteen goddesses of learning. In many temples the Indras or kings of gods in Jain cosmography are regularly worshiped. A pantheon has evolved with four classes of deities or superhuman beings to whom homage is given: residential, peripatetic, stellar, and heavenly beings. Each caste and each family has its own deity, and these deities are sometimes found in Jain temples. In the other direction, many of the Hindu gods and goddesses (for instance, Ganesa, Skanda, Bhairava, Hanuman, and Sarasvati) have become objects of Jain worship, at times represented in Jain temples with conventional idols. "Lastly, sacred animals, trees, places, and emblems and temples, idols and scriptures are considered as worthy of reverence by Jainas" (ibid., pp. 236-38).[14]

Ethical injunctions become highly complex and shade from moderation to severity as one passes from precepts for laity to those for monks. Rules are relative to one's status and one's capacity (Sangave, 1959, p. 232).

Like all religious bodies, particularly the more ancient ones, Jains have undergone internal fission both on grounds of doctrine and of disputed practice, producing both major and minor divisions. Though shrouded in the mists of history, these schisms are probably crystallizations of factional controversies over all such issues. The discussion above has already alluded to the two major

---

14. Sangave (1959, p. 238) notes that such "irreligious practices" are opposed in modern times by "faithful Jainas."

divisions of Digambaras and Svetambaras. Later the Digambaras subdivided into the major subsects of Bisapanthi, Terapanthi, and Tarapanthi or Samaiyapanthi, and the two minor subsects Gumanapanthi and Totapanthi; the Svetambaras split into the subsects of (1) Pujera or Murtipujaka or Deravasi or Mandiramargi, (2) Sthanakvasi or Dhundiya or Bistola or Sadhumargi, and (3) Terapanthi. The Sthanakvasi have already received attention.

A marked trend toward localism appeared among Jain believers who gathered as small bands of disciples in locations separated from their fellow believers elsewhere. Some of these circles (Samgha) became self-perpetuating like the Mula Samgha, Dravida Samgha, Kashtha Samgha, or Mathura Samgha among the Digambaras. Gachchas were still smaller divisions arising from those originally grouped around separate Jain teachers; among the Svetambaras a teacher named Udyotana Suri created eighty-four Acharyas (teachers) from his disciples and each of them established his own Gachcha. There are several lists of the Gachchas among the Svetambaras (which do not agree on the names assigned), and a more recent compilation mentions 111 Gachchas, admitting, however, that many of them have died out (Sangave, 1959, pp. 54-61).

CASTE DEVELOPMENTS

There is very little doubt that early Jainism was anticaste in at least two senses: admission into lay or ascetic orders was open to members of any caste whatever, and castes were considered so unimportant that Jain literature before the tenth century A.D. did not refer to castes in the religious community (Sangave, 1959, p. 329). This is not the same as affirming that the Jain religion abolished caste altogether or prohibited its members from declaring caste membership, a policy that would have been futile among converts from Hinduism.

By the twentieth century, however, there were traditionally eighty-four castes in the Jain community, though in point of fact the number was well over a hundred, most of them confined to the Digambaras alone or the Svetambaras alone, although five castes are represented in both sects (the Osavala, Poravada, Humbada, Narasimgapura, and Nema). Altogether there were eighty-seven castes and subcastes among the Digambaras and thirty-eight among the Svetambaras (ibid., pp. 73, 75). How did this elaboration come about?

Two different explanations are given by the Jains themselves. An orthodox view propounded by some Acharyas focuses on the vocational element as the kernel of caste. These religious teachers contend that, in contradiction of the Brahmanical view that occupations are hereditary, Jainism asserted from the first that it is not birth but activities that determine one's status in society and that it is open to any Jain to change his life activity if he sees fit. Conforming this conception with the Jain path toward salvation, they maintain that among the fifty-three rites (Kriyas) enjoined upon the believer, the eighteenth is the so-called Varna-labha, that is, entering a caste category. It is permissible for a person of lower varna (someone, for instance, in the first stage of the householder's career) to approach leading members of a higher varna and request admission therein. When the leaders accede to his wishes, he becomes a bona fide member of the upper varna and attains the same status as all other members of that varna. Presumably this change would be based on the choice of a proper vocation which the individual feels is more suitable to his capacities than his former work. On this interpretation, the Jain devotee was free to follow any occupation he liked; in any case, it made no difference to his religious observances, which were shared with all coreligionists (Sangave, 1959, pp. 69-70).

The other explanation is far more simple. Since early Jain books do not give importance to castes but refer to them simply as a form of social practice, "The castes are therefore not ancient at all; and it is most likely that they might have been formed during the last one thousand years." The Digambaras take this position, and Swami Atmananda of the Svetambaras contends that castes did not exist in early Jainism but were later organized by the Acharyas. The Sthanakvasi monks agree that caste was not legitimized by Jainism as a religion (Sangave, 1959, p. 75). In contradistinction to the orthodox view, this explanation may be called the plain or direct view.

There is probably some truth in both contentions. Although the orthodox view has appeared rather late, it could help to explain the present predominance of the Vaisyas among Jains as a circumstance produced over time when the community became more urbanized and the examples of successful mercantile migration to various parts of India became a pattern to be emulated by laymen seeking upward mobility. However, the orthodox view is naive in describing caste change in terms of a humble request alone. As for the direct view, it is on solid ground when it emphasizes the essential indifference (rather than opposition) to caste in the teachings of Parsva and Mahavira, as well as in early Jain literature, but again it gives no hypothesis to explain the apparent tenacity of caste practice after as much as a thousand years had passed. Nor does it give reasons to account for the convergence in merchant castes, since the "majority of the Jainas consider themselves as Vaisyas and there are practically no Sudras among Jainas," yet, "The predominance of Vaisyas is, historically speaking, a comparatively recent development because in ancient times Jainas were found in all classes and especially among the Kshatriyas" (Sangave, 1959, pp. 82, 277). There is fairly wide agreement among Jains today that caste in their community has social but not religious sanction.

It is perhaps significant that the barrier of widow remarriage is the chief point of difference between northern Jain castes and those of the Deccan, where the same restrictions on this practice do not hold. There is apparently strong correlation with income levels, with the poorer sections allowing widow remarriage, for we read that "while Jainas in the North are rich and follow commercial activities on a big scale, those in the Deccan are comparatively poor and are mostly agriculturalists and petty traders" (Sangave, 1959, p. 101).[15]

Theoretically, castes restrict social intercourse and marriage and control kinship units within the religious community. There are also instances where Hindu and Jain castes overlap. A number of Hindu castes have Jain sections or

---

15. In addition to the endogamous structure of castes, the Jains also (at least in some cases) developed exogamous gotras, rationalizing them through the metaphysical doctrine of karma (Sangave, 1959, p. 159).

divisions, as, for example, the Devamgas with thirty-three endogamous divisions, the tenth being a Jain division.

Doctrinally speaking, castes have no special religious significance, but they have become so intertwined with sacred practices that the two are almost fused. The great majority of temple land grants date back to a time when Jainism was the state religion; since most of the temples belong to individual castes and are managed or regulated by their panchayats, the interconnection is very close.[16] As castes dwindle in size, anomalies may occur; the tiny Kathanera caste, for instance, has only three hundred members but owns twelve temples altogether. Conversely there are much larger castes that own no property at all (Sangave, 1959, pp. 72, 343).

In the past there was relative equality among castes, and even today there is certainly no fixed hierarchy among them. Yet variations like Visa and Dasa,[17] or the levels based on widow remarriage, create relative differences of greater and lesser respectability. Stevenson reported the following notice on Hatthisimha's temple in Ahmedabad: "Low-caste servants in attendance on visitors, and dogs cannot be allowed to enter the temple" (Stevenson, 1915, 293n). Such instances are comparatively rare, however, and Jain leaders like Swami Atmananda maintain that Jainism theoretically regards all its followers as equals, so that there ought to be no objection for any Jain believer to accept food from any other; in fact, this was the practice in the past. The realistic situation today, however, is best summarized by Sangave (1959, pp. 80, 81) in these words: ". . . among some Jaina castes we find a feeling of superiority over other castes or particular divisions of a caste due to differences in moral standards, social practices, customs and manners."

PARALLEL CURRENTS

The penchant for elaboration reveals itself in many other areas of life among the Jains: in pilgrimages, temple architecture, rituals and ceremonies, hierarchies of priests and ascetics, sacred literature and religious journals, fasts and festivals, dietary rules and food customs, superstitions — in fact, in every avenue of belief and custom. It is unnecessary to pursue these in detail here except to observe that within its limited sphere as a minority religious community, Jainism shows multiform patterns and complexities that parallel in their own way the more massive amplifications of the Hindu system. Though maintaining itself as a distinctive subsystem, Jainism has incorporated both cultural and institutional features of the surrounding Hinduism to a far greater degree than other minorities, and in this sense is less separative and less distinctive than others. At the same time, in its continuing series of emendations and refinements of parallel patterns of belief and conduct, Jainism has produced a labyrinthian web of elements that appear esoteric and often confusing to outsiders. The passion for

16. A few temples are owned by wealthy individuals or local resident trustees, but their number is so small as to be negligible (Sangave, 1959, p. 343).

17. "Visa" means twenty in the score: that is, pure blood. "Dasa" means ten in the score: that is, half-caste.

elaboration and the accumulation of fresh elements is everywhere apparent. Any observer, trying to make sense of the Jaina system runs up against the twelve lay vows, the eighteen kinds of sin (the seventh of which has eight forms), the nine categories of fundamental truths, the seven (or eight) classes of Jiva (which may go up to fourteen classes), the division of each color by the two smells, five flavors, and eight touches, et cetera, until there are 560 divisions of pudgala (matter), nine chief ways of laying up merit, and forty-two ways in which the reward of this merit can be reaped. Again there are the eighty-two results of sin, the four emotions which tie the soul to the cycle of rebirth, the fifty-seven ways of impeding karma, the eight rules for controlling the mind and body, the twenty-two troubles, the ten duties of monks, the five rules of conduct, the twelve great reflections, the four kinds of bondage, the six exterior austerities, the six interior austerities, fifteen different kinds of Siddha (beings attaining moksha), and so on and on (Stevenson, 1915, p. 109 and Chap. VII passim).

The same propensity exerted in other directions has produced a voluminous religious literature, most of it still unedited or translated, and, in architecture, some of the most exquisitely wrought temples in all India, from the Arcadian setting of Mount Abu in Rajasthan to the metropolitan din of dynamic Calcutta.[18]

VESTIGIAL ILL-TREATMENT

With the Jains occupying a relatively favored position in the status system of India, it is conceivable that they might be free from any and all sorts of persecution or discrimination. On the whole this is true, but there are occasional flare-ups of religious fanaticism on the part of highly orthodox Hindus that occasionally erupt in a minor way as though to reaffirm forcibly the dominance of the majority religion. The following will serve as an example of this kind:

> ... orthodox Hindus were waging a spirited battle against what they saw as a threat to the status quo in Acharya Tulsi's controversial Jain interpretation of the Ramayana. His Agni Pariksha ... had incurred the wrath of Sanatanis (traditionalists) in Raipur and other parts of Madhya Pradesh ... but the government's ban wasn't enough to placate the militant Sanatan Dharma Sabha, which continued to clamour noisily for withdrawal of the offending volume and an unconditional apology from the Acharya for hurting their sensibilities. In response to a call by Mahant Vaishnava Das, shops, bazars and cinemas in Raipur closed for a day in protest at the Acharya's continued presence in the town. The same day, the Jain muni was persuaded to forego a fast he had planned to stage in protest at hooliganism by a Sanatan Dharma mob the previous week. It wasn't entirely the fault of Swami Karapatri, the All-India Dharma Sangh president, who had addressed the crowd shortly before. He had called for a non-violent agitation until Acharya Tulsi owned his mistake. The immediate response of the audience was an attempt to set fire to a

---

18. "Nearly 90 percent of Jaina temples are the gifts of single wealthy individuals" (Sangave, 1959, p. 390).

building where some of Acharya's women followers were staying. Foiled in that endeavour by the fire brigade, the crowd rampaged through the town, stoning houses, including the one occupied by Acharya Tulsi's lawyer. [*Overseas Hindustan Times*, Oct. 31, 1970]

Such sporadic incidents are only far-off echoes of the massive persecutions inflicted on the Jains during the medieval period and occur so rarely today that they surprise the public when they happen. Complaints about discrimination against them, so commonly found among other minorities, are rare or non-existent among Jains. Interviews uniformly bring denials that discrimination in employment, promotion, or housing exists at all. Occasions like the Raipur outburst, therefore, do not produce noticeable anxiety in the Jain community.

PUBLIC AFFAIRS AND THE POLITICAL ARENA

There is a noticeable contrast between the highly politicized Sikhs and the almost quietistic calm among the Jains. Neither in the British period nor after independence did the Jains ask for separate electorates, and in the movement for swaraj, it is significant that "the Jainas liberally contributed, not as a community but in their individual capacities, man-power, financial resources and silent support and good wishes" (Sangave, 1959, p. 372). During the years before the split of 1969 in the Congress party, well-informed Jains reported that the great majority of the Jain electorate voted for Congress candidates. Since 1969, with the Old Congress maintaining its stronghold in Gujarat and Karnataka, it is possible that a good many Jain votes (coming so largely from the merchant group) may have held to a conservative position and cast their lot with the Old Congress or the Swatantra, but this is pure conjecture and needs supporting evidence from public opinion polls. It is based on the impression, widely held among Jains, that socialism is something of a threat and a source of worry for the future.

All indications are that Jains vote and participate in elections quite proportionally to their numbers, and do so as individuals rather than in collective blocs, but they do not entirely lack group mobilization in the political field. In areas with a heavy concentration of Jains, it would be surprising if the community neglected this fulcrum of power altogether. Were they to do so, they would be an unparalleled exception to all other groups. What apparently happens is a covert combination of economic support coupled with electoral backing for Jain candidates. Thus, in areas of northern Madhya Pradesh, "Jain candidates for parliament or state legislatures do fall back on the support of their community for finance and propaganda. The savings from a Pancha Kalyanaka celebration in a Jaina dominated village were collected in the name of charity for a primary school for religious instruction, but the sum actually helped a Jain candidate of Congress (New) to contest and win the election" (Ravindra K. Jain, personal communication).

Throughout India as a whole, however, there is only occasional clustering of Jains in substantial population groupings, and therefore they are too ineffective numerically to have electoral impact. When to their deficiency of numbers is added the essential individual ethic that characterizes their religious *Weltanschauung,* their political weight is quite unimpressive.[19]

HOW MUCH PLURALISM?

This question breaks down into two parts: How much enclosure do the Jains already have? How much separateness do they want, and how is this regarded by the dominant group? The first query is factual and structural; the second is normative and cultural.

Empirically, the Jains maintain enclosure first by endogamy. Although among some castes like the Agarvala this restriction breaks down, for the Jains as a whole, caste and kinship bonds maintain what is probably a greater separation from the Hindu community than is true of the Sikhs, though the Sikhs also have breaks in the barriers. Relative adherence to endogamous rules, however, still awaits more thorough research. The same could be said for attendance at religious temples. Certainly the Hindu and the Jain devotee will frequent different temples and worship separately; institutionally, each will go his independent way. The line distinguishing the Jain practice from the Sikh is not too sharp, since the Sikh gurdwara is similarly for members of the religious minority and not a place the Hindu feels free to visit. Also separatist in character are the Gurukalas or residential schools established by Jains, where young people of the community prepare for higher education while keeping a strictly Jain religious life. When Gurukalas are impractical, Jains set up boardinghouses or hostels adjacent to centers of secular education, where students of their own community can congregate together. In Bombay and Ahmedabad there are cooperative apartments and housing societies that keep Jains in enclaves considerably insulated from outside contacts. Likewise there are myriads of associations for caste or gachcha members of local areas, and broader-based provincial sabhas or all-India organizations both Svetambara and Digambara. The net effect of such associations is to maintain distinct boundary lines between the Jain community and the larger Hindu world outside, although they suffer some reproach because they "have not created a sense of oneness among all Jains. On the contrary they have fostered separatist tendencies" (Sangave, 1959, p. 294). In other words, they serve not only to separate Jain from Hindu but Jain from Jain.

In terms of both organization and ideology, enclosure of the minority has consequences. The predominance of ascetic values serves as a stimulus to withdrawal from the world and hence from believers of other faiths. A recently noted "general awakening in the Jaina community" (Sangave, 1959, p. 354) has a rejuvenating effect by putting great stress on unique characteristics of the community that deserve to be fostered and preserved. This emphasis reinforces the inward-facing tendencies already established structurally. Consistent with the process is the overriding fact that Jainism is no longer a proselytizing faith but one that is highly self-contained by its very nature.

---

19. Locally, of course, Jains may have a good deal of influence in factional politics, as Rodney Jones (1974) describes for the city of Bhopal.

At the same time there are marked countertrends. Even though religion and caste endogamy are operative, strict observance of the practice has already broken down and, if informants are to be believed, the relaxing of endogamous rules gains new adherents with each passing year. In those cases where castes of the same name exist among both Jains and Hindus, amalgamation is already occurring among larger rather than smaller castes. And, although religious institutions display a structural separation of Jain and Hindu worshipers, the same is not true of the ceremonial officiant who, in the case of the Svetambaras, is a Brahman priest. Ritual among the *Mandirmargi* (idol worshipers) has incorporated so much of Hindu practice that the two are more and more similar: the Jain householder is now enjoined to perform an eightfold worship with images of the Tirthankaras or, in a good many cases, images of popular Hindu gods in the temple. This worship includes bathing the idol with water, sprinkling it with sandalwood paste or saffron, offering flowers before it or garlanding it, burning incense before it, offering rice, sweetmeats, fruits and nuts — all of which are Hindu modes of worship that bear witness to the assimilative process (Sangave, 1959, pp. 241-42).

Other boundary breaks occur when Jains celebrate popular Hindu festivals like Holi, Dasera, Sitalasatama (festival of the goddess of smallpox), Virapasali (when brothers and sisters give gifts to each other), Makarasankranti (when laymen bestow gifts on the poor and give fodder to cattle), Molakata (when girls abstain from food to obtain a kind husband), and even the final rites of Sraddha when Jains eat especially good food (Stevenson, 1926, pp. 878-79).[20] Such celebrations pull the Jains unmistakably within the Hindu orbit.

In comparison with the Sikhs who are not only highly concentrated in a single state but cherish a language of their own, the Jains have no such ecological density and wherever they reside in India, they speak the language of the area. Nor do they have a distinctive dress marking them off from the majority as the Sikhs do. In all these details the Jains are incorporated more fully into the larger society than are the Sikhs. An assimilative unity of outlook and convergence of social practice has led to a widespread popular view well expressed by Shri Shri Prakasa:

> ... as Hindus and Jains have mixed up socially, and as both observe the same castes and divide themselves up in the selfsame gotras, and as apart from a few details, their domestic life is alike, there have always been intermarriages among them; (they) have always had a common social life without any clashes or conflicts; and so it has never occurred to themselves and any one else to regard them as separate religious entities. In a country where even small groups tend to live in watertight compartments, the way Hindus and Jains have lived together, is a most pleasing and helpful feature of the variegated texture of our national life. [Choudhury, 1956, p. iv]

This idea, however rosy and optimistic, seems fairly typical of the public's ideology about the Jains. It even finds its way into census enumerations where

---

20. There are even popular sayings that jokingly accuse people of becoming Jains so as to eat festal dainties (Stevenson, 1926).

Sangave finds indications that interviewers have included Jains among the Hindus (Choudhury, 1956, p. 301).

The more the observer examines the place of Jains in Indian society, the more dialectical their relation to the total system appears. Separate in some respects, encompassed in others, enclosed on the one hand, but open to ample involvement with the dominant group on the other, the Jains' status is not clear-cut and unequivocal but, instead, is ambiguous and almost enigmatic. Integration of this minority is no simple matter.

Instead of an explicit, relatively fixed position at one of the four poles pictured in our original paradigm (Fig. 1.2), the situation in which contemporary Jains find themselves is a shifting one best characterized as an alternation between assimilative and separatist tendencies. Ambivalence exists on both sides of the superordinate-subordinate line, with each side changing positions according to circumstances. For example, in interviews, Jain respondents gave three answers instead of one to the question of whether Jains want to remain separate from the majority. Some said Yes, some said No, and some were uncertain. It is hard to escape the impression that some of these answers would have been different if the contact had been made on a different day. Conviction was absent and hesitancy common. Similar variation can be found in the non-Jain dominant community as well. Compare, for example, the assimilative ideology in the quote from Choudhury above with Nehru's statement that Jains "are a distinct religious community and (the) constitution does not in any way affect this well-recognised position" (quoted in Sangave, 1959, p. 426). Consequently, members of both the dominant group and the minority have held opposite views on the enclosure of Jains from the wider society. Although the structural features of Jain separation are at an intermediate position, normative views (how superordinates and subordinates see the situation in terms of what *should* be) are fluctuating and variable.[21]

PROSPECTS

The future of the Jain community seems assured but fraught with uncertainties. The secularism of Western thought in urban centers has proved itself a danger, particularly among those educated in leading colleges and universities. Erosion of belief and practice is common on all sides. Death fasts and other fasts are being dropped, intercaste marriages are increasing, prejudice against widow remarriage is declining (there is now a Jaina Widow Remarriage Association), many Jains no longer perform the Samskaras (ceremonies), and a large number of Jains receive no religious instruction at all (Sangave, 1959, pp. 321, 324, 340, 353, 359, 363). Interviews with leaders in the Jain

---

21. Since it is reported that in the 1940s and 1950s "there is a growing tendency to eradicate every non-Jaina element from the Jaina community" (Sangave, 1959, p. 427), this could well be an indication that there is a deliberate effort to stem the tide of indifference and secularism — a trend quite on the manifest level among Jains, though the opposite tendencies toward assimilation have been latent and often unrecognized. Certainly the Jains have had ample time in over 2,000 years to absorb much, even though the pace is glacially slow.

community, all of whom have higher education, reveal the fact that their children no longer seem interested in the religion of their ancestors, neither reading religious literature nor observing the most elementary practices enjoined upon the laymen. It is worth remembering, too, that "there are practically no new converts to Jainism. Not only that the non-Jainas are not brought into the fold of Jainas but every year thousands of Jainas become non-Jainas" (ibid., pp. 414-15). Informants report that many well-educated Jains of the younger generation do not believe there is any future for their religious community.

The high degree of divisiveness within the Jains is also something of a threat to collective existence. Sects and subsects, castes and subcastes fragment the larger whole into exclusive and often segregated units, and relations of mutual avoidance or hostility develop between them. For example, higher education is fostered among the Jains of a younger generation by scholarships exclusive to members of a particular caste or subcaste of one locality, and boardinghouses are also reserved for those of special sect or subsect. "The Mahavira Jaina Vidyalaya of Bombay is probably the biggest Jaina institution giving residential accommodation and scholarships to the students, but it is exclusively reserved for the Murtipujaka Svetambara Jainas only. In educational centres like Bombay and Poona there are separate Boarding Houses for the Digambara, Svetambara, and Sthanakvasi Jaina students and though they are situated very near each other, still there is hardly any communication among them" (Sangave, 1959, p. 297). Castes operating separately from each other also produce extreme disparities of education because of their differential wealth; those who are comparatively poor are unable to furnish much support for their younger members who desire higher education, and this process becomes cumulative as the educational achievements of the poorer castes continue to be low. At the other end of the scale the richer castes exult in the fact that their educational level is constantly rising as they provide generous financial backing for the young of their own caste background. Resulting inequalities further divide the Jain community in a way that potentially embitters its less fortunate members (ibid., p. 328).

Internal dissension is manifest in other ways. It has already been mentioned that most of the Tirthakshetras (sacred places of pilgrimage) belong to one major sect or to the other (Digambara or Svetambara); only four or five are claimed equally by both (see Table 5.1, above). The fact that these sacred shrines are common to the two sects must not be interpreted to mean that they have complete consensus on the issue. "Even those few common sacred places have, for all these years, become a constant bone of contention between the two sects as each sect tries to establish its claim of ownership over them by both fair and foul means. Crores of rupees have been spent by both the parties on litigation on these cases" (Sangave, 1959, p. 417). Not only the two main sects but each one of the many subsects regards itself as the only true representative of Jainism while judging all others as false and erroneous. In earlier times there were marriages between members of different sects, but recently there is endogamy in both sect and subsect (ibid., p. 418). So strong is the sectarian feeling "that the various sects and sub-sects not only hate one another but try to grab what the others have got. Naturally the Jainas think always of their sub-sect or sect and never of Jainism as a whole. . . . Thus it is quite evident that the Jainas have been segregated into different hostile camps on religious grounds. As a consequence we find that there is nothing like religious unity among the followers of Jainism and this undoubtedly hinders the progress of the Jaina community" (ibid., pp. 410-11, 418). Often the existence of internal organizations and societies within a religious community is interpreted as a sign of a flourishing social life and an overall vitality of the group as a whole. Although such associations exist in profusion among Jains, some of them initiating reform of traditional practices like bride price, child marriage, and the like, their base is likely to be narrow: a single caste, subcaste, sect, or subsect. Again, the total effect is divisive; rather than serving morale and unity among all Jains, "they have fostered separatist tendencies" (ibid., p. 294).

In some respects, therefore, prospects for the future look bleak. If it turns out that the birthrate is falling to the extent viewed with alarm by Sangave for the year 1941, this would be a reliable sign of the community's decline. I have already stated reasons for thinking that the projected decrease did not occur by 1971 and therefore reject that possibility as an immediate danger. As for the inroads of secularism, they are real enough but counteracted on all sides by traditional pressures of sect and caste which, no matter how divisive, keep alive a commitment to the ascetic ideal and agree in this, that the monks must be supported to bear lasting witness to the life of self-denial and austerity that India has always honored. The record of sobriety, moderation, and temperateness that gives the Jains the lowest crime rate of any community (Sangave, 1959, p. 229) is witness to a persistence in pursuit of their ideal that is not easily discouraged. The central value of ahimsa, whatever its accretions or exaggerations, is crucial to the life of the Jain community and forms the basis for their many charitable institutions like dispensaries and hospitals, Dharmasalas, educational centers, and libraries. It forms a dominant motive for the many public-spirited gifts bestowed by Jain philanthropists for the welfare of the nation and acts as a source of pride to the community as a whole. "There is no humanitarian cause which does not get sympathetic help from the Jainas" (ibid., p. 288). If the "inflexible conservatism" of the Jains noted by some writers is as strong as it is reputed to be and if it is centered about the ideal of ahimsa, the community will have a continuing function in the life of India that cannot easily perish.

BIBLIOGRAPHY

Basham, A. L., *History and Doctrines of the Ajivikas,* London, Luzac, 1951.

Choudhury, P. C., Roy, *Jainism in Bihar,* Patna, privately published, 1956.

Hoernle, A. F. R., "Ajivikas," in *Encyclopedia of Religion and Ethics,* vol. 1, edited by James Hastings, New York, Charles Scribner's Sons, 1926.

Hume, Robert Ernest, *The World's Living Religions,* Edinburgh, T. and T. Clark, 1924.

Jacobi, Hermann, "Jainism," *Encyclopedia of Religion and Ethics,* vol. 7, edited by James Hastings, Edinburgh, T. and T. Clark, 1914.

Jaini, Jagmanderlal, *Outlines of Jainism,* Cambridge, Cambridge University Press, 1940.

Jones, Rodney, *Urban Politics in India,* Berkeley, University of California Press, 1974.

Linton, Ralph, *The Study of Man,* New York, D. Appleton-Century Co., 1936.

Moore, George Foot, *History of Religions,* vol. 1, New York, Charles Scribner's Sons, 1925.

Nevaskar, Balwant, *Capitalists Without Capitalism, The Jains of India and the Quakers of the West,* Westport, Connecticut, Greenwood Publishing Corporation, 1971.

Sangave, Vilas Adinath, *Jaina Community, A Social Survey,* Bombay, Popular Book Depot, 1959.

Stevenson, (Mrs.) Sinclair, "Festivals and Fasts, Jain," in *Encyclopedia of Religion and Ethics,* vol. 5, edited by James Hastings, New York, Charles Scribner's Sons, 1926.

Stevenson, (Mrs.) Sinclair, *The Heart of Jainism,* London, Oxford University Press, 1915.

Trimberg, Thomas A., *The Marwaris: From Traders to Industrialists*, New Delhi, Vikras Publishing Co., 1976.

Chapter 6

Sikhs: A Mobilized Minority

Although one of India's smallest minorities, consituting less than 2 percent of the population in 1971,[1] the Sikhs have an influence far exceeding their numbers. Unlike other minorities, however (though here we must except the Scheduled Tribes), the orbit of the Sikhs has been primarily regional; the very fact that they are colloquially entitled "Punjabis" shows that their repute has a local character in spite of their recent dispersion into other parts of the subcontinent and overseas. Because of their self-chosen visibility they are probably India's most physically conspicuous minority, a position enhanced by their historical exploits in military and athletic encounters. Such popular images, however widely diffused, are likely to leave only superficial impressions unless the Sikhs' structural position in Indian society is more fully explored.

A RELIGIOPOLITICAL COMMUNITY

In some ways the status of the Sikhs in India is a marginal one because of the circumstances of their origin. In comparative terms, the Sikhs like the Jains belong in the sixth intergroup sequence, noted above as religious cleavage. Because the Sikhs' historical origin and development came so much later, they are the second minority in the sequence to receive attention in this volume. The growth and communalization of such religious bodies creates subsocieties that, in the proper political climate, become minorities. There is little doubt that the Sikhs moved farther in their organization of a total community than the Jains. In terms of comparative religion, Sikhism is one of the world's living faiths, developed from the life and teachings of the founder Guru Nanak into an institutionalized form of worship in gurdwaras that are quite distinct from Hindu temples. A purely religious view of the Sikhs does scant justice, however, to the full-bodied reality of the minority community as it exists today. For, like

---

1. In census terms it is 1.89 percent, and the total population of Sikhs is 10,378,797 (Census of India 1971, Series 1, Paper 2 of 1972, Religion).

the Muslims of the prepartition era, the Sikhs have fused religion and politics into an indissoluble whole – a phenomenon unique in contemporary India. In this respect they come perilously close to violating the avowed principle of a secular state supposedly governing the nation, but their unabashed boldness and zeal have won political successes that no other community has actually gained. To a considerable extent their victories are a function of their localism, since accession to their demands could be made without affecting the life of the entire nation. Consequently, before tracing their development, it is helpful to bear in mind a few demographic realities that define Sikh ecology.

CONCENTRATION AND DISPERSION

Of the 10,378,797 Sikhs in India, 8,159,972, or some 78 percent, live in the Punjab.[2] The overlap between this statistic and the rural Sikh population is extensive, for a little calculation from the census data shows that 80.96 percent of the Sikhs live in rural areas. Thus the overwhelming majority of Sikhs are Punjabi farmers. The largest concentrations of Sikhs elsewhere in India (200,000 or over in each case) are in Uttar Pradesh, Rajasthan, and Delhi, only Delhi showing urban predominance among minority residents. In descending order then come Jammu and Kashmir (105,873), Maharashtra (101,762), Madhya Pradesh (98,973), Bihar (61,520), and West Bengal (35,084). The number dispersed in other states is decidedly smaller and of lesser account. A series of diminutive settlements abroad demands brief mention also. "There are Sikh temples, associations and schools in London, Stockton, Vancouver, Iran, Afghanistan, East Africa, Bangkok, Malaysia, Sumatra, Japan, Australia, Philippines and scores of other places" (Parkash Singh, 1964, p. 84).

In the decennium 1961 to 1971 the Sikh population in India grew from 7,845,915 to 10,378,797 for a percentage increase of 32.28, while the all-India increase was only 24.8. And in comparison with other religious communities, the Sikhs had a growth rate surpassing every other except the Christians; for example:

Religious Community	Percentage Increase, 1961-71
Buddhists	17.20
Hindus	23.69
Jains	28.48
Muslims	30.85
Sikhs	32.28
Christians	32.60

---

2. The Punjab has had boundary changes making each census slightly non-comparable with the previous one. Thus in 1961 the state had 86 percent of all the Sikhs in India. Only three of India's eleven states in 1969 had the names and boundaries which they had in 1950 (Oren, 1969, p. 39).

Within the Punjab, the Muslims had a majority until partition in 1947. Some idea of the shift in population by religious groups can be gained from the following enumeration (from Oren, 1969, p. 60):

Religious Community	Punjab, 1921	Indian Punjab, 1961	Punjabi Suba,[3] 1966
Hindus	35.1%	63.7%	45.0%
Sikhs	12.4	33.3	52.9
Muslims	51.0	1.9	—
Christians	1.3	0.7	2.6
Others	0.2	0.3	—

By linguistic areas the major differences in 1961 (from Nayar, 1966, pp. 18-19) were:

Hindi-speaking region: 8.8 million population, or 43.3 percent of the state total.

Punjabi-speaking region: 11.4 million population, or 56.3 percent of the state total.

Hindus: 88.1 percent of the population in the Hindi-speaking region.

Sikhs: 8.0 percent of the population in the Hindi-speaking region.

Hindus: 44.9 percent of the population in the Punjabi-speaking region.

Sikhs: 52.8 percent of the population in the Punjabi-speaking region.

I have yet to obtain comparable figures for Punjabi Suba. To put the Punjab in perspective, however, it is well to emphasize that in 1961 it had a population of only 20.3 million, which was a scant 4.6 percent of the nation's total, and it had a comparable geographic area, 4 percent of India's total. Thus, the population density of the Punjab was 430 persons to the square mile compared with the all-India average of 373 (Nayar, 1966, p. 293). Worth noting, too, is the fact that the per capita income in the Punjab during 1960-61 was 451 rupees compared with a national average of 333. The Punjab is third highest among the states in per capita income, preceded only by Maharashtra with a figure of 468, and West Bengal with 464. Unemployment in the Punjab is also much lower than in most states. "In short, the Punjab occupies a privileged economic position among the states in India" (ibid., p. 295). Much of this prosperity is attributed to the skill and industriousness of Sikh farmers, whose yields per acre are not uncommonly three to four times greater than the average yields elsewhere in India's agricultural regions (Parkash Singh, 1964, p. 85).

ORIGINS AND THEIR SIGNIFICANCE

The founder of the Sikh order was Guru Nanak, whose life and teachings swerved so gently yet firmly away from conventional Hinduism at the close of the fifteenth and opening of the sixteenth century A.D. Like the reformers Gautama and Mahavira who preceded him, Nanak sought for a path to salvation

---

3. The (partially) autonomous state of the Punjab with boundaries drawn so as to permit a Sikh plurality. This issue and its eventual resolution are discussed later in this chapter.

that freed believers from dependence on Brahman priests and their legalistic controls. To the people of his day, Nanak was an apostle of liberation and religious freedom, who blended religious devotion with the familiar round of everyday life in a strange yet welcome way. No doubt it was the magnetism of the Guru that made his doctrine impelling, for a summary of it, as briefly outlined by later authorities, seems moderate and practical in a common-sense way, rather than exciting or alluring. However, the essential teachings clearly foreshadow the later directions taken by the movement.[4]

Although the details of his life are obscured by the accretions of popular piety, Nanak, who lived from 1469 to 1539[5] in western Punjab was in the employ of a local Muslim official in Sultanpur where he received a divine call and devoted the next few years to travel, visiting both Hindu and Muslim shrines. By the time of his return he had a number of disciples, one of whom was affluent enough to donate land where an entire village, Kartarpur, was built. Here Guru Nanak lived the rest of his life with disciples around him and, near the end, appointed one of them (Angad) as successor Guru.

The teachings of Guru Nanak were for the many, not for his faithful band alone. For him the aim of salvation was union with God (bhakti marga), which transcended the cycle of birth and death and was available to everyone, since the divine presence was all-pervasive. God as immanent was already present in the human heart, the Word, and the Guru. It was through these manifestations, particularly the guiding word of the Guru, that the pathway to divine union was made clear to the devout. But manifestation is not incarnation. God as Nirankar is the formless or qualityless (Nirguna) one in his primal aspect, but He is also conditional and manifest (saguna). Yet, though the Nirguna implies saguna, this does not in any way involve incarnation or the figure of an avatar. To be incarnated means to be involved in death, and the deity is not so involved. By rejecting this Hindu doctrine, Nanak felt free to press on toward a more universalistic conception above and beyond both Hinduism and Islam, though they were approximations to it. The view here is somewhat paradoxical. On the one hand, he declared that God is not only Brahma and Vishnu but Allah and Sahib. On the other, he tended to reject both Hinduism and Islam rather than to synthesize them or fuse them together; on this negative side of his doctrine, he asserted that Brahma, Vishnu, and Siva are "creatures of God, deprived of all functions and subject to maya and to death" (McLeod, 1968, p. 166).[6]

Nanak's negativism was perhaps more pragmatic than theological, however. He denounced attachment or dependence on birth, scriptures, ceremonies,

---

4. Major accounts of the life and teachings of Nanak, as of the founders of religion in all lands, are overlaid by hagiography and miraculous tales. Fortunately, the onerous task of separating historical wheat from legendary chaff has been admirably conducted by W. H. McLeod (1968) to whom the present account is wholly indebted.

5. Although the celebrations in honor of Guru Nanak's birth are always held in November, the probabilities are that he was born in April. The date of his death previously given as 1538 is now placed at 1539 (McLeod, 1968, pp. 94, 99).

6. The major vestigial trace of Hinduism left in Nanak's doctrine was the belief in transmigration. More important than karma, in his view, however, was Nadar or divine grace (McLeod, 1968, p. 205)

ascetic practices, idolatry, visits to places of pilgrimage, the hermit life in jungles, and reverence for Brahmans – all were useless for they did not bring men closer to God. This meant, too, the rejection of caste because "caste and status are futile." While family attachments were also to be avoided, this must not be misunderstood. "It is the attachment, not the family itself, which is to be spurned." As Nanak affirmed, "even surrounded by wife and sons one can attain salvation"[7] (McLeod, 1968, p. 212).

While Nanak's doctrines were many-sided and rich in variety, the one element fateful for the future was the nonascetic, lay-centered insistence on the values of everyday life, the this-worldliness of religious devotion. Nanak demanded that every one of his followers should earn his own living and never beg like an ascetic. His corresponding stress on the need of the people in the religious community for common life, common praise, the kirtan or corporate singing of devotional songs, all gave to the early Sikhs a nisus toward communal living that has had far-reaching consequences. The feeling of "one for all and all for one" enunciated at the beginning has never totally disappeared among later Sikhs, however overlaid with factionalism. The esprit de corps among the Sikhs throughout their history, gaining added momentum in later years, has few parallels in other religious bodies, whether in India or elsewhere.

PATTERNS OF COLLECTIVE DEVELOPMENT

In its beginning years, the Sikh brotherhood was a quietistic sect, self-contained though adaptive to the political currents of the day. Maintaining cohesive strength through the leadership and organizational skill of the Gurus (each one appointed by his predecessor strictly on the basis of merit),[8] the association grew and flourished, proving a strong attraction for both Muslims and Hindus who found it a welcome escape from fanaticism and ceremonialism, from caste restrictions and priestly domination. The egalitarian strain, so prominent in Nanak's teaching, became embodied in a new Sikh institution (founded by the third Guru, Amar Das) in the langar or community kitchen where all who wished to come, high caste or low caste, Muslim or Hindu, would eat together freely under the auspices of the brotherhood. It is reported that Akbar himself was a guest at the first langar (Satindra Singh, 1969, p. 8).

A historical account of Sikh community growth cannot be attempted here, but some of the structural changes require mention. For nearly two centuries, the dominance of the Guru remained firm; including Nanak as the founder and first Guru, there were ten such teacher-mentors in all:

Guru Nanak,	1469-1539
Guru Angad,	1504-1552
Guru Amar Das,	1469-1574

---

7. Nanak had a wife and two sons; indications are that he maintained these family relationships up to the time of his death.

8. With the exception of the eighth Guru, a product of nepotism, who was too young when he took office to exhibit his later capabilities.

Guru Ram Das,	1534-1581
Guru Arjun,	1563-1606
Guru Hargobind,	1595-1644
Guru Har Rai,	1630-1661
Guru Hari Krishen,	1656-1664
Guru Tegh Bahadur,	1621-1675
Guru Gobind Singh,	1666-1708

As the number of the faithful increased, it was typical of many Gurus to add new institutional features to the common life. Thus Angad, the second Guru, introduced the Gurmukhi script which eventually became the vehicle of the Punjabi language. Amar Das, the third Guru, not only founded the langar but set up territorial divisions or parishes with agents or masands to supervise them and collect contributions. He also created rituals for birth and death ceremonies, abolished purdah, tabooed sati, and encouraged marriage between castes. The fifth Guru, Arjun, was responsible for the building of Sikhism's major shrine, the Hari Mandir of Amritsar, and for rationalizing the collections into tithes gathered by masands and delivered at specified dates to headquarters. He also compiled the first official canon of the faith, the Adi Granth, consisting of sayings and liturgical ritual attributed to Nanak, together with much religious poetry of the period including a number of works by Kabir. This holy book he installed in the Hari Mandir.

By this time the organization of the Sikh community was becoming conspicuous and it soon aroused the suspicions of the Muslim ruler Jehangir, who perceived, rightly or wrongly, a growing center of power within the royal realm which, if not curbed, could challenge the emperor's authority. Such suspicions were confirmed when Jehangir's son Khusro, estranged from his father and beginning a rebellion of his own, obtained a blessing from Guru Arjun. In retaliation, Jehangir imposed a heavy fine on Arjun, who boldly refused to pay and, as a result, was tortured to death by Jehangir's minions. This was the first of many martyrdoms to come and had portentous consequences: first, it strengthened "this-worldly" tendencies, diverting the weight away from quietism and mysticism to political affairs; and second, it began a series of conflicts with Muslim officialdom which lasted far into the future, in striking contrast with the religious and theological rapprochement with Islam that characterized the teachings of Nanak.

Both these trends took firm root in the activities and policies of the sixth Guru, Hargobind, who carried two swords as emblems of spiritual and temporal power, built the Akal Takht (Throne of the Timeless), organized a militia, and built a fortress in Amritsar. Imprisoned for a time, he fled to the mountain foothills upon his release and preached defiant messages of war against despotic rule. Thousands of volunteers were thus attracted to his military forces, most of them Jats of the central Punjab (Satindra Singh, 1969, p. 10).[9]

---

9. Though proof is lacking, it is quite possible that the primacy of Jats in the Sikh community dates from this period.

Since the seventh and eighth Gurus were figureheads with little influence, the balance of power in the Sikh community shifted, for a time, to the hands of informal leaders called masands, who then began to use the funds they collected for their own personal gratification. Bereft of strong leadership, many of the more nominal Sikhs reverted back into the surrounding Hindu community, a process never wholly discontinued in future years. However, the ninth Guru, Tegh Bahadur, brought revitalization to the adherents of the faith; in fact, he was something of a missionary who traveled almost as far as Burma to win converts to Nanak's teachings. Like Hargobind in doctrine, if not in action, he expounded the message of Sikhism in such a way as to give it a strong flavor of opposition to tyranny in all its forms. This attracted the attention of Aurangzeb who reacted swiftly, brought Guru Tegh Bahadur to trial in Delhi, and had the court sentence him to death in 1675. His quartered body was then delivered to his son, Gobind Rai, then but nine years old.[10]

VALIDATION OF MILITANCY

Waiting thirty years before he chose a line of action that would provide vengeance for the death of his father and at the same time enlist religious motives for resistance to imperial oppression, Guru Gobind took a unique and decisive step that altered the entire course of the Sikh community. It put the seal of approval on the militant doctrines of Hargobind, giving them a conspicuous embodiment that came to symbolize the Sikhs in perpetuity. Guru Govind prepared a dramatic scene to announce his decision:

> . . . he invited all his Sikhs to a big gathering at Anandpur on the occasion of Baishakhi. From all parts of the country the disciples responded to his call enthusiastically. When the meeting was at its full, he appeared with a drawn sword from a neighboring tent and shouted, "Is there anyone who would lay down his life for protecting righteousness (Dharma)?" After three such calls one Daya Ram Khatri of Lahore got up and offered his head. The Guru dragged him to the tent. There was a thud and the Guru came out with blood dripping from his sword and made the same call again. Dharma, a Jat from Hariana, offered himself for the sacrifice. The call was repeated three times more and Mohkam Chand, a Chhipa of Dwarka; Himmat, a Jhiwar (water carrier) of Jagan Nath Puri and Sahib Chand a barber of Bedar offered themselves. The congregation was astonished when they saw all the five Sikhs clad in new uniforms entering the Assembly. The Guru prepared Amrit with his double-edged sword (Khanda) and baptized them into the order of the Khalsa. When he had done that he stood with folded hands before them and implored them to baptize him also in the same way so that he may also become a member of the same brotherhood. This action on his part made the Gurdas exclaim:

---

10. Tradition has it that Tegh Bahadur's "quartered body was snatched from a Muslim crowd in Delhi's Chandni Chowk by three chuhras (Untouchables) and carried back to Tegh Bahadur's son, the great Guru Govind Singh. As a reward for their effort the sweepers were admitted to the Khalsa and bestowed with the title of 'Mazbhi': faithful. They thus became a special sub-caste of outcastes in the Sikh community, and in fact distinguish among themselves between recent and historic converts to the faith." (Cohen, 1969, p. 455 n. Cohen credits this account to H. A. Rose, 1914.)

"Hail, Hail to Guru Govind Singh
who himself is the Guru and himself the disciple."
The tenth Guru thus merged himself into the Khalsa. [Bhai Jodh
Singh, 1967, pp. 43-44, by permission]

Significantly, the thousands of Sikhs present at the festival were all initiated
into the same order by the original "Five Beloved," regardless of caste, and all
those so installed followed the example of the Guru in taking the name "Singh"
(lion) which became one of the major signs proclaiming their membership in the
new order of the Khalsa (pure) (I. P. Singh, 1967, p. 70). In addition, the "five
emblems" were made obligatory for each member to wear: (1) Kes, unshorn hair
and beard; (2) Kanga, comb; (3) Kachh, knee-length pair of breeches; (4) Karah,
steel bracelet; and (5) Kirpan, sword. The Khalsa now became a league of
warriors pledged to fight for the faith against the tyranny of all rulers who
would try to oppress or exterminate them. Customs like sati, infanticide, and
pilgrimage were tabooed, and personal habits like wine drinking and the use of
tobacco were outlawed. From this time on, the Khalsa brotherhood, sometimes
known as the Keshadharis (bearded ones) became the truly orthodox Sikhs,
while others, namely the Sahajdharis,[11] took a secondary place in. the
community. Somewhat later, Guru Gobind Singh issued a decree that the reign
of the Gurus was ending and that the authority would be transferred to the
corporate community and to the Adi Granth. This would accord "a religious
sanction to the corporate decisions of the Khalsa. . . . A unique authority was
thereby conferred upon the scripture compiled by Guru Arjun and as a result the
inner strength of the community was further consolidated" (McLeod, 1968,
p. 2).[12]
    There is little question that the transformation of the Sikhs into a
religiomilitary fraternity was for the express purpose, at the time, of giving them
striking power against Moghul rulers, particularly Aurangzeb whose hostility
toward the Sikhs was unconcealed. Defiant as he was toward the ruler, Gobind
Singh insisted to the last on the oneness of the two religions in their aim and
devotion. One of his famous utterances was: "Hindus and Muslims are one. . . .
So are the Hindu Puja and the Muslim namaz. Men are all one!" (Harbans Singh,
1969, p. 226).

FROM PLURAL TO UNIFIED RULE

After the death of the tenth Guru, the new dispensation made it inevitable
that authority, ambiguously transferred to the entire community, would spread

---

11. Sahaj means beatitude or the state of union with the divine. Possibly a contrast with
the warriors is suggested by a name that could be translated as "the mystical ones." In
popular usage, however, it has simply come to mean the shaven who are therefore non-
orthodox.

12. Guru Gobind Singh added a good deal of new material to the original Adi Granth
and this resulted in the larger canon known as the Granth Sahib or Noble Book of the
Sikhs (Farquhar, 1967, p. 337). Perhaps his designation of the Adi Granth as authoritative was to give it a new preeminence, but this is pure conjecture.

over numerous local units, where it would become divided and localized. For a time this is what happened. When it is remembered that Muslim rule after Aurangzeb was uneven and sporadic, with numerous petty kingdoms, it is little wonder that the Sikh response to this was equally diverse and scattered. What emerged from the conflict of forces in the Punjab was the formation of guerrilla forces or irregular troops among the Sikhs. These military units were called misls, and each one was led by a local chief whose power depended on his ability to protect the community of the faithful by successful raids on the Muslim forces in his territory. Thus, the plurality of the misls matched the plurality of the sultanates during the eighteenth century in the period of weakening Muslim rule. Very possibly this flexible mode of response to political domination was more effective at the time than the centralized rule of a single Guru. At all events the Sikh and Muslim communities of the era were structurally moving in opposite directions. While the most noticeable feature of Muslim rule was the constant rupture between warring states, the Sikhs, at first divided in response to plural enemy forces, were finally united in opposition by a most powerful chieftain, Ranjit Singh of the Sukerchakia misl, who established his ascendancy over other chiefs by diplomacy, selective use of force, and personal charisma. A military leader of unusual skill and energy, Ranjit Singh extended the borders of the Sikh domains to most of northern India, to Jammu and Kashmir, and to what was later known as the North-West Frontier Province — almost an empire of his own. It is not surprising that so many Sikhs of a later day look back with nostalgia to the reign of Ranjit Singh as the golden age of their past. It was not until the death of Ranjit Singh in 1839, and consequent dissension among his successors, that the British were able to subdue the Punjab and consolidate their hold on the northern dominions of India.

CASTE, COVERT AND OVERT

Like Buddhism and Jainism which preceded it, Sikhism in its original form was (at least in public utterances) anticaste as well as anti-Brahman; this was exemplified in the doctrines of Nanak. With the passage of time, caste eventually became embedded to a greater degree in the structure of the Sikh community, though to a lesser degree than occurred among the Jains. How can the growth of caste practices be explained?

It is impossible to pinpoint with accuracy the precise steps that brought about this change or give corresponding dates, but Niharranjan Ray has provided a plausible hypothesis to account for the adaptation of the early Sikh community to the jati system. Stripped of its many details, his thesis is that the socioeconomic systems of the villages were organized around the different functions of agriculture, trade, commerce, arts, and crafts. This organization had already crystallized into a hierarchical institution sanctified by religion, which placed the priest in the uppermost stratum. The interweaving of religious and economic elements gave to this system a firmness and stability sufficient to withstand the shocks of conquests and upheavals so characteristic of the era. Consequently, when reformers inveighed against the caste system, their attacks on such an impregnable bastion were like throwing pebbles at a castle. It was futile to mount an offensive against the productive system of an entire society for the socioeconomic elements were so strongly knit together that alternatives were out of the question. Eventually, therefore, all opponents of the jati system consciously or unconsciously came to terms with it for they were caught up in the "inexorable laws of social economy" that governed the preindustrial religioproductive system. It follows that only with the advent of a genuinely alternative productive system is there an opportunity to break with the jati hierarchy decisively (Ray, 1970, pp. 110-12).

Reference has already been made above to the massive influx of Jats into Hargobind's army in the seventeenth century, and the numerical preponderance of Jats among Sikhs could well stem from this beginning. Since the Jats were originally a Sudra jati, this would identify the growth of Sikhs with lower caste recruitment. As B. R. Nayar (1966, p. 57) puts it, "Though then considered of a caste lower than the Brahmans and Kshatriyas, the Jat Sikhs later acquired political power and became the ruling class and eclipsed in social status the so-called higher castes." It is worth noting, however, that every one of the ten Gurus had a Kshatriya origin.

Farquhar (1967, p. 337) declares that caste "disappeared" with the organization of the Khalsa. This is only a half-truth. The obverse also has its validity, which this comment on the Khalsa makes evident:

> All those initiated take on the name 'Singh.' They are declared as sons of Guru Gobind Singh and his consort Mata Sahib Kaur.[13] Their birthplace becomes Anandpur . . . and their caste becomes Sodhi Khatri, the same as that of Guru Gobind Singh. He declared that caste was an after-growth in the Hindu social system, and that nobody could call himself a true Sikh unless he gave up the prejudice of caste. . . . He not only tried to make one caste out of four but removed all unevenness of religious privileges. In the Khalsa brotherhood the lowest was equal to the highest. [I. P. Singh, 1967, pp. 70-71]

From the latter point of view, this was not caste abolition but caste fusion with an egalitarian lift upward rather than a leveling downward, or so runs the rhetoric. It is reported (though no dates are given) that some members of the priestly and trading castes refused to interdine with members of the Khalsa and so refused to join the latter (Oren, 1969, p. 63). And as Niharranjan Ray (1970, pp. 34-35) notes, in the era contemporary with the tenth Guru, Sikh society was differentiated into two gross divisions: the Sardars or upper group, comprising tillers of the soil, artisans, and craftsmen; and the Mazhbis, which had such menials as scavengers, sweepers, and leather workers — a pattern somewhat similar to that found in Punjabi villages today. In fact, it is a familiar theme that Sikhism itself was from the first "a peoples' movement, in which the leaders were thrown up by the masses of peasants, artisans and other classes ranking low in the Hindu caste classification" (Talib, 1967, p. 51).

Shifts in the caste balance occurred from time to time. Thus, during the regime of Ranjit Singh and continuing through the first years of British

---

13. Guru Gobind Singh had two wives (Bhai Jodh Singh, 1967, p. 324).

dominance, many Khatris and Aroras of the Vaisya caste were converted to Sikhism, and, in spite of the numerical strength of the Jats, "the Sikh personnel of all the higher services, civil or military, had become predominantly non-Jat" (Khushwant Singh, 1953, p. 181). Later the balance swung back toward Jat ascendancy again, as will appear in the discussion below.[14] By the middle of the twentieth century, if Daleke village is an adequate microcosm, Sikhs in the agricultural settlements of the Punjab had a caste hierarchy almost as complex as could be found in Hindu villages of the same region, complete with Scheduled Castes which receive very little attention in early literature.[15] In spite of the retention of caste practices in Sikhism, it is important to emphasize that caste is probably less important in the Punjab than in other parts of India, with the exception of highly urbanized sectors. This lack of stress is partly due to the Muslim invasions of the north and the widespread adoption of Islam (with its repugnance of caste) by many lower status Hindu groups (Oren, 1969, pp. 61-62). No doubt the relative unconcern about caste is a part of the often cavalier attitude toward endogamy, toward dining restrictions (as in the langar), and toward traditional servility toward Brahmans, all of which were endemic in Sikhism from early times. As a result, the mantle of caste was worn lightly and jati membership was a secondary matter except when factionalism arose; even then it attained only temporary prominence followed by later neglect.

THE EQUIVOCAL BRITISH IMPACT

Imposition of British rule brought unexpected consequences. Defeat of Khalsa forces released thousands of soldiers to penury, dacoity, or thuggery.[16] But by the 1850s, the British began recruiting Sikhs into the colonial army and "may well have preserved Sikhism in the process" (Cohen, 1969, p. 460). At times the proportion of Sikhs in the military rose as high as 33 percent (Nayar, 1966, pp. 64-65). After World War I when agitation to remove corrupt and Hinduizing priests (mahants) from the gurdwaras[17] gave origin to the Akali Dal (army of immortals) — a cadre of recruits to take over and "purify" the temples — this was opposed by the British as a violation of law and order. But loyalty to the British was not lightly relinquished by the Sikh community as a whole and continued in some circles up to the time of independence.[18]

---

14. It is interesting to observe that the Jats traditionally practiced widow-remarriage (Oren, 1969, p. 63).

15. Because of a number of comments below, I will not enter into details here. See Indera Paul Singh, 1967, pp. 69-86, and his earlier volume of 1959. The most complete account is presented by E. Marenco (1953).

16. The British only gave the coup de grace to disintegration of the Sikh kingdom that followed the death of Ranjit Singh when his seven sons, born of different women, together with relatives and hangers-on, squabbled over the succession (Khushwant Singh, 1966, p. 5).

17. For details on the internal decay of the gurdwaras, see Nayar (1966, p. 195).

18. The extent of pro-British sentiment may be understood in the light of two leading organizations in the Sikh community: (1) the Singh Sabha, established among aristocratic

By supporting the traditional mahants of the gurdwaras, the British unwittingly reinforced a temporary relapse into Hinduism.

From the 1860s to about 1910, the British engineered a series of irrigation canals in the Punjab that opened up literally millions of acres for new cultivation. This project paid off in increased revenue for a time, but the long-term effects were less reassuring. A proliferation of moneylenders and a disproportionate number of Jat land purchasers resulted in overall caste domination and in 61.3 percent of the land being owned by 15.5 percent of the people by 1927 (Khushwant Singh, 1966, p. 154). Furthermore, years of drought and famine in the early twentieth century nullified the effects of irrigation. It was during this time that waves of Sikh emigrants departed for Canada, the United States, and different parts of Asia (ibid., pp. 149, 156, and Chap. 12).

SWARAJ AND PARTITION

As nationalist agitation moved toward independence, Sikh community fortunes became more and more identified with political rather than religious organization. No doubt this was a residual result of gurdwara reform which freed the group to pursue other aims. But it was also a consequence of charismatic leadership that directed the activities of Sikhs into activistic channels soon to become normative and all-pervasive. These channels partly absorbed the contagion of public excitement during the years of crusade against the colonial yoke — an era when mild or modest demands would scarcely have been heard.

By the 1930s, a new leader emerged in the Akali Dal, one who left an indelible imprint on the movement and in many ways became a symbol of the entire Sikh community. This was Master Tara Singh who remained the dominant figure for an entire generation, in many ways the most fateful years for the community as a whole. To understand his program and his influence,[19] it is necessary to appreciate the changing situation in the Punjab.

Most important of all, the pre-partition Punjab had a strong Muslim majority. Even as early as 1921 the state was registered as 51 percent Muslim, 35.1 percent Hindu, 12.4 percent Sikh, 1.3 percent Christian, and 0.2 percent

---

circles over the turn of the century, which founded a variety of schools for the spread of literacy and distinctive Sikh doctrines (including Khalsa College in Amritsar); (2) the Shiromani Gurdwara Prabandhak Committee (SGPC). This second association, formed in 1920, came to have semiofficial status and gave birth to the Akali Dal which then became a full-fledged political party. The formation of the Akali Dal "marked the transfer of political leadership from the landed aristocracy to the Sikh middle classes" (Nayar, 1966, p. 67). The Singh Saba held quite steadily to a pro-British orientation, whereas the Akali Dal was not consistent in this respect.

19. Tara Singh was a convert to the faith and was not born into it. Like a number of converts to this and other doctrines, he proved "plus royaliste que le roi," a zealot considered a fanatic by his enemies. At birth (1885) he was the son of a Hindu of the Malhotra caste, educated first at Rawalpindi in his pre-college career when he was converted to Sikhism. He then attended Khalsa College in Amritsar, graduating in 1907 and taking a teaching position in the Khalsa High School at Lyallpur; hence the title "Master" which became a permanent part of his cognomen afterwards (Khushwant Singh, 1966, 200, n. 12).

"other" (Oren, 1969, p. 60). In such a milieu the Sikhs could hardly expect to cut a prominent figure politically except by manipulating the balance of power. By the terms of the Montagu-Chelmsford Reforms of 1919, the Sikhs received not only separate electorates but 18.5 percent of seats in the provincial legislature (clearly more than their share), while Muslims received 50 percent and Hindus 30 percent (Nayar, 1966, p. 77). During the 1920s the Sikhs worked out an understanding with the nationalists. "A reciprocal relationship thus developed between the two movements: the Akali movement became a part of the nationalist movement and, in return, received the blessings of the Congress leadership in its objectives" (ibid., p. 76).

The Akali Dal, under the leadership of Master Tara Singh, then developed a central ideology that defined its future direction. A major doctrine of this ideology was an insistence on the necessity for the Sikh community to act as a unified political organization if Sikhism as a religion was to survive. Religious wisdom had to go hand in hand with political power, or the community would perish. Master Tara Singh gave this idea his usual pungent expression by declaring, "The Khalsa Panth will either be a ruler or a rebel. It has no third role to play." This had an important logical implication, namely, "Akali hostility to the secular state and to the idea that Sikhs should be members of other political organizations" (Nayar, 1966, pp. 68-70). The inseparability of religion and politics now became a fixed dogma of the party and, in this respect, paralleled the views of the Muslims. In 1932 a new allocation of seats was made under the Communal Award which gave 19 percent representation to the Sikhs in the Punjab legislature. The Akali Dal was not satisfied and asked for more. In 1937 when some non-Akali Sikhs joined with the Unionist party[20] to form a ministry in the Punjab, the Akali Dal called them traitors (a word that became a permanent part of the Akali Dal vocabulary) and enemies of the Panth. Thereafter the Dal reacted and worked closely with the Congress, even for a time asking fellow members to join that party. "Many of its functionaries came to occupy important positions in the Congress organization." This collaboration "continued until 1939, when differences began to develop and the Dal moved away from the Congress." When World War II broke out, Tara Singh, then a member of the working committee of the Punjab Congress party and of the All India Congress Committee defied the Congress decision not to cooperate with the British in the war effort. He "met with the British Viceroy of India in October 1939, then resigned from the Congress party and actively engaged in the recruitment of Sikhs to the British Army in India through the Khalsa Defense League" (ibid., pp. 78-80).

With the arrival of the Quit India movement against the British in 1942, Master Tara Singh avoided taking a position but permitted his followers to choose their own path. The Sikh position in the Punjab was not an easy one, with the majority of Muslims supporting Jinnah's drive for a separate Pakistan while Hindus espoused a complete rupture with the British and were more and more willing, by the 1940s at any rate, to grant concessions to the Muslim League. Being in a complete minority the Sikhs, on the principle of *sauve qui peut,* made their own declaration of autonomy. At that time the western

---

20. A coalition of Muslims and Hindus, dominated largely by the former.

districts of the Punjab were strongly Muslim, the eastern were Hindu, while the center sections had the most Sikhs; during the period of uncertainty the Akali Dal, under Tara Singh's direction, began agitating for Azad Punjab (a state of their own), where the maximum population would be Sikh but no religious community could form a majority. The purpose of this demand was naturally to seek a balance of power in a newly constituted political entity. On March 22, 1946, the Akali Dal officially demanded Sikhistan, for by that time Pakistan began to appear as a live possibility.[21]

World War II having come to an end, Indian soldiers in the British army were quickly demobilized because the possibility of disaffection in the colonial troops was augmented by nationalist agitation from the Gandhi movement. Consequently, it was in the 1940s that communal military organizations grew apace. Hindus with their Mahasabha developed a striking arm known as the Vir Dal; the Muslim League had its armed force and the Akali Dal soon launched its own, known as the Akali Fauj. Demobilized soldiers from the colonial troops served as the trainers of all these fighting forces, stepping up the potentials for local violence to dangerous levels (Lambert, 1951, pp. 201, 203-04). The anomalous position of the Sikhs reached its height in May of 1946 when Master Tara Singh in desperation called for a morcha (procession) against all enemies at once: British, the Congress, and the Muslims (ibid., p. 203).

As the machinery of state government broke down in the Punjab, riots broke out between Muslims and Sikhs; in Rawalpindi and the surrounding areas, Muslims attacked Sikhs; eastern Punjab saw the Sikhs attacking Muslims in retaliation. Extensive use of private armies increased the casualties, and in the heat of anti-Muslim passions, Hindus and Sikhs were drawn together. Casualties reached hundreds of thousands in the Punjab where the carnage was greatest. Mass migrations spread the contagion of violence as 6 million non-Muslims moved across the line from newly carved areas of Pakistan to India while 6.5 million Muslims migrated in the other direction to their recently created homeland.[22] Unfortunately for the Sikhs, the boundary marked out by partition cut through the heart of their most populous regions "leaving the wealthy canal colonies and half the central Sikh concentration in Pakistan. As usual there was no one coherent voice speaking for the Sikhs" (Lambert, 1951, pp. 215, 204). In terms of pre-independence Punjab, partition gave 66 percent of the total area and 80 percent of the irrigated area to Pakistan while ceding them 52 percent of the population (Nayar, 1966, p. 293).

The effects of partition on the Sikh community were traumatic but not catastrophic. As the Punjab in postpartition India shrank to smaller proportions, Sikh refugees migrated to many other areas of India, particularly in the north,[23]

---

21. A few days previously the SGPC came out for a policy of a separate state for the Sikhs, to be carved out of the Punjab then existing. The temper of the times can be gathered from a hysterical announcement of Jat farmers in Bharatpur a year later demanding a Jatistan (Lambert, 1951, pp. 203, 210).

22. The corresponding figures for the Punjab alone were 4,351,477 and 4,286,755 (Khushwant Singh, 1966, p. 284).

23. See the demographic introduction to this chapter.

and literally thousands of them went abroad to settle in small communities. However, over three-fourths of the Sikh migrants stayed in Malwa, the ancestral home of the religion.[24] Throughout the agricultural regions, a leveling process took place as strict ceilings of thirty acres were imposed on landholding and allotments of identical size were given to people of all occupations and backgrounds. Although this policy eliminated much of the landlordism, it simultaneously acted as a spur to diversify crops and expand into undeveloped activities like animal husbandry and poultry raising. Farmers unable to find a place in the Punjab migrated to more barren regions and began to cultivate where none had done so before, as in the Terai section of Uttar Pradesh and "jungle" areas of Madhya Pradesh or Rajasthan. Though hardships were severe, the entrepreneurial ethic, so widely developed in Sikh communities, stimulated new ventures and adaptations to both rural and urban conditions (Khushwant Singh, 1966, pp. 285-87).

Politically, however, matters were less satisfactory. It became quite apparent that the Sikh community, scattered as it was, could easily lose its impact as a political force. As Master Tara Singh put it, in somewhat bitter vein, "The Hindus got Hindustan, the Muslims got Pakistan, what did the Sikhs get?" Their gain numerically, in spite of the Muslim exodus, was nothing dramatic. According to the census of 1951, the religious breakdown (from Khushwant Singh, 1966, p. 292) was as follows:

	Hindus	Sikhs	Other
Punjab	63.5%	33.4%	3.1%
PEPSU[25]	48.8	49.3	1.9
Punjab + PEPSU	62.3	35.0	2.7

ALTERNATION OF POLITICAL TACTICS

After independence the Sikhs faced a political situation quite different from the one that preceded 1947. Gone was the separate electorate, one party rule was magnified almost to the point of monopoly, the ideal of secularism was in the saddle, constituents were in scattered disarray, and the religious community still disorganized after the upheavals of partition. During this period of flux, the

---

24. This is a reminder of another and important traditional "cultural classification the Sikhs make among themselves based on geographical location: Malwa Sikhs, those Sikhs south of the Sutlej river; Doaba Sikhs, those Sikhs between the Sutlej and Beas rivers; Majha Sikhs, those Sikhs northwest of the Beas river. The staunchest (most pakka) Sikhs are reputed to come from the Majha area, which includes the Golden Temple. Sikhs here are reputed to observe the symbols and religion of Sikhism more closely; the other two groups accord to the Majhas their superior status, but each place themselves second in this triarchy" (H. Izmerlian, Jr., personal correspondence).

25. PEPSU stands for Patiala and the East Punjab States Union, a temporary alignment of a few princely states lasting from 1948 to 1956, when the central government abolished it as a separate entity and merged it with East Punjab. (See Khushwant Singh, 1966, p. 288).

crucial question was: "How could the Sikhs retain their distinct and separate identity in a state nominally pledged to secularism but in actual practice increasingly Hindu?" (Khushwant Singh, 1966, p. 294).

The initial response to this question was to pursue whatever community aims could strengthen its identity by infiltrating the dominant party and working through its machinery. In the first Congress rule of the Punjab (1948-49), Sikh members of the Congress party, apparently under strong influence of Akali Dal leaders, succeeded in pushing through three important concessions for their constituency: (1) the "services formula," (2) the "parity formula," and (3) the "Sachar formula." The first two of these were semiofficial agreements, while the third was an informal pact signed by two Hindu and two Sikh leaders in the Congress party, a quasi-contract that came to have the force of law.

The "services formula" established numerical proportions of Hindus and Sikhs in the bureaucracy of the Punjab government, with the Sikh share somewhat larger than their proportion in the population. Ministers refused to say what these proportions were. The "parity formula" arranged matters so that the number of Sikhs and Hindus in the ministry would be equal although the Sikhs formed only a third of the population. The "Sachar formula" provided details for the teaching of Punjabi and Hindi in different areas of the Punjab. Under this formula the Punjabi-speaking region was an area of high Sikh concentration, actually a majority. However, the Hindi-speaking region was divided, with one sector in the north and the other in the southeast.[26] And once it was officially accepted that two linguistic regions existed, Tara Singh pressed his advantage by demanding that linguistic regions be made into politically autonomous areas. And although it is an open question whether he could foresee the results so far in advance, the actual consequences of the Sachar formula to make the study of Punjabi compulsory as a second language in Hindi-speaking areas, naturally had the effect of making Hindi speakers seek the autonomy of their own areas to escape the necessity of learning Punjabi under duress. This in turn would complement the drive of Punjabi-speakers (overwhelmingly Sikhs) to have a region of *their* own as well. In time the effect would be a squeeze play (Nayar, 1966, pp. 217-20).

Gian Singh Rarewala, the chief minister of PEPSU, believed that "new occasions teach new duties," and so he proposed that the Akali Dal should abandon the political arena and take up strictly religious matters, allowing its members "to join the progressive and national forces and take full part in the rebuilding of the country." In so doing, it could once and for all escape the onus of communalism. Enraged by this doctrine, Master Tara Singh branded it as treachery and betrayal, taking the issue to the entire Dal which, under his influence, expelled Rarewala and four of his supporters from the organization. Although Rarewala had been condemned, his proposal had alerted the Akali Dal to a situation in which, for the time being, the Sikh party could not possibly win on its own. It had to continue working through the Congress organization. Some of Rarewala's ideas bore fruit a few months later (October 1956), when the Akali Dal seemingly reversed itself, advising its members to join the Congress party while asserting that the Dal "would in future concentrate and confine

---

26. For details of the Sachar formula, see Khushwant Singh (1966, pp. 295-96).

itself to religious, educational, cultural, social, and economic betterment of the Sikhs" (Nayar, 1966, pp. 224-27). This resolution proved to be only a temporary retreat. Congress did not give the Sikhs sufficient candidates to satisfy the Dal, and after the latter had won three postindependence elections within the SGPC, Tara Singh then felt he had sufficient support to demand Punjabi Suba or a separate state. At first this claim was made on a linguistic rather than a religious basis, so as not to contradict openly the ideal of the secular state (furthermore linguistic autonomy had already been legitimized).

Of all the opponents of Sikh separatism, Nehru was perhaps the most prominent; accordingly, he became the target of the Dal's wrath when he came to Patiala for a speaking engagement in 1953. As he rose to give his address, Akalis in the audience began a systematic effort to shout him down, using slogans such as, "We shall wrest Punjabi Suba," and "Long live Master Tara Singh!" Soon Tara Singh himself joined them and shouted, "I will not allow Mr. Nehru to speak." As the tumult rose, Nehru had to retire without finishing his speech, and the meeting broke up in wild disorder as the crowd attacked police with brickbats (Nayar, 1966, p. 240). Agitations and demonstrations became the order of the day for the Akali Dal, triggering off reciprocal commotion from Hindu opponents. In 1955, as the Dal campaigned for Punjabi Suba in the elections, while the Hindu associations vigorously opposed it, the shouting of slogans by Sikh and Hindu demonstrators led to tense situations where each side began shouting and throwing stones at the processions of the other. The Punjab government countered by banning the shouting of slogans. Responding to this challenge, Tara Singh organized a massive demonstration, replete with slogans, and made an initial speech at the Golden Temple where he defiantly offered himself for arrest. For nearly two months thereafter, additional volunteers kept a steady stream of Sikhs coming to take his place until 12,000 had been arrested and the Punjab government felt compelled to rescind its order (Nayar, 1966, pp. 241-44; Khushwant Singh, 1966, p. 297, n. 12).

By October 1955, the States Reorganization Commission made a report in which it ruled against Punjabi Suba as an unjustified cleavage of the Indian Union. Again the Akali Dal protested, sending a number of leaders to Delhi for additional conferences with Congress stalwarts including Nehru, without success. In an apparent effort to placate the Sikhs, the Congress party held its next annual meeting at Amritsar in February 1956 where the Akalis kept up the pressure by organizing a procession three miles long, with Tara Singh proudly seated on an elephant. Negotiations begun at Amritsar continued at New Delhi and eventually produced a new concession, the so-called "regional formula" accepted by the Dal on March 11, 1956. This formula divided the Punjab legislature into MLAs from Punjabi-speaking regions and MLAs from Hindi-speaking regions. To make decisions, any issues affecting either region separately would then be considered first by the elected representatives of that region prior to its consideration by the entire assembly. The effect was to give even more official sanction for making the Punjab a bilingual state, for, in addition, the regional formula set up departments of Hindi and Punjabi in the state government and projected plans for a Punjabi University, later established in 1962 (Khushwant Singh, 1966, pp. 297-98).

At this point it seemed that agitation would cease because, after the regional formula was adopted, Akalis were again permitted to join the Congress party and "the Akali Dal gave a solemn undertaking to refrain from political activity thereafter"; this promise was not kept, for Tara Singh soon "revived the Akali Dal as an opposition party . . . in repudiation of the settlement under which most of the Akali leaders functioned within the Congress party and government" (Nayar, 1966, p. 247). Again the demand for Punjabi Suba was revived, and this time Tara Singh planned a mammoth procession to march all the way from Amritsar to Delhi on behalf of their goal. His fellow-Sikh and Chief Minister in the Punjab, Pratap Singh Kairon, intervened, however, by invoking the Preventative Detention Act to have Tara Singh arrested for "indulging in such activities so as to arouse religious sentiments of the Sikhs against the Hindus." Large-scale arrests of other Akali Dal leaders occurred simultaneously (ibid., p. 249).

During Tara Singh's incarceration and for a short time thereafter (during 1960 and 1961), a younger standard-bearer of the Dal took over temporary leadership. This was Sant Fateh Singh, who proved as vigorous and militant in his demands as the old Master.[27] Fateh Singh himself also went to New Delhi to plead with Nehru for Punjabi Suba. The talks ended in failure but prompted a counter-proposal from the central government that promised to give a more sympathetic hearing to Punjabi Suba if a majority of those, even in Punjabi-speaking areas of the Punjab, would endorse such a policy in the 1962 elections. This was a shrewd move. The Akalis felt that they could not attain this majority, and so they eventually ignored the proposal, convinced that the government would yield to greater pressure anyway. Therefore Master Tara Singh began a fast-unto-death with a fanfare of publicity on August 15, 1961, and Fateh Singh arranged further talks with Nehru to follow up the pressure. All in vain. Nehru and the government stood firm behind the decision of the inquiry commission denying Akali demands; in response to fresh appeals by Fateh Singh, Nehru replied only that "the Punjab was socially, linguistically, and economically a single unit, and a further division would do great damage to the state" (Nayar, 1966, pp. 255-56). By 1961, PEPSU had been added to the Punjab and the population elements were as follows:

Hindus	63.7%
Sikhs	33.3
Muslims	1.9
Christians	0.7
Others	0.3

THE GROWTH OF FACTIONALISM

For over a generation there was a noticeable rift between Sikh leaders who were Congress adherents and the dominant ranks of the Akali Dal. After independence, the number of Sikhs allying themselves with the Congress quite

---

27. For comparative purposes it may be well to note that Sant Fateh Singh was a Gujar (farming jati), whereas Tara Singh, as already noted, came from a Khatri background. Does this mean that there was some aversion to trading castes among the rural Jats, who were the strength of the Dal, so that no other Khatri after Tara Singh could be elected leader and one from the farming castes stood a better chance? (See Oren, 1969, pp. 81-83.)

naturally increased, for therein lay power. To the Akali Dal chieftains who accused them of opportunism, they could reply that the Congress was an all-India party, not a provincial one, and that it embodied the secular ideal in contrast with communal aims of a religious party. To this internal division was now added another.

When Master Tara Singh began his widely proclaimed fast-unto-death, he declared that he would not break his fast until the central government bestowed Punjabi Suba on the Sikh community. Sant Fateh Singh and other Akali political figures continued their talks in New Delhi but without success. Finally they agreed to the appointment of an inquiry commission on the government's terms. Because of the delay in setting up this commission, it was widely assumed that it would prove fatal to the life of Tara Singh, who would not be able to endure further deprivation. To the surprise of everyone, Tara Singh abruptly ended his fast on October 1, 1961, just forty-eight days after beginning it, explaining that "he had given up the fast as the Sikh mediators had told him that his life was important for Sikh unity, for if he died, 'the Panth will disintegrate and with it will finish Punjabi Suba'. . . . they have ended my fast but not my pledge to sacrifice my life for Punjabi Suba. Now either I shall die or see my pledge to achieve Punjabi Suba honoured" (quoted in Nayar, 1966, p. 260).

The breaking of Tara Singh's fast precipitated strong criticism in the Sikh community. Many asserted that by this act he had broken a solemn pledge both to the Akali Dal and to all fellow-Sikhs. A five-member ad hoc committee in the Dal found Tara Singh guilty of violating his oath and prescribed a number of punishments for him. Sant Fateh Singh sided with the committee, and, although Tara Singh was again elected president of the SGPC, his influence among the Akalis began to dwindle. By 1962, Sant Fateh Singh had established a rival faction in the party. He even "set up his own Shiromani Akali Dal and characterized the Akali Dal under Tara Singh's leadership as a bogus organization" (Nayar, 1966, pp. 194, 262). This split within the Akali Dal proved to be far more than a polarization of loyalty to two personally attractive leaders. It soon became apparent that Tara Singh and Fateh Singh had widely different ideological leanings on social issues that drove them into opposing alliances with other political parties in the national arena.

The Sant faction claimed to be progressive, favored nationalization of banks or insurance companies – in general, a movement toward socialism. "By 1967 the Sant Akali Dal was arranging electoral alliances with the two Communist Parties, the Samyukta Socialist Party, and even with the Republican Party. . . . The Tara Singh Akali Dal was arranging such understandings with the Swatantra Party, which has little support in the Punjab, and the Jan Sangh, the Party most bitterly opposed to the creation of the Punjabi Suba" (Oren, 1969, p. 300).

After the death of Tara Singh in 1967, his faction remained very much alive. Nearly four years later, in January 1971, supporters of the Tara Singh division of the Akali Dal, seized the Sisgant Gurdwara in the heart of Delhi, charging that the Sant Fateh Singh group had mishandled gurdwara funds and therefore would have to be replaced. Somewhat later, other followers of the Tara Singh faction captured Gurdwara Bangla Sahib using the same tactics. In both cases, the police intervened and met only token resistance. However, Mrs. Nirlep Kaur, president of the Gurdwara Reform Committee, denounced the police for committing sacrilege against the sacred shrines by throwing tear-gas shells into the holy precincts and breaking in with force. She further declared that the Reform Committee (obviously an arm of the Tara Singh faction) had been forced to take drastic action because officials of the SGPC failed to have elections to the committee for several years.[28] This is one incident out of many to show that the factions have continued to oppose one another in spite of the death of one of their leaders.

Factionalism appears in other guises. The more aristocratic elements among the Sikhs have never reconciled themselves to the democratic methods of the SGPC. While the Chief Khalsa Diwan supported Punjabi Suba in 1960-61 and again in 1965-66, this did not make it pro-Akali Dal. For example, the Chief Khalsa Diwan claims that the Sikh Gurdwara Act "has placed the Gurdwaras under the control of illiterate peasants and their agents, the leaders of the Akali Dal, who are, according to the Chief Khalsa Diwan, men of little learning and less character. It wishes the Gurdwaras to be under a less democratic form of control more attuned to the paternalistic character of the Chief Khalsa Diwan" (Oren, 1969, p. 196).

It should also be mentioned that the Scheduled Caste Sikhs have steadfastly opposed the Akali Dal, particularly in its demand for Punjabi Suba. These outcaste groups have felt that to subject themselves to the rule of the Jats in a Sikh state would alter the power balance decidedly against them; they have therefore voted with other parties in opposition to the Akalis (Oren, 1969, p. 111). This constitutes another important cleavage in the Sikh community.

THE FIGHT AGAINST ODDS

Before concluding this chapter, it is important to examine again the relationship of the Sikh minority to the society as a whole. One assumption of this study is that the historical sequence that an ethnic group shares with others in its rise and development will reveal similarities of outcome, because the patterns of historical succession resemble each other for two or more ethnic groups having the same sequence. In the present case, that sequence is religious cleavage. Yet the evolution of the Sikh community belies our assumption when compared with the growth of the Jains, who were born out of a similar religious divergence. One could hardly imagine a greater contrast than the Sikhs and Jains display, the former entering political and military arenas with zest and eagerness, the latter remaining passive and generally apolitical; the Sikhs courting autonomy and separateness while the Jains take on protective coloration and move toward assimilation. Such antitheses can hardly be attributed to a common origin in religious reform. Some intervening factor must account for such striking differences. I submit that the most likely component distinguishing the two cases is the value system of each group. As already observed, the message of Nanak who founded the Sikh faith had a strong secular dimension. He spoke out strongly against the ascetic life, insisted on his followers earning their way and

---

28. Reported in *Overseas Hindustan Times,* January 23, 1971.

subsisting on worldly occupations, maintaining a family life with full responsibilities, and refusing to support an order of holy men set aside from the rest of the community. It was this initial outlook that made it possible for the tenth Guru, under severe persecution, to organize a warrior band who then symbolized the survival and perpetuation of the religious community. The fight against odds has remained a dominant self-image of the Sikh community whether in war or political rivalry. On the contrary, Jainism, with an other-worldly ideal, refused to fight persecution, adhered to ahimsa, gave higher standing to ascetic monks than to laymen, and inhibited tendencies toward political or military activism. (An added factor is no doubt the diminutive size of the community which could hardly have made a broad impact on Hindu society in any case.)

The Khalsa image of the fight against odds was the stimulus that strengthened Guru Govind Singh to win unexpected victories against larger Muslim forces, that fortified the troops of Ranjit Singh as they carved out an unlikely empire in northwest India and Afghanistan, that energized the jathas that took over gurdwaras from "usurpers" even against the weight of British official action, that gave to Sikh battalions, wherever found, their aura of invincibility, that spurred initiative and thrust to survive economically after the catastrophic losses of partition, and that kindled the implausible drive for Punjabi Suba that always appeared as a lost cause — until it was won. This basic value stance permeates Sikh culture and makes for the invigorating atmosphere that serves as a tonic for the faint-hearted.

THE PATH TO AUTONOMY

Throughout the 1960s, when the agitation for Punjabi Suba was at its height, public opposition to Akali demands stemmed not merely from an ideological commitment to the secular state but also from a growing fear that the Sikhs in a state of their own, bordering on Pakistan, would collaborate with that country to the detriment of India. It was not lost on Indian public opinion that there were "enthusiastic receptions given to visiting Akali leaders in Pakistan" which "only served to intensify such a fear [of secession]" (Nayar, 1966, p. 52).

With the coming of the first Indo-Pakistan war in 1965, Sikhs distinguished themselves on the field of battle. The heaviest casualties among the Indians appeared to be those of Sikh officers and enlisted men. Yet it was undeniable that Pakistani broadcasts beamed at India were full of appeals to win over the loyalty of Sikhs in the following vein: "The Sikhs are our brothers. Their Guru Nanak went on a pilgrimage to Mecca. . . . Sikhistan is the birthright of the Sikhs. The people of Pakistan fully support the demand of the Sikhs for an independent state of their own and will help to rid them of the imperialist Hindu yoke" (Khushwant Singh, 1969, p. 159).[29] There were definite fears that the

---

29. Public uneasiness might have been greater with realization of the close ties that often *did* exist between Sikh officers in India and Muslim officers in Pakistan. As one Sikh Colonel confided to Khushwant Singh during a cease-fire in 1965. "I know the Colonel on the other side. We passed out of the academy the same year and fought together in

Sikhs might come to an understanding with the Pakistanis as a result of such propaganda.

Apprehension over the loss of Sikh loyalty and admiration at the exploits of Sikh soldiery in battle both played their part in weakening public opposition to Punjabi Suba. The death of Nehru and the removal of Pratap Singh Kairon from office, together with his subsequent assassination, eliminated two of the staunchest foes from the scene. As hostilities between India and Pakistan came to an end, "One thing that the short war . . . emphasized more than anything else was the importance of the Sikh people. Indians were compelled to admit that Sikhs were the chief defenders of their country" (Khushwant Singh, 1969, p. 159). The central government in New Delhi appointed a new cabinet and parliamentary committee to reconsider the whole issue of Punjabi Suba. In this changed atmosphere, when Sant Fateh Singh threw himself into the balance and threatened self-immolation if Punjabi Suba was not granted, he met with more response. There was a definite turning point in governmental policy. The year 1966 put the final touches on a twofold change in the configuration of northern India that granted most of the Akali demands. In the first place, the non-Sikh part of the Punjab was converted into a new Hindi-speaking state of Haryana; secondly, the remainder finally became the Punjabi-speaking state of the Punjab. The goal was won (Lamb, 1968, pp. 186, 263). However, the two states shared the capital of Chandigarh, and this remained a bone of contention until 1970 when it was eventually awarded to the Punjab.

This does not mean that the Sikhs have an overwhelming majority in what is now their "home" state. In fact, their numerical edge over the Hindus is a narrow one, with Sikhs being 52.9 percent of the Punjab population and Hindus being 45 percent as of 1966 (Oren, 1969, p. 60). Linguistic issues remain to create conflict, and linguistic dominance is probably less pronounced than it is in the "linguistic states" of Maharashtra and Gujarat.

THE ISSUE OF INTEGRATION

The relation of the Sikh community to Indian society as a whole can be judged eventually on criteria of participation and assimilation. The former can be assessed in part by the occupational status of Sikhs throughout India in conjunction with what knowledge we have about employment discrimination practiced against Sikhs. However, employment data are not systematically collected for Sikhs, as they are for the Scheduled Castes, whose priorities are written into law. As for assimilation, there are even fewer objective indices. Thus, we must depend, for the time being, on qualitative assessments.

Macroanalysis reveals a major bifurcation in the Sikh community. On the one hand are Sikhs of the Punjab with only a minority of urban dwellers. On the other are Sikhs of the diaspora throughout the rest of India and scattered

---

the Second World War. I know old Anwar does not want to kill me any more than I want to kill him. We were like twins. All my closest friends were Muslims. It's these bloody politicians who cause the mischief. They make speeches, we shed our blood" (Khushwant Singh, 1969, p. 166).

remnants in other countries of the world, an aggregate that is almost entirely urban. Restricting observations to India alone, it appears that 86 percent of the Sikh population in 1961 lived in the Punjab and that 14 percent lived outside the state. To answer a question on the rate of participation or assimilation for the Sikh community would require that the Punjabi and non-Punjabi Sikhs be examined separately on these dimensions. Future research is greatly needed to tell us how great the differences are in these two segments of Sikhism. Tentatively, it is possible to assert that there are significant differentials in comparing the two.

Sikhs in the Punjab participate freely at all levels of the economy and have a disproportionate share of their members in the upper strata of state government positions. Even before Punjabi Suba, when they had no more than 33 percent of the population, they had 50 percent of the cabinet ministers, 27.7 percent of other ministers, and 42.2 percent of the MLAs (Oren, 1969, p. 293). The predominance is considerably higher in the early 1970s. In other parts of India, informants report that Sikhs find it harder to get jobs in the private sector than in the public sector except at the lower levels. Others report that Sikhs work for non-Sikh employers in the smaller firms rather than the larger ones. It appears that skilled or white collar workers among Sikhs are happier in foreign corporations where they experience less discrimination and better treatment in general. In the New Delhi bureaucracy they are represented primarily in the lower levels but, in the absence of statistics, it is impossible to determine the proportion. In the Union Cabinet formed after the landslide vote for Indira Ghandi in March 1971, only one Sikh was included among thirty-five members in the Council of Ministers; this proportion is not too different from Sikh representation in the total population, however.[30]

Discrimination occurs. Some Sikhs living outside the Punjab complain that it is more difficult for them to rent than it is for a Hindu, especially in south India. There are more separate mohallas of Sikhs in Lucknow or Delhi than can be found in the Punjab cities, or so we are told. The charge is made that Sikhs find promotion difficult in Hindu or Parsi firms; there are other businesses in which this does not occur, of course, such as transportation and commerce, in which Sikhs are in proprietary positions (particularly in Delhi). One grievance mentioned by an informant from Amritsar was that he was prevented from visiting a Hindu temple in Benares because he was a Sikh, which he found to be a regular practice.

On the basis of quite scanty evidence, therefore, the tentative conclusion is that Sikhs in the Punjab are free to enter economic and political activities without serious restrictions but that in areas outside that state are subject to various forms of mild discrimination,[31] considerably less, however, than Muslims, or particularly the Scheduled Castes might experience.[32] As already indicated,

---

30. Reported in *India News,* March 26, 1971. Thanks are due to Professor K. N. Sharma for establishing this identity.

31. All-India research on employment discrimination (in comparative terms) is not only lacking but highly unlikely in the immediate future.

32. Migration of Sikhs into northern cities after partition was so extensive that it aroused prejudiced attitudes. Old Lucknow residents say quite openly, "Lucknow used to be quite a pleasant place to live till the Punjabis came."

the Sikhs as a whole are well above the poverty level, and there is consensus both within and without their community that Sikhs, whatever their income, maintain a higher standard of living for themselves, and more lavish habits of consumption than Hindus at the same economic level. In this respect, the distinction between Punjabi and non-Punjabi Sikhs has very little relevance.

With respect to assimilation, the Sikh community as a whole undoubtedly prefers both religious and political autonomy, as their history shows. For the Hindu community that surrounds them, the question is not so easily answered. In a sense, the dominant Hindu community has never fully accepted the ideal of autonomy or separatism as the last word for the Sikhs. Distinguishing first between religious and political integration, it is noteworthy that on religious issues the Hindus have been ambivalent. Not all have accepted the militant views of the Arya Samaj that Sikhs should be brought back into the fold, a forthright assimilationist doctrine strongly centripetal in its leanings. Nevertheless, the Hindu public seems inclined to accept a milder form of belief that could have similar long-term consequences. Thus the notion is widespread that the underlying basic tenets of Sikhism *are* fundamentally Hindu; proof of this proposition is the assertion that the writings of Hindu saints are found throughout the Adi Granth. Buttressing this theme is the affirmation that Guru Nanak had no intention of starting a new religion but was only trying to purify the old. It was really quite unnecessary for any separation to occur in the first place; the Sikhs are essentially a part of the Hindu community like the Jains, Arya Samajists, and other sects (Nayar, 1966, p. 61). At times one can hear Sikh leaders themselves, in a burst of public rhetoric, reinforcing such assimilationist views. "Hindus and Sikhs are at the root one and are like twin brothers. They interdine, intermarry, have all social relations with each other, have common culture and customs, have common shrines and temples" (ibid., p. 72).[33]

That an actual process of assimilation is occurring can hardly be doubted, though this does not mean final absorption into Hinduism. Many educated Sikh youth are defecting from religion. There seems to be a decline of religious observance in Sikh homes, themes from cinema tunes are used for hymns in a number of Sikh shrines, and the dominance of the Keshadhari is not what it once was. Even in the villages have appeared a goodly number of partly shaved men who returned there from jail sentences brought on by Akali agitation (Nayar, 1966, pp. 103, 106). Khushwant Singh (1953, p. 180) outlines the assimilationist process when it does occur, as passing through four stages: (1) Orthodox Sikh, (2) Unorthodox Sikh, (3) Sahajdhari Sikh, and (4) Hindu. The fourth stage, however, could be adherence to secular or non-religious views just as well.

It is obvious, at least in the eyes of Sikh leaders, that the Sahajdharis constitute a category at least halfway to Hinduism. The actual percentage of Sikhs who are Sahajdharis is at present unknown, though British census figures in 1932 listed them as 262,000 out of a total 4 million Sikhs at the time or some 6 percent of the entire community (Oren, 1969, p. 63). Probabilities are that the

---

33. Although the Akali movement encouraged centrifugal tendencies, Tara Singh himself once said, "The Sikhs are Hindus and I feel they are so. But I do not say so, as in that case the Hindus would absorb the Sikhs." Nayar (1966, p. 72) comments, "At election time, Akali candidates tell Hindu audiences that there is no difference between Hindus and Sikhs except that the Sikhs wear unshorn hair."

proportion is higher today when the extent of migration and urbanization is taken into account.[34] An Akali complaint against the central government is that it permits Sikhs in the army to be clean shaven and have hair cuts. This, they feel, is tantamount to letting the army recruits assimilate to Hinduism (ibid., p. 133). Leaders in the SGPC and their colleagues in positions of responsibility in the community at Amritsar exude confidence about the ability of the Khalsa to resist assimilation, while those who live outside the Punjab are not so sure. Wherever there are Sikhs as a scattered group in other areas there is more apostasy, and wherever they remain concentrated they tend to preserve their way of life intact (Khushwant Singh, 1966, p. 304).

On the basis of evidence now available, the most likely conclusion is that the Sikhs alternate between yielding to pervasive assimilative forces and reasserting substantial autonomy. To the extent that they can make the Punjab a separate haven where they maintain both religious and political separatism *and* this is reciprocated by the larger Hindu community, the result would be a cultural pluralist integration. However, in the 1971 landslide election, a Congress victory in the Punjab shattered the political cohesion of the Akali Dal, and even with the achievement of Punjabi Suba, the process still seems to be moving in an assimilative direction.[35] It may be that the attainment of political autonomy has led, paradoxically, to more complete incorporation as an unexpected consequence. On the religious issue, however, there is little doubt that Punjabi Suba will be a powerful bulwark against assimilation, though not an absolute one. Outside the Punjab, on the other hand, increasing Hinduization and secularization will take place. This will have limited impact so long as the overwhelming majority of Sikhs remain Punjabis as well as devout farmers. The dominant community, on the whole, probably accepts the Punjab autonomy that makes this situation possible as the best compromise available under the circumstances.

---

34. The Gurdwaras Act of 1925 included Sahajdharis in its definition of Sikhs, which meant that they were eligible to vote for elected members of the SGPC and could themselves be so elected. In the late 1960s when Oren did his research, no Sahajdhari was a member of the SGPC or a Sikh member of the Punjab assembly. On the other hand, Sahajdharis seem to come from trading castes and from urbanites generally. They often intermarry with Hindus. Curiously, "The Hindus of Sind were more or less Sahajdharis and yet they are certainly not thought of as Sikhs by anyone today" (Oren, 1969, p. 134).

35. As reported in *Overseas Hindustan Times,* April 17, 1971.

BIBLIOGRAPHY

Cohen, Stephen P., "The Untouchable Soldier: Caste, Politics and the Indian Army," *Journal of Asian Studies* 28 (May 1969), 453-68.

Farquhar, J. N., *Modern Religious Movements in India,* Delhi, Munshiram Manoharlal, 1st Indian edition, 1967.

Lamb, Beatrice Pitney, *India, A World in Transition,* 3rd ed. rev., New York, Frederick A. Praeger, 1968.

Lambert, Richard D., Hindu-Muslim Riots, unpublished Ph.D. dissertation, University of Pennsylvania, 1951.

McLeod, W. H., *Guru Nanak and the Sikh Religion*, London, Oxford at the Clarendon Press, 1968.

Marenco, E., Caste and Class among the Sikhs of Northwest India, unpublished Ph.D. dissertation, Columbia University, 1953.

Nayar, Baldev Raj, *Minority Politics in the Punjab*, Princeton, Princeton University Press, 1966.

Oren, Stephen A., Religious Groups as Political Organizations: A Comparative Analysis of Three Indian States, unpublished Ph.D. dissertation, Columbia University, 1969.

Ray, Niharranjan, *The Sikh Gurus and the Sikh Society: A Study in Social Analysis*, Patiala, Punjabi University, 1970.

Rose, H. A. (comp.), *A Glossary of the Tribes and Castes of the Punjab and North-West Frontier Province*, vol. 3, Lahore, Punjab Government, 1914.

Singh, Bhai Jodh, "Structure and Character of Sikh Society," in *Sikhism and Indian Society*, Transactions of the Indian Institute of Advanced Study, vol. 4, Simla, Rashtrapati Nivas, 1967.

Singh, Harbans, *Guru Nanak and Origins of the Sikh Faith*, Bombay, Asia Publishing House, 1969.

Singh, Indera Paul, *A Sikh Village in Traditional India*, Illinois, Philadelphia, 1959.

Singh, Indera Paul, "Caste in a Sikh Village," in *Sikhism and Indian Society, Transactions of the Indian Institute of Advanced Study*, vol. 4, Simla, Rashtrapati Nivas, 1967.

Singh, Khushwant, *The Sikhs*, London, George Allen and Unwin, 1953.

Singh, Khushwant, *A History of the Sikhs*, vol. 2: 1839-1964, Princeton, Princeton University Press, 1966.

Singh, Khushwant, *Khushwant Singh's India*, edited by Rahul Singh, Bombay, IBH Publishing Co., 1969.

Singh, S. Parkash, "Contemporary Sikhism," *Religion and Society* 11 (No. 1, 1964), 83-92.

Singh, Satindra, "Guru Nanak and his Sikhs," *Illustrated Weekly of India* 90 (No. 47, November 23, 1969), 8-13.

Talib, Gurbacham Singh, "Evolution of the Heroic Character," in *Sikhism and Indian Society, Transactions of the Indian Institute of Advanced Study*, vol. 4, Simla, Rashtrapati Nivas, 1967.

Chapter 7

People of Allah:
The Conspicuous Minority

Most citizens of India seem to think of Muslims automatically whenever someone mentions minorities. Probably the number who are unaware that there is any other minority runs into the millions. In the English-language newspapers, the term "minorities," even when used in the plural, is often enough a euphemism for Muslims, and everyone understands instantly what is meant. Fitting this national thought pattern admirably is G. S. Ghurye's treatise, *Social Tensions in India* (1968), where the author devotes eight chapters out of fourteen to Muslims who therefore capture, if they do not monopolize, attention.[1] Scheduled Castes and Scheduled Tribes may be the victims of indifference; not so the Muslims. History has already cast them in a conspicuous role, and, even after the wheel of fortune has depressed their lot, they cannot escape the glare of public gaze. If, as many contend, there is a "Muslim problem" in India, it is due to overexposure as much as to any other single factor. The purpose of this brief summary is to minimize the dramatic features of Hindu-Muslim relations in favor of a more structural analysis.

SEQUENCE AND ETHOS

Like other minorities, the Muslims rise from one of the six intergroup sequences outlined in Chapter 1. The fifth sequence, colonization, is the one presently applicable, with the proviso that "colonization" (a dominant form of conquest in the nineteenth and twentieth centuries) is used as a convenient term denoting all forms of foreign rule over a territory. In premodern times it was a

---

1. This book is quite intemperate in its attacks on Muslims, among whom it registers no redeeming features. On the other side of the ledger, it is regrettable that M.R.A. Baig's *The Muslim Dilemma in India* (Delhi, Vikas, 1974) appeared too late for its insights to be incorporated here.

form of hegemony in which the conquering ruler set up his court in the newly won kingdom. It was preeminently in the role of conquerors that the Muslims came to India and thus took their rise from an older sequence replaced by the more recent pattern of colonization.

Stripped of extraneous details, the Muslim presence in India has shown a marked shift from the status of an elite to that of a powerless minority. Reversal of roles is the bedrock reality that cannot be overlooked in any appraisal since it has left an indelible imprint on the beliefs and attitudes of Indian Muslims, particularly in the north.[2] The experience of deprivation has had a shattering effect, and reactions to this experience, when coupled with the responses from the Hindu community, have shaped the fluctuations between conflict and integration ever since the birth of Indian independence. Above and beyond this central fact are innumerable cultural and social realities that modify its harsh effects. A number of these modifications deserve attention.

First, since the Muslims are a religious minority, it is necessary to give a brief account of the origin and spread of Islam. Founded by the prophet Mohammed (A.D. 570-632), it is the last of the monotheistic faiths to be born in the Middle East. Its basic watchword is "There is no God but Allah and Mohammed is his prophet." Mohammed himself regarded his role as a successor and culminating figure in a whole line of religious leaders such as Moses and Jesus. Christianity, however, had but little influence among the Arabian tribes of his day, most of which were relatively isolated in desert surroundings; it was common for each tribe to have its own special god along with numerous magical practices. Because he was a visionary of the familiar sort who claimed that the deity spoke through him, Mohammed received a respectful hearing. And because of his extraordinary charisma along with the supertribal and universal message of his revelations, Mohammed's influence and doctrines spread from tribe to tribe with unprecedented speed.

It is not without importance that Islam was born in an area pervaded by nomadic culture. Throughout Arabia and the Middle East, nomads and pastoralists set up a social order of the greatest simplicity; each tribe displayed a rough equality of male adults with only the sheikh as supreme leader. At times the sheikh passed the office to his son; in the constant raids and feuds of desert warfare, however, nothing could save a weak or unworthy sheikh from being deposed by another whose power was legitimated in battle. Once the sheikh was accepted, however, his word was law and his rule unquestioned. Loyalty was the

---

2. It is worth mentioning that even though most Muslims (northern especially) have the self-image of conquerors, a quite large proportion are the descendants of converts from Hinduism. And even during Moghul rule, probably no more than a small part of Muslims were a ruling elite, while there were simultaneously a number of Hindu princes with considerable power and many Hindu merchants. The sense of disinheritance so common among Muslims today has a curious but interesting parallel internationally, where the British have seen their worldwide empire dwindle to a shadow of its former supremacy. The position of the British is therefore such that they can empathize freely with the present Muslims of India. Even in the nineteenth century, the British appeared to have a greater sense of kinship with the Muslim upper class than with the comparable Hindu class, partly because of a shared aristocratic ethos and partly because there were fewer religious impediments to social intercourse (such as interdining).

supreme virtue — to the sheikh and to the tribe. Beyond these limits there were no moral obligations, with the possible exception of the law of hospitality which lost its validity after three days.

The nomad lived on the produce of his flocks, on his sheep, goats, or camels. Not only did he avoid planting and sowing, but he looked down on agriculturalists as sedentary weaklings who could and should be despoiled to enrich the tribesman. Conquerors who succumbed to the seductions of settled life were, in the nomad's opinion, enfeebled and forced to yield dominion to whatever desert marauders attacked the oasis settlements. The freedom and movement of desert life with its invigorating hardships, enforced vigilance, sustained solidarity, intermittent warfare, and the sporadic joys of freebooting — these were the savor of life for men of the desert from Mesopotamia to Morocco.

It was in this cultural milieu that Mohammed gave his message to the world, and its values, along with the nomadic style of life, colored and shaped the universal doctrines of early Islam. This truth has been obscured because Mohammed himself was a Mecca merchant who spread much of his message through city centers, because his ideas were cosmopolitan in comparison with those current in his day, and because his followers spread the word and set up their rule in metropolitan centers like Baghdad, Damascus, and Cairo. One of India's outstanding Muslim scholars has indeed insisted that "Islam has, in all countries, promoted urban life, and Muslim civilization has everywhere been essentially urban in character" (Mujeeb, 1967, p. 10).

Apart from the term "essentially," Mujeeb's assertion is formally correct. Yet one may ask whether it is not a half-truth at best. The original cities of Islam and those that shaped its cultural preferences have been centers whose founders were nomads rather than agriculturalists. The latter have tended to occupy a lower position in the Muslim scale of values than Hindu culture has assigned them. At the birth of Islam, Medina, Mohammed's adopted home city, was a metropolis of tribesmen who had moved to town or whose forbears had done so, and Mohammed himself, as a member of the Quraish tribe, tended sheep in his youth, had his revelation in a desert cave, and did not leave his smaller hometown of Mecca for the larger city of Medina until forced to flee for his life in his fifty-second year.

Mohammed's plea for social equality was, in a curious way, a reiteration at a refined level of the rough and ready proto-democracy of tribal existence transposed to urban living where so often wealth, luxury, and ostentation were accompanied by poverty and want for the great bulk of the people. The prophet's prohibition of usury, his justification for appropriating wealth by the government, and his denunciation of hoarding brought down the wrath of merchants and traders on him in Mecca. Immured in their local beliefs and practices, Meccan priests and their orthodox followers demanded that he perform a miracle to prove the validity of his doctrines, a requirement he refused to fulfill because he claimed no divinity or supernatural powers. Driven out of Mecca in haste, he journeyed to Medina in A.D. 622, the year from which the Muslim calendar now begins.

For present purposes it is unnecessary to pursue the history of Islam and its rapid growth. About the founder it is important to remember that he opposed the local mores by forbidding idolatry, sorcery, superstition, and well-entrenched forms of exploitation; in his ideas about kinship and marriage he accepted the local proprieties up to a point, but departed from them sufficiently to grant women the right of divorce and inheritance of half the male share in paternal property, both of which were rather startling novelties in that milieu.

Once the message of Islam proved itself a liberating force and a Great Tradition capable of displacing little traditions of the surrounding tribes, it spread like wildfire under the early caliphs (who were to the plural converted Muslim tribes what the sheikhs were to pre-Islamic local tribes, except that under the new dispensation the caliphs were tacitly granted both spiritual and temporal rule). In actuality the caliphs became martial leaders who spread the Muslim dominion by the power of the sword from Persia to Spain. Eventually, later military rulers received more or less permissive grants of power from the dominant caliphs of the time until the caliphate became a subject of rivalry and discord following the eighth century. After that time it was the temporal rulers who gained the ascendancy in Muslim lands.

PASSAGE TO INDIA

In the Middle East and along the coasts of northern Africa where desert culture was preeminent, the Muslims converted entire populations. Although accused of making these conversions by force and coercion, they had the indigenous nomadic culture as their invisible but powerful ally. In numberless ways there were common understandings between the invading armies of Islam and the wandering tribes they subjugated. However, as Muslim forces proceeded beyond desert confines to agricultural regions of the Spanish northwest or the Indian southeast, they lost the ability to win over majority populations for the faith. Neither in Spain nor in India have Muslims constituted more than 25 to 30 percent of the population, and in Spain they were eliminated entirely.

In India the influx of Muslims was sporadic and intermittent. It can be summarized briefly under three headings: (1) Arab migrations to the Malabar coast from the seventh century; (2) the isolated conquest of Sindh from the eighth century; and (3) waves of invasion from the eleventh to eighteenth centuries by Turks, Afghans, Mughal Turks, and Persians. The Arab migrations were peaceful penetrations by traders, commercial adventurers who began coming long before the birth of Mohammed but who later imported the new faith during the seventh and eighth centuries. These entrepreneurs not only dotted the coast with mosques but apparently won over the confidence of Hindu upper caste elites who gave daughters in marriage to the newcomers, particularly when they became settled residents. Descendants of these marriages now form a large Muslim community in Kerala known as *Moplahs* from the Malayalam term *mapilla* for son-in-law.

The conquest of Sindh in A.D. 712 by Mohammed-bin-Quasim, commander owing allegiance to a Damascus Omayyad caliph, was an event disconnected from the rest of India; its chief importance lay in the fact that it was the first of the Muslim military invasions. Unlike the others, which succeeded each other in wavelike fashion, the subjugation of Sindh was unrelated to the mainstream of Indian history.

In contrast, the series of invasions by Muslim armies entering India through the Punjab, beginning with the attack by Mohammed of Ghazni in the eleventh century and concluding with Persian incursions at the breakup of the Mughal Empire in the eighteenth century, constituted the fulcrum of authority in the subcontinent throughout the period. Muslim rule, whatever its vacillations, was rarely, and then not successfully, challenged in the seven centuries that marked it dominion.

VARIATIONS IN ISLAMIC RULE AND PRACTICE

It would be a mistake to regard the invasion of Muslim conquerors as monolithic, a kind of foreign juggernaut rolling over India like a gigantic machine. As Percival Spear so well remarks,

> The Islamic faith, in fact, was brought into India at various times and places by different groups and in different forms. . . . Turkish Islam was very different from Arabic Islam and Afghan Islam different again. Further, Muslims were influenced by their cultural surroundings. In particular Persian culture from abroad and Hindu ideas from within India have modified and variegated the Islamic complex. Indian Islam is a necklace of racial, cultural, and political pearls strung on the thread of religion. One cannot appreciate the necklace merely by studying the thread. [Spear, 1967, pp. 30-31]

One of the major variations was the method of making converts. From the eleventh century to the time of the Mughals in the sixteenth century, force was a prominent feature of proselytizing. For example, we read of ten thousand men of a Hindu army commanded by Hardat who surrendered in a body and "proclaimed anxiety for conversion" (Titus, 1959, pp. 21-22). It also seems likely that the mass conversions, in which entire caste groups or tribes like local Rajputs, Jats, Gujars, and Meos went over to Islam collectively, were responding to military victories by the newcomers (Spear, 1967, p. 33). At the same time there is considerable evidence that zealots of Islam were capturing converts from lower Hindu castes between the eleventh and fifteenth centuries, possibly even into the sixteenth (Titus, 1959, pp. 46-47). This activity may have been responsible for the many rural conversions in scattered regions of present-day Uttar Pradesh and Bihar. The largest mass conversions took place after the Muslim conquest of Bengal in the thirteenth and fourteenth centuries, when nearly the whole countryside went over to Islam, ostensibly to escape their low caste position (Spear, 1967, p. 34).[3] From some accounts it appears that sufis (mystics, saints) were prominent among Muslim missionaries in various parts of

---

3. "Some say that this province had only recently been forcefully reconverted from Buddhism to Hinduism and hence the willingness to escape to Islam" (Theodore P. Wright, Jr., personal correspondence).

India. "Influenced by the sufi missionaries like Jalaluddin Bukhari (13th century) entire tribes in Punjab and Sind embraced Islam" (Hyder, 1969, p. 12).

Conversion, then, took not single but multiple forms. Significantly, we are told that the first Turkish conquerors themselves were newly won converts to the faith who were suspected of trying to prove their devotion by fanaticism (Spear, 1967, p. 32). On the other hand, Akbar (1556-1605) during his reign encouraged leaders of all faiths to disseminate their doctrines at his court, approved and practiced religious intermarriage, and promoted Hindus to high positions in his personal entourage. During his reign, the Muslim legalists temporarily lost their power.

Between the simple faith of Mohammed and the later complex super-structure of Islamic kingdoms was a yawning gulf. As one writer notes, "The egalitarian society created by Mohammed and the first Four Caliphs gave way to lavish imperialism" (Hyder, 1969, p. 11). In the process of development, codification of law (Shari'ah) took place, and, although Islam had abolished priesthood, a viable substitute for it appeared in the *maulvis* (theologians) and *faqihs* (jurists) who arose to interpret the meaning of the Quran and the Shari'ah. Occupying a different function were the *ulema* (scholars) who, because of their greater erudition, displayed a wider variety of opinions and doctrines, some of which might appear quite heterodox. One could almost say that in Islam, the contrast and frequent conflict between Sufis and maulvis, or between faqihs and ulema, are reminiscent of the opposition between priest and prophet in ancient Israel.

The abundant growth of legalism in Islam was followed by two derivative tendencies that had considerable impact on the Muslim world, particularly in India. First was the practice of ulema and maulvis at the royal court to interpret the sacred law in support of whatever decision the ruler might make. When one such scholar was asked why he did not denounce an unjust ruler, he replied that the ruler's sword was sharper than his tongue (Karandikar, 1968, pp. 41-42). As the temporal authority of the caliph passed more and more to the sultans, the restraints of religion seemed to be weakened by heightened royal authority.

A second tendency was for legal interpreters to make later sayings or writings of the canon supersede earlier ones. A later verse of the Quran could abrogate an earlier one that appeared to contradict it, and later sayings and traditions (Hadith) of the Prophet could cancel out those that had gone before. As-Shafi, who propounded this form of interpretation, laid the groundwork of classical Muslim law with this principle, and his views became highly influential in spite of the fact that Shafi is only one of the four schools of orthodox Islam. On the basis of his interpretation, it became possible to annul Mohammed's earlier saying in the Quran, "Begin not hostilities. Lo! Allah loveth not aggressors," in favor of his later injunction given during war against the Meccans: "Fight them! Allah will chastise them at your hands and He will lay them low and give you victory over them, and He will heal the breasts of folk who are believers." It was the same As-Shafi who laid down the corresponding doctrine that the only way for Muslims (if they were powerful enough) to deal with unbelievers would be to serve an ultimatum: "Death or Islam" (Karandikar, 1968, pp. 45-47). There were many who opposed this idea, a number of them

Sufis, but Shafi's theory became widely accepted as justifiable, in view of the exigencies of rule.[4]

Structural changes in social organization of Muslim communities followed the conquests and setting up of new kingdoms and sultanates. An earlier emphasis on the emancipation of women, so marked in the sayings of Mohammed, gave way under Byzantine influence to the purdah system of seclusion (particularly in the upper classes), a custom taken over by the higher castes in India.[5] Distribution of wealth by government action was eroded in favor of increasing accumulation of riches by rulers who taxed their subjects methodically. The simple man-to-man leadership of the Prophet's day was displaced by inheritance of rule in the Arab Omayyad dynasty of Damascus (661-750) and strongly reinforced later by Persian notions of hereditary kingship. An army of courtiers and hangers-on was augmented by a multitude of artisans and tradesmen in the royal cities together with the serried ranks of the military forces.

Early relations with Kafirs or unbelievers were mild, and the social pressures on them to convert to Islam quite often avoided compulsion; non-Muslims living under Islamic rule had a unique place as zimmis or God's responsibility. They were to receive special protection until they saw the light, and they were excused from military service by paying the jiziya or substitute tax. Over time, under the influence of the legalists, canon law made it incumbent on a Muslim ruler to extend the rule of Islam by force, the world now being divided into dar-ul-Islam (abode of Islam) and dar-ul-Harb (abode of war) with each kingdom of necessity belonging to one category or the other. With the elaboration of this doctrine, rulers were supposed to transform every dar-ul-Harb into dar-ul-Islam through jihad or holy war. Those who submitted but did not go on to conversion became zimmis who had to pay the jiziya and the kharaj (land tax), both of which became discriminatory. For those who refused to pay, there was only one alternative: to fight. It must be recognized, however, that in India the Muslim armies were too small in relation to the large Hindu population for such stringent rules to be enforced. In addition, the military was greatly dependent on Hindu farmers of the countryside to provide their food. Hence the prescriptions were notably relaxed (Titus, 1959, pp. 18-19).

From the relative social equality of early Islam, the movement toward social stratification continued to ramify. It was only natural, at first, that those directly descended from the family of the Prophet should have high esteem in

---

4. Less influential, though grudgingly admitted and selectively applied, was the doctrine of a third alternative or "tolerated minority" (dhimmi). Originally reserved for "people of the book" (Ahl-i-Kitab) like Christians and Jews, this provision was extended, *faute de mieux,* to Hindus in practice, since there were far too many of them to make the "death or Islam" choice a practical expedient. Interestingly, Akbar, who did not accept the legalists' doctrine, was unopposed at court because of the first tendency just mentioned, that is, for ulema to accept any dictates of the contemporary ruler. Hence, Muslim kingdoms and sultanates eventually reflected the doctrinal views of the monarch, whether liberal or conservative.

5. The position of women, relatively high in the Vedic period, had already been greatly lowered by the time of Manu (about 200 B.C.). Later, the Muslim influence only exaggerated an already existent trend and chiefly in the upper echelons of society. (See Khushwant Singh, 1969, pp. 74-76.)

the community; they came to be known as Sayyid. Those of Arabian ancestry, presumably those who came from the earliest cadre of converts, had a coveted place just below that of the Sayyids; such were called Sheikhs. In India, where the Mughal dynasty was the most illustrious during the Islamic period, the descendants of Mughal families have come to occupy a position next to the Arabs in order of prestige. Below them, at a somewhat greater distance, are those who trace their lineage to tribes from the North-West Frontier and Afghanistan, being known as Pathans. This fourfold division of Sayyid, Sheikh, Mughal and Pathan marks off the upper or "noble" (Ashraf) division of Indian Muslims (Titus, 1959, pp. 176-77). The rest or commoners are "ajlaf" and probably descended from the families of Indian converts from the lower castes. Endogamy is practiced to a considerable extent in each division, but there is not the rigidity of caste. This third mode of ranking based on the caste position of converts to the faith has an ambiguous complexity described by Titus (ibid., p. 176) in the following words (probably these divisions have their major origin in rural rather than urban populations):

> . . . as the converts from various classes and castes of Hindus came in, from Brahmans and Rajputs to the lowest outcastes, and as the lower caste groups continued to live mostly in their ancestral villages, it was inevitable that there should continue among those Hindu converts the same general feeling of aloofness the one from the other. . . . Therefore today it is not astonishing that we should find it the common practice to regard Muslims as belonging to two social groups: the Sharif zats (high castes) and the ajlaf zats (low castes).

These are nothing more than an approximation to Hindu castes. The mode of worship is not caste-bound as is so often true among the non-Muslims. To put it plainly: in the mosque, all believers are equal; in the cities, there is little stress on caste position (money takes a more prominent place); it is in the rural areas that many caste lines remain. As already noted, however, the leading Indian Muslims are urban dwellers. Among twentieth century Muslims in the subcontinent, caste is less important than ancestry, and the two do not tend to coalesce, as they do among Hindus.

MUSLIM-HINDU CONTRASTS

A brief comparison of Semitic and Indian religion is necessary before proceeding further. The three major faiths originating in the Semitic-language areas (Judaism, Christianity, and Islam) have emphasized monotheism by *exclusion.* "Thou shalt have no other gods before me," or "There is no God but Allah, and Mohammed is His prophet." Indian religion takes the opposite view. Popular polytheism from Vedic times to the twentieth century has been resolved by regarding all lesser gods as manifestations of Brahma; in other words, monism by *inclusion.* While Islam (together with Judaism and Christianity) elevates the one God by denying the many, Hinduism uses the many to approach the One. In this sense, Islam has a hard edge of intolerance, Hinduism the soft yielding of tolerance. In a very real sense the tolerance of Hinduism becomes universalized because it regards the gods of all peoples and all religions as manifestations of Brahma; without exception they are each and every one partial revelations of divine truth.[6]

In the matter of conduct, universalism is replaced by pluralism in the Hindu view of the world, while Semitic religions dichotomize morality in terms of right and wrong with a wide gulf fixed between them. Hindu morality, on the other hand, is situational and a function of one's caste position. Thus, what is right for a member of jati A will not necessarily be right for a member of jati B, even though they are in the same varna. To keep the dharma or duty of one's caste position makes a man a good Hindu, no matter what he believes about the gods; in fact, he may be an atheist without his belief affecting his status. In the case of Islam, however, the same morality applies to everyone regardless of position. Ethics is essentially egalitarian. In the mosque, high and low, prince and pauper, are alike before Allah. For the Muslim, right belief and right action are equally important and the same for all. For the Hindu, however, right action is such an overwhelming issue (affecting eons of transmigration) that it pushes belief in the gods into quite a secondary place. This makes right action particularistic for the Hindu rather than universalistic, depending on the status fixed at the time of birth; this, in turn, reflects the cumulation of karma from past lives in previous births.

These contrasts between two religious traditions are, of course, highly simplified for purposes of exposition. There are schools of thought in both Islam and Hinduism that show variations from the above picture and contradict it in many details. And, as secularism grows, the sharp edges of such antitheses become blurred. However, I submit that the central tendencies of the two major faiths are not far removed from the outline just presented and that recognizing these elemental differences can aid the reader to understand the responses that members of each religious community make toward the other.

ECLIPSE AND READJUSTMENT

In the space of two centuries, Indian Muslims have suffered two major setbacks, one at British hands, displacing their rule in India, the other with heavy losses of members and leaders to Pakistan during (and after) the prolonged chain of events that finally culminated in partition.[7] British colonialism had the following results:

> Partly owing to blind resentment and partly to the natural conservatism and narrowmindedness of the (Muslim) feudal classes, they could not see

---

6. Toward the end of the chapter, it will become clear that Hinduism has its own unique form of intolerance.

7. There were other causes for the decline of Muslim hegemony, of course, such as the weakening of Muslim principalities by local victories of Mahratta and Sikh armies that helped to fractionate Muslim dominion still further into fragments ill-equipped to resist British military power. Also, the loss of Muslim leadership to Pakistan after partition was less marked in south India than in the north.

anything good in the culture of the new rulers and regarded their own culture as superior to it in every way. . . . the ulama and the sufis . . . hated Western culture even more intensely than the classes mentioned above. . . . The study of the English language and modern sciences had been permitted by a broad-minded religious leader like Shah Abdul Aziz, but according to many ulama it was not permissible. In short, the attitude of Muslims in the South and West towards the new rulers and the new age was that of cautious compromise and, in northern India, on the part of the ulama and the masses one of bitter resentment and hostility. [S. A. Husain, 1965, pp. 19-20, 22; by permission]

The upshot of these events was the failure of Muslim children in the changed atmosphere to get education in the English language and in the sciences. While the Hindus, particularly the upper castes, availed themselves eagerly of the new English medium so as to fill the offices of administrative services in all provinces, Muslims lagged behind under the influence of religious leaders to whom Western education was anathema. Even the fervent pleas of Sir Syed Ahmed Khan, who helped establish Aligarh University as a center of higher education for spreading modern ideas and the scientific outlook for Muslim students of middle and upper classes, had little effect on the community as a whole. Sir Syed's religious colleagues were, for the most part, simply estranged by his Anglophilia and rejected his attempts to renovate Muslim education. Paradoxically, most of the Muslim League leaders who founded Pakistan were followers of Sir Syed, and their departure from India retarded modernization for the community who remained.

The second major blow to the Muslim community was partition itself. It may be that Pakistanis do not consider it in this light today, but for Indian Muslims it has meant further reduction in status, along with all the personal tragedies that made the experience a disaster. The process of partition was a series of bloody massacres that left a million dead and fourteen million homeless (Husain, 1965, p. 122). Two-thirds of the Muslims throughout the subcontinent found themselves in Pakistan, leaving one-third in postpartition India, where they constituted approximately 11 percent of the population in 1971 (it was nearer 25 percent of undivided India). The proportion of Muslims in residual India has hovered around 10 percent since the time of partition, the number reaching 61,417,934 in 1971.[8]

The effects of partition were more catastrophic in most ways than the aftermath of British occupation, as the Muslims underwent dismemberment and massacre in addition to loss of prestige along with economic and political reverses. Sheer survival became a serious problem. Reservations made by the British for Muslims in government services were quickly abolished, and jobs could only be secured by competition in an atmosphere of suspicion that Muslims were disloyal to the nation. Muslim industrialists and businessmen who had supported the Muslim League hurried to Pakistan where they could take advantage of the vacuum left behind by the departure of Hindu and Sikh commercial classes driven out by the wave of violence engulfing both regions of the subcontinent.

---

8. Census of India 1971, Series 1, Paper 2 of 1972, Religion.

Serious hardships to business also resulted from the Evacuee Property Law passed soon after independence. This Law provided

> that no intending Muslim evacuee would be allowed to sell his property in India. This had the beneficial effect of arresting the course of Muslim emigration but it did great damage to Muslim businessmen, because, according to the general social pattern in India, the Muslim families had generally joint properties and business establishments and it was not customary to divide them. Now under the Evacuee Property Act, if a single member of a family migrated to Pakistan the whole property was put in charge of the official custodian and the remaining members of that family could neither sell their shares of the property nor raise loans on them. Besides, the term 'intending evacuee' was so widely interpreted that at one stage almost all Muslims were covered by it and their properties declared unsaleable. Obviously this put many people to great difficulty, but for the business classes of Muslims, it was simply disastrous, because it became impossible for them to borrow money in time of need and this often sounded the death-knell of their business. [Husain, 1965, pp. 131-32; by permission]

Civil service employment also declined. In Hyderabad and other princely states, along with a number of northern provinces, Muslims had had the lion's share of government services, and many of them were zamindari as well. After independence, the institution of zamindari was abolished and the princely states dissolved; this impoverished a large, if not major, share of upper and middle classes. Since the livelihood for literally millions of their fellow-Muslims in the poorer classes had been dependent on the prosperity of such elite groups, the resulting unemployment became endemic, and the white-collar groups were especially hard hit.

Political losses were equally serious. Before independence, Muslims enjoyed the privilege of separate electorates where they could nominate and elect representatives of their own choosing. In later years they had their own political party, the Muslim League, which spoke increasingly for the entire community. Because of the limited franchise of prepartition days, only about 10 percent of the Muslims voted, and the task of marshaling support under the circumstances was not too difficult; voters were, for the most part, the articulate middle and upper classes who had sufficient means to be eligible electors[9] (Husain, 1965, pp. 116-17). After independence, with universal franchise and joint electorates,

---

9. These facts refute the absurd allegation of the Jan Sangh party in the six-point program adopted at their Patna convention in December 1969, where they charged that the Muslims needed Indianising "because over 93 percent of them had voted for the Muslim League and Pakistan before partition" (*Times of India,* Dec. 28, 1969). Since only 10 percent of the Muslims voted at all, the accusation is obviously manufactured for propaganda purposes. And, as a later commentator pointed out, in the last Muslim election where there was a separate electorate (1946), the Muslim League secured only 74.4 percent of the vote. Furthermore, only a little more than a third of those who voted in that election came from areas now in India; some of them have since migrated to Pakistan, and others have died. So even among the Muslim *voters* (who were themselves but 10 percent of all Muslims in pre-independence India), less than a third are resident in present-day India (letter of Gopal Krishna to the *Times of India,* Jan. 2, 1970).

it became more difficult to organize political participation for any purpose of long-range significance.

Since the main strength (and aggressiveness) of pre-independence Muslim League was in the north, particularly Uttar Pradesh, and since the League itself was frequently blamed for partition, public opinion has been hostile to attempts to revive the organization. In Kerala and Madras, far from the borders and with less of their leadership drained off to Pakistan, the League has been maintained as a going concern. Farther north, resistance has been strong. Attempts to set up the League in a few northern cities during 1959 were unsuccessful, a number of conveners being arrested (Wright, 1966b, p. 592, n. 83).[10] The Muslim Majlis (with Muslim League support) played something of a role in the 1967 election, and the Muslim League reappeared with limited effectiveness in West Bengal and Uttar Pradesh during the election of 1971. In sum, Muslim efforts to reestablish political strength have been relatively weak.

It appears that decline in status has followed the deteriorating economic and political fortunes, although evidence on this question is less clear. The growth of the Jan Sangh is certainly one indication of widespread belief in the northern states that the Muslims in India were in some way responsible for partition, with the former Muslim League and its intransigent leader M. A. Jinnah as symbols of disunity and contention. There has been a violent reaction from the trauma of partition with its unspeakable carnage, the memory of which will haunt India for a yet indeterminate future. Indirectly, this attitude implies a serious denigration of the entire Muslim community because of its influence in bringing about India's worst catastrophe. Hindus may not share the overt hostility of the Jan Sangh, but they may quite agree that Muslims before partition were over-privileged and must now make it on their own; a certain grim satisfaction accompanies this attitude, and it implies recognition of a decline in Muslim prestige. In a way, the downgrading of status can be traced to the time of mass migrations attendant on partition. In the words of one observer:

> For many true Muslims the greatest spiritual anguish. . . was that they had to see hundreds of thousands of Sikh and Hindu refugees from West and East Pakistan in a deplorable plight, driven from their homes and wandering about in quest of shelter and to hear the bitter and biting words that all this was done to them by Muslims. . . . The sparks of hatred and revenge in the eyes of their old non-Muslim neighbors aroused in them a strange and complex feeling. [Husain, 1965, p. 128; by permission]

If this description is a valid one, it indicates Muslim recognition that they are tainted with social guilt in the eyes of the larger community and must now accustom themselves to lower standing than was previously theirs because of public disparagement. Conversely, the opinion seems widespread in the dominant group that the creation of a separate state of their own in Pakistan should satisfy the Muslims and that now they ought to be reconciled to a

---

10. This precarious political position made the Muslims even more vulnerable to internal rivalries in their midst. For example, in the 1959 arrests for Muslim League activity, one League authority admitted "that two factions within the Calcutta office denounced each other as Pakistani agents to the government" (Wright, 1966b, p. 592, n. 83).

secondary place in Indian society (Siddiqi, 1970, p. 30). Since status is an affair of social definition, postpartition views of Muslims as declining in social position are widely accepted by the public.

DEMOGRAPHIC REALITIES

Although the Muslims have a greater proportion of urban dwellers than do the Hindus, it is important to recognize that the Muslim population of India is predominantly rural. According to the 1971 census, the total Muslim population was 61,417,934 of which 43,732,953 (71.21 percent) were rural and 17,684,981 (28.79 percent) urban.[11]

There is a popular belief that Muslims are increasing their population much more rapidly than Hindus, a notion based on the correct observation that the rate of increase for Muslims as shown by the census is greater than the corresponding rate for Hindus. Those who regard the Muslims as a continuing threat to all Hindus draw conclusions from official statistics that appear so alarming that they tend to inflame public opinion. Such leaders in the Hindu community as Shankaracharya of Sharda Dwarka Peeth, Tarkateerth Raghunath Shastri Kokje, and Shri Sudhir Hendre (who is president of the All-India Anti-Family Planning Action Committee) have made statements to the effect that family planning is covertly forced on Hindus while Muslims are allowed to procreate without limitation. If the present discrepancy in the rate of population increase for the two communities continues, they declare, the inroads of family planning may eventually reduce the Hindus to a minority in their own land. What are the facts?

Table 7.1 shows that it is not only the Muslims who have a higher growth rate than the Hindus but also the Sikhs and the Christians, the latter having the highest rate of all. Secondly, the proportional relations of growth do not vary appreciably from one decennium to another; that is, when the Hindu rate increases in 1961-71, so does the Muslim rate and the other two rates (while the Christian rate remains the highest of all four). At all events the discrepancy between growth rates is but a few percentage points. What is really significant is how little the family planning programs affected the total growth rates in view of the fact that *all* of them rise in the second decennium. Comparatively speaking, the Hindu rise in the growth rate was somewhat less than the corresponding one for Muslims. There appear to be two reasons for this. Though the difference is not great, at least one well-informed writer reports that in the 1960s, if one is to judge by the opinions expressed by columnists in Urdu newspapers, those who oppose family planning appear to be in the majority in the Muslim community. At least they predominate in the media of public opinion (Chishti, 1968, 43 n.). The same cannot be said of the Hindu community, where there is no such unity of views and where the program for family planning began its vigorous campaign only in the mid-sixties under the Third Plan. Resistance to family planning was less unanimous among Hindus

---

11. Figures taken from Census of India 1971, Series 1, Paper 2 of 1972, Religion, Statement, Distribution of Population by Religion 1961-71.

TABLE 7.1

**Growth Rates of Four Major Religious Communities
During Two Decennia***

Community	Decennium 1951-61 Growth Rate, %	Decennium 1961-71 Growth Rate, %
Hindus	20.29	23.69
Muslims	25.61	30.85
Christians	27.35	32.60
Sikhs	25.13	32.28

*After Pethe, 1973, p. 77.

than among Muslims, if we are to judge from this sort of evidence, which helps to account for the discrepancy between the two communities.[12]

If we note that there is a marked differential between the Hindus and *all* other communities, the latter having rates of growth uniformly higher, demographers seem fairly well agreed that a fundamental reason for this gap is that Hindus regard widow remarriage as not respectable and hence do not practice it; the other religious communities allow it and hence have a higher fertility. When it is estimated that about one-tenth of Hindu women are widowed and do not bear after they attain that status (though owing to relatively early marriage, they are in the child-bearing ages), this decreases the fertility of the Hindu population appreciably.

As for the assertion that family planning programs are somehow forced on Hindu communities while ignoring Muslims, field studies and reports from independent researches show that such programs are carried out for all communities and that religious membership does not halt operations at any special boundary of this sort. In the regions where these studies have been pursued and the effects of family planning are measured, there is no evidence that fertility levels are significantly related to either religion or caste, nor is knowledge of birth control or willingness to learn about family planning. All religious groups are now practicing family planning, although regional differences occur in the rate such practices are adopted. Certain areas show Hindus with higher adoption rates, whereas others show Muslims leading the way. In Tamil Nadu, one study showed the Muslims with a much higher adoption rate than Hindus, and research in Karnataka showed the Christians far ahead. It can hardly be assumed that only the Hindus will see the advantages of family planning and eventually make greater use of it than members of other religious communities.

It is also important to recognize that the formerly strong resistance to family planning among Muslims is beginning to break down. For instance, the Imam of Jamma Musjid in Delhi, along with a number of other leaders, has issued a 'Fatwa' or religious ruling in support of family planning by employing proof

---

12. However, there is no corresponding evidence (to my knowledge) about Sikh or Christian communities.

texts from the Quran and the Sunnah (traditions of the prophet Mohammed). This could well mark the turn of the tide among Muslim believers in favor of family limitation and in any case will be a strong influence in that direction (Pethe, 1973). Muslim urban predominance over Hindus should also be a factor leading to more rapid family limitation among Muslims.

Such considerations make it quite clear that the fears of a few Hindu zealots that Muslims will overpopulate the subcontinent are groundless.[13]

A glance at Muslim populations in other countries of the world comes as a surprise to most Indians when comparisons are made. India has a Muslim population practically equal to that of all the west Asian (Middle Eastern) nations put together, the latter totaling 64 million, while the figure for India in 1971 was 61 million. Surprisingly, there are only two nations in the world with a larger Muslim population than India: one of them is Pakistan with 90 million; the other is Indonesia with some 85 million. Likewise it is astonishing to most observers to discover that the People's Republic of China has as many Muslims in her domain as there are in all of India; the numbers given are equal. The Soviet Union has a smaller number (only 35 million), and the entire continent of Africa contains slightly over 100 million. In terms of national Muslim populations, India is tied with China in third place, that is, with the third largest Muslim population of any country anywhere (Hyder, 1969, p. 13).

LIVING IN AN ENCLAVE

The degree of enclosure is quite high for the Muslim community. Endogamy is enforced to nearly the same degree as it is between castes. Ecological concentration is especially high in the cities, where Muslims occupy numerous mohallas of their own where they carry on most of their neighboring. Some argue that such urban concentrations increased after 1947 for security reasons; whether this is true or not, such reasons are realistic for preserving the mohallas since they often do serve as havens of protection.

Institutional duplication is marked, though not absolute. Religious institutions are separate from those in the rest of society with the exception of wayside shrines that are sometimes employed by both Hindus and Muslims of the locality. Family life is quite separate from that of the Hindus and socializes children in certain distinctive ways. Purdah is far more widespread among Muslims, and women are strictly guarded from everyday relations with outsiders to a greater degree than exists in most Hindu families. Yet within the household the Muslim family eats together, even with the servants on many occasions. There is less veneration of the older generation than is normally present in Hindu

---

13. Another assertion often made is that the continued practice of polygyny among Muslims tends to keep their birth rate higher. This disregards the marked decline of polygyny among adherents of Islam. Also demographic reasoning shows that even when practiced, polygyny would make little difference, for "as long as the proportion of females in the reproductive age group who are married is more or less stable, there is no reason to believe that fertility would be higher whether four women are married to four different men or all to one man" (Pethe, 1973, p. 77).

families. Though the evidence is not conclusive, it seems probable that among Muslims the male at marriage is more likely to set up a separate household and to be less encompassed within the parental family than is characteristic of the Hindus. Such features may help to account for a strong masculinity syndrome among males, though historically this phenomenon can be traced back to Arabian culture in its desert setting. No doubt polygyny seems especially consistent with all these trends, but in spite of traditional permissiveness on this issue, there is very little evidence of polygyny in the present generation. Economic pressures, if nothing else, reduce the likelihood of such a pattern.

Educational institutions also set boundary lines within which Muslims are set apart, at least in the primary grades when Muslim children attend Quaranic schools where they recite verses from their sacred scriptures until they learn whole passages by heart. This gives a unique direction to their socialization patterns at an impressionable age, even though many of them go on to secondary school with non-Muslims.

Some associational clustering also takes place among Muslims, although voluntary organizations are few. In this respect they are characteristic of Indian society as a whole, where nonascriptive clubs or formally organized societies are rare except among middle-class, western-educated groups. At this level there are occasional recreational clubs for Muslim youth in the cities, a natural outcome of residential concentration in the cities. A limited number of Muslim professionals break across the line into all-India organizations, since they have wider contacts with upper class clients and colleagues; some, therefore, join associations that cut across religious lines such as Rotary, Lions, or specialized professional and business organizations.

Informants report that separation of Muslims and Hindus is more clear-cut in the cities than in rural areas. In the cities, ecological patterning makes for rigidity of group definition where the dividing line is quite distinct, both residentially and socially. This sharp separation is less true in the villages, where Hindu and Muslim domiciles are adjacent or in the same area, and socializing across religious lines is the usual pattern among neighbors who know each other well. One may surmise that, historically, mass conversions to Islam taking place in the villages were not uniformly successful but affected limited sectors or scattered families here and there.[14] Since the new converts did not migrate and therefore kept their place in the village economy, continuing with their customary tasks, their relationships with neighbors continued on a primary group basis. In a good many, perhaps most, of these cases, retention of traditional Hindu practices (for instance, observation of Hindu festivals such as Dussehra or Divali) was quite common (Titus, 1959, pp. 170ff.; Mandelbaum, 1970, pp. 546-51).

---

14. There are, of course, a few all-Muslim villages even today, but they are so rare that they constitute exceptional cases where, in the past, the wave of conversion rolled over them completely. Syncretism with Hindu practices was common here too. Intermediate types, like the Meos of Rajasthan, also occurred. The Meos are a former robber caste, claiming descent from the Rajputs, who were converted and reconverted in the wake of different Muslim invasions, yet kept many of their old Hindu customs. After independence, because of local prejudice, they were alienated from Hindu society and, paradoxically, became more completely Islamized (Aggarwal, 1966).

DOMINANT GROUP CONTROL

Because of the variations in ecological concentration in rural as compared with urban areas, Muslims seem much more free from harassment and violence in agricultural villages than in the cities, where anti-Muslim riots have frequently erupted. In this respect, Muslim experience is the opposite of that befalling the Scheduled Castes, who encounter their major violence in rural areas, as already noted. In such cases it appears that increased visibility of the minority group makes it a more convenient target. If it is true that Muslims in the villages are residentially scattered and mixed with homes belonging to members of various castes, they would be, for that reason, less conspicuous than the dwellings of the Scheduled Castes in a separate section by themselves. In the transitional changes accompanying political activity since independence, any challenge of traditional authority by the Scheduled Castes in the village brings down upon them the wrath of caste Hindus, who strongly resist efforts to change their status. Attacks on their peripheral settlements are made easy by the well-defined boundaries that set them off. In the cities, however, it is the Muslims in their mohallas who are highly visible, while the Scheduled Castes are more dispersed and unexposed. And it is not so much an attempt by Muslims as a minority to dispute their status that incites the Hindus to action against them in the cities, but the massive presence of Muslims in a phalanx (rather than as neighbors) that serves as a constant source of irritation or threat quite unbearable to a population only recently migrated from the villages where such densities of Muslims were unthinkable. Agitators thus have a convenient (and permanent) stimulus to which they can point when they wish to arouse the masses into action against what they picture as a ubiquitous menace. It is then predictable that violence can be triggered quickly in the urban milieu and that it will find a natural target in the visible Muslim minority.

A quite different but significant mode of dominant group control consists of a set of laws permitting the police to arrest and hold without trial, certain categories of offenders or suspected offenders. The best-known legislation of this character is the Preventive Detention Act of 1950 which accords to police forces the authority to incarcerate for up to a full year any persons who are believed to be a danger to state security, a threat to public order, or a menace to the continued provision of services needed by the community at large. The terms of reference of the Act are so broad that it can be used as a bludgeon against a wide variety of suspected persons and is employed quite commonly against those known to incite or support open violence habitually, "communal" seditionists and provocateurs, actual spies working in the service of a foreign power, fifth columnists who are Indian citizens, and all those known to be manifestly addicted to violence (Bayley, 1969, p. 265). From this list it is easy to observe how readily such categories could be applied to Muslims, particularly in the wake of two Indo-Pakistani wars. Even after the first of these conflicts, there is evidence that Muslims felt the Preventive Detention Act was used indiscriminately against them;[15] it can be definitely inferred from the fact that one of the

---

15. With the Chinese invasion of 1962, a new decree that was even more drastic in operation, the Defense of India Rules, was also put into effect. Its purpose was primarily to immobilize any Chinese who might have been acting as fifth columnists in India during the

major political demands made by Muslim groups even before the Bangladesh episode[16] was the repeal of the Preventive Detention Act (Wright, 1966a; Smith, 1963, p. 108), an appeal successfully thwarted by being widely ignored.

RELATIVE POSITION OF MUSLIMS IN THE SOCIAL STRUCTURE

Since the rural population of India has shown a decline in standard of living in the 1960s (Bardhan, 1973), we can only infer that the Muslims (with a rural majority) shared this reduction. There are no separate figures to substantiate this conclusion, however.[17] It is hard to escape the impression that the number of self-employed among Muslims is unusually high.

Muslims have no reserved places in the educational system or in the services such as those available to the Scheduled Castes and Tribes. Market for commodities created by artisans is no longer what it was, and the younger generation shuns the long discipline of apprenticeship; consequently, the number of Muslim artisans has dwindled to a small number of older workers who recognize their precarious position at the end of the line.[18] In the cities, therefore, Muslims entering industrial occupations do so commonly at the unskilled level. If the situation at Ahmedabad is any criterion, skilled workers have a definite advantage in the mills, while the unskilled are subject to the hazards of intermittent employment (Roy Burman, 1970, pp. 36-37). As a result, the Muslim workers who most need the work are also most vulnerable to unemployment.

There is some evidence that Muslims have a better chance to get jobs in private rather than in public sectors. As one informant declared, "In private business merit counts for something and Muslims are known as good workmen; but in government employment, nepotism is almost total." Although this statement is exaggerated, it seems to be true that Muslims expect more favorable reception when they seek white-collar employment in the capitalist economy rather than in the state economy. But even in the private sector there are difficulties because the candidate obtains little help from those of his own religious affiliation. In the majority of cases he is likely to apply to a Hindu (or at least a non-Muslim) employer for a position, and there is considerable likelihood that he will run up against family or caste preferences.

---

conflict. For a discussion of this set of rules, see Chapter 12 below. The "emergency decrees" of 1975 simply extended these sweeping powers, which were then applied indiscriminately to anti-Congress leaders of many types. See Chapter 13 for brief mention.

16. The Bangladesh episode occurred in 1970-71 when East Pakistan declared its independence from the western sector of the country, which then launched an unsuccessful preventive attack. Owing largely to the intervention of India, the move for independence was won and East Pakistan emerged as a new nation adopting the name of Bangladesh (Bengal nation).

17. Theodore Wright suggests that one reason the economic condition of Muslims has not been studied is because it would be considered communal and would lend itself to more demands for reservations (personal correspondence).

18. An attempt to revive some of these skills among Muslim children is being made by a few carpet manufacturers observed in northern India, but with quite limited results.

In government service there has been a marked decline in the number of Muslims occupying bureaucratic positions after partition. In pre-independence India, Muslims had more than their share in the Indian Civil Service under British sponsorship; Hindu proportion in such positions may have been reduced in the 1920s because Gandhi urged his followers to stay away from such forms of collaboration whereas the Muslim League did not. At any rate, the great majority of Muslim officials in New Delhi, particularly at the higher levels, migrated to Pakistan with the change in regime. Since then there is definite evidence that the number of Muslims in what is renamed the Indian Administrative Service is now down to less than half the proportion the Muslims bear to the total population (Wright, 1966a; Smith, 1963, p. 117, n. 60). As still another observer declares, "A recent survey showed that barely 2 per cent of Government officials at the highest level were Moslems. . . . Outright discrimination is more clearly shown on the lower rungs of the bureaucracy. Moslems account for less than one-half of one per cent of the clerks and messengers of the central Government here. These figures are not published by the Government, and discussion of what to do about the problem is virtually nil. The official position often seems to be that the problem does not exist" (Lelyveld, 1968).

Widespread abandonment of Urdu by all branches of government (with the possible exception of Hyderabad) has also made it difficult for a great many Muslim candidates who have Urdu as their mother tongue to take competitive examinations for government posts. This is one factor accounting for the fact that very few Muslims take the examinations at all; another is a constant fear of discrimination if they do take them (though this is often not as prevalent as they assume). Possibly the demoralization of the Muslim community has something to do with the situation for, as Lelyveld comments, "Moslems accounted for only 1.5 per cent of those who competed for these posts, though they represent 11 per cent of the population" (Lelyveld, 1968). The lack of competent candidates from the Muslim community "has often been noted by persons who are on the selection boards" (Ahmad, 1970, p. 27).[19]

The economic weakness of the Muslim community must also be seen in the context of the total society where development is slow, wages are low, and unemployment on the rise. With jobs scarce everywhere, it is perhaps inevitable that those who can dispense them see to it that only the persons closest to them get such opportunities.

> Under such conditions parochial loyalties to family, caste, religious community, provincial origin and language, take precedence over the needs of competence, complete objectivity and fairness in employment. . . . This is obviously perceived by the minority members as discrimination against them. The demoralizing influence of such perception is that people give up the struggle to improve their competence. Consequently, whenever

---

19. Another possible disability in the competition for such positions may be the "Nawabi" mentality of the north Indian Muslim, that is, "the self-image, however incorrect, of an aristocrat who is generous and for whom the Puritan virtues are infra dig" (Theodore Wright, personal correspondence).

opportunity is available, they are left behind. Thus the 'self-fulfilling' prophecy comes true.[20]

In the field of education, we have already seen how the opposition to Western culture in general, and British in particular, led to their rejection in the nineteenth century — a trend opposed with limited success by Sir Syed Ahmad Khan. The effects of this community refusal are still being felt, with the additional difficulty, so marked since partition, of pursuing education in Urdu which, in independent India, isolates the group from its neighbors.[21] Although literacy figures are not obtainable for the Muslims as a whole, they are still stigmatized as "an educationally backward group" (Latifi, 1968, p. 39). In this, as in so many other ways, the community occupies a salient low status.

MOBILITY AND ITS IMPEDIMENTS

There are many ways in which the paths to advancement are blocked for Muslims in their upward climb to higher positions in society. This becomes clear when we look at the analogue of Figure 3.1 on modes of mobility (Chap. 3) and Figure 4.2 (Chap. 4). In Figure 7.1 I have redrawn the figure for the Muslim community so as to bring out both parallel and different features when compared with the Scheduled Castes and the Scheduled Tribes. The most obvious change is that the sector for the upper left-hand corner is missing. In Figure 3.1, this sector is labeled "Sanskritization," and in Figure 4.2 the caption is "Hinduisation." Obviously neither of these choices makes sense to the Muslims, who have no intention of giving up their religious allegiance.[22] Such cultural emulation by Muslims as a whole is not a viable alternative as it is for the Scheduled Castes or Scheduled Tribes for whom the option is perceived as a clear gain.[23] Not so for the Muslims who already have a built-in aversion to the "idolatry" of their Hindu neighbors in spite of occasional holiday participation in popular religious festivals. Conversions of Hindus to Islam have been many; conversions of Muslims to Hinduism are extremely few. After all, Hinduism is

---

20. Ahmad (1970, p. 28). A sidelight on this situation is revealed by a number of informants who maintain that only the most competent college students among the Muslims even try for competitive examinations in India and that those with second- or third-class records, often go to Pakistan, where communal partiality is assumed to work for them. Recent restrictions on entrance to Pakistan have nearly closed this outlet.

21. A curious exception is the cinema which, for some reason, is permeated with Urdu culture and language; here many actors, actresses, and directors seem to be Muslim.

22. The Arya Samaj has made it possible for adherents of Islam to become Hindu by means of the *shuddhi* ceremony, also used for Christians. While theoretically this is supposed to raise the convert to the status of the twice-born Hindu, religious public opinion does not always legitimize this sort of mobility manipulation in sacred terms (Jones, 1968, pp. 47ff.).

23. It is true that Muslims emulate their *own* elite but, since this imitation is not out-group oriented, it does not receive any place in the figure (Mandelbaum, 1970, p. 556).

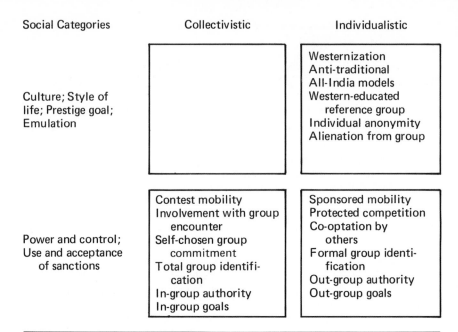

Social Categories	Collectivistic	Individualistic
Culture; Style of life; Prestige goal; Emulation		Westernization Anti-traditional All-India models Western-educated reference group Individual anonymity Alienation from group
Power and control; Use and acceptance of sanctions	Contest mobility Involvement with group encounter Self-chosen group commitment Total group identification In-group authority In-group goals	Sponsored mobility Protected competition Co-optation by others Formal group identification Out-group authority Out-group goals

Fig. 7.1 Modes of Mobility for Muslims

not a proselytizing religion in spite of all the efforts put forth by the Arya Samaj,[24] and the probability of mass conversions from Islam are not much above zero.

Since the collectivistic cultural path to mobility is practically impossible, what chance is there that one of the three other alternatives might prove productive? A choice of Westernization is far less attractive to the Muslims as a whole than to the Hindus, who have had their vanguard in this procession since the middle of the nineteenth century. A relatively sympathetic interpreter of Islam among the Hindus has this to say of the modernists and liberals in the Muslim community:

> Liberals in the prepartition period and after partition have displayed a lack of moral courage, have developed a snobbish outlook and seem to address only to either the highly educated Muslims or the Western scholars. The general Muslim propensity to stick to old habits, customs and Personal Law is based on some genuine and some false fears of an aggressive posture of Hindu nationalism. It breeds suspicion and hatred and results in reactionary conservatism and fanaticism. Moin Shakir[25] ruefully notes that the people are very much under the sway of the orthodox and fanatical ulama. For them even liberalism is too revolutionary to accept. They look

24. Jones declares that the activities of the Arya Samaj have changed the character of Hinduism by making it a *pracharakdharm* or propagandistic faith. This probably overstates the case since the Arya Samaj program is an exception to the whole tenor of Hinduism.

25. Muslim publicist.

upon the liberals as free thinkers and deviationists. [Karandikar, 1968, p. 377; by permission]

To adopt the goal of Westernization, it is necessary to achieve higher education, especially in English medium. As already noted, the depressed economic level of the Muslim community together with lack of reserved admissions, special scholarships or freeships, all combine to reduce the chances of Muslim youth to attain a university education. These circumstances may be less prevalent in the southern states, where there are a number of affluent leaders, men who, for example, founded the Muslim Educational Association of Madras and New College for Muslim students in 1951 to replace the old Muhammedan College that became overrun with non-Muslim students after independence and after new legislation that opened it to all (Wright, 1966b, p. 599, n. 127). In the north, of the two universities catering to Muslims, Aligarh is 35 to 40 percent Hindu while Jamia Millia in Delhi is 60 percent Hindu (as reported by officials of the two universities). Thus, to a marked degree, Muslims are not fully represented even in their own institutions of higher learning, and the road to Westernization is either undesirable or highly inaccessible as a living option for the overwhelming majority of Muslims.

What then of the political alternatives, the potentials for either contest or sponsored mobility? Contest mobility is best illustrated by the formation of the Muslim League in pre-independence days when group solidarity expressed itself through it as a minority-controlled party. However, as already emphasized, this outlet is hardly feasible in north India today, where Hindu memories of the fervent pleas for a separate state coupled with the unspeakable carnage that accompanied the triumphal march to Pakistan combine to create widespread sensitivity that refuses to countenance legitimacy of the League's rebirth, even when it has made a feeble reappearance. Two Indo-Pakistani wars and the Bangladesh crisis have augmented these initial suspicions.

Vestigial remains of the Muslim League still exist in Tamil Nadu to some degree and more strongly in Kerala. A reason for this differential is that when a substantial Muslim area of what was then a part of Madras state was cut off and attached to Kerala, the Muslim proportion of the population rose from 8 percent in Madras to 16 percent in Kerala (Wright, 1966a, p. 257). However, since the Muslim population of Madras and Kerala combined is less than 10 percent of all Muslims in India, it is still fair to say that the road to a political party of their own has serious obstacles in nearly the whole of India.

Theodore P. Wright, Jr., believes that, in the long run, south India may be a better test of a Muslim minority's adjustment to a secular state than the north, where the trauma of partition and proximity to Pakistan distort intergroup relations. As he points out, Muslims and Hindus in the south have had more relaxed and normal relations because: (1) Islam entered the area peacefully as Arab traders, not as conquering armies; (2) for the most part, Muslims and Hindus in the south speak the vernacular of their region rather than a separate language (like Urdu in the north); (3) the few Muslim rulers that were in the south historically dominated only small areas and then in brief rule; (4) less of the southern Muslim leadership was drained off to Pakistan in 1947; (5) there has been almost no communal rioting in the south; (6) local areas in Kerala with an absolute Muslim majority are too far from Pakistan to arouse Hindu fears.

Wright's argument holds up well except for his inclusion of Gujarat in the south; the Ahmedabad riots there in September 1969 would cancel out point 5. With Gujarat omitted, however, his outline is persuasive. (See Wright, 1966b; for further discussion, see Schermerhorn, 1971, pp. 37-47).

Since the nationwide rebirth of the Muslim League is not likely, a political pressure group composed of dissident elements has taken its place. The All-India Muslim Majlis-e-Mushawarat (Consultative Council) was organized on August 9, 1964, and includes members from former leaders of the Muslim League, from the Jama'at-e-Islami which openly opposed the formation of Pakistan in the past, and a number of "nationalists" who were either strong Congress supporters from pre-independence days or affiliated with the Muslim front for the Congress party, the Jami'atul-'Ulama'-e-Hind. As a loose confederation, the Majlis urged Muslim voters not to operate directly by supporting any single party but indirectly "by extending support to individual parliamentary and legislative assembly candidates from different political parties, primarily according to the candidates' attitudes toward the Muslim community." Thus, it was recommended that they vote for candidates who satisfied three conditions: that they be free from caste or communal narrow-mindedness, that they subscribe to democratic and secular principles, and that they regard all citizens as brethren regardless of religion or other special group affiliation and be broadly in agreement with the People's Manifesto issued by the Majlis. Candidates who met these conditions were asked to sign a pledge to support the nine points of the Manifesto and work for their adoption if elected.

A study of Majlis efforts before 1968 shows quite clearly that their political effects were equivocal. At the outset, the organization was critical of the Congress as taking Muslim votes for granted. They did succeed in increasing non-Congress membership for Muslims both in the Lok Sabha and in state assemblies (at least this outcome was attributed to the Majlis) from 1962 to 1967. At the same time, even by the end of that period, a plurality of Muslim legislators remained Congress members both at the Centre and in the states. Furthermore, the Congress party made it quite evident in all these campaigns that they did not welcome Majlis support. Finally, close scrutiny of the electoral process showed that the Majlis often disregarded their own criteria when endorsing candidates (Quraishi, 1968).

To summarize briefly: the path of contest mobility is strewn with difficulties, and there is no unified political leadership that can be supported by organized voting for the entire Muslim community on an all-India basis. The first major factor preventing such unity is internal divisions within the Muslim community, which rule out any unified program of social action. Karandikar (1968, pp. 377-78) gives Anwar Moazzam's realistic summary of the situation:

> He feels that the disintegration of the Indian Muslim community among several divisions based on race, schools of law, sufi orders and new puritanical thought have made it very difficult for the modern thinkers to help the community emerge as a homogeneous and progressive entity. This is because each sub-division has different views on education, status of women, civil laws etc. and each looks upon other groups as not true Muslims. [By permission]

The second reason why contest mobility fails is the determined opposition of public opinion (and especially superpatriotic parties like the Jan Sangh who help to keep the issue alive) to the formation or re-formation of a Muslim political party on an all-India basis. Reappearance of the Muslim League in scattered remnants here and there have led to the usual accusations of "communalism" from such sources.[26]

Turning now to sponsored mobility, the last chance remaining in the alternate series, we find that this pattern occurs with great frequency in the political arena. Muslim candidates are sponsored most often by the Congress party but with increasing frequency by other parties as well (Quraishi, 1968, pp. 984-85). This is most likely to occur where there are sizeable Muslim populations, and in these areas co-optation pays off for the political party selecting the candidate. However, Muslim leaders are quite aware that such elections are not necessarily rewarding for their community as a whole.

Two of these leaders express candidly what many of their colleagues probably feel. M. Z. Safraz declares, for example, that "Muslim legislators are generally too weak and too helpless. They dare not speak in support of Muslim demands and grievances lest they should be termed communalists. Muslim legislators elected with Hindu votes dare not incur the displeasure of their voters." In like vein, M. M. Anwar asserts, "Under the present system of joint electorates the Hindu society has no opportunity to get to know the real mind of the Muslim community because most of the Muslims whom they have adopted in this secular state have naturally got to be considered as the show boys of the majority community" (quoted in Karandikar, 1968, pp. 333-34).

The realities of power allow such grievances to be manipulated; knowledge of this fact may then prevent the taking of action on them. As one political observer perceptively remarked, "If the political importance of a group, within the ruling party for example, were to depend on its capacity to reflect Muslim grievances, the group would inevitably develop a vested interest in keeping these grievances alive" (Gupta, 1962, p. 381). To the extent that the ruling party is aware of such potentials, it is motivated to play the role of protector to any minority large enough to make its vote count; if the grievances are redressed, however, the role of the protector eventually disappears with them. So by failing to redress grievances, by making sympathetic noises to the minority in public while assuring majority members in private that minority claims are too extreme to be tolerated, a ruling party can withstand, and even turn to its account, widespread mistreatment of the minority, whether mild or violent. Whether this actually occurs on a substantially wide scale or not, many Muslims suspect that it is the case and are correspondingly cynical about their political future.

The upshot of the matter is that sponsored mobility as a political phenomenon may lead to higher status for a few chosen legislators without advancing the interests of the group in any appreciable way. Hence, when

---

26. The term "communal" is India's favorite epithet for tarring political opponents with the stain of ill repute. Its wholesale use in this fashion prevents people from employing it in any sense except an invidious one. The political air would be greatly clarified if the term "communal" were banned from public discourse, which is why it is generally avoided throughout political exposition in these pages.

scholars or publicists prepare impressive lists of the Muslim candidates elected over a number of years, they may contribute to group pride, but they signify no more than a Pyrrhic victory.

Of the four roads to mobility, then, the first is empty, the second and third blocked by community forces, and the fourth rewarding for a chosen few but generally fruitless for the group.

IDEOLOGY AND INTEGRATION

Again it is necessary to raise the question that has occupied major attention in the discussion of each minority group's locus in the total society: What are the views of both the dominant group and of the minority on the kind of policy that should be adopted by the minority in relation to the national whole? Should it remain separate, "join the main stream," or find some other position at variance with both of these?

Perhaps the most influential of the contrasting views on this problem are first those of the Jan Sangh and then those of the unreconstructed Pakistan ideologues. The former have popularized the view that Muslims at present are not full-fledged loyal citizens of the country and need "Indianizing" to purge them of disloyal tendencies. The latter are bitter-end followers of Jinnah who still cling to the notion that Muslims and Hindus are not merely two religious groups but two nations that must be separated spatially and geographically because of their inherent incompatibility. The Jan Sanghis are assimilationists, the Jinnah followers are secessionists.[27]

In the intergroup arena, these two extravagant ideologies feed on each other and produce a vicious circle of hostility and antagonism. Conflicts that arise from the confrontation of such incompatible views do not quite fall into Lewis Coser's dichotomy of realistic versus nonrealistic conflict (Coser, 1956, pp. 48ff.). They are not strictly realistic because they do not emerge primarily from a clash of interests. Neither side states its position in economic terms or even as a struggle for power. Conversely, it is not a purely nonrealistic conflict either, for no matter how much tension is released by each of the opponents, there is basically a conviction that the values at stake are so precious that they are ultimate and final; hence, to compromise would be to give up what the group really lives for. Perhaps we could call such conflicts *destiny conflicts* to distinguish them from realistic and nonrealistic types. To outsiders they will always appear nonrealistic, and, when exploited for secondary purposes like winning elections, they can perhaps be regarded as pseudorealistic. But as destiny conflicts, they arise over a clash of irreconcilable values and thus attack the foundations of consensus, as James Coleman shows in a different setting (Coleman, 1957).

The two opposing ideologies just discussed correspond to the alternative: forced assimilation with resistance. On the one side are the Jan Sanghis

---

27. There is an even more extreme Muslim doctrine held by the Jamaat-i-Islami who dream of converting India to Islam, however unrealistic this may appear to others. But this view is hardly influential enough to have major impact on Muslim public opinion in an increasingly secular world.

demanding Muslim assimilation — a clearly centripetal appeal. On the other are the Muslim adherents of the two-nation theory, who would apparently still like to defect — a pronounced centrifugal viewpoint. In neither case have we any hard data to tell us how representative each set of ideological followers actually is. What is of interest to the outside observer is that each of these two sides seems to view the *other* as representative. The more likely probability is that both conjectures are highly distorted and false when regarded as typical of community opinion as a whole.[28]

There is, however, a great deal of difference in the visibility of the two groups. Those desirous of having or joining a separate Pakistan have been so thoroughly discredited in public opinion that they feel forced to express themselves only in private and among intimates. Jan Sangh members are quite the reverse; not only are they voluble and unrestrained in communicating their views, but they make good use of such public utterances to garner votes. Their political influence can be partly judged, at least, by the fact that they are the only political party in India that increased its percentage of the popular vote and augmented its number of parliamentary and assembly seats quite steadily from 1952 to 1967 (Baxter, 1969, p. 1).

If integration of the Muslims into Indian society is to occur, it is most likely to do so when forced assimilation ceases to be a viable alternative and limited but sanctioned autonomy replaces it (as is, after all, implied by a secular state). This consummation is unlikely unless two conditions are met: First, in some way Muslims must demonstrate that the overwhelming majority of their number have but a single political allegiance: to India, their native land. By implication this would mean public repudiation of the two-nation theory and those Muslim leaders who still cling to it.[29] Second, demands for assimilation (Indianization)[30] must be relinquished, since they are unnecessary if the first condition is met.

Needless to say, these conditions are not likely to be fulfilled in the near future. The practical difficulties for implementing the first alternative are almost inconceivable since there is no organization or authority that can speak for all Muslims, or even for a majority thereof. The writer is convinced, after considerable interviewing in the Muslim community, that those who continue to believe in the two-nation theory are of the older generation who will soon pass from the scene and who, at present, have quite limited influence on the thinking of other Muslims. Nor must it be forgotten that many ulema, including the Deoband school, opposed the two-nation theory when it was unpopular to do so, that is, just before partition. As for the middle and younger aged groups

---

28. Only a well-designed national public opinion poll could give a definitive answer to such a question. The views expressed here are based on interviews with community leaders, press reports, and journal articles by reliable authorities.

29. This does not mean that Muslims need renounce familial feelings for their relatives in Pakistan or Bangladesh, or cease to be concerned about their safety in the future.

30. If Indianization is interpreted to mean Hinduization or compulsory conversion, it violates Part III, Article 25, of the Constitution. Further, interpreting Indianization to mean that political allegiance must always and under all conditions supersede religious allegiance in India is also of doubtful constitutionality in a supposedly secular state, but might require separate court judgments in particular cases.

today, they appear to be definitely loyal to India, although their allegiance is at times sorely strained by the recurrence of riots in which Muslims are all too often the chief victims. After Ahmedabad, where hundreds of Muslims perished in September 1969, West Pakistan may look like a haven of refuge. (See my monograph, *Communal Violence in India, A Case Study,* 1976.)

On the other side of the ledger, there is little indication that the demand for "Indianization" will be dropped unless it clearly results in traceable loss of votes for the Jan Sangh. This is not likely to happen as long as the demand for Indianization touches a responsive chord in the Hindu community.[31] Customarily, the Hindus are reputed to show great tolerance for other religions, a tradition that has already been emphasized in this chapter. But the obverse of Hindu tolerance is a curious intolerance of all who do not accept the pantheistic doctrine that all religions are indifferently equal and, hence, that Hinduism, which recognizes this broad-minded truth, is definitely superior. To put it another way, all proselytizing religions are energetically rejected and opposed if they do not give up proselytizing and allow their god to take a place in the Hindu pantheon along with Siva, Vishnu, and the rest. As Ashok Rudra points out, even Buddhism was later neutralized by making Buddha an avatar of Vishnu. He goes on to say that "Hinduism has been tolerant only of such other ways of life and systems of thought and values which consented to let themselves be Hinduised in their fundamentals" (Rudra, 1965, p. 25).

Thus, a major reason why destiny conflicts are so endemic in the relations between Hindus and Muslims is that Hinduism (or Brahmanism, if you will) has failed to absorb Islam as it has other religions like Indian Buddhism. The same is true for Christianity, as we shall see in the next chapter. Both Islam and Christianity have their own forms of intolerance in their insistence on monotheism by exclusion, as already mentioned. It is religions like these that Hinduism finds unreasonable, unamenable to absorption, and hence abhorrent. There is almost a caste aversion to such religions – a feeling that even Gandhi, with all his universalism, could not escape. It is reliably reported that Gandhi was greatly perturbed when Premier Nehru's sister, Madame Pandit, resolved to marry a Muslim; subsequently, Gandhi hastened to her side and argued so vehemently against the union that she finally surrendered and gave up her plans. Intercaste marriage Gandhi could encourage, but marriage with a Muslim – never.

Such deep-seated antipathies on the Hindu side, when added to the repugnance for idolatry on the Muslim side, quite dispel the idea that future integration of Muslims is easily facilitated by the harmonious atmosphere of tolerance that hangs like a fragrance over Hindu society – a notion apparently accepted by no less an authority than Max Weber,[32] at least for the ancient

---

31. Wars with China and with Pakistan have created fluctuations in public opinion that influence these main trends in divergent ways as well. In 1962 it is likely that some Muslims hoped the war with China would produce a common enemy that could bind Hindus and Muslims together, but the two Indo-Pakistani wars ruined this possibility. Conversely, a number of Hindus after Bangladesh could well have hoped that the partition of Pakistan would fragment Indian Muslim opinion still further between Urdu speakers and Bengali speakers (T. Wright, personal correspondence).

32. See the quotation from Weber in Smith (1963, pp. 61-62).

period. Europeans and their descendants can hardly be surprised at this reservoir of deep antagonism when they recall the Thirty Years' War in central Europe, which had to occur before a secular state could take root. Nothing similar is occurring in India today. As for the past, it is also well to remember that armies of Hindus fought other Hindus more often than they fought Muslims, and, conversely, armies of Muslims fought each other more often than they fought Hindus.[33] These homely truths must be recalled by those who have only counsels of despair to offer.

---

33. Statement given to the author by a historian who wished to remain anonymous.

BIBLIOGRAPHY

Aggarwal, Partap Chand, Cultural Change and Widening Integration Among the Meos of North India, unpublished Ph.D. dissertation, Cornell University, 1966.

Ahmad, Abad, "Economic Participation," Seminar 125 (January 1970), 26-29.

Baig, M. R. A., "Enlightened Communalism," Seminar 125 (January 1970), 12-14.

Baig, M. R. A., *The Muslim Dilemma in India,* Delhi, Vikas Publishing House, 1974.

Bardhan, Pranab K., "On the Incidence of Poverty in Rural India," *Political and Economic Weekly* 8 (Nos. 4, 5, and 6, Annual Number, February 1973), 245-254.

Baxter, George, *Jana Sangh: A Biography of an Indian Political Party,* Philadelphia, University of Pennsylvania Press, 1969.

Bayley, David H., *The Police and Political Development in India,* Princeton, Princeton University Press, 1969.

Chishti, Anees, "Review of Hindustani Muslim Siyasat. . . ," Seminar 106 (June 1968), 42-44.

Coleman, James, *Community Conflict,* New York, Free Press, 1957.

Coser, Lewis A., *The Functions of Social Conflict,* Glencoe, Ill., Free Press, 1956.

Ghurye, G. S., *Social Tensions in India,* Bombay, Popular Prakashan, 1968.

Gupta, Raghuraj, *Hindu-Muslim Relations,* Lucknow, Ethnographic and Folk Culture Society, U. P., 1976.

Gupta, Sisir, "Moslems in Indian Politics, 1947-60," *India Quarterly* 18 (Oct.-Dec. 1962), 355-81.

Husain, S. Abid, *The Destiny of Indian Muslims,* New York, Asia Publishing House, 1965.

Hyder, Qurratulain, "Muslims and their Heritage," *Illustrated Weekly of India,* 90 (No. 50, December 14, 1969), 8-13.

India, a Reference Annual, 1968. New Delhi, Publications Division, Ministry of Information and Broadcasting, Government of India, 1968.

Jones, Kenneth W., "Communalism in the Punjab," *Journal of Asian Studies* 28 (No. 1, November 1968), 39-54.

Karandikar, M. A., *Islam in India's Transition to Modernity,* Bombay, Orient Longmans, 1968.

Krishna, Gopal, "Framework of Politics," Seminar 106 (June 1968), 32-35.

Kulke, Eckehard, *The Parsees in India: A Minority as Agent of Social Change,* Munich, Weltforum Verlag, 1974.

Latifi, Daniel, "Tasks Ahead," Seminar 106 (June 1968), 36-41.

Lelyveld, Joseph, "India's 55 Million Moslems Living in Rejection and Isolation," *New York Times,* October 28, 1968.

Mandelbaum, David, *Society in India,* vol. 2: *Change and Continuity,* Chapter 29, Berkeley, University of California Press, 1970.

Miller, Roland E., *Mappila Muslims of Kerala: A Study in Islamic Trends,* Madras, Orient Longmans, 1976.

Mujeeb, M., *The Indian Muslims,* London, George Allen & Unwin, 1967.

Myrdal, Gunnar, *Asian Drama, An Inquiry Into the Poverty of Nations,* 3 vols., New York, Pantheon Books, 1968.

Pethe, Vasani P., "Hindus, Muslims and the Demographic Balance in India," *Economic and Political Weekly* 8 (No. 2, January 13, 1973), 75-78.

Quraishi, Zaheer Masoon, "Electoral Strategy of a Minority Pressure Group: The Muslim Majlis-e-Mushawarat," *Asian Survey* 8 (December 1968), 976-87.

Roy Burman, B. K., "Social Profile," Seminar 125 (January 1970), 33-38.

Rudra, Ashok, "Myth of Tolerance," Seminar 67 (March 1965), 22-25.

Schermerhorn, R. A., "The Locale of Hindu-Muslim Riots," *Indian Journal of Politics* 1 (January-June 1971), 37-47.

Schermerhorn, R. A., *Communal Violence in India, A Case Study,* edited by Syed Z. Abedin, Kalamazoo, Michigan, Consultative Committee of Indian Muslims, 1976.

Siddiqi, Nejatullah, "Identity," Seminar 125 (January 1970), 30-32.

Singh, Baljit, *Next Step in Village India,* New York, Asia Publishing House, 1961.

Singh, Khushwant, *India: A Mirror for its Monsters and Monstrosities,* Bombay, IBH Publishing Co., 1969.

Smith, Donald Eugene, *India as a Secular State*, Princeton, Princeton University Press, 1963.

Spear, Percival, "The Position of the Muslims Before and After Partition," in *India and Ceylon: Unity and Diversity,* edited by Philip Mason, London, Oxford University Press, 1967.

Titus, Murray T., *Islam in India and Pakistan,* Calcutta, Y.M.C.A. Publishing House, rev. ed., 1959.

Wright, Theodore P. Jr., "The Effectiveness of Muslim Representation in India," in *South Asian Politics and Religion,* edited by Donald E. Smith, Princeton, Princeton University Press, 1966a.

Wright, Theodore P. Jr., "The Muslim League in South India Independence: A Study in Minority Group Political Strategies," *American Political Science Review* 60 (No. 3, September 1966b), 579-99.

Chapter 8

Christians: Obscure Marginals

Among the well-defined minorities of India, Christians occupy an anomalous position. Though composed of Indian nationals, they are stereotyped as foreign or alien-oriented; though relatively well-educated, they may be slighted as low caste; because they are proselytizers, Hindus regard them with disdain as violating the ideal of universal tolerance. This composite of qualities appears to the great majority as an enigma — an enigma that can be ignored, since there are so few Christians. Many towns and villages do not include a single Christian, and in the cities it is possible for most citizens to spend their days without ever encountering (recognizably at least) any Christian whatever. The noticeable tendency among Christians themselves to remain inconspicuous as adherents of their religion contributes to their invisibility as a community.

The census of 1971 lists the Christian population as 14,223,382, or 2.60 percent of India's people. This proportion is relatively insignificant in comparison with the Muslims, who form over 11 percent. As indicated in the first chapter, Christians (as well as Muslims) are here considered as arising from the fifth intergroup sequence of colonization or conquest. Though the situation is not so clear-cut in the case of the Christians, there is more than an accidental connection between the growth of their community and the authority of a foreign power. In the fifteenth and sixteenth centuries, the Portuguese conquerors on the west coast regarded forcible assimilation to the Christian faith as the accepted policy of rule. While this procedure was in no way matched by later British strategy, which was generally tolerant in a laissez-faire way, it is significant that it was precisely at the height of British colonial power in the late nineteenth and early twentieth centuries that conversions to Christianity reached their peak in India. As the country became independent of her alien yoke, new accessions to the Christian faith declined to the vanishing point. In view of these developments, it is hardly any wonder that the Indian public has concluded that adherence to Christianity and the presence of a European power are causally linked or that Christianity is a Western importation that could not take root in India without the shield of foreign protection.

While this popular view disregards much of the historical evidence, it is nevertheless an accepted social definition of the Christian community and, as such, a primordial element of the intergroup arena impossible to ignore.

CHRISTIANITY'S EARLY ENTRANCE INTO INDIA

The record seems to show that the first appearance of Christians on the Indian subcontinent was that of individual missionaries rather than complete families. Initially, this was a form of infiltration rather than a full-fledged migration. Historical evidence indicates the possibility that two of Jesus's apostles began proselytizing in India during the first century A.D., St. Bartholomew in North Konkan (coastal region of modern Maharashtra) and St. Thomas in Malabar or present-day Kerala (Baptista, 1967, Chap. 1).[1] Some scholars question the historicity of these events. At any rate, a number of Christians migrated to Malabar from their religious center of Edessa in Mesopotamia during the fourth century A.D., when they were persecuted by the Persians and fled to set up a new community. These Christians were the founding fathers of the Syrian Church of India, and their numbers were later augmented by scattered adherents to the faith as well as by a limited number of converts in India. However, not much is heard of the Christian community again until the latter part of the fifteenth century, when the Portuguese under Vasco da Gama occupied Goa. Christianizing the populations they conquered was official policy and was put into effect in those areas of Malabar overrun from nearby Goa. The process was aided by the work of the famous Roman Catholic missionary, Francis Xavier, who made many converts during his brief stay in India in the year 1542. It is even reported that by 1556 there were 300,000 Roman Catholic Christians in India. By 1599 the Portuguese Catholics exerted great pressure on the Syrian Christians to take the oath of allegiance to the See of Rome and finally won them over; later, however, when the Dutch, Danes, and French challenged the Portuguese dominion, a large part of the Syrian Christians broke away again and reestablished their independence (Schermerhorn, 1933, pp. 62-63).

It would be wearisome to follow here the many divisions and schisms within Christianity, whether in India or the rest of the world. Sufficient to note that many of the divisions that developed elsewhere were transferred to the Indian scene. The Protestants arrived much later than the Catholics, making their first appearance as chaplains of the East India Trading Company during the years 1667-1700. This cadre made few conversions. Then in 1705 the Danish government sent out a number of German Pietists as official missionaries to south India, and in the latter part of the eighteenth century, William Carey, the founder of the Baptist Missionary Society, began work in Bengal, followed by Alexander Duff from the Established Church of Scotland and others of lesser prominence. The number of converts made by these men was very small, and it was a policy of the East India Trading Company until well into the nineteenth

---

1. If this be fully proved, Christianity would have appeared in India long before its existence in England and Ireland.

century to resist the inroads of missionaries. In fact, official policy forbade their entrance, and so William Carey elected to come out in another role. He was the superintendent of an indigo plantation, teacher, translator, and publisher, only later appearing as a preacher (Schermerhorn, 1933, pp. 63-65).

The East India Company drew rather lucrative profits from pilgrim taxes at both Hindu and Muslim shrines and hence had a vested interest in keeping Christian missionaries out. They also went so far as to exclude Christians from the ranks of Indian officials in their service and in Mysore even debarred Christians from courts of justice. However, Parliament in London began to weaken the powers of the East India Company after evangelical groups in Britain publicly demanded freedom of entrance for missionaries into India as a whole. By 1813, Parliament nullified Company restrictions on the admission of missionaries and, from that date, Christian representatives entered in ever-increasing numbers, first from England or the continent and then from the United States. It was in the first wave that Alexander Duff entered. His name is important because he influenced and later joined forces with Ram Mohun Roy in the effort to promote Western learning. By 1835, partly as a result of Duff's influence, English was made the medium of instruction in all institutions of higher learning receiving financial aid from the East India Trading Company. This policy carried over into later periods and was perhaps the most important source for the spread of Western education in the subcontinent (Schermerhorn, 1933, pp. 61-64; Lamb, 1968, pp. 116-17).

CHRISTIANITY'S APPEAL TO SUBMERGED PEOPLES

Although in Malabar (coastal region of modern Kerala) and parts of the Madras presidency, Christians gained adherents from upper castes even in early times, the spread of their religion was more rapid during the nineteenth and twentieth centuries to groups on the margin or to "outsiders" who were in Indian society but not of it. I refer especially to tribal populations and the many castes below the Sudra line.

The British encouraged missionary activity both in the "excluded areas" of the northeast border and the Chotanagpur region toward the center.[2] From 1812 to the end of the century, Christian leaders from abroad carried on protected proselytizing and the multiplying of schools with great effect in the mountain zones (Bareh, 1965, pp. 159-60). Missions in Chotanagpur had a later start (1845) and made substantially fewer converts among the tribals, although they initiated measures to protect cultivators in their rights as landholders.

Such activities naturally nettled the Hindu zamindars, who now saw in Christianity not only an enemy to their religion but to their economic profits. It is therefore significant that "During the Mutiny of 1857, the missionaries were advised by the Government officials to leave Ranchi and in their absence the Church property was destroyed, looted, and the Christian converts were badly persecuted. It was at the time that a bomb was thrown over the Lutheran Church at Ranchi. However, the missionaries returned to Ranchi after the

2. For the dissimilar colonial policies applied to these tribal areas, see Chapter 4, above.

situation returned to normal. Commissioner Dalton of Chotanagpur became the special friend of the missionaries and the Mission began to flourish" (Sahay, 1968, p. 294).[3]

The depressed classes constitute the second sector within which the Christians made greatest inroads. This activity showed its greatest development after the Mutiny. One commentator notes, "The Mutiny resulted in the destruction of nearly all of the mission stations in North India. Although the Indian Christians were few in number, they were loyal to the British, and the result of the Mutiny was to establish a lasting friendship and spirit of cooperation between the government of India and the missionary agencies. After the government had been taken over by the crown in 1858, society was more stable and the modern missionary era in India really began" (Schermerhorn, 1933, p. 65).

THE MASS MOVEMENT

A few years later came the period of Christianity's greatest growth, the so-called "mass movement." Results in the Punjab illustrate the way in which it spread elsewhere. In that area the new converts came predominantly from the Chuhras and other outcastes; increase in the Christian population came from such Untouchables with only a sprinkling from the upper castes. How rapid the gains were can be shown by the following figures:[4]

	1881	1891	1901	1911	1921	1947
No. of Indian Christians in the Punjab	3,823	19,547	37,980	163,994	315,031	493,081
Increase during decade		15,751	18,433	126,041	189,017	
Percentage increase		415%	94%	331%	115%	21.4%

During the years noted in the above table, especially before the 1920s, conversion to Christianity in numerous cases could be described as a corporate act.

J. W. Pickett (1933, pp. 22-23), who made the most extensive study of these mass conversions, defines their general nature as follows: "The distinguishing features of Christian mass movements are a group decision favorable to Christianity and the consequent preservation of the converts' social integration. Whenever a group, larger than the family, accustomed to exercise a measure of control over the social and religious life of the individuals that compose it, accepts the Christian religion (or a large proportion accept it with the

3. I am indebted to Dr. K.N. Sahay for this and other sources describing early Christian missions in Chotanagpur.

4. Taken from Campbell (1961, p. 11).

encouragement of the group), the essential principle of the mass movement is manifest. . . . The group deciding for Christ ordinarily is composed of one caste, and often includes all the members of that caste in one, or more than one, village. But occasionally, members of two or more castes in one or several villages have combined in turning from old allegiances, beliefs and practices in religion to those which they have understood to be Christian."

If one report is to be believed, the Protestants gained more from such mass movements than the Roman Catholics. John R. Mott, for example, estimates that about half of the Roman Catholics in India are descendants of converts who became Christian in the mass movements, but that at least 80 percent of the Protestants belong in a similar category (Pickett, 1933, p. 5). Historically, the predominance of Catholics in Kerala and the south of India is due to the fact that their institutions have been there for centuries. However, during the period of the mass movement, it appears that group conversions did take place in some sections of the southwest coast. Pickett reports that a number of Sudra castes on the western shore, particularly among fisherman, joined the Roman Catholic faith in large numbers, though no figures or dates are given (ibid., p. 28). In the north, conversions to the Roman Catholic fold assumed a mass form chiefly among the tribals in Chotanagpur after the arrival of Father Lievens in 1885 (Sahay, 1968, p. 296). In three years time he is reported to have christened over 11,000 persons and attracted 40,000 catechumens who served 832 villages (Plattner, 1957, p. 121).

It is worth noting that many, if not most, of the princely states had no converts to Christianity during this period since it was common practice for the rajahs to keep out all missionaries (Levai, 1957, p. 19). Similarly, there were no significant mass conversions in the vicinity of British installations. Pickett notes that mass movements "have not generally developed where missionaries were most closely associated with the Government; American and Continental missions have been connected with more of these movements and with more converts than have British societies" (Pickett, 1933, p. 55).

The onrush of new adherents to Christianity was so great that there were even times when missionaries tried to stem the tide of converts where it seemed wholly artificial. In Bihar, after an incident in which Hindus attacked Muslims, the British levied a special tax on Hindus to meet the cost of damages while exempting Muslims and Christians from the assessment. Almost immediately "thousands of leather workers" applied for Christian baptism; church leaders stopped all such ceremonies for several months and petitioned the colonial government to announce that exemptions for the tax would be valid only for those Christians who were members of that community before the riots (Pickett, 1933, p. 54).

SOCIAL CONSEQUENCES OF MASS CONVERSIONS

Within the Christian community the rapid influx of members from outcaste populations created problems of assimilation and consolidation. Habituated to subjugation and exploitation, the new converts carried with them the habits of servility and obsequiousness that had proved so suitable in the past. As G. E. Phillips wrote, "The sense of pleasure which self-respecting men have in standing on their own feet is at first totally incomprehensible to pariahs. God made them, they think, to lean on others; if it were not so He would have created them in some other caste. Nothing annoys the missionary so much as the constant declaration by the village Christians that he is their father and their mother — a statement which is always the preface to some fresh appeal for help" (quoted in Heinrich, 1937, p. 4). And though there were notable exceptions, so many of the untouchable converts had lived all their lives in a climate of inferiority that they found it difficult to break with the self-image of impotence so fateful in their lives; the result was frequently a perpetuation of upper caste leadership and dominance in the Christian community itself. Thus, a seminary instructor gave unsolicited testimony that upper caste students did better work, were more confident, showed greater achievement, and did more long-range planning than did those of lower caste background.

Paradoxically, another phenomenon that appeared among the converts from the Scheduled Castes was a pattern of released aggression. Liberated suddenly from the weight of perpetual ill-usage, they gained heightened enjoyment from tormenting the powerless in their new environment. The missionary, priest, and church official were exempt from this treatment, but the local village pastors were not. Many of these leaders reported that they were subject to frequent harassment, especially when soliciting funds. "The inner struggle of the pastor, who found himself in the power of his parishioners as they sang, 'the old ass comes braying every other day,' and who had to win their cooperation, is not hard to imagine. He, too, encounters the authoritarianism of his depressed groups who desire to exercise authority in the one place where it seems possible" (Heinrich, 1937, p. 72). Likewise the anti-Brahman trends that burgeoned in Tamil Nadu had parallel repercussions in Christian groups. In the late 1950s, as a few Brahmans and upper caste members entered the Christian community in south India, a faculty member from a Christian seminary reported to the author that the students there who had come from the lower castes took particular delight in hazing the new Brahman colleagues who had just come in and in making life miserable for them in countless ways.

Dr. B.R. Ambedkar, acknowledged leader of the Scheduled Castes, opposed the conversion of his community to Christianity. He declared, "Many members of my own caste have become Christians and most of them do not commend Christianity to the remainder of us. Some have gone to boarding schools and have enjoyed high privilege. We think of them as finished products of your missionary effort and what sort of people are they? Selfish and self-centered. They don't care a snap of their finger what becomes of their former caste associates so long as they and their families, or they and the little group who have become Christians, get ahead. Indeed, their chief concern with reference to their old caste associates is to hide the fact that they were ever in the same community. I don't want to add to the number of such Christians" (quoted in Pickett, 1938, p. 23).

THE NEMESIS OF DEPENDENCY

Western priests and pastors who imported their version of Christianity into India brought, as a matter of course, a highly complex set of institutional patterns which seemed to them necessary for propagating and maintaining the faith. While Hinduism was loosely organized with only local priests and wandering sadhus as scattered, even straggling authority figures, the Christian panoply with its hierarchy of officials, discipline, law, and institutional structure stood out in sharp contrast. The proliferation of administrative arrangements that had taken centuries to develop in Western society with its emergent industrialism was now superimposed on Indian communities that had observed such intricate establishments chiefly in royal courts or colonial directorates. Gandhi was especially critical of this multifold Christian establishment and frequently harked back to the simplicity of Jesus and his Sermon on the Mount. Even the institutions of modern medicine, hospitals and clinics under Christian auspices, were targets of his criticism and he begged his Christian friends not to import all the paraphernalia of Western medicine into India for, in his words, "We cannot afford it" (Gandhi, 1957, pp. 223-24).

In the era of mass conversions, such institutional complexes developed unexpected functions. New converts, cut off from the web of economic ties in the jajmani system of local villages by informal excommunication were often unable to earn a living at their old occupations. To remove new Christians from ostracism or persecution in areas where they were well-known, the mission not infrequently took converts bodily into the compound or walled area surrounding a church or bungalow, providing simple jobs for the newcomers as subsistence. Growing need for servants, helpers, and assistants in the affairs of ecclesiastical, educational, and medical institutions made it possible to utilize such personnel on a fairly wide scale. Though many of the converts earned no more than a pittance, it was nevertheless more regular and abundant than they had ever earned before. This segregated process of "compound living," however, also left the convert unfitted to earn his way in the larger society, a problem that became painfully evident when any mission had to be closed. Starvation or near-starvation of the Christians promptly resulted. Only retrospectively did Western Christian leaders come to realize the full implications of their converts' former status as originally integrated members of a religious, occupational, and total village matrix. By leaving the Hindu community, these new Christians automatically cut their occupational ties to enter an imported and relatively isolated social system where their old skills were often unusable and new ones rarely trained. However, for a time, the multiplication of jobs needed in the highly complicated Christian institutions gave regular employment to many who needed it.

An unintended consequence of the mass movement into Christianity was, therefore, a dependency pattern partly aided by previous centuries of pariah living and partly fostered by the individualistic leader-follower pattern of the Christian community so antithetical to the closely interwoven structure of caste. The missionary became the "father and mother" who, in the early stages, not only provided but was expected to provide food, clothing, jobs, education, and medical care. On the one side was the missionary socialized in Western culture with its plentiful consumer goods, which for him were normative, setting up a whole series of aspirations which he then projected as "needs" of the new convert. On the other side was a new member of the Christian community suddenly awakened to indefinite expansion of aspiration levels for material commodities in the wake of his conversion and the pervasive influence of religious leaders from abroad. Since the series of new "needs" was continually expanding, it helped to perpetuate the dependency pattern far into the future.[5]

The priest or pastor with his European type bungalow, elaborate sets of hill stations for rest and recreation, special periods for furloughs in the home country, extraordinary schools for missionary children, and solicitous plans for retirement, all of which, considering the cultural background of the missionary, may have been necessary for his health and welfare in a subtropical region requiring painstaking adjustments, nevertheless had the effect of setting a standard of living extremely high in relative terms, while at the same time isolating missionaries from Indian society as a whole (Grant, 1959, p. 4). Thus, the representatives from Europe and America were more than proselytizers for a different faith; they were introducers of a foreign way of life and a type of education that reinforced it. Prestige became attached to Westernization almost imperceptibly as the newly converted Christians adopted the mode of life exemplified by religious leaders from abroad (in so far as this was possible). This life-style required, of course, a standard of living quite expensive by Indian standards (Joardar, 1949, pp. 55-56, 119, 149).

Authority figures from abroad not only had great prestige but the power that comes from disbursement of funds. Churches, schools, and hospitals were supported by finances from the West, as were the salaries of personnel both European and Indian. The power structure thus created within the Christian community proved difficult to dislodge in spite of very genuine efforts to do so; a residual dominance of the missionary continues to have its effects as long as there is power of the purse. To interpersonal dependency is therefore added an institutional dependency.

TRENDS IN EDUCATION

Education assumed a salient position among Christians. The leaders, strongly oriented in this direction, founded hundreds of schools, colleges, and institutes where generations of clerks, teachers, ministers, priests, and white collar workers were graduated for new positions in a rapidly urbanizing society. This process gave many Christians access to positions of prominence and authority in the civil service,[6] the army, railways, the communications system, universities, and provincial councils. Christians trained in mission schools achieved higher literacy rates (in English) than most groups and, under the British communal policy, gained many high ranking posts. Even though the great mass of Christians remained poor, the status of the entire group in the colonial period reflected the

---

5. "Compound living," though not uniformly adopted, was widely prevalent and had repercussions in the Christian community for decades. Ultimately, it gave rise to the many schemes for vocational training that belatedly appeared.

6. One ecclesiastical informant assured the author that before independence there was not one Hindu in the Delhi governmental bureaucracy, that most were Christians or Muslims. Although this claim is exaggerated, it rests on the observation that the British depended on Christian civil servants and felt assured of their loyalty. The effect of this circumstance on Indian nationalists was not lost.

prestige of Indian Christian personnel in the middle echelons of power where they rubbed shoulders on an equal plane with Brahmans and upper caste Hindus, often to the chagrin of the latter.

An unexpected, or at least unprepared for, result of the growth of educational institutions was the rush to Christian schools of Hindus, Parsis, Sikhs, tribal peoples, and even a few Muslims. The overweening importance of English instruction as a prerequisite for upward social mobility stimulated increasing numbers of non-Christians from wealthy or ambitious families to attend mission schools and colleges in the early twentieth century, beginning a trend that continued even after the departure of the British.

Particularly influential in this process was the novel emphasis, at least in India, on the education of women in Christian schools. Although at first this was too daring a step for Hindu girls, the barriers eventually came down when parents recognized that educated sons might well prefer educated wives and that families could maintain or at least control the subordinate status of women by properly arranged marriages along these lines. In time, families found a way to accommodate the forms of marriage to new conditions by the simple substitution of educational standing as equivalents for stated amounts of money in the dowry. A girl with a high school education would thus, let us say, be able to subtract 500 rupees from her dowry, and with a college education as much as 1,000 rupees or more. At the same time the girl, under these conditions, might have a chance to secure a "better" husband measured in terms of potential earning power correlative with *his* education. As adjustments of this kind were increasingly made, Hindu girls entered Christian schools at an accelerated pace, almost matching that of the boys.

The upshot of these trends was that thousands of non-Christian graduates before 1947 looked back to Christian schools as their alma maters, and this reservoir of good will (which included the families of graduates) was one upon which the Christian community could later draw.

AN ERA OF CRISIS

Beginning with the 1930s, not one but a whole series of crises befell the Christian minority. During this decade, the economic depression in the United States and Europe brought severe reductions in funds allotted to missions, churches, and schools abroad. Many institutions closed their doors while still more reduced staffs, lowered salaries, and decreased their services. A great many missionaries returned to the West and were not replaced. For a number of years the slowly rising tide of nationalism in the Christian community produced increasing demand for greater representation of Indian personnel in ecclesiastical offices. In the face of changed conditions, this policy was now strongly implemented — by necessity. But it occurred at a time when the usual flow of financial support dwindled and when Indian Christian leaders assuming new responsibilities were forced by circumstance to ask their own congregations for contributions. Not only were such lay bodies relatively impoverished, but the habits of dependency impeded changes of attitude required for self-support. Even before the depression, parishioners who abased themselves before the missionary sahib would turn on their own Indian pastors and humiliate them when the latter requested donations; few local ministers were willing to put themselves in a position where they would have to seek full support from the depressed classes among Christian laymen if there was any possibility that they could work for the mission and receive a regular salary. Now that Indian Christian leaders were thrown back on direct subjection and full support from village churches or *basti* settlements lacking mission finances, their lot became increasingly unhappy, and many left the service of the church altogether. Village after village lost its ecclesiastical leadership, while others temporized with occasional visits from religious ministrants in distant cities once a month to as little as once a year.

World War II proved to be an added blow, for it not only increased the rate at which the missionaries left, but in time so restricted all travel that replacements became almost an impossibility. Reinforcing these difficulties was the wave of Indian nationalism in the 1940s which deepened a number of internal divisions within the Christian community and made it more vulnerable to outside attack. As the Congress party refused to sanction the British war effort unless India was granted full independence, it became evident that Britain counted on her protected minorities in India to rally to the Allied cause. How this pressure divided opinion within the Sikh community at the time has already been noted above. The same type of internal schism now appeared among the Christians, where the older generation, most white collar workers, and a particularly vocal group of missionaries supported the British either openly or tacitly. Another group composed of pacifists and passive conservatives preferred to remain neutral. A third division (only a tiny handful of younger laymen, pastors, and missionaries) supported Gandhi and Nehru; their influence, however, was minimal.[7]

During this period of intense nationalism, the Christian community reaped the harvest of close attachment to the British along with preferences for foreign types of worship, architecture, dress, and other external symbols. Such ways, which showed the Western origin of the Indian church all too clearly, now made it the target of Indian patriots. The story of the missionary who tore a Gandhi cap from the head of an Indian convert with the remark that Christians had no right to be nationalists was an unmistakable clue to how far the denationalizing of Christianity had already gone (Grant, 1959, p. 5). That the great bulk of Christians should apparently be unmoved and stand aside while their Indian fellow-nationals who were sacrificing property or life itself for their country's freedom looked for help in the cause — help that was not forthcoming — turned the patriots against the Christians in fury. "They are no true Indians," was the taunt. In these turbulent days there were even British officials who saw which way the wind was blowing and no longer maintained their old close ties with missionaries; jobs for Christians in government services decreased considerably. As the movement for swaraj reached its peak, a backlash of nationalism

---

7. A Christian educational leader recounted to the writer an incident from this period concerning a missionary editor of an ecclesiastical journal who was prejudiced against Gandhi because of the latter's opposition to the British. When Gandhi's wife died, this editor would not allow any news of the event to appear in his publication.

eventually arose within the Christian community itself, where protests became vocal against the relatively high salaries of missionaries when compared with low stipends for local Christian workers. Insubordination grew among Christian lay and clergy ranks alike; demands for a more truly Indian church became more vocal on all sides (Joardar, 1949, pp. 304-07).

Within the church establishment, missionaries who were pro-British or at least passively neutral were in a position to appoint or elect Indian leaders for the community during this period. Not only did they favor the "safe" men in positions of responsibility, but the Indians looking for promotion found that they could often secure their goal by convincing the missionaries that they *were* safe. It therefore appeared that while the church was becoming Indianized in *color* of its official ranks, it continued to be Western in *outlook* as long as the new leaders perpetuated bureaucratic denominational viewpoints. These were men who had little or no influence in the wider Hindu society that became pervasively dominant after independence. Yet it is only fair to say that many, if not most, were able administrators whose abilities matched their counterparts in the new government quite favorably. The new officialdom in Delhi, however, tended to ignore them.

PUBLIC OPINION AT CROSS-PURPOSES

With the breakup of the colonial order, there were strong sentiments both for and against the Christians. At first the antagonism seemed stronger, as could have been predicted. S. V. Ramamurty attributes a good deal of this to the shift in social control that accompanied the new era. In his eyes, the communal prejudices of the colonial period "were to some extent fostered by the British rulers on the principle of divide and rule. But the play of such prejudices was kept under control so as not to affect the overall efficiency of administration. The prejudice of race, religion, caste, language, province, opinion, or property was all played upon before and allowed to operate but within limits. Now that British control has ceased, these group prejudices are running riot.... The loosening of administration is due to the loosening of control from an outside force without such force being replaced by that of an inner unity" (Ramamurty, 1951, pp. 164, 165). Long-nursed grievances mushroomed into demands for revenge, and, although Muslims received the lion's share of the backlash, Christians were the target for much of its deflected force. Not only did many hurl charges of unpatriotic conduct at members of the community, but old accusations about "rice Christians" were renewed. The uncomfortably accurate jibe at the Western ways of Christians now took on added sting in the midst of a blossoming renaissance of Indian dancing, music, and the arts.

Added to these charges against the Christians was the widespread belief that proselytism was a denial of Hindu tolerance and therefore inimical to the tranquillity of India. In the previous chapter I have noted that both Islam and Christianity make absolute claims for their respective faiths and therefore approve of vigorous efforts to convert others. This element of intolerance contradicts the Hindu doctrine of the equality of all faiths, which implies both even-handed tolerance and opposition to conversion, since the latter necessarily denies this premise and therefore constitutes an act unfriendly to the genius of India. Hindus of all types appear to agree on this ideology, from Gandhi to Radhakrishnan. For example, Gandhi (1957, p. 28) declared that it is Hinduism's freedom from dogma that appealed to him. It is not an exclusive religion. He commented that the Parliament of Religions is but an empty phrase if the Christians of that body look upon Hinduism as simply error or upon Christianity as having exclusive truth (ibid., p. 60). To make his position even more clear, he stated flatly, "I believe that there is no such thing as conversion from one faith to another in the accepted sense of the term" (ibid., p. 49).

This Gandhian view overlaps with that of the superpatriots who take a more ethnic view of Hinduism and declare that "Hinduism is for the Hindus as England is for the English." Such adherents see foreign missionaries in India simply as agents of an alien imperialism. One of them wrote, "Their exploitation of India has been even worse than that by the British government" (M.C. Parekh, quoted in Forman, 1956, p. 185). A spokesman for the RSS[8] was even more forthright: "There are only two courses open to foreign elements . . . either to merge themselves in the national race and adopt its culture [i.e. religion?] or to live at the sweet will of the national race" (quoted in Curran, 1951, p. 31). Militant Hindus, therefore, attacked the Christians with only slightly less fervor than they did the Muslims.

Conversely, there were currents directed toward a more favorable view of the Christian community. During the blood bath of partition when hundreds of thousands of refugees inundated northern India, Christians set up a number of centers where they gave temporary shelter, food, and clothing to displaced persons of all faiths. This relief task was performed "so well and so disinterestedly that even men like the late Sri V. J. Patel, who were not ordinarily sympathetic towards Christian missions, spoke very highly of them (the Christian workers). It was largely under the influence of Sri Patel that, in spite of some misgivings, the Constituent Assembly included in the new constitution the right 'to profess, practice, and propagate religion.' " (Asirvatham, 1957, p. 19).

It was also significant that Nehru, who was quite nonreligious and agnostic in his personal beliefs, at the same time held to a liberal view of the secular state and therefore was quite willing to support freedom of religion for Christians, not merely as coexistence but including the right to seek converts if they wished. In a statement he gave to the Catholic press, he declared that "any faith whose roots are strong and healthy should spread, and to interfere with that right to spread seems to me a blow at the roots themselves."[9] As one of the Christian leaders wrote of Nehru and his ideology in later years, ". . . by a strange irony it is this position which of them all is most unsympathetic to religion, that offers the greatest freedom for religious conversion" (Forman, 1956, p. 188). After independence, Gandhi himself, opposed as he was to proselytism, stated what he

---

8. Rashtriya Swayamasevak Sangh, a militant organization formed to fight for Hindu interests in the Nagpur street riots of 1924. Its growth spread to many other cities throughout upper India, where it established cadres for paramilitary training.

9. Quoted in the *Catholic Herald,* London, May 10, 1946.

thought the new policy should be, namely, "No legal hindrance can be put in the way of any Christian or of anybody preaching for the acceptance of his doctrine" (Gandhi, 1957, p. 220).[10] There is probably little doubt that, when the militants of the RSS were incriminated in the murder of Gandhi, their disrepute strengthened the hands of those who were opposed to them and who worked for the adoption of Article 25 in the Constitution affirming the right to "profess, practice, and propagate religion" (Forman, 1956, p. 189).

During the period of the Constituent Assembly and the adoption of the Constitution, the tide ran in favor of the Christian community, but there is evidence that this support for their civil rights was vulnerable, that it depended to a considerable extent on the actions of Nehru and a small but powerful elite trained under the old British system or in Christian schools. Not long after independence came attempts to whittle away the rights that had been formally granted without a corresponding change in public opinion. Concerning Article 25, "One of the earliest infringements upon it was an order of the Madhya Pradesh Government forbidding anyone to convert a person from one religion to another except in the presence of a magistrate. This was so obvious a denial of the right of propagation that informal appeals to the Central Government soon brought its recision" (Appasamy, 1951, p. 41).

Later the Madhya Pradesh legislature appointed a committee to investigate charges that Christians made conversions through compulsion, deception, and material incentives. The result was the highly publicized Nyogi Report of 1956 which marshaled evidence from both Christian literature and the testimony of witnesses that tended to support such charges. However, the rather obvious bias and animus of the Nyogi Committee were scored by Chief Justice Hidayatulla[11] in a public judgment, and as one cleric observes, "The Report was buried, the broad-minded Nehru seeing to the burial. . . . So long as Nehru was alive, these elements got short shrift. But times have changed" (Soares, 1969, p. 24). They changed sufficiently so that after Nehru's death, a renewal of provincial action against Christians occurred in Orissa, where the state legislative assembly passed an anticonversion act; the Madhya Pradesh government continued the process by doing the same (ibid.). The courts, however, have denied the validity of these acts.

Ironically, such complaints about conversions came at a time when Christian leaders were testifying on all sides that new adherents to the Christian church were rapidly dwindling in number. For example, even by the first flush of independence in 1949, it was reported that only ninety-three converts to Christianity were made in the city of Lucknow in nine years but that during the same period sixty-five Christian girls married outside the community and one Christian family publicly renounced its faith (Joardar, 1949, p. 53). By 1959, a

---

10. This marks a change of mind on Gandhi's part, for in an earlier statement he had already affirmed, "If I had power and could legislate, I should certainly stop all proselytizing" (Gandhi, 1957, p. 104). Likewise he maintained in that earlier period that former converts to Christianity should be welcomed back into the Hindu fold (en masse if necessary) without *shuddhi* (ibid., p. 83). Is it significant for such changes of mind that Gandhi's own son had a "so-called conversion to Islam"? (ibid., p. 135).

11. Quoted extensively in *Truth Shall Prevail* (1957, pp. viiiff.).

foreign observer who visited Christian centers in many different areas of India discovered that a great many Christian colleges had produced no converts whatever in decades (Grant, 1959, p. 17). Two researchers in 1966 reported on the Christian community in Delhi "that there have been few converts since the end of the mass movements nearly forty years ago and that the growth of the community since that time has been primarily from natural increase through births and from immigration"[12] (Alter and Singh, 1966, p. 132). From the Punjab another investigator stated positively that "The rate of growth of the Punjab rural church since 1925 has been equal to, but no greater than, the natural growth rate of other non-Christian village groups in similar circumstances" (Campbell, 1966, p. 155).[13] In view of such cumulative evidence from different regions, it is hard to avoid the conclusion that the widespread alarm about proselytism and conversion to Christianity are quite academic and based upon conditions that disappeared over a generation ago.

THE STATUS OF MISSIONARIES

Complaints against missionaries have crystallized into public policy since independence. There were no restrictions on the entrance of missionaries into British India during the latter part of the nineteenth and early part of the twentieth century. It was only necessary for the incoming alien to declare that he would in no way interfere with the authority of the colonial government. With the departure of the British, however, public distaste for the influx of foreigners propagating another religion became strong enough to result in the promulgation of new rules for admission or expulsion of such persons. In 1955 this new policy was codified with the following features:

(1) *Additions and replacements:* Those coming for the first time in augmentation of the existing strength of a mission or in replacement will be admitted into India if they possess outstanding qualifications or specialized experience in their lives.

(2) *Retiring missionaries:* Those returning from leave after they had been in India for five years or more will ordinarily be eligible for admission. Such of them as qualify will be granted 'No objection to return' endorsements at the time of leaving.

(3) *Border and tribal areas:* For reasons of security, new missionaries coming to work in border or tribal areas, wherever they are situated, will not be admitted.

(4) *Opening of new centres:* Missions in India do not at present apply specifically either to the State Government concerned or to the Government of India for permission to open new centres or institutions. This has resulted in the opening of a number of missionary centres without the knowledge of the State Government concerned or of the Government of India. Thus Government does not have the information

---

12. The reference is obviously to rural-urban migration.

13. Though similar surveys of south Indian Christians are not available, interviews with many leaders there confirm a similar lack of growth in the Christian community from Andhra to Kerala.

about missionary centres or about the missionaries working at such centres which is necessary for dealing with individual cases of missionaries and other missionary questions. A foreign mission desiring to open a new centre or institution will, therefore, apply to the State Government concerned, who will obtain the approval of the Government of India.

(5) *Missionaries from Commonwealth countries:* The admission of missionaries from Commonwealth countries will also, as far as possible, be dealt with on the same lines as foreign missionaries. [Jacob, 1958, p. 413]

The Deputy Home Minister is under pressure to make an annual report to the Lok Sabha on the number of missionaries entering and leaving India during the previous year. If the number of admissions is greater than it was in the previous year, the Minister comes under serious criticism from the superpatriots, and thus there is definite incentive to make sure the numbers are not too large. In this way, a premium is placed on denying visas to entrants and on expelling missionaries for causes that seem appropriate. Thus, "No missionary can get an entry permit unless the Government is satisfied that he is essential, the Government being the sole judge. Then only temporary residential permits are given, and the Government can at will refuse renewal or extension, no reason being given" (Soares, 1969, p. 24). A case in point is that of Father Ferrer in Manmad, Maharashtra, who was highly successful in developing new agricultural methods among the local peasants but also aided in extricating them from dependence on traditional moneylenders and the network of officials who might take advantage of them. The authorities reacted sharply to his policies, and, when Father Ferrer's permit expired, the State Government did not renew it and forced him to leave. At the time of his departure, followers and admirers marched all the way to Bombay to offer him tribute in open assembly (ibid., pp. 24-25). Newspaper publicity on the incident made it a *cause célèbre,* and eventually the Union Government allowed him to return on condition that he seek a new locale for his labors, which turned out to be Anantapur in Andhra Pradesh. Again, Father Ferrer ran afoul of local sentiment and was expelled from the state by the regime in Hyderabad, only to be rescued by the Union Government which overruled the state decree and allowed him to continue his social service activities in the area of Anantapur (*Overseas Hindustan Times,* August 28 and September 4, 1975).

There are other expellees, such as a number of Italian missionaries forced to leave the border areas of Assam on grounds of national security (Soares, 1969, pp. 24-25). Some of these men had been in India for as much as a generation, and church authorities regarded government action as arbitrary. It is doubtless possible, however, that an earlier furore over the way a Christian missionary supported Naga demands for independence in the 1950s (Mankekar, 1967, passim) had repercussions more than a decade later.

At all events, the same irony exists here as we have observed in the controversy over proselytism, where the number of converts decreased quite independently of government action. Similarly, the number of missionaries entering India was strongly on the decline years before independence, and the curve continued downward with the birth of the new nation when Indianization of the church became a dominant trend. Mission authorities report that the economic depression in the West and the aftermath of World War II reduced the number of missionaries coming to India between 1929 and 1945 to a mere trickle and that, with the withdrawal of colonial authority, nearly 95 percent of the British missionaries and a substantial majority of American missionaries returned home. After independence there were few of the older missionaries left except occasional figures in educational, agricultural, or medical institutions. Among the Protestants, it is reported that the few new missionaries entering India after independence tended to stay a shorter time and to return home after a single term of service. With Indianization, a number of missionaries of the older generation no longer wanted to remain because they were losing executive positions. The United Church of Northern India reports that the number of missionaries serving their denomination was reduced by 26 percent between 1957 and 1967 with the additional probability that most missionaries who resign or retire in the future will not be replaced (*United Church of Northern India Survey*, 1968, p. 147). Though comparable figures for Catholics are not available and the *Catholic Directory of India 1969* does not give the percentage of priests who are Indian, the national *Gazetteer* gives the following figures: Catholics have 6,500 ordained priests of which 5,000 are Indian; 20,000 nuns of which 17,000 are Indian; and over 70 archbishops and bishops, more than two-thirds of which are Indian. (Both Cardinals are Indian as well.) The same issue reports that Protestants of all denominations have 3,500 foreign Christian workers and 5,000 ordained Indian pastors (*Gazetteer*, 1965, p. 498). If these figures are correct, Indianization has proceeded farther among Catholics than among Protestants, though in both cases Indian ecclesiastics are now in the majority.[14] As the number of missionaries continues its decline, the controversy over foreign domination of the church may be expected to subside.

SEPARATE COMMUNITIES?

To what extent do Christians live in separate enclaves with definite boundaries setting them off from other citizens? *A priori* it is probable that such boundaries will be most explicit where the caste rules of Hinduism retain their restrictiveness and define those of other religions as ineligible for commensalism or marriage. Such precepts take added potency from the fact that so many Christians have ancestral origins among the outcastes. Probabilities are therefore high that most Christians will live in communities separated from Hindus by walls of social distance. Part of this stems from pressures of the larger society and part from the preference of Christians to maintain an exclusiveness of their own. The usual pattern is a high degree of enclosure among Christians, as in Delhi and the Punjab where "The Christian *quam* tends to be an ethnic community with a membership determined primarily by birth. It includes all who are born of Christian parents unless they openly reject this membership" (Alter and Singh, 1966, p. 130). The author of this comment notes the argument for self-segregation among Christians: namely, without such binding ties

---

14. The accuracy of these figures is open to question since the personnel of Catholic religious orders are not included.

provided by exclusive community consciousness and a close-knit solidarity, Christians would tend to drift back into the Hindu caste system (ibid., p. 80). Another cleric remarking on the inward-facing character of the Christian community declares that the growth of the church is almost entirely internal "and that the life is the somewhat introverted life of an army in trenches, rather than the aggressive life of an army on the march" (Campbell, 1966, p. 214). The impression gained from observation of Christian communities from Kerala to Uttar Pradesh is that members of the minority participate in at least three institutional spheres that are usually separate from those of other Indian citizens: educational, religious, and family structures. The main institutional bonds that tie them to the rest of society are the economic and, to a lesser degree, the political. Endogamy is still the rule in spite of frequent exceptions among well-educated Christian girls (Joardar, 1949, p. 53). Although Christians vote in local and national elections, interviews with their leaders make it quite clear that participation in politics is minimal and that detachment from politics is widespread. Though there are no comparative measurements, observation in urban areas at least suggests that the social enclosure of the Christians is not maximal, as it is among the Scheduled Castes, but exists to a high degree — comparable to the situation in the Muslim community.[15]

OCCUPATIONAL STRUCTURE

Although there are no studies of occupations among Christians as a whole, there are important clues. First of all, it is significant that slightly more than a fourth of Christians are urban while the ratio among Hindus is less than one-fifth. Among the states, Maharashtra has the highest proportion of urban Christians (over three times as many as rural adherents), while in Karnataka the ratio of rural to urban Christians is fairly even.[16] On an all-India basis, however, rural dominance is definitely established[17] in spite of the fact that rural membership is on the decline (Paul, 1959, p. 181).

Indications are that both urban and rural Christians are, on the whole, in the lower tier of the occupational ladder with the addition of a few professionals. In the villages, Christians are farm laborers, tenants, and peasant proprietors with a considerable number of stock raisers, milkmen, and herders in some areas. In the cities, most Christians tend to work for non-Christian employers with the great bulk as industrial operatives or in service occupations; a much smaller number are white collar workers or professionals.[18] There are practically no Christian

---

15. Interviews with Goan Christians in Bombay brought out the fact that, for them, all other Indians are "they" while only Goans were "we." The sense of separation and of superiority is especially strong here, as it is in Goa itself.

16. Census of India, 1971. Union Table C, VII, Religion, pp. 28-31.

17. The rural component is almost certainly higher than official figures show, since local census or revenue clerks frequently enter Christians on their records as "Harijan" or "backward class" without mentioning that they are Christian (Campbell, 1966, p. 187).

18. Data supplied by Lucknow church official in 1959.

entrepreneurs, partly, no doubt, because they lack the support of family and caste so prominent in the business community elsewhere.

Rural Christians tend to be in low-income occupations such as cultivators and laborers. There are some exceptions, as in Rajasthan where there are three notably Christian villages; the largest of them, Riploda, has 75 percent of the Christians owning land and forming a landholding stratum that could be called something like the "dominant caste" of that particular village (*United Church of North India Survey*, 1968, p. 280). In a number of Uttar Pradesh villages the economic status of Christians declined after their cooperative failed (Paul, 1959, p. 212). A Lucknow study shortly after independence clearly showed the Christians of that city to have the lowest per capita income of the ten communities in the metropolis, although the actual occupations are not specified (Joardar, 1949, p. 77). A study of Protestant Christians in Delhi about two decades later showed the occupational range given in Table 8.1.

Obviously the situation in Delhi is not representative because the capital accentuates the need for government employees which, in view of the high literacy of the Christians, skews the occupational profile in that direction. The high *percentage* of Christians in government offices may also give a mistaken picture of the proportion of bureaucratic positions occupied by Christians, which is admittedly low. Though actual figures are unavailable, Christian leaders report that the proportion of government workers from the Christian community in civil service jobs is actually less than 2 percent the Christians have of the total population. This is a marked contrast with the higher representation the Christians had in the colonial service before 1948. Another feature of Table 8.1 may give a false impression: since the occupations listed are those of *church members* rather than *baptized Christians*, the ratio of industrial workers is probably much lower than the actual numbers would show if a census of baptized Christians were available. There seems to be fairly wide consensus on the fact that Christian industrial workers are not attending churches in large numbers and that they are therefore invisible members of the Christian community. An interesting sidelight on the situation comes from a church survey as follows: "The Christian employees in one factory, where 25 percent on the labour force is Christian, said they did not dare to let the leaders of their local United Church of North India congregation know of their Trade Union activities because they thought these would be disapproved of. In another area a District Superintendent (a church official) was firm in the belief that Christians 'were not made for business' because of the danger of becoming involved in dishonest practices" (*United Church of Northern India Survey*, 1968, p. 68).[19]

The occupational categories shown in Table 8.2 for Christians of that denomination in Rajasthan towns (rural areas not included) are taken from the same source. Although this résumé is from only one state of northern India, when taken together with the Delhi study (Table 8.l), it suggests what was confirmed by church leaders in other parts of India: the occupational position of Christians in towns and cities is markedly higher in both income and status than that of rural Christians. Whether the discrepancy between town and country is

---

19. Hereafter, all references to this survey will be abbreviated UCNI.

TABLE 8.1

Occupations of Adult Church Members in Delhi in the 1960s*

Occupation	Percentage
Government service	43
Domestic service	21
Education	13
Medicine	11
Business	3
Industrial labor	2
Other	7

*Alter and Singh, 1966, p. 69.

TABLE 8.2

Occupations of Adult Members of the United Church of North India in Rajasthan Towns During the 1960s*

Occupations	Percentage
Doctors, nurses, compounders†	18
Teachers	18
Railway employees	30
Skilled and semiskilled factory workers	18
Clerks	5
Servants and laborers	8

*UCNI, p. 280.
†This term was not explained in the survey.

greater in this respect than it is for non-Christians is a question that requires further research.

Similarly, there is oral evidence but no survey data to prove discrimination against Christians in the urban job market. Informants among Christian leaders from many regions of India complained that their fellow communicants met with prejudice when applying for positions. As one ecclesiastic in Bangalore put it, the Hindus tell applicants quite openly, "You've had your day before. Now you have no British to protect you." Like members of other minorities, the Christians are also likely to lack the support of joint family or caste when they are candidates for jobs in the open market. The same informant declared that Christians were using Hindu surnames to hide their identity under these conditions.[20] Reports from Kerala where Christians are highly concentrated seem to show that there is less job discrimination there than elsewhere. There is

---

20. During the mass movement into Christianity, it was common practice for the newly baptized convert to be given a Christian name as a mark of his new status. Quite often this was a Biblical name like Abraham, Isaac, Jacob, or Ezekiel. Such names were proudly worn at the time and served to put the stamp of visibility on the new Christian. However, with the rise of nationalism and the coming of independence, the process has been reversed, as Christians seek to become more inconspicuous by assuming Hindu names again.

general agreement among informants that Christians are better represented in lower grade government positions than in the higher echelons and that they find promotion to upper positions more difficult than do non-Christians in both the public and private sector, particularly when their status is known. These comments need further corroboration.

SOCIAL MOBILITY

Strong emphasis on literacy and especially on higher education in the Christian community has made it possible for many members to rise in the social scale. As one cleric puts it, the church "has been and is an example of the most rapid rise from individual underprivileged status to high professional and technical status" (Campbell, 1966, p. 143).

As an illustration of vertical mobility, another writer traces changes over a single generation among Christians of one Protestant denomination in Delhi: ". . . a senior Methodist pastor has estimated that in 1930 more than 60 percent of the Methodists in Delhi were domestic servants or day labourers. Today [early 1960s], probably less than 25 percent of the Methodists in the city are in these occupational categories. A similar upward movement has taken place among Anglicans and Baptists. Many of those whose grandparents were cooks or cobblers are today members of the educated middle class. This rise in status may be attributed very largely to the training given in Christian schools and hostels" (Alter and Singh, 1966, p. 132).

A parallel instance occurs in the Punjab, where it is asserted that "No similar depressed class or caste can boast the number of high school, college, or post-graduate students that distinguishes this group in the Punjab. It has produced doctors, lawyers, professors, teachers, ministers, administrative officers, nurses, clerks and mechanics out of all proportion to its size and antecedents. From village sweeper to Ph.D. in two generations is not an uncommon story among Christians in the Punjab. It is most unusual among other similar social and economic communities. Unfortunately these marks of success of the rural community are also the source of its growing weakness. The best young men and women are leaving it. The educated seldom, if ever, return to it, the illiterate and backward are left in it" (Campbell, 1966, p. 181).

This mobility pattern reinforces and accentuates the rural-urban migration movement characteristic of Indian society as a whole. It is also instructive to compare mobility trends among Muslims and Christians by means of the paradigm advanced above (see Chap. 7, Fig. 6.1). In the case of the Christians this will take the form of Figure 8.1.

In previous examples of the paradigm, the upper left sector is marked "Sanskritization" for the Scheduled Castes and "Hinduization" for the Scheduled Tribes; it refers to group mobility resulting from the adoption of a way of life belonging to an external reference group with high prestige. In the case of the Muslims, this sector has been left blank because there is no such out-group emulation on their part and they do not regard Hinduizing as a viable possibility. The same can be said of the Christians; consequently, the upper left sector is also left blank. Although there may be cases where individual Christians

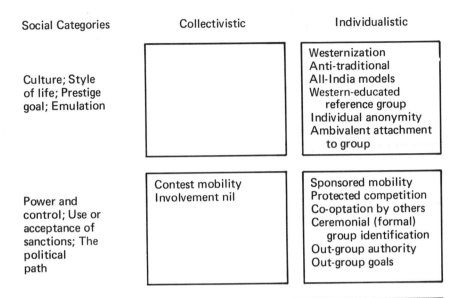

Social Categories	Collectivistic	Individualistic

Culture; Style of life; Prestige goal; Emulation		Westernization
		Anti-traditional
		All-India models
		Western-educated
		   reference group
		Individual anonymity
		Ambivalent attachment
		   to group

Power and control; Use or acceptance of sanctions; The political path	Contest mobility Involvement nil	Sponsored mobility Protected competition Co-optation by others Ceremonial (formal) group identification Out-group authority Out-group goals

Fig. 8.1 Modes of Mobility for Christians

turn Hindu, evidence does not suggest that such conversions are in any sense a group movement or a form of collective mobility, as the paradigm suggests. The path of Westernization is by far the most common one adopted by Christians, although it leads to heightened individualism and widespread loosening of group loyalties to the Christian community, particularly in areas where the concentration of Christians is minimal. In such areas the individual often conceals his Christian origin and may remain aloof from his religious colleagues.

In the sector marked "contest mobility," the Christians really have no place. In order to show a significant movement in this direction, Christians would have to organize a political party of their own or at least a political association or voting bloc within one of the major parties. With the exception of a few covert tendencies in this direction by some Kerala Christians, the religious community as a whole has not built any political structure of its own that could place candidates on the ballot for electoral contests. During the colonial regime, Christians had separate electorates, but after independence they renounced this privilege publicly. Since they constitute no more than two percent of the electorate, they cannot hope to place any candidates of their own or obtain the voting strength to elect them. Hence, there is no alternative but an acceptance of sponsored mobility in the political arena, that is, the co-optation of popular Christian figures by political parties who find this method a practical way to win elections in areas where Christians are residentially numerous. In 1970 a prominent ecclesiastic reported to me that there were twenty-two Christians in the Lok Sabha and that many of them came from tribal areas. Another large percentage came from southern India, where there is a greater concentration of Christians. It is rare, however, to find elected Christian representatives from northern India. The upshot of sponsored mobility is that a few Christians rise to limited prominence by becoming tools of an established party but that there is little effect on the mobility of the group.

The only really effective channel of mobility for Christians as a whole is, therefore, the ladder of Westernization through the educational process. A closer look at this operation reveals a number of differentials; education is not evenly spread. In the first place, it is quite limited in rural areas, as already hinted above.[21] In fact, one of the incentives for the cityward migration of rural Christians is the drawing power of mission schools for their children. A second differential involves the special educational advantages supplied by the government for Scheduled Castes. Here this question arises: Are Christians whose families stem from an outcaste background eligible for these special scholarships and should they claim the right for themselves? Interviews leave the impression that Catholics are more likely to give an affirmative answer to this question than Protestants, and Christians in the south more inclined in this direction than those in the north.[22]

Finally, there are strong indications that the upward mobility rate of Christians which seemed so high in the period immediately following the mass movement has slowed in recent years. At that earlier period, the initial status of converts was usually so low that there was literally no direction to go but up. In the 1970s, however, with new conversions at a standstill and greater internal differentiation among Christians at diverse stations on the scale of occupations, movement in an upward direction appears to be retarded. Furthermore, with the composition of schools changing in response to total population increase, there are not only growing numbers of Hindus in Christian schools but continual additions of Christians in government or Hindu schools (Alter and Singh, 1966, p. 111). This could have the effect of diminishing the number of scholarships available for Christians in the long run, thereby slowing the rate of mobility.

CHRISTIANITY AND REFORM

Latter-day criticism of the Christian minority cannot obscure the effects of its doctrines and practices on the pattern of Indian life. The humanitarian ethic of Christianity was influential in the British prohibition of sati and in constant attacks on infanticide, child marriage, the taboo on widow remarriage, and Untouchability. In the nineteenth century, Christians made common cause with reformers like Ram Mohun Roy, who took the offensive against these and similar practices. One might even make a case that the founder of the Arya Samaj, Dayanand Saraswati, in his outline of the new Vedic Hinduism, was trying to carry out some of the same reforms under the influence of the Brahmo

---

21. Nevertheless, M.S. Paul (1959, p. 87) reports that there were no illiterate Christians in any of seventeen "Christian" villages of Uttar Pradesh.

22. The survey of Delhi Protestants notes that most of them are opposed to registering as Harijans for educational benefits (Alter and Singh, 1966, p. 117). Worth noting, too, is the trend among Protestants in the north to establish more schools for girls than for boys (UCNI, p. 102; Alter and Singh, 1966, p. 102).

Samaj while rejecting its syncretism (Lamb, 1968, pp. 116-18). Later Vivekananda, influenced by Western Christian notions of social service, compounded these with the Indian values of renunciation and spiritual salvation. This tradition of reform continued with Gandhi himself, who frequently quoted Christian as well as Hindu scriptures to reinforce his program of welfare that transcended individual regeneration. As Beatrice Lamb puts it, "His compelling and revolutionary interest in social justice still haunts many Hindus for whom such a concept is both inconvenient and contrary to tradition" (ibid., p. 121).

In tribal regions, the efforts of missionaries to protect the Adivasis from the power of unscrupulous moneylenders and zamindars has already been noted. Though this has been criticized for using "materialistic motives" to win converts, it has had long-term effects in legislation, as when Father Hoffman was sufficiently influential to pressure the government of Bengal to pass the Chotanagpur Tenancy Act in 1908, a statute that gave four hundred Munda villages inalienable ownership of land originally theirs. Locally, the same priest established Credit Bank and Cooperative Societies that eventually held thousands of accounts for tribals in the area (Plattner, 1957, p. 122).

Service institutions established by Christians dot India from the Himalayas to Cape Comorin. A late compilation lists more than 150 colleges, 2,177 high schools, 214 technical schools, 153 teachers training schools, 620 hospitals, 670 dispensaries, 68 leprosy centers, 713 orphanages, 87 homes for the aged, 681 hostels and welfare organizations, 275 crèches, 44 agricultural settlements, 27 industrial centers, and several institutions for the blind, deaf and handicapped (Verghese, 1969, p. 8). This listing does not include primary schools, of which the Catholics alone have 5,367 (*Catholic Directory*, 1969, p. 3).[23] For a minority as of 1969 of thirteen million (seven million Catholics, five million Protestants, and one million Orthodox Syrians),[24] this showing is impressive. Many if not most of these institutions depend primarily on support from abroad. In this sense, there is still foreign domination; a very real question is whether the agencies would continue to operate without such aid.

PROSPECTS

What is the probable future of the Christian minority? An investigator in Lucknow whose research is both historical and cross-sectional makes a significant prediction: eventually the Christian community will divide into two sectors definable chiefly by economic standing. Those in the lower half of the income level will revert to the Hindu masses from which they or their ancestors originally came. Members of the upper half will throw off a number of their

---

23. The number of Protestant primary schools is not available to the author. For brief details on various service institutions, the reader can consult *The Catholic Directory of India 1969* and the *Christian Handbook of India 1959* (for the Protestants). There appears to be no more recent publication that gives a complete listing of Protestant denominational institutions.

24. Figures on the breakdown of internal divisions given by Verghese (1969, p. 8).

Western traits, adopt a wide range of Indian practices and a more Indianized style of life to become more literally Indian Christians (Joardar, 1949, p. 442).

As already mentioned, the prospects of growth in the Christian community from future conversions are unlikely. Clearly, natural increase now brings the only significant advance in numbers, even though it is worth noting that the decennial rate of increase is greater for the Christians than it is for any other religious faith, or for the national rate as a whole. Thus, the percentage increase for Hindus from 1961 to 1971 is 23.69, for Muslims 30.85, and for Christians 32.60, and the all-India rate for the total population was 24.8.[25] If Joardar's prediction about the future with a preponderance of Christians in the upper economic levels proves to be correct, there would be some slackening of the birthrate among them, and the greatest increase could be expected at the lowest levels among those who reverted to Hinduism.

Today the growth pattern among Christians is no longer affected by sizable increments from conversion, and the ratio of increase is only slightly above the national average. As one Christian leader complains, "An impartial survey of the Indian scene. . .compels one to admit the hard fact that we cannot look forward to any significant addition to the Christian population in India otherwise than by natural growth and that the Indian Christians should reconcile themselves to their position as a minority community in India" (quoted in Levai, 1957, pp. 52-53).

The maintenance of group separation may be expected to continue. It is a dominant trend in Indian culture to encyst its diversities. As J. W. Grant (1959, p. 21) declares, "India deals with foreign elements much as an oyster deals with a piece of grit. The invader is allowed to become a part of India, but he is prevented from contaminating the national life by a protective wall of social distance. Where China absorbs, India isolates. . . . New religions that enter India have a good chance of survival, but they often lose their ability to spread."

This process has continued longest in Kerala, where the Syrian Christians are now encysted in what is, to all intents and purposes, a position parallel with the Nayars and below the Brahmans in the regional caste system; those converted to Christianity in the last century are kept at arms' length as Pulayas who are still regarded as outcastes by Syrian Christians and treated as such, although they are fellow religionists (Alexander, 1967). In contemporary times, we are told, "It is now more than a century since conversion from backward classes to the Christian Church began in Kerala. In spite of the passage of a century and more, there are separate places of worship, separate congregations, separate cemeteries, etc., for the different caste sections of the same denomination within the church in various parts of Kerala" (Koshy, 1968, p. 23).[26]

It is quite possible and, in the long run probable, that the development of Christianity in Kerala is something of a model for the future, when India will accept the Christian community on the same basis that it has accepted others, that is, when the non-Hindu community assents to a separate and unique

---

25. Census of India, 1971, Union Table C, VII, Religion, pp. 28-31.

26. A succinct summary of Christian involvement with the caste system appears in Mandelbaum (1970, pp. 564-72).

position within the wider caste system. It is conceivable that urbanization and industrialization may act as deterrents, but it is more likely that they will slow the process rather than prevent it entirely. Interviews throughout India among both Hindus and Christians showed a decided preference for definite separation of the religious community rather than absorption or assimilation.[27]

In the case of the Christians, there is sufficient agreement both within and without the community that a cultural pluralist policy is acceptable, and, unless the Hindu militants become considerably stronger or their attention is deflected from its present focus on the Muslims, there is no reason to expect any change in the foreseeable future. What appears most likely is an unexciting course toward an inconspicuous but conceded semi-caste position and compliance with its demands.

In reply to my question, "What does integration mean to you?" a prominent Christian leader who had already expressed a desire for group separateness replied simply, "Just peace and quiet between communities."

---

27. Arya Samajists were not interviewed. They would doubtless prefer assimilation.

BIBLIOGRAPHY

Alexander, K. C., "The Problem of the Neo-Christians of Kerala," *Man in India* 47 (Oct.-Dec. 1967), 316-30.

Alter, James P., and Herbert Jai Singh, "The Church in Delhi," in *The Church as Christian Community: Three Studies of North Indian Churches*, edited by Victor E. W. Hayward, London, Lutterworth Press, 1966.

Appasamy, A. J., *The Christian Task in Independent India*, London, S.P.C.K., 1951.

Asirvatham, Eddy, "The Missionary in Present-Day India," in *Revolution in Missions*, edited by Blaise Levai, Vellore, South India, Popular Press, 1957.

Baptista, Elsie W., *The East Indians: Catholic Community of Bombay, Salsette and Bassein*, Bandra (Bombay 50), Bombay East Indian Association, 1967.

Bareh, Hamlet, *et al., Tribal Awakening*, Bangalore, Christian Institute for the Study of Religion and Society, 1965.

Campbell, Ernest Y., *The Church in the Punjab*, Nagpur, National Christian Council of India, 1961.

Campbell, Ernest Y., "The Church in the Punjab, Some Aspects of Life and Growth," in *The Church as Christian Community: Three Studies of North Indian Churches*, edited by Victor E. W. Hayward, London, Lutterworth Press, 1966.

The Catholic Directory of India 1969, Bombay, St. Paul Publications, 1970?

The Christian Handbook of India 1959, Nagpur, National Christian Council of India, 1960?

Curran, J. A., *Militant Hinduism in Indian Politics*, New York, Institute of Pacific Affairs, 1951.

Forman, C. W., "Freedom of Conversion, The Issue in India," *International Review of Missions* 45 (April 1956), 180-93.

Gandhi, Mohandas K., *Christian Missions, Their Place in India,* 2nd ed., edited by Bharatan Kumarappa, Ahmedabad, Navajivan Publishing House, 1957.

Gazetteer of India, Country and People, New Delhi, Publications Division, Ministry of Information and Broadcasting, Government of India, 1965.

Grant, John Webster, *God's People in India,* Toronto, Ryerson Press, 1959.

Heinrich, J. C., *The Psychology of a Suppressed People,* London, George Allen & Unwin, 1937.

Jacob, Kerula, "The Government of India and the Entry of Missionaries," *International Review of Missions* 47 (October 1958), 410-16.

Joardar, Noni Gopal Dev, "The Indian Christians of Lucknow," unpublished Ph.D. dissertation, Yale University, 1949.

Koshy, Ninan, *Caste in the Kerala Churches,* Social Research Series, No. 4, Bangalore, Christian Institute for the Study of Religion and Society, 1968.

Lamb, Beatrice Pitney, *India, A World in Transition,* 3rd ed. rev., New York, Frederick A. Praeger, 1968.

Levai, Blaise, ed., *Revolution in Missions: A Study Guide on the Subject,* Vellore, South India, Popular Press, 1957.

Mandelbaum, David G., *Society in India,* vol. 2: *Change and Continuity,* Berkeley, University of California Press, 1970.

Mankekar, D. R., *On the Slippery Slope in Nagaland,* Bombay, Manaktalas, 1967.

Parekh, M. C., *Christian Proselytism in India,* n.d., p. xiii, quoted in C. W. Forman, "Freedom of Conversion, The Issue in India," *International Review of Missions* 45 (April 1956), 180-93.

Paul, Marrel Christopher, "The Habitat, Economy and Society of Christian Villages in Uttar Pradesh," unpublished Ph.D. dissertation in geography, Agra University, 1959.

Pickett, J. Waskom, *Christ's Way to India's Heart,* Lucknow, Lucknow Publishing House, 1938.

Pickett, J. Waskom, *Christian Mass Movements in India,* New York, Abingdon Press, 1933.

Plattner, F. A., *Christian India,* London and New York, Thomas & Hudson, 1957.

Ramamurty, S. V., "Group Prejudices: Administration," in *Group Prejudices in India, A Symposium,* edited by Manilal B. Nanavati and C. V. Vakil, Bombay, Vora & Co., 1951.

Sahay, K. N., "Genesis and Development of the Early Christian Movement in Chotanagpur," *Journal of the Bihar Research Society,* Prof. S. H. Askari Felicitation Volume (1968), 286-312.

Schermerhorn, W. D., *The Christian Mission in the Modern World,* New York, Abingdon Press, 1933.

Schönherr, Siegfried, *Einflüsse von Modernizationsfaktoren auf die Föhrerrollen bei den Mundas,* Nürnberg Monograph, 1968.

Soares, A., "Foreign Missions in India," *Illustrated Weekly of India* 90 (December 28, 1969), 23-25.

Truth Shall Prevail, Reply to the Niyogi Committee, Bombay, Catholic Association of Bombay, 1957.

The United Church of Northern India Survey, 1968, Nagpur, 1969?

Verghese, Jamila, "The Saga of Christian Achievement," *Illustrated Weekly of India* 90 (No. 52, December 28, 1969), 8-13.

Chapter 9

Anglo-Indians:
An Uneasy Minority

The Anglo-Indians constitute the only Indian minority essentially definable in racial terms (Anthony, 1969, p. 8). Admittedly, tribal communities or the resident Chinese manifest a number of physical traits that set them off as distinguishable from most Indians, but these are not the characteristics that capture whatever attention is given to them; cultural differences from the Indian mode are equally, if not more, important. But in the case of the Anglo-Indians, it is the genetic mixture of members and their antecedents that characterize the group explicitly; cultural disparity, where it exists, gets secondary attention. For example, all Anglo-Indians are Christians,[1] but it is not this cultural feature that distinguishes them; were it so, they would have been included with the rest of the Christian community in the last chapter without being singled out. However, even within the Christian churches, Anglo-Indians remain a specially recognized subgroup set off from the rest by having membership in a group known to be biologically derived from both Indian and European ancestry while, at the same time, preferring a European style of life. This subgroup has major interpersonal relations within its own boundaries and usually practices endogamy.

In comparative terms, the Anglo-Indians are a consequence of the fifth intergroup sequence outlined in Chapter 1: colonization and its derivatives. Without the colonial expansion of Europe into tropical and semitropical regions, there would be no identifiable collective known as Anglo-Indians. Where explorers, adventurers, soldiers, and traders were single men, their influx into distant lands resulted in racial mixtures of many types: the mestizos of Latin America, the Colored of South Africa, the Burghers of Ceylon, the Anglo-Burmans of Burma, the Metis of Canada, the Eurasians[2] of Indonesia, as well as

---

1. Anglo-Indians, for the most part, belong to various Christian churches by affiliation rather than by conversion; their formal relationship with such religious organizations is derived from parental membership on the European side.

2. Actually the popular name for such racial mixture in India was also "Eurasian" in the nineteenth and early twentieth centuries. This was changed to "Anglo-Indian" as

the Anglo-Indians of India. Cross-cultural research on the varieties of racial mixtures throughout the world is summarized, in contemporary form, by Noel P. Gist and Anthony G. Dworkin in their recent volume, *The Blending of Races* (1972); this work serves as a socio-historical background for the present discussion.

The Indian Constitution, Article 366 (2), defines "Anglo-Indian" as follows:

> . . . "an Anglo-Indian" means a person whose father or any of whose other male progenitors in the male line is or was of European descent but who is domiciled within the territory of India and is or was born within such territory of parents habitually resident therein and not established there for temporary purposes only.

Although there is an obvious anachronism in this definition, it is a part of the accepted scheme of things in Indian thought which has its distinctive way of designating such persons. Thus, someone whose male parent was European and female parent was Indian would be classified as Anglo-Indian, but, if his male parent was Indian and female parent was European, he would not be accepted as Anglo-Indian but simply be labeled "Indian." Although the outsider may be critical of this obvious one-sidedness (which does, after all, smack of male chauvinism), for purposes of exposition it is necessary to adopt such a definition here (with certain qualifications to be mentioned in a moment) simply because it represents the current authoritative meaning ascribed to the term in the Indian setting.[3]

At least two provisos must be added. First, it is obvious that the words "is or was born within such territory" is inaccurate since it refers to the boundaries of present-day India, whereas there are Anglo-Indians now living within those boundaries who were either born in the undivided India before partition (that is, in either present-day Pakistan or Bangladesh) or whose parents were born there. In the second place, the Constitutional definition would encompass those whose parents were both European if they had been residing permanently in "Indian territory" or were born of European parents on both sides who lived permanently in that territory (in the enlarged sense used here, that is, including Pakistan and Bangladesh) in a previous generation. Such persons should be designated by the more exact term of Domiciled Europeans, which they have been called in the past. The effort to put them in the same category with

---

associations bearing the latter name became prominent, and in 1911 the community was officially designated "Anglo-Indian" in the Census (Anthony, 1969, p. 2). For the sake of simplicity, the present chapter will retain the label of "Anglo-Indian" when referring to earlier periods at the time "Eurasian" was more commonly used.

3. By the very nature of the case, neither this definition nor any other can make all persons denoted by the category clearly visible, since a good many have already "passed" into the European or the Indian population. More attention has been given to the former than the latter, but Gist rightly notes, "It seems probable that numbers of hybrid children, especially those born out of wedlock, were reared by their mothers and socialized into Indian society without close or continuous contacts with European cultures or people. To the extent that this occurred, these children, or subsequently their own offspring, were enveloped by the culture and social system of their mothers and thus disappeared as identifiable racial hybrids" (Gist, 1972, p. 40).

Anglo-Indians was rejected by the Anglo-Indians, however, when the major organization of the community changed its name from the Anglo-Indian and Domiciled European Association, All India and Burma, to the All-India Anglo-Indian Association (Gist and Wright, 1973, pp. 98, 100).[4]

Consequently it seems best, for present purposes, to define as Anglo-Indian those persons, one of whose male progenitors, past or present, was of European descent but whose progenitors on the female side included one of Indian descent or of mixed European and Indian descent ("Indian" referring here to indigenous residents of prepartition India). This usage is somewhat broader in geographic terms, while remaining narrower socially and racially, than the definition presented in the Constitution.

The size of the Anglo-Indian community has always been a matter of some uncertainty. Official statistics are subject to both losses and accretions due to false claims. As an early census report stated: "The actual figures of Europeans and of the Anglo-Indian 'Domiciled Community' are always somewhat doubtful, owing to the tendency of the latter to return themselves as Europeans[5] and of Indian Christians to claim to be Anglo-Indians."[6] While the population of India shows a gradual rise over time, census figures for the Anglo-Indians fluctuate between 100,000 and 138,000, at times increasing and at other times decreasing in decennial reports. Enumerations of the community began in 1911 and were discontinued after 1951. In 1951 the census listed fewer Anglo-Indians (111,637) than it gave for 1921 (113,090). Frank Anthony tried to settle the issue for 1961 by accepting the statistics for Indians who report English as their mother tongue (223,781) as the best indicator for computing the number of Anglo-Indians, though he acknowledges that some Goans could be included in such a list (Anthony, 1969, p. 9). What may be overlooked in this estimate is the indeterminate number of Nagas who gave their mother tongue as English in a state where English is the official language. If a large number so reported themselves, any figure in the 200,000s would be quite inflated. Still another factor inflates it: after independence, a substantial number of Anglo-Indians migrated to England, Canada, New Zealand, and Australia — no one knows how many, although in the 1960s, Gist received reports that more than half of the entire Anglo-Indian population moved abroad (Gist, 1967a, p. 371). Assuming

---

4. Frank Anthony accepts the children of Domiciled Europeans as Anglo-Indians but qualifies his statement as follows: "The definition of Anglo-Indian does not postulate mixture of Euro-Asian blood but merely requires European descent in the male line of parents habitually resident in India. Thus even assuming, contrary to the ethnic verities, that the original British families settled in India for two, three or more generations had no admixture of Indian blood they were and are Anglo-Indians. . . .As a one-time student of Anthropology, I have always been extremely doubtful of the validity of the ethnic purity claim of the so-called Domiciled Europeans. With inter-marriage between Britons and Anglo-Indian women, which represented the marital usage for about 200 years, few, if any, European families in India really escaped a touch of the Anglo-Indian tar brush" (Anthony, 1969, pp. 4, 5).

5. During the British period Europeans had, among other advantages, more political influence per voter than others (Hedin, 1934, p. 171).

6. Census of India 1921, I, Part I, 231.

that this migration actually occurred, how is it possible to maintain the highest estimate of 250,000 for the community at the end of the 1960s (Anthony, 1968, p. 11)?[7] Since emigration continued to drain off population well into the 1970s (Gist, 1972, p. 58), it seems doubtful that the present population of the Anglo-Indians exceeds 100,000 today and it could be somewhat smaller.

ON THE FRINGE

Probably more than any minority in India, the Anglo-Indians have a borderline position in society. The ambiguity of their status is not new today, but it takes somewhat different forms from those which it had in previous historical periods. Since independence the Anglo-Indians perceive that they are not accepted by the dominant group unless they adopt its values and style of life as their own. This, however, they feel unable to do because for generations they have maintained European standards of dress, diet, family life, education, and language. Now they lack reinforcement for their subculture from colonial authority and feel a continually increasing pressure to conform to Indian manners and folkways. As one observer put it:

> ... the Anglo-Indians are living between two cultural worlds and not really wanted in either, but wanting nevertheless to be a part of the European world — wanting this very strongly — and also wanting, but less strongly, to be a part of the world of Indian culture. [Gist, 1973, p. 135]

The dilemma of cultural priorities is thus an inescapable fact of everyday life. But the Anglo-Indians not only undergo equivocal *cultural* demands but *structural* rejection as well, since they are shut out from what Milton Gordon calls "large-scale entrance into cliques, clubs and institutions ... on primary group level" (Gordon, 1964, p. 71) of the dominant group. Gist interprets this dual status of the Anglo-Indians in terms of marginality and suggests that in independent India, the minority group is both culturally and socially marginal to the indigenous Indian community or communities (Gist, 1967a, p. 365).[8]

It was not always thus. The present borderline position of Anglo-Indians is a result of long development, of conditions in which their status frequently shifted, sometimes dramatically. It may best be understood after a brief review of preceding changes.

A PERIOD OF TOLERANCE

Racial mixtures in India came in the wake of colonial expansion with the appearance of Portuguese, Dutch, and French adventurers from the fifteenth to

---

7. Anthony gives no indication of whether his estimate takes emigration into account or whether it fails to do so.

8. Considering the caste structure of Indian society, the lack of group incorporation at Gordon's primary group level is less damaging to the ego than would be the case in the United States, where it might be perceived as more serious rejection. A norm of primary-group acceptance would be quite out of the question in India.

the seventeenth century (Gist and Wright, 1973, pp. 9-10), but the main nucleus of the later Anglo-Indians came from the union of British traders and soldiers with Indian women beginning in the latter part of the seventeenth century in eastern India. During this era of worldwide exploration, race prejudice was practically unknown (Hedin, 1934, p. 165), and liaisons with women of Asia, Africa, and the western hemisphere were the rule rather than the exception. Although the East India Company sent out a few batches of English women at the outset, this policy was discontinued (Gaikwad, 1967, p. 16), and the basic directive then announced in the Directors' letter to men of the Company during 1684: "The soldiers' wives shall come to their husbands, if they can find means to satisfy or pay the owners for their passage, and for such soldiers as are single men, if you could prudently induce them to marry Gentues, in imitation of ye dutch polliticks, and raise from them a stock of Protestant Mestizees. . . ." (ibid.).[9] As with soldiers everywhere, temporary unions were often preferred to permanent marital ties. East India Company officials who enriched themselves (the Nabobs) often found it convenient "to keep lower caste native girls as concubines. In the eighteenth century, there were few unmarried British men in Calcutta without a mistress. These mistresses were either lower caste Indians or of mixed descent" (ibid., p. 18). At the same time Indian princes frequently took pride in recruiting British officers to train and lead their troops. Many of these officers were granted great power and wealth, and it was not unusual for this to include "retinues of Indian girls" (ibid., p. 17).

Although not discouraging concubinage directly, the East India Company preferred to endorse marriage with Indian women quite explicitly, as in the following letter to the President of Madras sent by the Directors in 1678: "The marriage of our soldiers to the native women of Fort St. George is a matter of such consequence to posterity that we shall be content to encourage it at some expense, and have been thinking for the future to appoint a Pagoda [five rupees] to be paid to the mother of any child, that shall hereafter be born of any such future marriage, upon the day the child is christened, if you think this small encouragement will increase the number of such marriages" (quoted in Anthony, 1969, p. 12).

This period of toleration continued until 1786. There were almost no British women in the colonies; marital and extramarital unions with Indian women or those of mixed parentage were common, and official policy encouraged such bonds so long as they were permanent. Increasingly the rank and file of the military came from the mixed population; such men had many advantages. Knowing the habits and vernaculars of their region, able to disguise themselves as Indians when their pigmentation was suitable, and with the capacity to infiltrate the camps of Indian troops, they were important intelligence agents (Stark, 1926, p. 43). During the East India Company military campaigns, the British treated Anglo-Indians in all troops as equals. When their fathers were sufficiently

---

9. Note the term "Protestant." Already a number of British soldiers had found eligible women of Portuguese and French origin in the Madras area and married some of them, preferring Christians (though Catholics) to non-Christians. However, at this time in England, strong anti-Catholicism led to revulsion against any and all marriages with Catholics (Anthony, 1968, p. 12).

well-off, they sent their offspring to England for higher education and these came back to India as members of covenanted ranks in the civil service or as officers in British Regiments. Anglo-Indian young men who had less prosperous fathers and were unable to pursue further education in England could nevertheless enter military service at the Warrant Officer level or below. During those days they were categorized as British and, like all men so classified, were not permitted to purchase land for agricultural purposes or to live more than ten miles from a town or settlement. They shared in the ever-growing wealth of the British community and distinguished themselves in both civil and military service (Anthony, 1969, pp. 18-19).

PERIOD OF MALE EXCLUSION

After 1786, the directors of the East India Company and officers in upper ranks of the military establishment became suddenly aware of two social trends in their world which, when considered together, loomed like a threat to their dominance in India. First was the dawning recognition that "the new class of British citizen attained a numerical superiority over the imported Britisher in the country" (Stark, 1926, p. 42). Secondly, the news from Haiti seemed ominous. In that French island possession, leaders in the mixed racial population joined forces with the blacks to foment rebellion against their European masters. Although the situation in India was not quite an exact parallel, English officialdom was unable to rid itself of the suspicion that the "Indian born" British, now grown to unwieldy proportions, could easily ally themselves with Muslim or Hindu rulers to expel the whole colonial apparatus.

Four official edicts followed, abruptly changing the entire status of the mixed population by singling them out for severe restriction. The first edict in 1786 forbade any wards or orphans of British fathers and Indian or Anglo-Indian mothers to go to England for higher education. In 1792 the Directors of the East India Company published a second edict prohibiting the employment of any persons with Indian extraction in the upper or official cadres in civil, military, or marine branches of the Company's service. In 1795 a third edict excluded all persons of Indian extraction from any post whatever in the military service of the Company except certain noncombatant ranks like fifers, drummers, bandsmen, or farriers. Finally in 1808, all Anglo-Indians were summarily discharged from both high and low ranks of the regular British army (Anthony, 1969, pp. 20-22).

The consequences of these events were shattering for the men of mixed parentage. While a few with high standing in the military were able to take service with native princes and command regiments for their new masters, the great bulk of the men entered the ranks of the unemployed or took over what marginal work they could find. While the status of the men declined, the status of Anglo-Indian women rose appreciably as a result of the ever-increasing demand for Anglo-Indian wives from British officials in Company or military service. During this era it became a mark of prestige to marry Anglo-Indian rather than Indian women, a process aided by the steadily growing Anglo-Indian population. In the 1790s the Orphanage for Anglo-Indian girls adjoining

St. Stephen's Church in Calcutta became a Mecca for British single men; once a year it became the scene of an almost ritualized selective inspection of new eligibles. "For many years, its great hall was used for an annual ball given in the interest of men seeking wives from the girls in the orphanage or from among the new arrivals from England. Officers in the Upper Provinces were known to journey 500 miles to obtain a wife in this fashion" (Stark, 1926, p. 64).

On the other hand, the repressive character of the four edicts and the way they separated out the category of the mixed population for special treatment began to create a distinctive set of self-feelings among what was formerly but an aggregate of individuals. Before this time, each of these individuals with mixed ancestry thought of himself and was regarded by others as having a particularized identity rather than one belonging to a recognized group. Thus the "mixed group was not characterized as a separately identifiable unit" (Grimshaw, 1959, pp. 228-29). But as British officialdom began to deal with Anglo-Indians categorically and not just individually, this effect was reflexive in the way that persons of mixed ancestry looked at themselves as a group apart.[10] Thus, the four edicts helped to stimulate a new community consciousness that eventually became a permanent heritage. Acceptance of a common fate and a common label stamped the nucleus of a completely recognized community.

A PERIOD OF SHIFTING STATUS

The official ostracism imposed by the British on Anglo-Indian men had unexpected repercussions. Many Indian-born entered the armies of Mahratta, Mysore, and other princes, and eventually became integrated into their new military ranks. It was not long before skirmishes and occasional warfare broke out between these Indian forces and British regiments. The spectacle of their former colleagues conniving, mobilizing, and raising arms against them was too threatening to be endured. Colonial functionaries realized too late that by precipitate action they had driven their comrades in arms into the very posture of rebellion they had tried to prevent. Hastily they revoked the edicts of exclusion and called all Anglo-Indian soldiers back into British military services again under threat of severe sanctions for disobedience. In spite of inevitable grumbling and resentment, the estranged troopers returned to join their fellows and fight side by side against the Indian forces that had recently espoused them. However, after the end of these minor wars, the Anglo-Indians were summarily discharged again (Gaikwad, 1967, pp. 22-23). They were thus forced eventually into the ranks of destitution swelled by the already impoverished civilians.

Concurrent with these events was an increase in race prejudice in the ruling stratum. There seems little doubt that much of this can be attributed to the marked increase in the number of British women moving into India. A mere trickle of these women had come out to join their husbands in the late eighteenth and early nineteenth centuries, but their numbers steadily grew after the East India Company lifted their travel restrictions on both men and women in the new charter published during 1833 (Gist and Wright, 1973, p. 14). Gradual equalizing of the sex ratio in the British sector of India made it possible

---

10. This is the major postulate of Dorris L. Goodrich, 1952.

for newly arrived women of the community to become powerful arbiters of eligibles and ineligibles in the marriage market and eventually to eliminate competition from Anglo-Indian rivals. Anthony comments that "the British women evolved an insidious, almost viciously malicious social code directed to the elimination of this competition" and that "a wall of social exclusiveness was drawn increasingly around British society" (Anthony, 1969, p. 354). Two leading historians assert of this period, "It must be confessed that the growing number of English women who began to settle in India with their husbands increased the tendency of the white population to form . . . a caste" (Thompson and Garratt, 1934, p. 456). Exclusiveness soon produced closure in both family relations and those of clubs or associations. As happened in other colonial settings, "Color distinctions began to blot out other distinctions and racism became the defining perception of the social field" (Schermerhorn, 1970, p. 116). In the present case it was directed against both Indians and Anglo-Indians along with noticeable sensitivity to darker or lighter pigmentation.[11] In sum, the nineteenth century was the era in which Anglo-Indians came under the full stigma of the color bar.

As opportunities for British marriages were eventually eliminated, Anglo-Indian women found that men of their own mixed status were enduring severe financial handicap as they struggled to find a place in the economy in the wake of British rejection. Since many were totally unable to support a family, their female counterparts were more fortunate in being able to locate avenues of employment that gave them footholds for independent support. Anglo-Indian women (along with their Indian Christian associates) now found a demand for their services in occupations like nursing, teaching, and office work, where neither Hindu nor Muslim women were permitted to participate. Much of this work was carried out under Christian auspices in mission hospitals and schools, where English was the language of administration or instruction. Since English was their mother tongue learned at home, this gave Anglo-Indian women an advantage over their Indian Christian colleagues for whom English was a second language. The tradition of Anglo-Indian teachers, particularly in the primary grades, seems to have started in this period. As for clerical employment in Company offices and the numerous commercial firms that burgeoned in the nineteenth century, Anglo-Indian girls not only had the language facility needed but a network of interpersonal connections with military and civil personnel that provided entrée to this form of employment.

> As stenographers and secretaries they were especially useful to the British because of their competence in the English language as well as their occupational skills. Generally they had no hesitancy about accepting employment in an office among personnel who were mainly or entirely men — a work situation not usually acceptable to Hindu or Muslim women. Although Anglo-Indian women were not accepted as social equals by their British colleagues or superiors, they nevertheless had a symbolic function in an office setting in which female congeniality was an asset. [Gist and Wright, 1973, p. 65]

---

11. One is reminded here of the folk saying among American blacks, "White is right but brown is down. Black — stand back!"

After losing eligibility as marriage partners among their British associates during this period, they became targets of exploitation and clandestine relations instead. This helped to originate rumors about Anglo-Indian women of easy virtue that later became stereotyped.

As racism became more pronounced during the nineteenth century, the colonial apparatus faced a series of decisions on policy affecting mixed populations. In the light of similar situations in other parts of the world, Harry Hoetink summarizes the alternatives for colonial (which he calls "segmented") society:

> ... in the first phase of the development of every segmented society, mingling takes place. In this process one group arises which has mixed racial characteristics and a cultural heritage which is largely, or wholly, that of the dominant segment. At this point the dominant segment has to choose whether to continue to allot to this mixed group the social position of the lowest segment, or an intermediate position, or to accept it as its social equal. . . . No other choice is possible. [Hoetink, 1967, p. 102]

The Indian case shows quite clearly that the choice, however, may bring different decisions over time. In the first stages of Indian colonialism (and this holds for Portuguese, Dutch, French or English alike) there seemed no point in making invidious distinctions, and the dominant group accepted the mixed offspring as basically equal. This attitude may have been influenced by the fact that the mixed offspring were too small a group to constitute a threat, and some positive feelings may have trailed the experience of novel sexual relations as having exotic value. In time, however, the sense of equality was eroded, to be replaced by the notion of white supremacy and exclusiveness. As this happened, the mixed group was assigned a new and intermediate position.

Economic hardships prompted an appeal to Parliament for redress in 1829, but the only response was a formal declaration of equality for employment in the East India Company in 1833, a pronouncement never implemented (Anthony, 1969, pp. 48-49; Stark, 1926, pp. 122-23). Anglo-Indians formed a number of self-help organizations at the time, but they proved ineffective (Gist and Wright, 1973, p. 97).

A PERIOD OF TEMPORARY SECURITY

The Mutiny of 1857 proved to be a watershed in the life of the Anglo-Indian community. During hostilities, Anglo-Indians distinguished themselves in military exploits and proved themselves so valuable to colonial authorities in helping to suppress the uprising that the British singled them out for special rewards. As the government in London removed the authority of the East India Company and assumed direct responsibility for rule in India, they decided to provide a kind of bonus for services rendered. This took the form of reserved jobs in communications and internal security forces; it included such positions as locomotive engineers, firemen, brakemen, conductors, stationmasters, inspectors, auditors, guards, telegraph operators, navigation officers, engineers and mechanics, customs officials, postal employees, and police. In such roles

Anglo-Indians were especially serviceable to British interests because of their fluency in English, their loyalty to the regime, and, consequently, their ability to protect the lines of communication (Gist and Wright, 1973, p. 59).

> Within the railroad and telegraph systems they maintained a near monopoly of employment positions. Until 1878 every branch of the telegraph department was manned almost entirely by Anglo-Indians or Domiciled Europeans. . . . Shortly after the turn of the century the government made it an official policy that Anglo-Indian and Domiciled European employment within the telegraph system should not fall below two-thirds of the total, but in 1920 it had declined to approximately one-half. Customs, another service in which the community maintained a virtual monopoly, was staffed almost entirely by Anglo-Indians or Domiciled Europeans until 1920, but gradually became infiltrated by other Indians. [Gist and Wright, 1973, p. 17]

In the latter half of the nineteenth century, therefore, Anglo-Indians were able to gain a more comfortable standard of living as a result of guaranteed employment. Although they never fully matched the income of their British counterparts, they surpassed the incomes of most Indians and, more importantly, had the comforting assurance of steady, dependable earnings. As this condition lasted for more than a generation, it stabilized family life and encouraged more marriages within the community, which was now completely endogamous (Anthony, 1969, p. 8). Comparatively speaking, this was the golden age of the Anglo-Indians, and, to the extent that it was economically feasible, they emulated the style of life set by English residents, often including the use of Indian servants in the home and a fair share of conspicuous consumption in conviviality and recreation.

Many of the work roles in this era were such as to demand a high school education, and a number of schools were established expressly for the purpose of educating Anglo-Indian or European children. Some of them were endowed and supported by wealthy patrons such as the La Martinière institutions, some supported under church auspices like the St. Xavier Colleges, and some under joint church and government sponsorship like the Bishop Cotton schools. In the late nineteenth century both young men and young women of the community had the benefit of education in schools, nearly all of which had high standards of academic excellence (Gist and Wright, 1973, p. 115).

Such privileges were bought at a price. In the job market the Anglo-Indians became more and more dependent on occupations controlled by the British. This was to prove a serious weakness under changed conditions. Furthermore the advantages in their favor had a cumulative effect on Indians in the wider community, and most of them strengthened Indian antagonism. From the time of the Mutiny when Anglo-Indian soldiers took the field against both Muslim and Hindu troops, to the occupation of reserved jobs from which Indians were excluded, came the recognition that members of this supposedly separate community were "lackeys of imperialism" taking bread out of the mouths of the indigenous population. Such feelings were exacerbated with the realization that railway employees had responsibility to act as militia. As an Anglo-Indian school principal reported:

On the railways Anglo-Indians cannot get posts unless they agree beforehand to join the Auxiliary Force (India). In most of our schools cadet companies are maintained in which the boys are compelled to enroll. When they leave school they automatically join the Auxiliary Force (India). If riots break out in towns, where no military are stationed, the Auxiliary Force is called out and often has to fire on and kill the rioters. This naturally tends to cause hatred on the part of the Indian towards the Anglo-Indian. [Weston, 1938, p. 116] [12]

Growing insulation of Anglo-Indians, in school and at work, from their Indian neighbors, and strong identification with the British way of life tended to magnify the self-conception of community members as somehow superior to Indians. Subject to race prejudice and social ostracism from the British, Anglo-Indians were able to relieve their feelings of frustration by passing on the imputation of racial inferiority to Indians whom they now saw as beneath them. "It was common in my boyhood days to hear Anglo-Indians talk of Indians as 'niggers' " (Weston, 1938, p. 137). This sort of superiority complex heightened the enmity of Indians toward the mixed population and built up a reservoir of ill-will that inevitably showed itself in the turbulent years to follow.

Although the period of temporary security was one of relative affluence and lasted well into the 1920s, it did not assure well-being to everyone. In the 1890s, a state commission in Bengal found 19 percent of Anglo-Indians of that state "in utter destitution and living on public or private charity," and as late as 1918-19 another commission put the figure at 17 percent (Hedin, 1934, p. 173).

From the turn of the twentieth century as Indian nationalism picked up momentum, pressure on the British to admit more Indians to railway and telegraph services resulted in gradual infiltration of the reserved posts by Indian candidates. This was offset in World War I by sweeping enlistments of Anglo-Indians in the military forces, even estimated to be 75 percent of "the available manpower" (Anthony, 1969, p. 130). But after the close of the War, the Montagu-Chelmsford Reforms in 1919 gave proportionately more Indians higher posts in such sectors as Indian Audits and Accounts Department, or Posts and Telegraphs, and even made a university degree a prerequisite for some of these posts. This displaced a good many Anglo-Indians since an overwhelming majority had not advanced beyond the high school level, there being little need for university training in the vocations open to them. On the other hand, many Brahmans and high caste Hindus in well-placed circumstances, along with Parsis and some Indian Christians, had continued their education to the university level. Displaced Anglo-Indians after 1919 often crowded into railway employment, where school requirements were not so high. It was reported that in the 1920s

... they have succeeded in gaining some 5,000 additional positions in that department [railway] only by dint of the bitterest competition with Indians. . . . The Anglo-Indians claim also that many Goanese and Indian

---

12. Although this was written in 1938, it describes the duties of Auxiliary service that go back to a much earlier day. (Cf. Anthony, 1969, p. 129.)

Christians pass themselves off as Anglo-Indians for purposes of employment, but probably the loss by this source in actual number of positions held is fully balanced by Anglo-Indians passing as Europeans. [Hedin, 1934, p. 174]

On the whole the 1920s marked the waning of an era when Anglo-Indians were comparatively well-off, and, as Indianization of the services continued to grow, they were forced into greater economic competition for which, in many respects, they were ill-prepared.

It was during this period of competition that the community became the scene of efforts to consolidate a number of organizations to fortify group interests. A national trend was finally embodied in a conference of five local Anglo-Indian societies in April 1926, when three of the five amalgamated under the direction of Sir Henry Gidney, a charismatic physician who rapidly became the recognized leader of Anglo-Indians throughout the land. The unified society, then called the Anglo-Indian and Domiciled European Association, All-India and Burma, became the dominant organization of the community, and it was joined in 1929 by the local Allahabad group, the fourth society to merge, leaving only the Madras association permanently outside (Anthony, 1969, p. 92).

AN ERA OF ADVERSITY AND AGITATION

From the 1930s to the end of World War II, India passed through tumultuous social changes in the struggle for swaraj. In the alternating roles of bystander, resister, and reluctant tolerator of such changes, the Anglo-Indian community lost much of the ground they may have gained in the previous era of good fortune. Most harmful of all, at the outset, was an economic depression of worldwide dimensions which crippled British trade and commerce; this led to the discharge of numerous employees and lowering of wages for others. Because of their exposed position, Anglo-Indians were highly vulnerable to these changes. Weston comments on how the youth were affected at this time:

> . . . young men like these have been forced to accept woefully inadequate wages rather than starve. Anglo-Indian and Domiciled European young men, whose education cost their parents on an average over Rs. 50 per mensem, are, today, told they can only be engaged in the Loco Department of the Railways on a pittance of Rs. 10 p.m. or about 5d. per diem; this, because the Indian can subsist on the wages and we are told to take it or leave it, as there are thousands of Indians ready to accept such appointments. [Weston, 1938, p. 119]

Starvation wages were debilitating; unemployment was worse. Weston (ibid., p. 108) continues:

> In my boyhood days[13] a lad in the 6th Standard of about 14 years of age, with no more than a knowledge of the 3 R's was able to get employment

---

13. Apparently the 1890s.

easily on the railways or in the telegraph department, and unemployment was unheard of. Today [14] young men of my community with a good high school education, and some with degrees, are roaming the streets in search of employment, and unemployment is rife. Hundreds of the community are to be found today in all the large towns begging for their daily bread.

As more and more Indians displaced Anglo-Indians in various services,

The cumulative effect of this policy has been that, while in 1921, before the Montagu-Chelmsford Reforms began to operate, there were fewer than 1,000 unemployed Anglo-Indians and Domiciled Europeans in India, today after a decade of the operation of the Reforms and the introduction of Indianization of the Services nearly 20,000 or more than one-third of the total able-bodied men of the community are unemployed, the majority of them being homeless and in rags, roaming the streets in quest of food. [15]

During these years of reversal, Sir Henry Gidney organized the forces of the community so that they could speak with a united voice in the Association, becoming the champion of Anglo-Indian rights before the bar of British opinion. For a time he was a prominent member of the Central Legislative Assembly at Delhi, where he defended the interests of his constituency and led deputations before the Secretary of State for India, as well as the Simon Commission; he then took up the cudgels for Anglo-Indians at all three Round Table Conferences in London. As a result of his strenuous efforts in their behalf, the Government of India in 1934 affirmed the right of Anglo-Indians to the following types of employment: "reservations of 2½ per cent of the direct recruitment to the superior railway service, 40 per cent in the telegraphist cadre, 3 per cent of all vacancies in the Appraiser Department of the Customs which were filled by direct recruitment, and 8 per cent on the Railways in posts with which the Community had past association. As hitherto, there was a 50 per cent reservation for the community in the Preventive cadre of the Customs service" (Anthony, 1969, p. 107). Sir Henry was also influential by helping to keep in force many of the grants for Anglo-Indian education.

It was in the 1930s when the nationalist fervor in India reached a new peak, when a program of civil disobedience launched by Congress gained rapid acceptance, and when boycotts, hartals,[16] and demonstrations became more and more frequent. To the Anglo-Indian people, such disturbances raised the specter of a double threat — one in the present and another in the future. In the present, a rising tide of outbursts against the government required suppression, and Anglo-Indians still in official positions like the railways, the Auxiliary Force, or the police were therefore under orders to shoot down demonstrators, if necessary, and thus raise the level of hostility against both themselves and their

---

14. 1938.

15. Weston (1938, p. 118). In his desire to point up contrasts, Weston either overlooks or does not know the extent of poverty in the earlier period, a condition already noted above, at least for Bengal. This may be due to Weston's local position in Bangalore and his lack of familiarity with urban disorganization in Calcutta.

16. Hartals are closings of small shops by protesting shopkeepers.

community. If colonial power were in complete control, such antagonism could be borne with equanimity, but such was clearly not the case. Legitimacy and authority were rapidly diminishing, and it was common knowledge that a transfer of power was in the offing. This was the future fear. In the changes to come, Anglo-Indians recognized that they would lose all protections of their present position and be thrown on the mercy of a Hindu majority. Forebodings of an uncertain status in independent India mounted as the Congress party chalked up fresh victories.

Sir Henry Gidney, highly sensitive to the winds of public opinion, uttered a note of warning in one of his addresses to an audience of Anglo-Indians by declaring, "If we are to be acceptable to the future India, we must at once completely reorientate our ideas, our outlook and our objects in life, especially our educational system; so that we may become more sons of India than aliens, as we are now regarded by all Indians, thanks to our educational system which is entirely alien to Indian nationalism and aspirations" (quoted in Weston, 1938, p. 130).

There is little evidence that such changes in Anglo-Indian schools actually took place until after independence, and Gidney's caveat probably had little effect at the time. That Anglo-Indians could rapidly reverse the habits of a lifetime was too much to expect. Especially was this true when internal dissensions, widespread poverty, and an embattled position in tumultuous India conspired to bewilder and confuse the community on all sides. It was truly a period of anomie for the group, and it was not difficult for apathy to alternate with arrogance or servility, depending on the circumstances.

The intermediary (and therefore marginal) position of Anglo-Indians was reflected in the ambiguity of British law at the time, and the contradictory definitions it assigned to the mixed population. "For purposes of employment under the Government, and inclusion in schemes of Indianization, members of the Anglo-Indian and Domiciled European Community are statutory natives of India. For purposes of education and internal security, their status in so far as it admits of definition approximates that of European British subjects" (Indian Statutory Commission XVIII, 527, quoted in Hedin, 1934, p. 171). Significantly, the second half of this statement lacks the definiteness of the first, which apparently gave British authorities considerable leeway to change the treatment of individual cases.

The disabilities of the community during these years of adversity weighed more heavily on the men than on the women, whose chances for employment continued to remain somewhat better. It was not until World War II that the men found a channel of escape when the proportion of enlistments equaled the volume of recruits joining up in 1914-18 (Anthony, 1969, p. 130). But the contradictions of British policy were especially evident in the armed services, where Anglo-Indians were officially supposed to be non-Europeans (ibid., p. 97). Yet during wartime emergencies when the English needed more manpower, they put strong pressure on Anglo-Indians, when possible, to declare themselves "Europeans." During World War II, selective racism apparently lay behind the program of encouraging Anglo-Indians to join the services as European Emergency Commissioned Officers (90 percent of these were Anglo-Indian); on the other hand, Anglo-Indians were prohibited from joining the Air Force if they tried to enlist in India; England reserved that branch for British only. Yet approximately 4,000 Anglo-Indians, by the simple expedient of travel to England, were accepted into the RAF as bona fide English recruits (ibid., pp. 132, 154-55).

In India, the British tried valiantly to increase their own quota of recruits by padding it with Anglo-Indians. Relating his own experience of those days, Frank Anthony testifies, "I protested over and over again to the military authorities that their recruiting officers deliberately encouraged and even compelled Anglo-Indians to register themselves as Europeans. I can cite case after case. When a lad would go to a recruiting officer and say, 'I am Anglo-Indian,' the recruiting officer would say, 'Go back. Think over it and come back tomorrow and enroll yourself as a European.' He went back and the next day he was recruited as a European" (Anthony, 1969, p. 171). What is tacitly understood in this account is that only lighter skinned members of the community were forced into this position. Also Anthony's report is one-sided in the sense that it places all responsibility for "passing" to undue influence deliberately applied by English authorities; yet there were also cases (some of them reported to the author by informants) where initiative came from the Anglo-Indian himself to escape his community both in war and in peace when the opportunity arose: whether by enlistment, by movement to another city in India, or by migration to countries of the British Commonwealth. The prevailing racism put a premium on renegadism for those of lighter pigmentation.[17] Certainly the chances for superior jobs, income, and advancement for those who "passed" were attractions hard to resist. However, the hostility of most Indians to the British war effort created a critical dilemma for Anglo-Indian males, caught in a squeeze play from which there was no escape.

The turbulent years leading up to independence were, therefore, for the Anglo-Indian people a time of ever-renewed anxiety.

INDEPENDENCE AND AFTERMATH

As the Indians took over the reins of government, there was some apprehension among Anglo-Indians that even the reserved jobs they had left would be suddenly lost to them. This was prevented, however, by political foresight. After Gidney's death in 1942, the leadership of the Anglo-Indian Association fell upon the shoulders of Frank Anthony, whose special legal talents were especially valuable during the difficult days of transition including the prophetic debates of the Constituent Assembly of which he was a member. Largely because of his efforts, provision was made in the new Constitution (Articles 333 and 334) for representation of Anglo-Indians by nomination to the

---

17. Weston writes: "Those who are fair will deny that they are Anglo-Indians and register themselves as Europeans. Some of our best young men from our schools in India go to England to complete their education and when they return to India for work they claim that they are arriving in India for the first time. Pathetic stories are told of parents who have sacrificed their all for their sons to educate them in England and who have been disowned by their sons on their return to India" (Weston, 1938, pp. 166-67).

Lok Sabha and to the state assemblies for a period of twenty years,[18] while appointments to the railway, customs, postal and telegraph services were to be kept at the current level for Anglo-Indians but reduced by 10 percent every two years until all reservations ceased (Article 336). This prevented a sudden disruption of employment for those still dependent on government service and allowed for adjustment to other occupational categories during the period of transition that lasted until 1960.

Though their numbers were doubtless small, there were some Anglo-Indians who had served in the British bureaucracy for many years but after the departure of colonial authority regarded allegiance to India as overriding all other considerations. Such public servants were willing to carry on for the new government at any sacrifice to themselves and cast themselves on the mercy of Indian public opinion. Their sentiments were well stated by Mr. Ralph Stracey, a prominent civil servant writing from Calcutta in 1947:

> India, we should not love thee; thou hast spurned
> Our mothers, outcaste beyond the pale
> Of law and social contact, to bewail
> Their landless state; unmercifully turned
> Thy proud face from us, children of thy night,
> And left us gazing by the endless seas
> To distant England where Man's liberties
> Are cherished more than birth, religion, might.
>
> Oh cruel woman, thou has done these harms
> To thine own sons! Yet, in our hearts forlorn
> Is love for thee imperishable! Come,
> Take us at last, oh Mother, to thine arms,
> Nourish us at thy breast as doth become
> A kindly mother to her latest born![19]

Such sentiments were probably not shared by more than a small minority. Much more common were strong fears that Anglo-Indians would lose both political and economic security in independent India. As a consequence, substantial numbers began to migrate to England, Canada, Australia, and New Zealand. Informants affirm that the women have been the most avid advocates of departure, giving as their reason that they want to clear out "for the sake of the children." They also testify that the younger generation migrates in disproportionate numbers, while Gist and Wright assert that middle and upper classes predominate (Gist and Wright, 1973, p. 20). Although many issues in the newspapers are disregarded by Anglo-Indians, the antennae of the community are sensitive to public events that appear to threaten the group as a whole. Each national crisis precipitates a new wave of migration to other countries; after the departure of the British and the uproar of partition which triggered the largest wave of exiles, smaller migrations have responded to events like the death of Nehru in 1964 and the loss of Congress party support at state levels in 1967. In the latter case, the British Immigration Act which raised new barriers for those who wished to enter England, deflected the channel of would-be migrants to

---

18. This was later renewed.

19. Used by permission of the author.

Australia and Canada, where the trend took on greatest proportions after 1968. Although the Australian and Canadian restrictions were not so severe as the revised rules in Britain, they nevertheless called for unusual scrutiny of the individual case; this was especially true in Australia, since it was the policy of that country to have an official from the Australian High Commission interview personally every single Anglo-Indian applicant for a visa before stamping the emigrant's documents. This procedure has led to a suspicion that Australian functionaries may be screening applicants on the basis of color, a supposition steadfastly denied by the authorities. Whether it is true or no, interviews among interested parties confirm the view that the emigrants tended to be on the lighter side of the color scale.[20]

Although only limited research has been done on the integration of these migrants in the United Kingdom, preliminary interviews reveal that they have made a reasonably good adjustment to their new environment, have steady employment, and live in fairly comfortable circumstances.[21] Most of them had the initial advantage of relatives and friends who preceded them and helped to furnish useful contacts with prospective employers and landlords. Whether those who settled in distant Commonwealth countries were equally fortunate is still a matter for further exploration.[22]

Those who remained in India have not suffered the persecution that they half-expected, but they have had the sense of being the last remnant of a much larger and more substantial community — an impression reinforced by a constant stream of letters from abroad. The specter of unemployment remains an ever-nagging concern, particularly for the men. The basis of this worry is shown in Table 9.1, which gives the results of a sample survey of some 10 percent of Anglo-Indian households in Calcutta during 1957-58.

Assuming that this sample is fairly representative of the Anglo-Indian residents in Calcutta in the 1950s, 23 percent of the total are at the poverty level, if Rs. 100 or less per month is taken as the defining boundary. If we place the upper limit at Rs. 200, the percentage living in poverty rises to 47 percent.

---

20. India increased the difficulty of migration by the announcement of new currency regulations. An informant, telling of the difficulties suffered by members of his own family who migrated to Australia reported to the writer that before April 1, 1968, an Anglo-Indian migrant, like all others, was permitted to take as many as Rs. 50,000 out of the country. After that date, the amount was reduced to Rs. 69 (with some exceptions).

21. Reported to the writer by Noel P. Gist in personal correspondence. His interviewing took place in England during the summer of 1964. . . . It is of momentary interest that Frank Anthony, by using a dramatic example of a prestigeful Anglo-Indian who was unable to find recognition for his talents in London but was forced to work as an obscure clerk, gave the impression that migrants suffered a loss of status and were therefore unhappy to have left India (Anthony, 1969, p. 212). If single cases could prove a point, one could select an opposite extreme like the instance of a young Anglo-Indian popular singer, totally unknown and unsuccessful, who migrated to England; by the eventual expedient of changing his name to Englebert Humperdinck, he catapulted to stardom.

22. As migrants do the world over, Anglo-Indians going abroad wrote home glowing accounts of their new opportunities and experiences. These were reported to the writer by a number of recipients of such letters. Need to discount such reports is a common feature of migration analysis.

TABLE 9.1

Distribution of Monthly Household
Incomes Among Anglo-Indians in Calcutta*

Monthly Income Groups in Rupees	Number of Households	Percentage of Total
50 or less	36	7.3
51-100	77	15.7
101-200	118	24.0
201-400	124	25.3
401-750	80	16.3
750 or over	56	11.4

*From Pilot Survey of the Socio-Economic Conditions of the Anglo-Indian Community, 1957-58, Calcutta: Baptist Mission Press, 1958, quoted in Gist and Wright, 1973, p. 90.

In either case, the proportion is large and the effects on morale serious. These figures, too, are for India's largest city where employment prospects are many and diverse compared with smaller towns. In the many railway centers after the 1940s, the narrow range of occupations coupled with a decreasing proportion of even that limited number, created hardships difficult to appreciate. At times this cleavage in the community has isolated an entire stratum from activities among more favorably placed community members and has led to apathy, defeatism, and sometimes resentment against their own leadership for ignoring them (Gist and Wright, 1973, p. 91).

FAMILY, MARRIAGE, AND SEX ROLES

Restricted opportunities in employment have had serious repercussions on the family life of Anglo-Indians. Even at higher status levels it is evident that members of the minority have been paying the price of disproportionate numbers historically in intermediate statuses (such as military and railway occupations). The cost of such protected jobs of primarily higher manual skills, and of subordinate clerkships as well, was a certain satisfaction with minimal or average educational standards that eventually inhibited upward mobility. The few Anglo-Indians with university training did find a vacuum near the top of some civil service offices immediately after the exodus of Muslims following partition, but this was not to be repeated. Almost all adults in the Anglo-Indian community are high school graduates or less; matriculation is the limit for all but a favored few. This educational level undoubtedly lies behind the remark of their recognized leader when he commented that the Anglo-Indians were not a "reading community" [comment in *Review* 60 (Nov./Dec. 1969), pp. 6-7]. It helps to explain the complaint of a number of respondents, namely, that scholarships for higher education, sometimes even secondary education, go a-begging among the people. Part of this seems to result from skepticism about the chances at higher levels of business or bureaucratic occupations in a Hindu-dominated society, where the number of university graduates is so large that Hindus cannot find employment for their own people, even with the aid of caste and family ties. There are, of course, new occupational patterns. It is reported that occupations requiring secrecy sometimes require candidates who do not have ties with larger communal groups where loyalty might cause them to divulge such secrets. Patent attorney offices are one example. In other cases an Anglo-Indian worker is kept on to train the boss's son to get ahead in the business and thus serve an instrumental function. At other times, when young men from the Anglo-Indian minority have made a name for themselves in sports, they find certain doors of employment opening for them. But these are scarce items.

The overwhelming majority of Anglo-Indians lack the capital or the experience to go into business for themselves. One reason, if informants are to be believed, is the relatively high standard of living (requiring more expenditure for consumer goods than among Indian families at the same income level). This is another holdover from the colonial period[23] which has its effects here as it does among the Indian Christians mentioned above. The lack of savings and the amount of relatively lavish spending receive a good deal of comment from community members themselves (Gist and Wright, 1973, pp. 54-55, 90-91). At the same time, informants report that Anglo-Indians avoid the trade unions or trade union occupations. There are exceptional cases where an Anglo-Indian with a fairly high position in a British firm, merely by hanging on when the British leave, can rise to the level of a chief executive, but only one such case was reported by Gist after sampling the employment market in both Bangalore and Calcutta (ibid., p. 63). Apparently, it was this same manager who stated that "Anglo-Indian workers declined to take a job in the company because the work was unskilled, which they regarded as degrading, or at least beneath their cherished station in life" (ibid.).

Such conditions have greater impact on the men than on the women. Lack of access to steady and rewarding employment erodes the very element in the male role that might endow it with respect and dignity, namely, that of being provider and manager of the home. Economic handicaps and often intermittent employment give him an image within his family environment as an improvident ne'er-do-well who is tolerated if not wholly approved and who tries to fill the provident role without notable success. Away from home and occupation (if he has the latter), he stresses hypermasculinity as displayed in athletics, club life, and the military, which he has a tendency to idealize. Historically, the most prestigeful role for males has been the military, and, even when civil service or bureaucratic activity preponderates, a strong preference for military roles remains as Anglo-Indians have participated actively in one war after another, in both British and Indian armed services. The English gentleman has been much admired among Anglo-Indians over the years, serving as a kind of role model;

---

23. Looking back nostalgically, one Anglo-Indian educator reminisced, "At one time each Anglo-Indian family could rent a fair-sized house with a large compound. Today two or three families are occupying one house. At one time Anglo-Indians hired many servants and generally kept a car or a carriage and horse. Today most families can afford one servant only and no car or carriage, but the 'bus' has to be indulged in. A large number of the community spend anything from one-third to one-half their salaries on alcoholic drinks" (Weston, 1938, p. 166).

chief concerns of the English gentleman were war, hunting, and sports, all of them requiring more than average leisure for their pursuit. Although agriculture and statesmanship of the British gentry were inimitable because Anglo-Indians were excluded from these fields, the disdain for manual unskilled labor could be imitated successfully, especially in Indian society where it resonated with Indian high caste sentiments and saved men from the ultimate degradation. The British model was not without influence at both upper and lower positions of the social scale.[24] At lower levels, however, it could well contribute its share to the burden of unemployment by helping to legitimate the image of men of leisure, a role that continued to be valued by males, in spite of its disadvantages, while it was potentially distasteful to an increasing number of females who saw it as threatening their future when their men were unable to support them.

While the male role veered toward a leisure model, the female role moved toward a work model. As already noted, Anglo-Indian women were formerly in great demand as nurses, teachers, and office workers. Since independence they have played a decreasing role in the first two vocations. In the case of nursing they are losing out because the demand for nurses who have command of the vernacular (rather than English) is definitely growing, and, to a large degree, these positions are increasingly filled by Indian Christian women who have command of the local language. As for teaching, there is great dissatisfaction with the extremely low salaries that are paid. "Actually, Anglo-Indian girls with limited secretarial training can commonly command a beginning salary higher than many professionally-trained teachers receive after years of service" (Gist and Wright, 1973, p. 66). Not only does this attract an increasing number to secretarial positions, but in recent years there has been expansion in service occupations where command of English is required and where role demands are favorable to females, that is, airline stewardesses, sales personnel in large mercantile establishments, receptionists of all kinds, models, night club entertainers, and the like. To put it quite bluntly, employment opportunities are considerably greater for women than for men (ibid., p. 153). Such "conflicting images have worked to the disadvantage, and often humiliation, of the Anglo-Indian men who may be forced to rely on their wives for family support" (ibid.).

Such intrafamily relationships lead to stereotyping on both sides, to the embarrassment of the men, all too often defined as weak, unreliable, or undependable characters who cannot support a wife properly.[25] Conversely, the girls are characterized as reliant, independent, and efficient workers who are enterprising and ambitious enough to support themselves and others. Because of these sex role images, there are many parents who prefer not to have their daughters marry too soon in order that they may continue to support their families of origin. Conversely, girls often tend to refuse marriage with men of their own community in the belief that they will not be able to support wives

---

24. Thus, it appears significant when the foremost leader of the community describes with relish and detail his participation in a hunting party with the Maharajah of Bikaner which reads like the diary of a British sahib from earlier days (Anthony, 1969, pp. 247ff.).

25. One respondent tried to explain this to me by asserting that Anglo-Indian mothers mollycoddle their sons but not their daughters.

and children steadily. Not only does the habit linger on (reinforced as it is by the racial ideology already mentioned) of marrying Europeans if at all possible, but both Gist's informants and my own report an increase of exogamous marriage by females. Such marriages are often to Indian Christians but also occur with westernized Sikhs, Hindus, Parsis, and even Muslims (Gist and Wright, 1973, pp. 78-81). The extent of this exogamy is somewhat limited, but it is undoubtedly on the increase and could eventually jeopardize the chances of Anglo-Indian males to find suitable partners, especially when it is remembered that liberally inclined Hindu or Muslim parents are willing for their sons to marry out, especially if the bride is fair,[26] but do not allow the same latitude to their daughters.

Seen in historical perspective, the marked autonomy and independence of Anglo-Indian women in a society of highly sheltered females has given rise to a popular conception of them as somehow deviant. After they were excluded from polite society by the influx of British women in the nineteenth century, they attained a new status of forbidden fruit for British men. Especially where an Anglo-Indian woman was fair of complexion and attractive in appearance, she found herself, in spite of her exclusion and even partly because of it, in greater demand than ever: first by Anglo-Indian men of both darker and lighter hue, and second by British men who had been accustomed to consider such women as eligibles and now found it difficult to renounce all relations with them entirely. Among these colonials were those who were single and preferred a dalliance but could not manage it with women from England who were either too few or too distant; those who were married were not infrequently annoyed by, while reacting against, the jealous strictness with which their wives excluded Anglo-Indian women from polite society. In many commercial and business houses, Anglo-Indian girls were secretaries, bookkeepers, or stenographers. Respondents tell of parties after office hours where conviviality, dancing, and festive enjoyment were a diversion in which lines of authority could be forgotten for the time. For many British men far from home, these were the only occasions for merrymaking in which both sexes could participate; it was unthinkable that Hindu or Muslim women could take part, and English women were not only few in number but usually controlled and restrained by husbands, families, or Victorian conventions.

Being the center of attraction for men of their own community and for British men as well was an experience of special privilege for such Anglo-Indian girls. When indulged, humored, and catered to on all sides, they were the target for exploitation and blandishments of men who had no more than a temporary interest. Intrigues and entanglements were inevitable as the transiency of such affairs in the India of that day was enough to start tongues wagging and produce a stereotype of the Anglo-Indian woman as a cocotte. This trend of thought was strengthened by the visibility of the Kareya quarter in Calcutta where the bordellos were noticeably Anglo-Indian (Chaudhuri, 1965, p. 315).[27] Although

---

26. See the exposition of the way that a parallel color consciousness developed among the Aryans of India from very early times in N.C. Chaudhuri (1965, pp. 184ff.).

27. The obvious relish with which Chaudhuri describes this area, the practitioners themselves, and the clients has led Frank Anthony to refer to such lucubrations as "penny-shovelling exercises in near pornography" (Anthony, 1969, p. iii).

the actual amount of promiscuity in the community as a whole cannot have been large, particularly outside Calcutta, the stereotype of the Anglo-Indian wayward woman became firmly fixed and a common theme for novelists. By the simple expedient of earning her way, the Anglo-Indian woman has faced a double handicap: responsibility for family support on the one hand and a certain amount of public stigma on the other. To her family and friends she is the efficient, skillful office worker whose relatively generous earnings are the mainstay of the home. To the wider society she is an employee who dresses in European style, is worldly wise in the arts of makeup, has many and continuous contacts with men outside the home, and a freedom in social affairs denied to her Indian sisters. Among the latter are naturally Hindu or Muslim women, desirous of emancipation, who cannot help but regard the freedom of movement enjoyed by their Anglo-Indian sisters with considerable envy but are able to conceal it well by condemning them as profligate demimondes. The persistence of this view was revealed to me when, in 1969, I was informed by an Anglo-Indian clergyman that in order to migrate to Australia, every young woman from the Anglo-Indian minority applying for a visa was required to have a character reference as one of her documents. This voucher or warrant was not required of the men. Such long-lived stereotypes of the women are bound to have serious impact on the role, status, and self-conception of female community members.

SOCIAL PARTICIPATION

Entrance of Anglo-Indians into secondary relationships outside the family are circumscribed by the downward escalator of mobility since independence (Gist and Wright, 1973, pp. 91-92), the loss of leadership through emigration which drew off many with higher incomes, education, and life prospects,[28] and the barriers of discrimination and lingering suspicion still remaining in the behavior and attitudes of the majority. In important respects, the public life of Anglo-Indians is therefore circumscribed and confined.

In terms of stratification there appears to be a massive stratum of lower income impoverished members, a decidedly shrunken middle class, and an even smaller upper income group. With this type of community structure, it is predictable that the organized associational life will show limited development. Here, as elsewhere, the lower stratum generally is least likely to exhibit participation in formal organizations (Hodges, 1964, p. 105). The lack of communitywide inclusion shows up clearly in the All-India Anglo-Indian Association "whose membership includes most of the prominent Anglo-Indians in positions of power" (Gist and Wright, 1973, p. 89). Not only has this organization become an elite enclave (with a limited number of rank-and-file followers), but it does not necessarily attract a representative membership. Gist and Wright report, "Out of an Anglo-Indian population of 10,000 in Bangalore in 1967, only about 400 were members, approximately the same ratio of membership to total population two decades earlier. Wright found in his New

---

28. On the basis of prevailing reports from informants, their departing relatives and friends were also predominantly in the younger adult employed group in their forties or under.

Delhi study that of 176 adults interviewed, 47 percent of the males and 42 percent of the females were members of the Association. As in the Bangalore survey, the sample is probably not statistically representative of the entire community" (ibid., p. 102). Anglo-Indians in lower strata are especially critical of the Association for neglecting the welfare needs of the indigent (ibid., p. 104).

Similar trends exist in the churches. While all Anglo-Indians are nominally Christian, there are more Catholics than Protestants among them and respondents attest to limited attendance.[29] The abundance of impoverished slum dwellers in the cities includes many who are alienated entirely from the churches while others are attracted to evangelical sects where fundamentalist views are disseminated. But it seems fairly certain that more churchgoers come from the middle classes than from the indigent strata near the bottom of class levels (ibid., p. 111), which again makes participation oligarchical.

The process repeats itself in the schools. Although, for its size, the Anglo-Indian community sponsors the most educational institutions (300 altogether) and those of the very highest caliber in the entire society,[30] in a period of declining income, the entire system is caught in a squeeze. Teachers and administrators alike have kept alive a tradition of uncompromising quality education, which has so appealed to the elite families of Hindu, Sikh, Parsi, and other communities that their children now constitute a majority of the pupils while the Anglo-Indian contingent has shrunk to between 2 and 20 percent in most schools.[31]

Recreational life is declining to a considerable degree. A number of the clubs that have furnished congenial surroundings for athletics and social gatherings of all kinds have been patronized mainly by those of middle or upper income levels; since independence, these social clubs have admitted an increasing clientele from other communities (Gist and Wright, 1973, pp. 141-45). Anglo-Indian athletes who often had more than their share on All-India teams in the 1920s have only minor representation today. As a result of the migration, a number of outstanding players, particularly in hockey, found their way to Commonwealth teams abroad, particularly in Australia (Anthony, 1969, pp. 231-32).

On the political front there seems to be widespread agreement among informants of different levels that Anglo-Indians are not politically active or assertive, either as individuals or as a group. To be sure, the minority is so miniscule that even high-powered organization on its part could show little impact as a pressure group. It simply lacks the votes to constitute a balance of power. Entirely apart from lack of numbers, however, respondents declare that

---

29. Gone are the days when English-speaking congregations were predominantly Anglo-Indian and the training-ground for young missionaries (Weston, 1938, p. 55). During colonial times, "In the Anglican churches seats were arranged in order of priority — men of European descent came first, the Anglo-Indian behind them, and the last seats were meant for the Christians with cutaneous pigments" (Mukerji, 1964, p. 143).

30. Below the university level.

31. A few exceptions like St. Patrick's School and Orphanage in Bangalore or St. Paul's School in Calcutta have over half their student population Anglo-Indian, but they are unrepresentative (Gist and Wright, 1973, pp. 119-20).

political interest is either low or nonexistent; as one professional testified to the author, most Anglo-Indians have quite other interests. In reading the newspapers, they turn first to the sports page and later, if at all, to domestic or world news. The same values appear in radio listening, where Ceylon programs are turned on most of the time (mostly American or European popular music) "because Anglo-Indians don't like Indian music and don't bother listening to the news bulletins."

However, the apolitical stance of most Anglo-Indians has historical roots. During much of the colonial era, the community looked to British authority to protect its interests and, when that proved unavailing, transferred reliance to single national leaders like Gidney and Anthony whose place in the seats of power made it possible for them to defend the concerns of their colleagues by wresting concessions from reluctant governments. After independence, Anglo-Indians have not elected their representatives in Parliament or the assemblies but have nominated candidates in caucuses who are then appointed either by the president of India or the state governors. This latter arrangement only applies in those states with the largest concentrations of Anglo-Indians, which include Andhra Pradesh, Bihar, Madhya Pradesh, Tamil Nadu, Maharashtra, Karnataka, Uttar Pradesh, and West Bengal (Gist and Wright, 1973, p. 110). On the whole, political (and often other) decision making has been delegated to strong leaders as a mode of adjustment to political realities. For example, one delegate to the national convention of the All-India Anglo-Indian Association in October 1969 stated, ". . . some very valuable suggestions and resolutions were adopted, but after they left the meeting, they usually left it to Mr. Anthony and the central office to do the work."[32] The impression is widespread that political concerns are best left in the hands of those who have some leverage and know where best to apply it. This attitude undoubtedly has cumulative and circular effects as the rank and file relinquish political initiative to the chief while he, in turn, is encouraged by adulation to regard his own ventures as beyond criticism since they are made on behalf of the community as a whole.[33]

A PLURALIST ENCLAVE?

In the process of colonization, the rulers were accustomed to confronting a preexistent ethnic pluralism; in the case of India the British encountered Muslims, Sikhs, Jains, tribals, and Hindus as distinct groupings, each requiring administrative arrangements suitable for its special needs. Anglo-Indians differed from all the rest because they had no prior presence[34] calling for immediate

---

32. Quoted from minutes of the meeting in *The Review* 60 (Nov.-Dec., 1969, p. 4).

33. Most of the criticisms of the Association and its leadership come from nonmembers who frequently assert that it neglects economic aid and welfare for those in need (Gist and Wright, 1973, pp. 102-04).

34. To simplify the account, I omit mention of the Portuguese, Dutch, and French predecessors here, recognizing that a more complete version would extend the same categories to their forms of domination.

recognition. They were not an indigenous phenomenon but a derivative one, growing out of the colonizing process itself. As an emergent resulting from the confluence of peoples, the Anglo-Indians had an ambiguous status that has never been completely resolved. Racial features of this equivocal position have already received attention; what remains is to consider the pluralist elements that help to clarify the distinctiveness of the group.

Historical development of the Anglo-Indian community reveals alternating effects of cultural and social pluralism. Cultural pluralism was displayed in language, values, and norms; social pluralism in segmentary boundaries shutting out common participation with outsiders.

In the seventeenth and early eighteenth centuries before the mixed population had a marked numerical growth, neither cultural nor social pluralism had more than a minimal growth. Since males of the mestizo category were useful as scouts and soldiers, it was rewarding for them to be bicultural so as to play dual roles as interpreters, spies, and other go-betweens in the service of the company's military forces. At this time there was neither cultural nor social pluralism. This condition began to change rapidly in the 1790s when the British separated the mixed group from their own by fiat, excluding them from the armed forces. Social pluralism imposed from without resulted. Apart from the few officers and men who found employment in the armies of Indian princes, it is safe to say that the mixed population from the 1790s to the 1830s, thrown back on the indigenous Indian population, found themselves rejected there too, as aliens and unacceptable castoffs from the colonial masters. As this double social pluralism impinged on them from both sides, the mixed group found reinforcement of their status in heightened group consciousness and solidarity. Yet as a protective device they made a number of gains by stressing a one-sided cultural pluralism, that is, by adopting to the hilt both the language and customs of the colonial rulers in order to preserve a position in commercial and administrative circles. Zealous adoption of British manners and style of life also enabled those defined as racially acceptable (lighter colored) to find positions of higher responsibility in official ranks where they "passed" if they were men, or married into such ranks with similar consequences if they were women.

As increasing numbers of British women entered the colonies between the 1830s and the 1860s, social pluralism was reinforced by ostracism in clubs and recreational life until it reached a high point in the latter nineteenth century when endogamy among Anglo-Indians became practically the rule, when ecological concentration increased, particularly in the railway colonies, when institutional duplication particularly in education (though less in religion) grew considerably, and associational clustering in clubs and benefit associations became the order of the day. At the same time, cultural pluralism remained relatively constant since language, mores, and family patterns remained those of the dominant group rather than of the surrounding society. This condition lasted until well into the twentieth century, when social pluralism was augmented by Indianization of the services that accompanied the drive toward swaraj.[35] The

---

35. Gist describes the same phenomenon by employing the concept of marginality and remarks that the Anglo-Indians were socially marginal to the British but both culturally and socially marginal to Indians (Gist and Wright, 1973, p. 36).

anomaly of the Anglo-Indian position during this period was reflected in the ambiguity of British law which assigned them a threefold status: "Natives of India for the purpose of employment, European British subjects for certain defence purposes, and non-Europeans vis-à-vis the British Army" (Anthony, 1969, p. 97).

Immediately after independence, advantages of cultural congruence with the British declined sharply, and the Anglo-Indians occupied a new exposed condition where the dissimilarity of cultural values between themselves and the dominant Hindus became a glaring defect. The gap of double pluralism, social and cultural, was suddenly deepened as it became evident to the majority that the minority group refused to give up the language and ways of life of the former rulers who had retreated only to leave their spokesmen behind to remind the newly liberated of the symbols and values that governed in earlier days when India was in servitude to a foreign power. Attacks on the English language were frequent and bitter, particularly by the Hindi enthusiasts in northern India over a period of years (Anthony, 1969, Chap. XI). At the same time, social pluralism gained new strength as upper caste Hindus set up a number of barriers to Anglo-Indian employment in both public and private sectors, while Anglo-Indians withdrew more and more into the protective environment of their social clubs. In order to keep out Anglo-Indians, Hindus were forced to develop new rigidity and clarity of group definition which would make it possible to identify Anglo-Indians in order that discrimination could exclude them. In self-defense, Anglo-Indians increased endogamous practice, ecological concentration, and especially associational clustering, as they fortified the social clubs and the national Association to increase their solidarity. The ebb and flow of these forces appear to parallel the crises that threaten the community. The coming of independence, the death of Nehru, the attacks on English-medium schools, the waves of migration, and other such crucial events set up actions to increase the degrees of enclosure (social pluralism). Concurrently there are forces in the opposite direction (such as increased contacts in school between Anglo-Indian and Indian children and a minor trend toward exogamy) which have the potential for dialectical counteraction. What are the implications for integration?

None of the four ideal types (assimilation, sanctioned autonomy, forced segregation, or forced assimilation) quite fits the minority position of the Anglo-Indians in contemporary India. There are too many differences of opinion on policies for the minority within the dominant group, and subordinates are also divided on major issues. Because of their cultural pluralism (the preference in this case for patterns identified with England or the West — in language, family organization, religion, courtship practices, recreational enjoyments, et cetera) — Anglo-Indians are not interested in assimilating culturally but desire to preserve their style of life. In this respect, they display centrifugal tendencies. Acceptance of this position by caste Hindus would create mutuality by recognizing the minority desire and legitimating it. In a sense, this is the function served by the caste system, and accepting the Anglo-Indians as another caste or castelike community would put the seal of approval on a live-and-let-live policy with definite integrative features. However, it is quite clear that the upper castes are not in agreement on such a program. Such influential groups as the superpatriots, the militants of the Arya Samaj, and the Hindi enthusiasts (all of whom are pushing in the same direction) take a centripetal stand and press for an assimilative ideal. The most common expression of this ideal, vis-à-vis the Anglo-Indians, is in agitation for the use of Hindi in all schools to the abandonment of English and for the Indianization of the services, both public and private. Other sections of the dominant group are either passively tolerant or lean toward a centrifugal position and are willing to permit the Anglo-Indians (and other minorities as well) to maintain their own culture or way of life without interference. Those with the latter persuasion are relatively inactive or quiescent, while the advocates of absorption are energetic, vigorous, and forceful. Geographically, the latter are more numerous and influential in north India, while the others are more characteristic of the south. One could almost say that the alternative of cultural pluralism is more publicly acceptable in the south while forced assimilation is more popular in the north. The responses of informants confirm the greater ease that Anglo-Indians in the south seem to have with their Hindu neighbors in comparison with Anglo-Indians in the north.[36]

However, when Anglo-Indians face a situation in which assimilation is more or less forced on them, their chief line of defense is to show that they have enough bonds with all other Indians really to belong. Thus, to demonstrate that Anglo-Indian schools implement the official three-language formula[37] in the schools when others do not is to give evidence of loyalty to an all-India ideal widely accepted for national integration (Anthony, 1969, pp. 423-24). Another defense is to cite the innumerable officers and enlisted men from the Anglo-Indian community who distinguished themselves for special deeds of bravery in wars against Pakistan (ibid., pp. 450-76). Such appeals doubtless have their value but, since they are insufficiently reported in the mass media (in such a way as to identify Anglo-Indians as such), they have quite limited effect.

The future then is uncertain. Political realities will have a strong and probably determinative influence in the years to come. In the past, the Congress party has had a secular tradition of live-and-let-live for all minorities including the Anglo-Indians. However, even with landslide electoral victories like those of 1970 and 1972, these triumphs mask a great many internal disagreements and schisms that can quickly surface in times of adversity (for instance, during the famines and takeover of wheat trade by the government in 1973). Hence, there is no assurance that a final approval of community autonomy will soon be reached for the Anglo-Indians, for that would be a likely occurrence only in times of relative internal peace and tranquillity. The immediate future does not promise such a time. Since some victories for the Anglo-Indian community have been won in the least promising of times in the past, however, the same could happen again, given the type of leaders who can again exploit crises in their favor.

---

36. Based on a very limited set of impressions taken from a small number of cases. It also assumes that most Anglo-Indians would favor a cultural pluralist solution.

37. In the three-language formula, all students learn the link language (English), the language of the region, and Hindi.

BIBLIOGRAPHY

Anthony, Frank, "A Strategy for National Integration," *The Review* 59 (No. 10, October 1968), 9-14.

Anthony, Frank, *Britain's Betrayal in India. The Story of the Anglo-Indian Community,* Bombay, Allied Publishers, 1969.

Chaudhuri, N. C., *The Continent of Circe, An Essay on the Peoples of India,* Bombay, Jaico Publishing House, 1965.

Gaikwad, V. R., *The Anglo-Indians: A Study in the Problems and Processes Involved in Emotional and Cultural Integration,* Bombay, Asia Publishing House, 1967.

Gist, Noel P., "Cultural vs. Social Marginality: The Anglo-Indian Case," *Phylon* 28 (Winter 1967a), 361-375.

Gist, Noel P., "Conditions of Inter-Group Relations: The Anglo-Indians," *International Journal of Comparative Sociology* 8 (September 1967b), 199-208.

Gist, Noel P., "The Anglo-Indians of India," in *The Blending of Races: Marginality and Identity in World Perspective,* edited by Noel P. Gist and Anthony G. Dworkin, New York, Interscience (John Wiley & Sons), 1972.

Gist, Noel P., and Roy Dean Wright, *Marginality and Identity, Anglo-Indians as a Racially-Mixed Minority in India,* Publication 3, Monographs and Theoretical Studies in Sociology and Anthropology in Honour of Nels Anderson (General Editor, K. Ishwaran), Leiden, E. J. Brill, 1973.

Goodrich, Dorris L., The Making of an Ethnic Group: The Eurasian Community in India, unpublished Ph.D. dissertation, University of California, Berkeley, 1952.

Gordon, Milton M., *Assimilation in American Life,* New York, Oxford University Press, 1964.

Grimshaw, Allen D., "The Anglo-Indian Community: The Integration of a Marginal Group," *Journal of Asian Studies* 18 (February 1959), 227-40.

Hedin, Elmer L., "The Anglo-Indian Community," *American Journal of Sociology* 40 (September 1934), 165-79.

Hodges, Harold M., *Social Stratification, Class in America,* Cambridge, Mass., Schenkman Publishing Co., 1964.

Hoetink, Harry, *The Two Variants in Caribbean Race Relations: A Contribution to the Sociology of Segmented Societies,* translated by Eva M. Hooykas, London and New York, Oxford University Press, 1967.

Mukerji, Nirod, *Standing at the Cross-Roads; An Analytical Approach to the Basic Problems of Psychosocial Integration,* Bombay, Allied Publishers, 1964.

Schermerhorn, R. A., *Comparative Ethnic Relations: A Framework for Theory and Research,* New York, Random House, 1970.

Stark, Herbert A., *Hostages to India,* Calcutta, Calcutta Fine Art Corrage, 1926.

Thompson, Edward J., and G. T. Garratt, *Rise and Fulfillment of British Rule in India,* London, Macmillan, 1934.

van den Berghe, Pierre L., ed., *Africa, Social Problems of Change and Conflict,* San Francisco, Chandler Publishing Co., 1965.

van den Berghe, Pierre L., "Some Analytical Problems in the Study of Plural Societies," unpublished paper (mimeographed), 1967.

Weston, C. N., *Anglo-Indian Revolutionaries of the Methodist Episcopal Church,* Bangalore, Scripture Literature Press, 1938.

Chapter 10

Jews: A Disappearing Minority

This and succeeding chapters will turn attention to minorities whose origin lies outside of India but whose ancestors made their entrance into the subcontinent at time periods quite distinct from each other. For the sake of convenience, the minorities of migration, bygone and recent, are now considered in chronological order of their incoming: Jews first, then Parsis, and Chinese last of all. The first two, as religious minorities, came on the Indian scene before secularism had taken root and, as devotees of spiritual values (albeit in a separate tradition), were not so much a threat as they were fellow pilgrims in the search for salvation. Religious competition was out of the question since neither Jews nor Parsis proselyted for converts, thus proving themselves in accord with the special Hindu ideal of tolerance reported above in Chapters 7 and 8. Both these minorities, therefore, had an initial advantage in their chances for integration when compared with the later Chinese arrivals, whose chief mark of identity was nationality in a more secular age where this distinction was one of potential separateness and a certain irreconcilability. Ties of nationality also had political consequences in the international arena that could quickly appear threatening to the state; a minority with such ties would pose more difficult problems of integration, especially in India.

To begin with the Jews, they constitute the smallest of all the ethnic minorities considered in this volume and, in addition, are shrinking in size by means of emigration even more rapidly than the Anglo-Indians. As will become evident, the reasons for departure are the opposite of those motivating the Anglo-Indians, the Jews responding to a pull and the Anglo-Indians to a push. The issues that initiate movement abroad on the part of Indian Jews are of extra-Indian significance, but it is such issues that give them sufficient importance, as a minority, to receive equal attention with other ethnic communities in India in spite of their insignificant size. As the world's most prominent "perennial minority," the Jews invite comparative analysis in a very special sense.[1] It is not only their significance for India but historic and

---

1. This need for comparative studies helps to explain the appearance and success of *The Jewish Journal of Sociology* (London) in its seventeenth year of publication as of 1976.

cross-cultural factors of worldwide import that focus attention on the Jews. However, the implications of their Indian experience for their modes of response to other societies can only be hinted at in such a brief review as the present one.

The Jewish population of India, even at the peak of its growth in the late 1940s, did not exceed 26,000 (Strizower, 1971, p. 5). In the 1961 census, this figure had dropped to 18,533 with slightly more females than males. Of this total, 16,743 or 88 percent were urban dwellers. In terms of concentration, the great bulk of the Jewish population reside in three states of India as shown by the following enumeration:[2]

Maharashtra	15,591
West Bengal	1,191
Kerala	370
	17,142

This leaves 1,411 who lived in other parts of India such as Ahmedabad, Delhi, Madras, and some smaller cities. The threefold division into Maharashtra, West Bengal, and Kerala points to the three major subcommunities of the Jews that are nearly separate enclaves in themselves: the Bene Israel, the Baghdadi Jews, and the Cochin Jews. Of these three divisions, the Bene Israel live chiefly in Bombay, the Cochin Jews in Kerala, and the Baghdadi group is rather unequally divided between Bombay and Calcutta. There are, in addition, a few hundred European Jews who came to India from Austria and Germany after Hitler's rise to power in the 1930s (Strizower, 1971, pp. 5-6). Neither the Baghdadis nor the European Jews in India have received much attention from scholars, but both the Bene Israel and the Cochin Jews have been the subject of research by historians and anthropologists. Hence, what follows will refer primarily to the two subcommunities that have been in the spotlight, although my brief contacts with the Baghdadis of Calcutta have resulted in a limited number of observations below.

ORIGINS AND RELIGIOUS BACKGROUND

Like the Parsis, the Jews of India originally migrated to south Asia from more northern regions but at an earlier date. Unlike the Parsis, however, Jews can trace their appearance in the subcontinent to several migrations rather than to a single one. Precisely when these took place is still something of a moot point. Unlike most other peoples of the ancient world, Jews were identified with many lands rather than with a fixed location. Traditionally, they ascribe this circumstance to the Diaspora, or dispersion of the Jewish population to surrounding areas after the destruction of Jerusalem and the Temple by the Romans in A.D. 70. But any critical reading of the historical record makes it clear that this was but one Diaspora of many. The term "wandering Jew" is more than a mere metaphor. Even superficial examination of the record reveals at least seven times when, because of invasions by conquering armies or severe persecution followed by flight, Jews were displaced from their homes in the

---

2. Census of India 1961, Vol. I, Part II-c (i), Social and Cultural Tables, Supplement to Table C VII, Religion. Figures for the 1971 Census have not been available to the author.

ancient world and forced to move elsewhere. If each of these occasions could be dignified by the term "Diaspora," the following list would appear:

Diaspora 1. Fall of Israel to Tiglath Pileser, 734 B.C. Some migration to Assyria and other parts of the ancient world.

Diaspora 2. Fall of Israel to Sargon, 722 B.C. Similar migration.

Diaspora 3. Fall of Jerusalem to Nebuchadnezzar, 586 B.C. Elites of the Jewish population carried captive to Babylon.

Diaspora 4. Persian conquest of Babylonia by Cyrus, 538 B.C. Many Jews allowed to return to Jerusalem or migrate elsewhere. A number remained in Babylon.

Diaspora 5. Alexander conquers Syria in the fourth century B.C. Some exodus of Jews to Egypt and other Mediterranean areas.

Diaspora 6. Romans destroy the temple and city of Jerusalem, A.D. 70. A major scattering of Jews in every direction.

Diaspora 7. Sassanid Persians persecute and massacre Jews, chiefly in Babylon. Jews flee in many directions, some of them southward, fifth century A.D.
[G. F. Moore, 1932, pp. 18-20, 24-25, 31-32, 51, and 66; C. Roth, 1969, p. 122]

Since trade connections with India were known as far back as Solomon's day (tenth century B.C.), some accounts of the first Malabar Jews say that they came with Solomon's fleet of merchantmen; others trace the origin to descendants of captives taken to Assyria in the eighth century B.C.; there is also the surmise that the first arrivals were offspring of the Babylonian captives, which would trace back to the sixth century B.C.; still a different version speaks of antecedents considerably later, that is, the fourth century A.D., this time from a group in the western Mediterranean who came from forbears escaping after the destruction of the Temple in A.D. 70. The Cochin Jews themselves have a tradition that their progenitors came directly to the Malabar coast in the first century A.D., immediately after the destruction of the Temple (Strizower, 1962, pp. 89-90). A modern Jewish historian, however, after describing how the Jews of Babylon were slaughtered by the Persian king Firus in the fifth century A.D., declares it to be "probable" that the Jewish colonies of Malabar were "due to refugees who fled eastward from Mesopotamia at this period of crisis"[3] (Roth, 1969, p. 122). This allows for a leeway of thirteen centuries within which the date could be set.

As for the Bene Israel of Bombay, they believe that they are descended from the Ten Tribes of Israel, especially those avoiding capture and deportation by the Assyrians as announced in II Kings 18:11.[4] Tradition has it that these Israelites migrated to many other countries, India being only one of an extensive list. A similar exodus of those deported to Assyria also took place, but the Bene Israel do not trace ancestry to them. Nevertheless, one of their own chroniclers derives the group from a Jewish migration of the Greek period in Palestinian history, about 175 B.C.[5] (K. S. Kehimkar, quoted in Strizower, 1962, p. 52).

---

3. Corresponding to Diaspora 7.

4. Corresponding to Diaspora 2.

5. May be regarded as a continuation of Diaspora 5.

On the basis of such conflicting evidence, it seems unprofitable to speculate further about the obscure origin of the Indian Jews. All one can say is that hard historical evidence is within closer reach for the Cochin Jews than for the Bene Israel. The Cochin group has an engraved copper plate given to a prominent Jewish leader by a Hindu ruler centuries ago. Some authorities date this plate at about A.D. 750, and internal evidence shows that there must have been a flourishing Jewish community for some time before this to make such a beneficence possible (Fischel, 1967, p. 231). Hence, the Malabar community could be dated back a century or two earlier at most. Thus, it would still be possible for the original immigrants to have come from *any of the seven Diaspora* already mentioned, which makes our uncertainty fairly obvious. Data for the Bene Israel are still more ephemeral, and they do not permit a *terminus ad quem* as do the clues available in Cochin.

The religion of the Jews is an ethical monotheism based on the notion of a historic covenant with the deity made by Moses who revealed the terms of the covenant and the statutes confirming it (the Ten Commandments) to the Hebrew people, who then regarded themselves as specially chosen to manifest the divine will to others.[6] Like the Muslims, the Hebrews had strong roots in desert nomadism, and in their early history were warrior tribes who conquered most of Palestine, only gradually giving up their pastoral economy for agriculture. But as wealth and prosperity increased and the gap between rich and poor grew wider, a number of prophets appeared preaching the fierce egalitarianism of the desert as a message of the deity. As Palestine was invaded by foreign armies and the Palestinians scattered, these ethical precepts of the prophets were crystallized into laws to govern day-to-day activities of the people even when they were far from their ancestral home. Priests and scribes eventually ascribed antiquity to these laws, imputing them to Mosaic times and affixing them to the original covenant. This practice led to legalism in religion, but the principles pervading the law were prophetic and strongly ethical. During the times of exile, an important change in the form of worship occurred. It was no longer possible to have a central temple for celebration of the national religion, such as existed in Jerusalem or Samaria. A new and more flexible form of worship evolved, one adapted to the devotion of the faithful in any and all lands. This was the synagogue.[7] As Max Dimont has put it:

> On the soil of Babylon the Jews created two new ideas which have since become the possessions of mankind. Instead of a temple for sacrifice, the Jews built synagogues for religious assembly; instead of rituals for God, the Jews offered prayers to God.[8] The synagogue became the prototype

---

6. This is not to assert that Moses was the *founder* of what later became Judaism (that position is traditionally ascribed to Abraham), but it serves to focus attention on the *Mosaic covenant* which, among the many covenants mentioned in the Old Testament, played such a crucial role in setting the direction for religious development for the Jewish people.

7. This inadequately brief sketch is based on modern historical analysis as presented by a number of writers. A longer, excellent summary is found in Moore (1932, Chaps. I-III inclusive).

8. This dichotomy is perhaps too sharp. Prayers offered in unison or together may well become a permanent part of ceremonial or ritual.

for the church of the Christians and the mosque of the Moslems; prayer became the universal symbol of devotion to God. Through synagogue and prayer, the Jew no longer was tied to any specific priesthood, temple or country. He could set up shop in any land and be in direct communication with God — without intermediaries. The Jewish religion, which had been immobile and rigid, now became an exportable commodity, resilient and invisible. Survival of the Jews in captivity and in dispersion was assured. [Dimont, 1962, p. 68]

COLOR AND CONSANGUINITY

The great majority of Indian Jews are brown in color, varying on a continuum from lighter to darker shades within that category. As Schifra Strizower remarks on the issue, "... Jews everywhere resemble in physical features the people among whom they have been living for centuries; and it is somewhat difficult to believe that Jews with dark skins living in countries inhabited by people with dark skins brought their skin colour with them, while Jews with light skins acquired their skin colour through intermarriage" (Strizower, 1971, pp. 27-28). One can only interpret this to mean that in spite of Jewish law imposing endogamy upon adherents of Judaism as early as the Babylonian captivity, frequent wandering of migrants, with or without family companions, made a choice of Jewish marital partners well-nigh impossible for those settling in an area for the first time. Any one of several alternatives (each governed by local conditions) could then be chosen: (1) temporary liaisons, (2) concubinage, often semi-permanent, (3) outright intermarriage in defiance of Jewish law, or (4) marriage following conversion of the partner (usually the bride) to Judaism. Jewish migrants were likely, however, to regard these alternatives as temporary measures to be superseded as soon as their religious community grew to a size that would permit the Jewish law of endogamy to operate normally. If the group was initially quite small, this process could take as much as several centuries, during which time the physical features of the community would resemble more and more the characteristics of the surrounding population. If modern scholarship is correct, this is the sort of process that seems probable not only in India but in European areas as well (if skin color is taken as the distinguishing mark), for the oldest Jewish legislative writings outside the Pentateuch (the Mishnah) declare that Jews "are neither white nor black but of the intermediate shade" (Strizower, 1971, p. 28).

The Jews of Cochin, about whom we have somewhat more definite information, are divided into endogamous subgroups which David Mandelbaum (1939, p. 424) calls castes: the black Jews, the white Jews, and the brown Jews. Members of the three groups designate themselves by the names (1) Malabar Jews, (2) *meyuchasim,* and (3) *m'shuhararim,* respectively. The term "black Jews," which found its way unaccountably into English is a definite misnomer because this group (a definite majority) displays many shades of brown with darker hues predominating but no black whatsoever. And to speak of the third group as "brown Jews," as though it is their *color* that separates them from coreligionists is to dwell on a nondistinguishing feature. Although racial terms in popular usage have come to be employed in English, the real division is a matter of *social relations,* and these relations are but imperfectly reflected in color variations. In simpler terms, the Malabar Jews (English: "black Jews") are descendants of the earliest Jewish settlers; the *meyuchasim* (English: "white Jews") are descendants of Jewish settlers who arrived at a later time; and the *m'shuhararim* (English: "brown Jews") are the "underprivileged descendants of the manumitted offspring of unions between Cochin Jews and their slave concubines; they are also divided into two groups, one of which is attached to the white Jews and the other to the black Jews according to descent" (Strizower, 1962, pp. 100-01).

These endogamous divisions among the Cochin Jews are thus distinguishable both historically and genetically. The so-called "black Jews" (Malabar Jews) can be traced back to the earliest Jewish migrants who came to the shores of southwest India before the eighth century A.D. Mandelbaum hypothesizes that these earliest arrivals "made a number of converts to Judaism from among their slaves and servants.[9] . . . The colony was probably founded by stranded merchants and a few stray families who filtered through the barriers in the way of a passage to India . . . it is likely that with the passage of centuries, and with rare recruits from outside Jewry, the original Jewish stock became thoroughly mixed with that of the native converts" (Mandelbaum, 1939, pp. 446-47). Blood tests show, significantly, that the "black Jews" have blood which is very similar to that of the Hindu population of Kerala, whereas the blood of "white Jews" is quite different serologically (ibid., p. 446).

There are substantial reasons for believing that the "white Jews" or *meyuchasim* are descended from later arrivals to the settlement at Cochin. We know, for example, that the earliest Malabar Jewish group of any size was at Cranganore but that they were forced to leave that city because of Portuguese persecution and the natural destruction of harbor facilities by a monsoon flood. History also records the visit of a Jewish delegation from Amsterdam to Cochin headed by De Paiva, who enumerates twenty-five heads of families among the white Jews, only two of whom came from Cranganore. The rest were families known to have come from Europe or the Middle East in the sixteenth or seventeenth centuries. Like all descendants of migrants, the white Jews like to claim antiquity for their ancestors, but this event in the late seventeenth century contradicts their allegation. Strizower concludes, "Thus the White Jews' claim to the lineage of the Cranganore principality rests on only two families – both of which are no longer to be found in Cochin. Moreover, the White Jews' synagogue is still called the Paradesi, the *foreign* synagogue" (Strizower, 1962, p. 103).

For this and other reasons which cannot be outlined here, the strongest probability is that white Jews came from Mediterranean and northern European areas in the sixteenth century or later but held themselves aloof from the Malabar Jews already on the scene, refusing to intermarry with them. Consequently, the so-called white Jews retained a lighter complexion on the whole. This does not mean that they are white as a Caucasian would view them

---

9. Under normal conditions (that is, a fully developed community with a fairly well-balanced sex ratio), a Jewish group would have no need for proselytizing and would frown on its practice. Only in exceptional circumstances (like a serious deficiency of Jewish eligibles for marital partners) would conversion of outsiders be practiced, and even then in the case of potential mates only, as in the fourth alternative mentioned above.

today because, even in the seventeenth century, De Paiva reported back to his Amsterdam colleagues that the Jews of Cochin (ancestors of today's "white" Jews) had a color which "is brown, caused no doubt by the climate, for they are entirely separated from the Malibari (Jews) of rank because it is a great disgrace to intermarry with them. They do not eat of what the Malabari Jews kill, nor do they celebrate *minyan*[10] in their company. They allege that the Malabaries are sons of slaves. . . . But in all things the two observe the same rites and ceremonies" (quoted in Mandelbaum, 1939, p. 434).

The third group or the so-called brown Jews *(m'shuhararim)* are recognized by all as having a dual status, some subordinate to the white Jews and some to the black Jews, being descendants of slaves and servants of each Jewish "caste," respectively. It is assumed, of course, that such slaves and servants were all converts to the faith. But by the twentieth century, at least, the position of the *m'shuhararim* attached to the white Jews was clearly manifest to all, while the corresponding status of the black Jews' *m'shuhararim* was covert and nearly invisible.

From time immemorial the *m'shuhararim* attached to the white Jews were denied the right to sit on benches in the synagogue, have their marriages solemnized there, or be buried in their cemetery. These provisions were annulled after a Gandhilike demonstration, and all rights of participation were eventually granted even though intermarriage is still frowned on by custom (Strizower, 1962, pp. 112-13). However, the black Jews have apparently integrated their *m'shuhararim* so successfully that outsiders cannot single them out, though the black Jews themselves are quite aware of who they are (ibid., pp. 114-15). The extent to which endogamy separates the two groups is uncertain because it goes unmentioned. Since the number of black Jews far outnumbers the white, there must be more *m'shuhararim* belonging to the former than to the latter; nevertheless, they are not identifiable. Thus, in the census of 1931 there were 1451 Jews in Cochin, of which 144 were white Jews and 1307 black Jews. This would leave a remainder of only nineteen Jews (Mandelbaum, 1939, p. 451), which, coincidentally, was about the size of the *m'shuhararim* belonging to the white Jews. However, assuming that the nineteen belong there, what has happened to the enumeration of the *m'shuhararim* belonging to the black Jews? Have they simply disappeared? The answer is an unsatisfactory one: the Jewish community as a whole simply did not report on the *m'shuhararim* as a separate category, and so we are left with only conjecture. However, the matter is of little consequence today for the simple reason that the Cochin community is rapidly dwindling as the inhabitants migrate to Israel; by 1970 it is estimated that the total number of Jews in Cochin declined to 250 (Strizower, 1971, p. 5).

Among the Bene Israel of Bombay, there has been a semicaste division paralleling the distinctions in Cochin Jewry except that the historical chronology for each subgroup is reversed. In Bombay, too, there was a "white" group and a "black" group, which were called Gora and Kala, respectively. The Gora claim to be the pure descendants of the traditional seven couples shipwrecked on the

---

10. Probably this should read, "nor do they include them in a minyan of their own." Technically a minyan is a collection of ten Jewish males over thirteen years of age which is the minimal number of people necessary to establish a religious community and hold synagogue services (Dimont, 1962, p. 124).

Konkan coast centuries ago who were the original Bene Israel of India, while the Kala are known to be from a mixed lineage of Bene Israel men with non-Bene Israel women. In contrast with Cochin, where the "white" group is from a more recent set of arrivals, the "white" Bene Israel or Gora of Bombay are descended, or at least claim descent, from the very earliest settlers.[11] For a long time the Kala, as offspring of intermarriages, were assigned a lowly status which even took on overtones of ritual pollution in the Hindu mode, since there were injunctions against touching their utensils, interdining with them, or intermarriage with their members. Although they were permitted entry to the synagogue, Kala could not wear the Tallith or ritual garment, and they received the sanctified wine of the ceremony only after the Gora had been served. However, by the late nineteenth century, such inequalities in the synagogue were abolished — the precise manner of their demise apparently unknown. Some of the other restrictions took longer to die, but today all such open avoidances are regarded as inexcusable social errors. Only a few covert residual forms remain. As one Gora respondent told the visiting anthropologist, "We are all equal! But when it comes to marriage, most Gora don't like their children to marry Kala. Yet there have been some marriages between Gora and Kala in recent years. What to do? But don't mention that I discussed the subject with you!" (Strizower, 1971, p. 30).

Another contrast with Cochin is the fact that "white" Jews in that city are a tiny minority heavily outnumbered by "black" Jews, while in Bombay the so-called "white" Jews or Gora form the overwhelming majority of the Bene Israel. Stated otherwise, it is equally true to say that the descendants of earliest settlers predominate numerically in both Jewish communities and that the color designation "white" is erroneous in both cases. And the Gora themselves take the following position (in a sort of collective quote): "It is not skin colour which tells us who is Kala. It is known in the community who is Kala. There are some Gora who are a little dark — but not because of mixed unions! Poverty and the excessive heat of India greatly affected the fair complexion of our ancestors" (Strizower, 1971, p. 27). However, the fact that there is so little actual difference between the skin color of the two groups (both a decided brown with variations) has led Strizower to conclude, "It would seem, therefore, that Kala are the offspring of mixed unions which for some reason or other have been *remembered,* while unions between the ancestors of the Gora and non-Bene Israel have been *forgotten* — perhaps the ancestors of the Kala contracted unions with non-Bene Israel later than did those of the Gora [italics added]" (ibid., p. 28).

Later arrivals in Bombay, the Baghdadi Jews, have notably lighter complexions than the Bene Israel, and, from their first appearance, the Baghdadis kept the Bene Israel out of their synagogue and forbade intermarriage as well.[12]

---

11. It must be admitted that the "white" Jews of Cochin also claim the earliest ancestors there, but historians do not recognize this claim as valid.

12. Baghdadis, of course, deny that this ostracism was due to color consciousness but attribute it to failure of the Bene Israel to keep certain basic Jewish laws and adhere to them. Evidently, the Baghdadis were unable to convince Louis Rabinowitz who visited Bombay in 1952 and investigated the relations between the two divisions of Jewry, for he stresses skin color as a key factor in such exclusions (Strizower, 1971, p. 47).

Baghdadis found it to their advantage during the British period to identify themselves with the European element rather than with their darker coreligionists, the Bene Israel. With the coming of independence the situation changed drastically; although there was no complete reversal of roles, at least the prestige of lighter skin color no longer played a decisive part, but insulation of the two groups from each other is still the common pattern (Strizower, 1971, p. 47).

MARGINAL TRADING PEOPLES?

Over a generation ago, the late Howard Becker submitted a constructed type[13] defining a category of ethnic groups, as follows:

> The preliminary hypothesis may then be that a number of traits ordinarily regarded as specifically Jewish in the "racial" sense are not the result of biological transmission, but of a peculiar socio-cultural heritage. If the researcher turns first to the past in the quest for data, he may focus on the early contacts with the Phoenicians and other traders, as well as on the "caravaneering" facilitated by the surviving nomadic pattern. Next, perhaps, he may concentrate on the "middleman" locations characteristic of the Jews before as well as after the Diaspora; the ghettoes were splendidly placed for the development of extensive trade with many lands. Once more, he may direct his lens toward the dual ethic separating the members of the in-group from those of the out-group — on the one hand, the "chosen people"; on the other, the unclean Gentile . . . . Looking for like phenomena in nearby areas our investigator may then discover that the Armenians are strikingly similar to the Jews. . . . [Becker, 1940, p. 31]

Becker called these groups "the marginal trading peoples," exemplified by Jews, Armenians, Parsis, Greeks in Egypt, and Border Scots.[14] The purpose of this constructed type, as of others created in like fashion, is to enable the investigator to have an initially plausible guide for study of a people which reveals them not in their uniqueness but rather in their likeness to others similarly placed.

Are the Jews of India a marginal trading people? Any scrutiny of their history and development raises grave doubts about the imputation of this label. Significantly, Becker fails to note that the societies entered by Jews differ in the degree of their permeability. "The permeability of a group is the ease with which a person can become a participant" (Lasswell and Kaplan, 1950, p. 35). There are some societies in which the opportunities for newly arriving traders are open and flexible; others, however, have this occupational niche fairly well closed. It seems not only possible but probable that India, during the time of early Jewish migration, approximately near the middle of the first millenium A.D., was a classical caste society in which Vaisya status was protected by closure against those lacking the proper ancestry. It is true that coastal areas were partly exempt from such restrictions, since maritime trade brought in a number of foreigners.

---

13. One form of Max Weber's "ideal type." See Weber (1947, pp. 109-10).

14. On Becker's hypothesis many others could be added: Syrians and Lebanese in East Africa, Arabs on the Malabar coast, overseas Chinese in southeast Asia, et cetera.

But should these foreign elements attempt permanent settlement, vested interests would be more likely to protect those who already had strong proprietary interests. Leaving speculation aside, we know that in both Malabar and the Konkan, descendants of the earliest Jewish settlers have been reported in many other occupations besides that of merchant. Early in the eighteenth century, a Protestant chaplain visiting Cochin reported that the "black" Jews were engaged in a variety of occupations, mainly agriculture and cattle raising, though a few were selling products like butter and poultry (Mandelbaum, 1939, p. 435). Even had their ancestors been traders, there is no solid evidence that their descendants were also. There is some reason to believe that the ancestors of "white" Jews in Cochin were traders, but in the seventeenth century De Paiva, the emissary from Holland, reported that "the mercantile status of the Jews is no longer what it was." And in the latter half of the nineteenth century, the "white" Jews of Cochin suffered grave economic loss as the import trades were taken away from the traders that were left (ibid., pp. 434, 437).

In the Konkan area near Bombay, the first Bene Israel settlers may have been traders (there are no data to prove or disprove the point), but by the time there are confirmed historical reports of the Konkan Jewish community, a great many were in one of the lowliest occupations recognized by the Hindus, namely that of oil-pressing, while the rest were in agricultural pursuits with a sprinkling of carpenters (Strizower, 1971, pp. 22-23). In the rural areas then occupied by the Bene Israel, the great probability is that trading opportunities were rare and already appropriated by the Banias.

Openings for commerce and trade were more promising where foreign powers established hegemony over ports and coastal areas. The growth of Parsi enterprises following the arrival of the British in Bombay is a prime example. To a lesser extent, this theme with variations occurred among the Jews as well. While a few traders were apparently included in the first wave of settlers to Cochin, other occupations were represented also. With the coming of the Portuguese, it might be expected that new opportunities for trade would arise, but this possibility is ruled out by the fact that the Portuguese persecuted the Jews relentlessly (waves of the Inquisition had not yet receded), and it was not until the Dutch took over in 1663 that freedom for Jews opened the way for new mercantile enterprises. By 1723 it was reported that "white" Jews were chiefly traders connected with the Dutch company, while "black" Jews (the majority) continued in more rural pursuits (Mandelbaum, 1939, p. 435). Though the reasons for change were obscure, we are told that in the British period, particularly the last half of the nineteenth century, the "white" Jews of Cochin suffered economic loss as the import trades were taken away from them "and they earned a livelihood by collecting hides from the interior, making casks, and book-binding. The black Jews were then sawyers, carpenters, masons, produce merchants, and only a few of both classes were sufficiently well off to be money lenders" (ibid., p. 437).

In Maharashtra a somewhat similar pattern appeared. Although direct confirmation is unavailable, inferential evidence shows that it was only with the advent of the British to Bombay that the Jews established themselves as entrepreneurs. And it was not the Bene Israel who entered this category to any marked degree but rather the newly entering Baghdadis, who did not have the handicap of an already lowly position as Telis or oil-pressers on the caste scale. "For the Baghdadi community soon outstripped the Bene Israel in a number of ways. The leaders of the Baghdadi community pioneered in industry, providing employment for many thousands of people. They built museums and public libraries. They subsidized the religious, educational, and charitable services of their community. Moreover, Bene Israel relate, 'The Baghdadis shared the privileges of the Europeans in India' " (Strizower, 1971, p. 42).

Entrance into business and commerce occurred far less frequently among the Bene Israel, who also migrated to Bombay in British times, beginning in 1746. But the chances which they seized were not so much those of enterprise as of military and civil service. The heyday of Bene Israel enlistment in the Army was from 1750 to 1857, and after that time, being unable to furnish regiments of their own since their smaller numbers prevented it,[15] they turned their attention to such ancillary services as the medical corps, accounts, or service corps (B. J. Israel, personal communication). The garrison census at Aden in 1872 listed 1,435 Jews from India, the majority being Bene Israel with a smaller element of Baghdadis. The records showed that there were Bene Israel among "other service personnel such as military accounts clerks and draftsmen, sub-engineers, overseers and mistries of the Public Works Department, Commissariat and medical service employees and skilled artisans such as masons and carpenters who were recruited in Bombay on high wages" (Samuel, 1963, pp. 60-61). Most of the artisans were presumably civilians attached to the military. But they are a clue to the kind of occupations the Bene Israel were following in Bombay, where they were entering many of the same bureaucratic positions that opened up to the Anglo-Indians during that period — for instance, in the railways, customs, postal and telegraph services — positions which gave them security and a certain status (Strizower, 1971, p. 139).

Since independence, there is a widespread belief among the Bene Israel that most of their adult workers are employed as white collar workers in both private and public employment. Thus, they "tend to refer to themselves, and are frequently referred to by their Indian neighbors, as a clerk caste. Indeed, some Bene Israel who had heard that Jews elsewhere were frequently in businesses of their own exclaimed, 'How very strange! How very unlike Jews to go into business!' " (Strizower, 1971, p. 77). This stereotype of a community of clerks and office workers is, however, not substantiated by actual census figures. In 1961, Greater Bombay had a total Jewish population of 12,366, of whom the total workers were 3,765 (2,924 or 47 percent of the males, and 841 or 14 percent of the females). Thus, men below the age of retirement were almost fully employed, whereas a comparatively small proportion of women were employed. Enumeration by categories is given in Table 10.1. These figures show conclusively that the majority of the men in the work force were in blue collar occupations rather than in offices. "Most men are employed in factories and workshops (mainly as mechanics) followed by commercial employment (mainly clerical). Professional employment and the public services come lowest in the

---

15. As noted above in Chapter 6, the British eventually formed "class regiments," each homogeneously composed of members from the same caste or religious community.

TABLE 10.1

Occupational Distribution of the Jewish Work Force, Greater Bombay, 1961*

Occupation	Male	Female
Cultivation, agricultural labor, mining, quarrying, fisheries, etc.	4	1
Household industry	12	15
Manufacture other than household industry	1,210	195
Construction	58	7
Trade and commerce	780	80
Transport, storage, and communications	474	67
Other services	386	476

*Compiled from the 1961 census by B. J. Israel. I am indebted to Mr. Israel for this compilation and for extensive communication on the Jewish community.

scale in the general category 'Other Services' and in this category more women than men are employed. Presumably the category includes teachers and nurses as well as lawyers and doctors" (Israel, 1963, p. 22). The census does not distinguish between Baghdadis and Bene Israel; on the generally agreed supposition that the Baghdadis have a larger proportion of entrepreneurs (managers and proprietors) in the upper echelons, along with more than their share of professionals, this would reduce the number in "trade and commerce" among the Bene Israel to a lower figure than is shown by the census enumeration; it would also mean that their *percentage* of manufacturing employees is still higher than the table indicates. Their reputation as a "clerk caste," therefore, is not a function of their numbers, as popularly supposed. It will soon be shown that it is more a symbol of their influence.

If respondents are to be believed, the Baghdadis have more than their share in business and commerce, both in Bombay and in Calcutta. In Calcutta, the occupational distribution is reported to be unique, since a substantial percentage of the Baghdadis work for the same mammoth firm, B. N. Elias & Co. This might well mean that the number of white collar workers is at a high level, though there are no statistics available for proof. If, as is popularly supposed, the Baghdadis are more firmly established in higher commercial and business positions than are the Bene Israel, this is in large part a legacy from the special status the Baghdadis won for themselves by migrating to India under the British Raj.

Returning to Becker's thesis, we are forced to conclude that it is impossible to apply his category of "marginal trading people" to the Jews of India as a whole. Only a few "white" Jews of Cochin and a fairly large number of Baghdadis would qualify, with some scattered "black" Jews of Cochin and a tiny number of Bene Israel. The great majority, however, are not commerciants or traders, owing to historical circumstances that closed many such opportunities to them in India. The stereotype so often held of the typical Jew as a petty trader, trafficking with Gentiles in the continuous give and take of bargaining, is therefore irrelevant for Indian Jews as a whole. It simply does not fit.

RESIDENTIAL CONCENTRATION

Throughout their urban settlements in Cochin and Bombay, the Jews have tended to cluster in their own neighborhoods. One reason for this has doubtless been to remain within walking distance of a synagogue (Orthodox Jewish law forbids riding to a house of worship on holy days), but there are also other motives for flocking together — at least in Cochin. In Malabar, where Jews first lived in Cranganore and other coastal towns of that day, the Portuguese Inquisition became a threat to all Jews of the territory in Goa after 1560; they therefore moved to Cochin, where they were protected by the local Raja. Significantly, such a large number of Jews migrated to that city that the Raja was jokingly called "king of the Jews" by his local subjects. This ruler gave the Jewish refugees a piece of land next to his palace; this land has remained the Jewish quarter for four centuries. As reported in 1938, and confirmed by the present author in 1969, Jews still live in the one long, narrow street laid out for them in 1568, the lower end containing the Riverside (Kadavumbagham) synagogue of the "black" Jews, while in the upper part of the street, where the houses make a better appearance, live the "white" Jews who have their own synagogue, the Paradesi, in their sector. In between are houses of the lowly *m'shuhararim,* most of whom attach themselves to the "black" Jews at the lower reaches of the street (see Mandelbaum, 1939, pp. 430, 440).

In Bombay, where the same need to escape persecution did not exist, the clustering of Jews can probably be accounted for by the mixed motives of conformity to Jewish law and the demands of congeniality or prestige. The history of this process has not been documented as it was in Cochin, but respondents report that the great majority of Bene Israel are concentrated in the so-called Dongri area at a conjunction of Byculla, Nagpada, Mazgaon, and Umarkhadi, where a number of low-income Hindus and Muslims live. A smaller number have moved out to middle class and upper class neighborhoods, producing the approximate patterns given in Table 10.2. The "best residential areas" are chiefly Malabar Hill and Colaba. In addition to those who live in Bombay, there are a sizable number who live at the fringes of Greater Bombay in small clusters comprising the remainder of the minority community in the metropolitan area. Though detailed information of the same type is not available for Baghdadi Jews of Calcutta, reports from a community leader in 1969 state that there were only about 400 left at that time, the largest number of families living in adjacent areas near the center of the city.

UNIQUENESS OF BENE ISRAEL

In contrast to the Cochin Jews, the Bene Israel of Bombay have a curious deficiency in their background; their ancestors, so far as they can discover, lacked knowledge of the Pentateuch, the Talmud, traditional synagogue ritual familiar to Jews elsewhere, and even Hebrew. As compared with coreligionists in other lands, they were an unlettered group adhering to mere fragments of

TABLE 10.2

Residential Neighborhoods of the Jews in
Greater Bombay: Alternative Estimates*

Type of Neighborhood	1951 (estimate by Strizower)	1961 (estimate by Israel)	1970 (estimate by Israel)
Communal neighborhood	7,800	7,242	6,000
Areas similar to communal neighborhood	1,500	1,980	1,000
Middle class suburbs	900	2,291	1,500
Best residential areas	300	853	500
	10,500	12,366	9,000

*The Strizower figures are given in her volume (1971, p. 59), and I have added her totals of Bene Israel, Baghdadi, and European Jews to give the total for all Jews, which corresponds with the items in Israel's estimates. I have assigned Strizower's figures to the date 1951 because she made her study before the 1961 census was taken and would therefore have used the 1951 statistics as her baseline. B. J. Israel's figures were supplied in personal correspondence; those for 1961 are solidly based on the 1961 census, whereas those for 1970 are more conjectural (note allowance for emigration).

ancient Jewish practice: (1) observance of the Sabbath as a day of rest;[16] (2) keeping of a few Holy Days; (3) some dietary regulations; (4) circumcision; and (5) recitation of the Shema or confession of faith (Strizower, 1971, pp. 5, 13-14). Beyond these practices, they were unfamiliar with the rich legal and ceremonial elaborations that were an integral part of Judaism elsewhere.[17]

The origins of the Bene Israel are still obscure. Their own tradition has it that they are descended from members of the lost Ten Tribes of Israel who were shipwrecked on the Konkan coast before the beginning of the Christian era. Seven couples were supposed to have survived the shipwreck, and it is claimed that their offspring became the Bene Israel.[18] There are many other conjectures about the early Jewish migrations but none of them seems conclusive. Even though it is not necessary to accept the tradition that the first arrivals on the

---

16. Those who became oil-pressers were known to their Hindu neighbors as the *Shanwar Teli*, or Saturday oil-pressers, because they refused to carry out their duties on the seventh day or Sabbath.

17. They seem also to have failed to know or observe a number of marriage laws, which is an important reason Baghdadis have given for remaining separate from them (denying, of course, any race prejudice). This issue was raised again in Israel (Strizower, 1971, pp. 4, 47, 95-96, 167-68).

18. The original migration would thus have been over 2,000 years ago, possibly at the time of Diaspora 3 (see above). Most historians are doubtful about this. Also, the story of the shipwreck is so similar to a Purana myth of earlier times (referring also to the Konkan coast) that the coincidence needs a good deal of explanation (Strizower, 1971, Chap. 2; Israel, 1963, p. 4).

Konkan coast came before the Christian era, it is quite possible that these early Jewish migrants predated the development of Sephardic ritual, the latter being coterminous with the Moorish golden age (eleventh century A.D.). Whoever they were and whatever may have been their origin, it is clear that they were effectively isolated from the rest of Jewry for a considerable period. After their arrival in India, this seclusion continued until the eighteenth century, when a visitor from Cochin Jewry, David Ezekiel Rahabi,[19] took it upon himself to teach and instruct a number of the Bene Israel in the fundamentals of Jewish observance. He was the first of a succession of teachers from Cochin who influenced the people to organize their religious life into the more ritualistic forms familiar to Jews elsewhere. By 1796 "the centre of Bene Israel religious life shifted to Bombay City with the establishment of the synagogue. . . (though) effective control remained with the lay leaders of the community in the absence of a rabbinate" (Israel, 1963, p. 8).

Although from this time on the Bene Israel drew closer to the mainstream of Jewish life, they nevertheless remained unique in a number of respects. Quite unlike Jews of other communities, they lacked a tradition of Jewish learning, there were no hereditary priests in the community, they did not practice the Bar Mitzvah or confirmation of the Jewish male, nor did they observe the usual custom of avoiding travel on the Sabbath; not all practiced the dietary regulations, and those working outside the home did not hesitate to practice occupations that required them to work on the Sabbath (Strizower, 1971, pp. 116, 124, 125, 164).[20]

ACCULTURATION

The Cochin Jews and the Bene Israel who have lived in India for hundreds of years have adopted Indian languages, customs, diet, and dress, not indiscriminately but selectively. In Cochin the Jews have adopted Malayalam as their mother tongue and practice many caste customs among themselves with the "white" Jews excluding "black" Jews from their synagogue and the "black" Jews retaliating in kind. Endogamy is strictly enforced within each group [Mandelbaum (1970, p. 491) boldly calls them "jatis"], and "blacks" as well as "whites" have prevented marriage with their own *m'shurararim*. Most adult Jews in Cochin eat opium and chew betel; the orthodox diet regulation which prohibits the mixing of milk and meat dishes has come to mean that meat curries

---

19. An old Bene Israel tradition refers to another David Rahabi who came to the Konkan nine hundred years ago, taught the people Hebrew prayers, and appointed three young men to supervise Jewish ritual. The descendants of these men became known as Kazis (judges). The historicity of this tradition is doubtful. B.J. Israel suggests that the name of the eighteenth century teacher from Cochin may have been assigned later to the legendary one and that the term "Kazi" was probably borrowed from the Muslims among whom the Bene Israel lived for some time (Israel, 1963, pp. 2-3).

20. Bene Israel also relied more than most Jews on their own individual reading of the Old Testament for personal interpretation, a heritage from Christian missionaries in Bombay who translated the Bible into Marathi and had many close ties with the local Jewish community (Israel, 1963, pp. 10-11).

are not to be mixed with milk curries (Mandelbaum, 1939, pp. 425-26, 430ff., 437, 452, 424). Indian dress, too, is worn, though more commonly by women than men.

Similar elements appear among the Bene Israel. They claim Marathi as their mother tongue in Bombay, though a few in the country districts speak Gujerati. And since the Bene Israel lived under the rule of the Marathis and the Muslim Sidi of the old Janjira state, Hindu and Muslim influences have both left their imprint on the community. It is possible that the name "Bene Israel" itself is indirectly a reflection of Muslim bias against the term Jew (Yehudi) and the attempt under Muslim rule to adopt a name less offensive to the dominant group at the time. It is significant that no other Jews made a similar change in their official name.[21] Perhaps the term Kaji is really of Muslim origin, as already noted. B. J. Israel writes, "The Konkan Muslims have Kajis and also use the word as a surname. Our synagogues are 'Masjids' not 'Mandirs'. . . . Our Fast is a 'Roza' not an 'Upavas' and we used Muslim rather than Hindu kinship terms" (personal correspondence). He also asserts that Muslim customs were adopted more frequently by the Bene Israel than were the Hindu, mentioning the adoption of Muslim laws of inheritance, some marriage and funeral customs, and the cult of the prophet Elijah as harbinger of the Messiah, an apparent imitation of the cults of Muslim saints (Israel, 1963, pp. 5, 6).

Hindu cultural influences are strongly marked as well. As already mentioned above, the Bene Israel have a varied set of caste practices. Before arriving in Bombay they were designated by the caste name Shanwar Teli, and their own internal division between Gora and Kala has been, in the past, a castelike separation with mutual avoidance and endogamy, though the lines are less sharp in recent years. Their interrelationship is outlined as follows:

> Nevertheless, Gora and Kala cannot legitimately be considered to have formed a fully fledged caste system. Relations between them were not conceived of as preordained or even as necessary. There was no interdependence. Certainly Gora did not need the services of Kala. True, Kala worshipped in the synagogue of the Gora; but had they desired it, Kala could have established their own place of worship – as the underprivileged Meshuhararim once did in Cochin. Gora and Kala come closest to the subcaste pattern; coexisting but not complementary to one another. [Strizower, 1971, p. 30]

The Bene Israel have also taken on a few patterns of conduct that are characteristic of higher Hindu castes, such as prohibition of beef eating and strong disapproval of widow remarriage. So ingrained is the latter injunction that one Bene Israel informant declared, ". . . we know that widow remarriage is not prohibited in the Bible. . . . But don't you think that the Hindu attitude to widow remarriage goes one better than the Bible? . . . . And is not this a good thing?" (Strizower, 1971, p. 26). Residual features of the joint household continue, with one married son remaining in the parental home. Apparently this

---

21. Such, at any rate, is the suggestion made by H.S. Kehimkar (nineteenth century), often regarded by members of the community as the semi-official historian of their group (Strizower, 1971, p. 18, notes 5 and 6).

son is more likely to be the youngest, as the custom is practiced today. The matter of arranged marriages, so common in the community, is not specifically Indian, however, but a feature of Jewish marriages traditionally practiced elsewhere. Though women of the Bene Israel probably receive somewhat more education than Hindu and Muslim women, their status is guarded and segregated in the fashion common to other Indian communities. "It would never do for Bene Israel girls to roam about as freely as do the boys – and most certainly not in the company of boys. Bene Israel say that girls found lingering about in the company of boys and chatting freely with them would damage their reputation beyond repair – 'And who would offer for them then?' . . . . For girls are expected to help their mothers in the home; and as they marry early – in their late teens – they are very soon occupied with their own household affairs" (ibid., p. 149).

India has left another significant mark, though more strikingly on the Bene Israel than on Cochin Jews. Long residence of the Bene Israel in rural areas, isolated from their fellow Jews and from the cosmopolitan currents flowing through the cities, fixed their occupations in the lower range throughout the back districts and in no more than intermediate position in Bombay; it was thus unnecessary for more than a few especially ambitious men to have higher education, and the synagogues themselves had no rabbis. Unlike many Jewish communities abroad where there is a distinctive elite devoting itself solely to the advancement of Jewish learning (Torah, Talmud, and the traditions), there is no such group of scholars among the Bene Israel; in this respect, "their status system is a replica in miniature of what exists in the wider world, lacking the complexity peculiar to the status system of many other Jewish communities" (Strizower, 1971, p. 164). Conditions differ in Cochin, however. There the "black" Jews have more men learned in the Talmud than is true of the "white" Jews, and it is "black" Jews who are frequently used as officiants among the Bene Israel of Bombay (Mandelbaum, 1939, p. 442). It is not certain, however, that such learned men form a recognizable elite even though they receive high esteem and respect from their fellow Jews.

ORGANIZATIONS AND ASSOCIATIONS

Outside the synagogues there is little evidence that the Jews of Cochin have a flourishing associational life. No other institution appears to be needed, especially when the number of adherents is so small. For the Jews of that city, the synagogue "is an all-encompassing shelter and it is a psychic balance wheel," integrating the group (Mandelbaum, 1939, p. 453). In Bombay, however, the situation differs markedly. Because of larger numbers and the diverse demands of an urban milieu, the Bene Israel have a luxuriant growth of organizations expressing a wide variety of interests and values. These may be conveniently classified into four types: religious, educational, philanthropic, and sociable.

In the 1970s, the Bene Israel had four synagogues and three prayer halls in Bombay, while the Baghdadis had two synagogues of their own. [Prayer halls are one or two rooms rented for purposes of worship, whereas synagogues occupy entire buildings for the same purpose (Strizower, 1971, pp. 109-10).]

The Bene Israel also maintain the Israelite School (formerly known as the Sir Elly Kadoorie School) with instruction in Marathi, substituting Hebrew for Sanskrit and preparing students through the secondary level. In the 1970s, this school was on the decline, losing enrollment and constantly in debt (B. J. Israel, in foreword to Strizower, 1971, p. x; Strizower, 1971, 1971, p. 137).

Three philanthropic ventures deserve mention. First is the Bene Israel Home for Destitutes and Orphans, established to keep potential beggars off the street; at last report, the institution's inmates had dwindled in number to twenty orphans and six adults, the adults doing the maintenance work (Strizower, 1971, p. 140; B. J. Israel, personal correspondence). The second is the Stree Mandal, a women's association conducting a needlework class for orphans in the Home and occasionally organizing meetings "where the educated women would lecture the less-educated ones" (Strizower, 1971, p. 142). Third is the Jewish Cooperative Credit Society which, after an initial burst of activity, gradually lost favor and eventually applied to the Registrar of Cooperative Societies for its own dissolution (B. J. Israel, personal correspondence).

Not so easy to categorize are the sociable clubs like the Israelite School Maccabean Fellowship of 250 members which arranges recreational and ceremonial festivities for the entire Bene Israel community, and the Zionist meetings under the aegis of a Jewish-agency-subsidized teacher who encourages the study of Hebrew while publicizing the achievements and prospects of Israel for settlement. It is worth noting that Zionist activities are practically the only ones in which Bene Israel and Baghdadis cooperate, though at times the two groups separate even here (Strizower, 1971, p. 153).

The organization of the Bene Israel in a certain respect is quite unlike that of Jewish minorities elsewhere. In Jewish communities outside of India, it is the affluent and highly educated element (particularly professionals) who have constituted an elite leading the way while others followed. Such is not the case among the Bene Israel, for among them − in all their communal organizations, particularly within the synagogues − business executives and professionals are not elected to office and lack the status of official leadership. "For there is a certain antagonism between the university-educated Bene Israel and the clerks as well as a recognition that the former are much too preoccupied with secular affairs to give sufficient time and energy to the business of the synagogues. Nowadays, then, it is the clerk element which is in charge of the synagogues − and therefore of much of communal life. . . . Thus it is the rank and file[22] which controls not only the synagogue but also the home for orphans and destitute, the great part of the offices of the school and the cooperative society" (Strizower, 1971, pp. 118, 130). The dominant leaders, therefore, come from the stratum sociologically identifiable as the lower middle class. In terms of social values, two illustrations will bring out the implications of this relationship in the group, one revealing who is looked down on, the other who is looked up

---

22. It appears to be an exaggeration to call the clerks "the rank and file" when they are far less numerous than industrial workers at the factory level, as noted above. Strizower neglects any discussion of the latter group. It may be that the clerks have assumed positions of leadership partly in view of their higher prestige vis-à-vis the blue-collar operatives below them in the occupational scale.

to. Beginning with the first, a characteristic term for those of low degree among the Bene Israel is "carpenters." This may be a throwback to the period when the community migrated from rural areas to Bombay with some attaining white collar positions while others remained at the level of menial workers. By looking down on "carpenters," those in the clerk category could simultaneously emphasize their Westernized middle-class orientation and the typical Indian upper caste disdain for manual work. But whatever the reason, "Bene Israel tend to brand those of whom they disapprove as 'carpenters' – uneducated, unsuccessful, noisy and quarrelsome" (ibid., p. 156).

Conversely, the clerks explicitly look up to the wealthier and more successful business or professional men even while excluding them from leadership positions in voluntary organizations. Thus, on the occasion of a celebration for the opening of the new holiday home in the country, a good many prosperous Bene Israel stayed in hotels and did not mingle with the crowd or eat with them but simply attended the formal opening ceremony. However, when the wealthy men and their wives appeared, members apparently from the clerk status in the assembled crowd spoke to Schifra Strizower and, as the latter reported, they "drew my attention to the personality and position of those who had achieved the status of a career: 'Notice their refinement! Observe their beautiful manners!' . . . . They certainly did not seem to feel equal with those whose education and attainments involved them in a different world" (Strizower, 1971, p. 157). Quite possibly, those making such comments were women, since their confinement to the domestic scene distinguished them from their husbands who had more opportunity to observe such upper status persons through contacts in business or the bureaucracies. The deference expressed, however, was probably not confined to one sex.

As for the Baghdadis, during the early 1970s they had two synagogues in Bombay and four in Calcutta, all of them orthodox; in Calcutta an elected management committee called the Manhigim administered the Maghem Synagogue (*Order of Service,* 1960). The structure in Calcutta has been called "the largest synagogue in the East." Baghdadis have one school in Bombay and two in Calcutta (one for boys and one for girls), all of them English medium; the one in Bombay has a headmaster and part of the teaching staff taken from the Bene Israel community (Strizower, 1971, p. 69). It is a fair inference that the clustering in business and professional occupations more characteristic of the Baghdadi group precludes their entrance into the ill-paid ranks of primary and secondary school teachers. Teachers are more on the clerk level where the Bene Israel "belong." In Calcutta, where the author was unable to obtain complete data, the girls' school had an Indian non-Jewish principal and, like many of the English-medium schools under Christian auspices, had far more students from outside the minority community than from within (there were two hundred non-Jews to thirty Jews). However, this was in 1969 when the exodus of Calcutta Jews to Israel had already decimated the community. The associational life of the Baghdadis in Bombay and Calcutta has not been studied, but since the group was far inferior in numbers to Bene Israel, there was much less opportunity to organize; furthermore, the constant traffic with other communities in the wider world of trade and industry encouraged membership in such noncommunal business organizations as Rotary International and Lions for some Baghdadis. As already mentioned, wealthier members were noted for their charitable works; best known was David Sassoon who arrived in Bombay during the early years of the nineteenth century (Japheth, 1966, p. 3) and who founded the famous Library and Reading Room which bears his name in the 1840s.[23] There is definite need for more thorough research on the Baghdadi group, who came to India not only from Baghdad, the capital of Iraq, but also from Aden, Afghanistan, and Iran. It should be mentioned parenthetically that there are special occasions on which the Bene Israel call in priests from the Baghdadi community to perform ceremonies such as the "Redemption of the First-Born Son" or the "Blessing of the Priest" on the High Holy Days (Strizower, 1971, pp. 79, 67-68).

INTEGRATION INTO INDIAN SOCIETY

Both the Cochin Jews and the Bene Israel adopted a policy of live and let live with their Indian neighbors. Whether this attitude is cause or effect of the notable Hindu tolerance of Jewish freedom in India is hard to say. In Cochin, almost from the first, Hindu rulers found the Jews worthy persons and accorded them special privileges. And while the Bene Israel of the Konkan were not so highly favored, they nevertheless found a comfortable niche in the occupational system, as they did later in Bombay. Eventually taking a semicaste status in the larger society, they have been integrated in the cultural pluralist pattern they have preferred in so many other societies.

I interpret this to mean that the dominant elite of India — the caste Hindus — find the presence of the Jews acceptable when the latter maintain a cultural autonomy that resembles the familiar caste pattern of Indian society. Similarly, the Jews' preference for religious and cultural separateness (with preferential acculturation) encounters no serious opposition from the Hindus. The fact that they do not fear persecution and are on familiar terms with their neighbors is evidence of the congruent reciprocity of views that defines their position. "They have no fear for their communal survival, nor do they feel the need to justify their community's existence. And it may well be that it is this factor which accounts for the comparative equanimity with which they face the failures of many of their communal undertakings" (Strizower, 1971, p. 165).

A curious manifestation of this posture, but a quite understandable one, is the political stance of the Jews. In this respect they act much like the Christians (and some of the Parsis) by showing a definitely limited interest in political activity and voting Congress as a way of staying on the safe side. This point of view, marked among the Bene Israel, has its roots in an earlier historical decision. In 1917, interested members of the community convened a communal assembly bearing the name of the Bene Israel Conference. During this meeting, those in attendance split over the issue of including "politics" in their deliberations. Forces opting for nonpolitical discussions won the vote of the assembly; in protest, the opposing members withdrew and formed a rival organization calling

---

23. A Sassoon family also appears in Calcutta, represented on the Board of Management of the Maghen David Synagogue. (See *Order of Service*, 1960, pp. 14, 15.)

itself the All-India Israelite League. At its meeting in Karachi in 1918, the League delegated eight members to present an address to Mr. Edwin Samuel Montagu, Secretary of State for India, supporting the scheme for reform proposed by the Indian National Congress and the All-India Muslim League while opposing separate electorates for any community except the Muslims. This address received wide publicity, but there is reason to believe that it stimulated the Bene Israel Conference, in opposition, to send a secret message to British authorities, saying that the address sent them by the Israelite League did not represent the true wishes of the Jewish community. At any rate, the Bene Israel Conference, dominant in numbers, espoused a policy of neutrality on such political issues, and this became the stance of the community as a whole. Significantly enough, such neutrality amounted in effect to support for the British who could wish for nothing better than neutrality at the time. "Not to make political demands was to support the status quo and, in fact, the Bene Israel remained loyalists till 1947 and they genuinely regretted the departure of the British" (B. J. Israel, personal communication).

This factional split in 1917-18 was fateful for the Bene Israel. "It is said that it was the unseemly manoeuvres and counter-manoeuvres of the educated members of the community on the platforms of the Bene Israel Conference and the All-India Israelite League which deprived them of the trust of the rank and file. Unable to believe any longer in the purity of motives of the educated section, the rank and file decided to take over communal control" (Strizower, 1971, p. 130). It is significant that, from the time when the clerk section gained the power of decision in the community, we hear no political pronouncements from them. Part of this may be due to the covert leanings toward the British which were best kept out of sight after independence. Part was the conclusion that *no* public stand on political questions might be definitely preferable to *divided counsels* (with the washing of community linen in public). There is also a touch of cynicism involved for, as Strizower observes, "I did not get the impression that informants were merely careful in their political utterances, but rather that they held that politics are the concern of the educated and wealthy; others involved in the strenuous struggle for economic survival as they are had best leave politics alone" (ibid., p. 73).

Thus, informants from the Bene Israel (and some from the Baghdadis as well) assured me that the Jews of India have little to do with politics and hint that this lack of involvement is simply a way of remaining as inconspicuous as possible. There are times, of course, when the indiscernible become discernible, as when an outstanding Jew attains national prominence: when a Bene Israel like Dr. E. Moses becomes Mayor of Bombay (1937-38) or when a Baghdadi like Major General J. Jacob becomes Chief of Staff to the Commanding Officer of the Eastern Command. No publicity machinery bruits such items to the world, and it is quite likely that the majority of Jews prefer it that way. With the caste and communal rivalries that so often dominate the political scene, the Jews have opted out instead of playing the game of coalition. In view of their diminutive electorate, this choice is quite inevitable. Thus, when the Shiv Sena shuts down the city of Bombay, the Jews remain inconspicuous, along with the Parsis and the Christians who, after all, consider themselves powerless before the juggernaut of massive coercion on behalf of Maharashtrian job monopolies. Though in other respects the Bene Israel identify themselves with the Maharashtrians, they are secretly offended by a forced uniformity that threatens any minorities whatsoever. There is doubtless a fear that a mass movement like the Shiv Sena might crystallize around a preference for Maharashtrian *Hindus,* which would then deny to the Bene Israel their native status.

A VANISHING MINORITY

A final assessment must emphasize, however, that emigration is depleting the ranks of Jews in India, no matter what city or subcommunity is considered. Since the formation of the state of Israel, a drive to join coreligionists in Palestine has taken on cumulative force. The process has not been all-inclusive, however, but selective. As might be expected, young adults have led the procession, having fewer vested interests to protect; those who remain are, on the whole, older and more settled. In Cochin it has been the "black" Jews who migrated first, and nearly all of them have already gone; as for the "white" Jews, they have delayed their decision longer, but apparently more of them contemplate migration to Canada and Australia instead of to Israel (Strizower, 1971, p. 81, n. 12). Cochin Jewry has practically disappeared. Even as early as 1962, it was reported that 95 percent of their population had already emigrated (Strizower, 1962, p. 124). As late as 1970 it was estimated that the number of white Jews who remained in the city (many too old to migrate) had dwindled to 90 (Strizower, 1971, p. 81, n. 12). In Bombay the Bene Israel air the grievance that it is much easier for the Baghdadis to be admitted to Israel than for the Bene Israel (ibid., p. 81, n. 13). There appears to be some basis for this charge since the chief Rabbi of Israel, after some importuning, announced that he was having the background of the Bene Israel investigated to see whether they were fit marriage partners, that is, were "pure" Jews or not.[24] It was only the Bene Israel who had to be singled out by being investigated "as far back as possible." This attitude provoked indignation and bitterness among the Bene Israel. Some already in Israel asked to be repatriated, and a few actually went back to India in the early 1950s[25] (Strizower, 1966, pp. 124-26, 141-43). Eventually, however, the Israelis treated the Bene Israel on equal terms with all other Jews (Strizower, 1971, p. 167), just as they had with Yemenites and all other "Oriental" Jews whose skins were somewhat darker than those of the Ashkenazim (at least this became official policy). Jews from Bombay encountered some practical difficulties: the Bene Israel white-collar workers, for instance, were placed on Kibbutzim where they found the adjustment to agricultural labor created severe hardships for those accustomed to office work indoors. Many left the rural cooperatives for Beer Sheba, where they made up a new enclave of their own. In

---

24. The fact that Baghdadis had made these charges before Striozwer, 1971, pp. 44-45) led to the suspicion that it was they who alerted the Chief Rabbi of Israel to the problem.

25. Why were no such questions raised about the black Jews of Cochin? We do not know, but questions about their authentic status as Jews were raised as early as the sixteenth century and eventually their bona fide position was legitimated. This process was repeated in the nineteenth century (Mandelbaum, 1939, pp. 431-32).

a way they were both more Westernized (particularly those who spoke English) and at the same time more Oriental (speaking Marathi) than the acculturated Israelis. They were also, significantly, the only Jewish group in Israel who had never experienced persecution or discrimination (Strizower, 1966, pp. 134-35).

Why do they leave India? What accounts for the steady drain to Israel? One factor appears to be a "decline of confidence" in the ability of Jews to compete for economic positions in the urban economy without the aid of family or caste to support their chances. Another is acceptance of Zionist ideology, which tells them that their first loyalty should now be to Israel. Also, "They expect that Israel will prove as indulgent a parent as the India of British days" (Strizower, 1971, p. 167). Those deciding to migrate receive the kind of financial assistance from the Jewish Agency that makes their journey possible (ibid., p. 72). Many freely predict that in ten to twenty years there will be no Jewish minority in India. As the process snowballs, a new motive is added: to join the relatives and friends who have already preceded them. And so the perpetual wanderings that brought the Jews to India many centuries ago are now repeating themselves in the expectant hope that this time the journey will lead to a permanent home.

BIBLIOGRAPHY

Becker, Howard, "Constructive Typology in the Social Sciences," in *Contemporary Social Theory,* edited by Harry Elmer Barnes, Howard Becker, and Frances Bennett Becker, New York, D. Appleton-Century Co., 1940.

Dimont, Max I., *Jews, God and History,* New York, Simon & Schuster, 1962.

Fischel, Walter J., "The Exploration of the Jewish Antiquities of Cochin on the Malabar Coast," *Journal of the American Oriental Society* 87 (No. 3, Sept. 15, 1967), 230-48.

Israel, Benjamin J., *Religious Evolution Among the Bene Israel of India Since 1750,* Bombay, 1963.

Japheth, M. D., *The Jews of India, a Brief Survey,* Bombay, 1966.

Lasswell, Harold D., and Abraham Kaplan, *Power and Society, A Framework for Political Inquiry,* New Haven, Yale University Press, 1950.

Mandelbaum, David G., "The Jewish Way of Life in Cochin," *Jewish Social Studies* 1 (October 1939), 423-60.

Mandelbaum, David G., *Society in India,* vol. 2, Berkeley, University of California Press, 1970.

Moore, George Foot, *History of Religions,* vol. 2, New York, Charles Scribner's Sons, 1932.

Order of Service held on February 7, 1960, on the occasion of the Seventy-Fifth Anniversary Celebration of the Dedication of the Maghen David Synagogue, Calcutta.

Roth, Cecil, *A Short History of the Jewish People,* new rev. ed., enlarged, London, East and West Library, 1969.

Samuel, Shellim, *A Treatise on the Origin and Early History of the Beni-Israel of Maharashtra State,* Bombay, 1963.

Sklare, Marshall, *Conservative Judaism,* Glencoe, Free Press, 1955.

Strizower, Schifra, *Exotic Jewish Communities,* London, Thomas Yoseloff, 1962.

Strizower, Schifra, "The Bene Israel in Israel," *Middle Eastern Studies* 2 (January 1966), 123-43.

Strizower, Schifra, *The Bene Israel of Bombay,* New York, Schocken Books, 1971.

Weber, Max, *The Theory of Social and Economic Organization,* translated by A. M. Henderson and Talcott Parsons, Glencoe, Free Press and Falcon's Wing Press, 1947.

Chapter 11

Parsis:
Asian Puritans In Transition

Unlike the stereotyped image of a minority, the Parsis are neither the objects of visible discrimination nor notably subservient; they are near the top of the status scale, commanding esteem from both high and low.

In terms of sheer numbers, they seem inconsequential. The 1971 census gives their total for all of India as only 91,266. They are almost entirely urban dwellers and, unlike the Anglo-Indians who are more widely scattered, they are concentrated chiefly in two states, Maharashtra and Gujarat (the former Bombay State). The Parsi population of Maharashtra is 72,266 and that of Gujarat 15,131. Females predominate over males in both states in contrast to other minorities throughout India, which show a surplus of males.[1] There are dispersed pockets of Parsis in other Indian cities, some even with their own fire temples, but a list of such cities is not available.

Greater Bombay has the highest urban concentration of the community with over 90 percent of the Parsis living in Maharashtra; of these, again, females had a slightly higher proportion. Outside of India the largest number of Zoroastrians is in Iran, with 26,000 in 1971.[2] The next largest group appears in Pakistan with 5,412. Other scattered remnants include 1,000 or more in each of the following areas: Africa, North America, and Europe (Desai, 1964, pp. 18, 24).[3]

Before their migration to Bombay following British colonial penetration, the overwhelming majority of Parsis in India occupied rural areas of what is now Gujarat, and for most intents and purposes it is fairly accurate to say that

1. Census of India 1971, Series 1, Paper 2 of 1972, Religion, Section II, Introductory Note, and Union Table CVII, Religion, Appendix, p. 32.

2. According to Mr. Fariborz Nassimil, Secretary of the Anjuman in Teheran (Nov. 27, 1971). Information kindly furnished by Dr. Ketayun Gould, personal correspondence.

3. The author is greatly indebted to Mr. S.F. Desai for making available his demographic studies and other important documentation for the Parsi community.

Gujarati is their mother tongue, although a high percentage speak English or are bilingual. Literacy in the Bombay constituency reaches 90 percent, with the females leading the males by a fraction of 1 percent (Desai, 1964, p. 28). No other minority in India displays female ascendancy of this sort; the status of women is unusually high in Parsi social life. Although occupational statistics are lacking for the contemporary period, it seems safe to say that the middle classes are overrepresented, with a fairly large number of white-collar office personnel, professionals, and executives. However, as we shall see, this situation needs to be placed in proper perspective.

According to the framework outlined in Chapter 1 above, it is important to remember that the Parsi minority in India came into existence through the channel of our fourth sequence, migration, and to emphasize equally the fact that their migration took place as early as the eighth century A.D. At that time a small band of devotees from Iran were sufficiently loyal to their faith to leave their homeland where, had they remained, severe persecution and forced conversion would have been their lot. The bond that held these pilgrims together was faith in Ahura Mazda, the god of their fathers revealed through the words of Zoroaster, a zealous prophet to the ancient Iranians.

ZOROASTRIAN RELIGION

The Iranians and Indo-Aryans originally lived in the same area of central Asia just north of the Hindu Kush mountains, and philologists have found many linguistic links between them. For example, in religious terminology, the Mithra of the Iranians is the Mitra of the Vedas. The juice of a plant used in ritual ceremonies has the same name in both cultures: Soma or Haoma. Priests who tend the sacred fire are called Athravan in Persian and Atharvan in old Sanskrit. As the peoples of that area migrated southward into what is now India, they transformed the religion of nature deities into a more metaphysical and speculative form; for other peoples of the same strain who migrated westward into the Persian steppes and beyond, religion took a more practical and ethical turn. Zoroaster was the pioneer in this latter change. He can best be understood as a prophet with a fourfold mission: to combat the old nature religion, to oppose the corrupt popular religion currently replacing it, to support and strengthen agricultural practices in their struggle against invasions by the nomads, and to espouse the demands of an ethical deity whose requirements for individual conduct were stringent. The first mission, attacking nature religion, was accomplished by identifying the traditional Indo-Iranian gods with devils or daevas (as happened to Indra and Nasatya, for example). Secondly, Zoroaster's attack on popular religion consisted of denouncing the priests, necromancers, and magicians who attached themselves to princely rulers and used their wiles to justify evil deeds of their masters and the judges who served them. The third mandate was deeply rooted in the attempt to make his people establish gardens and fruitful fields even in wastelands or desert country by hard, unremitting toil. In the struggle to maintain the agricultural villages of the Mazdeans against the nomadic Turanians who constantly attacked, Zoroaster saw the conflict of deities in which Ahura Mazda would triumph as the prime mover of civilizing forces. Finally, he regarded Ahura Mazda as the source of order (Asha) in the world, the foe of every evil, and the power making for righteousness among men. The meaning of life was interpreted as the constant warfare against evil by means of good thoughts, good words, and good deeds, a conflict in which Ahura Mazda was continually overcoming the destructive deeds of Ahriman, prince of darkness, as man could overcome the sins of injustice, corruption, cruelty, and lies by obedience to the supreme lord. For Zoroaster, his message appeared as a personal revelation, demanding for himself and others a path of ethical commitment by accepting the way of truth and goodness and Ahura Mazda as the supreme source of that demand.[4]

This clarion call fell at first on deaf ears. It was ten years before Zoroaster found his first convert, that being, ironically, his first cousin. Later, by sheer persistence, he finally made a break-through in Bactria where he converted King Vishtaspa; from this ruler and his royal court, the message of the new religion spread to Media and the rest of Persia. Reliable accounts of detailed religious growth after the death of Zoroaster are hard to come by. One authority observes, "How generally Zoroastrianism was the religion of the Iranian peoples before the rise of the Persian empire,[5] there is no means of determining; only about Media have we testimony that it was the dominant, if not the exclusive, religion of the country, whose priests, the Magi, were a powerful hereditary class" (Moore, 1925, p. 372).

It appears likely that the task of preserving the Zoroastrian religion was then taken over by priests who, as they did in the Judaic faith, immobilized and transfixed the flaming words of the prophet by converting them into a set of rules and ceremonies. As Max Weber put it, years ago, "The bearers of charisma, the oracles of prophets, or the edicts of charismatic war lords alone could integrate 'new' laws into the circle of what was upheld by tradition. Just as revelation and the sword were the two extraordinary powers, so were they the two typical innovators. In typical fashion, however, both succumbed to routinization as soon as their work was done" (Weber, 1946, p. 297). The Gathas themselves do not contain any instructions for worship since, for Zoroaster, worship was a spontaneous act (Moore, 1925, p. 370). Later priests, however, could not leave public prayer to chance but promoted ordinances to regulate the acts of devotion.

It was not only the priesthood, however, but the eventful course of many Persian dynasties — Achaemenian, Parthian, and Sasanian — which gave a

---

4. This deceptively brief statement of Zoroaster's original message as reflected in the only words we have from him directly (in the Gathas) is synthesized from the works of several scholars, such as G.F. Moore, 1925; A.V.W. Jackson, 1901 and 1928; M.N. Dhalla, 1938; D.F. Karaka, 1884; and S.K.H. Katrak, 1965. The major collection of sacred Zoroastrian writings is the Avesta in four parts: (1) the Yasna, including five Gathas; (2) the Visparad, containing invocations; (3) the Vendidad (sanitary and moral laws); and (4) the Khordah-Avesta (laudations). Many other books in the canon have been lost or destroyed.

5. Probably this refers to the rule of Cyrus the Great in the sixth century B.C. The fact that Zoroastrianism was so firmly and widely established by that time has led many scholars to place Zoroaster's date much earlier. A favorite date is near 1,000 B.C. (Dhalla, 1938, p. xxxi), though others place it as late as 660-583 B.C. on the basis of different evidence (Jackson, 1928, pp. 17-18). The actual period of the prophet's lifetime is still a moot point.

continually changing coloration to the Zoroastrian faith. Details must be omitted here, but four salient trends of religious development need emphasis to bring out the lifeways of Parsis who migrated to India: (1) the movement toward national identity; (2) enlargement of the supernatural realm; (3) drift toward priestly hierarchy and authority; and (4) prominence of distinctive rituals that highlight uniqueness of the faith.

In ancient Iran, as in the rest of the contemporary world, the fate of a people was bound up with the destiny of the ruler. Hence, when Zoroaster converted the Bactrian king, his faith became identified with the power and influence of the ruler. "Zoroaster sets his hope of the triumph of the good world on a good sovereign. . . . By converting kings and people, it became the national religion of the Iranian people and the Achaemenian kings" (Moore, 1925, pp. 366-70). Thus, in the manner of the day, Darius, at the height of Iranian power, had these words carved in stone: "By the grace of Ahura Mazda, I am king. Ahura Mazda gave me the kingdom" (quoted in Katrak, 1965, p. 59). Such allegiance to the supreme deity of Zoroastrianism (with some linguistic changes that need not be considered here) continued down to the Sasanian dynasty which finally succumbed to the Arabs in the seventh century A.D. Even when the devotees of the ancient faith were driven into hiding or exile by the arrival of the Muslims, refugees continued to regard their religion as belonging to a people; this identity remained in spite of later ordeals. A modern Parsi scholar-priest sums up the matter in these words, "Though possessed of all the best elements that fitted it to be a world creed, Zoroastrianism has never shown any signs of becoming a universal religion. In the midst of the vicissitude of fortune, it has become a national religion at best" (Dhalla, 1938, p. 18).

In the second place, the proliferation of supernatural beings became, for a time, a conspicuous trend. From the very first, Ahura Mazda is represented as having ministers or "Holy Immortals" who carry out his will: Vohu Mano (good mind), Asha (right order), and others. These Amesha Spentas, so called in the non-Gathic books, are personified attributes of the deity who are eventually assigned a life of their own, some even receiving special worship like Vohu Mano, who had fire temples in Cappadocia during the first century B.C. In later times, each of the divinities is presented as regnant over some portion of nature or some month of the year. Though Ahura Mazda remains supreme, the immortal ones (later called Yazatas) are worshiped along with him, leading one authority to call the system a "monarchical polytheism" (Moore, 1925, p. 374).[6] Later Zoroastrianism retains the Amesha Spentas, although they come to occupy a subordinate place somewhat like angels in the Christian world view.

The growth of a priestly hierarchy was the third development. How soon the priesthood became hereditary is not known, but it was fairly early in Zoroastrian history. By the Sasanian period (A.D. 226-637), the priests had upper and lower ranks, with the High Priests frequently occupying such offices as prime minister, ambassador, chief justice, religious teacher, and author; in fact, they were second in rank only to the king himself. Eventually the priestly hierarchy crystallized

---

6. A genuine polytheism flourished in Iran alongside Mazdaism in the fifth to fourth centuries B.C., when Mithra and Anahita were worshiped as well as Ahura Mazda; however, this phenomenon was apparently temporary (Moore, 1925, p. 372).

into a threefold division. At the bottom were the Erwads, who could don the white turban but perform only three ceremonies; above them came the Mobeds, who had to undergo more purification rites but in turn could perform a number of higher ceremonies forbidden to the Erwads. In the top position were the Dasturs who, in addition to performing any ceremonies, were supervisors of the Mobeds, giving them their instructions and commanding them what to do. These distinctions continue to the present day (Katrak, 1965, pp. 233-34).

A fourth change occurred after Zoroaster gave priority to some rituals over others, and it is these rituals that are now regarded as distinctive of Zoroastrianism, both by the faithful and by outside observers. The use of fire as a sacred symbol, and exposure of the dead constitute the best known examples. There seems good reason to believe that the cult of fire preceded Zoroaster and that he may have accepted it as a token of the divine, but in the early books there is more mention of the Haoma (sacred drink) sacrifice. It is not until we come to the Vendidad, a later compilation, that stress is laid on keeping of the holy fire, which must be fed with clean wood, incense, and the sprout of a pomegranate tree. In the same book are instructions for keeping up the fire on the domestic hearth, which is also sacred (Jackson, 1928, p. 197). It seems a plausible hypothesis that the growth of the priesthood was closely connected with increased emphasis on tending the sacred fire which became a priestly function. As for funeral ceremonies, they too were pre-Zoroastrian but confined to Magian customs; even Zoroaster seems to have ignored the practice, if we can judge by the Gathas. Neither the Achaemenian nor the later Parthian peoples originally exposed their dead. How this came to be a distinctive practice of the later religion is explained by Moore, as follows: "The Achaemeni⸱ kings were buried in tombs, a mode of disposing of the dead abhorrent to the sacred law of the Vendidad,[7] but seemingly not condemned in the Gathas. Herodotus affirms of his own observation that the exposure of the dead was practiced by the Magi, but adds: 'the Persians envelop the body in wax and bury it in the earth,' and Strabo makes the same distinction; the Magians alone leave the bodies to the beasts of prey. The exposure of the dead on raised platforms is not infrequent among wandering tribes, and has of itself nothing to do with a fear of polluting the earth, which might seem to be equally well attained by coating the body in wax. We can only infer that the former was no prescription of primitive Zoroastrianism, but a custom — doubtless very old — of a particular region or tribe which in Sasanian times succeeded in being made law" (Moore, 1925, pp. 372-73). Again it seems plausible to conclude that such funeral customs became widespread *pari passu* with the growth of the priesthood.

ESCAPE TO INDIA

With the overthrow of the Sasanian kingdom in the seventh century A.D., the conquering Arabs compelled the Iranians to accept Islam or face extinction (Karaka, 1884, vol. 1, p. 23). Tradition relates that a small band of Zoroastrians

---

7. This sacred book did not appear until about a thousand years after Zoroaster (Katrak, 1965, p. 222).

escaped to the mountains of Khorasan, where they remained for about a century protected from attack; eventually, however, they suffered persecution and fled again, not once but many times. As they moved south, they halted at the island of Hormoz in the Persian Gulf, then at the port of Diu where they stayed temporarily only to push on again to Sanjan, some twenty-five miles south of Daman, where they established a more permanent settlement after negotiations with the local ruler. The date of their arrival is given as A.D. 716.

When the Hindu prince, Jadi Rana, inquired who the newcomers were, the Dastur who led the group is said to have made the following reply: "We call ourselves Parsis, being the inhabitants of Pars, a province in Iran, and our language is known as Farsi." To elucidate the religion of the group, the Dastur presented sixteen "schlocks" or distichs outlining selected elements of their faith that presumably would appeal most to the local ruler[8] — items such as the use of incense, perfumes, and flowers in religious ceremonies, observing rituals for the relief of ancestors, and even exaggerating enough to say, "We are worshippers of the cow." A later Parsi historian recognizes the extravagance of these statements but justifies them as follows, "It must, however, be frankly stated, that the first Zoroastrian refugees in India played the part of dissemblers, and that these distichs were framed with the view of gaining the favour of the Hindu Rana" (Karaka, 1884, vol. 1, p. 31).

The prince finally gave the pilgrims permission to stay in his kingdom subject to the following conditions:

1. That the Parsis would adopt the language of his country (Gujarati) and cease to speak that of their forefathers.
2. That they would adopt the customs of his country.
3. That they would renounce arms of any sort, that they had been carrying, on their landing on the shores of India.
4. That they would perform the marriage ceremonies of their children at night in conformity with the practice of the Hindus.
5. That they would not slaughter cows and would respect the sentiments of the Hindus in that matter.

To these conditions the Parsi newcomers consented, and thus began their residence in India, a stay that became a permanent settlement (Katrak, 1965, p. 110). Another sign that the Parsis were quite willing to conciliate the Hindus was the abandonment of all attempts to proselytize or gain new converts. This was a severe break with earlier tradition which encouraged believers to proclaim the faith of Zoroaster to the entire world (Dhalla, 1938, p. 325).[9] Precisely

---

8. In their previous stay in Diu which supposedly lasted nineteen years, the Parsi pilgrims became familiar with both the language and the customs of that region, a circumstance that stood them in good stead when appealing for tolerance to the Hindu ruler in Sanjan (Katrak, 1965, pp.108-09).

9. In one of the later sacred books, the Dinkart, there is even encouragement of the use of force for the conversion of nonbelievers (Dhalla, 1938, p. 325). In origin, Zoroastrianism was intolerant in the sense that it conceived itself to be the only true religion. In this it resembled both Islam and Christianity (Moore, 1925, p. 371), as discussed in Chapters 7 and 8.

when the decision was made to relinquish their claims to convert others, history does not reveal. Since such a resolution was consistent with the other compromises made with the Hindu ruler on their arrival, it could have been part of the Parsis' initial adjustment. But whenever it happened, it brought the Parsis closer to Hindu tradition and transformed their community into a corporate entity partly approaching a caste.

RISE OF THE ENTREPRENEURS

The Parsi community soon migrated from Sanjan to Navsari and Surat, where they remained as farmers and toddy-drawers for eight centuries or more (Menant, 1924, p. 642).[10] After the fifteenth century, local rulers, both Muslim and Hindu, appointed desais or tax farmers from the Parsi community, finding them men of probity who stood outside the particularisms of caste. Later, Portuguese, Dutch, and British colonialists, for similar reasons, selected outstanding Parsi men to be their compradors or brokers. Such figures pointed the way for the business leaders who followed (Karaka, 1884, vol. 1, pp. 4, 9).

In matters of doctrine, Robert E. Kennedy, Jr., contends that the Parsis, like the Puritans described by Max Weber in his *Protestant Ethic and the Spirit of Capitalism,* had a rational and pragmatic ideology that predisposed them to entrepreneurship. He draws on R. K. Merton's study of *Science, Technology and Society in Seventeenth Century England,* especially Merton's suggestion that Puritans believed in an underlying order in nature, while accepting a standard of verification that can be made by the senses. When these ideas are coupled with two values enjoined by their religion – that is, "the desire to accumulate rather than to consume material goods, and the desire to maximize one's material prosperity" – the resulting combination heightens the tendency (with opportunity, of course) to "select financial vocations in favor of other possible pursuits." The probability of such an outcome is even greater when the idea takes strong root that physical work has a kind of intrinsic value.

All these notions, Kennedy avers, are to be found in classical Zoroastrianism. The underlying order in nature is called *Asha* in 185 out of 256 verses in the Gathas. Asha represents the divine law and moral order in the world and is related to the ancient Sanskrit rite referring to the immutable laws governing the movements of natural bodies. Also common in the Gathas is approval of efforts to increase prosperity, signifying that the increase of wealth becomes proof that one is following asha. For the wicked, however, there is lack of prosperity. The Zoroastrian is also urged in the Gathas not only to acquire but to maintain wealth; this is emphasized several times and therefore validates the second value, which is accumulation rather than consumption of material goods. Zoroastrians win salvation through exertions that aim to establish the Kingdom of Order. This verifies the final value, that material work has ethical connotation and is intrinsically good. When all these factors are compounded together, the resulting

---

10. There are even reports that Akbar invited a Dastur from Navsari to Delhi, bestowing on him 2,000 acres of land as a royal gift. From Iran came another visiting Dastur in 1597, with whom the monarch was so impressed that he built a Zoroastrian temple with the sacred fire to be kept burning continuously (Karaka, 1884, vol. 2, p. 3).

ideology stimulates a search for financial success as an attainable good, provided the proper occasion is at hand. Such occasions rarely occurred during the first centuries of Parsi settlement in Gujarat, but Kennedy notes that, even at the close of the eleventh century, Parsis were among the leading traders of Cambay (Kennedy, 1962, pp. 11-17). Commercial opportunities of the ports with their increasing sea traffic began a series of trading ventures that multiplied in scope and volume with the burgeoning of European companies, which served as employers and models simultaneously.

Objective factors during the seventeenth to the nineteenth century were especially propitious for the full development of a Parsi business ethic. To place the matter in perspective, it must be recognized that the opportunities for Indians to take advantage of the growing commerce and trade of the eighteenth century were far greater in Bombay than in Calcutta. In the latter city the British monopolized the raw materials industries of jute, tea, and indigo, together with the export trade of these commodities to London. Indians were hardly able to get much of a foothold in these closely regulated markets until well into the twentieth century (McKelvey, 1962, p. 128). In Bombay, however, cotton was the major commodity, a crop handled at least in large part by Indian interests from the start. This was also true in Gujarat, already the most economically advanced region of indigenous trade where the British could profit without in any sense cornering the markets. In Bombay, far more than in Calcutta, it was likewise the case that a brisk trade with Chinese ports became a major source of growing wealth. "Bombay's cotton and opium for the most part went east and hence could be handled by Indians, unaffected by the British monopoly of trade between India and Britain which involved most of Calcutta's exports" (Lamb, 1955, p. 103).

Another objective condition favoring Parsi gains in the scramble for commercial success in that era was their freedom from some of the impediments that prevented local Hindus from taking full advantage of the new opportunities. I refer especially to the factors of community and caste. Parsi writers emphasize the rigidity of caste restrictions and mention the taboos on normal social relations with outsiders in commensality, or other regulations like those governing Untouchability (Katrak, 1965, p. 116).[11] The merchant castes or Banias of Gujarat were often limited to the towns where they lived; jatis were local and tended to keep their members geographically confined. Since no such restraints were laid upon the Parsis, they had greater mobility and the number of their competitors was limited as well (Karaka, 1884, vol. 2, p. 243).[12]

Hindu authorities like Guha, however, deny the importance of such restrictions but stress an entirely different dimension of social relations among the Hindus: that is, the administrative and multidimensional community ties

---

11. However, in their many centuries of living among the Hindus, the Parsis took over a number of Hindu customs. Precisely what the usage was, we are not certain, but it is reported that to eat with unbelievers used to be considered sinful and, as a result, Sir Jamshedji Jijibhai once declined to dine with the Governor of Bombay (Menant, 1924, p. 648).

12. Yet it is worth mention that by the eighteenth century, Parsi merchants adopted the dress of the Banias, which they retained until quite recent times (Menant, 1924, p. 645).

that bound the non-Parsis in a web of inescapable obligations. "The strength of the Parsis lay in their relative non-involvement in earlier civil and military administrations — run by Hindus and Muslims — and the concomitant advantages, such as a claim to special favour from the new masters. . . . leadership motivations in these communities[13] were bound to be diverse and complicated. There were too many demands on their emerging leaderships. Parsis were, on the other hand, relatively free from such diverse social commitments. As demands on their leaders were not many-sided, they could devote their entire energies to economic self-help" (Guha, Nov. 1970, p. 1935).

A related condition that favored the Parsis was a set of diversified opportunities for capital accumulation not open to Hindus. In early years of British occupation, the Parsis could draw on their monopoly of brewing and liquor selling (ibid.), occupations that were abhorrent and polluting to the Banias. Later on, many of the Parsis migrating to Bombay found shipbuilding a congenial occupation and one in great demand. Here again, the customs of merchant-caste Hindus were so firmly set against any type of manual labor that to engage in carpentry was quite unthinkable. The Parsis, however, had no such inhibitions. Guha asserts that "Parsis were known to be expert shipbuilders right from the 17th century. Besides the Company-owned Bombay dockyards, there were also in our period small private shipbuilding yards all along the western coasts. On the Bombay dockyards, some 500 ship carpenters, mostly Parsis, worked in 1781, under Parsi master builders. Their number increased to a thousand or so by the turn of the century and 2,000 by 1847" (Guha, Aug. 1970, p. M109). As for companies devoted entirely to shipbuilding, by 1881 Parsis accounted for twenty-six of the forty-six shipbuilding firms in Bombay (Karaka, 1884, vol. 2, p. 98), the rest being chiefly British. Thus, a good deal of the growing wealth of the Parsis came from the profits of shipbuilding, where they amassed sufficient capital for other ventures.

It seems likely, also, that the example of hereditary desais furnished a community model of intermediary roles that had considerable influence for Parsis migrating to Bombay when they were forced to abandon agricultural pursuits. As the desais or tax farmers had proved themselves successful go-betweens joining rulers to ruled, so the possibilities of exploiting the new conditions of sovereignty suggested modes of accommodation already familiar in pattern. Even before the eighteenth century, the Parsis acted as go-betweens, agents, and brokers for Dutch, French, and Portuguese traders; they therefore experienced no difficulty in transferring allegiance to the conquering British who followed. Their mode of adaptation was to avoid direct competition with the British but to seek out ways to collaborate as brokers, junior partners, and clients.[14] They apprenticed their wards with European firms, thereby learning new business methods highly advantageous in the changed commercial climate. They also aided the British in crucial sectors of enterprise by seeking out sources

---

13. The reference here is to both Bohras from the Muslims and Banias from the Hindus.

14. They did not always take second place, however, "In 1854, C.N. Davar, a Parsi banker and trader with many British contacts, built the first cotton textile mill" (Lamb, 1955, p. 104).

of raw cotton supplies in the interior[15] and having them transported to the exchange center where they could be transshipped to the textile industry in England. Conversely, they introduced and distributed British-made goods to the Indian market.

Such middleman positions contributed to early banking success as well. In the first years of the nineteenth century, the Meherjis, who became famous Parsi bankers, "hailed from a family with a farming background and were revenue-farmers for Bassein under the late Peshwas. Under early British rule, they were appointed as revenue-farmers for sea and land customs of some districts of Maharashtra. They were also engaged in raw cotton imports on a large scale. In 1830 they were invited by the Nizam to open banking operations in his territories. During the decade 1835-1845, their direct advances to the Nizam amounted to at least Rs. 18 million. However, the Nizam's inability to repay caused the failure of their firm in 1851. When the European-dominated Bank of Bombay was established in 1840, one-third of its 333 shareholders were Parsis, contributing 23.6 per cent of the Bank's share capital" (Guha, Aug. 1970, p. M113).[16]

Apparently, too, the Parsis had considerable aptitude for languages and applied themselves in that direction, for we read in more than one source that they developed special fluency in the use of English (Karaka, 1884, vol. 1, p. xxvi). During the early period of capitalist growth they became known as Dobhashias. This word is a compound of "Do" (two) and "Bhashas" (languages), that is, those who knew two languages (Katrak, 1965, p. 116). This term came to mean a commissioned agent for a European firm and the word was shortened to Dubash by the British.[17] By the census of 1881, Zoroastrians had 146 out of a total of 159 dubashas listed among the commercial occupations (Karaka, 1884, vol. 1, pp. 98-99).

From a dependent and middleman position in the burgeoning economy, the Parsis worked their way up through symbiosis to independence. Dissatisfied with subordinate roles, a number of Parsi entrepreneurs utilized the larger ships of the British and opened up trade routes to Burma, Calcutta, Persia, Arabia, and China (Kennedy, 1962, p. 17). In some cases, the Parsis put Europeans in charge of their ships. In other ventures, the Parsis who had accumulated capital lent their money while the British put up their imposing names, and the joint enterprises "worked miracles in the colonial business world" (Guha, Aug. 1970, p. M115). Such interdependent relations with European enterprisers increased in size and scope, concurrently raising the status of Parsis to positions of economic and even social equality. As Helen Lamb has observed, the Parsis became "Britain's economic and political middlemen in dealing with the Hindu population, receiving valuable contracts and concessions in return. Wealthy Parsis adopted

---

15. Parsi enterprise was especially active in the south where their "merchant-capital penetrated far and wide in the cotton-growing area of the Deccan, in the form of advances to the cotton-growers" (Guha, Aug. 1970, p. M113).

16. The Hindu percentage, coincidentally, was only 6.2 (Guha, Aug. 1970, p. M113).

17. A number of Parsi families have retained "Dubash" as a surname to this day (Katrak, 1965, p. 116).

Western education, sports and dress, and sometimes even dined with the British. This roughly equal relationship helped them to enter the industrial field since it made it possible to hire British engineers and technicians — members of the ruling race — who were necessary for the operations of their textile plants in the initial stages" (Lamb, 1955, p. 104; by permission). There is a hint here, though no more, that an element of racial preference may have been involved; to the extent that Parsis were fairer-skinned than their Hindu neighbors, it would then be easier to favor them in the transactions that took place.

The largest Parsi fortunes were those founded on the early trade with China. Thus Sir Jamsetji Jijibhoy gained his fabulous wealth through trade in cotton and opium with the Far East in the latter part of the eighteenth and early part of the nineteenth century. Not only by his wealth but by his philanthropy did he symbolize a whole generation of early Parsi capitalists who built hospitals, schools, rest houses, and the like in great profusion. It is reported of Sir Jamsetji, for example, that his gifts to charity totaled £273,333 sterling and that his outstanding generosity gained him a British knighthood (Katrak, 1965, pp. 150-51). Perhaps best known among the Parsi capitalists of the same era were the Tatas who, as a family, were especially outstanding, Nusserwonji leading the way with traffic in opium and cotton, while his son Jamsetji followed with the establishment of the Empress Cotton Mills.

Below these towering peaks of prosperity there were lesser ones of significant size. In fact, by 1881 the occupational structure of the Parsi community as a whole reflected a significant shift. The census of Bombay City for that year listed the Parsi male occupations other than "miscellaneous" as 1,940 professional, 2,079 domestic, 3,317 commercial, and 3,610 industrial (Karaka, 1884, vol. 1, p. 99).[18] It was already possible by that date to regard the bulk of the Parsi population as Bombay dwellers, since the census of 1881 reported that 70.3 percent of them were born in that city (Seal, 1968, p. 82, n. 3). By 1884 a leading commentator noted, somewhat sadly, "The Parsi today are not men of the country; they have become essentially men of the towns. . . . When other avocations brought riches sooner the Parsis gave up their investment in lands" (Karaka, 1884, vol. 1, p. 100).

THE GOLDEN AGE

A flowering of Parsi culture and enlightenment accompanied the economic prosperity of the nineteenth and early twentieth centuries, and it is during this epoch that the most influential currents of change were released in the community. Most of these were made possible by the expenditure of new wealth belonging to the leading enterprisers of the era and their philanthropic zeal to see it used in constructive ways.

---

18. The number of "miscellaneous" occupations was by far the highest, reaching 13,737. Counting these we can then state that commercial and industrial occupations constituted more than a third of all male Parsi occupations in Bombay at the time. This was a fantastically high proportion for the India of that day, and even today. As for female occupations, over 90 percent were reported "miscellaneous" in 1881, a category quite unrevealing.

By the 1850s, associational life in Bombay was flourishing; its direction toward "enlightenment" and reform may be judged from the following testimony of Dadabhai Naoroji, the Parsi editor of *Rast Goftas (Truth Teller)*, a prominent journal of the day:

> The six or seven years before I eventually came to England in 1855 ... were full of all sorts of reforms, social, educational, political, religious, etc. ... Female Education, Free Association of Women with Men at public, social and other gatherings, Infant Schools, Students' Literary and Scientific Society, Societies for the Diffusion of Useful Knowledge in the Vernacular, Parsi Reform, Abolition of Child Marriages, Remarriage of Widows among Hindus, and Parsi Religious Reform Society, were some of the problems tackled, movements set on foot, and institutions inaugurated by a band of young men fresh from college. ... Such were the first fruits of the English education given at Elphinstone College.[19]

The Parsis were thus forging ahead in many fields of education. By 1931, for example, Parsis led all communities in India with the highest percentage of its members literate in English (50.4 percent), almost twice that of the next highest indigenous group, the Jews, who registered 26.4 percent (Davis, 1951, p. 185). This was the culmination of a trend starting in the early nineteenth century, when English schools, taught mainly by Anglo-Indians and retired soldiers, were started in Bombay with Parsis predominating among the pupils. After the retirement of Montstuart Elphinstone from the Company, many Indians, with Parsis leading the way, subscribed funds for the college which bears the General's name; until the latter part of the nineteenth century, Parsis had an enrollment that either surpassed that of the Hindus in the College or at least equaled it. Much the same tendency occurred at St. Xavier's School founded by the Catholics. In order to open up educational opportunities for less fortunate Parsis, Sir Jamshedji Jijibhai contributed generous funds to establish schools for them, both in Bombay and the outlying country areas (Karaka, 1884, vol. 1, pp. 281-83, 285, 288-90).

Female education and the emancipation of women also made great strides during the golden age. Unlike many other communities who send out male migrants to the cities in advance of their women, "It is a well-known characteristic of the Parsis that they never move singly; they always bring with them their wives and children, nay even their whole families which in those days were joint families" (Desai, 1948, p. 7). Hence the women were also subject to early urbanization. The many centuries of rural living in Hindu society had led to abandonment of Iranian customs, and so we find the adoption of the conjugal family, late marriage, and the high status of women. With the movement of Parsi families into nineteenth century Bombay, acculturation to the British mode became the order of the day. Joint families took longer to disappear, but as early as 1777 the Parsi Panchayet issued an edict against infant marriages, and by 1884 it became a matter of comment that Parsi ladies started to go out with their husbands and even stroll about on foot. Female education began auspiciously in

---

19. From "A Chapter in Autobiography," *Speeches and Writings of Dadabhai Naoroji* (Madras, 1910), p. 656, quoted in Seal, 1968, p. 197.

1849 with the establishment of girls' schools which had instruction in the vernacular (Gujarati) before transferring to English. In the latter part of the nineteenth century, many Parsi ladies took the lead in female education, some even training to be doctors. As an index of their emancipation, it is remarked that they had no objection to being treated by male doctors, a somewhat daring step unmatched in Hindu society (Karaka, 1884, vol. 1, pp. 123, 127, 129-30, 173, 299, 303, 324; vol. 2, p. 270).

The growth of philanthropy during the nineteenth century was phenomenal, both within the Parsi community and in service to those of the wider society as well. The Parsi Panchayet, beginning as a charity organization "giving help to the indigent and in maintaining Dokhmas or Towers of Silence or other institution of public worship" became next a "sociojudicial force," then finally a superwelfare agency managing numerous trusts for community needs. The affluent members of the community displayed to the full the sentiments of *noblesse oblige* founded on religious adjuncts that went back to the Gathas: for instance, "Happiness unto him who renders happiness to others." Instead of ostentatious display, the wealthier Parsis vied with each other in creating trust funds for schools, hospitals, residential and housing colonies for their members, and social services of all kinds for the less fortunate (Desai, 1963, pp. 8-14). However, the munificence of Parsi business leaders was not confined to their own religious colleagues. They made liberal gifts for institutions that would benefit others regardless of creed, color, or caste, as the following (all established wholly or in largest part by Parsi philanthropy) will attest:

The Engineering College at Poona
The Mr. Nadirshaw Edulji Dinshaw Engineering College at Karachi
The Victoria Jubilee Technical Institute, Bombay
The Elphinstone College, Bombay
The Sydenham College of Commerce, Bombay
The Grant Medical College, Bombay
The Sir Kavasji Jehangir University Hall, Bombay
The Sir Jamsetji Jeejeebhoy School of Art, Bombay
The J. N. Petit Institute (popularly known as the Petit Library), Bombay
The Deccan College, Poona
The Indian Institute of Science, Bangalore
Tata Institute of Social Sciences

[Katrak, 1965, pp. 165-66]

Although the major gains of the community were made in commerce and industry during the golden age, it gradually became apparent that the political field needed closer attention. "Till about the middle of the 19th century the Parsees were quite indifferent towards Politics" (Katrak, 1965, p. 175). But the fact that a renewal of the charter for the East India Company fell due in 1853 led to the organizing of associations in Calcutta, Madras, and Bombay, all of them originating proposals to influence the British parliament toward more favorable provisions for India in the revised charter. Parsis were outstanding leaders in this new political venture embodied in the Bombay Association, born in 1852; the organization's first order of business was to petition Parliament about the charter. Two vice-presidents and the honorary president of the

Association were Parsis, and Parsi alumni from Elphinstone College made and seconded the motion for a resolution establishing the organization, with their Parsi colleagues from the College giving strong support to the new political activism (Seal, 1968, p. 198). In the meanwhile, leaders like Dadabhai Naoroji were getting practical experience in the political arena. Going to England on an economic mission, he became interested in promoting simultaneous examinations for the Civil Service of India in London and in India; after a long lobbying fight he won a victory for this policy in the House of Commons. As he gained increasing prominence and influence, he was appointed Dewan of Baroda to straighten out its finances and, on successfully passing this test, was elected to the Bombay Corporation and then later was offered a seat on the Bombay Legislative Council. On returning to England, he made several attempts and finally succeeded in being elected to the House of Commons in 1892, the first Indian to win this honor (Katrak, 1965, pp. 176-77).

Even before his victory in England, Naoroji had been elected the first president of the Indian National Congress at their organization in 1885, and, in line with the moderate ideology of that body at the time, he held that the best interests of India would be served by appealing to the British people directly, not against British rule (for which there was faith in its policies of fairness and justice)[20] but against the arbitrary and warped decisions of the English bureaucracy in the subcontinent. Naoroji stated his view succinctly as follows: "With regard to Home Rule ... I am a warm Home Ruler for Ireland, but neither myself nor any other Indian is asking for any such Home Rule for India. You must have seen from the Report of the Congress that our demands are far more moderate, in fact only a further development of existing institutions (the Legislative Councils)" (letter to Wilson, quoted in Seal, 1968, p. 280). More radical elements in Maharashtra led by Tilak, who encouraged violence against the British, were never countenanced by Parsi leaders; most prominent among these leaders was Pherozshah Mehta, the so-called "uncrowned king of Bombay," a man of commanding influence in both municipal and Presidency councils. Significantly, too, while Tilak was leading his rebellion against British rule *in toto,* he "was sentenced by a Parsi judge to a long term of imprisonment. Thereafter his influence waned; the minds of men turned to more constructive fields, and as long as Pherozshah Mehta lived he dared not put his nose into Bombay." So wrote a retired British public servant (Reed, 1952, p. 167). Being loyal to the Crown as most of the community were, Parsis were known to be exponents of moderate nationalism that sought no more than greater representation in the existing councils of the day.

INTIMATIONS OF DECLINE

The long road upward in wealth, power, and influence could not continue indefinitely. Even during the affluent years of the golden age, there were signs of

---

20. The pro-British attitude of the Parsi community as a whole was well displayed during the Mutiny of 1857, which called forth the strongest support of prominent Parsis for the colonial rulers at the time. Many Parsis suffered with the British at the hands of the mutineers (Karaka, 1884, vol. 2, p. 282).

contrary forces that one day would have to be reckoned with. As the Parsis shifted their vocations from brokers to entrepreneurs, outsiders came to fill up their places, and soon these others became rivals and competitors. Even as early as 1884, a prominent Parsi historian complained that the position of the Parsis "in the commercial community of today is not what it was a quarter of a century ago. . . . (In fact) the native merchants and dealers, who are chiefly Hindus of Kutch and Kathiawar, have so far advanced, under British auspices, in education and knowledge that they can now deal directly with Europeans. The Parsi middleman is consequently no longer a necessity as he was in days of yore." The Khojas in particular became keen business rivals, and eventually the Jews displaced Parsis in the China trade (Karaka, 1884, vol. 2, pp. 257-59). The running current of competition flowed alongside of the Parsi business and industrial stream; most important of all, it was a rising current.

In spite of the marked success of so many Parsi entrepreneurs, the community as a whole did not display a consistent or general rise in prosperity. A few wealthy families like the Tatas were able to make the transition by reinvesting their fortunes from textiles in such wide open and highly lucrative forms of heavy industry as steel, engineering products, and electric power.[21] Most Parsi businessmen were unwilling or unable to take advantage of these opportunities, however, and were faced by gradual overcrowding in textiles and related industries. Like capitalist growth elsewhere, developments within the Parsi community showed the usual differentiation into extremes of wealth and poverty with uneven gradations in between. The élan of business initiative was also hampered by unique economic conditions that followed independence when the government concentrated on controlling inflation and expanding agricultural production. This led to

> decline in prices, rising unemployment and lack of effective demand for the purchase of goods Indian business is able to produce. . . . Thus the economy experienced a consolidation of the previous wave of industrial expansion rather than an upsurge of new activity which might have facilitated the emergence of new groups into industry. . . . The industrial base is small; factories provided only 5.8 per cent of India's national income in 1950-51. It is overweighted in textiles and deficient in basic heavy industry components in relation to more ambitious development schemes. . . . New elements trying to break into industry may be discouraged on the one hand by the power exercised over the modern banking system by leading families, and on the other by the social welfare regulations, particularly onerous for those less well-endowed financially. [Lamb, 1955, pp. 112, 115; by permission]

---

21. The versatility of the Tatas in starting new corporations is legendary. One relevant anecdote will serve. In the case of the Western Ghats, a mountainous formation in Maharashtra, "there is a fall of eighteen hundred feet to plain level and the market of Bombay City less than a hundred miles away. 'Store this water,' cried Gostling, 'and put down your turbines and generators at the foot of the hills.' 'Store this water I will' replied Tata; and his sons did. Bombay is now one of the most completely electrified cities in the world. . . . There are thousands of tenement rooms with but a single light; electric power does much to relieve the burden on the poor" (Reed, 1952, p. 127).

In these changed conditions, fewer and fewer Parsis entered the ranks of businessmen as time went on, while more and more sought out occupations that would bring security without risk in white collar jobs as well as the professions (Lamb, 1955, p. 111). The number of people working for wages clearly increased and, although there are no recent figures on occupational distribution, a visit to Parsi community institutions in Bombay such as I was able to make in 1970 revealed a sizable number of apartments and tenements supported by Parsi-established trusts for low income and indigent members of the community. These features of Parsi life attracted attention as early as the 1950s and gave rise to the following observations:

> Community feeling may be stronger among the less successful members of the business communities. Many poor Parsis, for instance, attend Parsi schools and inhabit Parsi subsidized tenements along with their fellows; wealthy Parsis have been attending cosmopolitan educational institutions for the last hundred years. Those chambers of commerce which are organized by small traders are frequently limited to one community, as are the traditional money market bazaars. At the other extreme one finds members of old Gujarati and Parsi industrial families marrying out of their group and forsaking business for diplomacy and the professions. [Lamb, 1955, pp. 108-09; by permission]

Patterns of rapid social change that culminated in the worldwide depression of the 1930s and the new alignments of internal forces after independence finally made it obvious that the golden age of the Parsis was over. Some details of the decline now claim our attention.

RELIGIOUS CONTROVERSIES

When the Parsis first migrated to India, the natural leaders of the community were the priests; by the nineteenth century the religious functionaries had been displaced by elders among the businessmen. This transition was gradual, partly because Zoroastrianism was a religion of deeds rather than creeds. Ancient beliefs were of less moment than ancient practices, and ethical demands remained central. Individual worship and practices of devotion at home or in the open air were fully as important, if not more so, than congregational ceremonies at the fire temples presided over by priests. In time, however, the prosperity of prominent leaders and the universal spread of Western education in the community created a gulf between priesthood and laity that is still unbridged.

As a learned Dastur of the modern school has put it:

> The Parsi priesthood had long before degenerated into ignorance. The situation was not keenly felt so long as the laity was equally illiterate. But now when the latter sought enlightenment, the clergy had kept less and less abreast of the times. During the long period of twelve centuries, very few priests rose above mediocrity. The priest hitherto had acted as an intercessor between the layman and Ormazd,[22] and through elaborate

---

22. Later Avestan term for Ahura Mazda, the new term widely adopted in all Parsi literature.

ritual had undertaken to gain for him divine help, being duly paid to recite penitential prayers for the expiation of the sins of the living, and to sacrifice for the purchase of paradise for the dead. The youth of the new school argued that there was no more need of the Mobed's mediation between him and his Heavenly Father. He demanded that the priest should act as a moral preceptor, a spiritual ministrant to his soul. This, in those times, the priest could not do. He could not widen his religious outlook and adapt himself to the demand of the younger generation. The youth now grew up without religious instruction and gradually gravitated towards indifferentism. [Dhalla, 1938, pp. 484-85]

Perhaps indifferentism is too weak a term to describe the viewpoint of modern Parsi youth who, as Katrak reports, are quite active in their criticism of ancient practices upheld by the priests. He states that many young Parsis, imbued with ideas absorbed from Western education, attack the use of prayers in the ancient Avestan language which no one understands today; even translations into Gujarati and English would not be sufficient, they say, because of so many obscure allusions and ambiguities in such prayers. Far better, they believe, for learned scholars or Dasturs to rewrite such prayers in the modern idiom so that they will have meaning for worshipers in the twentieth century. The youth also object to the frequent and expensive ceremonies carried on for the benefit of souls of the dead; not only is this considered a waste of money but a useless exercise. How can anyone with a scientific world view maintain that prayers and ritual can have any effect on the fate of a dead person? Even the Prophet maintained that punishments and rewards were intrinsic to the acts of the believer and not to what others do for him. In addition, the youth are especially critical of Parsi funerals and the disposal of the dead. Certain restrictions and prohibitions connected with such ceremonies are censured. For example, from the moment of death until the body is laid in the tower of silence, a dog is brought in two or three times before the corpse; however, no non-Parsi is allowed to be in the presence of the body. The youth of the community are therefore beginning to ask why a dog is permitted such a view[23] when intimate friends of the deceased are forbidden to pay their last respects in contemplation of the remains.

As for the final disposal of the body, not only the youth but Western-educated laity argue that it surely makes no difference to the dead person what happens to his body, whether it is exposed, buried, cast into the sea, or even cremated. Hence an increasing number are becoming convinced that no one method (like exposure in a tower of silence) should be practiced to the exclusion of all others. In certain cities where a modern faction prevails, the dead are actually buried and there is no tower of silence. In other localities, both practices are prevalent, but in these circumstances the Parsi Panchayet has asked the priests not to say prayers over the dead who are buried rather than exposed. This prohibition helps to maintain the older forms against too rapid change,

---

23. In ancient times, apparently, it was believed that the glance of a dog was a terror to demons and therefore could dispel the presence of evil spirits that hovered over the dead (Moore, 1925, p. 391). Later tradition has it that the presence of a dog will somehow ease the passing of the soul to heaven (Gould, personal correspondence).

though it stems the tide only to a partial degree. There are even a few radicals who argue for cremation, but this will probably make no headway because the pollution of fire through dead bodies is such a repugnant taboo that it is abhorrent to the community (Gould, personal correspondence).

The youth of today also inveigh against traditional customs by contending that there is nothing wrong about smoking, or going bareheaded in the temples. Ancient belief had it that smoking is a way to pollute fire and hence is a sacrilege and that going bareheaded in the fire temples might allow some hairs to fall in the sacrificial viands used in sacred ceremonies and thus pollute the food so that it would be seriously desecrated. The younger generation can see no rationale for these beliefs in the twentieth century and wants to discard them. Much the same attitude is held toward the traditional initiation ritual at puberty when the boy or girl is invested with the sacred Sudra (undergarment) and Kusti (thread); this is more and more regarded as a mere formal exercise that has no modern significance. The part of the ceremony most criticized is perhaps the offering of Nirang or Ab-e-Zar (golden water) to the neophyte; the word is a euphemism for urine of an albino bull which is both drunk and applied to the body. Today's youth looks upon the practice with extreme distaste, and some are beginning to insist on substituting Homa (consecrated juice of pomegranate leaves) instead (Katrak, 1965, pp. 259-63 passim).

Modern Parsi scholars also began to arrange the ancient Zoroastrian texts into chronological order on the basis of historical criticism.

> Tradition, they argued, attributed to Zoroaster doctrines that he never preached. They advocated a return to the original purity of the faith by stripping off the accretions that had gathered round the pure canon of the prophet, thus removing the haze of ignorance and bigotry that had overclouded the light of their excellent religion. All this was highly sacrilegious to orthodox ears. [Dhalla, 1938, pp. 488-89]

In Bombay there are two Parsi newspapers, one of which takes a conservative stand on religious topics, the *Jama-Jamshed,* while the other, the *Kaiser-i-Hind,* takes a more liberal point of view.[24] They continue doctrinal controversies in their columns on a regular basis.

CONSEQUENCES OF A PURITAN ETHIC

A result of Parsi business success was a gradual trend toward consumerism, a trend which Weber emphasized in the growing affluence of Puritans in Europe (Weber, 1948, p. 175). That this universal tendency appears in the twentieth century Parsi community is reflected in the comments of a prominent leader on the occasion of a World Zoroastrian Congress. He declares:

24. Jehangir Patel, a Yale graduate and editor of an English-language journal called *Parsiana,* comments, "Basically we are two communities – an urban, reformist, sophisticated community, and a die-hard, very orthodox group that controls our institutions and trusts" (quoted in Weintraub, 1975).

As history has proved time and again, every nation and community which has become economically prosperous has tended to take to a life of ease and comfort which in its turn has led to deterioration in its economic condition. The Zoroastrians in India seem to be passing through that phase. It is not that no Zoroastrian young man is hard-working, but the fact remains that given the choice the modern young man will rather spend one hour in a picture house than earn a few extra rupees. By the same token, no modern young man with even a small capital will want to risk that capital by venturing out either in trade, commerce or industry, but would either like to live upon his capital or invest it in safe security, even though the return may be small. . . . No religious group in India probably is so much in pursuit of pleasure or prestige as ours. The poorest envy and want to copy the standard of living of the richest, and wealth has come to acquire a status symbol such as is out of all proportion to its intrinsic worth. [Sahukar, 1964, p. 13]

Nearly twenty years before, Sir Homi Mody of Parsi fame noted the community trend in somewhat different terms when he said of the minority shortly after independence, "We have an idle rich class, contributing little to the general well-being of the community beyond indiscriminate charity, and our poor are getting poorer and losing their self-respect" (Mody, foreword, 1948, p. xi).

TWENTIETH CENTURY READJUSTMENTS

It is unrealistic, however, to attribute the slow economic decline of the Parsis solely to the altered motives of a leisure class. Conditions in the wider society changed too rapidly to be controlled. As already indicated above, chances for advancement soon became seriously limited and the economic depression of the 1930s reduced even successful enterprisers to penury. In the early 1940s it was estimated by the leading statistician of the community that the proportion of Parsis actually in poverty reached 40 percent and that, in contrast with earlier conditions where widows led the list of those receiving charity contributions, couples with children led the list of recipients, being 33 percent of all those given aid by the Parsi Panchayet. In but two years' time, the cost of living index for the working class went up from 150 to 200 percent. The number of Parsi unemployed kept rising in the late 1930s and early 1940s, and all of the unemployed were over thirty years of age (Desai, 1945, pp. 3, 6, 9, 21).

National independence increased the number of obstacles to be overcome. Parsis lost whatever patronage they earlier received from the British (Sahukar, 1964, p. 12). Jobs became increasingly scarce, not because there was open and deliberate discrimination against hiring Parsis but because, in a labor market crowded with new undergraduates, those with family and caste connections made full use of them to the exclusion of Parsis — unless the latter could gain similar advantages in Parsi firms which were, in any case, far less numerous than others. The employment situation since independence has been well stated in these words, written originally in reference to the Muslims but in many ways equally applicable to other minorities: "The imagined discrimination is real enough but it is not anti-Muslim so much as pro-caste-community-language-region. Thus Hindus employ Hindus, Muslims Muslims, Christians Christians,

Parsees Parsees, and so on. Within this, Tamils employ Tamils, Bengalis Bengalis, Jats Jats, Brahmins Brahmins, and so on again. In a shortage situation, every group inclines to favour its own kind" (Verghese, 1971, p. 9).

In addition, the experiment of prohibition had a shattering impact on those Parsis still living in rural areas. "It is a well-known fact that most of the Parsis who owned agricultural lands also had toddy and liquor shops. With the advent of partial prohibition in 1939 and complete prohibition 10 years later most of the Parsis lost their principal means of livelihood and they had to fall back on agriculture. Being not conversant with agricultural practices they had to depend on servants or hired labour to carry out agricultural operations" (Desai, 1963, pp. 26-27). A study made in one of these rural communities showed that 48 percent of the Parsi families there were formerly in toddy or liquor trade and that prohibition, introduced in 1947-48, worked severe hardship on the village. Their dilemma was exacerbated by the Lenders' Act and Agricultural Debtors Relief Act under which agricultural credit was especially hard to secure, and restrictions on the right to sell land were most severe. Irrigation was lacking, and the land had suffered four years of drought by the time the study was made. Former owners of toddy and liquor shops now forced to depend on agriculture were handicapped in a number of ways. Other communities worked their women in the fields, but the Parsis had never done so and were too proud to change. In order to succeed properly, the men would also have needed to do field work, but they did not have sufficient experience and tried to work servants rather than family members. Social and religious expenses were considerably higher for Parsis than for Hindus of the village. Many impoverished Parsis were subsisting on donations and doles from the Godavara Parsi Anjuman Trust; "penury and misery" were rampant. The researcher estimated that seven out of ten Parsis in the local community had insufficient income for their families (Shah, 1955).

In the cities the actual number of those in business and industry were being affected by new government policies, for "world over, the tendency is towards clipping the wings of merchant princes and industrial kings and more so in India, with its avowed State policy of evolving a socialist pattern of society" (Sahukar, 1964, p. 14). A notably bourgeois community like the Parsis suffers especially from such a policy. At the same time there are vocations rarely chosen by the younger generation today: the civil service, because "amongst the lower middle classes there is not enough awareness of the openings of employment in the services"; in the lesser lines of retail business, because "there are two main reasons why most of our people avoid the retail trade and service industries — they are disinclined to work hard for long hours, and it is wrongly presumed that a small trader or tradesman has an inferior social status" (ibid., pp. 14-15). A wider range of vocations appears to be needed to maintain the economic health of the community.

WELFARE

One of the by-products of economic decline among Parsis has been a marked increase in the efficiency and rational ordering of welfare services on a scale to be found in no other minority group of India. The impulse to take care of their own has proceeded far beyond the philanthropic generosity of an upper crust which first established the pattern; it has now broadened to a democratic agency in which all joined forces to extend benevolent services more widely.

> The hoary panchayat of India became in the hands of the Parsis an effective instrument of community organization and development on the basis of self-help and self-reliance, every member, rich or poor, contributing his mite to the Anjuman funds or 'community chest'. . . . The apex of these local Anjumans has been the Parsi Panchayat of Bombay, the custodian of the funds of most of the Parsi panchayats of India and a few from abroad. . . . Although all the wants of its needy members may not be met adequately, one can say that no deserving Parsi need go hungry, no Parsi child need grow up without minimum education and no sick Parsi need suffer for want of medical care. [Bulsara, 1969, p. 11]

The number and variety of service agencies are impressive (Desai, 1963, pp. 13-30 passim).

POPULATION TRENDS

The Parsi community in India is probably the only one for which we have sufficient demographic data to make relatively firm conclusions about the future.[25] This is due to the notable studies of S. F. Desai, former secretary of the Bombay Panchayet. For many years he has been a major protagonist for new eugenic programs among Parsis without, on the whole, much success. The grounds for his conclusions, however, and the evidence he adduces, are fairly decisive, whatever the deductions from his factual data may be. Taking the Bombay Parsis as the population for which there are the most complete vital statistics, Desai shows that from 1901 to 1943, while the rates of birth and death fluctuated somewhat, the overall trend was down for both rates. Whereas in 1901 the crude birthrate for Parsis was 24.5 per 1,000 and the crude death rate 30.5, by 1943 they had equalized at a lower level, with the crude birthrate at 15.8 and the crude death rate at 15.6. By this time, then, the population was stationary, failing to replace itself. In the same report, he shows that the number of Parsi children zero to five years of age per 10,000 of each sex was reduced by nearly a half between 1881 and 1931. Thus, the mean age of the Parsi population of Bombay is shown to be about seven years older than the mean age of the Indian population (Desai, 1945, pp. 40, 41, 43, 50). It is definitely Desai's aim to show that internal statistics of this kind presaged a long-term decline even when totals did not always reveal it. For example, if we look beyond the Bombay statistics to all-India figures, a visible decline for the Parsi population does not appear until 1961, though it is quite evident from Desai's data that a trend toward continual decrease started much earlier. Sum totals for Parsi inhabitants in India as a whole are as follows (note that before 1951 areas now in Pakistan were included): 1891, 89,887; 1901, 93,952; 1911, 100,096; 1921, 101,778; 1931, 111,853; 1941, 114,890; 1951, 111,791; 1961, 100,772; 1971, 91,266. There are no declines here except in the last twenty years, though the period 1911-21 showed a miniscule rise of only 1.6 percent.

---

25. Up to 1951 there were fairly adequate figures in Kingsley Davis (1951) on major trends, but this study has not been updated.

Desai's compilation of 1948 shows that the birthrate of Parsis in Bombay City took an upward trend from a low point of 15.8 in 1943 to 20.1 in 1946 (Desai, 1948, p. 29). The reason for this increase is obscure (end of the war baby boom?), although it proved to be temporary. On the basis of a different computation, that is, how many children are needed per 1,000 families to obtain population replacement, the number is estimated as 5.896 per family. Desai then declares, "We are short of this expectation by more than 60 per cent. Obviously the Parsis are on the decrease, unless the marriage rate goes up again and not only marriage rate but also reproduction rate" (ibid., p. 51). In the frontispiece of this volume, Desai presents a logistic curve based on data available to him in the late 1940s; this curve shows "that by 1961 the population will have reached its maximum and that thereafter it will remain comparatively steady unless special measures are taken in time to check the tendency" (ibid., p. i). Events were to show that this estimate was definitely conservative and that the downturn would come even earlier, as the totals in the above paragraph reveal.

In his last public pronouncement, Desai carries forward the annual statistics for Parsi births and deaths in the city of Bombay; before the year 1955 there is an excess of births over deaths, but in that year the balance tipped in the opposite direction, so that for every year, 1955 through 1962, there were more deaths than births. By 1962 the birthrate was as low as 12.3 and the death rate was 14.3. Instead of the downtrend coming in 1961, as shown by the earlier logistic curve, it seems to have started in 1955, and the failure of replacement becomes more obvious with each passing year.

A final set of figures to clinch this conclusion (if such is needed) is one showing the age distribution of the Parsi population compared with the all-India ratio. Here it is even more obvious that the deficit of children and the surplus of aged among Parsis is a stark and ineluctable fact. While in India as a whole the percentage of those in ages zero to fifteen reaches 40 percent, among Parsis it is as low as 18 percent. In the age groups from sixteen to fifty the two figures are about equal, with the all-India percentage being 54 and the Parsi, 52. In older ages, the differential is again a striking one: 6 percent of the all-India population is fifty-one years of age or older, whereas 30 percent of the Parsis are in that age group (Desai, 1964, p. 30).[26] The almost complete urbanization, spread of Western education, and high standard of living associated with middle-class status have had noticeable effects, one of which has been abandonment of the joint family that had been a Hindu legacy for centuries. All left their toll on population growth (Katrak, 1965, p. 220).[27] Concerning the overall decline,

---

26. Since cancer seems to appear disproportionately in the age group after fifty, it is significant that Parsis in Bombay are reported to have an overall cancer morbidity nearly three times higher than the rate of Hindus in the same city (*Overseas Hindustan Times,* Dec. 9, 1976).

27. Desai, like many eugenicists, contends that differential birthrates, the highest coming from lower income groups, involve a deterioration in "quality." Even in the early days of independence he warned that "we shall continue to witness a slow accretion of the lower classes in the lowest stratum, a diminution of the medium classes at a steady pace and a quick throwing out of the rich and higher middle classes, who fail to leave any issue behind to continue the line" (Desai, 1964, p. 73), and he repeats his admonition in his later analysis (Desai, 1964, p. 23). However, since scientists are not agreed that there is any deterioration in the germ plasm among the lower classes, the eugenicists' alarm may be quite unjustified. (Cf. Horton and Leslie, 1970, pp. 272-74.)

Desai (1964, p. 22) concludes that "In the end . . . depopulation is worse than overpopulation for a community like the Parsis."

Under these conditions, it becomes more and more difficult for the community to enforce endogamy, a traditional mode of survival for both Parsis and Jews. One of Desai's tables, based on the 1961 census for Bombay, shows a preponderance of women over men between the ages of twenty and thirty-nine. As he notes in his discussion, "This is just a marriageable age and if suitable husbands are not found, women would tend to get married outside" (Desai, 1964, pp. 21, 29). Such a tendency is already observable in the marriage statistics from Bombay, which indicate that during the years 1955 to 1962 there were 101 Parsi males who married non-Parsi females and 117 Parsi females who married non-Parsi males (ibid., pp. 31-32). Since the females are somewhat more exogamous, Desai comments that "there is a preponderance of females marrying outside and females marrying outside means lesser number of children born in the community" (ibid., p. 21).

The latter assertion is not true, however, unless we assume that the children of exogamous Parsi males would be counted among the Parsis, whereas those of exogamous Parsi females would not. Such indeed *is* the rule among Parsis, but it is unique to their community and cannot be assumed as a matter of course without recognizing this peculiarity.[28] "The Parsee women marry non-Zoroastrian boys of their choice, despite the fact that by that daring step they are being excommunicated[29] and their children are not accepted as Parsees. The modern young Parsee girls are further irritated by the fact that even when the alien boys of their choice show their willingness to be converted to the Zoroastrian fold, the community has sternly barred their entrance for all time" (Katrak, 1965, p. 265). What cannot be inferred from this statement is that the rule forbidding children of exogamous Parsi women to become Parsi is a *religious* regulation embodied in the sacred texts or the utterance of an authoritative body like the Panchayet. Such is not the case, as Katrak himself makes clear in another passage where he shows that it had quite a different origin historically. The regulation asserting that children of exogamous Parsi females may not become Parsis but that children of exogamous Parsi males *may* become Parsis originated in the judgment of a British court, the High Court of Judicature, Bombay, delivered on November 27, 1908,[30] when it decided the case of a Parsi man who had married a French woman and wanted to admit both her and her

---

28. Among the Jews, for example, apart from the strictures of the most orthodox, the admission of children into the Jewish faith, when one parent has been a Gentile, is simply dependent on the latter's conversion to Judaism.

29. This assertion is incorrect. The issue of excommunication must be sharply separated from the issue of whether children shall be admitted into the faith or not. With regard to the first, a ruling of the Parsi community dating from the middle 1950s is that if a Parsi female marries a non-Parsi in a civil ceremony and not a religious ceremony and has not, herself, converted to another faith, she is still entitled to all the privileges and rites of the Parsi community, although her children may not become Parsis (K. Gould, personal communication). Thus, it is an error to assert that she will be excommunicated.

30. This was Suit No. 639 of 1906, which shows that the Court had the case under advisement for two years pending the decision. I am indebted to Mr. Jamshid Cawasji Katrak of the Bombay Parsi Panchayet for these and other details regarding the Court judgment.

children into the Parsi faith. Evidence produced in that court showed that ancient Zoroastrians had not only married outside the faith but in doing so were adjudged meritorious since it brought outsiders to the knowledge of the true religion (Katrak, 1965, pp. 263-65). No doubt most of the cases reviewed were those of *males* who married out (kings were especially prominent in this regard), which may account for the judgment being delivered on behalf of males only.

Females, however, have not accepted this verdict without resistance. In recent years,

> . . . at Karachi, nine Parsee girls of marriageable age, and with a college education, wrote a letter to the High Priest of the Parsees in that city to enquire if he had any objection to their marrying boys from outside of their community. If so, on what grounds? If on religious grounds, could he kindly quote to them Chapter and verse of the Zoroastrian sacred scriptures, which so far as they know have never prohibited marriages between Zoroastrians and non-Zoroastrians. They remained anonymous by signing the letter, 'Nine Parsee Girls.' This clearly shows the spirit the modern young Parsee girls possess, with their modern education. [Katrak, 1965, p. 266]

While this illustration comes from nearby Pakistan rather than from India, it displays an attitude and viewpoint that cannot but have its counterpart in Bombay.[31]

If it eventually becomes possible through legal means for both men and women who marry exogamously to bring up their children in the Parsi religion, at least one step would have been taken to halt the population decline. Desai also suggests the encouragement of earlier marriages, larger families, and arranging more contacts for those of marriageable age among Parsi youth including those in other settlements like Iran (Desai, 1964, p. 22). It is doubtful whether his suggestion to "decentralize population from a highly industrialised city like Bombay" would be effective when it is realized that other similar communities like the Jews have always had a higher rate of exogamy outside the large metropolitan centers. Furthermore, other authorities note that Parsis who have already migrated elsewhere have lost their solidarity. In Burma, Malaya, Africa, Hong Kong, Europe, and the United States, it is reported by an outstanding Parsi social worker that the Parsis in these scattered areas are "not living in well-organised and well-knit, highly cooperating bodies but mostly as individual families, economically rich but socio-religiously rather poor. Even in Iran and India disintegration of communities had sent Zoroastrians away from their home towns into other towns and villages" (Yeganegi, 1966, p. 7).

WIDER PERSPECTIVES

By portraying some details of the economic and demographic decline of the Parsi community, I am not in the least suggesting that this is the paramount or

---

31. A Parsi informant reported to me in 1970 that a court case was pending in south India where a Parsi woman who married outside her community was suing for the right to bring up her children as Parsis. I have been unable to obtain further news on this case or any judgment delivered on it. One thing is certain: if the judgment goes against the woman, there will be other similar suits elsewhere.

overruling feature of the community. It would be fairly easy to make out a case for the precise opposite and show that, in all its visible or manifest features, it is the most vigorous, enterprising, and well-organized ethnic group in all India. It is only behind the scenes or in the covert elements of Parsi society that it is possible to find such traces of devolution. If not the most prosperous community in the nation, it is still one of the most prosperous. Over and above this achievement, it has made sure that its less fortunate members do not become a burden on the wider society. After visiting the housing units set aside for the more poverty-stricken of their fellows, I can only concur with the assertion of a prominent Parsi leader that "even the poorest among the Zoroastrians in India are probably better off than the poorest non-Zoroastrians in some parts of India like Bihar or Orissa or Kerala or Madras" (Sahukar, 1964, p. 12). Perhaps many internal features of vulnerability in Parsi society are simply the obverse of their inordinate success, in a word the nemesis of triumphant bourgeois anywhere.

To raise the question of integration into the larger society is, in the Parsi case, to encounter the greatest unanimity on the issue I have yet discovered for any minority dealt with in these pages. To a man, the Parsis interviewed agreed that they preferred separation from the rest of Indian society in religion and marriage but not in other social relations. Non-Parsis concurred that the Parsis had the right amount of autonomy and were therefore "integrated" properly into the nation as a whole.[32] It is significant, of course, that Parsis do not participate in politics as a body; their tiny size precludes such activity, though it is conceivable that with organization they might, at times, swing the balance of power in the Bombay electorate. But this is not their public style. Individual political leaders like Masani of the Swatantra party may attain national influence, but there is no Parsi party or even Voters League. Even prominent figures in the superpatriotic Jan Sangh like Vajpayee have commended the Parsis for being truly integrated into India, the intimation being: here is one minority that does not need Indianization.

It is plain that the preference for a cultural pluralist solution shows remarkable consensus among both Parsis and Hindus. Throughout their long history in India, the Parsis have been singularly free from conflict or persecution initiated by outsiders. On only two occasions have they actually been attacked, one by a Bania with hired mercenaries of Kolis and Rajputs in Cambay during the seventeenth century A.D., and the other by a Rajput ruler in the eighteenth century at Variav. Both of these were quite minor incidents and had no significant repercussions (Katrak, 1965, p. 140). Having neither military nor political cadres, the Parsis have lived peaceably with their neighbors since their initial oath to the Hindu chief of Sanjan in the eighth century. Mutual respect and tolerance have characterized both Hindus and Parsis in their encounter with each other, their intermingling often marked by self-effacement. In many respects the position of the Parsis is so secure because it resembles the

---

32. Only one non-Parsi respondent (a woman) tried to demur on this issue. She resented openly the Parsi rule that forbids the entrance of non-Parsis into fire temples, considering this an unjustifiable separation of Zoroastrians from fellow-citizens in India. No other complaint of this kind was encountered, and I suspect that it was idiomatic, though only further exploration could ascertain this.

self-contained and inner-facing life of the caste; this phenomenon is familiar enough to be accepted on all sides. If the Parsis are a caste, even metaphorically, they are without question the most urbanized, Westernized, and secularized caste yet to appear. While most minorities in India are to be contrasted with the dominant elite, the Parsis (many of them, at least) seem to have joined it. In the more popular use of the label, one could almost say that they are no longer a minority at all.

Since the days of British dominance, the modern sector of the Parsis have accepted in large measure the rationalist ideas of the enlightenment and the world view of liberalism-cum-utilitarianism. This identifies them with that sector of the elite termed "conditionally Westernized" in Chapter 1 above: English educated, seekers of Western culture, secular minded or agnostic in religious belief, scoffing at traditional religious doctrines and astrology, secularists in politics, convinced parliamentarians, and eschewing the use of mass violence of all kinds in domestic politics.[33] Since the conditionally Westernized are estimated at less than 10 percent of the dominant elite in India, they are vulnerable to the power of the 90 percent, or "parochial neo-traditionals," who are educated in the vernacular, attracted more to regional culture than to Western culture, retaining domestic caste restrictions, paying homage to all types of religious figures (including astrologers), accepting social techniques like satyagraha, gherao, or boycott for attaining political aims as a last resort, and suspecting minorities of disloyalty to the nation. It is this latter group of parochial neo-traditionals who are potentially the more influential sector of the national elite, and the modern Parsis have yet to learn (along with other conditionally Westernized) how to come to terms with such strongly assertive forces.[34] One thing is certain: the old tendency to universalize progress in Western terms is becoming less and less acceptable to the neo-traditionals; it is also doubtful whether it can furnish desirable guidance for Indian society as a whole. It can do service only for the few (Joshi, 1970, pp. 35, 37). With this fact of life, the Parsis, too, must come to terms, and this may require facing in new directions. Possibly the very exclusiveness and separation from the wider society has given the Parsis a way out of the dilemma that so many urbanites seem to confront. Yet the demographic decline remains as a major unsolved problem, and the question remains whether this obstacle can be overcome without some new adjustment like the revitalization of their religion in new forms.

---

33. It is worth mentioning, however, that the former Commander-in-Chief of the Armed Forces was a Parsi, General Sam Manekshaw.

34. Research would be rewarding on the impact of the Shiv Sena on the Parsi way of life in Bombay, for example. This might give an inkling of the way Parsis will react to neo-traditionals in the future.

BIBLIOGRAPHY

Bulsara, Jal E., "The Parsis," *Illustrated Weekly of India* 90 (August 31, 1969), 9-11.

Davis, Kingsley, *The Population of India and Pakistan,* Princeton, N. J., Princeton University Press, 1951.

Desai, Sapur Faredun, *A Changing Social Structure, Being a Collection of Data Submitted to ad hoc Committees Appointed by the Conference of Trusts,* Bombay, 1945.

Desai, Sapur Faredun, *A Community at the Cross-Road,* Bombay, New Book Co., 1948.

Desai, Sapur Faredun, *The Parsi Panchayet and Its Working,* Bombay, 1963.

Desai, Sapur Faredun, "Statistics of World Zoroastrians With Special Reference to Indian Zoroastrians," in *The Second World Zoroastrian Congress,* Report, Part II, Papers, Bombay, 1964.

Dhalla, Maneckji Nusservanji, *History of Zoroastrianism,* New York, Oxford University Press, 1938.

Guha, Amalendu, "Parsi Seths as Entrepreneurs, 1750-1850," *Economic and Political Weekly* 5 (Aug. 29, 1970), M107-M115.

Guha, Amalendu, "Comprador Role of Parsi Seths, 1750-1850," *Economic and Political Weekly* 5 (Nov. 28, 1970), 1933-36.

Horton, Paul B., and Gerald R. Leslie, *The Sociology of Social Problems,* New York, Appleton-Century-Crofts, 1970.

Jackson, A. V. Williams, *Zoroaster, the Prophet of Ancient Iran,* New York, Macmillan Co., 1901.

Jackson, A. V. Williams, *Zoroastrian Studies, The Iranian Religion and Various Monographs,* New York, Columbia University Press, 1928.

Joshi, R. C., "Myths Old and New," in *Minorities in Nation-Building, International Experience, Proceedings of a Seminar Organised by the India International Centre,* New Delhi, 1970.

Karaka, Dosabhai Framji, *History of the Parsis, Including their Manners, Customs, Religion and Present Position,* London, Macmillan & Co., 2 vols., 1884.

Katrak, Sohrab K. H., *Who are the Parsees?* Karachi, Pakistan Herald Press, 1965.

Kennedy, Robert E., Jr., "The Protestant Ethic and the Parsis," *American Journal of Sociology* 68 (July 1962), 11-20.

Lamb, Helen B., "The Indian Business Communities and the Evolution of an Industrialist Class," *Pacific Affairs* 28 (No. 2, June 1955), 101-16.

McKelvey, William Warren, Environmental Influences on Two Indian Business Communities, M.S. thesis, Massachusetts Institute of Technology, 1962.

Menant, D., "Parsis," in *Encyclopedia of Religion and Ethics,* edited by James Hastings, New York, Charles Scribner's Sons, 1924, vol. 9, pp. 640-50.

Mody, Sir H. P., "Foreword," in A. F. Desai, *A Community at the Cross-Road,* Bombay, New Book Co., 1948.

Moore, George Foot, *History of Religions* (rev. ed.), vol. 1, New York, Charles Scribner's Sons, 1925.

Reed, Sir Stanley, *The India I Knew, 1897-1947,* London, Odhams Press, 1952.

Sahukar, Nariman D., "Promotion of Economic Welfare," Paper II in *The Second World Zoroastrian Congress,* Report, Part II, Papers, Bombay, 1964.

Seal, Anil, *The Emergence of Indian Nationalism, Competition and Collaboration in the Later Nineteenth Century,* Cambridge at the University Press, 1968.

Shah, Buddhischandra V., *The Godavari Parsis, A Socio-Economic Study of a Rural Community in South Gujarat,* Surat, Godavara Parsi Anjuman Trust, 1955.

Verghese, B. G., "Bangla Desh and the Crisis of Identity," *Overseas Hindustan Times,* July 3, 1971.

Weber, Max, *The Protestant Ethic and the Spirit of Capitalism,* translated by Talcott Parsons, London, George Allen & Unwin Ltd., 1948.

Weber, Max, *From Max Weber,* translated and edited by H. H. Gerth and C. Wright Mills, New York, Oxford University Press, 1946.

Weintraub, Bernard, "The Indian Parsis: Waning, Troubled," *New York Times,* March 6, 1975.

Yeganegi, Mrs. Farangis, "Need for Systematic Contacts Between Zoroastrians All Over the World," Paper I, Part II in *The Second World Zoroastrian Congress,* Report, Part II, Papers, Bombay, 1966.

Chapter 12

The Chinese:
A Unique Nationality Group

As in the case of the Jews and Parsis, the Chinese in India trace their origin to immigration. But unlike the Jews, Chinese are marked by three characteristics that make them unique in the subcontinent. (1) They are recent migrants or descendants of migrants whose history extends back scarcely a hundred years. (2) They are defined in terms of nationality, with linguistic boundaries that set them apart from India and affiliate them with a different national culture. (3) They have escaped the attention of scientific investigators in the subcontinent, which means that they exist behind a wall of ignorance separating them from both the Indian public and the world of scholarship as well.[1] Any attempt, such as this one, to rescue them from their double obscurity cannot hope to be more than provisional. Whatever flare-up of notice they may have received in 1962[2] has temporarily receded, although it has left unmistakable residues behind — many of them still disabling the daily life of Chinese citizens in India.

DEMOGRAPHIC UNCERTAINTIES

Because there has been so little immigration to India during the last century, the census has understandably tended to neglect many refinements of categories defining the newcomers, such as those commonly found in countries like Brazil or the United States;[3] India had no need for such intricate distinctions and

---

1. The third feature also distinguishes them from the recently arrived Tibetans in north India who have been at least minimally studied. The Chinese minority in India has received some attention in Taipei where a set of documents entitled "Records of Overseas Chinese in India" is on file — in Chinese (Chang, 1968, p. 93).

2. Date of hostilities between India and China in the Himalayan region.

3. For instance, "foreign born," "country of birth," "country of parentage," "first generation," "second generation," "foreign stock," "foreign stock of mixed parentage," "male-female ratio of foreign born and foreign stock," "urban or rural residence of foreign born and foreign stock," "occupational characteristics of foreign born or foreign stock," et cetera.

consequently used only the most gross differentiae, so gross in some cases that their ambiguity remains a constant puzzlement.

For example, the 1961 census refers to the Chinese once as "Chinese speakers" and once simply as "Chinese" under the category of "Non-Indian Nationals." In the first case, the census enumerates 14,607 "Chinese speakers," 8,697 males and 5,910 females. In the second case, we are told that there are 5,710 "Chinese" in India, 3,352 males and 2,358 females.[4] Each of the two totals, 14,607 and 5,710 is then broken down by states of residence, the overwhelming majority in West Bengal (10,384 "Chinese speakers") with the next largest contingent in Maharashtra (2,032 "Chinese speakers").

The simplest interpretation of these figures is that there are 5,710 foreign-born Chinese in India and 14,607 residents of Chinese stock (first generation plus descendants of earlier migrant generations). But a third entry in the same census report, standing by itself and without state breakdowns, is one where Chinese are listed by "place of birth" (in this case, China) but with a quite different total of 8,095. There are no footnotes to explain the differences between this total and the other two. But if 8,095 is accepted at face value for first-generation immigrants (definitely implied by the explicit category "place of birth"), then the 5,710 figure ("Chinese") does *not* have this meaning. What is its denotation? Apparently quite uncertain.

Complications multiply. *India News* of May 8, 1970, reports that, as of November 1969, "more than 7,000 Chinese were registered as residents in India," but there is no indication to tell us whether these are citizens, immigrants, or transients. If this total corresponds to the "Non-Indian nationals" (5,710, the second category listed above), there is no necessary discrepancy provided that the question of "foreign born" is bypassed, for the number could reasonably increase from 5,000 to 7,000 in eight years or the time interval between the 1961 census and the *India News* figures for 1969. However, this assumption is precarious and will not bear much weight. Ordinarily police registration (which seems to be the referent of the *India News* statistic of 7,000) is applied to foreigners, and on this assumption there would be a decrease from 8,000 to 7,000 since the foreign-born in 1961 are listed as 8,095. This possibility is a live one, too, because we know from other sources that a considerable number of Chinese emigrated after the "incident" of 1962. This leaves us with two contradictory possibilities, each of which is plausible but unproved.

Alternatives increase. Still another estimate was published by the Overseas Chinese Affairs Commission of Taipei in 1964. Their figures include all generations of Chinese abroad and refer to ethnic membership regardless of citizenship status. On this basis they give the Chinese population of India in 1964 as 53,252, by far the largest number mentioned by any authority (Chang, 1968, p. 99). This has strong evidential value since the Nationalist government of Formosa has access to sources of information only available to a long-established fact-finding center staffed by Chinese speakers who are enabled to verify documents and records from overseas settlements which are often unintelligible

---

4. Census of India, 1961, Vol. I, Part II-c(ii) and (iii). I am indebted to Deputy-Registrar General, Dr. B. K. Roy Burman, for furnishing these and accompanying figures by state residence.

to local authorities. The Taipei statistics heighten the probability that all official totals of the Chinese population given by Indian authorities are substantial undercounts.

The only safe conclusion is that the Chinese population of India is not certainly known but that it numbers somewhere between 14,000 and 53,000 including first, second, and later generations.[5] What percentage of these are citizens is anybody's guess. But on the supposition that the great majority are second or later generations, this would mean that such a majority are also citizens, since the Constitution of India tacitly accepts the *jus soli*[6] for its people as stated in these words: "At the commencement of this constitution [1950], every person who has his domicile in the territory of India and —

(a) who was born in the territory of India; or
(b) either of whose parents was born in the territory of India; or
(c) who has been ordinarily resident in the territory of India for not less than five years immediately preceding such commencement,

shall be a citizen of India" (Part III, article 5).

Informants report that nearly all those of Chinese ancestry now resident in India were born within the country, and, if this estimate is correct, the overwhelming majority of them are legally defined citizens.[7]

CHINESE MIGRATION: PATTERN AND SOURCE

In the case of the Chinese, we face a migration that differs from that of the Jews and Parsis in the following respects:

1. It is recent. As a collective movement, it dates chiefly from the last century.
2. Part of it consisted of contract labor transfers where people were shifted in bunches or lots with minimal initiative on their part.
3. Another part of it was composed of voluntary migrants who came as individuals or families on their own.[8]
4. Those who came were a fragment of a historic civilization identified in modern times as a nation, not a body of religious believers as such.
5. The Chinese in India were a marginal fraction of the most massive migration in Asian history during the last century and a half. It is

---

5. 1971 Census reports available to the author have contained no data on Chinese residents.

6. The *jus soli* defines as citizens all those born within a defined (national) territory; the opposing doctrine, the *jus sanguinis,* defines as citizens all those related by blood to *previous* citizens, regardless of where those so defined were born or currently reside.

7. The worldwide depression of the 1930s stopped most emigration and, after the Communist regime gained control in 1949, "the People's Republic normally kept its citizens inside" (Williams, 1966, p. 75).

8. Numbers 2 and 3 make up two of the five major subtypes of migration given more attention in Schermerhorn, 1970, pp. 98ff.

estimated that the overseas Chinese outside the mainland numbered 16,420,000 in the late 1960s, exclusive of those in Hong Kong, Macao, and Taiwan (Chang, 1968, p. 97).

6. Like most other Chinese migrants of the era, those arriving in India reached their destination for the most part during the rule of a colonial power and made their initial adjustments to that authority.

Although limitations of space prohibit detailed attention to each of these factors, it is necessary to focus attention on those elements shared by these migrants with millions of their fellow-countrymen, particularly the overseas Chinese in southeast Asia where the bulk of them settled.

Historically, the Chinese spread their cultural influence in two ways: by conquest and by migration. The classical people of China — the Han — had their geographic center along the Yellow River spreading from there northward to what later became the Great Wall, and westward nearly to the borders of Tibet. It was the Han peoples who disseminated the culture of their relatively urban civilization southward by conquest as far as modern Vietnam and Thailand, both of which were consequently Sinicized to a considerable degree. In the area between the original Han kingdom and present-day Indochina, there were hundreds of mountain and forest tribes, some of which were overrun by Han conquests while others remained untouched. The provinces of Kwangtung (Canton) and Kwangsi (Wuchow) were among those permeated by Han culture, and it is these southern states, together with Fukien, from which the bulk of later emigrants departed between the seventeenth and nineteenth centuries. A number of factors influenced their decision to leave their homes behind, but the crucial influence was the Manchu dynasty which overwhelmingly defeated the northern legions and smashed its way southward to bring the rest of the Empire to its knees. The brutal Manchus denuded a coastal zone in Kwangtung, Fukien, and Chekiang, burning down the villages as they advanced. In this seventeenth century conquest, some of the displaced people on the coast were given property if they left their homes and moved to the interior; the rest, both fearing and despising the Manchus, sought refuge overseas (Wiens, 1954, pp. xi-40; Purcell, 1965, p. 24). These southern coastal provinces never fully recovered their agricultural productivity; emigration became almost a tradition there. Recurrent hardships of the area are summarized by Chang as "poverty, rural unemployment, civil war and famine. . . . ," while the attractions abroad were "employment opportunities created by the exploitation and development of the tropical world by European countries and by the shortage of manual laborers in highly developed countries. The occupations of the Chinese abroad were therefore largely determined by the needs of the country to which they moved" (Chang, 1968, p. 104).

OVERSEAS CHINESE MIGRATION: STAGES AND DEVELOPMENT

The movement of Chinese into all of southeast Asia and south Asia falls naturally into the following periods:

I.   Era preceding mass migration. Seventeenth century to 1875.

II. Mass migration.
    1. The thriving colonial age. 1875-1920s.
    2. The decline of colonialism. 1920s to World War II.
III. Limited migration.
    1. Post-colonial independence — pre-Communist phase. 1941-49.
    2. Post-colonial independence — post-Communist phase. 1949-present.[9]

Each of these periods left its mark on the Chinese migrant populations. Common to nearly all stages were the initial characteristics of the migrants summarized neatly by Williams' definition of an overseas Chinese: ". . . an overseas Chinese is a person of some Chinese ancestry who views residence abroad as compatible with Chinese cultural identity and less certainly with some remote Chinese political orientation. The overseas Chinese considers his expatriation the result of his own or his forbears' economic strivings. He regards himself as a member of the overseas Chinese people, which is, in turn, part of the greater Chinese nation, and is so regarded by those around him" (Williams, 1966, p. 6). This was, however, not a self-conception that appeared in full bloom but a product of stages I and II, continuing into stage III.

In era I, before mass migration began, the sojourn of southern Chinese abroad was first to kingdoms governed by native rulers of the pre-colonial epoch. During those years, the Chinese lived in tiny ghettoes and carried on limited trade. Their numbers increased appreciably in the latter part of this first period when Europeans were establishing a foothold for later and more consolidated colonial empires. It was not, however, until the final quarter of the nineteenth century that the full establishment of colonial economic organization came into being and when the demand for expanded labor forces for mines, plantations, and commercial undertakings reached its height; and it was in this era that Chinese migration reached its flood tide. As it became a mass movement, more women went abroad to join husbands and families, bringing the sex ratio in Chinese settlements abroad closer to a balance. This added natural population increase to the number swelled by migration itself but served at the same time to halt assimilation into local groups, as the Chinese now fashioned more separate enclaves of their own. The process was augmented after the Nationalist revolution of the Kuomintang in 1911 when the new rulers on the mainland initiated a militant ideology for the nation and its representatives abroad; the *jus sanguinis* became a dogma with the watchword, "where there are Chinese, there is China." Nationalistic pride spread from the mainland to overseas settlements and produced a plethora of Chinese schools, chambers of commerce, and other separate institutions that kept Chinese culture alive at the cost of provoking resentment among local populations, especially when the Chinese enclaves controlled increasing sectors of the economy with some conspicuous display of wealth.

---

9. In India this last phase can be divided again into the period 1949-62 (the era of the approving catch phrase "Hindi Chini bhai bhai") and a later one, 1962 to the present, that is, from the Indo-Chinese armed conflict through the period of the second Indo-Pakistani war. In this latter period the attitude toward China was reversed into an almost frozen posture of alienation.

A smoldering hostility toward the Chinese on the part of indigenous populations was strengthened by the rise of local nationalisms as colonial regimes weakened with the worldwide depression of the 1930s, and popular leaders sought to wrest political power from colonial rulers as well as economic power from overseas Chinese merchants, traders, and industrialists. Harassment of the minorities mounted on all sides. With the arrival of World War II and the Japanese occupation of China, the new regime tried to capture local nationalisms without noticeable success; in this period of transition it became quite clear that European colonialism was drawing to a close, but the shape of things to come was quite obscure. Indigenous nationalisms continued to increase their strength while the overseas Chinese communities, subject to hostility from both local patriots and the Japanese invaders, not infrequently suffered attacks from both sides. As the war closed and the local areas became independent, aggression from Japanese conquerors abated, but offensives from new local governments increased sporadically. As the communists dislodged the Kuomintang from the seats of power on the mainland, this provoked a crisis of loyalties among the Chinese abroad who strove to keep channels of communication and mutual exchange open both to Taipei and to Peking (Purcell, 1965, pp. xi-xv).

The trends noted so far affected overseas Chinese throughout the whole of southeast Asia, particularly in Burma, Thailand, Vietnam, Cambodia, Laos, Malaya (with Singapore), Sarawak, Borneo, Indonesia, Portuguese Timor, and the Philippines. The vast majority of their fellow Chinese abroad settled in these areas, and only a tiny fraction of the migrants came to India. What the latter shared in culture and historical development with their conationals abroad and what was unique to their experience in India can be pieced together precariously; documentation is weak and the investigator limited to separate and often unrelated items. Putting them together will result in alternate composites, each of which will depend on the organizing inventiveness of those who examine the fragments. What follows is one of these versions, and it will serve us hypothetically until more complete ones follow.[10]

THE CHINESE IN INDIA: A SPECIAL CASE?

Like the rest of the overseas Chinese, those who migrated to India came chiefly from the provinces of southeast China (Kwangtung, Hunan, Kiangsi, and Fukien) and the languages spoken by the majority of present-day Chinese in Calcutta as well as the rest of India is either Cantonese or Hakka.

Apart from a few early Buddhist pilgrims, the first Chinese reported to have arrived in India was a merchant from Fukien province named Ah Chi, who brought a gift of tea to one of the native princes of West Bengal in the eighteenth century and eventually founded a small town by the name of Ah Chi Po where an old Chinese temple still exists. However, this preceded any migration

---

10. An additional difficulty is that countless pieces of information are missing; thus, it is safer to speak of all the "known" fragments in English sources. More thorough research based on Chinese sources is sorely needed.

in numbers. "Except for a few Buddhist pilgrims, India did not attract Chinese migrants until after 1865, when the British launched an economic program for India with the introduction of tea plantations and of railroad and highway projects. The first group of Chinese, brought in from Hong Kong and Macao,[11] worked as tea planters, as tea-box makers in Assam, and as road-builders in Bengal" (quoted from Taipei records in Chang, 1968, p. 93). In the same era (the latter part of the nineteenth century), a contingent of Cantonese migrated to Calcutta; being skilled woodworkers and carpenters, they had no difficulty establishing themselves and became the nucleus of the Chinese community of the city. At the close of the nineteenth century, a much larger group from China entered Calcutta. These were, almost without exception, unskilled workers of Hakka origin; when they discovered that the Hindus avoided leather work and shoemaking, they gradually took it up and trained themselves in the skills associated with the different stages of leather preparation. By the 1960s there were between 7,000 and 8,000 Hakkas in the Calcutta area, most of them dependent on the tannery industry. A large number of Chinese bootmakers and as many as a hundred Chinese dentists[12] are scattered throughout other cities of India.

Although there is no social history of the Chinese minority in India, extensive studies of other Chinese communities in the Nanyang (domain of overseas Chinese) furnish a number of parallels so common and widespread that they throw a great deal of light on developments in the Chinese community in Hindustan. One significant difference was in the type of colonial rule: from as early as the eighteenth century, it was the British, rather than the Spanish or Dutch, who especially attracted Chinese settlers to their colonies (Purcell, 1965, p. 25). But as already noted, the bulk of Chinese migration came in the heyday of the colonial era, and thus the Chinese ordinarily settled in areas where there were alien governmental structures superimposed on the institutions of local peoples. The colonial authorities regarded the migrants chiefly as utilitarian instruments of the economy, traders, agents, or manual workers, and had no interest in them as a people or in their cultural habits. Conversely, however, the Chinese, in order to play their role as useful workers for the ruling regime, developed a working knowledge of indigenous customs and mores quite unknown to the Europeans; at the same time they were soon more knowledgeable about the dominant whites than the Europeans were about them. It was uniformly true that the colonial masters "were almost completely ignorant of the Chinese language and mores, and the Chinese were happy that it should be so" (Purcell, 1951, p. 659). This placed the migrant Chinese behind a screen of invisibility and helped to account for their reputation as inscrutable, though there was no real mystery involved: neither the Europeans nor the local Asians bothered to look. On the other hand, the Chinese, who scrutinized both sides intently and became bilingual or trilingual in the process, were in excellent position to profit by this superior knowledge. It is therefore not surprising that

---

11. Many of the mobile Chinese in these cities stemmed from the provinces of southeast China already mentioned.

12. Informants report that the latter have come from Ipoh, a city in Malaya.

they showed rapid adaptation and noticeable upward mobility during the colonial era.

The many Chinese immigrant settlements throughout the Nanyang were anything but homogeneous. Each one "was not a complete unit of China transplanted, but fragments from various settings placed together in one spot. Different tribes and classes were put into unwonted juxtaposition. . . ." (Purcell, 1951, p. 660). This applies to Calcutta where Cantonese and Hakka rub shoulders together but constitute to this day a mosaic rather than an amalgam. The consequence is a set of diverse loyalties and orientations. Expectations of uniformity entertained by outsiders are completely false. Chinese settlements abroad, whether in Burma, Malaya or Indonesia, are in no way monolithic in views or attitudes (Williams, 1966, p. 4). A local respondent in Calcutta comments immediately on internal factionalism among the Chinese throughout the city. Probably most Chinese communities in the Nanyang were anything but close-knit except when under attack.

After 1911 the Nationalist government of China tried to centralize control of all its people abroad, encouraged its consuls everywhere to register population lists, and sent emissaries overseas to examine both the social and commercial activities of the Chinese of the territories, and to direct their educational institutions by means of common curricula introduced across the board. Such agents also furnished grants-in-aid in an attempt to maintain control over the school systems and to prevent their dependence on local governments. These measures created resentment in many colonies and apprehensions of an *imperium in imperio* (Purcell, 1951, p. 668).

It is probable that the Chinese community of Calcutta escaped these forms of control; their full impact could not have been felt, judging from the current predominance of Christian mission schools over those of indigenous Chinese sponsorship. Geographic realities help to account for this fact, since the Chinese of India were far removed from their fellow-nationals in both southeast Asia and the mainland. They appear to have been, from the beginning, outside the mainstream of the Nanyang, a marginal group who could easily have escaped the attention of Nationalist officials, or regarded as so insignificant in numbers as to warrant little effort to keep them in line.

We are handicapped, in any case, by the absence of annual or decennial immigration figures for the Chinese population of India. Without such data we cannot infer the extent of social intercourse with the mainland over the years, or how much demographic growth was due to migration and how much to natural increase. There are only a few clues from observations of Nanyang Chinese elsewhere. For southeast Asia it appears that population growth between the 1940s and 1960s (disregarding the migration slowdown of the 1960s) was of the order of 3 percent per year, possibly a bit less (Purcell, 1965, pp. 2-3). This rate of increase is generally regarded as high. Another authority comments that, apart from Burma, all the Chinese settlements in southeast Asia are composed overwhelmingly of Chinese born of local origin rather than in China proper. So high is the birthrate, that in one city where statistics are fairly reliable (Singapore), evidence shows fully half its inhabitants of Chinese ancestry under fifteen years of age. Reports are that their parents have no memory of mainland China (Williams, 1966, p. 75).

Whether these trends apply equally to the Chinese population of India is still uncertain; the problem requires more intensive research than it has received so far. Considerable emigration from India occurred in the 1960s as will be noted later, but there seems to be no special reason why the natural increase should be noticeably different from that observed throughout southeast Asia. There is little, if any, miscegenation with local Hindus, where caste restrictions set up strong barriers. Endogamous preferences are also strong among the Chinese themselves, and informants report that there are a number of cases where males of the minority community have traveled as far abroad as Taipei and Hong Kong to find suitable brides. Another demographic clue comes from the Chinese of Semarang who have been intensively studied; there the enlarged family is changing to the conjugal or nuclear type, women are more emancipated, and young people have more voice in the choice of marriage partners than was traditionally the case (D. E. Wilmott, 1960, quoted in Purcell, 1965, p. 34). Such secularizing processes have the effect of reducing birthrates and the size of families. A similar process is apparently at work in Calcutta where greater freedom of women's roles is shown by the increasing entry of Chinese girls into the work force as typists or stenographers.

The relation of Chinese communities to governmental authorities during the colonial era was equable and accommodating. "By and large, the Chinese were very law-abiding and gave the ruling Powers little trouble. Schlegel was right when he said that the Chinese were 'easy to govern.' Indeed this quality has brought them, at times, into the contempt of rough European individualists who have dismissed this tractableness as the characteristic of 'sheep' " (Purcell, 1951, p. 660). On the whole, most overseas Chinese settlements adopted a more or less deliberate policy that left politics and government in other hands without seeking to participate actively in it.[13] Cynics could say that these decisions developed *faute de mieux* since the Chinese were never given political responsibilities anyway; consequently, they performed those duties the various governments allowed them to do — functions quite outside the political realm (ibid., p. 663).

After World War II, emigration of Chinese from the mainland came to a rather abrupt halt (except for surreptitious leakage into ports like Macao and Hong Kong). Lack of fresh recruits from home base has therefore allowed each of the overseas communities more of a chance to develop autonomously in its own way. Outsiders have often stereotyped the inhabitants of such settlements as affluent merchants engaging in lucrative trade. This is a mistaken idea. "For every overseas Chinese commercial giant, there are thousands of petty traders, and for every small shopkeeper or itinerant peddler, there are scores of laborers" (Williams, 1966, p. 20). Even cursory acquaintance with the Chinese community of Calcutta reveals the same type of occupational distribution.

Since the 1940s there has also been change in the leadership structure of many communities in the Nanyang. "Today the semi-literate *nouveau riche* is passing from the ranks of leadership. . . . While in the first twentieth century decades the respected members of an overseas community were rich merchants

---

13. An older dictum had it that "the Chinese don't mind who holds the cow so long as they milk it."

who embraced Chinese nationalism, to add to their stature and influence, physicians, lawyers, editors, labor union officers, teachers, industrialists, traders, and career politicians are currently pushing aside the old leadership." Such men see the progress of their community bound up with that of the countries in which they live and are more open to rapprochement with people of the land and their aspirations (Williams, 1966, p. 88). The extent to which this evolution has occurred in India is somewhat uncertain, but secular changes are moving in the same direction. Contacts with conationals abroad reinforcing traditional patterns are increasingly cut off, and the chances for new leadership are correspondingly enhanced.

Significantly, since the communist regime has been regnant on the mainland, the opportunity for Chinese abroad who have accumulated even modest means to return back to their native province (or that of their ancestors) has quite disappeared.[14] The Peking government has prohibited the unrestricted flow of coffins to mainland provinces for burial; the communists are firmly convinced that the old burial practices took too much land out of cultivation and hence, from an economic point of view, were a definite waste. This creates still another rupture of the connections between Chinese abroad and their ancestral homeland (Williams, 1966, pp. 78-79). Such effects of communist rule, however, were minor. More important ones must now claim attention.

THE COMMUNIST ERA IN CHINA: ITS LARGER CONSEQUENCES IN THE NANYANG

When observers interpret the People's Republic of China as a center of subversion constantly seeking to overthrow the governments of south and southeast Asia by infiltration and revolutionary doctrine, they neglect some of the hard evidence openly available. From the time when Mao took the reins of power in Peking, from 1949 to the Cultural Revolution of 1967, the Chinese communists reversed many policies of the Kuomintang and relaxed the hold of the central government over Chinese compatriots abroad. Peking organized a new agency having the title The Overseas Chinese Affairs Commission; its director, Liao Ch'eng Chih, adopted a policy encouraging overseas Chinese to remain apolitical, even discouraging governmental studies among Chinese organizations and schools, since this might make local regimes (as he said in his own words) "think that we were going to carry out revolutions and 'subversive activities' locally and 'impair diplomatic relations'" (Fitzgerald, 1969, pp. 103-04). The Kuomintang generously encouraged Chinese language schools abroad, but the communists did not. The Nationalists held firmly to the idea that all persons born of Chinese parents abroad were blood members of the Chinese nation regardless of their birthplace, but "Peking abandoned the concept of *jus sanguinis*... embodied in the KMT Nationality Law of 1929"

---

14. Some exceptions occurred as in Indonesia, where many Chinese were forcibly expelled and accepted repatriation from the People's Republic of China, though there seems to be some doubt whether individual families were typically sent to the precise areas from which their ancestors came (Williams, 1966, p. 78).

(ibid., pp. 111-12). Chinese in the Nanyang were urged to become loyal citizens of the land in which they were living. Another authority puts the matter more strongly, "Now Peking prefers to treat the Chinese abroad as an embarrassing nuisance complicating the implementation of grand strategy" (Williams, 1966, p. 29). Historically, of course, the Chinese overseas contributed liberally to the Nationalist revolution of 1911 and to the Kuomintang government that followed it. But in stark contrast, "the Communists owe the overseas Chinese nothing. Mao Tse-Tung's revolution was not nurtured by expatriates. Peking's current willingness to neglect most of the Chinese abroad may be in part explained by this historical circumstance. . ." (ibid., p. 52). In time, the communist regime encouraged overseas Chinese in Indonesia and Burma to become apolitical citizens and even to intermarry with local residents (Purcell, 1965, p. xv; Fitzgerald, 1969, pp. 106, 117).

In cases where amicable relations between overseas Chinese and the newly formed independent regimes of their environing areas are impossible to maintain, the People's Republic of China not only promises to serve as a sanctuary for those who want to leave when danger threatens but has actually implemented that decision. Thus, in Indonesia where local violence against Chinese became endemic after independence, over 100,000 persons of Chinese ancestry were repatriated to the mainland. Between 1951 and 1966, it is reported that at least 200,000 overseas Chinese repatriated themselves (Williams, 1966, pp. 65-66).[15] By accepting these conationals without demur, the Peking regime demonstrated its willingness to remove any irritants with the governments of newly organized nations, to adopt certain humanitarian measures, and to develop unhampered friendship with nationalist leaders abroad.

Though the Cultural Revolution of 1967 in China produced some criticism of such tolerance, there is little evidence that it brought any immediate change in policy (Fitzgerald, 1969, pp. 104, 122). One deviation from this broad program of conciliation, however, has importance for the Chinese community in India. Although the Peking regime was not the center of mass subversion it was popularly supposed to be, it nevertheless did encourage intervention in local affairs of foreign countries under one condition: "Only the Chinese in countries hostile to the People's Republic . . . are called upon to be disobedient to their governments. Elsewhere, Chinese are encouraged to be inconspicuous, decent settlers" (Williams, 1966, p. 69).[16] This exception to the dominant policy placed the Chinese minority of India in an embarrassing position in 1962.

---

15. In a very real sense, this process represented a severe strain on the communist government and a sacrifice on their part, because the repatriates had to be not only clothed and fed but ideologically assimilated as well; the latter proved most difficult because of the markedly individualistic habits and attitudes of the refugees, who often resisted the collective patterns and doctrines imposed on them (Williams, 1966, pp. 66-67).

16. A noticeable change in the international balance of power sometimes affects Chinese policy more radically. Thus, after the capture of Saigon by North Vietnam in May 1975, an official in Kuala Lumpur reported a massive increase in insurgency forces, ostensibly supported by Peking (Tuohy, 1975).

INDO-CHINESE HOSTILITIES AND THEIR REPERCUSSIONS

In the fall of 1962, Chinese armies invaded Indian territory[17] beginning with light forces on September 8 and a mass attack on October 20, continuing until the following month. To the Indian public and to government officials, this was perceived as a sudden, premeditated, and wholly unprovoked attack,[18] and it aroused the country to a fever heat of martial enthusiasm surpassing all previous experience. Demonstrations against the Chinese took place in all the major cities, and Chinese officials in both Delhi and Peking charged that Chinese stores throughout India were smashed and looted, that Chinese nationals were beaten and insulted, and that Indian crowds gathered before the Chinese embassy and consulates shouting noisy threats and imprecations (notes in White Paper No. VIII, 1963).

On October 28, 1962, approximately 1,000 Chinese held a meeting in the Choon Ye Thong Church of Calcutta, with Mr. K. C. Yap presiding. The meeting by acclamation condemned the Chinese invasion of India and publicly declared loyalty to the government at New Delhi.[19] At that time it was reported that there were 15,000 Chinese in Calcutta and that 12,000 of these were "stateless"; that is, they held neither Peking or Kuomintang passports. The same report announced that four hundred Chinese of Calcutta had acquired Indian citizenship and three hundred more had applied for it by that date. There were also hints that some Chinese were compelled to apply for Peking passports, although the source of this information was not mentioned (*Statesman,* Oct. 29, 1962).

Regarding the situation as opportune for fifth columnists, the Government of India initiated several countermoves. The main ones were as follows:

1. On October 25, 1962, the Government of India issued an order forbidding any Chinese national from leaving his local area or to absent himself from his registered address for more than 24 hours without permission from the Registration officer who in turn was empowered to use his own discretion.
2. On October 30, 1962, President Radhakrishnan issued an ordinance (amending the Foreigners' Law of 1946) which now made the provisions of that law applicable in a special way to any persons of non-Indian origin who at birth were citizens or subjects of any country now at war with India or committing aggression against her.
3. On the same date the President issued a parallel order affirming that no person of non-Indian origin who at birth was a citizen or subject of a country subsequently committing aggression against India or assisting in

---

17. Boundary disputes preceded military action, and the Chinese therefore asserted that they were trying to reclaim their own territory. Cf. S.P. Varma, 1965.

18. For the long incubation period and stimuli to aggression on both sides, see Lamb, 1968, pp. 332-38.

19. Referred to later in White Paper No. VIII, 1963, p. 112.

this act, could henceforth petition any Indian court for the enforcement of his constitutional rights under Articles 21 and 22 of the Constitution which guard individuals against arbitrary violation of their rights.[20]

4. Somewhat later the Government of India prohibited any Chinese national from leaving the country except by special permit and then only from specified cities: Bombay, Calcutta, Madras, or New Delhi.

5. The Government of India also authorized the formation of internment camps for arrested foreigners (in the nature of the case, Chinese) and transported such persons to the camps. Between October 26, 1962, and the latter part of 1963, the Government interned more than 2,130 Chinese (including 1,313 in Assam and 817 in West Bengal). Eventually the foreigners interned included those "reasonably suspected" of committing or about to commit acts assisting a country at war with India or aggressing against her.

6. Such internees or enemy foreigners were no longer permitted to sell or transfer any property without the approval of the Custodian of Enemy Property for India who legally assumed power of attorney for such persons and was under regulations governing the sale, management, and disposal of all property of persons interned or paroled (Schoenfeld, 1963, pp. 221-35).[21]

7. Chinese passing through Indian ports were not allowed to come ashore without a permit and this was issued to them only within their last twenty-four hours in port (Chinese informant).[22]

Technically these measures were designed for the foreign-born, but there is agreement among the Chinese interviewed that such measures were not infrequently applied to those of Chinese ancestry whether born in India or not. After all, no official could observe the difference, and it was easy for him to conclude that a given person was concealing his origin, in case of doubt. Furthermore, proof of Indian birth was not in the possession of most suspects, and, had it been sought in time of public clamor, it could hardly have been secured. In the popular outcry against the enemy, all Chinese were indistinguishable, and this contagion could hardly fail to make its way into the ranks of officialdom, particularly at the lower levels where the agents of enforcement were likely to share the sentiments of the crowd and display their patriotism with the best of them. Hence it is not certain how many Chinese detainees were actually foreign-born or India-born. Probably this will never be known.

---

20. This meant all Chinese-born who later became Indian citizens were now to be treated as foreigners.

21. On the assumption of communist sympathy with the Chinese, the Government of India simultaneously detained a considerable number of Indian communists (especially from Kerala) and even included three socialist leaders in Delhi. Since both the Centre and the states have jurisdiction over civil rights, Home Minister Shastri ruled that detainees could be released on orders from the Chief Ministers of the various states, and they eventually obtained release by this route (Schoenfeld, 1963, pp. 234-35).

22. Later this was rescinded for Singapore Chinese when Lee Kuan Yew threatened to treat all Indian travelers in Singapore the same way (Chinese informant).

Chinese propaganda organs on the mainland complained vigorously against the treatment of Chinese nationals in India. A highly voluble statement of these grievances appeared in the following statement by a writer for the subsidized Chinese press:

> Thousands of innocent Chinese, including a large number of old people, women and children, have been thrown into concentration camps . . . . India's concentration camps are in desolate enclaves in Rajasthan and other places. Those incarcerated there were robbed of their property and money and were not even allowed to take along extra clothing. . . . Half of the Chinese nationals interned in the camps have fallen ill as a result of ill-treatment but they received no medical care. . . . Many have lost contact with their families. Those Chinese nationals who have not been interned stand in daily fear of arrest and loss of property. Indian police may burst into their homes at any time to conduct a search and subject them to blackmail, extortion and other malpractices. The Indian authorities have besides employed economic and other discriminatory measures against Chinese nationals so that many of them have lost their jobs; others have found it impossible any longer to operate their shops or other businesses, and their property has been frozen. Those who have been deprived of the means of earning a living have, furthermore, been prohibited from selling their property. The Indian authorities have promulgated the fantastic regulation that any Chinese national who sells his property will be subject to a five-year prison term and the same punishment will be meted out to those who buy such property. Under the pressure of these draconian measures, some Chinese have become mentally deranged; others have committed suicide.[23] [Chou Pao-Ju, 1962, p. 10]

While it is difficult either to substantiate or refute such charges in detail, the actual process of detention (which started in the winter months) was undoubtedly accompanied by serious hardships, especially for those accustomed to urban residence — a substantial proportion. The Indian Ministry of External Affairs, in answer to a Chinese government complaint about the detention process, replied on December 13, 1962:

> The Chinese note of 24th November has referred to internment of Chinese nationals in Assam State and five districts of West Bengal. It became necessary for the Government of India to remove all Chinese nationals from that region along with others who were security risks when Chinese aggressors had been moving threateningly towards these areas. This was done in pursuance of the requirements of security and defence of the country against foreign aggression.

In the same note the Ministry responded to the Chinese charge that the Chinese nationals were put under harsh surveillance by Indian authorities with the statement:

---

23. This merely repeats and expands on similar statements in the note from the Ministry of Foreign Affairs, Peking, to the Embassy of India in China, December 18, 1962. See White Paper No. VIII, 1963, pp. 105-06.

The maintenance of law and order and public security assumes greater significance when the country concerned has been subjected to external aggression. Several orders were promulgated by the Government of India under the Defence of India Regulations placing restrictions on Indian nationals in order to safeguard the security of the country endangered by massive Chinese invasion. The Foreigners Law (Application and Amendment) Ordinance 1962, was also promulgated with the same end in view. The promulgation of this Ordinance is a matter solely within the sovereign jurisdiction of the Government of India. [White Paper No. VIII, 1963, p. 104]

On November 21, 1962, China suddenly made a unilateral offer of a ceasefire and announced that on December 1 they would pull their troops back 12.5 miles behind the positions of actual control. Though this territorial solution was not satisfactory, the war came to an abrupt end. Negotiations then began on the status of the internees within India. The Chinese Government in its note of December 18, 1962, announced that it "decided to send ships to India to bring back those Chinese nationals who are either interned or unable to continue to earn their living in India as a result of other forms of persecution and who wish to return to their motherland" (White Paper No. VIII, 1963, p. 107).

To this the Indian Government replied in its note of December 31, 1962:

The cases of these Chinese internees are being reviewed from time to time. Only those who constitute serious risk to national security will continue under detention. The Government of India are also prepared to give necessary facilities to Chinese nationals in India, who wish to return to China of their own free will. These facilities will, in the first instance, be limited to holders of passports issued by the Government of the People's Republic of China who have no criminal or civil complaints pending against them. These Chinese nationals returning to China will be allowed to take back the sale proceeds of any property that they may have in accordance with the prevailing Indian regulations on the subject. The Government of India presume that similar facilities for repatriation etc. will be extended by the Chinese Government on a reciprocal basis to Indian nationals in China who wish to return to India.[24] [White Paper No. VIII, 1963, p. 112]

Repatriation did occur, but the details are obscure. Informants in Calcutta during 1969 reported that more than three thousand Chinese "left the country" in the wake of the Indo-Chinese hostilities, but the time and manner of their departure were only vaguely indicated. How many were detainees, how many left in Chinese vessels, and the date of their journey, all are matters of conjecture.

---

24. In the same note, the Indian government also replied to charges of harshness and severity in the internment camps by asserting: "The officially accredited representative of the International Committee of the Red Cross in India has also visited the camp and was fully satisfied with the arrangements made. It may be stressed for the information of the Chinese Government that the facilities accorded to these internees are in full conformity with the scales prescribed by the Geneva Conventions of 1949 to which the Chinese Government are also a signatory" (ibid.).

One thing, however, seems certain: delays in the release of detainees were incessant. Over two thousand Chinese nationals entered the internment facilities in November or December of 1962. After the close of the war, releases were slow and intermittent. The avowed policy of the Indian Government was to continue holding only those who seemed to constitute a threat to national security. This meant that a hard core of the prisoners could be denied release indefinitely. Confirmation of this appraisal was furnished by the Peking radio which officially broadcast the following message almost two years later in October 1964: "We are extremely indignant over the persecution of Chinese nationals by the Indian government. We resolutely demand the release of several hundred Chinese nationals who are being detained by the Indian government" (Williams, 1966, p. 68). The drop in the number of internees from around two thousand to "several hundred" in two years may indicate that in the later period there was still some suspicion attached to the remainder in the camps, possibly uncertainty on what to do with them, or inertia which relieved the pressure of making bureaucratic decisions.

There are some indications that inertia continues to affect the relationship between Government officials and the Chinese rank and file within India. Restrictions imposed in wartime against the freedom of travel for Chinese nationals (extended in practice to the India born) are allowed to continue without any sign of their termination. The most noticeable sign of dissatisfaction in the Chinese community, so far as I was able to discover in 1969, was resentment over travel regulations. One informant, to illustrate his own experience in this regard, produced the following letter written by himself to the proper agency in New Delhi during 1967 and gave permission for its publication.[25] (The writer is an India-born Chinese.)

To the Proper Authority
New Delhi

Dear Sir:

On – – – 1967 I wrote to the Foreigners Registration office in X^{26} for permission to travel to Delhi with my wife and two small children to interview the Immigration Attache for Canada, 7 Link Road, New Delhi.

The local authorities inform me that sanction has to come from the Delhi Police before a travel permit could be issued. I have waited 20 days and still no news, up to this moment.

In view of my previous experiences, I am doubtful whether my request to travel will be granted in time for my proposed departure for Delhi on the – – of – –. May I request your help and sympathetic consideration in this matter.

You will appreciate my difficulties when I briefly mention the following instances.

---

25. Names, specific dates, and places concealed or omitted to ensure confidentiality.

26. The Chinese writer's city of residence.

1) On – – – I applied for permission to go to – – – on business in connection with purchases for my shop. The request was refused on – – – (a month and 6 days later).

2) In the month of – – – in – – – I requested for permission to visit X with my wife for one days sightseeing, travelling by Government Tourist Bus. Application was refused at the end of that month.

3) My wife requested for permission to attend her sister's wedding in X. She applied 6 weeks before the marriage date. No sanction was received even after the date of the wedding. Reason was "X authorities did not send a reply." My wife's train reservation had to be cancelled, and her ticket refunded at a loss. The disappointment involved can be imaginable.

4) On – – – I applied for permission to go to X to buy equipment from a European closing his business. Because of Import control, new equipment of that type is impossible to buy. Now that this chance was offered to me, I wanted to go to X and buy the things before someone else in my line of business heard about it. After waiting for 3 anxious weeks, and sending several reminders, the permit was not yet granted. By that time the opportunity was lost. I cancelled my request in my letter dated – – – (the following month).

5) On – – – at 9 A.M. my wife received a shocking Telegram from her family in X, informing her of the death of her father. I applied for permission to leave for X immediately with my wife to attend the funeral. Along with my application I had enclosed the original copy of the telegram. My request to leave this city even on such an urgent matter was not granted. The reason was "X authorities had to send their approval before we were allowed to go." The authorities here were kind enough to send out a wireless message to X. Sanction was granted on – – –, 2 weeks after the burial.

Any help you can render to make travelling a little less difficult will be most gratefully appreciated.

Thanking you.

Yours faithfully,

———————

Restrictions of this kind have had marked effects on the enclosure of the Chinese community in India. Not all of the results can be laid at the door of the Indo-China war itself; the diplomatic aftermath had serious consequences as well. During the first Indo-Pakistani war of 1965, "China . . . accused India of aggression against Pakistan and declared publicly that she would aid Pakistan. She did not actually intervene, but mutual accusations of border violations continued" (Lamb, 1968, p. 338). Much the same sequence of events was repeated during the second Indo-Pakistani war of 1971. Reiterated denunciations of India's actions from Peking have helped to keep India's attitudes of enmity alive, and, in this climate of opinion, the Chinese minority of India, rightly or wrongly, remains a target of suspicion. In this respect, the situation in India is unique throughout the Nanyang. Not one other nation in south or southeast Asia has been overtly attacked by Chinese armed forces or has experienced the Chinese joining a diplomatic alliance against them; consequently, none has felt the same severe provocation to maintain a continual antagonism toward the Chinese[27] (at least collectively, if not on an individual basis).

Repercussions within the Chinese community in India were predictably strong. Confidential interviews reveal that internal factions, at least in Calcutta, clustered around two types of divisions, one provincial (Cantonese versus Hakka) and one ideological (communist versus Nationalist or Kuomintang). A preliminary assessment makes it appear that the Hakka lean more toward the Kuomintang and that the relatively small group leaning toward the communists comes chiefly from the Cantonese camp, though most of the latter seem to be uncommitted. This is a sensitive area and not really open to the investigator. Throughout the Nanyang as a whole, Williams estimates that about 10 percent of the overseas Chinese are procommunist and 10 percent pro-Nationalist, with the other 80 percent avoiding open commitment (Williams, 1966, p. 21).

Throughout southeast Asia, the trend in overseas Chinese communities has been to direct more attention than formerly to public issues of the countries where they live. "Increasingly and inevitably, the elites of the isolated overseas Chinese have turned their faces toward local problems and policies. . . . The new overseas Chinese leadership, only now taking shape, is less and less concerned with establishing reputations as men devoted to China. The emphasis of these men is on guiding their compatriots toward the best possible accommodation within the societies and states of southeast Asia" (Williams, 1966, p. 84). It appears quite likely that this process has had a lesser development in India, where a continuing public animus against the Chinese exists and where there are so many restrictions on their mobility. Informants also report that from their earliest years in school, Chinese children in Calcutta find themselves the object of intermittent attacks from others in their classes. Minor clashes occur between Chinese and Indian children on the school grounds, and some Indian children like to torment their Chinese playmates from time to time. Whatever clashes occur are hushed up and do not receive any publicity.

Another complaint among the Chinese is that the Calcutta city improvement program in 1957, which required the demolition of old buildings, had the effect of pushing many people out of their homes in Chinatown. In addition to the regulations limiting their travel, still newer legislation prohibits private firms from employing Chinese in "protected areas," that is, those closely related to national defense such as steel, types of large manufacture, and transport. There is little if any promotion for Chinese working in offices of Indian firms. Many Chinese are therefore limited to remaining "babus and typists," as one informant put it. However, there seems to be a good deal of agreement that a very large number, if not a majority, of Chinese in the labor force are working for other Chinese or are self-employed. Research on the occupational structure is badly

---

27. The source of conflict in attacks on Chinese in places like Malaya and Indonesia was quite different: domination of the economy or, in Malaya at least, danger of a Chinese majority developing. Needless to say, neither of these factors had the slightest influence within India, where hostility toward the minority was more the product of outside forces.

needed. While a number of Chinese prefer the self-segregation implied by working for fellow-ethnics, there is no question that a great number feel themselves driven to it and that it may have a depressing effect on the economic welfare of the community.

THE CALCUTTA CHINESE: SURVIVAL STRUGGLES

In Calcutta it appears that the Chinese are less a community than a loose alliance of three subgroupings: the Cantonese of the central city, the Hakka of Tangra, and the Hakka of Dhapa, both the Hakka groups being satellite industrial suburbs. In Calcutta proper the Cantonese before 1957 were chiefly concentrated in Chinatown and had at least the nucleus of a genuine community life. With the coming of urban renewal, most of Chinatown's buildings were demolished, the residents scattered, and individual families atomized by seeking to find separate homes in different locations wherever rents were available. The resulting dispersion destroyed the major concentration, although there now seem to be plural clusters of Cantonese in areas around Chinese restaurants in various parts of the central city. The Cantonese, however, did not join their countrymen in the industrial suburbs.

In contrast, the Hakkas established themselves from the first in the outer ring of the city, where land was cheap and industry could gain a foothold. Over the years the Tangra and Dhapa areas developed through two stages into a fairly large industrial complex. In the first stage a few entrepreneurs set up individual tanneries, each with its own manual techniques, labor from a single family, and a small but rapidly growing market. As the demand for leather products increased, the process moved into a second phase where consolidation of small firms into larger ones, greater use of technology, and increased collaboration between the larger units boosted the efficiency of operation. By the late 1960s there were at least one hundred separate tanneries, some large, some small, and two hundred small traders in tannery goods serving as middlemen between the producers or processors and wholesale or retail outlets dealing in finished leather goods. Owners, managers, and traders were all members of the Chinese Tannery Owners Association which coordinated their efforts, helped to expand markets, and provided credit when needed. Every member was required to contribute to a revolving fund and could borrow from the fund proportionally to his volume of business. The Association today is at least partly a welfare society as well, since it manages an ample supply of funds. It is not, however, either a union or a trust but a loose confederation among individual producers and traders, each of which maintains an often fierce independence otherwise. The larger operations are concentrated in Tangra near the office of the Association, while the smaller and less impressive firms are found in Dhapa which has the great bulk (reportedly six thousand) of the Hakka Chinese.

Although this network of tannery operations is impressive, it furnishes little more than a bare living for the great majority who engage in it. As the network has grown, it has provided a low-level security to a continually enlarging group without raising the standard of living appreciably for more than a few top managers. A generally low economic level also seems characteristic of the

Cantonese in the central city with the exception of a few who parlayed a woodworking business into a source of substantial wealth. The average Chinese family in Calcutta proper, however, according to one local authority, has an income of about Rs. 400 per month for a family of four. It seems likely, too, that cultural emphasis on eating well with a variety of foods (many imported) puts pressure on Chinese families to spend more for groceries than their Hindu neighbors, thus leaving less for rent and other necessities. While the general estimate is that there are twenty to thirty Chinese restaurants within the city limits of Calcutta, very few of these are sufficiently equipped to handle a middle-class clientele. Many such establishments are family affairs, holes in the wall, or servers of snacks rather than full-fledged restaurants. Some of the larger ones are so organized that either Indians or Europeans own the licenses for the premises, while it is the Chinese who prepare the food, serve the tables, and do the rest of the actual work. The hold of the local Chinese on commercial life seems tenuous indeed compared with their more notable successes in Thailand or Malaya, where their population base is substantial.[28] The narrow commercial foothold of the Chinese in Calcutta may be at least partly due to the marked success of the Marwaris in the city, who began their grip on the retail and exchange business of Bengal as far back as the nineteenth century (Seal, 1968, p. 50n.). Another reason may be the relatively low educational level of the Chinese community. While fully literate, they did not usually progress beyond the primary or intermediate levels of the educational system. Some freeships were given them in mission schools, but these rarely extended to the college or university level, and the few wealthy Chinese did not indulge in extensive philanthropy, particularly in this direction. The consequences are that the Chinese in Calcutta proper have been distributed in manual occupations, office work, or employment in ineffectual family businesses.[29] Those with prestige among the Chinese are those who can dispense jobs, although the elders retain much traditional respect. After 1962 it has been difficult for any Chinese to secure a position with a Hindu firm.

INTEGRATION OF THE COMMUNITY

Are the Chinese integrated into Indian society? The question seems disingenuous. To say *yes* when there is discrimination against them in employment, when travel restrictions on their movement survives more than a decade of unreal peace, when their citizenship status as defined by the

---

28. The impact of the Indo-Chinese war on the organization of a Chinese restaurant in New Delhi is illustrative, though it has unique features. Reports have it that before 1962 this restaurant was known as the Golden Dragon. During hostilities or immediately afterward, the Chinese management was ejected and replaced by Indian. However, the Chinese cooks were retained and the entire operation camouflaged when the restaurant was rechristened The Mikado, giving it a Japanese veneer that would not clash with the public's sensibilities about the Chinese.

29. Leaders of the community seem agreed that vocational education is a prime need for Chinese youth. They do not mention university training.

Constitution is simply ignored by Government officials, and where enmity toward their country of origin is a dominant current of public opinion, making them a target of constant suspicion — to say *yes* when all these conditions exist is to stretch credulity.

On the other hand, to say *no* and to deny their integration is to contradict the view of integration already expounded above (Chap. 1) as "a process whereby units or elements of a society are brought into an active and coordinated compliance with the ongoing activities and objectives of the dominant group in that society." There we asserted that an index of compliance would be an agreement of the dominant group with the goals (centripetal or centrifugal) embraced by the subordinates. Thus, if the minority desired to remain separate in important respects and the dominant group also wished it to have a partially separate existence, this would constitute sanctioned autonomy or cultural pluralism symbolized by alternative B in Figure 1.2, Chapter 1. According to the paradigm, concurrence by both parties on the societal goals of the subordinate group facilitates integration.

In the case before us, we are therefore confronted by a seeming paradox, where both the dominant group (caste Hindus) and the subordinates (Chinese) coincide in the view that the minority shall remain insulated and apart. This agreement is not one of mutual regard but of mutual distrust. The dominant group appears to have smoldering hostility toward the subordinates as a residue from military conflict in 1962; this enmity has led them to restrict free movement of the Chinese outside their residential quarters. Conversely, the minority experiences an ill-concealed apprehension that they may suffer future attacks unless they remain in protected seclusion. Joint effects of both attitudes bring about a high degree of enclosure, which can then be termed *integration by mutual avoidance.* Doubtless some observers would deny that this is integration at all, because it is not like that of the Parsis and Jews whose separatism marks a condition of reciprocal tolerance and goodwill in their relations with the dominant group.

However, I submit that integration cannot be confined exclusively to a condition of harmony or amity but is a dimension having degrees of more or less. If consensus and mutual accord denote a high degree of integration, suspended hostility is simply a lower degree. For over half a century, sociology has labeled this latter condition "accommodation," namely:

> Accommodation is the natural issue of conflicts. In an accommodation, the antagonism of the hostile elements is, for the time being, regulated, and conflict disappears as overt action although it remains latent as a potential force. With a change in the situation, the adjustment that had hitherto successfully held in control the antagonistic forces fails. There is confusion and unrest which may issue in open conflict. [Park and Burgess, 1921, p. 665]

In this sense we can say that integration is therefore a process that includes not only social avoidances arising from mutual respect but also those rooted in mutual aversion, since both of these prevent overt conflict from shattering the outward peace between the two parties. In the second, or accommodative, form we have integration in its lowest common denominator, where it is behavioral assent without attitudinal accord. In this limited sense, it is quite possible without contradiction to say that the Chinese are integrated into Indian society. But it must be added that this is a low level of integration with pervasive elements of strain.

There are, however, tangible feelers in a more positive direction. During interviews with a number of Chinese informants, I could not help noticing ambivalence on the question of integration among some adults who played down their latent antagonism and displayed a sort of reluctant desire for acceptance by the larger Hindu community. Resentful withdrawal vies with a yearned-for participation.[30] How widespread this attitude is it is impossible to say, but it seems undeniable that any mode of adjustment the Chinese can achieve in the present climate of opinion depends more on political decisions in Peking and New Delhi than on internal cultural or social changes.

From the legal point of view, the relationship between the Chinese and the indigenous Indian population cannot be resolved while the present laxity and indifference toward clarifying the status of citizenship remains. As noted earlier, the Constitution of India plainly enunciates the principle of *jus soli,* according to which anyone born on Indian soil or whose parents were so born is *ipso facto* a citizen. One question is therefore whether the ordinances of 1962 and the accompanying emergency actions were applied to those of Chinese ancestry whether citizens or not.[31] A second question is whether the travel and job restrictions being applied to "Chinese nationals" affect those who are legally citizens and hence endowed with equal protection under the laws. Even a superficial acquaintance with the Chinese of Calcutta reveals anomalies that are puzzling to a legal view of the situation. On the one hand, it is reported that all Hakka are second or later generation in India, and, on the other, that between two and three hundred Hakka were naturalized on January 26, 1950. In the same Hakka community, one of the leaders stated that no Chinese person there was accorded citizen status between 1962 and 1965. The same respondent (in 1969) declared emphatically that it was still impossible for anyone to cross the boundary line of his residential suburb and enter another *unless he were a citizen.* However, the business man who wrote the letter quoted above, and whose movements were severely restricted, was India-born and hence, as the constitution clearly states, a citizen. Another prominent member of the Chinese community in Calcutta remarks confidentially that the Indians are ambivalent about according citizenship to the Chinese. This comment is bewildering, since the overwhelming majority of those with Chinese ancestry is reported to be born in India; so why should the question of *granting* citizenship arise? From a purely legal standpoint, the issue is quite superfluous when such persons have a constitutional citizenship already by reason of the *jus soli.*

---

30. Ties with the China homeland grow weaker and weaker; they would lose most of their strength, were it not necessary to regard Peking as a protector of last resort.

31. This is what happened to those of Japanese ancestry in the United States who were removed to internment camps during World War II whether legally citizens or not. (Cf. Schermerhorn, 1949, Chap. 10.)

Legal clarification of the problem is impossible until the issue is carried to the Supreme Court of India. And in the 1970s during the general uncertainty following the Emergency, any initiative to begin the legal process in this direction is quite unlikely.[32]

---

32. An anthropologist of European ancestry but born in India who read these lines is convinced that Indian authorities simply do not take the concept of citizenship seriously, and hence it should not be regarded as a problem. He writes, "Formal naturalization does not mean anything. Whether Chinese fill in a bit of paper or not, as long as the local administrators classify one as not belonging to a recognisable Indian community, this is all that matters. An example of the same sort of thing can be seen in respect to Tensing's autobiography where he describes his confusion as to his nationality after climbing Everest. Although born and partly brought up in Tibet, he regarded himself as a Sherpa and the Indians certainly regard him as an Indian even though his parents and he himself were not born in India. The Sherpas are a recognised Indian community. I am sure any Sherpa could easily obtain an Indian passport" (William H. Newell, personal correspondence). Whether in the long run the Chinese of India will be willing to leave matters in this ambiguous state is then the question.

BIBLIOGRAPHY

Chang, Sen-Dou, "The Distribution and Occupations of Overseas Chinese," *Geographic Review* 58 (No. 1, Jan. 1968), 89-107.

Chou, Pao-Ju, "India's Concentration Camps," *Peking Review* 5 (No. 52, Dec. 28, 1962), 10-12.

Fitzgerald, Stephen, "Overseas Chinese Affairs and the Cultural Revolution," *China Quarterly* (No. 40, Oct.-Dec. 1969), 103-126.

Lamb, Beatrice Pitney, *India, A World in Transition,* 3rd ed., rev., New York, Frederick A. Praeger, 1968.

Park, R. E., and E. W. Burgess, *Introduction to the Science of Sociology,* Chicago, University of Chicago Press, 1921.

Purcell, Victor, *The Chinese in Southeast Asia,* 1st ed., London, Oxford University Press, 1951.

Purcell, Victor, *The Chinese in Southeast Asia,* 2nd ed., London, Oxford University Press, 1965.

Schermerhorn, R. A., *These Our People, Minorities in American Culture,* Boston, D.C. Heath, 1949.

Schermerhorn, R. A., *Comparative Ethnic Relations,* New York, Random House, 1970.

Schoenfeld, Benjamin N., "Emergency Rule in India," *Pacific Affairs* 36 (No. 3, Fall 1963), 221-37.

Seal, Anil, *The Emergency of Indian Nationalism,* Cambridge at the University Press, 1968.

Tuohy, William, "Indochina Outcome Leaves Rest of Region Confused," *Los Angeles Times,* May 25, 1975.

Varma, S. P., *Struggle for the Himalayas: A Study in Sino-Indian Relations,* Jullundur, Ambala, Delhi, University Publishers, 1965.

White Paper No. VIII, Notes, Memoranda and Letters Exchanged Between the Governments of India and China, October 1962-January 1963. Ministry of External Affairs, Government of India, New Delhi, 1963.

Wiens, Harold J., *China's March Toward the Tropics,* Hamden, Conn., Shoe String Press, 1954.

Williams, Lee, *The Future of the Overseas Chinese in Southeast Asia,* New York, McGraw-Hill, 1966.

Chapter 13

Panorama

Like all societies, India oscillates between periods of stability and periods of rapid change. In comprehensive terms, the major changes in her history have been initiated by Aryan, Muslim, and British invasions, each followed by consolidation of authority and consequent stability. But here the similarity ends. The aftermath of the first onslaught by the Aryans was a long-term, massive transformation of the entire social structure into hierarchical forms buttressed by a pervasive world view — a social order resilient but resistant to change. Once formed, this caste system and its Brahmanic doctrines became the elemental ground of social organization whose patterns remained for over a thousand years amidst the rise and fall of innumerable local kingdoms.

The Muslim incursions superimposed a new set of rulers with a contrasting set of beliefs, but their effects on social organization were minor compared with the monumental changes resulting from Aryan impact. The caste system remained firm, even making inroads on the new conquerors. Muslim proselytizers gained a number of converts to the faith but few indeed compared with the voluminous Hindu population. Also the brevity of Muslim sovereignty (perhaps four centuries) could not match the millennium of Brahmanic civilization. Finally, as the unity of Muslim rule was dissolved into a multiplicity of petty kingdoms, its structural effects on Indian society were decidedly weakened.

The British colonial regime brought a series of changes that, though moderate and partial at first, proved cumulative and increasingly rapid as time went on. Even after the rulers withdrew from the subcontinent entirely, the dynamic of their practices and institutions continued to penetrate and redirect the energies of Indians in every walk of life. Departure of the colonial power after two centuries of dominance did not usher in an era of stability but an accelerating process of change which continues unabated still today. By departing at the moment of widespread violence after setting in motion the kinetic forces of Western industrial society so dissimilar to Oriental culture, the British initiated shock waves of influence that continue to agitate India without transforming it.

The integration of ethnic minorities into Indian society must be viewed in the context of this recent period with its incessant change. It is an era of transition with the *terminus ad quem* obscure, although official adoption of five-year plans ostensibly furnishes unidirectional goals of "development." But when attention shifts from a narrow economic focus to a broader perspective, where cross currents are simultaneously visible, their immediate and delayed effects on minorities are clearly exposed. A few conspicuous change elements deserve mention.

Massive migrations during partition brought into northern India hundreds of thousands of Hindus fleeing from their homes in the old Punjab into areas where Muslims made up as much as a fifth or more of the settled population. Forced to become refugees by Muslims in their previous homes, they harbored lasting hostility toward Muslims, who now were comfortably settled while they were homeless vagrants with no place to go. Once such migrating Hindus found a resting place, it was natural for them to harbor hatred and revenge for members of a minority community whose policies and actions had disrupted their lives. Thus "if in such an area [of northern India] there is a liberal sprinkling of post-partition migrants from Pakistan then the area is positively combustible, in the communal sense" (Mathur, n.d., p. 20). These migrations help to explain why enmity against Muslims stays alive in north India and why attention on "minorities" so often concentrates on Muslims to the neglect of other groups.

A second change with important consequences is India's adoption of late industrial models for early ones. By a curious twist of history, the era in which the new nation came into being was a period whose legacy to the new political standard-bearers was a singular amalgam of Harold Laski, Ramsay McDonald, William H. Beveridge, and a roseate view of the Soviet Union popularized by Sidney and Beatrice Webb. Significantly, it was a labor government with a socialist slant that finally arranged to pass the reins of authority to India. The result has been an inexperienced bureaucracy directing an industrial economy with more attention to labor, welfare, and licensing regulations than to processes of investment (Lamb, 1955, pp. 112, 115), with the result that the industrial base developed slowly while targets of the five-year plans have been monotonously unrealized. Land reforms and technical changes in agriculture have raised productivity — but not enough to prevent famine in times of drought and flood or to erase the deep economic disparities. Hence poverty steadily increases in the countryside (Bardhan, 1973), and the army of landless laborers continues to grow.[1] These changes have placed additional burdens on the minorities at the bottom of the economic heap, that is, on the Scheduled Tribes and Scheduled Castes.

Poverty on the land has driven millions to the cities in search of employment which the slowly developing industrial sector was unable to furnish. Unemployed masses of unskilled laborers choked the streets and alleys of Calcutta, Bombay, Madras, and lesser cities, their numbers eventually augmented by a fresh flood of unemployed graduates from the burgeoning colleges and universities. It is futile to describe this process by the use of the familiar Western

---

1. Census of India 1971, Series 1, Paper 1 of 1971. Supplement, Provisional Population Totals, pp. 62-63 and 66-67.

category of "urbanization," when in 1971, 80 percent of the population was still resident in villages while only 20 percent was in cities and towns.[2] Rural-urban migrants themselves are no more than superficially urbanized. It would not be difficult to build a case for an opposite hypothesis, that is, the ruralization of the cities. Flocks of goats or sheep are driven on boulevards where they block traffic; pedestrians in rural fashion wander aimlessly from one side of the road to another, oblivious of any vehicles bearing down on them; roadside shrines spring up unexpectedly in open city squares; and squatters settle in empty lots, often cooking their food or furnishing warmth by burning dried dung gathered from the streets by women and children who follow bullocks, cows, and other domestic animals on foraging expeditions. Transplanting rural mores to unfamiliar urban settings is a commonplace occurrence — a kind of change to counteract change, as it were. Such reversals within larger currents of movement are so familiar as to escape notice.

Suspicion of all strangers, so deeply ingrained in every village (Wiser and Wiser, 1963) is not abandoned upon migration to the cities. "Urbanization" does not erase these suspicions but only renders them more diffuse, making them into a sort of cultural miasma of distrust that permeates social relations at all levels.[3] Commentators have noted a comparable pattern among southern Italians whose circle of safety was the extended family and all others were strangers or potential enemies with whom intimate relations and confidences could not be shared (Banfield, 1958). A caste society like India perpetuates and continually renews this culture of distrust as long as the majority of its members are socialized in a village milieu. For example, in the making of contracts there is often severe anxiety as to whether the other party will carry out his obligation. In the many factions and coalitions on the political scene, there is also constant (and often well-founded) apprehension that loyalties and promises are undependable. Social networks keep changing their shape and form. "Crossing the aisle" with its sudden shift of party allegiance is both a result of basic distrust and a source of future mistrust. Commenting on this national atmosphere, Rajni Kothari observes:

> . . . it is interesting that so far trust and camaraderie have best come out in settings where it was possible to submit to a charismatic and transcendental authority rather than where people of the same stature had to work together. Gandhi provided this in a unique manner — and was himself remarkably free of any sense of threat from others — so did Nehru. But even Nehru was suspicious of leaders who rose to national stature and appeared to challenge his position in the country. [Kothari, 1970, pp. 267-68]

In such an atmosphere, concerted effort of any kind is difficult. A third party must intervene to initiate restraint, concessions, or adjustments and to

---

2. *India, A Reference Annual*, 1974, p. 13. Kingsley Davis estimates that if a developing nation is to industrialize while its population is still dominantly agricultural, it needs to move some 60 percent of the people from the rural areas to the cities (Davis, 1971, pp. 378-79).

3. G.M. Carstairs (1957) attributes this climate of distrust to psychodynamic factors.

play the role of facilitator. Adversary processes can be inhibited in this way through submission to such figures as a ritual authority, landlord, panchayat chief, charismatic figure, or, collectively, to the rule of a dominant caste in the village or region. When such third parties are not available and polarization of conflict occurs, persons may then align themselves with the patron or group that benefits them the most. In situations of fluid change, opposing factions may be highly unstable and commitment to them consequently fickle. When the relationships are more structural (that is, repeatable, buttressed by customary norms), the factions may last for generations. Although factions can surface at any time, they seem to proliferate in periods of rapid change. R. W. Nicholas's statement that "In most Indian villages . . . political competition is organized by factions" (Nicholas, 1968, p. 317) is a revealing symptom of significant changes taking place in Indian society.

Under such fluid conditions, pragmatic adjustments predominate over ideological commitments. This means that they are instrumental, ad hoc, and of uncertain duration. "Pragmatic rules are characterized by instability and continuous emergence even in times of relative stability, but most markedly when fundamental social change is underway" (Nicholas, 1968, p. 311). Such change was ushered in by independence.

IMPLICATIONS OF THE FRANCHISE

In pre-independence India it is doubtful whether much more than 10 percent of the population ever voted, for property and communal restrictions were relatively confining. Suddenly, with the adoption of the new Constitution, the franchise was thrown open to all without limit, unlocking forces hitherto held in check. Every variety of human grouping outside the strictly political ones — family, caste, faction, village, region, religion, linguistic division, and so on — now became endowed with special potency since it could get to be the center of loyalties given new dynamism through electoral expression. Other unfamiliar but official social units were superimposed: the "self-governing" bodies at village, block, and district levels, plus more distant ones like the state or national union. Uniting the official and unofficial structures was still another secondary formation — the party — pointing the way for group action and enlisting the often confused and bewildered citizen to make choices with others during periodic whirlwinds of public agitation. While these secondary units did not necessarily demand day-to-day commitments like those of family and caste, they nevertheless required recurrent expressions of preference for electoral candidates. Suffrage then became the stirrer of events and the occasion to push them in one direction or another, and, as political campaigns became longer and longer, the very atmosphere was charged with inescapable bargainings, schemings, and commitments. Agitation was soon normative.

In this perpetual ferment, it seems plausible to say that the smaller the political units, the greater the caste influence. At such local levels, political choices are highly sensitive to caste loyalties and caste association seems to flourish (Rudolph and Rudolph, 1967, p. 95). In village centers, dominant upper castes can take charge and march Untouchables to the polls, as the Thakurs did in a community in Uttar Pradesh (Gould, 1965). It is, however, also true to say that political parties, by their very presence, weaken caste bonds by manipulating factional divisions within them and that this process is likely to continue for an indefinite future (Rudolph and Rudolph, 1967, p. 97). Furthermore, the secret ballot itself has the potential to block the spyglass of surveillance which upper castes have used to control the lower, enabling the latter to mobilize forces secretly so as to capture the local seats of power (Béteille, 1965).

Above the local level the process becomes more complicated, where

> ... politicians must have recourse to the representation of independent interests and to ideological and programmatic appeals through more manifest and specialized political structures, particularly the political party. At these levels, independent political calculations begin to split, combine or fuse castes of all ranks. [Rudolph and Rudolph, 1967, p. 81]

The dialectic of change thus makes the political process kaleidoscopic. Fission occurs at all levels: splits within caste, village, party, state assembly, and national Parliament. Matching its divisive force are fusions: factional coalitions, caste federations, contagious swarming around charismatic figures,[4] formation of autonomous subsystems or networks operating at intermediate levels (Kothari, 1970, p. 91), and party coalitions at all levels.

Since both fissions and fusions are temporary, some cancel each other out, some reinforce one another, and others (particularly those with more permanence) serve as centers of persistence around which the others swirl. Some of these centers are conspicuous and highly visible; during the early years of the Republic, they were the Congress party and Premier Nehru himself. Other centers, however, were less perceptible, dormant, and underlying sources of influence that went unremarked by most observers. It is to these latter that we now turn.

THE PERENNIAL ELITE

In the torrent of change that overtook India with the introduction of Western ideas and methods, it must not be forgotten that limits and boundaries on this change were imposed by the colonial power itself. Although elements of laissez-faire were introduced into the system, we have already noted that the popular image of an open field for advancement, whatever its validity may have been for frontier societies, has little pertinence for India. Especially before the welfare state took hold in England, the British, as B. B. Misra points out, wanted the emerging middle class in the subcontinent to be a stratum of imitators rather than innovators with new values and methods. The new education was to "satisfy the needs of an already developed economy" and the serried ranks of the civil service. "This perpetuated traditional literary education as a virtual monopoly of the upper castes of Hindu society. . . . government servants and lawyers, college teachers and doctors, constitute the bulk of the Indian middle

---

4. *Personalismo* is not confined to Latin American nations.

classes. The mercantile and industrial elements which dominate the composition of the Western middle classes are still a minority" and the latter are mainly limited to the larger cities (Misra, 1961, pp. 11-12). And as the upper caste elite moved into these positions of power, this process restricted the rise of those who entered the competition too late or who came from underprivileged groups:

> Historically the expansion of business in India had proceeded from the top downwards, not from the bottom upwards. An Indian plutocracy had even earlier formed a separate caste by itself, and those who carried on business under them did so as their subordinate and servile agents, not as free merchants. . . . Indeed the directors of Indian industries were persons who must generally be classified as members of the upper rather than the middle classes. [Misra, 1961, p. 251] . . . . social stratification first proceeded from legal, educational, and administrative changes, not economic diversification. Of the professions, law became by far the most important and powerful; and it was not until after the first two decades of the present century that the technical and business professions slowly began to rise to importance. [Ibid., p. 343]

Thus, the underlying power structure of the caste Hindus, so strong in pre-colonial times, was encouraged and perpetuated by the colonial power itself in the economic field. And, if this restrictive set of circumstances severely limited upward mobility for Hindus at lower and intermediate levels of the caste scale, it must, *a fortiori*, have had even greater inhibiting effects on members of minorities who lack the nepotic advantages of the upper castes. There are certain exceptions, of course. Parsis rode the colonial wave to many positions of preferment, while Jains, with their representatives in upper strata for centuries, were able to escape the worst consequences of economic immobility. In the expanded opportunities of urbanization under British rule, the Jews also made considerable headway, and in rural sections the irrigated fertility of the Punjab opened up improved chances for capital accumulation among Sikhs as well. Apart from these four communities, however, minorities of India have displayed glacially slow ascent in their standard of living.

Ascendant in the pre-colonial era, the upper caste elite made economic gains under the British and were able to consolidate these after independence.

In the political arena, the same dominant group maintained itself. It was from this element, particularly the Westernized division, that the Constituent Assembly was organized to formulate the Indian Constitution. The statesmen deliberating in the proceedings had already participated in the march toward swaraj, using as their tool against the British the very ideas of popular freedom and representative government that the latter adopted for themselves. Determined to show that they would extend the principles of liberty as far as any and all democracies of the world, the new constitution-makers adopted in full the egalitarian ideal of citizenship. This meant (as the preliminary pages of Chapter 1 have noted) that they replaced the *equivalent* mode of incorporation by that of the *uniform* mode. Under the former (which the British had legitimated in their Indian possessions), Muslims and some other ethnic groups could vote only in separate electorates. Their citizen status was derivative from their ethnic status. Under the new Constitution, this derivative mode was abolished and citizenship was thrown open to all, regardless of ethnic membership. All were equal under the law and all were eligible to participate in the electoral process without regard to their accident of birth. A new normative model supplanted the old.

What few observers noted at the time was the paradox of upper echelon leaders at the very apex of the power structure in the new India, solemnly affirming equalitarian ideals as the basis for future political activity. Nicholas comments on the contrast:

> The moral principle that guided the framers of the Indian constitution. . . is flatly contradictory to that of the villagers. The constitution holds that "all men are created equal," that all citizens of India should have equal rights, including the right to participate in political activity, and that hierarchical social relations are inherently evil. The egalitarian principle is embodied in a set of laws designed for uniform enforcement throughout the Indian republic. [Nicholas, 1968, p. 310]

The pragmatic, ad hoc operations of the elite in politics are theoretically a form of mediation between two clashing principles or social demands: the egalitarian ideal and the hierarchical model. Universal suffrage forces such leaders to act as if equality were real though, through it all, pragmatic alignments of caste, faction, and leader-follower networks permit an age-old preference for hierarchical pattern to reassert itself behind the facade of ever-shifting incumbency. The resulting fluctuation of officeholders obscures the fixity of social origins from which power figures are recruited − that is, the upper castes.[5] It is this set of higher varna levels which, as a composite, constitutes the dominant group vis-à-vis the minorities. In the foreground is an easily discernible multiplicity of ever-changing leaders, loyalties, factions, alliances, and networks of influence which give the impression of never-ending flux. In the background, however, is an order of permanence, an enduring center from which actors advance to play their roles − the elite structure. In terms of origin, *plus ça change, plus c'est la même chose.* The underlying formation of dominance in Indian society formed by caste Hindus persists throughout the turbulence of any and all agitations. From this center the *leadership personnel* for every endeavor is recruited: magnates and trade-union officers, Swantantra and communist parties, cabinet officers and administrative chiefs, university faculties and student members, professionals and bureaucrats, landlords and petty police. As the stratification system in the cities shifts balance from caste to class, it is still those from the upper echelons of caste who climb to higher positions in class.[6] Both at village and national levels, twice-born castes form the ruling strata; the hierarchical structure is thereby preserved, however covertly. Within that structure, the fulcrum of power seems to shift from the "conditionally Westernized" to the

---

5. This must be qualified for south India where there is a "relative absence of twice-born castes" (Rudolph and Rudolph, 1967, p. 76). Although technically at upper levels of the Sudra category, a number of these castes perform functionally substitute roles of dominance.

6. "Climb" is therefore an inapt term for many; "glide into" would be more appropriate.

"parochial neo-traditionals,"[7] from the more cosmopolitan to the more nationalistic, from parttime officeholders on leave from academic and legal occupations to fulltime political professionals whose entire life is spent in party activity or legislation.[8] These "new men of power" have sufficient experience manipulating social networks to achieve outstanding results in the struggle for party success. But their elite origins remain unchanged, and their unspoken assumption of superiority is a mode of thought so deeply ingrained in religious tradition and daily practice that the ideal of equality, in comparison, is little more than a veneer. The pervasive sentiment is a sort of legitimized condescension.

It is an easy step from this conclusion, for those committed to Marxian analysis (or its analogue in C. Wright Mills), to make out a persuasive case for increasing polarization between an oppressive upper class and a victimized lower mass throughout the subcontinent — all screened from view by the diversionary tactics of noisy politicians in between. To uphold such a view, it is necessary to sharpen the image of the ruling strata so that their repressive and exploitative actions overshadow all else. This would carry the logic of class conflict to its definitive conclusion. To turn from logic to empirical observation, however, if we examine closely the Great Traditions of India which are a legacy of dominant castes to the entire civilization, we find them embodying a much more flexible Weltanschauung, which

> was not only highly permissive and accommodative, but also self-consciously pluralistic. . . . Indeed the democratic ideology fitted very nicely Indians' predilection for the autonomy of social and primordial institutions, the legitimacy of intermediate structures between state and society, the freedom to retain local identities, and the tolerance of cultural and religious diversities. [Kothari, 1970, p. 253]

In light of this historical observation it is safe to conclude that the ascendancy of India's dominant group is muted and disguised. This does not make it any the less real.

SALIENT MINORITIES

A systematic comparison of our ten minorities will properly stress three dimensions that bring out their likeness and difference as these have significance for twentieth century India. These three elements are size, separateness, and mode of affiliation.

With respect to size, the minorities fall into three major clusters: large, intermediate, and small. Large minorities are Scheduled Castes, Muslims, and Scheduled Tribes, each with 7 to 14 percent of the population. Intermediate

---

7. See Chap. 1, pp. 19-20 above.

8. This is more applicable to Congress politicians than to those of other parties. See Kothari, 1970, pp. 205-10.

minorities are Christians and Sikhs, each with 1 to 3 percent. Small minorities are Jains, Anglo-Indians, Chinese, Parsis, and Jews, each with less than 1 percent. A quick glance at Table 13.1 brings out the details.

By reason of their size, those of the first cluster occupy a place of real importance. Since their percentage of the population hovers around the 10 percent level, they call to mind Stanislav Andreski's generalization:

> As an approximate rule, there is a critical ratio which is most conducive to popular persecutions, and which seems to lie around 10 per cent. With this ratio the non-dominant minority is very conspicuous, has many points of friction with the majority, but is still small enough to be persecuted with ease. Harassing a minority of 30 or 40 per cent often entails great danger, whereas a minority of 1 or 2 per cent (provided that it is not particularly conspicuous for other reasons) can more easily escape the attention of the majority unless it is put into the limelight by organized hostile propaganda. [Andreski, 1964, p. 296]

Such factors certainly have relevance in India, but they are modified by demographic and historical singularities.

First of all, Andreski seems to assume, without stating it openly, that his general proposition is valid where there is only a single minority in the 10 percent range. In India, however, there are three such minorities; thus, public attention is at least partly diluted by the simultaneous claims of almost equally large competing groups, and the tendency to single out any one of them for discrimination or persecution is lessened.[9] Such a tendency, if it exists, must then be explained by referral to unique or especially prominent historical influences. I believe the tendency does exist by reason of the agitations of partition and the influx of tormented Hindus fleeing across the border from menacing tides of Muslims in Pakistani territory. The flood of bitterness and rancor that followed has made the Muslims a major target of enmity in the years that followed. At the same time, societal conditions in India have turned attention away from the other two large minorities: the Scheduled Tribes because they are often so out of sight as to be out of mind, and the Scheduled Castes, regarded as so lowly and degraded that it is ill-mannered to pay them much attention. Both Scheduled Tribes and Scheduled Castes are also defined (by the public as well as in the Constitution itself) as "backward" or "weaker" sections of the people who are, with whatever reluctance, given special privileges that are supposed to bring them up to a level with others in the society. A special agency with its own Commissioner is set up to supervise the process of

---

9. Louis Wirth made this singling-out process the distinguishing mark of his oft-quoted definition: "We may define a minority as a group of people who, because of their physical or cultural characteristics, are singled out from the others in which they live for differential and unequal treatment, and who therefore regard themselves as objects of collective discrimination" (Wirth, 1945, p. 347). This gives the impression that numerical minorities *who are not singled out* must be excluded from the category of minority groups altogether. By disregarding the size and number of such groups, Wirth bypasses the variable characteristics of the singling-out process and the corresponding feelings of being objects of discrimination, both of which may sink to near zero when size of groups decreases and the number of groups *increases.*

TABLE 13.1
Numerical Clusters of Indian Minorities by Magnitude, 1971

Size	Minority	Total Number	Percentage of Population
Large	Scheduled Castes	79,995,896	14
	Muslims	61,417,934	11.21
	Scheduled Tribes	38,015,162	6.94
Intermediate	Christians	14,223,382	2.6
	Sikhs	10,378,797	1.89
Small	Jains	2,604,646	0.48
	Anglo-Indians	250,000	0.05
	Parsis	91,226	0.0167
	Chinese	53,000	0.0097
	Jews	16,000	0.0029

overcoming backwardness; delegating such problems to government hands then disposes of them so that they can be forgotten. Unintentionally, this constitutes a built-in mechanism for reducing the attention that might otherwise focus on these plebeian minorities; a corresponding overmeasure is then left for the Muslims. Augmenting this emphasis is the "organized hostile propaganda" mentioned by Andreski which places them in an unfavorable light; certain elements of the Jan Sangh and RSS continue this pattern of propaganda against Muslims perennially. Such agitation, however, is not foisted upon an innocent public de novo but simply deepens a channel of antagonism already dug by centuries of divisiveness and the upheavals of partition. It is therefore no accident that any public reference to "minorities" or "the minority question" carries an almost automatic assumption that Muslims are meant; others remain in the shadow or are ignored.[10] Conversely, the Scheduled Castes and Scheduled Tribes, in popular thought at least, are not so much regarded as minorities but as simply unfortunate or uncouth varieties of people. While the dominant group looks *down* on them, they look *across* at Muslims, whose potential equality is not just a matter of legal definition but a condition buttressed by religion and a high culture that have defined India's distinctiveness in the past and, in a limited but real sense, continue to do so in the present.

Each of these three minorities falls within the approximate range of Andreski's 10 percent and therefore inside his vulnerable zone of targetability for attack. And when the combined population of all three reaches close to a third of India's inhabitants (31.85 percent), it seems justifiable to give them the title of the *salient minorities.*

---

10. In her "coup" of 1975, Indira Gandhi stressed new programs for ameliorating the lot of tribals and Untouchables but omitted mention of the Muslims. Condescension soft-pedaled hostility toward inferiors and legitimated charity for them. Not so for potential equals like the Muslims.

STRUCTURAL PLURALISM

It turns out that the second dimension of separateness focuses on the same three minorities. In any attempt to discover the extent to which each of the ten ethnic groups is separated from members of the larger society (termed here "the degree of enclosure"), we necessarily proceed with the use of common indicators. They are, in this case, endogamy, ecological concentration, institutional duplication, associational clustering, rigidity and clarity of group definition, and segmentary relations of members with outsiders (Schermerhorn, 1970, pp. 125-27; van den Berghe, 1965, pp. 78-79). If it were possible to arrange the minority groups in a continuous series from higher to lower degrees of seclusion or insulation, this would give us a reliable estimate of the degree of enclosure based on numerical calculation. Unfortunately, only one of these indicators (associational clustering) is properly quantifiable (with data lacking to implement it, however), and so it is possible to give only an estimate here, based on judgmental inferences from historical sources, empirical observation of communities, and statements from informants. In reckoning the factor of institutional duplication, I am taking into account family, religion, education, recreation, economic activities, and political activities. To these I am adding language as a structural element of parallel importance in keeping groups separate. Reviewing the comparative enclosure of the ten minority groups under discussion, I would arrange them in the following continuous order from the highest degree of enclosure at the top to the lowest at the bottom:

Scheduled Tribes
Chinese
Muslims
Scheduled Castes
Anglo-Indians
Christians
Sikhs
Jews
Parsis
Jains

As in the case of stratification analysis, there will be more agreement among observers on the items at extremes of the continuum than the items in between, and I would expect considerable dissent on the intervening cases of the list. However, comments on the first and last in the series will at least illustrate briefly the mode of analysis I have employed. The Scheduled Tribes are hypothesized to have the greatest structural separation from the rest of the society because their endogamous practices are stringently observed, they are geographically clustered in regions or settlements relatively inaccessible to the rest of the population, they speak languages or dialects strikingly different from those in adjacent districts, practice religious customs at variance with Hinduism, and engage in forms of recreation unique to them and their own members. In other institutions such as education, the economy, and the polity, they participate with outsiders to a variable degree. (See Fig. 4.1 above). The percentage of tribal children in government schools may be increasing but is difficult to determine; a considerable number attend mission schools, but under present conditions this attendance is unlikely to increase. Education organized by outsiders cannot be expected to produce lasting effects, however, unless subsequent rewards for acculturation are certain. As for gaining a living, probably the majority of tribals remain outside the usual modes of peasant agriculture, employing simpler methods of their own. Moni Nag makes the confident assertion that between tribals and nontribals

> ... the difference in the modes of subsistence appears to be the most striking and easily recognizable one, at least in the Indian situation. The fact that the shifting cultivation is not just merely a matter of technology but represents a distinctive way of life and has close interrelation with other aspects of culture has been pointed out by a number of Indian ethnographers. Some of them have even opposed the introduction of intensive cultivation among them on the plea that such a change would bring about too much disruption in their ways of life (V. Elwin, 1939: 106-31). [Nag, 1967, p. 194]

Although a few tribes have accepted more intensive agriculture and some others have entered the industrial labor force, Nag gives the impression that by and large the Scheduled Tribes practice an economy of their own separate from that of Indian society as a whole.

The same, of course, cannot be claimed for the polity which is the one institution that necessarily holds together any modern society, including that of India,[11] though it may do so in more coercive fashion for tribal subjects who participate (when they do) more awkwardly and with less habituation than other citizens. At the same time there are internal forms of social control that could be classed as "political" in a number of tribal units, thus duplicating the larger polity on a smaller (but possibly more effective) scale. Associational clustering is more of an urban phenomenon and has little relevance for Adivasis who are about 95 percent rural, so that this factor can be disregarded. Finally, rigidity and clarity of group definition along with segmentary relations with outsiders are especially marked in practically all tribal areas.

This multiplicative analysis clearly supports the conclusion that the Scheduled Tribes have the highest degree of enclosure of the ten minorities in our list. Logically speaking, extreme enclosure is simply the obverse of negative incorporation;[12] thus, if the evidence so far is convincing, it is plausible to assert that tribals are less integrated into the societal fabric of India than are other ethnic groups. This conclusion is hardly surprising.

At the other end of the continuum, Jains have the lowest degree of enclosure and the highest degree of incorporation of the ten minorities. Endogamous barriers between them and Hindus at the same caste level (or bearing the

---

11. M.G. Smith emphasizes the role of the political institution as the one indispensable unifying factor in all societies, especially when societal consensus is lacking (1960, p. 772).

12. This does not refer, except by indirection, to acculturation or assimilation, which denote the cultural dimension rather than barriers that separate distinguishable groups. That structural and cultural factors combine empirically cannot be denied, but there are advantages in keeping the analytic distinction between them quite clear.

identical caste name) have broken down to a considerable degree.(See pp. 118-19 above.) Ecological concentration is limited for Jains; they are found with dispersed and scattered residence in mixed areas. There are no linguistic barriers between Jains and their neighbors. Family structure is almost identical – the incidence of joint families, patriarchal dominance, rules of inheritance, and so on, is like that of their Hindu counterparts. Religious beliefs and practices, while occurring in separate temples, are linked in various ways, as among the Svetambaras who employ Brahmans to perform the ceremonies.[13] The ascetic ideal is accepted on both sides of the religious line. Jains also share recreation patterns with the larger society in the celebration of popular Hindu festivals. In education, Jain youth attend both government schools and Gurukalas (residential schools) for pupils of their own community in areas of greatest Jain population. In college or university education there seem to be no separate institutions of instruction for Jains, although some of their students may live in separate boarding houses of their own during the time of their attendance. As for the economy, Jains participate, as do Hindus, through merchant caste affiliation, and an increasing number are joining the Hindus in white collar bureaucratic occupations as well. In Calcutta they form a substantial part of the Marwari network of shops and corporations. Politically, they play an inconspicuous but meaningful role as conservative voters whose numbers are too small in most districts to affect the balance of power; this does not prevent them from taking full part in the duties of citizenship. At the same time, Jains have a large number of caste associations, provincial sabhas, and all-India organizations; locally, they also have a few cooperative apartment and housing societies. These tend to preserve, to a limited degree, a clarity of group definition in the urban scene and, for the selected members of such organizations, segmentary relations with outsiders.

In sum, the Jains, while manifesting the lowest degree of enclosure, nevertheless maintain some boundary lines and are in no danger of absorption into the larger Hindu community. Among the younger generation there is definitely a greater potential for assimilation into a growing secular urban mass.

When we compare the list of minorities by size (Table 13.1) with the continuous series based on the degree of enclosure (p. 324), the parallels, though not precisely the same, are strikingly similar. In both cases the upper extreme is represented by the Scheduled Tribes, the Scheduled Castes, and the Muslims, although in the category of structural pluralism, the Chinese must be added. The Chinese population is so inconsequential, however, that they constitute India's smallest minority except for the rapidly disappearing Jews, reducing Chinese visibility to near zero. If, for this reason, we tentatively subtract them from the upper extreme, we arrive at the same salient minorities revealed by numerical comparison. The outcome is paradoxical: the very minorities whose presence is most conspicuous because of their size are least noticeable because of their segregation.

This paradox raises further questions: At whose behest is the segregation established? Is it self-imposed or other-imposed? What preferences accompany these relationships? At the close of each chapter above, these issues received

---

13. See above, p. 110. Significant, too, in its way, is the fact that the Digambaras have outcaste groups that parallel those among Hindus.

major attention under the heading "Reciprocal Goal Definition" (see Fig. 1.2); that is, what do the dominants and minorities regard as legitimate aims for the minorities? The question refers to an ideology of what *ought to be* in the relationship of each minority to the society as a whole. This relationship may reasonably be called normative mode of affiliation.

NORMATIVE MODE OF AFFILIATION

Here again we seek for a continuum: Which minorities show a high degree of consensus with the dominant group on the mode of affiliation appropriate for them in relationship with the larger society? Shall it be assimilation, autonomy, or some other form? Conversely, which minorities show a low degree of consensus with the dominant group on this issue? And which groups occupy an intermediate position? In Table 13.2 we find significant parallels with previous groupings on different dimensions.

Beginning this time with the ethnic communities at the lower end of the scale (in Table 13.2) we find that the minorities at that extreme are the ones whose integration into Indian society is most problematic. Significantly, they are the very groups already designated as salient minorities in terms of size[14] and enclosure. In reflecting on the mode of affiliation, however, it is not enough to center attention on minorities by themselves; it is equally important to contemplate simultaneously the role of the dominant group. In a previous colonial dominion, special historical appreciation is also required.

In the colonial empires of Asia and southeast Asia, the changeover to independence was spearheaded by a local elite able to mobilize the masses to overturn the foreign power and promote the creation of their own nation. This transfer of power was often disorderly, accompanied by sudden changes in the predominance of local groups. Guy Hunter made this comment on the situation:

> For at midnight on Independence Day the old order which held society together vanished. For an instant of time, until a new order appeared, society reverted to the disparate small groups which had composed it before the colonial conquest. Nationalism, as the counterpart of new independence, is a vision of this new order; an attempt to impose upon the welter of events and human groupings disclosed by the failure of authority some new protecting framework within which a unitary social organism can take shape. [Hunter, 1966, p. 74]

As the dominance of a national elite replaces that of a foreign elite, the internal balance between multiple ethnic groups assumes a new alignment. The colonial authority must at least make a show of neutrality toward local groups, a policy that often prompts them to show special favors toward minorities to weight the balance against majorities or especially powerful corporate units. Of course, this public display of justice can well be a convenient mask for a divide-and-rule policy. In any case, colonial sovereignty inevitably entails selective partiality toward some groups rather than others. Then independence brings a new set of

---

14. Here, of course, the Chinese constitute an exception.

TABLE 13.2

**Degree of Consensus of Minorities and Dominant Groups on the Mode of
Affiliation Preferable for Each Minority in India During the 1970s**

High Degree of Consensus	Intermediate Degree of Consensus	Low Degree of Consensus*
Jains	Sikhs	Scheduled Tribes
Parsis	Christians	Scheduled Castes
Jews	Anglo-Indians	Chinese
		Muslims

*Alternatively, formal consensus combined with hostility and mutual avoidance.

partialities, namely those favored by the indigenous elite. A new balance is struck, sometimes influenced by power considerations and sometimes by open retaliation against hated colonial favorites now stripped of their former protection.

In the case of India, the British imperialists, for reasons of state, gave special privileges to the largest minority in the land — the Muslims — as a counterweight to the massive influence of Hindus in the Congress party. These privileges took the form of a separate electorate on the one hand and extensive representation in all ranks of the bureaucracy and police force on the other. The Sikhs contributed far more than their share of military recruits and were highly favored for this reason. Although ambivalent toward the Anglo-Indians, the colonial authority utilized their manpower almost monopolistically in areas where security for the regime needed safeguarding: in railway personnel, telegraph and customs services, the parttime militia, and as infantrymen and pilots during both world wars.

The British had an unspoken but subterranean affinity based on cultural congruence with these three minorities. The ideals of the English upper classes combined macho qualities in sport, hunting, or the chase with military virtues and courtly conduct in "society," together with preference for direct, straightforward, sometimes blunt relations with one's peers and unabashed lordliness or imperiousness with one's inferiors. Such cultural traits made the British more at home with Muslims, Sikhs, and Anglo-Indians than with most Hindus, whose behavior tended to be more tactful, discreet, and sometimes more devious. It must also be remembered that the British could eat and drink freely with the members of these three minorities without the barrier of caste prohibitions, and a certain camaraderie resulted. Similar rapport occurred with the rajahs, whose subculture was the same, and in social intercourse with Kshatriyas generally.

Relationships of the British with other minorities were more equivocal. Benevolence toward fellow Christians was combined with a certain aloofness toward lower class converts; conversely, ecclesiastics, especially missionaries, sought to ingratiate themselves by siding with imperial authority during nationalist agitation. Dealings with Untouchables were quite impersonal and largely derived from the British attempt to set up a legal system granting equal rights to all; an offshoot of this venture was the establishment of compensatory measures that would raise the social and educational levels of the Scheduled Castes in the form of "protective discrimination." Tribal relations were managed on the familiar British principle of indirect rule with as much autonomy permitted as would be consistent with "law and order." Finally, when inaugurating the dependent economy of the colony which furnished raw materials for the industry of Manchester and Leeds, the British found their greatest support among the commercial-minded Parsis, followed by the Jews, and to a lesser extent among the Jains who were more inhibited by caste restrictions. Very little is known about transactions with the Chinese before independence except for scattered references on the coolie trade on tea plantations and in one or two seaports.

This set of internal balances in the colony showed its most drastic change after independence in the position of the Muslims, who not only lost nearly two-thirds of their members to Pakistan (including the most educated and skilled leaders) but plummeted to the unenviable position of India's most freely hated minority, which could now be forced to assume reversal of roles with severe loss of former privileges. Then, because of national excitement over the clash between Gandhi and Ambedkar on issues of policy for the Untouchables and the ensuing agitation in the Constituent Assembly on the problem, the Scheduled Castes, after independence, attained greater prominence under the new administrative arrangements they received. By derivation, the Scheduled Tribes followed the same path. In the latter case, however, another element was added; intermittent waves of anxiety occurred in the dominant group when border tribes made guerrilla attacks on the army while apparently enjoying logistical support from Chinese in the north.

All things considered, the transfer of power from colonial elite to national elite has therefore resulted in the very alignment of subordinate ethnic communities that we have already noted as the three salient minorities: Scheduled Castes, Scheduled Tribes, and Muslims. In each case, however, the historical influences producing the result have been different. In the Muslim example, the power transfer resulted in a reversal of *status role,* but their *prominence* remained high. For the Untouchables and tribals, the new setting of authority left the *status* element relative unchanged but raised their *prominence* several notches. Marked antagonism toward Chinese did not appear until after independence and the incidence of hostilities in 1962. Although that occurrence gave them additional prominence, their diminutive size prevented their having the impact of the three salient minorities.

Anglo-Indians and Christians generally lost whatever favoritism they enjoyed under British sovereignty and experienced considerable (though not extreme) downgrading of status after independence. Sikhs, too, suffered a mild reversal. Their clamor for special privileges in Punjabi Suba left the dominant group wary and cautious in other dealings with them, although their military exploits in

Pakistani wars won approval. Moderate changes of this kind place these three minorities in the same intermediate position already assigned them by reason of size and enclosure (including Anglo-Indians together with other Christians).

As for the remaining minorities — Parsis, Jews, and Jains — they seem to have experienced the least change of all after the new nationalistic alignments. This is at first surprising since both Parsis and Jews had protected positions in the colonial era and, with few exceptions, favored the foreign power during the drive for swaraj. However, this inclination was more covert than overt and was accompanied by a rapid and astute shift of allegiance after independence. It occurred, too, chiefly in Bombay, the most cosmopolitan city of India, where loyalties were probably less sharp and compromises more common than elsewhere. Also, their philanthropies to Indian institutions stood them in good stead with the new regime. Jains, who showed less partiality toward the British, displayed more diplomatic skill in relations with them while requiring less need to prove themselves vis-à-vis the Indian public after independence.

At all events, by their very inconspicuous character and their shrewd adaptability to changing circumstances, Parsis, Jews, and Jains remained at the same approximate status level both before and after the birth of the new nation. This again makes them congruent with the scale position noted above under the dimensions of size and enclosure.

NEHRU AND POST-NEHRU

After independence, dominants of the new regime were an indigenous oligarchy within the system and, to that extent, unavoidably partisan. New modes of adjustment to authority were required of minorities and, by the nature of the case, were often ad hoc or pragmatic. The ruling strata, on their side, were accustomed to positions of privilege even under the aegis of colonial administration — positions that were buttressed by their ascendant influence in the Congress party. As the national government came into power, the same ruling strata were forced to assume the obligations of authority with the shaky ideology of democratic equality enshrined in the Constitution and through the cumbersome mechanisms of mass electoral participation. To assume complete and peremptory command would have been much easier than to perform the uncertain balancing act of being leaders with superior wisdom and, simultaneously, servants of the masses. This duality of role required a nimbleness of response that soon took the form of manipulation of both electoral and governmental machinery, a form of action quite as pragmatic and ad hoc in its way as the adaptive behavior of minorities on their side. Ambivalence, therefore, became a pervasive feature of intergroup relations.

In the first euphoric glow of swaraj, the sacrificial example of Gandhi, the reflected idealism of Congress leadership, and the diffuse contagion of national accord swept all before them. As this rosy haze dissolved and the everyday tasks of making the new regime into a viable system became the consuming preoccupation of the leadership, unity in direction and goals was maintained for a time by the charisma of Nehru, whose commitment to the norm of equal citizenship rights was resolute and firm. Not only Nehru but the like-minded elite who shared his authority in the early days of the Republic were for the most part British-educated or Westernized professionals. As the need for greater entrée into public life grew with the burgeoning of electoral politics, however, a different stratum was tapped, this time from literate upper caste members of the emerging middle classes. Bifurcation of caste Hindus into conditionally Westernized and parochial neo-traditionals took place on a wide scale, the types described above in Chapter 1 (pp. 19-20). For both of these subdivisions, the need to make the national system workable (a definitely altruistic norm) combined with the drive to win elections at all costs (an egoistic goal).[15]

The conditionally Westernized, allied with Nehru ideologically and bound to him by personal loyalty, were the chief supporters of the "secular state"[16] and its ideal of equality before the law (uniform incorporation). Christians, Anglo-Indians, and Muslims all report that they felt safer and less threatened by the new political alignments as long as Nehru was alive and that they felt more vulnerable after his death. The dwindling number of pro-Nehru adherents in politics and the steady growth in the ranks of parochial neo-traditionals in a newer generation created a changed political climate. In this new atmosphere, Christians, Anglo-Indians, and Muslims have adopted forms of self-protection that would stir up the least antagonism among the neo-traditionals. Since the Anglo-Indians share membership in the Christians' community, the two-in-one have responded in a similar way by opting for a kind of apolitical passivity. Muslims, on the other hand, have been more active and have adopted a number of coalition alliances with party groups and factions in electoral politics, as their larger numbers make possible.

Reactions of the other minorities can be at least partly understood by referring to Nehru's influence. Until his death in 1964, Nehru symbolized the government and its policies for these groups who were either ambivalent or

---

15. Cf. Rajni Kothari's analysis of two parallel types which he credits with different social skills. On the one hand were the people who were "Brahminic," adept in dealings with Western administrators and in establishing organizations to promote social causes. On the other were "men from commercial and peasant proprietor occupations, occupations that had always called for a high level of interpersonal skills, a pragmatic and bargaining approach to problems, and an ability to marshal a new type of solidarity among their own caste, often based on a reinterpretation of their traditional status and a populist and anti-elitist ideology" (Kothari, 1970, p. 237). Although Kothari refers to two types of leadership here, my assertion is simply that there are comparable population elements among caste Hindus as a whole, both of them having high prestige (however different the norms) while together they form a substantially real power structure vis-à-vis the minorities. To the extent that the two subdivisions remain linked, neither will lose social control in the national system.

16. I am using "secular state" loosely here, as it is conventionally employed. Strictly speaking this term is a misnomer, since the state in India can set up departments controlling and superintending the administration of certain religious institutions including places of worship. The state can appoint officers with powers to direct religious authorities as to how their institutions will be administered. The state also has large powers over the scale of expenditures and can determine how much money will be required for the performance of religious rites and ceremonies, and is authorized to make additions or alterations in the budgets of a good many religious institutions. This would make it a jurisdictional rather than a secular state. See Luthera, 1964.

opposed to his views, at least to the extent that they were aware of them.[17] Among the salient minorities, the Scheduled Castes were doubtful of Nehru's sympathy for their plight when his opinion was widely quoted that there was no Untouchable problem but only an economic problem. Leaders in the Republican party were inherently opposed to such a view as neglecting the religiously defined segregation and ostracism of Scheduled Castes which they did not regard as simple matters of poverty or economic oppression. The Untouchable political candidates co-opted into the Congress did not openly oppose Nehru's opinions but presumably regarded them with serious doubts. However, the ideology of Congress party spokesmen which grandly enunciated principles of equality and justice for rural masses and underprivileged castes was so widely disseminated, while the nominations it made from the Scheduled Castes were so great, that the party could count on Untouchable support at least until 1967, whatever subsurface doubts about Nehru may have existed.

The response of Scheduled Tribes to Nehru's leadership was even more uncertain; as is evident from his public utterances (see Chap. 4 above), Nehru fully accepted cultural autonomy for tribal peoples. The latter could not help but recognize, however, that these liberal views were not necessarily consonant with "planned development" in the outlying areas or with the attitude of dominant Hindus in such areas (reflected, as they were, in the supercilious posture of block development officers, schoolteachers, and other government representatives who were trying intentionally to "uplift" their charges). It is a defensible thesis that, even if Nehru's views had been widely known among Adivasis, it could only have had the effect of proving his impotence in getting them adopted in actual government planning.

Although the Sikhs were divided in their attitudes toward Nehru, the majority (who followed the dictates of the Akali Dal) regarded him as an arch-obstructionist who stubbornly opposed their program of Punjabi Suba. For a time he appeared to them as a *bête noire* whose very appearance triggered agitations and demonstrations to overpower and drown out his influence. Although the political issue of Punjabi autonomy was finally settled in their favor, it was not, however, until after Nehru's death. Though the Sikhs obtained most of their demands, a good many members of the community continued to nurse wounded feelings from the protracted conflict in which so many blows were exchanged. Caste Hindus of the dominant group, however, considered the case closed and turned attention elsewhere; this attitude, however, has been

---

17. The reader may well object to this bird's-eye view of the situation and assert that most members of Scheduled Castes and Tribes, by reason of illiteracy and seclusion, could not have had any opinions on the subject whatever. There is some validity to this demurrer. However, seasoned observers report that (1) national and state elections opened up communication channels to the most unlikely local situations; (2) transistor radios aided the process; (3) there were few areas of India that Nehru (and other Congress leaders) did not visit – opportunities for *darshan* (adoring gaze) were great; (4) educated political leaders from the minorities often articulated desires and goals of their constituents in simplified and popular forms; (5) grapevine channels of communication operated with a swiftness surpassed only by the radio; (6) messages directed at the masses were black-white, good-bad, right-wrong uncomplicated ideas which became the common currency of gossip in the villages; (7) it was easier to disseminate opinions about a person like Nehru than about an institution like government.

interpreted by Punjabis as neglect of Sikh interests, so that they initiate fresh agitations intermittently as though to make sure that the minority will not lose its conspicuous publicity.

Thus, the integration of each minority community into the web of contemporary India is clearly a derivative from the Nehru years and can be better understood in the light of his influence. When we examine the paradigm of integration first set forth in our initial chapter, it must be emphasized that its relationships are those of the post-Nehru period and are not necessarily valid for an earlier time. A scrutiny of Figure 13.1 (a variation of Fig. 1.2) will make this clear.

INTEGRATION AND CONFLICT: THE FUNCTIONS OF A PARADIGM

The rationale for this paradigm (Fig. 1.2, with Fig. 13.1) is the assumption that, for each minority, agreement with the dominant group either on a centripetal mode of affiliation (C_p) or a centrifugal (C_f) will be a sign that integration as a process is succeeding. Agreement on the centripetal mode (assimilation and/or incorporation) is represented by the letter A, while agreement on the centrifugal mode (cultural pluralism and/or sanctioned autonomy) is labeled B. Conversely, it is assumed that when any minority is in disagreement with the dominant group on its mode of affiliation, it will assume one of two types — either as in C, where the subordinates seek some form of assimilation which is denied them by the dominant group; or as in D, where the minority seeks to maintain its distinctive way of life whereas the dominant group wants the minority to abandon its ethos and accept the customs of the surrounding people. Such disagreements (C or D) imply a process of conflict that counteracts integrative forces. The purpose of this paradigm is to indicate the exclusive logical alternatives of an action system, here expressed as A, B, C, or D, each with its special relationship.

One of the aims of this research is to test the validity of this paradigm. Table 13.2, p. 328, above, represents the first stage in the testing process. It shows that the logical alternatives apparently prevail in those cases where there is a high degree of consensus (thus A or B) but that there are intermediate degrees of consensus, which would imply that the alternatives are uncertain rather than clear-cut. To complete the picture, a low degree of consensus (supposedly identical with disagreement, and hence C or D) is listed alternatively in the same column as "formal consensus combined with hostility and mutual avoidance," which signifies A or B while denying the imputed process of integration that is supposed to accompany these alternatives.

Such evidence leads to the conclusion that Figure 1.2 (and its variation in Fig. 13.1) does not give us logical alternatives *which exhaust the possibilities* of analysis. We therefore turn to a closer look at our empirical results as the second stage for testing the adequacy of the paradigm.

Interview data support the conclusion that Jains, Parsis, and Jews are all considered well-integrated by the dominant group and so regard themselves. There is reciprocal tolerance and goodwill on both sides based on a "live and let live" ideology (B), which is at least partly based on caste norms that embody the

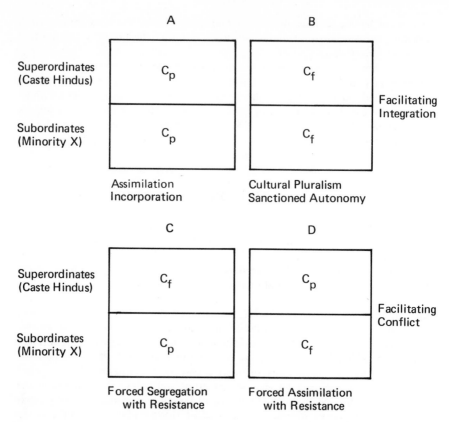

C_p = Ideology preferring centripetal goals for subordinates.

C_f = Ideology preferring centrifugal goals for subordinates.

Fig. 13.1   Normative Modes of Affiliation Expressing Legitimate Aims for Subordinate Groups

B ideal. Certainly the Jains, because of their indigenous origin and pivotal sharing of religious values with the larger Hindu community, are accorded a closeness not given any other religious minorities, not even the Sikhs, and the demands of endogamy are relaxed more often for the Jains whose internal jat divisions so frequently have names and practices paralleling their Hindu counterparts. Although this factor is lacking among Parsis and Jews, who maintain a conventional endogamy for the most part, it would not be overstretching the truth to say that for all three of these communities their integration into Indian society as a whole is assumed without the question of uniform incorporation being raised at all. Even to bring up the issue of citizenship in their case seems irrelevant; it is not merely a formal question (since members of all groups are officially individual citizens by assignment), it seems like no question at all because those who belong to any one of these three minorities are accepted as having assured ascriptive status without any need to screen their credentials politically.

It is probably no accident that Parsis and Jews are the smallest of the nonindigenous religious minorities, while the Jains are the smallest of the indigenous ones. Hence they are not potentially threatening because of their size.

However, our interviews show that a further refinement is necessary. There seems to be a significant division into communities that clearly fit the B relationship — Jews and Parsis — and a type uncertainly poised between the A and B types, as seems to be the case for the Jains (cf. Chap. 5, pp. 124ff.). For them, an assimilative process has been operative for literally thousands of years, and its result has been to generate an internal plurality of jati that parallel those of the surrounding Hindu society. The frequent breakdown of endogamous and commensal rules for transactions between members on both sides of the religious line has reduced the distinctive observability of Jains for many Hindus, who not infrequently deny that the former are a genuinely separate religious body, while some census interviewers have (quite inadvertently) included Jains within the Hindu population (pp. 123-24). For the caste Hindu observer, Jains appear different and yet the same. Conversely, when Jains are asked whether they want to remain separate from the majority or not, they give answers of all three kinds: yes, no, and uncertain. Thus, ambivalence appears on both sides of the line.

But it is the ambivalence of closeness rather than that of distance. It occurs *within* a fully developed integrative process rather than *between* groups sparring for competitive advantage. To use a dramaturgical example, it is as if the caste Hindus were observing Jains in a theater where the proscenium arch slowly dissolves to be replaced by a theater-in-the-round, where the line between audience and players breaks down; eventually the play merges into "real life," which, in turn, becomes more dramatic. In any event, the distinction between them may become meaningless. In time, it becomes a matter of indifference whether the line is observed or not. For many caste Hindu families it is consequently accepted without a qualm when younger members announce intentions to marry Jain partners; not too long ago, this might have been regarded as a daring step. No longer. Such changes are, of course, facilitated by increasing secular trends in the cities along with the spread of higher education.

The unique example of the Jains reveals an unsuspected sidelight on the way we can interpret the central paradigm. In this instance, we seem to have come across a form of integration which is neither assimilation (A), nor sanctioned autonomy (B), but one somewhere between, where increased closeness created by centuries of acculturation has occurred, where the lines between dominant and subordinate ethnics have become blurred and indistinct without wholly disappearing. It can be called the "integration of diffuse envelopment." Even at this macro level, there is a dialectic of intimacy rather than a dialectic of social struggle.

Turning, then, to the intermediate cases of Christians, Anglo-Indians, and Sikhs, we find mixed results. Echoes of underlying conflict between the Hindu community and the Christians are dying away. A generation has passed since the entanglement of Christianity with colonial authority provoked resentment and anger against an "alien" religion. Disdain for the lower caste position of converts or taunts against "rice Christians" are seldom heard today, when most adherents of the Christian faith are second or third generation. Displeasure over proselytizing has lost its point now that conversions from Hinduism are rare,[18] although vestigial remains of suspicion and mistrust come to the surface once a year in the Lok Sabha when the annual report on influx of missionaries is sharply criticized if it shows any increase over the previous year.

Within the Christian minority, the preference for a separate and self-contained community life is clearly observable. Vis-à-vis the larger society, Christians remain prudently inconspicuous. Their employment in the cities, and hence their economic survival, is usually dependent on Hindu employers, but notably on an individual basis. In family life, worship, and gregarious social intercourse, they remain insulated from outsiders.[19] Apart from voting blocs in Kerala, they have shunned organized political activity. No doubt as a protective measure, they have voted with Congress as the ruling party; this has brought them occasional nominations for office in case they have a prominent leader who can serve as a vote bank. Consequently, they are represented in the Lok Sabha and the state assemblies in solitary fashion but out of the limelight.

The B pattern for Christians, then, has a qualitative meaning all its own. Lacking the mutual cordiality so evident in the case of Jains, Parsis, and Jews, or the ill-concealed antagonism of the Chinese example, the integration of Christians is marked by a psychology of "letting sleeping dogs lie." In other words, a stability of instability, which can remain unshaken as long as there are other foci of national attention that appear more urgent. Such foci are not likely to be lacking in the immediate future.

As for the Anglo-Indians, in spite of the fact that they are all Christians, they are a unique subcommunity with a more ambiguous position in the social arena. As noted above (pp. 235-36), their case reflects an oscillation between a B policy and a D. Whenever the dominant group of caste Hindus turns its attention to the Anglo-Indians (admittedly seldom), it regards their attempt to preserve a European way of life as a painful reminder of colonial superiority conceits, even

---

18. Curiously, there has been little public comment on the fact that Christians have shown a higher rate of natural increase than any minority religion reported by the census. During the period 1961-71, Hindus had a percentage increase of 23.69, Jains 28.48, Muslims 30.85, Sikhs 32.28, and Christians 32.60 (Census of India 1971, Series 1, Paper 2 of 1972. Religion). The only cry of alarm roused by these figures relates to the Muslims (note discussion above, pp. 167-68), a sign that this is a sensitive area of public concern, while the growth of the Christian population is not. Why the increase among Christians is the highest of all has not, to my knowledge, been satisfactorily explained. The most likely hypothesis, I submit, has to do with medical care rather than with fertility rates, which should not show great differentials. But in the Christian community, the widespread use of doctors and hospitals, the disproportionate number of nurses, and the community concern to furnish health facilities for its members will have the effect of lowering mortality rates at all ages. Such life-preserving amenities are less prevalent among other religious minorities and still less among the Scheduled Castes, whose rate of increase is just below the national average with a figure of 24.18 while the all-India rate was 24.8.

19. Proliferation into subcommunities, Roman Catholic and multiple Protestant denominations, must also be taken into account.

when dismissing it as pretentious posturing. Especially galling to the neo-traditionals is the inability or unwillingness of so many Anglo-Indians to speak the vernacular language of the region where they live. This flaunts publicly their un-Indian and alien character for others to see and awakens the desire to make them conform at any cost. However, this emotional demand for a kind of assimilation contradicts a deep-seated bias toward cultural permissiveness. The result is an all-too-likely ambivalence toward Anglo-Indians not too far removed from annoyance. Throughout India as a whole, however, there is no well-established modal agreement among members of the dominant group on a permanent policy toward Anglo-Indians. The pressure for them to conform, at least linguistically, is much greater in northern India than in the south, where resistance to the spread of Hindi as a national language is still marked.

Anglo-Indians themselves, as a completely urban minority lacking a tradition of entrepreneurship, prejudiced against manual labor in industry, and without the usual nepotic aids of the Hindu white-collar world, are highly vulnerable to the inroads of unemployment (at least among males) and apprehensive about future discrimination against them. In the past, this has provoked many to migrate to Commonwealth countries; in the present, it leads an uncounted number to consider exit from India as a living option. There is little agreement on this policy, however. Some community members are fully committed to remain in India and accept the consequences of greater Indianization; some only tolerate such an outcome under the harsh pressure of necessity; still others are biding their time until the chance for migration becomes a practical alternative.[20] A certain tentativeness of outlook pervades the community; predictably, political participation is inhibited among the rank and file while being delegated by default to one or two national leaders. This is hardly surprising when the minority is so tiny numerically that it is unable to muster electoral strength.

In sum, there are wavering shifts from a D to a B position without a stable resolution when the interaction between Anglo-Indians and the dominant Hindus is considered. This pattern of indecision is strengthened by the transitional currents of Indian society, where finality is a luxury too hazardous to afford on the road to a fully autonomous national state.[21]

Turning then to the Sikhs: in spite of the apparent resolution of Sikh militancy in the past, it is likewise possible to regard Sikh-Hindu relations as fluctuating between a D and a B relationship. However, the characteristic meaning of this fluidity has a different import. D tendencies appear in the form of inescapable public pressures toward uniformity in the apparent increase of intermarriage at certain caste levels, in public claims that Sikhs and Hindus are

---

20. It would be false to leave the impression that a predilection for emigration is confined to Anglo-Indians. Studies like those of Rashmi Desai (1963) show that immigrants to Britain from the subcontinent arrive from many elements of the Indian population. My own casual conversations with Westernized Hindu businessmen, particularly those in higher income brackets, have turned up a surprising number who report that their sons are planning to live permanently in Britain, Canada, or the United States.

21. The series of decrees following the emergency declaration of June 26, 1975, by Indira Gandhi was ostensibly an attempt to arrest the currents of social change in selected directions.

"essentially" one, and the multiplying number of Sahajdaris or unbearded males. A marked B trend is apparent, however, in the persistence of Gurdwara worship, the SGPC, the Akali Dal Party, and Punjabi Suba. Most leanings are clearly in the B direction, although secular trends have noticeably eroded them. Integration of the Sikh community based on hard-won compromise and a stolidly averted gaze from conflicts past and present are the earmarks of Sikh-Hindu relations in the 1970s.

Finally, there are the minorities with the most problematic integration which include the salient minorities of Muslims, Scheduled Castes, and Scheduled Tribes, plus the Chinese. Here recurring animosities from the near and distant past keep Muslims in a state of ill-concealed friction with the dominant group. As cultural contradictions between Hinduism and Islam have been aggravated by reversals of historic sovereignty, clashes of values are compounded with conflicts of power, each reinforcing the other. Islam is a religion whose missionary zeal rests on the assumption that it is the only true religion, a candid intolerance. In contrast, the Hindu pantheism regards all deities as having rightful but limited claims, an overt tolerance masking a disguised sense of superiority to the narrow-mindedness of proselytizing faiths, a less candid though real intolerance of quite a different character. With their centuries of imperial rule accompanied by mass conversions to their faith, the Muslims established habits of ascendancy and superiority twice shattered by outsiders — first by the alien British and second by former subject Hindus.

The sense of faded glories has in many ways paralyzed the will to action of the Muslim community, suffused them with a loss of purpose, and created a pervasive inertia their leaders find it hard to overcome (Siddiqi, 1972, p. 17). Acceptance of separate living quarters, or mohallas, is less onerous than the accompanying realization of permanent weakness and subordinate status that goes with it. Beneath the surface of group passivity is a fierce pride fed by historical memories and religious adjuration. Apparent acceptance of a B pattern by Muslims is thus mingled with reactions perceived by outsiders as touchiness or sensitivity to insult. The dominant Hindus, in turn, focus on a different set of memories, recalling with dismay and horror the holocaust of partition which they attribute to the recalcitrance of the Muslim League. As a consequence, present-day Hindus tend to regard Muslim attempts to organize politically as something of a threat (at least in north India). Neo-traditional leaders of the more militant type speak boldly of "Indianizing" the Muslims and, on occasion, manipulate mass action against them. Although the Muslim-Hindu pattern fluctuates between D and B, it differs from the situation of other minorities by reason of recurrent historical occasions of intergroup violence that have kept mutual antagonism alive in spite of the efforts of leaders on both sides to promote reconciliation of the "destiny conflicts" that have rocked India in the past.

When we examine the situation of the Scheduled Tribes, we find that, in many respects, it is the most complex one to be found among the salient minorities. Although government programs to combat illiteracy, raise educational standards, and promote the techniques of intensive agriculture among tribals are part and parcel of a D pattern promoting assimilation (often reinforced by public utterances asserting the common citizenship of all in the uniform mode of incorporation) and although this activity *sounds* egalitarian, it obviously embodies the attempt to eradicate cultural difference by superimposing a majority style of life on the daily habits of minority members. To the Adivasis, these proceedings appear as a Juggernaut of homogenization and are resisted. Nehru temporarily came to their aid in the policy of Tribal Panch Shila (permissive cultural pluralism) which, however, was neither widely accepted nor generally implemented. It turned out that the real, though unspoken, meaning of the D pattern was the long-range intent to bring the Scheduled Tribes into full-fledged membership of Indian society through the door of caste. To the extent that Adivasis accept this version, they put the stamp of approval on a modified B pattern (limited autonomy), and this has been the mode of adjustment for a number of ethnolinguistic groups. However, it has the disadvantage that the tribals in the process often have no recourse but to enter the caste system on its lowest rung as Untouchables.[22] This price is a heavy one to pay and is to be avoided for the obvious reason that the tribal member who, after all, stands outside the system — like a Muslim or a Christian (and he frequently is a Christian) — does not have the stigma of pollution ascribed to a member of the Scheduled Castes. In many ways, therefore, it is more desirable to remain a tribal outside the system than to enter it as a befouled Untouchable. The special benefits granted by the Constitution are just as valid in the one case as in the other, a circumstance that also inhibits any inclination to change.

Consequently, the B pattern of tribal autonomy with its advantages of educational and bureaucratic reservations along with special seats in the legislatures may understandably make greater appeal than the *alternative B* pattern of acculturation to caste practices, each with its unique forms and customs. Such acculturation requires burdensome changes in family, religious, and dietary customs[23] — perhaps even more in recreational festivity. Either way, however, there is no escape for any tribe from local-level economic competition on unequal terms, resulting in exploitation by dominant group members more sophisticated in the techniques of agriculture, trading, commerce, and industrial management — all pressure tactics that move in a D direction.[24]

Inertia and the advantages of immobility often appeal to Adivasis, but they have little attraction for Scheduled Castes who cannot stay as they are without paying heavy penalties. The backward pull of tradition, nostalgia for old familiar ways, or relaxing into the protective shell of a mother tongue mercifully secret from the prying inquisitiveness of outsiders — such defensive patterns, however useful they may be for tribals, are hardly practical for Untouchables whose

---

22. In a few exceptional cases, certain tribes have attempted the transition by the route of claiming still higher varna status. Interestingly enough, this is usually a Kshatriya preference (Galanter, 1966, p. 634, n. 3; Sinha, 1962; von Fürer-Haimendorf, 1967, p. 183). These and other variations in the adaptive process are summarized briefly above (pp. 92-95).

23. The usual changes. Marginal exceptions occur among highly Christianized groups and those more assimilated in the Western mode for other reasons.

24. Fluctuation between D and B as dominant-group policies affecting indigenous isolates also occur in other noncaste societies like Canada, with its diversity of tribal groups. See John White, 1972.

historic status has been one of stigma and disgrace. For them the chief advantages lie in change, not stubborn clinging to the past. More than for any other single minority, tradition is an enemy of the outcastes. In their case, too, the Constitution clashes more sharply with age-old beliefs than it does for other communities, since its explicit assertion of equality before the law runs directly counter to the hierarchical dogmas that have kept them at the bottom of the social order for centuries. It is, therefore, predictable that Untouchables will turn to the law for redress of grievances more often than other minorities; it is equally predictable that they will find such appeals unavailing as long as local power structures are impervious to national currents of change.

Unlike other minorities throughout India, Scheduled Castes face a C situation, since their segregation is not so much voluntary as imposed from without, blocking the way to innumerable life goals. More frustrating still is the uncertainty of their direction in case the barriers *should* be lifted. In a segmented society like India, where a caste location is a prerequisite for elemental social identification, attempts to escape a lower caste position typically take one of two forms: Sanskritization, in which the adoption of Brahmanic conventions gives an entire caste a more respectable position, or a rise in position through Westernized education, economic affluence, or both. The first alternative demands generations rather than years to make itself felt, and so the second wins by default. Its effects, however, are scattered and uncertain.

Thus, when Untouchables recognize that Sanskritization is hardly an attainable goal for them, there is divided opinion on the manner of integration. Some prefer to move from C to A, whether by maintaining and enlarging the number of educational privileges and job reservations that take many of their members into the "mainstream," or, sometimes in league with local communists, by sponsoring strikes for higher wages among agricultural laborers, confiscating properties of large landowners, or appropriating wastelands for themselves, all of which lift their members out of extreme poverty into a position more nearly comparable to that of other cultivators. On the other hand, there are quite different segments like the neo-Buddhists who take a B position by embracing a different religion that separates them sharply from the Hindu community in a semi-caste enclave that preserves ethnic particularism in a horizontal rather than a vertical dimension. A few political leaders espouse a still different B resolution by demanding villages, towns, or larger areas set aside for Scheduled Castes where their members could maintain self-subsistent regions free from outside interference.

Dominant castes, on their side, exhibit marked ambiguity and uncertainty in their views on integration policy for the Scheduled Castes. Doubts are growing about renewing reservations and privileges that threaten to run indefinitely; alarms are rife over demands for wage increases and the seizure of property. Incorporation or assimilation of the A type is, on the whole, quite unacceptable to the entrenched caste Hindus. Yet they perceive B alternatives in ambivalent fashion. The traditional position of the Scheduled Castes as below the four varnas in a separate enclosure of their own was actually a B pattern *par excellence.* If any other were to take its place, it would logically have to be a *substitute B,* and what that substitute could possibly be is decidedly an unsolved problem. Conversion to Buddhism is not fully acceptable to the dominant group, and the demand for a separate territory is so outrageous that it cannot be taken seriously. Thus, there seems to be certainty as to what the substitute can *not* be, but none whatever as to what it *can* be. Realistic contours of such a pattern are, at present, quite unimaginable; who can say what a novel autonomy would consist of when it would have to be consistent with the egalitarian demands of citizenship?

When this sort of impasse is reached, it is easier to dismiss the issue from attention than to struggle with an insoluble riddle. Mingled disdain and condescension toward the depressed classes are therefore augmented by complacency which avoids fruitless thought on the question. Slogans and rationalizations easily fill the void: for instance

> There is no Untouchability any longer — it is now abolished by law. (This to foreigners.)
>
> Scholarships and reservations are spoiling the Scheduled Castes.
>
> X from the Scheduled Castes has been chief minister in Andhra; Y is in the cabinet at the Centre, although he is from the Scheduled Castes. This shows that prejudice is breaking down.

Typically, then, the stance of the dominant group to the issue of integration for the Scheduled Castes is "selective inattention" combined with quiescence; this in turn allows the grievances of the minority to accumulate until they reach explosive proportions. Thus, the prediction that open strife will increase as the process continues is freely made; a leading sociologist declares, "In the past the Scheduled Castes had accepted their civic deprivations as a matter of course. Now that a spirit of challenge has been kindled among them, it is likely that conflicts between Harijans and dominant peasant castes will become more pervasive" (Béteille, 1967, p. 99).

In summary, the first point to be emphasized is that there are more minorities for whom integration is problematic and uncertain than there are minorities for whom consensus occurs on minority policy (if we include both the salient minorities and those with an intermediate position on at least three indicators); this verifies the dialectical proposition that processes of integration and conflict are more often compounded than identified separately.[25] Secondly, of the seven problematic cases, there are at least three for whom the probability of conflict or future violence seems greater than it is for the other minorities;

---

25. Tentatively predicted on theoretical grounds in my earlier volume (Schermerhorn, 1970, pp. 57-59). What now becomes more clear after exploring the multiethnic society of India is that this merging of opposing forces makes it impossible to insist that the four alternatives of the paradigm of affiliation exhaust the possibilities of interaction. Diverse combinations in the first instance necessarily entail diverse combinations in the second. If we really take social change seriously (therefore history), we must view society as structurally diachronic, dialectic, and open-ended rather than synchronic, univocal, and self-enclosed. Only in a system of the latter kind can a paradigm present an arrangement of *exclusive logical alternatives*. However, under the conditions of *any* empirical society, and especially one undergoing the massive changes characteristic of post-independence India, all we can expect of our paradigm is that it serve as a tool of analysis in which all the major variations of group interaction are specified and comprehended.

again, this is the familiar set of salient minorities, Muslims, Scheduled Castes, and Scheduled Tribes. For each of the three, disagreement with the dominant castes reaches more precarious levels than we find in the other four cases. The most obvious example is that of the Muslims, whose many conflicts with the Hindus since the conquests of the eleventh century have left a trail of animosity all too easily regenerated intermittently since it feeds on itself.[26] The Scheduled Castes find themselves suffocated by simultaneous engulfment into the nether regions of Hinduism and the lowest substratum of the peasantry. Since independence, legal enactments and the stimulus of enfranchisement have emboldened them to adopt a new activism, however sporadically. This, in turn, is sufficiently threatening to the dominant group that it is energetically suppressed. Such actions and reactions are apparently on the increase. On their part, the Scheduled Tribes, as outsiders who see absorption into a larger nation-state as a threat to their identity, do not hesitate to use protective guerrilla tactics, particularly in peripheral areas like the northeast where advantages of terrain are on their side. However, for the dominant group, this raises the specter of tribal alliance with a foreign power, and this threat limits drastically any concessions that could be made to the communities on the border. Pacification of such groups runs the gamut historically from military action to political appeasement without reaching the goal of full reconciliation. In more central regions of India the vulnerability of Scheduled Tribes to revolutionary appeals is a potential that is ever-present as long as alienation of their lands continues with the march of "progress" and their poverty level continues to be the lowest in India.

As already noted, accommodation between Chinese and the dominant group masks a common distrust and antagonism that are prevented from coming to the surface by the process of mutual avoidance. Some of the resemblances between the Chinese and the Muslim cases are striking. In both instances there is a relatively high level of mutual antagonism, a condition derived from overt hostilities between larger collectives with whom present-day members are still identified, and agreement on a B policy which turns out to be no more than a formal consensus on a live-and-let-live policy. It is stretching the term to call this consensus integrative, except that a truce is integrative. In other respects, however, the similarity breaks down. Particularly as a result of their diminutive size, inconspicuous position, vulnerability to external control, and inability to square accounts with an oppressor, the Chinese cannot be classified with the salient minorities. In India they occupy a quite unique position.

POVERTY AND IMMOBILITY

The salient minorities also lead the list in destitution and poor prospects for raising their status. In the three states (Madhya Pradesh, Rajasthan, and Gujarat) where comparative income figures were available to me, the Scheduled Tribes

---

26. The more one deals with macroanalysis in empirical terms, the more one is forced to the conclusion that residual historical animosities over time become full-fledged causal determinants in their own right, even though at first they may have had an epiphenomenal and purely derivative character. Social psychological processes like these are not as insubstantial as they are often supposed to be.

averaged an annual per capita income between Rs. 101 and 104 as compared with the national average of Rs. 330 (see p. 78 above). Not only do the tribals occupy some of the poorest lands for agriculture, they are continually losing what they have through alienation in spite of laws to the contrary. Scheduled Castes are similarly impoverished, although the evidence is more indirect in their case. Research in West Bengal and the Old Delta of Tanjore District, Tamil Nadu, show a considerable increase in the number of landless laborers who are Untouchables (see above, pp. 60-61; and Béteille, 1972, pp. 144-46). Since these day laborers in rural areas are the poorest farmers, it is significant that over one-third of the Scheduled Caste labor force in a representative sample is composed of landless laborers as compared with only 9 percent of the caste Hindus (Verba *et al.*, 1971, pp. 81-82). Furthermore, the proportion of landless laborers increased substantially in the intercensal period 1961-71, which definitely implies a corresponding growth in the number of Scheduled Caste members entering that category. For example, agricultural laborers were 16.71 percent of the total work force in India for the year 1961, but this percentage went up to 25.76 in 1971. Limiting this statistic to rural workers only, the corresponding figures are 18.87 percent for 1961 and 29.98 percent for 1971.[27] The implication is, however, indirectly, that poverty is increasing among Scheduled Castes, who make up a disproportionate share of landless laborers at the bottom of the ladder.

While the data for Muslims are hardly satisfactory, it is clear that their loss of favored position after independence was accompanied by loss of property and jobs on a large scale and that they shared the general economic decline of the rural areas (see above, pp. 164 and 172-73). If we are to believe reports from individual Muslim respondents, they also experience extensive discrimination and exclusion from job openings in the cities so that, before the second Indo-Pakistani war, Muslim youth regarded West Pakistan as a land of opportunity. Now that these doors are closed, unemployment becomes the alternative.

On the whole, therefore, it is a defensible thesis that the three salient minorities occupy a very low, if not the lowest, economic stratum in comparison with the other ethnic communities surveyed in these pages.

Turning attention from the question of indigence to that of social mobility, it is already evident from the foregoing discussion that the three salient minorities have experienced considerable downward mobility in the recent past. A propos of this issue, K. L. Sharma (1973, p. 69) asserts that the presence of both upward and downward mobility in a society is a sign of greater fluidity of structure than upward mobility considered by itself. He thus presents four possibilities that define the movement and direction of mobility in various social systems:

		Down	Up
a.	High downward and high upward mobility	(+	+)
b.	High downward and low upward mobility	(+	-)
c.	Low downward and high upward mobility	(-	+)
d.	Low downward and low upward mobility	(-	-)

27. Census of India 1971, Series 1, Paper 1 of 1971, Supplement. Provisional Population Totals.

Although it is impossible to enter into the details of Sharma's analysis, it is sufficient here to point out his implied conclusion that India corresponds to condition d. If this hypothesis is accepted, any query about upward mobility for the three salient minorities will begin with the assumption that the movement is slow — in keeping with the societal pace. Furthermore, conditions of research in India make it impossible to follow the familiar clue of intergenerational change because relevant statistics are unavailable.[28] Yet there is a strong compulsion to seek for clues to upward mobility for the simple reason that governments, particularly in developing societies, are so often judged on their ability to raise the life chances of their citizens (Apter, 1958, p. 221).

In earlier chapters I have tried to approach this problem by turning attention away from the *extent* of upward mobility to a paradigm indicating *modes* of mobility occurring among the three salient minorities. Since the paradigm applies in a somewhat different way to each of the communities, it reveals how obstacles to mobility and consequent methods of coping with them vary in the three cases (pp. 53, 89, 174). Without considering each individual case again, it is sufficient here to reiterate that, when one applies the four modes of Sanskritization, Westernization, contest mobility, and sponsored mobility to each salient minority, none of the modes holds out any appreciable encouragement for group advance.[29] Scheduled Castes have a modicum of advantage in Westernization because of educational privileges and, together with the Muslims, have a real potential for contest mobility (political mobilization) which could prove favorable for them only when national conditions permitted. For example, a series of economic crises would heighten the chances of either or both minorities to transfer allegiance to leftist parties in protest.

It is just such a crisis in the wake of severe famine that saw the rise of the Dalit Panthers in 1974 as a small but militant party of Untouchable youth in Bombay who modeled their activities after those of the early Black Panthers in the United States and whose ideology borrowed from both the younger Eldredge Cleaver and Karl Marx. As yet unclear on their long-range goals while preaching

---

28. With the exception of A.K. Das's (1968) investigation noted above (pp. 60-61). Significantly, that study highlights downward rather than upward mobility. K. L. Sharma points out that the usual index denoting movement of manual to non-manual workers is less applicable to India, where industrialization is occurring at a low rate (Sharma, 1973, p. 69). It must also be recognized that there is a built-in aversion to collecting economic data by community in the census since this might encourage "communalism."

29. The four modes do not exhaust the possibilities for upward mobility. Untouchable mass conversion to other religions is another avenue, now abandoned so far as Christianity is concerned (cf. pp. 42-43) but still continuing in the case of Buddhism, where 2,000 Jatavs followed Ambedkar into that faith on March 18, 1956, in Nagpur (cf. p. 65) while "several thousand" accepted Buddhism on March 22, 1973, in Delhi (Sharma, 1973, p. 68). The earlier action led to a legion of followers which then tapered off abruptly. Thus in 1951-61 the Buddhists had a growth rate of 2267.01 percent, but this dropped to an insignificant 17.20 percent in 1961-71 (Census of India 1971, Series 1, Paper of 1972, Religion. "Note on Individual Religions," p. 22). It is still too early to determine whether a similar spurt of growth will follow the Delhi mass movement. Parenthetically, it should be noted that Buddhist conversion is a form of collective cultural emulation analogous to Sanskritization and could be placed in the upper left-hand corner of the paradigm.

radical change, they devoted themselves to arousing their caste fellows in the villages to revolt against the poverty and misery of their lives. In a parliamentary by-election, their movement provided much of the voting strength that defeated a Congress candidate in favor of a communist rival — an upset that sent shock waves through the political ranks. An aftermath of repressive measures which fanned the flames of resentment and created new martyrs soon followed. One journalist[30] reports:

> Immediately afterward there were violent clashes between the Dalit Panthers and caste Hindus. The police, caste Hindus themselves, cracked Panther skulls savagely and killed one of the movement's leaders while leaving non-Untouchable rioters free to inflict damage. A humiliated Congress administration appears to have conspired with the caste prejudice of the police and the Hindu majority to ensure the brutal repression of the Dalit Panthers.

It is still too early to predict the future growth of the Dalit Panthers, which could eventually have revolutionary potential if mobilization is adroitly handled; the movement may also recede in radical momentum, as happened to the Black Panthers in the United States. Much depends on the response of the dominant group, particularly as expressed in the strategy of the Congress party. This party, however, is precluded from the kind of easy victory won from the tribals by the absorption of the Jharkhand party into the Congress. In 1974, both the interests and ideology of the kulaks who gave the Congress so much whole-hearted support were implacably opposed to the program of the Dalit Panthers who, in turn, sought the overthrow of landlords and prosperous farmers. Such natural enemies could hardly join forces in the same political organization.

In sum, the salient minorities show such limited group advance on any dimension that they are almost frozen in a position of immobility. Curiously, Muslims seem somewhat worse off in this respect than the Scheduled Castes and Scheduled Tribes, who at least have scholarships and constantly renewed reservations to propel some of their members in an upward direction. No such indulgences exist for Muslims.

FINAL REFLECTIONS

Resolving minority issues awaits the shift in priorities. Understandably, the dominant leadership still gives major attention to winning elections, economic development, and foreign relations. This results in national neglect of India's second priority problem: the potential disaffection or alienation of nearly 40 percent of her people which the minorities represent. The five-year plans have nothing to say of this issue, and there are few, if any, signs of a sustained interest in minority affairs in the literature of government agencies or of political

---

30. A.S. Abraham, "India's Untouchables, At Last, Are on the March," *Los Angeles Times,* April 29, 1974.

parties.[31] At times, patchwork reforms, when hastily inaugurated, are announced as though they have instantaneously reached their goal.[32] The social sciences likewise reflect the national preoccupation with development programs as economists, followed by political scientists and sociologists, devote major attention to questions related to the productive capacity possessed by the country, with hardly a backward glance at the ethnic communities so briefly sketched in these pages.[33]

The exigencies of electioneering force politicians to give minorities more attention when it appears necessary to curry favor or ward off threat: that is, (1) when a minority has numerical predominance in some local region; (2) when a minority, though small, holds the balance of power in a particular election; (3) when one or more members of a minority have popular appeal that

---

31. This directly contradicts my earlier hypothesis that in a pol-ec society (in which the polity controls the economy) "the strict control that government has over economic practices is likely to be matched with overt surveillance and constraint of ethnic groups in direct and deliberate ways" (Schermerhorn, 1970, p. 186). Instead, we find here a really striking disregard of ethnic groups except under special or emergency conditions. What is the source of this discrepancy? I submit that the mistake has been to disregard the variability inherent in the pol-ec category when deriving a predictive hypothesis from it. Once we fully recognize the pol-ec category as a variable consisting of degrees of more or less, the prediction quoted above has validity only at one end of the scale (the higher or more extreme end), that is, among the communist nations where control of the economy by government reaches its apogee. This control is a matter of lesser degree among societies claiming to be socialistic but with limited nationalization and control of the economy; consequently, the conditions for ethnic surveillance will vary also. For example, of the six characteristics listed as marking a pol-ec society (ibid., p. 182), communist nations exhibit all six while India has only three, which allows considerable leeway for a private sector and entails important limitations on the actual amount of vigilance or watchfulness devoted to plural groups or associations.

32. Such as the headline "An Evil Practice Goes" referring to the "abolition" of bonded labor by presidential ordinance of November 1975. Closer examination shows that this decree can only have effect if its enforcement clause is efficacious. That clause provides that violation of the law's provisions is punishable either by maximum prison sentence of up to three years or a fine up to the amount of Rs. 2,000, or both (*Overseas Hindustan Times,* November 6, 1975). This practice of setting a maximum penalty with *no minimum* – a ceiling with no floor – is also part of the enforcement clause in the Untouchability Offenses Act passed by the Lok Sabha in 1955 and bears heavy responsibility for the lack of success enjoyed by the Act in attempting to eradicate the practice of Untouchability (Galanter, 1969). It resulted in the common practice of levying light fines of 3 to 10 rupees which made a mockery of the Act and failed to give it the slightest value as deterrent (Report of the Commissioner for Scheduled Castes and Scheduled Tribes 1958-59, I 30; 1959-60, I 28-29, and Department of Social Welfare, Annual Report, 1966, p. 34). To repeat this legal performance is to compound futility while giving the public impression of a dramatic blow to free agricultural laborers from peonage.

33. Some exceptions do occur. Anthropologists by the very nature of their discipline are committed to the study of nonliterate communities that form the indigenous isolate sector of ethnic groups in the nation. However, since the general public has little interest in such groups beyond the exotic, the studies of ethnographers are chiefly written by and for specialists. Political scientists also have given at least a modicum of attention to minority groups – primarily, it would seem, because the political process requires constant adjustment to ethnic group participation at local and state levels. Sociologists have barely broken over the line – preliminary steps toward research in ethnic and minority groups were taken at the annual meeting of the Indian Sociological Society in Delhi in 1969.

transcends group lines and can be co-opted as vote banks; (4) when public accusations against a minority chime in with local prejudice against it; (5) when it is well advised to manipulate a minority split into factions so as to nullify its voting power; or (6) when it is feared that a minority is being made the tool of a foreign power. Apart from situations like these, however, the dominant stratum (as found in the leadership echelons of the political parties rooted in the upper castes) can safely ignore minority affairs in the long stretches between elections. Again, a second priority.[34]

Public projects dealing with minorities risk failure unless they are based on realistic premises. The assumption that India is a collection of peaceful little Gandhis cannot be sustained. Richard Lambert reports that there were thousands of communal riots from the 1850s until partition, when all restraints were thrown aside and a million victims died (Lambert, 1951). Nirad Chaudhuri gives ample evidence of India's violent past and then comments:

> The very extremism of the doctrine of non-violence as preached by the Hindus, taken with the practice of a degenerate compassion, should serve to indicate that both were a panic-stricken recoil from something equally extreme in the opposite direction. . . . The non-violence was as irrational as the violence. The pendulum always swings farthest when it has been at its highest level on the other side. . . . Even the word for non-violence in Sanskrit . . . which is *ahimsa,* shows that it is a corrective to a basic trait which is its opposite. The Hindus did not preach love of man as a positive virtue, but only abstention from violence and killing.[35] (Chaudhuri, 1965, pp. 129, 130)

Gandhi's own method, satyagraha, came to mean mass demonstrations of disobedience to be used in situations where legal and conventional methods for redressing grievances were unavailable or useless.

David H. Bayley has given this mode of action the suggestive title of "coercive public protest," displaying the following characteristics: (1) it is

---

34. This is not a condition peculiar to India. Two political scientists have remarked on the same neglect in other Asian regions by declaring that "Everywhere in Southeast Asia, the new national governments have tended to ignore the problem of the ethnic minorities once the foreign imperial power has been eliminated. Their concern for such minorities is aroused only when they fear that outside elements may be using minority grievances as an excuse to reestablish foreign rule" (Thompson and Adloff, 1941, p. 282). Issues of ethnic integration thus appear to be a low priority item in many Asian nations, or were in 1955. Pressure of events and increasing mobilization of minority interests have forced such problems into the spotlight, however, in a number of southeast Asian nations. For a more recent review of such trends, see Hunter, 1966, and Enloe, 1970.

35. This implies a certain volatility in personality organization, a precarious balance between forces almost equal in intensity. The slightest stimulus may therefore jar either one side or the other into action. Philip Slater has some significant passages on this phenomenon and remarks that a people may be "preoccupied" with the control side of the balance. "Rather than saying Germans are obedient or Anglo-Saxon societies stuffy or puritanical, it is more correct to say that Germans are preoccupied with issues of authority, Anglo-Saxons with the control of emotional and sexual expression, and so forth" (Slater, 1970, p. 3). Analogously, one might say that Hindus are preoccupied with *ahimsa,* if Chaudhuri's analysis is correct. The entire passage by Slater is highly suggestive along this line (pp. 3-5).

aggregative, that is, it deals with crowds or multitudes brought together from different strata or locations in the social order; (2) it is public, as opposed to clandestine or conspiratorial; and (3) it imposes a constraint upon government by its presence and actions. As a weapon it creates some disruption of social order, an emergency with which the forces of government must deal (Bayley, 1962). Though this was certainly not Gandhi's intention, the mass demonstrations which he led tapped a ready disposition for aggression and gave it full moral legitimation in the cause for independence. But the momentum of mass action could not be stopped.

> In its application to the Indian nationalist movement the Gandhian doctrine of non-violence led to some of the bloodiest riots, one of which compelled him in 1922 to call off the non-cooperation movement. [Chaudhuri, 1965, p. 130]

An important side effect of the Gandhian agitation was that the universal esteem for the Mahatma became transferred to his *method,* which in later years lacked Gandhi's restraining influence. Satyagraha in the form of mass demonstrations came to have a halo of prestige that somehow rubbed off on the participants, no matter who they were or what their aims happened to be.[36] The results have increased the climate of public violence. As M. N. Srinivas[37] comments:

> ... unless there is a consensus among political parties that street violence is something that will destroy the country, we can do nothing about it. ... The other dimension is the utter insensitiveness of our bureaucracy. So long as people do not take a matter to the streets, burn buses, cars, railway stations and post offices, the politicians and the bureaucracy do not wake up. This is tantamount to telling the people, "Please go and burn something. Then only will you get what you are asking for." This kind of lesson that the politicians and bureaucracy are teaching the people is destructive of democracy.

As agitations become more widespread and more explosive t he response of government becomes more repressive. Mass arrests become the "solution" to all such problems under the Maintenance of Internal Security Act and are justified in the name of law and order.[38]

---

36. Ashis Nandy (1970, p. 72) makes the same point in different terms: ". . . the experience of the nationalist movement, which proved the politics of *ahimsa* and *satyagraha* to be efficacious tools of pressure and mobilization, still tends to justify agitational strategies and leads to the under-evaluation of formal means of demand articulation and protest. Simultaneously, persistent implicit assumptions about Indian passivity and pacifism induces authorities to disregard demand management till extra-systematic pressures are applied. This reinforces the agitational strategy and heightens further the participating Indian's inner doubts about his capability to control and channel hostility."

37. "The Changing Mores of India." Interview with M.N. Srinivas by N.S. Jagganathan. The *Hindustan Times Weekly Review,* Sept. 14, 1969.

38. The crushing of agitational movements was effectively employed against Naxalites in Bengal when it is asserted that between thirty and forty thousand detainees in Indian prisons appeared to have little chance for coming to trial. A petition to the government of India for their release was organized by Dr. Hari Sharma, a prominent Marxist, and signed by 285 professionals and academics from many countries on August 15, 1974; this was ignored by New Delhi. Massive arrests of labor leaders with sixty thousand of the rank and

Such being the conditions of public life in the final quarter of the twentieth century, it would seem more rewarding to promote sustained policies of conflict prevention or conflict regulation with the minorities rather than to subdue protests by force after they have reached the explosive level. Although grievance committees are an accepted tool of labor relations, they are unheard of where minorities are concerned. Agencies equipped to hear complaints and to deal with them more promptly than is possible in long-drawn-out court battles are not beyond the ingenuity of skilled minds to construct. Lokayukta (ombudsman) arrangements are not unfamiliar in India, though they are not usually applied to cases of this sort.[39]

But any such agency will be ineffective in the long run if it is narrowly confined to the hearing of complaints. Sources of conflict that are wide ranging and in different stages of development call for a center where the process of negotiation and continuous adjustment of policy are required — for each minority. In the past, India has favored group autonomy in the form of caste, which was relatively static and hierarchical, with elite disregard of lower strata and with dharma (duty) limited to norms for each separate caste. Under the rapidly changing conditions of contemporary India briefly sketched at the beginning of this chapter, autonomy (the B solution) still retains its legitimacy as an ideal,[40] but this calls for a decided modification of the caste model. Instead of static, purely self-enclosed groups, new conditions necessitate constant interaction and adjustment to political processes and governmental agencies, although endogamy may retain its traditional hold. Instead of unquestioned hierarchy, the new ideal of egalitarianism embodied in Constitutional legal rights exemplifies the "uniform mode of incorporation" mentioned above (p. 9). However, this

---

file proved so successful in "settling" the railway strike of May 1974 that it is perhaps no wonder that wholesale incarceration of protesters became a favorite weapon of the regime. In her seizure of dictatorial power in June 1975 following the nationwide agitation of Jayaprakash Narayan and his followers, Indira Gandhi was realistically aware of what such sweeping demonstrations might mean to the body politic. In her speech to the nation, therefore, she declared, "We had no doubt that such a programme would have resulted in grave threat to public order and damage to economy beyond repair. This had to be prevented" (*Overseas Hindustan Times*, July 10, 1975).

Indira Gandhi made a speaking tour in western and central India during February 1976. The *Overseas Hindustan Times* of March 4, 1976, reported on it in part as follows: "During the several meetings she addressed, the Prime Minister made it clear that the days of 'satyagraha' were over and an era of discipline was being ushered in to make the nation strong and prosperous." This could well be the first official attempt to undermine the legitimacy of the Gandhian technique of satyagraha by name since independence.

39. Legislation establishing such an institution must be based on experience with previous tryouts of the same idea. More explicitly, it would have to avoid the failures of the Maharashtra Lokayukta (LA) and Upalokayukta (ULA) Act of 1972, a document with such slipshod provisions as to make it inherently unworkable. For example, Harish Bhanot declares that "the biggest joke of the Act is that the term action includes 'failure to act.' In view of this, inaction or wrong action by a Government department on an issue is also 'action taken' and no complaint relating to that can even be entertained by the LA and ULA." For this and other deficiencies, see his comments, *Overseas Hindustan Times*, Jan. 16, 1975.

40. Yet elsewhere in Asia, as in mainland China, the opposite preference for assimilation appears predominant. See Moseley (1973). The assimilative thrust of communist policy is noted by Enloe (1973, pp. 43, 45) and for Soviet Russia in my earlier volume (Schermerhorn, 1970, pp. 136-39).

ideal is an unworkable one if it does not take into account the diversity of ethos, internal structure, and development of the ten minorities described in these pages. "Equality before the law" turns out to be a necessary but not sufficient guide for policy in dealing with the minorities. "To treat all alike," which the egalitarian ideal calls for, is to treat each one differently, as every parent knows when he observes his own children. Identical norms cannot be applied to all since each has its own patterns and reactions. Equivalence is far more acceptable as a practical guide than equality, even though equality is a touchstone for equivalence.[41]

Designs for minority integration are, however, exercises in futility if they are not an integral part of larger plans for the transformation of society that come to terms with the indigence and penury of the masses. It is no longer completely academic to consider the possibility of revolution.[42] Even facing that eventuality, the social scientist who thinks of the future as a "crucial variable" will note that there are values in Indian life that could be tapped to make such a future transcend the mechanical imitation of Marxian centralization of the communist world. In fact, the contemporary international crisis has raised important criticisms of both capitalist and communist suppression of human cultural and spiritual creations. As Fred Polak observes, there has been a

> depersonalization of man and the technocratic mass culture in both East and West. The ascendancy of the mass un-man, and the decline of the *Homo humanus*.... Just as the liberal's evolutionary image of un-hampered progress has led to a concentration of economic life in extensive monopolistic organizations, so has the socialistic revolutionary image of systematic intervention led to similar patterns of vast socio-economic organizational networks; on the one hand a metamorphosis of independent entrepreneurs into many-headed megalo-concerns, on the other hand, a metamorphosis of socialistic pioneers into massive administrative bureaucracies. The capitalistic apparatus now has its managers and anonymous stockholders, and the socialist apparatus has its managers and masses. [Polak, 1973, pp. 255, 291]

Some compelling image of what India can be that no other society has achieved is required to galvanize people into action, harnessing the reservoirs of spontaneous response aroused by Gandhi's ideal of village autonomy — with a new technology no longer of the kind he rejected because he regarded it as part and parcel of materialism and industrial exploitation. At present it is quite

---

41. Thus, instead of equivalence being a *condition of citizenship* as M.G. Smith speaks of it, equivalence is here regarded as a *policy demand* necessitated by the need to adjust diverse programs in a multiethnic society to an overarching democratic ideal of equality. This cannot be accomplished purely by the mechanical setting up of differential laws such as those specifying reservation privileges of Scheduled Castes and Scheduled Tribes or those recognizing the personal law of the Muslims; an agency is required that will be responsive to the continuous changes of minority life as affected by sociopolitical processes. Flexibility is a necessity.

42. When Nehru was asked whether India would follow the example of China, he replied, "No, no. We Indians lack the inner self-discipline necessary to accept Communism. If we fail, we will break up into warring states" (quoted in Denis Warner, "Democracy or Break-up," *Des Moines Register*, July 20, 1975).

possible for India to appropriate selectively a host of technological inventions from a world pool of scientific achievement while refashioning them in the light of a wholly different image of man. The oft-mentioned possibility of leap-frogging over the monotony and tyrannical scourges of early industrialism and the later ossification of giant conglomerates — this possibility now genuinely exists. But it will require, as John Wren-Lewis makes clear, technology at the very highest level rather than the crude lower-level developments of early industrialism assumed by many to be the precursor of future "progress" repeating the whole sequence of the West — including its mistakes. However, the uses of new forms of energy, both atomic and solar, can make it possible to organize small units of manufacture at local levels where people can live on a small but human scale without the "dark, Satanic mills" that have cursed both capitalist and communist production; the new dispensation could thus afford workers the chance to maintain that close relationship to nature regarded by Gandhi as necessary for man's sanity.[43]

With the abundance of energy potentially available from such inexhaustible sources, it becomes possible to fashion small rather than massive machinery and to construct devices that awaken and test the ingenuity of the operator instead of deadening human responses on the assembly line or other forms of mechanical monotony. This would be a pattern of new handicraft available only through science — one in which machines would truly be made for man and not man for machines. Other possibilities burgeon as soon as imagination is turned in this direction, such as

> . . . small-scale (small enough for a home or local commune), sophisticated, multi-product, self-maintaining hydroponic systems for food production, with re-cycling of waste products, as an alternative to mass agriculture, mass crop protection, mass transport systems, mass commercial marketing and large-scale sewage disposal. We shall need to consider providing efficient, sophisticated preventive medicine (based, perhaps, on new kinds of food, drink, clothing and atmospheres which give a high sense of well-being while also building up the body's disease resistance) instead of massive medical services and drug production. [Wren-Lewis, 1974, p. 169]

India has the technologists capable of developing such feats, though most of them, like so many applied scientists and engineers "are apt to be among the most conformist, unquestioning members of the community," as Wren-Lewis charges. Also, something like 20 percent of India's engineering graduates seek for passports to go abroad and about half of those who migrate (likely to be the most talented half) do not return.[44] How many would respond to such a Utopian vision is, of course, problematic, especially if it called for the sacrifice of economic security which is theirs in the West. Both with this security diminishing?

The purpose of this digression is not to advance a plea for any particular future but simply to open up a sense of lively alternatives in place of the

---

43. This would be consistent with Jayaprakash Narayan's vision of a "communitarian" society with almost total decentralization of power.

44. "Bringing Back Indian Talent From Abroad," *Overseas Hindustan Times,* June 20, 1974, p. 4.

numbing forecasts of doom with which we are all familiar. Changes such as these in the system might be expected, however, to remove the oblivious neglect with which the elite now view the lower orders, and even lead to an intercaste dharma that would undergird the new order.

Whatever India's future may be, whether it be the division into smaller states, each becoming a national entity, as Bernard Cohn envisages (Cohn, 1971, pp. 161 ff.), the copy of a Maoist model as the Naxalites hope, cultural regions in a larger structure of intermediate societies of the developing world challenging the dominance of the affluent societies posited by Rajni Kothari (Kothari, 1974), a decentralized mosaic of technologically equipped small communities sketched above, or a continually reconstituted version of the present nation-state, it will always face the issue raised in this volume: the perennial task of integrating multiple ethnics into the society on a continually adaptive basis relative to the ever-shifting changes of history. Only a cadre dedicated to the task can keep it alive. Whether the likelihood of such a venture is compatible with the regime of the late 1970s is the ultimate question.

BIBLIOGRAPHY

Andreski, Stanislav, *The Uses of Comparative Sociology,* Berkeley, University of California Press, 1964.

Apter, David, "A Comparative Method for the Study of Politics," *American Journal of Sociology* 64 (November 1958), 221-37.

Banfield, Edward C., *The Moral Basis of a Backward Society,* Glencoe, Free Press, 1958.

Bardhan, P. K., "On the Incidence of Poverty in Rural India," *Political and Economic Weekly* 8 (Nos. 4, 5 and 6, Annual Number, February 1973), 245-54.

Bayley, David H., "The Pedagogy of Democracy: Coercive Public Protest in India," *American Political Science Review* 56 (September 1962), 663-72.

Béteille, André, *Caste, Class and Power,* Berkeley, University of California Press, 1965.

Béteille, André, "The Future of the Backward Classes: The Competing Demands of Status and Power," in *India and Ceylon: Unity and Diversity,* edited by Philip Mason, London, Oxford University Press, 1967.

Béteille, André, "Agrarian Relations in Tanjore District, South India," *Sociological Bulletin* 21 (No. 2, September 1972), 122-51.

Carstairs, G. Morris, *The Twice-Born: A Study of a Community of High Caste Hindus,* London, Hogarth Press, 1957.

Chaudhuri, N. C., *The Continent of Circe, An Essay on the Peoples of India,* Bombay, Jaico Publishing House, 1965.

Cohn, Bernard S., *India, the Social Anthropology of a Civilization,* Englewood Cliffs, N.J., Prentice-Hall Publishers, 1971.

Das, A. K., *Trends of Occupation Patterns Through Generations in Rural Areas of West Bengal,* Calcutta, Scheduled Castes and Tribes Welfare Department, Government of West Bengal, 1968.

Davis, Kingsley, "The World's Population Crisis," in *Contemporary Social Problems,* edited by R. K. Merton and Robert Nisbet, New York, Harcourt, Brace, Jovanovich, 1971.

Desai, Rashmi, *Indian Immigrants in Britain,* London, Oxford University Press, 1963.

Elwin, Verrier, *The Baiga,* London, John Murray, 1939.

Enloe, Cynthia H., *Multi-Ethnic Politics: The Case of Malaysia,* Berkeley, Center for South and Southeast Asia Studies, 1970.

Enloe, Cynthia H., *Ethnic Conflict and Political Development,* Boston, Little, Brown & Co., 1973.

Galanter, Marc, "The Problem of Group Membership, Some Reflections on the Judicial View of Indian Society," *Journal of the Indian Law Institute* 4 (July-September 1962), 331-58; republished in *Class, Status and Power, Social Stratification in Comparative Perspective*, 2nd ed., edited by Reinhard Bendix and Seymour M. Lipset, New York, Free Press, 1966.

Galanter, Marc, "Untouchability and the Law," *Economic and Political Weekly* 4 (Nos. 1 and 2, January 1969), 131-70.

Gould, Harold, "Traditionalism and Modernism in U.P.," in *Indian Voting Behavior,* edited by Myron Weiner and Rajni Kothari, Calcutta, K. L. Mukhopadhayay, 1965.

Hunter, Guy, *South-East Asia, Race, Culture and Nation,* London, Oxford University Press, 1966.

Kothari, Rajni, *Politics in India,* Boston, Little, Brown & Co., 1970.

Kothari, Rajni, *Footsteps into the Future,* New York, Free Press, 1974.

Lamb, Helen B., "The Indian Business Communities and the Evolution of an Industrialist Class," *Pacific Affairs* 28 (No. 2, June 1955), 101-16.

Lambert, Richard, Hindu-Muslim Riots, unpublished Ph.D. dissertation, University of Pennsylvania, 1951.

Luthera, Ved Prakash, *The Concept of the Secular State and India,* London, Oxford University Press, 1964.

Mathur, Girish, *Communal Violence, A Study in Political Perspective,* New Delhi, Sampradayikta Virodhi Committee, n.d.

Misra, B. B., *The Indian Middle Classes, Their Growth in Modern Times,* London, Oxford University Press, 1961.

Moseley, George V. H., III, *The Consolidation of the South China Frontier,* Berkeley, University of California Press, 1973.

Nag, Moni, "The Concept of Tribe in the Contemporary Socio-Political Context of India," in *Essays on the Problem of Tribe,* edited by June Helm, Proceedings of the 1967 Annual Spring Meeting of the American Ethnological Society, Seattle, University of Washington Press, 1968.

Nandy, Ashis, "The Culture of Indian Politics: A Stock Taking," *The Journal of Asian Studies* 30 (No. 1, November 1970), 57-79.

Nicholas, Ralph W., "Rules, Resources and Political Activity," in *Local Level Politics, Social and Cultural Perspectives,* edited by Marc J. Swartz, Chicago, Aldine Publishing Co., 1968.

Polak, Fred, *The Image of the Future,* translated by Elise Boulding, San Francisco and Washington, Jossey-Bass, 1973.

Rudolph, Lloyd I. and Susanne H. Rudolph, *The Modernity of Tradition: Political Development in India,* Chicago, University of Chicago Press, 1967.

Schermerhorn, R. A., *Comparative Ethnic Relations,* New York, Random House, 1970.

Sharma, K. L., "Downward Social Mobility: Some Observations," *Sociological Bulletin* 22 (1973, 1), 59-77.

Siddiqi, M. Nejatullah, "Indian Muslim Response to Indian Pluralism," in *The Muslim Minority in India,* edited by Syed Z. Abedin, Kalamazoo, Michigan, privately printed for Muslim Students' Association, 1972.

Sinha, Surajit, "Status Formation and Rajput Myth in Tribal Central India," *Man in India* 42 (1962), 35-80.

Slater, Philip E., *The Pursuit of Loneliness: American Culture at the Breaking Point,* Boston, Beacon Press, 1970.

Smith, M. G., "Social and Cultural Pluralism," *Annals of the New York Academy of Sciences* 83 (Art. 5, January 20, 1960), 763-77.

Thompson, Virginia, and Richard Adloff, *Minority Problems in Southeast Asia,* Stanford, Stanford University Press, 1941.

van den Berghe, Pierre L., "Toward a Sociology of Africa," in *Africa, Social Problems of Change and Conflict,* edited by Pierre L. van den Berghe, San Francisco, Chandler Publishing Co., 1965.

Verba, Sidney, Bashiruddin Ahmed, and Anil Bhatt, *Caste, Race and Politics,* Beverly Hills, Sage Publications, 1971.

von Fürer-Haimendorf, Christoph, "The Position of the Tribal Population in Modern India," in *India and Ceylon, Unity and Diversity,* edited by Philip Mason, London, Oxford University Press, 1967.

White, John, "Civil Rights and the Native American: A Paradox," paper presented at the American Anthropological Association Meeting, Toronto, December 1972.

Wirth, Louis, "The Problem of Minority Groups," in *The Science of Man in the World Crisis*, edited by Ralph Linton, New York, Columbia University Press, 1945.

Wiser, William H., and Charlotte Viall Wiser, *Behind Mud Walls,* Berkeley, University of California Press, 1963.

Wren-Louis, John, "Educating Scientists for Tomorrow," in *Learning for Tomorrow: The Role of the Future in Education,* edited by Alvin Toffler, New York, Vintage Books (A Division of Random House), 1974.

Appendix

1. Are the_____* growing at a faster rate or slower rate than the rest of the population, in your opinion?
   How do we know?

2. Do the_____form a close-knit community?
   If so, in what way?

3. Would you say that the_____have a strong political consciousness as a group?
   If so, what are some evidences of this?

4. If the_____ are a minority, what group do they regard as the majority or dominant group?

5. Are the rules pretty stringent among the _____ about marrying only within the group?
   If not, what is the case?

6. In the cities, do_____ tend to live in neighborhoods or mohallas by themselves?
   Are there patterns of dispersion?

7. What organizations do the_____ have that duplicate those of other groups?

8. Do the_____have their own clubs or associations?
   If so, tell of some typical ones.
   To what extent do _____ join clubs composed of outsiders?

9. On the whole, do the_____ form a strong in-group, keeping outsiders at arm's length?
   Can you illustrate?

10. Do the _____ have chiefly casual or impersonal relations with outsiders?
    Could you tell a little about how this operates?

11. Can the_____ get a job anywhere without discrimination if their group membership is known?
    If not, who would prevent them?

*Each blank to be filled in with the name of the minority being investigated.

12. Can the _____ get promoted as rapidly as anyone else in large firms or offices if their group membership is known?
    If not, who would prevent this?

13. Can the _____ rent a house anywhere if they have the money, assuming that their community is known?
    If not, who would prevent it?

14. Can the _____ get as much education as people of other communities?
    If not, what are the obstacles?

15. Do you think the _____ want to merge themselves into other groups so as to become invisible, or do they want to remain separate?
    How do we know?

16. Does the dominant group want the _____ to merge with a larger group or would it prefer that the _____ remain separate?
    I'd like to hear a little more about that.

17. Do you think the dominant group doubts the patriotism of the _____ ?
    How would you describe the situation?

18. Do you think the _____ participate in politics as much as members of other communities?
    Could you describe their political activities briefly?

19. In your opinion do the _____ participate in
    a. Agriculture as much as other communities?
    b. Trade as much as other communities?
    c. Industry as much as other communities?
    Would you have any idea where reliable statistics would be available on this subject?

20. In your opinion, do the _____ feel that their participation in national life as a whole is
    a. too little?
    b. too much?
    c. about right?
    Can you think of any reasons why they should feel this way?
    Your comments on this would be appreciated.

21. On the whole, do you think the _____ are fairly well satisfied with their participation in national life?
    I'd be interested to get your slant on this whole question.

22. What evidences of conflict would you say there have been between the _____ and other communities in the last year or so?
    If so, what communities were involved?
    Could you give me a few details about this? And perhaps reliable references?

23. If there has been such conflict, how much newspaper publicity has it received?
    Some people say that such news reports are often suppressed. What is your opinion on this? Any special reasons why you think so?
    If news accounts appeared, were they fair, in your opinion?
    Why do you say that?

24. On occasion of such conflicts
    a. is it difficult to tell who started them?
    b. or which side received the larger share of damage or casualties?
    Do you have decided opinions on this?
    If so, I'd be interested to hear them.

25. What would you say are the issues on which the _____ and the dominant group have the greatest disagreement?
 Greatest agreement?
 Would you venture to say why?

26. Do both members of the _____ and the dominant group mean the same thing by "national integration"?
 Why or why not?
 If different, I'd like to hear your explanation.

27. How does the occupational distribution of the _____ compare with that of other communities?
 Would you happen to know where precise figures are available on this?
 If there are noticeable differences in occupational distribution among the _____ when compared with others, would you draw any special conclusions from this? What conclusions?

28. In your opinion, are the _____ poorer, richer, or about average when their incomes are compared with those of other communities?
 What are some indications of this?
 Could you tell me where I could get reliable figures on the subject?

29. Do the _____ live in urban areas as much as the rest of the population?
 Rural areas?
 Would you happen to know where statistics are available on this?

30. Could you give me some idea how the _____ compare with the rest of India in literacy?
 Is it possible to get valid data on this?
 If so, where?

31. Another approach would be to ask whether schools are available for _____ to the same degree as for other communities?
 On the whole, would the _____ show a different level of schooling when compared with the rest of India? If so, in what way?
 Where might statistics be available on this?

32. Are there any *special* provisions made for the schooling of the _____?
 If so, what is the nature of these provisions?

33. Are there any special types of schooling that the _____ seem to want that is somewhat different from the usual demand? If so, what?
 How do you feel about this?

34. Have you happened to notice any features of family life among the _____ that seem different from that of most families in India?
 If so, how would you describe them?
 Do any of these items affect their relations with outsiders? If so, how?

35. To what extent have the _____ gained positions in the civil service or government posts?
 a. at local levels
 b. at state levels
 c. at national levels
 Would you say that they are spread evenly through the bureaucratic hierarchy? If not, where are they located?
 Have you any idea how their representation in government posts compares proportionately with their percentage of the population?
 If not, could raw figures be obtained on this subject from which such a proportion could be calculated? From what source?

36. Do you believe that the_____ are making any special demands on government?
    If so, what would they be?
    What political issues seem to arouse the _____ more than any others?
    Are these expressed through leaders only, or are demands embodied in some sort of organization?
    If the latter, could you describe it for me?

37. To what extent do the_____ participate in the activities of political parties?
    If so, which parties, mostly?
    Would you hazard a guess why?

38. To what extent are the_____ represented in elective office throughout India?
    Are they given either reserved seats or separate electorates?
    Has any study been made of this question?
    If so, what is it, and where is it available?

39. Do the_____ participate in voting, proportional to their numerical strength?
    If not, what do you think is the reason?

40. Do the_____ have clubs, societies, or voluntary associations of their own?
    If so, would you say they are many or few? How many?
    Examples?
    Are any of these real centers of opinion formation? Explain.

41. Do the_____ join clubs, societies or organizations that admit anybody?
    If not, is this because the_____ are too exclusive or because they are excluded by others? Other reasons?

42. Could you tell me anything about newspaper circulation among the _____?
    Chief papers?
    Languages?
    In your opinion, how much do these papers influence the thinking of the community?
    In what direction?

43. Is there any indication that radio listening is popular among the_____?
    If so, would you call this a growing trend? Further comments?
    What influence do you think that radio listening really has?

44. In Indian society as a whole, what would be your estimate of how the _____ are ranked by most other groups?
    Would you say their national status is high or low? How can we tell?
    What would be some proofs of this?

45. Do the_____ have a system of ranking *within* their community that is peculiarly their own?
    If so, what is the nature of it?
    Who would rank high and who would rank low? Could you give examples?

46. Do the_____ practice self-segregation?
    If so, in what way?
    Are they segregated by others? If so, how?

47. Is there any indication that others exclude _____ from certain occupations?
    If so, what occupations? Who is instrumental in doing this?

48. To what extent do you think discrimination is practiced against_____ in obtaining jobs?
    What about promotion after securing jobs?
    Are there any reliable data on this? If so, where can they be secured?

49. Are the_____ subject to any *de facto* restrictions in voting, party activity, or being elected to office?
    If so, what is the nature of such restrictions?

50. Is there any evidence that police discriminate against the_____ either by failing to provide protection, by harassment, excessive arrests or by brutality?
    Could you give any examples of this, if it exists?

51. Are_____ on the police force in districts where members of the community are quite numerous?
    If not, what would you think is the reason?
    Comments?

52. In your opinion, does the dominant group in this case have any beliefs or doctrines asserting their superiority?
    If so, what is the nature of such doctrines?

53. Does the dominant group in this case tend to stress the idea of national unity?
    Examples?
    As you see it, do you think they exaggerate this issue?
    Do the_____ think so? I'd be interested in why you say that.
    What are the indications, pro and con?

54. Have the_____ developed any protest themes — protest against an underprivileged position?
    If so, what forms do these themes take?
    Are any of these themes borrowed from political parties? Such as?

55. Have you heard any members of the_____ contrasting their roles or activities with those of dominant group members?
    If so, how?

56. Have you heard any of the_____ saying how they would like to have the members of the dominant group act toward them?
    If so, describe what was said in your own words.

57. How do the_____ and the dominant group get along in personal contacts
    a. in the villages?
    b. on buses and trains?
    c. on holidays?
    d. processions?
    e. in the Lok Sabha?

58. Do you think the_____ are moving toward national integration or away from it?
    Why do you think so? Explain.

Index